# RAISING OUR FUTURE

*Families, Schools, and Communities Joining Together*

A national resource guide of family support and education programs
for parents, educators, community leaders, and policy makers

**Harvard Family Research Project**
Heather B. Weiss, Director
Cambridge, Massachusetts

©1995 President and Fellows of Harvard College

Published by Harvard Family Research Project
Harvard Graduate School of Education
Longfellow Hall, Appian Way
Cambridge, MA 02138

Design: Helen Owens In Concert

*This project was funded by the Carnegie Corporation of New York, the John D. and Catherine T. MacArthur Foundation, and the Charles Stewart Mott Foundation. The contents of this publication are solely the responsibility of the Harvard Family Research Project.*

Library of Congress Catalog Card Number: 93-079081

ISBN 0-9630627-0-0

# CONTENTS

Aberdeen Preschool Project
Early Childhood Education and Assistance Program (ECEAP)
Early Childhood Family Education

**RESOURCE LIST**

**PROGRAM LISTINGS
BY DIFFERENT
CHARACTERISTICS**

Alphabetical Listing of Programs
State-by-State Listing of Programs
State-Sponsored Programs
Program Listing by Location; Urban, Suburban and Rural
Demographic Characteristics of Participants
Sources of Income
Administrative Relationship to the School District
Program Service Components
Program Service Delivery Sites

# ACKNOWLEDGMENTS

Many people and organizations contributed to the preparation of *Raising Our Future*. Foremost, are the family support program directors who provided us with information about their activities. They shared with us their memorable stories and also the strategies that make these programs work for schools and for children and families. Our research benefited from the dedication of a team of student assistants and the advice of editors and production consultants. Special thanks go to Helen Owens who collaborated with us on book design. We also appreciate the comments of Harold Howe III, Ruth Tichenor, and Kate Wrean, who shared with us their ideas of issues useful to policy makers and school leaders. However, we claim sole responsibility for the information and viewpoints contained in the book. Finally, *Raising Our Future* was supported by generous grants from the Charles Stewart Mott Foundation, the Carnegie Foundation, and the John D. and Catherine T. MacArthur Foundation.

# PREFACE

Over the past two decades, grass roots family support programs have moved from relative obscurity into the limelight of educational, health, and human service policy and practice. These programs offer information on childrearing, support groups, and a broad range of service referrals. From local beginnings in schools and community groups, family support programs have attracted increasing attention (Weiss, 1989; Bruner, 1994) and are at the heart of many efforts to build systems of family-focused services that are integrated, comprehensive, and preventive. They are now a key component of policy reform efforts, central to achieving diverse policy outcomes including:

- The promotion of children's school readiness and school achievement (Council of Chief State School Officers, 1989);

- Improving key indicators of children's health (Hill, 1992);

- Family preservation and prevention of the need for foster or institutional care (U.S. Department of Health & Human Services, 1994); and

- The enhancement of low-income parents' efforts to gain economic self-sufficiency while nurturing their children's development (Smith, Blank, & Collins, 1992).

**School Involvement in Family Support**

While no one institution or profession has monopolized the invention or sponsorship of family support programs, public schools have played a large and increasing role in their early development and subsequent expansion. Schools' current involvement dates back to the 1960s and that decade's concern for providing equal educational opportunity for poor children through the jump start of early childhood intervention. The Brookline Early Education Project (BEEP), a research and demonstration program developed by the Brookline Public Schools in the early 1970s, is illustrative of more comprehensive and continuous school efforts to support and educate parents to promote their young children's early school readiness and success (Hauser-Cram, 1991). BEEP provided monthly home visits, health and social service information, and referral services during the child's first three years, and then provided prekindergarten education. In the early 1980s, Missouri adapted the BEEP model for its statewide Parents as Teachers program. Many other districts nationwide, motivated by concerns about the growing numbers of children who seemed unprepared to succeed in kindergarten and elementary school, have since developed parent education and support programs.

## PRINCIPLES AND PRACTICES OF FAMILY SUPPORT

A set of core principles and practices form the standards for assessing whether policies, procedures, and activities are family supportive (Dunst, 1995; Weiss and Halpern, 1988). These principles include the following:

- Recognition that all families need support.

- A focus on promoting parenting competencies rather than diagnosing dysfunction.

- Communication of child development information in a context of respect for cultural values and preferences, and building on the strengths of families to care for their children.

- A developmental approach that provides opportunities for participants to enhance their personal growth, their parenting roles, and their contributions to the program and the community.

- Commitment to promote and strengthen informal support networks among families and to help families cope with extrafamilial factors that impinge on parenting.

Family support practices are characterized by the following features:

- Participation is voluntary.

- Services are flexible, responsive, and individualized.

- Staff and parents relate to each other as partners and equals.

- Parents have a voice in program policies and operations.

- Parent-to-parent networking and support are encouraged.

- Parenting support comes from multiple sources, from family members, volunteers, paraprofessionals, and other community resources or services.

As more and more family support programs for young children and families were being created in public schools, some critics argued that these programs would not function well with families or flourish under school sponsorship. Family support programs, they felt, were based on core principles and practices that were not commonly found in schools—specifically, partnerships with parents and the capacity to work with non-school organizations on behalf of families. Skeptics believed schools were rigid, bureaucratic, and averse to parent involvement to support programs so contrary to their nature and organizational culture. Even some proponents interested in making family support more widely available suggested that most school districts would never extend their services down to early childhood and outward to work with parents. Therefore, family support advocates would be wise to look elsewhere for organizational and fiscal support for their programs.

Others, including key policy makers and educational organizations, argued that parenting education and support were critical to school reform and ultimately to improved school outcomes. President Bush and then-Governor Bill Clinton, for example, formulated the ingredients necessary to achieve National Education Goal One—that by the year 2000, all children in America will start school ready to learn—to include parent education as well as early childhood education in the preschool years (U.S. Department of Education, Office of Elementary and Secondary Education, June, 1991). The Council of Chief State School Officers (1989) and the National Association of State Boards of Education (1991) also issued a series of policy reports recommending to their members and a wider national audience the development of early childhood family support and education programs within the context of school.

Given this emerging controversy about the widespread feasibility and viability of schools as one possible and substantial home for early

---

### EXAMPLES OF FAMILY SUPPORT PROGRAMS

#### Child Development
#### Programs of the Pomona Unified School District

The Child Development Program (CDP) is a districtwide initiative that provides comprehensive, high-quality, affordable child care and developmentally appropriate programs that serve a multicultural population: 35% of participants are Latino, 35% are African-American, 25% are white, and 5% are Asian-American. The program offers a range of child care and preschool programs, including two state preschool programs, a teenage parenting and infant daycare program, respite child care, and latchkey programs. Many of these programs also offer parent support meetings, opportunities for parent involvement, financial subsidies for child care, referrals to counseling services, and parent education classes.

#### Parents as Teachers Program

The Parents as Teachers program is a national program model that began in Missouri and is now being replicated and adapted across the country. As in other sites, the program in Hollister, a rural community in Missouri, promotes the parents' role as their children's first teachers by cultivating positive relationships between parents and parent educators. Parent educators make home visits to families on a monthly basis, during which they encourage positive interactions between parent and child and offer suggestions for activities that build on household resources. The Hollister program also provides a drop-in center, toy lending, parent support meetings, developmental screening, GED classes, and child care referrals.

---

childhood family support programs, the Harvard Family Research Project began conducting a series of related studies about school-affiliated family support programs in order to address three questions:

1) What kinds of programs are schools starting in order to work with parents of children from birth to age six to promote child development?

2) What can pioneering programs teach us about the challenges of developing and implementing these programs in conjunction with public schools?

3) Can schools link and work with other community services in order to develop more comprehensive services to strengthen and support families with young children?

To answer these questions and produce this as well as other related publications, we first conducted an exploratory national survey of school-affiliated programs. We asked a range of educators to nominate candidates and located over 120 programs across the country. Our follow

---

**AVANCE FAMILY SUPPORT AND EDUCATION PROGRAM**

Located in San Antonio, Texas, Avance serves a predominantly Hispanic population in a low-income community with high rates of unemployment, dropout, and teen pregnancy. The Avance program aims to foster parents' personal development and parenting skills through home visits, parent support groups, job placement assistance, and a variety of parenting, ESL, and GED classes. When necessary, the program also provides transportation, child care, counseling, and social service referrals.

---

up showed that 77 of them met the criteria of an operational program with a substantial parent education and support component for families with children between birth and age six. Each of these programs responded to a mail questionnaire and one or more staff members participated in a telephone interview about program development and implementation. We used the information gathered as the basis for conclusions in the analytical overview preceding the individual program profiles in this resource guide as well as other related publications (Weiss, 1988; 1989; 1990; Lopez & Hochberg, 1993; Harvard Family Research Project, 1994; Shartrand, Kreider, & Erickson-Warfield, 1994). We conducted short telephone interviews in 1993-1994 to confirm that each program was still operational and learned that four had closed due to budget cuts.

**What Information Does *Raising Our Future* Contain?**

*Raising Our Future* presents a national resource guide that characterizes the genre of programs being implemented in schools today to serve families with young children, from preschool to the early elementary grades. Nine chapters roughly plot a continuum of programs, from those that are relatively self-contained to those that are more comprehensive and interconnected to the school and broader community.

There are between six and eleven profiles contained in each chapter. A total of 73 profiles describe the array of service arrangements under school sponsorship and provide detailed information on a set of operational features such as services, curriculum, staffing, and funding. Taken together, they enrich our understanding of the key ingredients in building the capacity of schools to sponsor family support programs.

```
┌─────────────────────────────────────────────────────────────┐
│                    A CONTINUUM OF PROGRAMS                    │
│                                                              │
│       The 73 programs in Raising Our Future are roughly organized │
│    along a continuum that ranges from relatively self-contained programs │
│    to more comprehensive interconnected initiatives. The nine chapters │
│    are:                                                       │
│                                                              │
│       Chapter 1     Preschool and Early Childhood Programs with Parent Involvement │
│                                                              │
│       Chapter 2     Support for Special Needs Children and Their Parents │
│                                                              │
│       Chapter 3     Parent-School Partnerships for School Readiness and Enrichment │
│                                                              │
│       Chapter 4     Home Visits for Parenting Support         │
│                                                              │
│       Chapter 5     School- and Center-based Parenting Support │
│                                                              │
│       Chapter 6     Teens, Parenthood, and Child Development   │
│                                                              │
│       Chapter 7     Family Literacy and Intergenerational Skill Development │
│                                                              │
│       Chapter 8     Family Resource Centers                   │
│                                                              │
│       Chapter 9     Family, School, Community Partnerships     │
│                                                              │
└─────────────────────────────────────────────────────────────┘
```

## How to Read
## *Raising Our Future*

*Raising Our Future* is organized so that it can be read along four pathways:

**1. Straight through from cover to cover.** Reading through the book from cover to cover gives you a clear idea of how programs evolve, and the range and scope of services family support programs deliver in a wide variety of communities. A one-page overview begins each chapter and describes in general terms the programs' goals, services and development. This is followed by a "Programs in Brief" section that provides a quick overview of the programs profiled in that chapter, and serves as an easy-to-read mini-index.

**2. By chapter topic.** Readers can pick a chapter topic that fits the needs of their community, for example, Chapter 4: Home Visits for Parenting Support. The profiles in this chapter provide examples of programs designed with similar goals in mind, working in different contexts with a diverse range of resources. Readers can compare how programs handle implementation factors such as funding, curriculum, relationship to the schools, administrative structure, community links, and level of parent involvement.

**3. By program component.** Each profile is presented in the same format. Included are concise descriptions of a program's philosophy, services, funding, staff and budget, among other program elements. A reader could, for example, read the "parent involvement" section in each profile to get ideas about the different strategies used by each program. A reader could also study sections across profiles for ideas in areas such as "evaluation" or "outreach," and then choose the approaches that make sense for them.

**4. Start with the listings.** The listings organize *Raising Our Future*'s contents by state of operation, administrative relationship to the school district, funding sources, demographic characteristics of participants, program services, and other variables. Using the listings, readers can search by terms that describe aspects of each program, such as "urban," for those operating in urban areas, or "at risk," for programs that serve disadvantaged communities. For example, although Chapter 4 contains profiles of six programs for which home visits are a primary service, many programs in other chapters also offer home visitation services; a complete list of these programs can be found by looking up "home visits" in the index. An alphabetical listing of all 73 programs is also included.

*Raising Our Future* was written to share information about the relationship between families, schools and communities rather than to provide an endorsement of specific programs. The book celebrates the strength and innovation of family support and education programs. It also provides honest information about how and why initiatives work, or don't, and suggests the future directions in which family support programs will grow. All of the programs in *Raising Our Future* have provided a contact name and address, so that readers can request further information directly from the programs, or begin a dialogue about family support. In addition to the profiles in the body of the text, we have compiled a comprehensive Resource List at the end of the book, which presents descriptions of materials, reports, and curricula and how to order them. It is Harvard Family Research Project's hope and expectation that readers and programs will network with each other, crafting new relationships that offer opportunities for mutual learning and strong bases of support.

# OVERVIEW

As schools begin to realize the importance of family partnerships for children's school success, making the transition from theory into practice will involve building the capacity for family support and involvement. This overview has four sections:

I **Research on family processes and family-oriented interventions.** Presents why families are important to children's learning, what research tells us about family support programs to date, and key lessons from the 73 programs studied for this guide.

II **New frontline practices: Building relationships with families and the community.** Looks at how programs have forged ties with various constituencies and describes practical and necessary strategies.

III **Organizational capacity: Resources, evaluation, and collaboration.** Like the previous section, also relates what successful programs have done in these areas.

IV **Continuing challenges and opportunities for action.** Discusses whether schools are appropriate settings for family support programs and the advantages of sponsoring programs, looks at the ideal family support program model, and presents lessons from the programs profiled pertinent to program implementation including leadership and funding challenges.

This overview shares some of the many ideas that emerged from our interviews with program personnel. We believe the advice and experiences shared here will support the evolution of family support programs from a movement to a status quo component of schools, with potential to have a positive impact on children, families, schools, and the greater community.

# I. Research on Family Processes and Family-Oriented Interventions

Families matter. Over two decades of research indicate that families make a significant impact on children's learning. Studies have shown that "family processes"—parents' beliefs, attitudes, and practices—aid young children's later school performance. These processes fall into three broad categories:

- Recognizing the child as an active learner.

- Providing stimulating learning experiences, especially around language development.

- Matching teaching styles to the child's abilities, interests, and situations.

Additionally, certain features of the home environment ease children's adjustment to the rhythms of school life while also being conducive to home learning. Homes in which space and time are well-organized enable children to do well in school, for instance having routines for chores, meals, and bedtimes; monitoring television viewing; and providing time and space for quiet learning (Eastman, 1988). Because parental attitudes and behaviors are woven into multiple parent-child interactions, it is difficult to single out any one family process that can influence children's school-related abilities more than others (Powell, 1991). Rather, the overall quality of family practices acts as a catalyst and support for children's school success.

---

### Critical Parenting Features that Promote Children's Development

Douglas Powell (1991:ii) identified nine critical parenting features that include: (1) a view of child development as a complex process that involves the child as an active contributor to development; (2) a realistic, in-depth understanding of the child's abilities and interests; (3) asking the child questions that stimulate thinking and problem solving; (4) matching parental teaching styles to situations and the child's developmental level; (5) strengthening literacy experiences within routine family interactions; (6) making reading and writing materials accessible, limiting television, and visiting libraries and museums; (7) reading to the child in ways that encourage the child to respond to parent questions about the story; (8) encouraging the child to manipulate a variety of stimulating objects; and (9) a warm, responsive parenting style that also accepts the child's ideas and feelings.

---

Family interactions are critical to language development. In their early years, children learn informally and through everyday social exchanges with others (Scott-Jones, 1994). Language and literacy skills emerge through routine exposure to words, commands, stories, and conversations. Parents who use more advanced levels and styles of language and thought help their children achieve higher levels of literacy (Snow, 1987; 1993). These processes take the forms of a family's use of sophisticated vocabulary; talking and listening that encourage explanation (e.g., why people do things or how things work); and storytelling that involves narrative talk by the child (e.g., how a child feels about the story or what the child thinks will happen next). Because language is the primary means employed by formal education, children's language development is crucial to their school success (Ramey, Ramey, Gaines, & Blair, n.d.).

Children's adaptation to school depends not only on developing their cognitive skills but also on being able to get along with others. Nurturant parenting provides an emotionally secure base from which a child can explore the social world and develop friendships. By establishing routines, modelling acceptable behaviors, teaching children to control outbursts, and encouraging them to share with others, parents foster children's capacity to form positive social relationships with adults and peers, and to avoid behavior harmful to themselves and others (Carnegie Corporation of New York, 1994). Furthermore, parents play a direct role in designing and monitoring children's peer relationships. Studies have shown that children whose parents initiate peer contacts and play groups are more likely to develop the communication and social skills that prepare them for group oriented settings such as child care centers and schools (Ladd & Coleman, 1993). By exposing children to community settings such as libraries, parks, and recreational centers where they can spontaneously interact with peers, parents help children adapt to new situations. One outcome of such exposure is smoother transition to and from kindergarten (Ladd & Coleman, 1993).

Successful parenting styles and practices have been found among families with different socioeconomic and cultural backgrounds (Henderson & Berla, 1994). Studies have found that many low-income families provide the high expectations and stimulating literacy experiences that enable children to achieve in school (Snow, 1987), and that working-class African-American mothers of high achieving children play a supportive role in their children's learning (Scott-Jones, 1987). Furthermore, Latino parents from low socioeconomic backgrounds place a high value on formal education and use a variety of strategies to promote their children's learning and development. These strategies include stressing the importance of formal education and studying (Reese, Gallimore, Goldenberg, & Balzano, 1994); teaching children appropriate school behavior (Hidalgo, 1995); protecting children by monitoring their friendships and limiting the areas in which they play (Hidalgo, 1995); fostering open and nurturing relationships with children (Hidalgo, 1995); and helping children with homework (Reese, Gallimore, Goldenberg, & Balzano, 1994; Hidalgo, 1995).

Other studies, however, have highlighted a lack of congruence between how children are raised at home and the expectations they face at school, which can inhibit children's academic success in mainstream schools (Brice Heath, 1984; Swap, 1990; Wong Fillmore, 1990). This lack of congruence can be lessened if schools collaborate with parents, keeping them informed of their children's progress and offering advice and support in the context of respect and partnership. When such collaborations exist, parents are likely to develop the confidence to practice strategies that are conducive to children's school success (Edwards, 1995; Henderson & Berla, 1994).

Just as the child develops in a family context, the family is also influenced by social stresses and supports in its community (Bronfenbrenner, 1986). McLoyd (1990), for example, has outlined a model depicting the ways in which poverty creates stresses in the family that in turn inhibit nurturant parenting. Other studies show that social supports and community resources mediate the negative effects of poverty and help promote parenting practices related to children's healthy development (Gabarino & Sherman, 1980; Hashima & Amato, 1994). These findings suggest that programs that seek to change parenting practices among highly stressed families must provide, in addition to information about parenting and child development, a wide range of support services.

A growing body of research suggests that family processes more than socioeconomic status are correlated with children's school success (Eastman, 1988; Henderson & Berla, 1994). As we have seen, these processes include a stimulating home environment, high but realistic expectations for children's achievement, and parental involvement in children's education at school and in the community. The family's primacy does not absolve schools from providing quality learning environments and supporting parents in their childrearing functions. Rather, the compelling evidence of the family's all-important role in fostering children's learning offers schools a strategic opportunity to develop relevant and meaningful home-school partnerships.

## What We Know About Family Support Programs

Evidence from the evaluations of research and demonstration projects and a handful of community-based programs form the basis of what we know about family support programs. While we must be cautious about generalizing from a few evaluated models to the field as a whole (Weiss, 1994), certain common patterns and themes emerge from studies of family-focused interventions.

***Home visits, as a means of providing parents with child development information and social support during their children's earliest years, can have beneficial outcomes for children and their parents.*** The Parents as Teachers (Missouri) program, sponsored by school districts, has succeeded in promoting children's intellectual, language and social development, and identifying "at-risk" conditions that were corrected or improved over time (Pfannestiel & Selzer, 1985). Parents benefited in terms of increased knowledge of childrearing practices and the school districts also gained in terms of parents' positive regard of the school's outreach and responsiveness to young children.

The impact of home visiting is related to participant and program characteristics. In an extensive literature review, Olds and Kitzman (1993) found that some parents were more likely to benefit than others: home visiting had positive outcomes with parents with preterm or low birth weight infants, families with disabled and chronically ill children, and poor, unmarried, teenage parents and their children. These patterns led the authors to suggest that parents who perceived that they or their children were vulnerable and needed help were more likely to benefit from home visiting. Additionally, they cited important program characteristics that influenced the quality of home visiting programs. Programs that provided comprehensive services, were intensive and continuous over time, and were staffed by well-trained professionals were more likely to demonstrate success.

***Programs that offer direct services to children in addition to parenting sessions have a positive impact on children's cognitive development.*** In a review of early education interventions for disadvantaged children from birth to age three, Wasik and Karweit (1994) concluded that demonstration programs that worked intensively with children and with parents were the most effective in promoting children's early school success, the latter measured by IQ and language proficiency scores, special education referrals, and retention data. Effective programs, they found, provided organized child care experiences for children. Their staff met weekly or semiweekly with parents for more than a year to provide parenting sessions and sometimes job training. Furthermore, programs that provided continuity in elementary school were also more likely to maintain early gains and help disadvantaged children from falling behind.

***Family support programs are necessary but not sufficient for disadvantaged families*** (Weiss, 1993). A family's economic circumstances and access to formal and informal social supports also can affect parenting styles, family functioning, and child development (Bronfenbrenner, 1986). Thus, family support programs are interdependent with the larger community. Their effectiveness, in part, depends on the availability and quality of other resources that can support and enrich family life, such as child care and afterschool programs, recreational activities, and cultural events; services that can meet the needs and concerns of children and families, including housing, jobs, and health care; and, the capacity of programs to connect with these resources (Weiss, 1993). No single program can ensure that all children have the opportunity to build resiliency and reach their full potential. Family support programs are more likely to make a lasting impact when they are part of a broad effort to build a "village" of support and protection for all children and families. As one of the few interventions that connects with families during a child's earliest years, family support plays an especially important role in fostering positive links among families, schools, and communities.

***Programs that have a strong impact on children's development are rich and complex, and are designed to individualize support and services.*** Based on 25 years of scientific research, Ramey and Ramey (1992) concluded that effective programs:

- Begin earlier and continue longer.

- Interact more frequently with participants.

- Provide direct learning experiences to children.

- Offer comprehensive services to children and families.

- Tailor services to match children's learning styles and risk conditions.

- Provide continuing supports as children make the transition into elementary school.

- Build upon cultural beliefs, traditions, and practices.

***School-sponsored parenting programs must be open to broader changes in organization and culture.*** Studies show that home-school partnerships that make a difference in children's school achievement are "comprehensive, long-lasting, and well-planned" (Henderson, 1987:9). While programs for low-income families help reduce low achievement, they still do not boost children's performance to the levels of middle-class children (Henderson, 1987; 1994). This suggests that parent involvement programs alone are not enough to counteract the negative influences of disadvantaged communities. An alternative model to more narrowly focused parent involvement would embed it in efforts to change the political, educational, and social climate of schools. This systemic approach calls for a commitment to organize parents to work collectively on behalf of children and to restructure schools around democratic decision making (Comer, 1980; Cochran & Dean, 1991; Fine, 1993); a comprehensive curriculum revision that makes connections with students and their families, communities, and culture (Swap, 1990); and linking schools more effectively with community resources (Jehl & Kirst, 1992).

Family processes make an impact on children's school achievement and this is good reason for schools to sponsor family support programs. However, the findings from intervention studies also indicate the importance of program implementation processes and matching intervention strategies to the characteristics of the populations being served. The United States is a pluralistic and democratic society, and family programs that have flexible approaches and encourage parental input and partnerships stand better chances of success. At the same time, programs that are high in quality, meaning that they are intensive, continuous, and comprehensive, do have an impact on children and families. This is a challenge for schools and their community partners as they make decisions about the allocation of resources. Careful thought will be required to employ the best possible intervention strategies to meet community needs and also build on its assets.

## Lessons for the Future

The 73 programs took multiple pathways to supporting families. We questioned program personnel about issues such as planning, forming goals and objectives, collaboration, funding, and staffing. Despite variation in how they managed implementation issues a common set of lessons emerged. They are as follows:

*Involve multiple stakeholders in the planning process*. Giving voice to a range of perspectives during the planning stage ensures that critical information or viewpoints are not left out of program design. This will also engender support from a broad array of constituents.

*Base program design on community resources and concerns.* Having and using data are key to developing a program that is responsive to community conditions. Know the services your community already offers and find out what the specific needs and interests are for your participants.

*Build trusting relationships with children and families.* Continuous outreach, patience, flexibility, building on family strengths, and empowering families to make their own choices are important strategies for building trusting relationships.

*Involve parents in a variety of roles.* Providing a range of participation options for parents, from receiving services to advisory board membership, facilitates reciprocal relationships with parents and allows them to contribute on multiple levels.

***Strive to build and maintain community partnerships***. Working closely with the community through its service agencies, local associations, volunteers, and businesses is a necessity. Though competition and difficulty in operating policies and procedures can pose problems, persistent outreach can establish cooperative rather than competitive relationships.

***Hire and support caring, well-trained staff.*** Good programs are dependent on a good staff: people who are dedicated, flexible, creative, and supported. Professional development is essential to support the staff and strengthen service delivery.

***Involve public school teachers with programs.*** The involvement and support of teachers can be critical to program success. When teachers recognize the importance of home and community for the child, work more closely with parents and families, exchange information with family support staff, and build positive parent-teacher relationships, they help to ensure that early gains are not lost once children enter kindergarten.

***Evaluate to strengthen the program and build support.*** To be truly useful, evaluation has to serve the needs of local programs as well as their sponsors. Evaluations that help improve the quality of a program's work and illuminate the process of development among children and parents, are valued highly by directors and funders.

***Raise funds broadly, continuously, and creatively.*** A creative, strategic, and persistent funding plan is key to program survival and expansion. Engaging in networking and advocacy activities also helps to ensure continued funding of family-focused programs.

# II. New Frontline Practices: Building Relationships with Families and the Community

Family support programs offer a new service ideology of working with children and families, embodying a set of principles that govern relationships with families and the broader community. Foremost is the belief that all parents have strengths and that these healthy traits form the foundation on which to build parenting skills. Participants in these programs, often parents and sometimes grandparents, engage in an interactive learning process. Staff members respect parents' personal knowledge and act as facilitators rather than experts, encouraging parents to formulate and pursue their personal and parenting goals. They do extensive outreach to recruit participants, and also link with other community agencies for information, referrals, enrichment activities, and joint services. Below, we discuss five frontline practices that build relationships with families and the community, which emerged from examining the 73 programs in *Raising Our Future*:

- Planning integrates the perspectives of multiple stakeholders.

- Program design is based on community resources and concerns.

- Goals and objectives focus on building parenting skills and offering support.

- Building trusting relationships with children and families is central.

- Parents play many roles in family support programs.

Planning Integrates the Perspectives of Multiple Stakeholders

The origin and development of the programs surveyed followed a common start-up path comprised of first responding to an opportunity, mandate, or community need, and then forming a group or task force to plan the program. A striking pattern across programs was the extent of partnerships that were key to the start-up phase. Most planning teams involved a number of stakeholders, including, but not limited to, school personnel, community members, and social service providers (see Table 1).

| TABLE 1. STAKEHOLDERS INVOLVED IN PLANNING AND DESIGN | | |
|---|---|---|
| **School Personnel** | **Community Agencies** | **Other** |
| School Committee Members | Extension Services | Community Residents |
| Superintendents | Health departments | State education representatives |
| Principals | Community colleges | |
| Teachers | Special councils | |
| | Urban Leagues | |
| | Social service providers | |

Each group brings to the planning process its own perspective and strengths that can influence how the group collaborates, perceives the community, and formulates program goals. For example, personnel employed by the community often have the most insight about how to serve and work with residents, while community residents can make programs more responsive, add a "bottom up" perspective to program design, and foster community ownership over the program once it begins.

## Program Design Is Based on Community Resources and Concerns

Gathering information and understanding its implications are vital steps for developing a program that matches community needs and fills gaps in community services. Schools determined their communities' needs by various means: 9 programs used statistical or demographic data, 35 programs considered the perceptions of professionals working directly or indirectly with children or families, and 10 programs conducted needs assessments by collecting information on community organizations and community members.

Policy makers and practitioners often argue that putting family support programs under school auspices minimizes stigma because education is perceived as something needed by everyone, not simply high-risk families. However, based on needs assessments and limited resources, programs often are forced to focus their efforts on those with the greatest needs. Of the 73 programs profiled, 26 had "at-risk" criteria for children and 25 for parents.

Several strategies were used in conducting community needs assessments. Some of these approaches not only collected useful information, but offered programs the opportunities to network with other agencies, garner community support, and build ownership over the program. For example:

- Special task forces hired outside consultants.

- Community members canvassed door-to-door.

- Home visitors asked their clients about their needs.

- Schools distributed questionnaires to parents.

Programs have different approaches to assessing community needs and interests, each of which offers its own benefits and limitations. Demographic data can give a sense of the "big picture" problems in a community, and can help shape a more formal needs assessment. However, this approach does not often elicit the strengths, interests, and concerns of the community, which are essential ingredients in successful program planning. Asking professionals who work in the community about what services are and are not being met can also provide useful information.

In sum, most programs agreed that there was no substitute for directly asking community members about their needs and interests. Doing so will make them feel valued, create a sense of ownership over the program, and create a desire to participate once it has begun. However a community's concerns are assessed, the combined experience of the programs profiled is clear: Know the services your community already offers and find out what your participants' specific needs and interests are.

## CONDUCTING A NEEDS ASSESSMENT:

## Early Developmental Awareness Project (EDAP)

For their needs assessment, EDAP in Mequon, Wisconsin, interviewed community organizations as well as potential program participants. To find out about parents' needs and interests, the program did a telephone survey, aided by PTA volunteers, in which parents were asked about their interests and convenient times to attend sessions and workshops. The program also interviewed people at the Children's Hospital, public and social service agencies, kindergarten teachers, and other childhood service providers to find out what services already existed and to create a resource and referral file for their program. In this case, the needs assessment achieved several goals. First, it helped the program to make contacts with the community of service providers and parents. Second, it was a way to find out what other organizations were already doing so services would not be duplicated and referrals could be made to those organizations in the future. Finally, it was a vehicle to keep the program aligned with parents' needs and interests.

---

### TABLE 2.   COMMON GOALS ARTICULATED BY PROGRAMS

**Ensuring that families' basic needs are met.** This included providing quality child care services, health and nutrition services, a sense of safety, transportation to and from the program, and economic assistance. This assured that these factors would not constitute barriers to program participation or successful outcomes.

**Improving child development, behavior, and achievement.** Programs worked to improve children's academic achievement and school readiness, self-confidence, socialization skills, and behavior.

**Increasing parent involvement in school.** Increasing the level of parent involvement in schools aimed to improve children's academic achievement, alleviate discipline problems, and foster parents' ability to teach and advocate on behalf of their children. Programs informed parents about what schools should be providing; tried to reduce parents' negative feelings about schools and teachers; showed parents how their involvement in their children's learning can make a difference; and tried to show schools how parents could be resources.

**Improving the parent-child relationship and childrearing practices.** All programs sought to improve the parent-child relationship and promote the idea that parents are children's first and most important teachers. Services reinforced school activities at home by showing parents how to help children learn, how to provide a home learning environment, and by improving parents' confidence in their role as teacher. Building trust and enhancing communication between parent and child; increasing parents' knowledge of child development and their own child's strengths; improving childrearing practices and parenting skills all moved toward the broader goal of helping parents to better address their children's intellectual, social, and emotional needs.

**Working for prevention and early intervention.** Because family support programs are preventive in nature, many programs tried to identify potential problems and address them at the earliest possible moment to minimize, prevent, and/or correct their impact. Identifying children's developmental delays, educating parents about abuse and neglect, providing support to families under stress, preventing dropout, counseling, offering prenatal care, and identifying at-risk families were some strategies programs used.

**Improving social support and interpersonal networks.** Increasing social support for families and fostering a sense of community was another goal for programs, which was based on the premise that all parents and families need support, not only those under stress or at risk. Improving relationships among community residents, a program enhances the ability of a community to support itself, and to provide an environment conducive to child development. Program objectives included helping participants develop relationships so they can help each other during crises, making parents feel less alone by connecting them with others, and offering positive experiences for parents under stress.

**Increasing parent opportunities through skill building.** Some programs chose to improve a variety of behaviors, attitudes, and skills that are thought to have a strong influence on parenting and the home environment. Interventions to build social skills, increase parents' self-esteem, and help parents become more self-sufficient and employable, all focus on helping families improve their quality of life.

**Building Objectives Focus on Building Parenting Skills and Offering Support**

The family support programs in this book have a set of underlying assumptions and philosophies that shape the goals, objectives, and services they provide. Such philosophies are important in understanding the logic behind interventions and the positive changes that programs wish to effect in families.

The primary, overriding goal of all family support and education programs is to enhance and support the family's capacity to rear its children into healthy, productive, and responsible citizens. Since this goal can only be achieved over the long term and is difficult to measure, programs must first decide on concrete objectives and design interventions that match the specific needs and interests of their participants (see Table 2).

When deciding on a set of goals, programs must consider the needs and interests of the community to ensure that the two are consonant, or at least compatible. In a community where basic needs, such as nutrition, child care, transportation, and safety, are not being met, it will be difficult, if not impossible, to set increased parent involvement as a goal, for example. In this case, an objective will be for the family support program to become more comprehensive and link with community services to see that families' basic needs are being supported.

**Building Trusting Relationships with Children and Families Is Central**

The heart of family support programs is the web of relationships connecting staff with families, parents with children, and parents with other parents. Recurrent themes in program implementation are continuous outreach, overcoming negative images of the schools, building trusting relationships, and empowering parents. Program administrators related several useful insights for gaining a comfortable and productive rapport with participants.

***Outreach strategies are multistranded***. Outreach is seldom an easy task, which program directors confirmed. Initial recruits were parents who felt the need for information and support, and were ready to join. Program directors, however, cited the difficulty of reaching poor and isolated families, teenage parents, and minority families. Lack of transportation and child care, and parents' reluctance to leave home in unsafe neighborhoods sometimes prevented participation. Staff members adopted a broad-based strategy to reach eligible families (see Table 3). "We go into the community," says one director. "We'll go to a fast-food

| TABLE 3.  COMMON OUTREACH STRATEGIES |
|---|
| Networking with other agency personnel and providing them with information to gain referrals. |
| Using the media—local newspaper, radio and television—to publicize a program. |
| Sending out fliers, brochures and newsletters. |
| Making personal contacts by phone or home visits. |
| Making public presentations. |
| Working through the PTA and other parent groups. |
| Targeting specific age and ethnic groups for participation. |

place if parents don't want to meet us at home or come to the office." By far, a program's best recruiter was a satisfied participant. Fifty programs declared that word-of-mouth information was the single most important form of recruitment.

***The approach to working with parents is developmental.*** Programs accepted parents as they were and began a relationship from there. "Be patient, it's slow at first," advised one program director. "Have an attitude of 'What can I do to help you?' and not 'I have come to solve your problem.'" Staff members recognized that each family was at a different stage of development, and while the programs had general

---

**SUPPORTING AND EMPOWERING PARENTS**

**Jefferson County Teen Parent Program**

Lisbet Hornung offers the example of a young mother whose half-credit from the program allowed her to graduate from high school. With the support of her peers and Ms. Hornung, the woman became determined to go to college. Through participating in the program, this young parent gained the confidence to get out of an abusive relationship and is now considering counseling as a profession. Lisbet Hornung calls her an exemplary parent.

**Early Education Center**

In a recent Early Education Center newsletter, one parent of a child with multiple handicaps recounts her experience in the program over a five-year period. She writes that EEC helped her and her husband learn about their son's limits and potential in an atmosphere of encouragement and support. She learned to make informed decisions about his health and education and is happy to report that her son is now doing well in the public schools.

---

goals, the individual needs of families dictated a range of specific objectives. For example, teenage parents could choose how to receive parenting information: through attending workshops or special events, or through home visits. Only when teens felt ready for regular group sessions did they join.

In programs for children with special needs, staff members focused on helping parents realize their children's strengths. These parents often felt that their children were failures, so staff had to reassure parents, help them to recognize their children's potential, and teach them effective strategies for working with their children.

After participating in a program and seeing their children develop, parents also grow and change, and may want to focus more on their own development as parents and as individuals. Staff members had to be open-minded and encourage parents to try new directions. A director advised, "Listen to what parents say they want. Also, don't write off anything as a failure. What parents did not want two years ago, they may be ready for now. Parents change and so should your program."

*Parents often have good parenting practices
that they do not recognize.*

Staff members identified individual family strengths, told parents what they were, and encouraged them to share these practices with other parents. This has the benefit of reinforcing parents and boosting their self-esteem while helping other parents simultaneously. In fact, connecting parents to each other and building social networks are integral to these programs, and activities are designed to diminish social isolation and promote supportive relationships in the community.

*The goal is to have parents both request help
from their peers and provide help to each other.*

**Programs strive to balance helping and empowering relationships with parents in their decisions about childrearing.** A strong service orientation characterized programs, and staff goals were to help parents promote their child's development and deal with specific problems more effectively. Parents tried out games and stimulating activities with children, borrowed resources through lending libraries, and learned about children's growth and health. They learned alternative ways to discipline their children and some learned how to cope with the behaviors of children having special needs or learning disabilities. In some cases, a program's screening service was instrumental in diagnosing children with speech or hearing defects that had been treated as mental problems, thus assuaging the anxieties of parents. Typically, programs offered the following services:

- 73 included parenting and child development information.

- 63 sponsored joint activities for parents and children.

- 62 offered opportunities for parents to meet other parents.

- 62 provided information and referral to other community services.

- 52 maintained on-site parent resource libraries.

- 50 had home visiting programs.

- 50 ran health and nutrition education programs.

Staff members were dedicated to helping families, some spending extra time visiting parents, finding out what children needed, providing transportation to the welfare office or medical appointments, and helping homeless families find housing. They stated that for good parenting skills to take root, basic needs must be met and that parents must be referred to the appropriate sources.

Staff members were also conscious that their mission was to empower parents, not to make them dependent on programs. They faced the challenge of setting boundaries and determining the extent of their involvement with families. While some parents needed a lot of guidance and support in the beginning, the goal was always to help parents advocate for their children. Staff informed parents of alternatives, but parents were encouraged to make their own choices, thereby helping parents develop their self-confidence and decision-making skills.

***Programs give careful attention to curriculum development.*** Many programs combined nationally validated training and curriculum packages with in-house creations. This "eclectic approach" was reported by 27 programs that used multiple curricula and by 18 programs that combined a national model with in-house innovations. The programs were more likely to create their own parenting curricula (23 programs) than curricula for children (15 programs). For the early childhood component, program directors chose curricula that were "developmentally appropriate," "enriching," and "experiential." Teachers emphasized that curricula should not be "watered down kindergarten." Some turned to the *High/Scope* curriculum and guidelines of the National Association for the Education of Young Children.

For the parenting component, the directors favored curricula that maximized parent interaction and provided choices in parenting techniques. The most common program models were *Systematic Training for Effective Parenting* (STEP), *Active Parenting,* and Missouri's *Parents as Teachers* (PAT); others used models developed by state departments of education. However, these models were often modified and supplemented with locally produced materials. Staff revised curricula to match the daily practical experiences of parents with diverse backgrounds. For example, a family literacy program for migrants (many of whom could not read) used wordless readers so they could tell stories with their children and encourage the development of children's verbal skills.

Program directors felt that flexibility was the key to maintaining parent interest. For parents who had not finished school and felt intimidated by the classroom, programs minimized negative experiences by making parenting topics and titles accessible, rather than dauntingly intellectual. Sessions avoided lectures and devoted time to questions and

| TABLE 4   PARENTS' ROLES |
| --- |
| **Parent as customer.** A parent's role was most frequently as a participant in or a client of the programs. In this role, some parents were asked to give feedback on their own needs, interests, and assessment of how well the program was serving them. Though this was a central role, it offered parents the least amount of direct control over the program. |
| **Parent as supporter.** Parents supported programs in many ways, including soliciting and contributing funding and resources, donating materials and resources, assisting with grant proposals, and holding fundraisers. Parents were cited as the best program recruiters, and participated in conducting needs assessments. Many other supplemental activities were carried out by parent volunteers as well. |
| **Parent as staff member.** Parents both volunteered and were paid to deliver program services at the staff level. Some programs hired parent participants as aids, assistants, or teachers, and in one case, as a parent coordinator. Others had parents manage entire programs or aspects of programs. Parents were sometimes given the opportunity to attend staff inservice training on topics such as leadership, group facilitation, legal rights, and parenting education. |
| **Parent as advocate.** Parents sometimes exerted their influence in the political arena when program funding was threatened. They lobbied the board of education, wrote letters of support for federal grants, wrote to their state legislators on behalf of the program, and formed advocacy groups to represent their own needs and interests. |
| **Parent as initiator, planner, and decision maker.** In this role, parents exerted the most control over program operations. They initiated, planned, and designed programs or services, or assisted program personnel in doing so. Some parents initiated their own parent groups to network with and support each other. For example, one group of parents formed a support group to help each other with babysitting and shopping. |

answers. Many programs had parents help set the agenda for parenting sessions and suggest topics for discussion.

**Parents Play Many Roles in Family Support Programs**

Parents played a variety of roles in the programs we surveyed, ranging from participation to program design and implementation (see Table 4). Programs often had a range of options for parents that built on their skills, preferences, and needs. Some federally funded programs, such as Chapter 1 and Head Start, mandated certain types of parent participation.

In thinking about parent participation, it is important to consider how much voice, independence, and power parents have in the various roles that are offered to them. Will parents have an impact on program implementation? If so, will they *feel* this impact? Most importantly, do the options facilitate a reciprocal relationship between parent and program? The more "power" parents feel they have in their roles, the more ownership they will feel over the program, and the more supportive of the program they will be.

# III. Organizational Capacity: Resources, Evaluation, and Collaboration

Family support programs must develop the organizational capacity to work effectively with families, schools, and communities. Although they are part of school systems, the programs enjoy a degree of autonomy and localized decision making. Program directors have the discretion to build effective service delivery through staffing, training, fundraising, monitoring and evaluation, and collaboration with community agencies. However, they must also network, communicate, and coordinate their work with other school units so that family support becomes integral to the school, rather than just an add-on program.

The family support programs we studied were fairly new additions to their districts. Program directors hired their staff and arranged staff training, negotiated for space, developed community partnerships, and used information, especially from evaluations, to justify continuing support. What came across in this survey of programs was the importance of staff leadership to overcome challenges of the start-up phase. While school auspices were advantageous in terms of gaining access to school resources and expertise, these benefits did not come automatically, but required negotiation and compromise. Specifically, our analysis of programs revealed that:

- Quality programs depend on caring staff who are well-trained and supported.

- Collaboration between teachers and programs is mutually beneficial.

- Finding available and accessible facilities poses a challenge.

- Evaluation can strengthen and build support for programs.

- Forming community partnerships is difficult, but well worth the effort.

- Because programs operate in a climate of fiscal uncertainty, successful fundraising is broad-based and continuous.

**Quality Programs Depend on Caring Staff Who Are Well-Trained and Supported**

Good programs depend on good staffs: people who are dedicated, flexible, creative, and supported. Knowing how to attract, train, pay, and retain a qualified staff for the long term—staff qualified to work with young children and adults—is also important for school districts and states that sponsor family support programs. Thus, funding for staffing positions was a major issue. In some programs, staff members became part of the regular school staff and were on its salary scale; in programs that were part of community education, staff members were paid an hourly wage that accrued to an annual income that was less than that of a starting teacher in the K-12 system. Some staff members, especially paraprofessionals, were poorly paid and received no benefits — 21 programs did not extend benefits to low-level and paraprofessional staff. When directors were asked, "What changes would you make in your program if additional funds became available?" 33 responded in terms of staff-related issues. They wanted to make part-time positions full-time, increase the number of staff, raise salaries, and hire consultants for specialized issues.

There was a wide range of personnel in these family support programs, including coordinators, teachers, school nurses, speech therapists, parent educators, and clerical staff. Of the 73 programs, 52 employed paraprofessionals, most of whom were parent educators.

While personnel were hired based on their education and experience, program directors also rated personal qualities highly. Building relationships is central to family support programs, and strong interpersonal skills was a preferred qualification. One early childhood program director summed it up: "Your staff should have the ability to relate to children from birth to age five, and to relate to every type of parent from the eager to the intimidated, abused, and insecure parent." Directors often looked for those who had parenting experience, sensitivity to other cultures, and a belief that parents can make a difference in their children's educational success. Qualities that came up time and again were "flexible," "nonjudgmental," "understanding," "caring," and the ability to work as a team.

Professional development is essential to support staff and strengthen service delivery. Training programs evolved hand-in-hand with the experiences of staff members and the needs they identified. Often, preservice training on the substantive components of child development and family support was followed by inservice training on recruitment and group process skills. Multicultural training was also becoming part of the agenda as was training to work with service providers from other professions. As staff members became more adept in their work, inservice training focused on specialized issues—working with parents who have drug addictions or with children who have certain behavioral problems.

Collaboration between
Teachers and Programs Is
Mutually Beneficial

The role of public school teachers in family support programs varied. While some had little or no teacher involvement, many more had teachers who were integral to program operations. These teachers communicated regularly with family support staff; participated in program planning, administration, and advisory boards; presented workshops to parents; and made home visits to families.

The involvement and support of teachers can be critical to program success. Because teachers are often the most frequent contact person between schools and families, more attention should be given to how they can reinforce a family supportive ethos. Teachers can help ensure that early efforts are not lost once children enter kindergarten by reaffirming the importance of family and community to the child, working more closely with parents and families, exchanging information with family support staff, and building positive parent-teacher relationships.

Unfortunately, working with families and collaborating with other professionals is not an area in which most teachers have received instruction. Teachers need information, formal experiences, and support in these endeavors. Most school administrators, teachers, parents and teacher educators agree that teachers need to be prepared for work with parents (Williams, 1992). Teachers themselves often admit that they do not always know the best ways to involve parents in school (Bempechat, 1990). Teachers need to have a new set of skills, knowledge, and attitudes if they are to work more closely with families and communities. Currently, very few preservice teacher education programs prepare teachers for this challenge (Williams, 1992; Shartrand, Kreider, and Warfield, 1994).

At the inservice level, family support programs can play an important role. Their expertise in collaborating with other agencies, working with families, and building reciprocal, empowering relationships with them can be passed on. Such training should focus on the benefits of having parents who are involved in their children's education and supportive of school practices, showing that work with families can, in the long run, make the work of teachers and schools easier and more successful.

To build teachers' capacity to work with families, both preservice and inservice training efforts can focus on the following ideas: bridging gaps between home and school culture; assuming the best intentions on the part of parents; helping families with limited financial resources and support networks to meet their basic needs; empowering families by providing them with encouragement, respect, and a voice in decision making; and finally, providing opportunities to build "social capital" by engaging individuals in the life of the school, building trust among teachers and parents, and agreeing on mutual values and expectations for children.

Finding Available and Accessible Facilities Poses a Challenge

| DO's and DON'Ts for Program Success | |
|---|---|
| **DO's** | **DON'Ts** |
| 1) **DO** make facilities welcoming to parents; rethink old rules that may pose barriers to parental participation. | 1) **DON'T** impose unreasonable demands on parents, teachers, or staff members. |
| 2) **DO** prepare teachers and other school personnel to welcome and communicate with families. | 2) **DON'T** forget to involve custodial, secretarial, and other school support staff in training sessions. |
| 3) **DO** involve participants at every level, from decision making to community outreach. | 3) **DON'T** impose requirements or mandates that are likely to generate opposition from parents, teachers, or school personnel. |
| 4) **DO** offer a range of services for participation, recognizing that certain groups will prefer certain types of involvement. | 4) **DON'T** forget to involve fathers and extended family members, such as grandparents. |
| 5) **DO** choose curricula carefully; adapt whenever possible to meet the specific needs of your community. | 5) **DON'T** overload parents with too much information. |
| 6) **DO** be sensitive to cultural backgrounds of all families. | 6) **DON'T** use one strategy to involve everyone. |
| 7) **DO** keep attuned to changing family needs and preferences. | 7) **DON'T** assume that an established program cannot be improved. |
| 8) **DO** work collaboratively with community resources and agencies. | 8) **DON'T** expect results to come quickly or easily. |

Family support programs were located at a variety of locations, depending on community resources, level of community support, and program funding. Most programs occupied buildings and classrooms that were owned and operated by school districts. Though there were some problems associated with housing a program in a school, most programs mentioned the many advantages to doing so. Schools are often a focal point of the community, so activities associated with schools had an automatic stamp of approval: One program director summed it up: "Schools are where all the good stuff happens." Programs often utilized school facilities such as playgrounds, cafeterias, and buses. Schools were often centrally located and highly accessible, and were also more likely to be open during the evenings. Finally, both parents and children benefitted from having positive school experiences that occurred before children were enrolled in the elementary program.

*One program director summed it up: "Schools are where all the good stuff happens."*

For other programs being separate from, but still close to the school offered the best of both worlds. Parents who were wary of schools were more likely to participate in a program separate from the school: A space apart from school helped parents by "detraumatiz[ing] the transition to school." Also, tensions arising from sharing space were less common, and programs still reaped the benefits of being in an accessible location with many resources. One program near a school bussed parents and children to the school for breakfast and lunch. Overall, the major facilities-related challenges faced by programs were instability and space limitations, school vs. program tensions, and accessibility:

*Unstable and inadequate facilities*. Many programs had to move several times over several years. One program had to relocate its offices almost every year—according to the director, "We just got used to packing up every year, and not knowing whether we were going to move or not." Instability was sometimes compounded by facilities that were too small or inadequate. Space shortages, high noise levels, lack of rest rooms, lack of privacy, scattered sites, and repair and maintenance difficulties were problems cited by program directors. Space shortages caused services to be cut back and prevented successful programs from expanding. Several programs desired a centralized location from which they could offer all services, but instead had to offer them at scattered sites around the neighborhood.

*Us vs. them mentality*. When programs were in school buildings, tensions sometimes arose between the program, its participants, and the school. Parents of public school students sometimes perceived programs as taking away facilities from their children, principals and teachers sometimes resisted sharing space and resources, and participants sometimes were wary of programs located in a school. If the school incurred additional expenses, such as paying a janitor extra when the program used the building during the evenings, problems sometimes arose.

*Accessibility and hours of operation.* Securing convenient and accessible sites was an important issue as well. Some programs wanted to be closer to poorer neighborhoods so the hard-to-reach would come, while others thought this would inhibit the participation of families that were of more comfortable means. Another issue was how long facilities were willing to stay open. Family support programs needed a place that could be used during evenings and summers, and such details had to be negotiated with the schools or their libraries beforehand.

Unstable or inappropriate program sites inhibited program operations in several ways. According to one program director, "In order for the program to fly you need a room!" Unfortunately, many programs struggled to find a stable location from which to run their program and offer services. Frequent moves inhibited participation, because they caused confusion and contributed to participants' dropping out of the program. When unconventional site arrangements were made, as with one program that housed its resource library in a school office, parents were sometimes hesitant to come.

In contrast, when facilities were adequate, convenient, and pleasant, the site was a great asset that attracted participants to the program. According to one program, an inviting location made those who might not otherwise enter a school happy to come.

Programs that were not located in schools often relied on space donated by local community centers or churches. Sharing rooms, buildings, and resources with other programs worked out especially well when programs used their facilities at different times; that way, each could take advantage of the others' resources without undue conflict. Sharing space with other programs also built familiarity and a sense of community. One program located in the same building as a Head Start program reported that space-sharing fostered a sense of continuity for the children who moved on to Head Start at age four.

**Evaluation Can Strengthen and Build Support for Programs**

Program evaluation was implemented broadly to document program processes and their impact on children and families. Of the 73 programs surveyed, 71 had some form of evaluation. The term "evaluation" connoted various forms of knowledge gathering strategies, ranging from needs assessments, standardized tests for children, and feedback forms for parenting workshops to formal outcome studies. External evaluations were the exception and were likely to be funded by foundations. Data collection for monitoring compliance with state and federal requirements occurred more frequently. Program directors agreed that to help program development, evaluation had to be built into the program from the very beginning (see Table 5).

---

### TABLE 5.   PURPOSES OF EVALUATION

**To improve program implementation.** Evaluation helped program staff members assess whether or not they were meeting their goals, find out how well they were doing, and plan the direction of future programming. It became a source of brainstorming and the inspiration for new ideas. It was also a tool in the process of qualifying for accreditation. Program directors singled out two areas where evaluation was particularly important for program quality. The first had to do with evaluations enabling programs to be more responsive to parents' concerns. Programs could then follow up by making the changes requested, thus improving recruitment and attendance, and offering relevant and supported services. The second focused on identifying areas for staff training, especially for dealing with children's behavioral problems.

**To document outcomes.** Program directors and their staffs wanted to know that their efforts were having an impact on participants. Although programs served children and parents, the outcomes most frequently mentioned focused on children's development. Over the short term, changes were measured by administering standardized tests, as in Chapter 1 programs that did a pre- and post-test for children's reading competence. Some programs recorded services children were receiving and developed a profile of each child's progress. While programs expressed interest in tracking the children as they went through school, they did not have the funds for the task.

**To document outcomes.** Program directors and their staffs wanted to know that their efforts were having an impact on participants. Although programs served children and parents, the outcomes most frequently mentioned focused on children's development. Over the short term, changes were measured by administering standardized tests, as in Chapter 1 programs that did a pre- and post-test for children's reading competence. Some programs recorded services children were receiving and developed a profile of each child's progress. While programs expressed interest in tracking the children as they went through school, they did not have the funds for the task.

**To build support for continued program funding.** Evaluation data was used strategically to publicize the accomplishments of a program and to validate its importance before local as well as state funders. According to one director, the information "takes the air out of your opposition" and provides an important tool for advocacy.

*According to one director, the information
"takes the air our of your opposition" and
provides an important tool for advocacy.*

The value of an evaluation goes beyond its benefits for program development and continued support. It can also provide information to boost staff morale. "It authenticates what we do," said one program director. Considering that staff members of these programs are underpaid and work conditions can be stressful, an evaluation can be designed to empower staff members in their teaching and supporting roles.

While consensus existed on the value of evaluation, program directors also pinpointed two major issues.

***Lack of funds for evaluation.*** This was especially true for longitudinal evaluations and experimental designs, in contrast to the recordkeeping and information gathering done in-house.

***Lack of congruence between evaluation and program interests.*** One concern mentioned was the lack of consensus between evaluators and program staffs on what constituted meaningful information and outcomes. Some program directors felt that "evaluation does not capture what we really do." Outcome measures were limited to academic achievement scores (for children as well as adults in school) whereas staff looked for "affective and attitudinal" changes. For them, the "subjective evaluation" of participants about their program experiences and growth were as important as test scores. Furthermore, some program directors mentioned that it was hard to measure prevention. Another issue focused on the timing of evaluations. Some outcome evaluations were conducted at the start-up phase, which was too soon to measure change. By the time programs were ready to be evaluated, there was no money to carry out the work.

*A program director expressed the belief that
"To be truly useful, evaluation has to serve the
needs of local programs as well as their
sponsors."*

A program director expressed the belief that "To be truly useful, evaluation has to serve the needs of local programs as well as their sponsors." Directors valued evaluations that helped improve the quality of their work and illuminated the process of change and development among children and parents. They and their staffs had face-to-face contact with families and got to know them as human beings, with all their struggles and dreams. They knew how hard it could be to reach families, recruit them, support them, and obtain services they needed. This personal encounter with families shaped what they expected from evaluations: a document about how participants *experience* services and change over time *and* how families fare on education, health, self-sufficiency, and other outcomes. Evaluations tended to dismiss the human stories behind the numbers as "anecdotal information;" but for the staff members of many programs, these stories embodied the elusive transformations that were at the heart of their mission.

Family support programs do not operate in isolation but work closely with the community through its service agencies, local associations, volunteers, and businesses. Most of the programs reported success in establishing links with other agencies, but some encountered challenges, especially during the start-up phase. The most commonly cited barrier to working with other agencies was competition. Program directors cited that other agencies' feared their participants being taken away from them, especially in the early childhood programs. Programs with screening for children met resistance from pediatricians; school-based programs with parent centers for preschool children had to be careful about relationships with the PTA.

However, persistent outreach to clarify the goals and activities of the program helped to establish cooperative rather than competitive relationships. The programs worked to identify ways in which services could be complementary and could build on each other, leading to a range of partnerships, which resulted in:

- Connecting families to services beyond the scope of the programs.

- Supporting program development.

- Communicating, networking, and developing joint activities.

- Serving the community in new ways.

*Connecting families to services.* The programs brokered services for families and connected them to community agencies. They provided referrals for children's screening, health and medical services. The health-oriented referrals were particularly common in programs that served children with special needs and teen parents. Some staff members did not simply provide participants with the names of diagnostic centers or clinics, but helped parents make appointments, fill out forms, and even provided transportation or accompanied them on a first visit when needed. The programs helped families obtain a wide range of services: emergency food, clothing, public assistance, adult education and bilingual services, job training, child care, and transportation. They also referred parents to community activities that could enrich their lives and promote children's development. Parents and children were encouraged to enroll in sports and recreational offerings and to participate in library activities such as a family reading program.

*Supporting program development.* The initial phase of program development often involved the ideas and suggestions of parents, community leaders, and service agencies. In a handful of cases, lead organizations joined forces to put a program together. For example, one school district offered to be the administrative agent for a program while the chamber of commerce took care of fundraising and a community college worked on developing a curriculum and training teachers. More commonly, programs networked with other agencies to recruit participants and to tap resource speakers to inform parents and staff on issues they were concerned with, such as drug addiction and child abuse.

Because family support programs are often underfunded, agencies also collaborated to optimize their opportunities for training and knowledge development. Agencies split the cost of having experts come into the community for staff training. Some programs worked with community colleges and universities to receive assistance on staff development and evaluation. Local businesses, associations, and volunteers were also instrumental in providing financial and in-kind support for the programs. At least two programs relied on their communities to help finance a building; many more relied on churches, schools, and local associations to donate space.

***Communicating, networking, and developing joint activities.*** Because other agencies provided services for children and families, the family support programs sought to keep abreast of what was available in their communities. In some communities, there were regular county service provider meetings that family support staff joined. These meetings allowed the staff members to introduce their programs, to make sure that information provided to a common group of participants was consistent, and to avoid service duplication for individual families. Alternatively, family support programs hosted breakfasts or other formal meetings to provide information and allay any fears about "turf." Staff members also paid personal visits to agencies to form reciprocal referral arrangements.

Knowing the common issues service agencies confronted also led to creative problem solving. One program director, for example, developed a collaborative to deal with multicultural issues. She had parents, teachers, and experts on a given culture discuss with service providers appropriate ways of dealing with families having different values or expectations.

***Serving the community.*** As programs developed expertise, they were contracted by other agencies to provide training and services. They became resources for the community. One program received a request from ten local businesses to provide parenting education workshops at brown bag lunches for employees. Another program developed a session for fathers at the public library. The library benefitted from more people coming to the building and taking advantage of its resources, people who might not have done so had they not participated in the program. The program also benefitted because it had the opportunity to recruit library users.

At the same time, the family support programs attracted a wider circle of community members to share their knowledge and skills with program participants. Through intergenerational and volunteer projects, the programs became a springboard for greater community involvement and investment in children and families.

## Successful Fundraising Is Broad-based and Continuous

Family support and education programs were built and maintained from a patchwork of funding streams that are inadequate, fragmented and unstable (see Table 6). Of the 73 programs included in *Raising Our Future*, 35 secured funds from three or more sources. Thirty-six programs received the lion's share of funding from federal and state governments. Their sources of support came from state prekindergarten and dropout prevention funds, Chapter 1, Chapter 2, special education programs, adult education and vocational training, and the Bilingual Education Act.

---

**TABLE 6.   COMMON FUNDING ISSUES**

**Inadequate funding.** Many policy makers supported family-focused programs because they had much promise, but then failed to fund them at a level that allowed local programs to deliver on that promise. Not only were there not enough funds to serve eligible families, but program funds were not increased yearly to keep up with rising costs. Programs either had to retrench or spread their funds more thinly among children and families.

**Unstable funding.** Funding that seemed certain one year sometimes vanished the next. This was especially apparent for programs in states experiencing a fiscal crisis in the late 1980s. Additionally, programs that were funded from year to year were unable to plan effectively. They began operations without their program money in the bank or closed temporarily until funds came through. Only four of the programs felt that their funding was "secure" or "stable."

**Patchwork funding.** While securing funds from many sources allowed a program to fulfill dreams of expansion, it could also become a "nightmare." Keeping track of different operational and accounting requirements could be confusing for managers and staff workers. It was also puzzling to families, who saw differences in the services for which participants were eligible. Additionally, as programs expanded by pooling public and private funds, school supervisors feared having to pick up the costs of counterpart contributions or when funding ended.

**Fickleness of funding.** Seed money, especially from foundations, was available to develop innovative activities, but maintenance money was scarce. Keeping up with new funding trends was not always desirable when programs had a focused mission. Programs were often the victims of shifting priorities. School systems could move whatever discretionary money they did have to other pressing social problems. Or, when programs were funded by external sources, districts were reluctant to pick up their share of matching funds over time.

**Fundraising time.** Because funding was inadequate and unstable, directors and even some of the staff devoted large amounts of time to fundraising. This detracted from other managerial or direct service responsibilities they had.

---

The consequences of the uncertain pattern of funding expansion and contraction were difficulty in building and maintaining stable staffs and staff burnout resulting from the continual struggle to get enough funding. Families also suffered when they were unable to gain access to continued support and services, and return to staff whom they knew and trusted.

Securing adequate funding and resources for program operations is a continuing challenge for most of the programs we surveyed. Though most programs did mention funding as a major and ongoing issue, they developed a number of successful strategies that allowed them to stabilize their fiscal base and continue their work.

Developing a strategic funding plan was important, as was persistence. Program directors worked as individual fundraisers for their programs. They claimed to "never stop looking for funding." Nor were they easily discouraged. If a grant application was rejected one year, they reapplied at the next round. The directors also engaged in networking

---

**Funding Efforts That Paid Off**

The **Addison County Parent/Child Center** in Vermont raised $300,000 in local community money and none of it was from one major donor. It took a year of planning, a three month capital campaign, and a matching federal Community Development Block Grant.

The **Parent Child Preschool** at Fox Elementary School in Columbus, Georgia was not an official line item on the budget for the first five years of operation. Parents actively contacted the superintendent and asked for his support in funding the preschool and its parenting component. Now, the program is a line item in the school budget.

---

---

**TABLE 7. COMMON FUNDING STRATEGIES**

---

**Building community support.** Through business partnerships, local fundraisers and in-kind donations of goods and services, programs obtained needed resources. These contributions maintained modest as well as more substantial program components. Unless fundraising was part of a strategic capital campaign, local dollars often served as supplementary income rather than the primary sources of program support. Local funding was still important, as seed money or matching funds, to attract more substantial resources from state and federal programs.

**Soliciting parent contributions.** Parents supported the programs by paying sliding-scale fees, participating in fundraising and providing testimonials before state legislators on the impact of the program on their lives.

**Forming interagency linkages.** Working collaboratively with other agencies helped spread program costs and brought in new money. Program directors mentioned that agencies shared inservice training, provided space at minimal or no cost, outposted staff for more effective recruitment and service delivery, and joined forces to apply for new funds.

**Advocating continued funding at state and local levels.** Because the bulk of program funds were from external sources, program directors built local support to sustain state funding. Program directors approached influential community groups and local leaders who could lobby for the program, especially when funds were likely to be cut. They also talked to their legislators directly and asked parents for their support.

---

and advocacy activities to ensure continued funding of family-focused programs. They agreed that creative funding was the key to program survival and expansion (see Table 7).

# IV. Continuing Challenges and Opportunities for Action

Advantages to Schools Sponsoring Family Support Programs

Are schools appropriate organizations to deliver family support services? Our survey of 73 programs leads to an affirmative response. School settings are stable environments that allow programs to reach out to families and establish positive relationships with them, offer educational activities to both parents and children, and broker multiple services to families in need. In varying degrees, programs received administrative, financial, and technical support from schools while enjoying autonomy in programming decisions. This arrangement allowed programs to be flexible and to tailor services to match the interests and needs of families. Furthermore, nearly all the programs developed with community participation, a positive step toward building networks and institutions that work together for the healthy development of children and families.

While the attitudes of schools ranged from tolerance to strong support of these programs, the directors unanimously considered them beneficiaries of family programs. Directors cited a number of advantages for schools in sponsoring family support programs. Specifically, these advantages were:

*Increased parent involvement and support for schools.* Parents who were involved in programs before their children entered the public schools were described as being more supportive of and less intimidated by the schools. Their attitudes contributed to a positive image of the school in the community. Increased parent involvement in some cases alleviated children's discipline problems and saved the school money.

*Staff development opportunities.* Family support program staff sometimes had different skills and knowledge that could benefit teachers and administrators. For example, program personnel offered workshops to schools in areas such as conducting home visits and encouraging parent participation.

*A pilot for new ideas.* Family support programs sometimes had innovative instructional approaches and administrations that appealed to schools, such as team teaching, strong parent involvement, and non-graded classrooms. Seeing how a new idea was working in a real program made it easier for schools to implement those ideas. The program could act as a model for the school to learn from and could offer its expertise and experience to the school.

*School savings.* The directors perceived that family support programs saved their schools money in a variety ways: sharing the program's materials and expertise with other school departments, offering free staff development to school personnel, developing a group of parent volunteers for the schools, and reducing the number of children who needed special education services.

Challenges

In spite of the benefits schools receive from hosting family support programs, these programs are often fragile "add-ons" to a school system's basic services. As such, they confront a number of challenges. Although some schools have learned new ways to involve parents, others are still struggling to come to terms with being open to the community. Where the school climate is less welcoming, family support workers take the roles of advocates for families and change agents. One program coordinator summed up the situation: "Our charge is to educate the public school, not to have it put us in their mold." To their credit, these programs have avoided the rigidity of a bureaucratic system and instead offer a model of positive program-parent relationships.

Being on the margins of a school system, programs are particularly vulnerable to lack of funding, low staff salaries, and inadequate space. Many struggle to survive on soft money. Whenever there is a financial crunch, the program budgets are substantially reduced. Out of the original 77 programs we surveyed, four were eliminated by budget cuts. While start-up money is available, long-term, sustained funding is hard to come by. Program directors work hard to put together different federal, state, and private grants in order to survive.

Limited funds also translate into limited salaries for staff. One program director aptly describes the work of parent educators as "professionalization without adequate compensation." Programs are more likely to employ staff members under different salary scales and schedules. Program coordinators are on teachers' salary scales, but frontline workers are paraprofessionals who work part time and on a temporary, hourly basis. However, scarce funds are not the only issue. The larger system that imposes personnel rules and restrictions is also a concern. For example, parent educators' salaries in one program were pegged to that of teaching aides; their salary levels could not be raised even if the program had the funds to do so.

Programs often have little control or choice over where they are housed, or whether they will need to move from one year to the next. They usually must take what is available and affordable, regardless of whether the facilities are too small, inconvenient, or temporary. When programs are able to use school classrooms and facilities, programs are vulnerable to eviction when school district enrollment increases and space becomes limited.

The issues surrounding the implementation of family support programs reflect some of the broader, systemic problems schools and other service institutions confront: changes in family structure and conditions, lack of funds and other material resources, and reluctance to change the status quo. Within this context, directors have to be leaders and strategists. They spend time informing teachers, principals and school boards about the value of their work. They and their staffs give presentations before the school board, network with school counselors and teachers, and attend schoolwide staff meetings. They seek to connect their programs with pressing school concerns so as to build a constituency. A program's evaluation results and accomplishments also go a long way, and astute directors capitalize on their strengths. "Being new, we were treated like second class citizens," says a director, "but national recognition has put us on the forefront. Good results have helped and we are now held in high esteem, though we had to fight our way in." In the complex world of school politics, entrepreneurial leadership is crucial for program development.

## Lessons and Opportunities

The challenges raised above also generate lessons and opportunities for action. The experience of the 73 programs suggests a model worth striving for. Ideally, family support programs would be nurtured by the wider school climate in which they operate. This means that principals, teachers, and other school staff would share similar values about parents and forming partnerships with families, and concomitantly, provide status recognition of family support staff. Family support programs would be continuous from the early childhood years through K-12, and would be open to all families. Through these programs, schools would serve as brokers of services in the community, whether offered on-site or through well-designed referral systems. Community resources would also be brought in to enrich learning experiences, through partnerships with libraries, businesses, and senior volunteers. Programs would be of high quality, with opportunities for staff development and leadership training. Their implementation would be facilitated by stable and adequate funding. Taken together, these components form the nucleus of a strategy to be pursued by state and local education agencies in building strong connections among families, schools, and communities. To the extent that policy lays out the broad themes that guide program implementation, the following lessons are pertinent:

*Family support and parent involvement are integral to school reform.* Because learning occurs in the home, school and community, forming partnerships with families boosts children's opportunity to excel in school. No longer is it sufficient to focus on classroom improvement; this has to be supplemented with information, support, and communication with parents or other adult family members. Genuine partnership involves a two-way communication so that parents' voices are heard, respected, and acted upon, while schools can also expect parents to take responsible involvement in their children's schooling. Such a partnership holds the promise of creating what James Coleman calls "social capital," or the shared norms that foster children's educational motivation, effort, and achievement.

While a good portion of the programs in our survey tended to focus on disadvantaged families, every effort needs to be taken to make family support and involvement activities as inclusive as possible. All parents are interested in their children's success and benefit from information that will help them understand their children's development and provide the encouragement and motivation they need. Family support programs enable parents to complement more fully the role of teachers, not in the sense of their becoming experts in subject matter, but in terms of showing interest, stimulating connections between what is learned in school and what happens in the home or community, and promoting better communication among parents, teachers and students (Epstein, 1994).

*The family focused approach to children's learning has to be continuous through the elementary grades and high school.* The impact of early childhood intervention is often diminished as children move to elementary school. Children need rich learning environments and parent involvement throughout the school years. Unless there is continuity to early childhood family support and involvement, it would be difficult to make an impact on the family processes that contribute to children's achievement. District level administrators can increase the ability of schools to develop effective home-school partnerships by offering schools support, fundraising expertise, and technical assistance. At the site level, principals can facilitate flexible implementation of family support and parent involvement programs, and encourage the cooperation of teachers and program staff. The State of Missouri provides one example of leadership to promote continuity of family support. Its early childhood Parents as Teachers program is now complemented by Practical Parenting Partnerships, a program to maintain family support and involvement in the elementary grades.

*Programs have to be designed comprehensively.* To be effective, family support programs must be linked with a continuum of supports and services. Family support programs promote child development and reinforce parents' competence in childrearing. They are an example of "primary services" (Wynn, Costello, Halpern, & Richman, 1994), or those resources in a community that are available to children and families without special qualification (i.e., eligibility based on income or other criteria). Other examples of primary services are child care and afterschool programs, art, music, sports, and the activities offered by parks, libraries, and community centers. However, to meet the needs of the changing family, work, and material resource conditions of families, family support programs are taking the lead or participating in community efforts to create a network of comprehensive services. They have collaborated with other primary services to complement their activities and to enrich the social, recreational, and educational experiences of children and families. They also have performed a brokerage role, connecting families to "basic services" such as health, job-training, adult education and other forms of assistance that improve family functioning, and to "specialized services" such as mental health, child welfare, and special education.

*Collaboration can expand outreach and strengthen program quality.* The early childhood arena is characterized by the diversity of its service providers. Parents bring their children to schools, child care centers, Head Start, or family child care, or a combination of these. Forming collaborative relationships among these providers and with other health and social service agencies is challenging for a number of reasons. Even when various organizations come together with the best of intentions, basic differences in philosophy can make it difficult to work together. Organizations may also fear competition and act defensively to guard "turf." Collaboration is a time-consuming effort, especially when differences in organizational rules and regulations require many meetings to reconcile differences and secure waivers.

And yet collaboration holds the promise of creating a synergy to create a continuum from primary services to specialized services that promote child development and help families deal with problems. The potential benefits for programs and communities are great. Through reciprocal exchanges, programs with well-developed family support components can serve as mentors for child-serving agencies without a two-generation focus. Programs serving poor children can purchase slots from other agencies that will expose children to more heterogeneous environments. Programs for infants and toddlers can link up with preschool programs to provide continuity of educational and support services.

Important first steps are being taken to support collaboration. The 1994 Elementary and Secondary Education Act (ESEA) allows schools to use up to five percent of the funds they receive under ESEA to develop, implement or expand a coordinated service project to increase children's and parent's access to social, health, and education services. At the state level, Kentucky's education reform encourages schools to work with other community agencies such as child care services and Head Start to establish preschool programs.

*Staff training and professional development form the backbone of quality programs.* Professional development opportunities in family support and education programs build stronger staffs, improve salaries and compensation, and contribute to program quality and success. At present, there are no national professional standards or systems that prepare, develop, and license family support personnel. However, this may be changing, with certain states leading the way. At present, Minnesota's Parent Educator License and the Combined Early Childhood Family Education (ECFE) License are required for those working in the statewide ECFE programs. In addition, Minnesota has recently developed a strategic plan to build a statewide early childhood professional development system to facilitate career development for "personnel in early childhood care and education programs serving young children from birth through age eight and their families" (Beaton, 1994).

Until such plans have materialized, there are other creative steps programs can take to promote staff development in their organizations. Giving staff the opportunity to participate in inservice workshops that are on topics of interest to them, offering tuition assistance or release time for relevant classes at nearby colleges or universities, encouraging them to pursue related licenses, credentials, or certificates, paying for memberships to professional organizations such as the National Association for the Education of Young Children (NAEYC), and offering them opportunities to attend conferences in the field are just a few possibilities. Staff development opportunities such as these not only increase staff skills and knowledge about families and children, they show staff members that they are viewed as professionals, allow them to gain skills and qualifications that can lead to better compensation in their positions, and can increase morale. Such opportunities for growth can do much to compensate for low salaries common to the field, potentially reducing staff turnover and burnout, another important indicator of high quality family support programs.

*Program leadership has to be nurtured.* Preparing staff for management functions constitutes the single most important gap in preservice and inservice training. Family support directors often have been trained to be practitioners rather than managers, but they are charged with operating complex programs. Their responsibilities run the gamut of hiring and supervising staff, fundraising, advocating for their programs, coordinating with other school programs and community service agencies, and preparing program reports. Fundraising alone requires an entrepreneur's savvy combined with an accountant's precision. Outreach involves developing communication skills with a broad and diverse range of peers, including parents, teachers, school staff, and other community groups. To prepare people for the demands of management, a comprehensive training program must be developed, combining academic and apprenticeship components, to build the administrative and communication skills in this newly emerging profession.

*Programs need a solid fiscal base.* Family support programs are funded on the notion of a small investment yielding a high return rather than on matching the investment to the requirements of a quality program. This translates to inadequate funding at the local level and its many ramifications for staff compensation, outreach activities, service provision, and how much time directors spend putting together a patchwork of funds. Without a solid base, programs are hard pressed to make new advances but must play catch up. Instead of using new resources to fill gaps and offer innovative activities, they are used to replace funds that have run out. The question of how these programs can be financed adequately and over the long term will continue to be an issue; the manner in which they are addressed will be a measure of the political commitment to strengthening family, school, and community partnerships.

* * *

The genre of family support programs is evolving constantly and soon will progress beyond the range of programs presented in this book. These programs are moving into new territory, and with that comes both challenge and opportunity. To educate the child, parents and other family members, schools, and community agencies must redefine their roles to include partnerships that support child development from infancy through adolescence. To sustain gains, family support and education initiatives must be continuous over a child's life. We must build a solid bridge between programs and schools. While all the programs described in the following pages have linkages with other community services, they must go beyond incremental planning to develop a comprehensive system of services.

It is clear that school systems alone cannot take on all of the responsibility for enhancing child development and strengthening families. Nor can family support programs meet the entire range of needs they find in the communities they serve. Broad-based collaborations can go further than any single organization to offer the supports and services that contribute to healthy families.

*Raising Our Future* documents first-generation family support programs. We hope the lessons learned from them make it easier for the next generation of programs to face the inherent challenges of implementing a service plan. Moreover, if this first generation of programs is successful, then the next will have even more advocates—those who have experienced, directly or indirectly, the benefits of the programs. As schools, community groups, and public agencies work together, they are in a position to advocate for improvements in programs for children and families. Today's programs will have lasting impact by advancing the family support model and by helping succeeding generations of programs reach their potential.

**References**

Baumrind, D. (1989). Rearing competent children. In W. Damon (Ed.), *Child Development today and tomorrow* (pp. 349-378). San Francisco: Jossey-Bass Publishers.

Beaton, A. S. (April, 1994). *Early childhood care and education professional* development: Strategic plan. Minnesota Department of Human Services, Early Childhood Professional Development Strategic Planning Consortium Steering Committee.

Benard, B. (1992). Fostering resiliency in kids: Protective factors in the family, school, and community. *Prevention Forum, 12*(3), 1-16.

Bronfenbrenner, U. (1986). Ecology of the family as a context for human development: Research perspectives. *Developmental Psychology, 22*(6), 723-742.

Bruner, C. (1994). State government and family support: From marginal to mainstream. In S. L. Kagan & B. Weissbourd (Eds.), *Putting families first: America's family support movement and the challenge of change* (pp. 338-357). San Francisco: Jossey Bass Publishers.

Council of Chief State School Officers. (1989). *Family support, education and involvement.* Washington, DC: Author.

Dunst, C. J. (1994). *Key Characteristics and Features of Community-Based* Family Support Programs. Commisioned paper presented for the Best Practices Project, Family Resource Coalition, Chicago. Unpublished manuscript.

Eastman, G. (1988). *Family involvement in education.* Paper prepared for the Wisconsin Department of Public Instruction.

Fine, M. (1993). [Ap]parent involvement: Reflections on parents, power, and urban public schools. *Teachers College Record, 94*(4), 682-729.

Epstein, J. (1994). Theory to Practice: School and Family Partnerships Lead to School Improvement and Student Success. In C.L. Fagnano and B.Z. Werber (Eds.), *School, Family and Community Interaction* (pp. 39-54). Boulder: Westview Press.

Harvard Family Research Project. (1993). *Building villages to raise our children* (vols. 1-6). Cambridge, MA: Author.

Hauser-Cram, P. (1991). *Early education in the public schools: Lessons from a comprehensive birth-to-kindergarten program.* San Francisco: Jossey-Bass Publishers.

Henderson, A. (1987). *The evidence continues to grow: Parent involvement improves student achievement.* Washington DC: National Committee for Citizens in Education.

Herr, T. & Halpern, R. with Conrad, A. (1991). *Changing what counts: Re-thinking the journey out of welfare.* Evanston, IL: Center for Urban Affairs and Policy Research, Northwestern University.

Hidalgo, N. (1995). *Tracing varied paths to school success.* Brown Bag Lunch Seminar Presentation at the Center on Families, Communities, Schools, and Children's Learning, Boston University, May 17, 1995.

Hill, I. (1992). The role of medicaid and other government programs in providing medical care for children and pregnant women. *The Future of Children, 2*(2), 134-153.

Lopez, M. E., & Hochberg, M. (1993). *Paths to school readiness: An in-depth look at three early childhood programs.* Cambridge, MA: Harvard Family Research Project.

Musick, J. S. (1994, Fall). Directions: Capturing the childrearing context. *SRCD Newsletter.*

National Association of State Boards of Education. (1991). *Caring communities: Supporting young children and families.* Alexandria, VA: Author.

Olds, D. L. & Kitzman, H. (1993). Review of research on home visiting for pregnant women and parents of young children. *The Future of Children, 3*(3), 53-92.

Patton, M., et al. (1993). The aid to families in poverty program: A synthesis of themes, patterns, and lessons learned. Minneapolis, MN: The McKnight Foundation.

Powell, D. R. (1991). Strengthening parental contributions to school readiness and early school learning. Paper prepared for the Office of Educational Research and Improvement, U. S. Department of Education. (Department of Child Development and Family Studies, Purdue University, West Lafayette, IN 47907-1267).

Powell, D. (1994). Evaluating family support programs: Are we making progress? In S. L. Kagan & B. Weissbourd (Eds.), *Putting families first: America's family support movement and the challenge of change* (pp. 441-470). San Francisco: Jossey Bass Publishers.

Ramey, S. L. & Ramey, C. T. (1992). Early educational intervention with disadvantaged children: To what effect? *Applied and Preventive Psychology, 1*(3), 131-140.

Reese, L., Gallimore, R., Goldenberg, C., & Balzano, C. (1994). Immigrant Latino parents' future orientations for their children. In R. F. Macias & R. G. Garcia Ramos (Eds.), *Changing schools for changing students: An anthology of research on language minorities.* Santa Barbara, CA: University of California Linguistic Minority Research Institute.

Shartrand, A. M., Kreider, H. A., & Warfield, M. E. (1994). *Preparing teachers to involve parents: A national survey of teacher education programs.* Cambridge, MA: Harvard Family Research Project.

Smith, S., Blank, S., & Collins, R. (1992). *Pathways to self-sufficiency for two generations: Designing welfare-to-work programs that benefit children and strengthen families.* New York: Foundation for Child Development.

St. Pierre, R., Layzer, J., & Barnes, H. (1994). *Variation in the design, cost, and effectiveness of two-generational programs.* Paper presented for Eight Rutgers Invitiational Symposium on Education. New Dimensions for Policy and research in Early Childhood Care and Education, Princeton, NJ, October 27-28.

Snow, C. (1987). Factors influencing vocabulary and reading achievement in low-income children. In R. Appel (Ed.), *Togepaste taalwetenschap in artikelen special 2* (pp. 124-130). Amsterdam: Anela.

Snow, C. (1987). Families as social contexts for literacy development. In C. Dauite (Ed.), *The development of literacy through social interaction.* San Francisco, CA: Jossey Bass Publishers.

Swap, S. (1990). Parent involvement and success for all children: What we know now. Boston: Institute for Responsive Education.

U. S. Department of Education, Office of Elementary and Secondary Education. (1991). *Preparing young children for success: Guideposts for achieving our first national goal.* Washington DC: Author.

U. S. Department of Health and Human Services. (1994). *Federal guidance for family preservation and family support services* (P.L. 103-66). Washington DC: Author.

Wasik, B. A. & Karweit, N. L. (1994). Off to a good start: Effects of birth to three interventions on early school success. In R. E. Slavin, N. L. Karweit, & B. A. Wasik (Eds.), *Preventing early school failure: Research, policy, and practice* (pp. 13-57). Boston: Allyn and Bacon.

Weiss, H. B. (1988). *Family support and education programs in the public* schools: Opportunities and challenges. Paper prepared for the National Association of State Boards of Education. Cambridge, MA: Author.

Weiss, H. B. (1989). State family support and education programs: Lessons from the pioneers. *American Journal of Orthopsychiatry, 59*(1), 32-48.

Weiss, H. B. (1993). Home visits: Necessary but not sufficient. *The Future of Children, 3*(3), 113-128.

Weiss, H. B. (1994). *Model programs and best practices in parenting support.* Unpublished manuscript. Cambridge, MA: Harvard Family Research Project.

Weiss, H. B. & Halpern, R. (1990). *Community-based family support and education programs: Something old or something new?*

New York: Columbia University, National Center for Children in Poverty, 154 Haven Avenue, New York, NY.

Werner, E. E. and Smith, R. S. (1989). *Vulnerable but Invincible: A Longitudinal Study of Resilient Children and Youth.* New York: Adams, Bannister, Cox.

Wynn, J., Costello, J., Halpern, R., and Richman, H. (1994). *Children, Families, and Communities: A New Approach to Social Services.* University of Chicago: The Chapin Hall Center for Children.

# 1

# Preschool and Early Childhood Programs with Parent Involvement

The following programs offer intensive educational services to young children, particularly to children from educationally and financially disadvantaged families. Parents are encouraged, and sometimes mandated, to become involved in their children's lives, either through classroom participation or through child development and parenting workshops. Home visits often supplement preschool programs by focusing on helping parents create comforting, lively environments conducive to their children's development. Preschools offer opportunities for socialization and skill mastery. Additional support services to families include: screening, child care information and referrals, drop-in centers, counseling, adult literacy, resource libraries, and career development education.

# Programs in Brief

# Early Childhood Project

| | | |
|---|---|---|
| Networking | Home visits | Parenting/child development education |
| Newsletter | Preschool | Parent-child joint activities |
| | | Kindergarten |

**Contact:** Martha Lee, Coordinator

**Address:** Four Corners School
21 Ferrante Avenue
Greenfield, MA 01301
(413) 772-1375

**Established:** 1987, local initiative

**Budget '88-'89:** $105,000

**Sources:** Massachusetts Chapter 188 early childhood grant,
remedial skills grant

**Size:** 65 families (including 75 children)

**Area Served:** Greenfield, Massachusetts

**Auspices:** Elementary Education

**1990 Respondent:** Marcia Hunker, Coordinator

*The scholarship program, which includes four-year-olds and their parents, has added an unexpected bonus to the overall success of the program. The program benefitted by having a group begin school with a positive preschool experience. Many of the children who received scholarships would have been considered at risk because their parents could not afford quality daycare.*

## Community

Greenfield is a blue-collar community with a population of 25,000 located in the northwest corner of Massachusetts close to the Vermont border. Greenfield's economy has improved somewhat since 1985 when Aid to Families with Dependent Children (AFDC) was being received by 18 percent of the town's residents (compared with 11 percent in 1987). The biggest employers for the town's mainly white middle- to lower-income residents are Phoenix Mutual Insurance, Lunt Silver, and Greenfield Tap and Dye.

## Philosophy and Goals

The Early Childhood Project, formerly called the ABCs in Greenfield, is a child-centered, individualized program that provides a unified approach to educating children according to their own natural development and interests. Basic skills are taught through experiential learning in classrooms designed to stimulate curiosity. The Early Childhood Project demonstrates an alternative developmental model of instruction to preschool and early childhood educators.

## History and Origins

Mary Ann Clarkson, a public school principal and director of the project, recognized the need for an early childhood education program in Greenfield. She knew about available state grants for early childhood education and in 1987 gathered a group of school administrators, teachers, parents, and community members to meet with the Massachusetts Department of Education. They began researching a program for Greenfield and set out to turn around an old-fashioned curriculum, which "on any given day in the different public schools, each class in each grade would be working on the same problems in the same workbooks at the same time," explains Marcia Hunker, grant coordinator for the program. The group wanted a curriculum that taught basic skills but was "exciting, playful, and focused on the emotional and physical needs of very small people, not adults." Some teachers in the school system were resistant to change; others, according to Ms. Hunker, felt liberated by the program. In 1987, Greenfield received a Chapter 188 early childhood grant and a remedial skills grant and began the program with one developmental kindergarten class and a scholarship program that enabled eight four-year-olds from low-income families to attend a private nursery school with a similar developmental curriculum.

**Features**

The Early Childhood Project teaches basic skills and parent and child developmental education. It provides home visits to parents of four-year-olds, serves parents and children in three out of five kindergartens, and has a developmental outreach teacher who works with selected children needing remedial help in grades 1 to 3. Children in the project's developmental kindergartens use whole language and "inventive spelling," the phonetic writing of words that are important to them. "What's Cooking," a parent-child activity session, correlates good children's books with cooking activities to teach parents home activities. The book, *A Space Story,* served as the source for "planet salad" made by parents and children. The exercise reinforces counting, measuring, and mixing skills. Parent education in the program includes having a human development specialist come and talk to the community about developmental tasks and maturation rates in children.

**Participants**

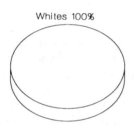

Whites 100%

Three of Greenfield's five kindergartens participate in the Early Childhood Project developmental classrooms. Children from lower-income families are eligible for scholarships to attend the First Church Nursery School. The project's developmental outreach teacher serves children in first through third grade needing extra help. Twenty-five percent of the parents participating in the program during the 1987-88 school year were single parents.

*Ms. Hunker says that the key to getting parents involved is through their children. In the past, parents in Greenfield were passive about education in the community. Now, they realize they can become involved and have an active say in what happens.*

**Parent Education**

Parent involvement and education varies from site to site. In an area where parents are struggling financially and have time constraints, parent education involves teaching them about their privileges and responsibilities in the education of their children. In higher-income neighborhoods, parents spend more time assisting teachers and networking with each other. They participate in field trips and initiate classroom activities.

**Curriculum**

The Early Childhood Project curriculum is based on the Bank Street College of Education developmental model, is supplemented by teachers' ideas and projects, and is modified to support the developmental needs and interests of individual children.

**Sites**

The Early Childhood Project's three developmental kindergartens are located in Greenfield's public school classrooms. The nursery school is located at the First Church. The kindergarten sites are stable; bus transportation is provided to all children except preschoolers.

**Parent Involvement**

Parents have been an important part of the Early Childhood Project from the very beginning. They helped write the original grant proposal to the state and canvassed the community door-to-door with a needs assessment survey of families with three-year-olds. Parents participate in joint parent-child activities and, as stipulated in the early childhood education grant, serve on the project's advisory board. "We pay attention to the parents on the board," says Ms. Hunker. "We poll their opinions on how the grant is doing and where we are going." The Early Childhood Project staff believes parent involvement is essential to a child's education. Ms. Hunker says that the key to getting parents involved is through their children. In the past, parents in Greenfield were passive about education in the community. Now, they realize they can become involved and have an active say in what happens.

**Outreach**

According to Marcia Hunker, the Early Childhood Project has no trouble attracting participants. Parents with children already involved in the program are active in outreach. The project sends out a bimonthly newsletter to parents, child care providers, school board members, and the advisory board. It also has a freelance reporter on its advisory council who develops news stories and gets media coverage for the program.

**Staff**

| Job Title | PD | Vol | FT | PT | Educ Req | Status | Benefits |
|-----------|----|-----|----|----|----------|--------|----------|
| Director | 1 | - | - | 1 | Post-Graduate Courses or Degree | Other Contract | Yes |
| Coordinator | 1 | - | - | 1 | College Degree | K-12 Contract | Yes |
| Nursery Teacher | 1 | - | - | 1 | College Degree | Hourly Non-Contract | No |
| Teachers | 4 | - | 4 | - | College Degree | K-12 Contract | Yes |
| Aides | 2 | - | 2 | - | High School Diploma | Hourly Contract | Yes |
| Secretary | 1 | - | - | 1 | High School Diploma | Hourly Contract | Yes |
| Library Assistant | 1 | - | - | 1 | High School Diploma | Hourly Contract | Yes |
| Parents and Student Teachers | - | Varies | - | - | None | - | No |

**State/District Requirements**

For all teachers, certification and college degree; for the director, postgraduate degree.

**Preferred Background**

None.

**Employee Education and Training Represented**

Infant and toddler education; prekindergarten and early childhood education; elementary education; education, grades 7 to 12; special education; parent educator; health and nutrition; child development and family studies; development and fundraising; research and evaluation.

## Administration

Marcia Hunker, the program coordinator, oversees several different classrooms and grants. She reports to the principal of the North Parish and Four Corners schools, who serves as director of the program and in turn reports to the superintendent of schools. The Early Childhood Project is administered exclusively within the public school system and involves developmental nursery school, kindergarten, one first grade teacher, a second grade teacher, and the developmental outreach teacher. The Massachusetts Department of Education monitors the program. An advisory board composed of parents, the project staff, the public school staff, representatives from public agencies, and the community is responsible for developing and implementing parent evenings and fundraising efforts. The board also provides suggestions and evaluates the program.

## Relationship to the Schools

Communication between the Early Childhood Project and the Four Corners and North Parish schools is active and often beneficial, notes the coordinator. The school system contributes classroom space and some equipment and pays program teachers. The developmental approach offers new ideas to Greenfield teachers, a number of whom have observed the program in action. Ms. Hunker makes presentations to school administrators, principals, and others in the system who are interested in early childhood education. Despite the mutually productive partnership between the school and the program, Ms. Hunker notes that the program would have more autonomy if it had a separate identity.

## Community Links

The Early Childhood Project exchanges information with other public agencies, and several staff members participate on interagency councils and committees.

## Funding

State, 100 percent.

## In-Kind Resources

Greenfield Public Schools provides paid staff, transportation, consultation and staff development, and administrative and clerical support. The schools also provide space, volunteer staff, access to equipment, computers, telephones, materials and supplies, and periodic direct service to program participants.

## Funding History

Although funding for the project increased by 10 percent in its first six months, state deficits froze Chapter 188 grant money at its 1989 level. The grant application for 1990 emphasized in-kind contributions. Ms. Hunker plans to reach out to the business community for additional funding for the nursery school program.

## Objectives

The Early Childhood Project emphasizes community education and involvement in a developmental program for four- and five-year-olds. The outreach teacher brings enriched classroom experiences to remedial students. The project provides activities for four-year-olds, allowing children to develop cognitively, physically, and emotionally.

## Evaluation

A required evaluation of the Early Childhood Project revealed a strongly positive outlook following the program's first year. Frances B. Elwell, an early childhood educator, commended the program for actively including children in their own educational process. "I feel that we've been fairly successful because we started very small and have grown," notes Ms. Hunker. "We had a strong base of support. It's hard to bring change unless you have people who want to change." In its second year, the program did a self-evaluation with assistance from the Massachusetts Department of Education. Recent recommendations include limiting enrollment to keep the outreach teacher's workload manageable, revising pre- and posttesting instruments, and doing quarterly (rather than monthly) children's progress reports. The remedial program has been highly successful, says Ms. Hunker. Children are developing more positive feelings about themselves, show improved test scores, and have started to read and write outside of the classroom. The project will continue to do annual evaluations.

**Replication**

The Early Childhood Project is based on the Follow Through Program in Brattleboro, Vermont.

**Materials Available**

A brochure and two videotapes of the Early Childhood Project are available from the Four Corners School.

# ADEPT Child Care Enrichment Services of the New Orleans Public Schools

*ADEPT is especially crucial to one dual-career family with twin seven-year-olds, because although one twin is active and needs no special care, the other is profoundly handicapped, attends special education classes, and is mobile only with crutches. At ADEPT, both can share experiences with other children and participate in games and activities under the supervision of trained personnel. ADEPT's integrated child care program gives both handicapped and nonhandicapped children the benefits of experiencing and accepting differences among themselves.*

| | | |
|---|---|---|
| Advocacy | Lending library | Parent support group |
| Networking | Crisis intervention | Physical education/gymnastics |
| Hotline | Itinerant educators | Parenting/child development education |
| Newsletter | Tutoring referral | Alcohol/drug abuse program |
| Child care | Individual counseling | Health/nutrition education |

**Contact:** Sandra McCullum, Assistant Program Specialist

**Address:** ADEPT
4100 Touro Street
New Orleans, LA 70122
(504) 286-2983

**Established:** 1981, school district initiative

**Budget '88-'89:** $652,000 total budget (child care program: $461,000; alcohol and drug prevention: $191,000)

**Sources:** Federal grant and client fees

**Size:** 2,620 families

**Area Served:** New Orleans Parish Schools

**Auspices:** Student Support Services of New Orleans Parish Schools

**1990 Respondent:** Nancy Torcson, Founder

## Community

ADEPT is located in New Orleans Parish, an impoverished school system whose academic and financial resources have been drained by a large network of parochial and private schools. According to ADEPT's founder and former director, Nancy Torcson, housing projects and lavish neighborhoods form a "checkerboard demography." Recent declines in the oil and shipping industries, which provided livelihoods for unskilled laborers and high school dropouts, have increased unemployment. Sixty-five percent of the city's population is black, 25 percent white, and 10 percent Hispanic. In the inner-city schools, 85 percent of the students and teachers are black.

## Philosophy and Goals

ADEPT has a preventive focus. Ms. Torcson describes ADEPT's approach as one in which "play encourages freedom, spontaneity, and confidence." ADEPT seeks to provide enriched before- and afterschool experiences in which children master challenges and develop self-confidence through supervised activities.

## History and Origins

In 1978, Nancy Torcson was running an informal child care business while studying at Tulane University. She moved her program into a neighborhood elementary school and subsequently approached the New Orleans Parish superintendent about using the schools as a base for a comprehensive daycare program. Her proposal was immediately accepted and gained community support through a needs assessment; the city's receptivity to creative ideas and the social climate of the late 1970s made child care programs an attractive proposition. Objections arose from principals who were reluctant to accept the idea of using the school as a daycare base and who did not want outsiders using the buildings after hours. Those objections ceased when revenues proved the benefits of the program. ADEPT is now in its tenth year as a self-funded, citywide child care program.

**Features**

Activities are geared to giving children a sense of the options open to them, providing them with opportunities for success, and helping them build a positive self-image. Ms. Torcson notes that the program works with children "through art, writing, drama, sports, and homework tutorials. ADEPT's participants are given an opportunity to develop better interpersonal relations, discover a sense of self, and learn better communication skills."

**Cultural Arts Enrichment Program** includes physical education and gymnastics and brings itinerant crews of professional artists to afterschool programs throughout the city either once or twice a week, depending on the school's ability to pay.

A **24-hour emergency "safeline"** for parents and children up to age 18 serves New Orleans and two outlying parishes by responding to questions on childrearing and discipline and providing a tutoring and referral service for children.

**Alcohol and Drug Abuse Community Prevention Program (ADACPP)** operates under a federal block grant and meets daily for two hours after school. The program is available to children in preschool through sixth grade in specific, low-income schools.

**Latchkey Education Program,** films for parents with children in kindergarten through eighth grade, turns the sometimes unavoidable "latchkey" situation into a positive experience that promotes independence.

**Participants**

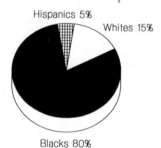

Hispanics 5%

Whites 15%

Blacks 80%

ADEPT serves preschool and elementary-age children in the New Orleans Parish Schools who need daycare. Special needs and high-risk populations are particularly welcome to the program, which is open to children as long as they can be mainstreamed. The average family participates for approximately four years; some are involved from preschool through the sixth grade and beyond. In general, these children come from working-class families. ADACPP participants are often latchkey children or children diagnosed by social workers as having low self-esteem due to family or drug problems. In 1988-89, 2,620 children were served. Eighty percent were black, 15 percent white, and 5 percent Hispanic. Approximately 35 percent of the participants were single parents.

*"Play encourages freedom, spontaneity, and confidence."*

**Parent Education**

Parents of student participants meet monthly for feedback interaction sessions. Once a semester, they are invited to a dramatic presentation hosted by speakers from various local drug awareness programs.

**Curriculum**

ADEPT uses *Me-Me Drug Prevention Program* (Kearny; Appleton, Wisconsin), which is available through the National Diffusion Network. The curriculum was intended for use by every classroom teacher, but in the ADEPT program, one teacher per school implements the curriculum with a limited number of participants. The child care enrichment component offers homework tutorials that are tailored to individual children's needs.

**Sites**

ADEPT's central offices are in the school district's central administration building; programs are held throughout the district. Child care services are available in 17 elementary schools, and the ADACPP reaches students in 40 elementary schools. In general, programs center themselves in cafeterias, which often open out onto playgrounds and are usually close to other necessary facilities. Classrooms are also available for tutoring, homework, and quiet reading.

**Parent Involvement**

Parents are not involved in the administration of the program.

**Outreach**

The hardest families to reach, says Ms. Torcson, remain those at poverty level who really need the service but are unable to afford even a sliding-scale fee. For these families, state and federal grants are available. ADEPT sends applications for scholarship grants to the New Orleans Parish Schools, and they are distributed throughout the schools. Word-of-mouth and parent-to-parent contacts are the most effective means of outreach, notes Ms. Torcson. Besides benefiting from television and newspaper coverage, ADEPT publishes the *ADEPT Update* and the annual *ADEPT Student Newsletter,* which contains photographs, drawings and notes by the children. The parent-teacher association also helps to publicize the program.

**Staff**

ADEPT employs a staff of 200, including school-site coordinators who teach, act as liaisons between ADEPT and the schools, and offer support to ADEPT's specially trained artists and substitute teachers.

| Job Title | PD | Vol | FT | PT | Educ Req | Status | Benefits |
|---|---|---|---|---|---|---|---|
| Program Specialist | 1 | - | 1 | - | Post-Graduate Courses or Degree | Other Contract | Yes |
| ADEPT Coordinators | 17 | - | - | 17 | High School Diploma | Hourly Non-Contract | Yes |
| ADEPT Support Teachers | 55 | - | - | 55 | High School Diploma | Hourly Non-Contract | Yes |
| ADEPT Lead Teachers | 16 | - | - | 16 | High School Diploma | Hourly Non-Contract | Yes |
| ADEPT Art Specialists | 7 | - | - | 7 | Some College | Hourly Non-Contract | Yes |
| ADACPP Counselors | 7 | - | - | 7 | Some College | Hourly Non-Contract | Yes |
| ADACPP Drama Teacher | 1 | - | - | 1 | Some College | Hourly Non-Contract | Yes |
| ADACPP Facilitators | 8 | - | - | 8 | College Degree | Hourly Non-Contract | Yes |
| ADACPP Coordinators | 24 | - | - | 24 | College Degree | Hourly Non-Contract | Yes |

| State/District Requirements | None. |
| --- | --- |
| Preferred Background | There are no state requirements, but ADEPT prefers coordinators to be qualified to teach as well as serve in administrative roles. |
| Employee Education and Training Represented | Prekindergarten and early childhood education; elementary education; child care; nursing; child development and family studies. |
| Administration | The assistant program specialist reports to the director of student support services of the New Orleans Parish School Board. The specialists for guidance and early childhood development are closely involved with the program, as are school-site principals and selected teachers whose input is vital to the delivery of services to the students. |
| Relationship to the Schools | "As the program has grown, so has school district responsiveness," comments Ms. Torcson. The schools help the program with computerized payroll for the ADEPT staff and diagnostic services for children. Some teachers work both for ADEPT and the schools, fostering closer relationships between teachers and parents. Approximately 60 public elementary schools participate in the program, providing space and equipment. |
| Community Links | ADEPT coordinates joint staff participation with public agencies and shares resources whenever possible. The Junior League headquarters was used for a talk sponsored by ADEPT on molested children, for instance. |
| Funding | Client fees, 71 percent; federal funding through the Office of Prevention and Recovery from Alcohol and Drug Abuse, 29 percent. |
| | Fees charged to parents range from $18 to $31 per month for beforeschool care and $20 to $65 per month for afterschool care, depending on intensity of services and reductions if the child is eligible for the free or reduced-price lunch program. Total costs per child per month may range from $38 per month for part-time before- and afterschool care for a student on a free lunch to $96 per month for full-time before- and afterschool care for students whose lunch is not subsidized. |
| In-Kind Resources | The school system donates space and supplies, including video and sound equipment; businesses offer computer paper, wood, and a variety of art materials. |
| Funding History | "Except for fee-based programs in extremely poor neighborhoods where federal block grants are necessary to cover program costs, virtually every program is solvent," says Ms. Torcson, "down to the last Crayola." |

*Activities are geared to giving children a sense of the options open to them, providing them with opportunities for success, and helping them build a positive self-image.*

| | |
|---|---|
| **Objectives** | The program seeks to help children extend their interpersonal relationships and to develop children's self-esteem, sense of belonging, respect for others, and confidence in their ability to learn. Ms. Torcson adds that she hopes ADEPT will always retain its family-centered approach by preserving close relationships between parents and teachers through potluck suppers, special programs, and evening meetings. |
| | ADACPP aims to provide substance-abuse education to teachers and help students make constructive decisions when confronted with destructive influences. It hopes families will learn parenting skills and that the community at large will become aware of substance-abuse prevention efforts and available community resources. |
| **Evaluation** | ADEPT, which is not supported by grants, does not require evaluation. When parental concerns arise, issues are handled individually. However, parents are always encouraged to give ADEPT feedback regarding service delivery. "Evaluation," says Ms. Torcson, "is our growing tool." |
| | Financed by a grant, ADACPP is evaluated annually by the New Orleans Parish School Board's Department of Accountability. Staff members circulate survey questionnaires, collect participation data, and review ADACPP's performance according to the guidelines specified in the grant requirements. |
| **Replication** | ADEPT has received national attention in the *New York Times* and has been sought out by other school districts as a model. |
| **Materials Available** | None. |

# Chapter 1 Preschool and Parenting Program

Networking
Home visits
Preschool
Toy lending
Newsletter
Hotline

Resource library
Parent support groups
Individual counseling
Health/nutrition education
Health care referral

Parenting/child development education
Parent-child joint activities
Community services info/referral
Developmental exams/screening
Child care info/referral

| | |
|---|---|
| **Contact:** | Dr. Helen Kurtz, District Early Childhood Specialist |
| **Address:** | Professional Development Center |
| | Scottsdale Public Schools |
| | Scottsdale, AZ 85250 |
| | (602) 852-2263 |
| **Established:** | Phased in from 1968 to 1983, local initiative |
| **Budget '88-'89:** | $162,588 total budget for three related programs (Home-Base: $56,015; prekindergarten: $52,073; PANDA: $54,500) |
| **Sources:** | Federal Chapter 1 funds, state allocations |
| **Size:** | 90 families |
| **Area Served:** | Scottsdale School District |
| **Auspices:** | District Pupil Services |

*Four-year-old Ricky entered the prekindergarten program extremely timid, with limited communication skills and such a poor self-image he did not know whether he was a boy or a girl. At first he would cower in the corner and cry, but a lot of praise and a rich, stimulating environment allowed Ricky to grow and develop. His end-of-year screenings revealed remarkable progress; his verbal skills had skyrocketed, and teachers are confident that he will meet with success in kindergarten.*

## Community

Scottsdale is an exclusive resort town, distinguished by valley, desert, and mountain landscape, yet the community contains extremes of affluence and poverty. The school district serves an ethnically diverse population; 19 languages are represented and minorities make up 27 percent of the target population. The academic future of the majority of children from non-English-speaking families is considered in jeopardy. Four of Scottsdale's 15 elementary schools qualify to receive Chapter 1 funds. In the Yavapai Elementary School, which houses the Chapter 1 programs for the district, half of the children come from single-parent households; nearly half receive subsidized lunches.

## Philosophy and Goals

The Chapter 1 Preschool and Parenting Program's three components, Home-Base, prekindergarten, and the special needs program, PANDA (Program for Assessed Needs in Developmental Areas), work collectively to diminish the need for special education services to children by encouraging active learning, risk taking, and decision making.

Chapter 1 intervention programs encourage parent involvement to assure a more successful educational future for targeted children. Through Home-Base and the prekindergarten, the program models techniques of positive parenting and effective teaching. Goals include helping educationally disadvantaged families create a stimulating environment for their toddlers. Learning, the program emphasizes, should be the shared responsibility of the child, the school, the home, and the community.

## History and Origins

In 1968, a federal Chapter 1 grant funded the prekindergarten program for high-risk children of minority and educationally disadvantaged families. The impetus for the program came from within the system. It was unique in the area and pulled in children from neighboring districts. Ten years later, Scottsdale added a home-based component for two- to three-year-olds. In 1982, anticipating a new federal law that would mandate special education for preschoolers, the district collaborated with a local special education evaluation agency to sponsor PANDA. In 1983, the school system adopted PANDA to serve preschoolers with special needs throughout the district.

## Features

Home-Base and the prekindergarten create a two-tiered approach to early intervention: families with two- and three-year-olds identified as at risk through diagnostic screening using the Developmental Indicators for the Assessment of Learning (DIAL-R) receive home visits followed by prekindergarten for four-year-olds.

**Home-Base** provides weekly home visits by a certified teacher and registered nurse to help families cultivate an atmosphere conducive to early learning in the home. Once a month, parent and child come to school and participate in a group activity with other Home-Base families. The program promotes access to health care by referral.

**Chapter 1 Prekindergarten** provides children with the skills and concepts necessary for successful entry into the district's kindergarten program. Four-year-olds (either graduates of Home-Base or new students identified through the DIAL-R) attend four half-day sessions weekly throughout the academic year, which prepare them for later schooling. Consistent with the approach of the elementary program, the prekindergarten program encourages active learning, risk taking, and decision making.

**PANDA** is a preschool designed to provide developmentally appropriate experiences for children between ages three and five who have handicaps in speech and language, vision, hearing, or physical or mental development.

## Participants

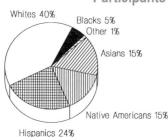

Whites 40%
Blacks 5%
Other 1%
Asians 15%
Native Americans 15%
Hispanics 24%

Eligibility for Chapter 1 programs is determined by the DIAL-R screening instrument for children ages two to four. Families with limited English proficiency are targeted for screening. PANDA participants are three- or four-year-olds whose multiple special needs require specific intervention. These children may be considered "educable" or "trainable" mentally handicapped or may have speech, visual, auditory, or other handicaps. In 1987-88, the Chapter 1 Preschool and Parenting Program served 78 children, 77 mothers, and 70 fathers; 9 percent single parents, 1 percent teen parents; 70 percent of the eligible population.

## Parent Education

All three programs incorporate informal opportunities for education in child development, health care, and nutrition. Parents assist as volunteers in the classroom or on field trips and are encouraged to observe their children in the school setting. They use the resource room in the Yavapai Elementary School, participate in a monthly "go to school day," and attend a spring workshop series. Home-Base and prekindergarten teachers model techniques of positive parenting and effective teaching.

## Curriculum

The prekindergarten program uses the *High/Scope* curriculum and district-prepared materials. The approach is experiential, with a lot of verbal interaction between English-speaking children and children for whom English is a second language. Home-Base is play-centered. Teachers set goals on the basis of observation and need. For instance, when over half of the three-year-olds were still drinking from bottles, a reasonable goal became helping mothers recognize the importance of developing such socializing skills as handling a cup. Field trips to playgrounds, malls, and dairies expose children to new challenges. "Some children had never seen steps," observes the director, Dr. Helen Kurtz. Materials are those commonly found in homes or in the wider neighborhood and are supplemented by the school's toy- and book-lending library.

## Sites

All three programs operate out of the Yavapai Elementary School and the homes of participating families. Site arrangements have been stable since the program's inception. An additional site for the PANDA program opened at Cherokee Elementary School in September 1989.

## Parent Involvement

Parents have a say in program planning through an annual needs survey, formal and informal parent conferences, volunteering in the classroom, and bimonthly meetings with the school psychologist and the behavioral specialist. During an initial home visit, prekindergartners' parents contract with teachers to participate actively in the program and to collaborate on home-learning activities. In addition, parents serve on advisory committees at both the district and school levels. "The program is responsive to parents' needs," says the director, " and receptive to what they have to offer. We always try to find something they feel important about and give them the opportunity to express that." Periodic luncheons in which everyone brings their own ethnic dishes "give mothers a chance to shine." Fathers work on playground equipment and gain a sense of pride and ownership. "The program is supportive and nonthreatening," she observes. "It tries to keep communication open, limit bureaucratic machinations, and streamline services so that parents have direct contact with teachers. There are direct phone lines to the program staff at school. We encourage suggestions."

## Outreach

Families learn of the program through community networks and former participants, in addition to media releases, elementary school newsletters, child-find activities, kindergarten registration and screening, and prekindergarten screening. The "missing population," as the director puts it, are new parents, generally non-English speakers, who do not yet have children in the system. The program is working on ways to initiate activities to find preschool children, particularly the handicapped, through mailings to social service agencies and pediatricians and through postings in libraries and Laundromats. A bicultural team has started to develop program materials for families whose first language is not English.

| Job Title | PD | Vol | FT | PT | Educ Req | Status | Benefits |
|---|---|---|---|---|---|---|---|
| Director | 1 | - | - | 1 | Post-Graduate Courses or Degree | K-12 Contract | Yes |
| Teachers | 3 | - | 3 | - | College Degree/ Post-Graduate Courses or Degree | K-12 Contract | Yes |
| Parent Training Specialists | 1 | - | 1 | - | College Degree | Hourly Contract | Yes |
| Speech/ Language Therapist | 1 | - | - | 1 | College Degree/ Post-Graduate Courses or Degree | K-12 Contract | Yes |
| Instructional Assistants | 2 | - | 2 | - | High School Diploma/ Some College | Hourly Non-Contract | Yes |
| Occupational Therapist | 1 | - | - | 1 | College Degree/ Post-Graduate Courses or Degree | Hourly Contract | No |
| Physical Therapist | 1 | - | - | 1 | College Degree/ Post-Graduate Courses or Degree | Hourly Contract | No |

**State/District Requirements**

For teachers, special education or elementary education certification; for speech and language specialists and occupational and physical therapists, state certification.

**Preferred Background**

For teachers, three to five years of experience in early childhood education; for instructional assistants, a high school diploma and early childhood experience; for speech and language pathologists, clinical competency and early childhood experience.

**Employee Education and Training Represented**

Infant and toddler education; prekindergarten and early childhood education; elementary education; education, grades 7 to 12; bilingual education; special education; parent educator; child care; health and nutrition; nursing; occupational and physical therapy; speech therapy; psychology; social work; child development and family studies; research and evaluation.

**Administration**

The early childhood specialist, who coordinates the two Chapter 1 programs and the special needs PANDA program, is responsible for special education services and curriculum development for preschool through third grade. The early childhood specialist position is new, and was established to "bridge the gap between pupil services, special education services, and elementary education," notes Dr. Kurtz. The position reports to the director of pupil services, and ultimately to the superintendent and the school board. "This is the first year the system has had an early childhood specialist, the first time the school has looked at early childhood across an age range. It is a different perspective. Philosophically, and through program implementation, the system has identified a real need," she says.

Relationship to the Schools

"It's ideal to be part of the system," says the director. "There are so many different support factors: administrative expertise, research facilities for data, good salaries and full benefits for the staff, no turnover problems. For the schools, early intervention can assure success." An early childhood planning team, including the special education teachers and coordinator, the curriculum specialists, and the school psychologist, coordinate early childhood services in the district. Their goal is to offer a continuum of services, including a staff daycare program and an English as a Second Language (ESL) preschool classroom. An interdisciplinary team facilitates the transition from Home-Base into the prekindergarten and kindergarten programs. "We literally hand them over to another teacher," observes Dr. Kurtz. Information goes directly to teachers, so they know what approaches work best with each family. "Teachers are not afraid to get involved with families . . . they are much less detached . . . . The teacher in the four- year-old program makes home visits to families every six weeks throughout the year . . . . When children move into the half-day kindergarten program there is a lot of interaction with parents to help make this a positive change."

> *"The program is responsive to parents' needs," says the director, "and receptive to what they have to offer. We always try to find something they feel important about and give them the opportunity to express that."*

Community Links

The program collects food, clothing, and bedding from community agencies for its Home-Base families. "We try to refer families out to social service agencies, when appropriate. For instance, one little girl's shoes were too small, and another had no coat . . . the teacher took them out to the local community center for recycled clothes," says Dr. Kurtz.

Funding

Federal Chapter 1 and preschool incentive grant, 83 percent; state grant under preschool handicap, 17 percent.

In-Kind Resources

Local school district provides speech and language services, administrative personnel, screening resources, psychological services, nursing, space, and utilities.

Funding History

Increasing school district support characterizes the program.

> *"Teachers are not afraid to get involved with families . . . they are much less detached . . . . The teacher in the four-year-old program*

*makes home visits to families every six weeks throughout the year . . . . "*

**Objectives**

Objectives include raising parents' awareness of what they can do for their children and preparing children for school. "We've increased the level of awareness of parents about what's available for their children in terms of the range of expertise and given them the ability to tap into the right resources . . . taught them how to get screening and pursue intervention . . . . "

**Evaluation**

The grant process demands that the program keep developmental checklists for two- and three-year-olds, log contact times and places, and take parent surveys for the prekindergarten and PANDA. The program has applied for accreditation, which will be determined through a National Association for the Education of Young Children (NAEYC) study of its objectives and implementation.

**Replication**

The program is unique.

**Materials Available**

None.

# Chapter 1 Pre-K Program of Clark County School District

| | | |
|---|---|---|
| Networking | Parent-child joint activities | Parenting/child development education |
| Preschool | Health/nutrition education | Community services info/referral |
| Home visits | Child care info/referral | Instructional meetings for parents |
| Newsletter | | |

**Contact:** Mary Neumann, Coordinator
Elise Ax, Assistant Superintendent, Chapter 1 Programs

**Address:** 2832 East Flamingo Road
Las Vegas, NV 89121
(702) 799-5190

**Established:** 1988, Chapter 1, federal initiative, preschool component

**Budget '88-'89:** $158,000 of statewide $5.1 million initiative

**Sources:** Federal Chapter 1 funds

**Size:** 30 children (at this site) out of the 5,090 served throughout the state

**Area Served:** Clark County, Nevada

**Auspices:** Clark County Schools

*"Most of our successes are judged by changes in the children,"* notes Mary Neumann. A mother of a Chapter 1 preschooler was afraid to come to school, would not allow home visits, and refused to attend instructional meetings. The child's teacher continued to invite her and started making headway with the son, who brought school ideas and projects home. Finally, the mother's response changed; she started attending weekly meetings and has since become a regular volunteer and an advocate for the prekindergarten program. According to Mary Neumann, in this case the child made the difference.

**Community**

Las Vegas, with a population of 219,250, is the largest city in Clark County. Situated in the southwest corner of Nevada near the California border, the city has a desert climate. The region's largest employers are the hotels, gaming industry, and chemical plants. Unemployment is close to the national average. The area population is 71 percent white, 15 percent black, 8 percent Hispanic, and 6 percent Native American and Asian.

**Philosophy and Goals**

The Chapter 1 Pre-K Program encourages parent involvement in education and plans activities for parents that will bridge the gap between school and home.

**History and Origins**

In 1965, the federal Educational Consolidation Improvement Act (ECIA) allocated funds to establish Chapter 1 programs for economically and educationally disadvantaged children in the schools. At first channeling these funds into services for high school students, Nevada gradually used the funds to extend Chapter 1 programs to the elementary grades. In 1988, Clark County initiated a Chapter 1 preschool as a pilot project in two schools. Elise Ax, assistant superintendent of compensatory education for Chapter 1, and Mary Neumann, Chapter 1 teacher consultant, developed the project proposal based on the Ypsilanti High/Scope model. The associate superintendent, who was a proponent of early childhood education and enthusiastic about the success of the Chapter 1 kindergarten programs, lent his support to the preschool initiative.

The Chapter 1 Pre-K Program is designed to assist four-year-olds and their parents by promoting cognitive, social, emotional, and physical development and language and communication skills. Students attend classes four hours daily. Each class of 15 children is staffed by a teacher and a teacher's aide. Chapter 1 teachers are required to design a parent involvement component. Assisted by the Chapter 1 administrative staff, teachers develop training activities for parents and primary caregivers.

**Home visits** to students' families occur twice; additional visits are scheduled if necessary. Advance notice is sent out to parents, a time set up, and the appointment confirmed twice. The school is notified when, where, and for how long the visit is scheduled. Ms. Neumann comments, "The purpose of the home visit is to give parents positive feedback and instruction." Teachers leave packets of educational materials for parents on subjects such as improving fine motor skills or learning how to use household objects to teach classification.

**Instructional meetings** for parents occur weekly for an hour, often at the end of the school day. Attendance varies from 3 to 20 parents. The program asks parents to suggest convenient meeting times. Teachers arrange for child care, or parents send their children home.

## Participants

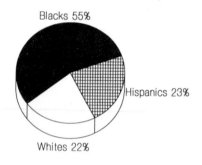

Blacks 55%

Hispanics 23%

Whites 22%

Children eligible for Chapter 1 have received a standardized developmental test score, or stanine, of 1, 2, or 3. Children most in need are the first to be accepted into Chapter 1 programs. "It is very important," says Mary Neumann, "to have Chapter 1 preschools. Otherwise, these kids wouldn't be able to attend preschool." Twenty-five percent of the parents in the entire program are single and 5 percent are teens.

*"Many district teachers, especially in kindergarten, are pleased by our curriculum and the 'risk-free' environment it promotes, where children are taught at their own level."*

## Parent Education

At weekly instructional meetings parents are encouraged to teach their children early learning concepts. The program helps parents of preschoolers further their own education by linking them to appropriate resources.

## Curriculum

The *Art of Parenting* and *Active Parenting* form the basis of the curriculum, supplemented by other materials including *Two-Step Direction,* which helps parents set clear expectations for their children. For the preschool, Ms. Neumann asserts, "The choice of teacher is very important, but equally important is the choice of curriculum. It must be developmentally appropriate, not a 'watered-down' kindergarten . . . . Many district teachers, especially in kindergarten, are pleased by our curriculum and the 'risk-free' environment it promotes, where children are taught at their own level."

## Sites

The Chapter 1 Pre-K Program is located in two schools; one in a predominantly black neighborhood, the other in a Hispanic neighborhood. Other Chapter 1 programs are scattered throughout the city's schools.

The program's main office and presentation rooms for special workshops are in a school district building, the home base for Chapter 1, its teacher consultants, and support staff.

**Parent Involvement**

Parents are asked to volunteer; Ms. Neumann says that in Nevada, however, volunteers have to be fingerprinted and very few Chapter 1 parents are willing to do that. She notes that "the few who do have become excellent volunteers and program advocates." A Chapter 1 district parent advisory committee, with representatives from every school advisory committee, meets quarterly to share information and host a speaker.

**Outreach**

In an effort to recruit children for the preschool program, letters were sent to the homes of Chapter 1 children who had younger siblings.

**Staff**

| Job Title | PD | Vol | FT | PT | Educ Req | Status | Benefits |
|-----------|----|----|----|----|----------|--------|----------|
| Director | 1 | - | 1 | - | Post-Graduate Courses or Degree | Other Contract | Yes |
| Teachers | 2 | - | 2 | - | Post-Graduate Courses or Degree | K-12 Contract | Yes |
| Teachers Aides | 2 | - | 2 | - | High School Diploma | Hourly Contract | Yes |

**State/District Requirements**

The administration and teaching staff must be certified by the state.

**Preferred Background**

None.

**Employee Education and Training Represented**

Prekindergarten and early childhood education; elementary education; education, grades 7 to 12; parent educator.

**Administration**

The Chapter 1 Pre-K Program is administered entirely within the public school system. The director reports to the assistant superintendent of schools of the Clark County School District. Other school departments involved include: personnel, accounting, data processing, transportation, instructional services units, elementary and secondary education, curriculum and instruction, research and development, purchasing, and school planning. The county Chapter 1 advisory board, composed of paid staff members and program participants, meets four times annually and is responsible for program planning and establishing relationships with community social service agencies.

**Relationship to the Schools**

The Chapter 1 Pre-K Program is part of the school system and maintains relationships with school nurses, psychologists, counselors, and elementary and secondary teachers. According to Ms. Neumann, the key person in running a successful Chapter 1 program is the principal. "A cooperative principal will go out of his way to accommodate the program and make good choices for teachers . . . ." She also notes that "part of a Chapter 1 teacher's job is to communicate with other teachers. We have set an example for staff training and development. After we train our teachers, they return to their schools and make presentations, both formally [at staff meetings] and informally [through conversations in staff lounges]. Principals have been very careful to place the best people in Chapter 1 staff positions. Our teachers help other teachers."

**Community Links**

The Chapter 1 Pre-K Program brings speakers in from the community and coordinates services with other agencies. Recently, a police representative addressed the county parent advisory board meeting about early signs of delinquent behavior.

A librarian interested in the program has opened the library weekly, at a special time, to read stories to children in the prekindergarten programs. Under the supervision of their preschool teachers, these children are also allowed to take books out.

*"Part of a Chapter 1 teacher's job is to communicate with other teachers. We have set an example for staff training and development. After we train our teachers, they return to their schools and make presentations."*

**Funding**

One hundred percent of the Clark County School District's Chapter 1 funds come from the federal government.

**Funding History**

The Educational Consolidation Improvement Act (ECIA) of 1965 channeled federal funds into school programs for economically and educationally disadvantaged children. These Chapter 1 monies have funded Clark County's preschool program since its inception in 1988.

**Objectives**

The program's objectives are to increase students' learning abilities, foster children's positive self-image, and prepare children for success in school and in life.

**Evaluation**

Chapter 1 requires formal pre- and postevaluations to indicate eligibility and to report on gains or setbacks.

**Replication**

The program has not been replicated.

**Materials Available**

None.

# Child Development Programs of the Pomona Unified School District

*Carlos, a Native American construction worker and the single parent of four children, was unable to find daycare for his infant. Forced to bring the child to work, he found himself changing diapers at the construction site. His child care problems were solved when his baby was placed in one of the program's infant centers, while his older children attended another center.*

| | | |
|---|---|---|
| Networking | Child care info/referral | Parent-child joint activities |
| Preschool | Referrals for medical care | Parenting/child development education |
| Child care | Parent involvement activities | Free meals for low-income child care |
| Newsletter | Community services info/referral | Health/nutrition education |
| Family therapy | Developmental exams/screening | Resource/toy-lending library |
| Crisis intervention | Mother/father support groups | Individual counseling |

**Contact:** Bill Ewing, Administrator, Child Development Programs

**Address:** 1707 North Town
Pomona, CA 91767
(909) 623-1461

**Established:** 1969, citizens' petition; joint initiative between school district and state

**Budget '88-'89:** $3,500,000

**Sources:** State government, federal government, client fees, in-kind contributions

**Size:** 1050 children

**Area Served:** Pomona Unified School District

**Auspices:** Pomona Unified School District Educational Services Department

### Community

Although in itself an urban center, Pomona is considered a suburb of Los Angeles. The population of 118,000 reflects a striking 36 percent population increase since 1986. In 1969 Pomona was viewed as a quiet, "citrus" community with many retired citizens. After the Watts riots, many black families moved to Pomona, the city experienced a "white flight," and the schools' populations shifted to reflect the new predominance of minorities. The schools are 56 percent Hispanic, 22 percent black, and 22 percent white.

### Philosophy and Goals

The Child Development Program (CDP) provides comprehensive, high-quality, affordable child care and developmentally appropriate programs that meet the needs of families from different income levels.

### History and Origins

Head Start came to the Pomona Unified School District in the mid-1960s and set the stage for the Child Development Program, which was started a few years later by a group of Pomona citizens who petitioned the Pomona Board of Education for a child care program to help low-income families. Spearheading the drive were homemakers and women involved in social service agencies, members of the Jewish community, and school personnel seeking solutions to potential racial conflicts. Three thousand people signed a petition to fund a child care program, which became a reality through a joint initiative of the California Department of Education and the Pomona Unified School District. State money funded building construction and the local school district provided funds for operation expenses and staff.

### Features

The Child Development Program is multifaceted.

**Children's Centers** provide daycare to children from infancy to age 13; one center remains open until midnight for parents who work or take classes late. Parents meet monthly to discuss parenting issues and share legislative information relevant to CDP's future expansion.

**Head Start State Preschool Program** and the **State Preschool Program** run for three hours a day, include biannual home visits, and require parent participation. For Head Start, parent education classes and parent involvement are federally mandated.

**School-Age Parenting Infant Development Program** provides quality child care for the infants of teen parents while parents attend regular classes and special parenting classes at an alternative high school. Teen participants also do practicum work in infant child care centers and may attend meetings on health and nutrition.

**Respite Child Care** is a short-term emergency program that locates and pays for child care for families in crisis. Parents meet with psychologists who make referrals for couples or individual counseling; parents are informed of CDP's child care and parent education resources.

**Latchkey Program**, **Alternative Payment Program**, and **Alternative Payment Latchkey Program** arrange and pay for child care and afterschool programs for children from low-income families. CDP also provides fee-based child care and child care referral to families who can afford to pay.

## Participants

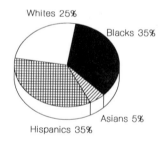

Whites 25%
Blacks 35%
Asians 5%
Hispanics 35%

According to Mr. Ewing, CDP administrator, the program preceded years of racial tension and responded to new residents' needs. He added that it took years to get Hispanics involved because they used an extended-family network for child care. As increasing numbers joined the job market they became involved in the program.

In 1987-88, 950 children, 300 mothers, and 200 fathers participated in the program's activities; approximately 25 percent were single parents and 3 percent were teen parents. Figures for 1988-89 are unavailable. Mr. Ewing notes that there is a long waiting list for child care in Pomona.

*Three thousand people signed a petition to fund a child care program, which became a reality through a joint initiative of the California Department of Education and the Pomona Unified School District.*

## Parent Education

Parents involved in CDP learn about child development through parent meetings and home visits; they are also encouraged to take courses from the school district's career and vocational education programs. Most parents in the Head Start program are unemployed, and for them the program represents the first step out of the home. Many of these families are non-English speaking. According to Bill Ewing, "Within two to three years, they turn into community leaders with good jobs."

**Curriculum**

The Children's Centers, the State Preschool Program, and the Head Start Preschool Program use the *High / Scope* curriculum. The School-Age Parenting Infant Development Program is adapting some of the High/Scope methodology to its existing informal curriculum.

**Sites**

The resource and referral program, Alternative Payment Program, Alternative Payment Latchkey Program, and Respite Child Care are administered in the CDP offices, a renovated parsonage. CDP's other sites are in public elementary schools, preschools, religious facilities, private home child care facilities, public secondary schools, an alternative high school, and community agencies.

**Parent Involvement**

Each children's center has a 12-member parent advisory group that does fundraising and plans events for children. Head Start's parent advisory board makes recommendations to the school board to hire and fire staff.

**Outreach**

The program has a large waiting list and does little additional recruitment. However, in an effort to reach more Hispanics, flyers are printed in Spanish and distributed in Hispanic neighborhoods.

**Staff**

| Job Title | PD | Vol | FT | PT | Educ Req | Status | Benefits |
|---|---|---|---|---|---|---|---|
| Management | 3 | - | 3 | - | Post-Graduate Courses or Degree | Other Contract | Yes |
| Head Teachers | 12 | - | 12 | - | Some College/ College Degree | Other Contract | Yes |
| Teachers | 28 | - | 24 | 4 | Some College/ College Degree | Other Contract | Yes |
| Psychologist | 1 | - | - | 1 | Post-Graduate Courses or Degree | Other Contract | Yes |
| Nurses | 2 | - | 1 | 1 | Post-Graduate Courses or Degree | Other Contract | Yes |
| Clerical | 6 | - | 5 | 1 | High School Diploma | Hourly Contract | Yes |
| Instructional Aides | 57 | - | 45 | 12 | High School Diploma | Hourly Contract | Yes |
| Custodial | 2 | - | 2 | - | High School Diploma | Hourly Contract | Yes |

**State/District Requirements**

Management staff members must have administrative credentials or a Children's Center supervision permit; head teachers must have a Children's Center permit and six units of administration and supervision; teachers are required to have Children's Center permits.

**Preferred Background**

The program looks for teachers who work well with both children and adults.

**Employee Education and Training Represented**

Infant and toddler education; prekindergarten and early childhood education; elementary education; bilingual education; special education; child care; medicine; health and nutrition; nursing; psychology; counseling; family therapy; social work; research and evaluation.

**Administration**

CDP's administrator reports to the assistant superintendent of educational services of the Pomona Unified School District. The program is administered solely within the school district. Monitoring agencies include the California Department of Education, Los Angeles County superintendent of schools, Community Care Licensing Department of Social Services, and Head Start Region IX.

**Community Links**

The program refers its participants to a wide array of medical and social service agencies, but most of its linkages are with schools and home child care providers. CDP has a contract with Greater Avenues to Independence (GAIN) to provide child care to families on welfare who are mandated to receive job training.

**Relationship to the Schools**

Bill Ewing writes, "We work with the principals, teachers, and the schools that will serve children in the program. In many instances our programs are located at the school a child will one day attend as a student."

**Funding**

State, 83 percent; federal, 15 percent; client paid fees, 1 percent; in-kind contributions, 1 percent. State monies fund the following programs: Children's Centers, State Preschool Program, Resource and Referral Program, Respite Child Care, Latchkey Program, Alternative Payment Program, and Alternative Payment Latchkey Program. State and federal monies support: Head Start State Preschool Program, GAIN, Child Care Food, Non-Subsidized Latchkey Program, and School-Age Parenting Infant Development. The school district dispenses the funds.

**In-Kind Resources**

The school district provides space and facilities; the Volunteer Action Agency provides volunteer staff.

**Funding History**

Funding is many times the program's original $100,000 budget in 1969.

**Objectives**

CDP addresses child care needs of families in the Pomona community and helps parents develop parenting skills and seek employment and job training.

**Evaluation**

The state requires external evaluations every three years and an annual self-evaluation for each of the programs. Bill Ewing asserts that "state evaluations haven't told us anything we didn't already know, but it helps to authenticate what we do. It keeps us together to see what we need to do to grow and reevaluate. Our annual self-evaluation reviews each program using a state-developed instrument designed to look at family development, the child's cognitive growth, and parent involvement. From this self-evaluation, we have seen that we need to train our staff to work more effectively with real behavior problems . . . We rate high in many areas of quality review — parent involvement, multicultural, health, positive self-image, parent education, and cognitive development." Each year surveys are sent out to parents involved in Children's Centers to determine their interests for future classes.

> *According to Mr. Ewing, the program preceded years of racial tension and responded to the new residents' needs.*

**Replication**

Program representatives from California, other states, and the Soviet Union have visited the Child Development Program with the intent of replicating its services.

**Materials Available**

A primer on school-age child care; description of the CDP's Mildly Ill Program. Other information is available upon request.

# Salem Early Childhood Center

The Salem Early Childhood Center works with teachers and parents to assist children with their adjustment to a new setting, new friends, and new challenges. During times of stress the program helps keep families intact. A homeless family at the center had to deal with a number of outside agencies including Head Start, Protective Services, the welfare office, and the school. Support from the center gave them the stability to find housing and carry on with their lives.

Child care
Networking
Warmline
Adult literacy
Toy lending
Preschool
Kindergarten

Medical care for children
Parent support groups
Newsletter
Resource library
Therapeutic assistance
Home visits

Parent-child joint activities
Parenting/child development education
Health/nutrition education
Developmental exams/screening
Child care info/referral
Referral to community agencies

| | |
|---|---|
| **Contact:** | Pamela Appleton<br>Director of Early Childhood Programs (Pre-K to Grade 2) |
| **Address:** | Memorial Drive<br>Salem, MA  01970<br>(508) 740-1181 |
| **Established:** | 1988, school initiative |
| **Budget '88-'89:** | $413,000 |
| **Sources:** | Local school district, state and federal funds, in-kind contributions, private foundations, and business donations |
| **Size:** | 153 families and 153 children |
| **Area Served:** | Salem, Massachusetts |
| **Auspices:** | Salem Public School System and the North Shore Community Action Program (Head Start) |

## Community

Salem is a small city approximately 25 miles north of Boston. A substantial number of low-income families, a significant blue-collar and white-collar population, and a cultural mix of Irish, Polish, Hispanic, and French-Canadian residents lend Salem the diversity and flavor of a large city. The average family income is approximately $17,000. Along with the rest of the state, Salem has shared in the recent period of prosperity, but the city was dealing with a budget deficit at the time the Salem Early Childhood Center was proposed.

## Philosophy and Goals

The Salem Early Childhood Center, formerly the Endicott Early Childhood Center, involves families in their children's education by providing appropriate services, information, programs, referrals, and opportunities for families to be involved in the schools at the building level. The program attempts to engage parents in dialogues concerning their children's progress and educational needs.

## History and Origins

In 1987, the Salem Public School System received a Chapter 188 grant to develop a program to assess the needs of its early childhood population. At the time, Head Start had a waiting list, and many children and their families were going unserved. Although the Chapter 188 grant helped pay for several openings in Head Start slated for Hispanic children, many children remained on the waiting list.

In January 1988, the superintendent of schools considered a plan presented by the director of early childhood programs to centralize all of the city's early childhood programs with the idea that pooling services would save money that could then be rechanneled to children's services. Although Salem was facing a budget deficit and new programs were hard to justify, funds were targeted to renovate an older school building to centralize existing services.

The initial $20,000 for the renovations came out of the regular transportation budget from funds no longer needed once all the early childhood services were united under one roof. Community-minded individuals and organizations, including the Bank of New England, the Salem Trust Commission, local developers, and contractors, provided the necessary support through grants, materials, and services. The program also received the support of the Department of Education, the school superintendent and administration, the Head Start director, and many others. By November 1988, despite prevailing doubts, rehabilitation of the school building was complete and the program in place.

**Features**

The Salem Early Childhood Center is composed of four subprograms that are part of the Salem Public School System. The North Shore Community Action Program/Head Start and the Campfire Boys and Girls Inc./After School Program are also housed at the center, but are administered by their respective agencies.

**Integrated Preschools and Kindergarten**, begun in September 1989, offers educational experiences for a diverse population of children in classrooms deliberately planned to allow the least restrictive environment possible. Children with special needs are grouped with mainstream children in a center-based, language-enriched program. The initiative is responsive to state and federal requirements to desegregate minority and low-income students and mainstream special needs students.

**Chapter 1 Preschool**, begun in March 1987, is a preschool for four-year-olds. The Chapter 1 attendance area residence requirement was waived when the school system contributed Chapter 188 funds to provide comparable services for eligible children in noneligible attendance areas, thus creating greater diversity within the classroom. Transportation is provided by Salem Public Schools.

The **Mother-Child Home Program**, begun in March 1988, provides home-based services to children aged 18 to 30 months, primarily from low-income families who receive Aid to Families with Dependent Children (AFDC). The primary objective is to increase the level of verbal interaction between mother and child, thus improving the child's academic skill level and lessening the need for remedial services upon entry into school.

**Parent Resource Center**, opened in November 1988 and funded by a grant from the Bank of New England in Essex, Massachusetts, serves children from birth to age seven and their families. The materials in the parent resource center are bilingual (Spanish and English). Parents have access to books, games, and interactive educational materials for home use.

**Campfire Boys and Girls Inc./After School Program** provides child care and educational services to children ages three to seven who are already taking part in a Salem Early Childhood Center program.

**North Shore Community Action Program/Head Start** provides a preschool experience for three- and four-year-olds from low-income families. The curriculum is based on individual need and encourages parents to participate in their children's education. In addition to educational services provided on site, home visits are made by teachers and mental health professionals. Transportation is provided.

## Participants

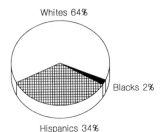

Whites 64%

Blacks 2%

Hispanics 34%

The main criteria for participation is residency in Salem. Other prerequisites for participation vary according to the subprogram. The Head Start program specifically targets three- and four-year-olds from low-income families. The Mother-Child Home Program targets low-income and AFDC dependent families. The director estimates that in 1988-89, 50 percent of all participants in the Salem Early Childhood Center were single and 10 percent were teens.

*Strong local support, instrumental in getting the program underway, has helped make the services well known to the community.*

## Parent Education

Parent education is accomplished through lectures, parent-child joint activities, a parent resource and toy-lending library, parent support groups and therapeutic services, a home visiting program, and the adult literacy program available through Salem High School. A monthly Parent Network Series (workshops and lectures) and monthly therapeutic group sessions offer parents a different kind of forum in which to air concerns or address dysfunctional behavior.

## Curriculum

The curriculum emphasizes language experience (and the "whole language" approach, originating in Australia), literacy acquisition, and socialization based on models endorsed by the National Association of the Education of Young Children (NAEYC) and current research. Kindergarten children use the IBM *Write to Read* program in English and in Spanish (VALE). Thematic units are enhanced by special events such as storytellers, puppet shows, nature and science programs, various cultural programs, and field trips, which are each chosen to match classroom activities and the needs and interests of children.

## Sites

The Salem Early Childhood Center occupies the Endicott School, which is situated in a low-income area of the city that is easily accessible. In less than a year, the center has outgrown its site, and some programming occasionally occurs at other locations. The school district is planning expansion, including an early childhood wing.

## Parent Involvement

According to Ms. Appleton, parent involvement, through donated services and materials, proved crucial to renovating the school building and getting the program off the ground. Many parents serve on the Early Childhood Advisory Council, mandated by Chapter 188, which had a hand in planning the coordination of early childhood services in Salem. Of 33 members, 8 are parents who participate in the program and 10 come from the community. Remaining board members are program and school personnel and representatives from private and public community agencies. The board meets five times a year to approve the budget, maintain relationships with community agencies, and act as an advisory group. Traditionally, parent involvement has been channeled through the Endicott Parent-Teacher Organization (PTO), which has jurisdiction over extracurricular activities and enrichment programs in addition to school fundraising efforts.

## Outreach

Strong local support, instrumental in getting the program underway, has helped make the services well known to the community. Advertisements for specific programs are placed in the local newspaper, and additional outreach efforts are made through bilingual social service agencies and within the school through the Department of Special Education and Chapter 1. Home visits reach low-income parents of children with severe developmental problems, who are sometimes reluctant to be involved in the program. Recruitment of transient Hispanic families is problematic.

## Staff

| Job Title | PD | Vol | FT | PT | Educ Req | Status | Benefits |
|---|---|---|---|---|---|---|---|
| Teachers (Public School) | 6 | - | 5 | 1 | College Degree | K-12 Contract | Yes |
| Teachers (Head Start) | 2 | - | 2 | - | Some College | Other Contract | Yes |
| Assistant Teachers/ Instructional Aides | 8 | - | 7 | 1 | High School Diploma/ Some College | Hourly Contract | Yes |
| Bilingual Outreach Parapro-fessional | 1 | - | 1 | - | Some College | Hourly Contract | Yes |
| Nurse | 1 | - | - | 1 | College Degree | Other Contract | No |
| Maintenance | 1 | - | - | 1 | High School Diploma | Hourly Contract | Yes |
| Volunteers | 10 | - | - | 10 | Some High School | - | No |
| Student Teachers | 4 | - | 4 | - | Some College | - | No |

## State/District Requirements

The Head Start program is responsible for hiring its own staff; the public school system requires the early childhood coordinator, teachers, and assistant teachers to meet Massachusetts Department of Education certification requirements.

## Preferred Background

Staff members should have knowledge of early childhood development, educational curriculum and teaching methods, and show evidence of continued professional growth. The program has had some difficulty recruiting bilingual staff members.

## Employee Education and Training Represented

Prekindergarten and early childhood education; elementary education; bilingual education administration; special education administration; parent educator; child care; medicine; health and nutrition; speech therapy; psychology; social work; child development and family studies; development and fundraising; research and evaluation.

## Administration

The public school programs are administered exclusively within the district, involving the Departments of Early Childhood Education, Equity Education, Special Education, and Language Arts and Chapter 1. The director meets with various school departments to coordinate efforts. Although the Head Start program is housed within the center, it is administered separately. The director of the center and the director of Head Start meet frequently and correspond regularly to coordinate administration.

**Relationship to the Schools**

Salem Early Childhood Center occupies a unique place within the Salem Public School System. Although the program has several funding streams from the private and corporate sector, the director holds the title of principal and the program has earned itself equal status with other public school departments.

**Community Links**

The program maintains strong ties to traditional human service agencies such as the Office for Children and the Departments of Education and Social Service. The program staff also works closely with the public library and local museums to design activities and educational programs for students and their families.

**Funding**

Funding comes through a variety of public agencies, which include the Salem Public School System, Chapter 1, Head Start, Chapter 636 (Equity Education), Departments of Education and Special Education, Chapter 188 discretionary funds, and Commonwealth inservice grants. Additional funding is provided through corporate and business donations, foundations and private agencies, private donations, and in-kind contributions.

**In-Kind Resources**

The volunteer staff provided by the parent organization; equipment by the Bank of New England and Salem Trust Commission; supplies and materials donated by local businesses.

**Funding History**

The Salem Early Childhood Center has an unusually diverse and creative array of funding sources. A blend of local, state, and federal grants gives the program flexibility in responding to families' needs. For example, federal and foundation funds have allowed the program to bring on staff two psychologists, a licensed counselor, and a university intern to provide comprehensive services to children and their families through Children's Friends and Family Services of Salem, a private agency in the city. Services include play therapy both in and outside of class, crisis intervention, individual and family therapy, and support groups. Since this is the first year the program has been in operation, no changes in funding are anticipated.

**Objectives**

Salem Early Childhood Center aims to coordinate delivery of comprehensive early childhood services to help children with wide variations in skills to reach their maximum potential. The program prepares children for the transition to the public schools and provides parents with the support and services vital to participation in their children's development and education.

**Evaluation**

An evaluation is planned for the end of the first year of operation. The Massachusetts Department of Education has initiated a more intensive three-year evaluation with Temple University called Project Impact to identify characteristics of programs which lead to positive outcomes for young children and their families.

**Replication**

The Mother-Child Home Program is an adaptation of the Verbal Interaction Project in Wantagh, Long Island, based upon the psychological research of Dr. Phyllis Levenstein and the Parent-Child Home Program in the Pittsfield, Massachusetts public schools. The Campfire Boys and Girls Inc./After School Program is an adaptation of the *Campfire After School Program Initiative*, available nationwide through Campfire, Inc. The Chapter 1 preschool is modeled on the Peabody Chapter 1 preschool in Peabody, Massachusetts.

**Materials Available**

*Writing to Read, Whole Language, Math Their Way* and information about the Salem Early Childhood Center are available from the director.

# Franklin Early Childhood Center

Kindergarten
Preschool
Networking
Child care
Newsletter

Parenting workshops
Parent support groups
Individual counseling
Child care info/referral
Resource library

Developmental exams/screening
Parent volunteer opportunities
Health/nutrition education
Community services info/referral
Parenting/child development education
Parent-child joint activities

| | |
|---|---|
| **Contact:** | Joyce McGinn, Principal/Program Director |
| **Address:** | Hewlett-Woodmere School District #14 |
| | 1180 Henrietta Place |
| | Hewlett, NY 11557-1100 |
| | (516) 374-8150 |
| **Established:** | 1978, state and local partnership; 1983, center established |
| **Budget '88-'89:** | Figures unavailable |
| **Sources:** | State, school district, and in-kind contributions (client fees for BEFORESCHOOL/AFTERSCHOOL) |
| **Size:** | 347 children and families |
| **Area Served:** | Hewlett-Woodmere School District |
| **Auspices:** | Instructional Services, Hewlett-Woodmere School District |

*One participant relates, "We speak two languages in our house and starting school was difficult for the children. They began school as prekindergartners and I think they are very successful now because of the extra help they received when they were very young . . . I have always volunteered to help with Italian-speaking families. We used to go house to house, the director and I, to talk to families and help them register in the program. Then I began working in the school as a monitor and helping the principal. I got more experience as the program grew bigger and I developed more skills in working with children. I enjoy being with children."*

## Community

Hewlett-Woodmere on Long Island's south shore is a traditional, middle-class, residential community comprised of several unincorporated and incorporated villages within the town of Hempstead. Hempstead's population of 40,404 includes a high percentage of well-educated adults. In the Hewlett-Woodmere School District, 93 percent of the high school graduates go to college. The community is mainly white; Hispanics, Asians, Pacific Islanders, and blacks make up 5 percent of the population. The seaside villages have an established air of solid, old-fashioned neighborhoods, good public works agencies, and a volunteer fire department. Country clubs dot the area and, with the exception of the area around Kennedy Airport that was rapidly built up in the 1950s and 1960s, industry has for the most part stayed away.

## Philosophy and Goals

The Franklin Early Childhood Center strives to involve parents in their children's education and to teach children to become self-confident learners. In keeping with the well-documented increase in the number of children enrolled in preschool, extended-day, and afterschool programs in the last eight years, Franklin Early Childhood Center's articulated goals include coordinating health, psychological, and social services to children through a centralized support system. The center also promotes early learning through innovative approaches that involve the "optimal use" of learning materials and collaboration among staff members. It assures social, ethnic, and economic integration and encourages parent involvement through parent education programs. The center operates on the theory that success in school is directly related to the emotional climate of the family and the degree of parent involvement at home and in school.

Franklin Early Childhood Center grew, program by program, into an established center within the Hewlett-Woodmere School District over 20 years. Hewlett-Woodmere's commitment to early childhood education began with a 1966 New York State-funded prekindergarten class for disadvantaged children. School district administrators wrote the proposal as a joint venture and saw the idea develop into an active program housed in an elementary school building. In 1975, the district closed one of its four elementary schools, but started a four-year-old cooperative prekindergarten through the Department of Community Services, instigated by the out-going superintendent. According to Joyce McGinn, director and principal of the Franklin Early Childhood Center, the program attracted the "lost group" of parents who couldn't afford private prekindergarten and yet didn't qualify for the state program. Ms. McGinn took charge of the cooperative prekindergarten, using parent volunteers to supplement teachers and aides in the classroom. She says that the program engaged parents who might otherwise have felt alienated from a bureaucracy they could never penetrate.

*The center operates on the theory that success in school is directly related to the emotional climate of the family and the degree of parent involvement at home and in school.*

In 1978, State Assemblyman Arthur Kremer backed a proposal for a comprehensive extended-day program, offered to all kindergarten children but aimed at families with parents who were going back to school or working. Again, school district administrators wrote a proposal for a $100,000 grant from the state. In the middle of that year they set up classes in the three elementary schools. Initially, the new program met with resistance from kindergarten teachers, who were unfamiliar with the idea. Over the years, says Ms. McGinn, things "got smoother," particularly when the program gathered under a separate umbrella in the Franklin School.

From the late 1970s on, the idea of offering a comprehensive package of educational programs to young children and services to families grew in a piecemeal fashion; each new program was supported by active community awareness of unmet needs, particularly those of nontraditional families: working and single-parent families, non-English-speaking homes, and so on. The biggest leap came with the Advisory Committee on School Reorganization in 1982, and the resulting transformation of the Franklin School into an early childhood center in 1983.

**Features**

The Franklin Early Childhood Center offers a comprehensive developmental early childhood program emphasizing parent involvement. In its commitment to effective early childhood education and continuity of experience in the public schools, the center brings together a number of previously established programs: Peninsula Education Nursery for Threes (PENT), New York State prekindergarten, kindergarten extended day, cooperative prekindergarten, AFTERSCHOOL, BEFORESCHOOL, regular kindergarten classes, readiness programs, and a parent-toddler program. Schedules and curricula are responsive to the needs of working and single parents, disadvantaged and developmentally delayed children, as well as traditional families and normal or precocious children. Services provided outside the classroom range from screening and diagnostic testing to special programs for strengths and needs, including English as a Second Language (ESL) and early intervention. Intellectual talents are addressed as seriously as disabilities and referrals to community resources and programs suggested.

## Participants

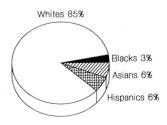

Whites 85%

Blacks 3%

Asians 6%

Hispanics 6%

The Franklin Early Childhood Center programs are open to prekindergarten- and kindergarten-age children and their parents who are residents of the Hewlett-Woodmere School District. Working parents qualify for the extended-day prekindergarten and BEFORESCHOOL and AFTERSCHOOL programs. Ms. McGinn feels the program reaches all residents who are eligible to participate. Fifteen percent of Franklin Early Childhood Center's participants are single parents.

*According to Joyce McGinn, director and principal of the Franklin Early Childhood Center, the program attracted the "lost group" of parents who couldn't afford private prekindergarten and yet didn't qualify for the state program.*

## Parent Education

The Being a Better Parent program brings together children under two years and their parents for joint activities and parent training. Training workshops prepare parents to participate in classrooms, and the Responsive Parenting Program offers parent training to all parents.

## Curriculum

Franklin Early Childhood Center is a developmental program based on the New York schools' prekindergarten curriculum. All curricula materials are developed by the Franklin Early Childhood Center staff. The program's educational style advocates learning by doing and uses the Sylvia Ashton-Warner experiential approach to reading.

## Sites

The Franklin Early Childhood Center is housed in a public elementary school in Franklin and includes 16 classrooms, a library, two cafeterias, special subject areas, a children's kitchen, an auditorium and gymnasium, playscape (interior playhouse and climbing equipment), outdoor playground, health office, and administrative offices. Transportation is provided by the school district for the New York State prekindergarten and kindergarten program. Parents provide transportation to the other programs.

## Parent Involvement

According to Ms. McGinn, participation in the center is a family affair. Approximately 60 percent of parents with kindergartners and 90 percent of parents with prekindergartners have participated in the classroom on a regular basis. In the classroom, parents take part in a careers program, sharing their careers with the children, and work as volunteer aides. In all aspects of their involvement in the program, from walking down the school hall to spending time at home with their children, parents are considered essential to the success of the program.

The center promotes its programs, services, and activities through district publicity, a school newsletter, and newspaper articles. The *New York Times* featured the Franklin Early Childhood Center in the Sunday Magazine section in 1986.

Franklin Early Childhood Center hires only certified teachers, all of whom have graduate degrees and have undergone extensive inservice training. District-trained paraprofessionals and volunteer parents assist the professional staff.

| Job Title | PD | Vol | FT | PT | Educ Req | Status | Benefits |
|---|---|---|---|---|---|---|---|
| New York State Pre-Kindergarten Teacher | 1 | - | 1 | - | Post-Graduate Courses or Degree | K-12 Contract | Yes |
| Kindergarten Teachers | 6 | - | 4 | 2 | Post-Graduate Courses or Degree | K-12 Contract | Yes |
| Cooperative Pre-Kindergarten Teachers | 5 | - | - | 5 | College Degree | Hourly Contract | Yes |
| Kindergarten Extended Day Teachers | 10 | - | - | 10 | College Degree | Hourly Contract | Yes |
| Pre-Kindergarten Extended Day Teachers | 4 | - | - | 4 | College Degree | Hourly Contract | Yes |
| Special Education Communication Class Teacher | 1 | - | - | 1 | Post-Graduate Courses or Degree | K-12 Contract | Yes |
| Peninsula Education Nursery for Threes Teacher | 1 | - | - | 1 | College Degree | Hourly Contract | Yes |
| Physical Education Teachers | 2 | - | 1 | 1 | Post-Graduate Courses or Degree | K-12 Contract | Yes |
| Librarian | 1 | - | - | 1 | Post-Graduate Courses or Degree | K-12 Contract | Yes |
| Nurse | 1 | - | 1 | - | College Degree | Other Contract | Yes |
| Social Worker | 1 | - | - | 1 | Post-Graduate Courses or Degree | K-12 Contract | Yes |
| Speech Specialist | 1 | - | - | 1 | Post-Graduate Courses or Degree | K-12 Contract | Yes |

**Staff**
(continued)

| Job Title | PD | Vol | FT | PT | Educ Req | Status | Benefits |
|---|---|---|---|---|---|---|---|
| English as a Second Language Specialist | 1 | - | - | 1 | Post-Graduate Courses or Degree | K-12 Contract | Yes |
| Center for Individual Help Specialists | 4 | - | - | 4 | Post-Graduate Courses or Degree | Hourly Contract | Yes |
| Reading Specialist | 1 | - | - | 1 | Post-Graduate Courses or Degree | Hourly Contract | Yes |
| Psychologist | 1 | - | - | 1 | Post-Graduate Courses or Degree | Other Contract | Yes |
| Aides | 26 | - | 4 | 22 | | Hourly Non-Contract | No |
| Be A Better Parent | 1 | - | - | 1 | College Degree | Other Contract | No |
| Before and After School Teacher | 1 | - | 1 | - | - | Hourly Non-Contract | - |
| Before and After School Aides | 5 | - | 5 | - | College Degree | Hourly Non-Contract | - |
| Clerical | 2 | - | 2 | - | - | Hourly Contract | Yes |
| Cafeteria Aides | 2 | - | - | 2 | - | Hourly Non-Contract | No |
| Bus Aides | 10 | - | - | 10 | - | Hourly Non-Contract | No |
| Student Interns | - | 8 | - | 8 | Some College | - | No |
| Volunteers | - | 16 | - | 16 | Some High School | - | No |
| National Council of Jewish Women Volunteers | - | 12 | - | 12 | - | - | No |

**State/District Requirements**

Teachers and specialists are required to have New York State certification in their respective fields.

**Preferred Background**

Franklin Early Childhood Center seeks caring, sensitive adults for all positions.

**Employee Education and Training Represented**

Prekindergarten and early childhood education; bilingual education; elementary education; special education; nursing; occupational and physical therapy; speech therapy; psychology; counseling; social work.

**Administration**

The director of Franklin Early Childhood Center reports to the deputy superintendent for instructional services in the Hewlett-Woodmere School District. The program is administered exclusively within the public education system.

| | |
|---|---|
| **Relationship to the Schools** | Administratively, fiscally, and physically, the center belongs to the public schools. |
| **Community Links** | BEFORESCHOOL is offered in cooperation with the Five Towns' Community Center. PENT is sponsored by the National Council of Jewish Women; Being a Better Parent is offered in conjunction with the Nassau Medical Center. The Hewlett-Woodmere School District has a strong interagency connection with Head Start, the YMCA, church and temple programs, daycare services, public and private agencies, other public schools, and private schools. Franklin Early Childhood Center has developed a children's services directory that lists all resources for children in public and nonpublic schools and in public and private agencies. Schools collaborate to provide inservice opportunities for teachers. Together, all of these organizations act as advocates for children. |
| **Funding** | The center is funded by the local school district, the state, client fees, and in-kind contributions (no percentages given). Franklin Early Childhood Center also receives a special legislative grant through the New York Bureau of Child Development, a New York State prekindergarten grant and federal Chapter 1 funding. |
| **In-Kind Resources** | Staff support services and transportation come from the National Council of Jewish Women for the PENT program and from a consultant with the Nassau Medical Center for the Being a Better Parent program. |
| **Funding History** | Funding for the center has been stable; state grants and district funding sources request annual written proposals. Special legislative grant funding for the center has increased by 50 percent since it began in 1983. |
| **Objectives** | The Franklin Early Childhood Center seeks parent involvement and quality education in the context of a comprehensive developmental early childhood program. |
| **Evaluation** | Evaluations for state grants occur yearly and, in addition, Ms. McGinn circulates questionnaires to prekindergarten and kindergarten parents, staff members, and students concerning the center's effectiveness in matching the environment and curriculum to children's sensory, cognitive, and physical development. Out of the teachers' survey the need for improved transition between kindergarten and first grade became apparent. |
| **Replication** | Other public school districts have visited and used portions of the program or curriculum. |
| **Materials Available** | Write to the program for more information. |

# Los Alamitos Child Development Center

| | | |
|---|---|---|
| Preschool | Health/nutrition education | Parenting/child development education |
| Toy lending | Parent discussion groups | Parent involvement opportunities |
| Home visits | Bilingual assistance | Developmental exams/screening |
| Newsletter | Resource library | Community services info/referral |
| Networking | Child care info/referral | Parent-child joint activities |

**Contact:** Barbara Halvorsen, Site Preschool Coordinator
Elaine Hamada, District Coordinator

**Address:** State Preschool Program
Los Alamitos Unified School District
11481 Foster Road
Los Alamitos, CA 90720
(310) 430-1021 ext. 337

**Established:** 1972, California state preschool grant

**Budget '88-'89:** $105,000

**Sources:** State and local school district funds

**Size:** 40 families at one site

**Area Served:** Los Alamitos, California

**Auspices:** Personnel and pupil services of Los Alamitos School District

**Community**

Los Alamitos, a stable, suburban community 25 miles outside of Los Angeles, is home to an armed forces reserve center. The majority of families participating in the preschool come from two military compounds in Los Alamitos.

**Philosophy and Goals**

The Los Alamitos Child Development Center, formerly the Los Alamitos State Preschool, aims to develop the "whole" child in an enriched educational environment. Hands-on experiences for children, parent participation, and the involvement of high school students as classroom aides are major components. The program encourages parent involvement in classroom activities and in support programs that reinforce learning at home. It fosters multicultural awareness, encourages differences in clothes, food, music, literature, games, and customs, and integrates these influences into the curriculum and activities.

**History and Origins**

In 1965, the California Department of Education established the statewide California State Preschool Initiative. Modeled after Head Start, the initiative provided a developmental preschool with opportunities for parent participation and education. The Los Alamitos Child Development Center began in 1972 with a grant proposal written by the assistant superintendent of the Los Alamitos School District. This local program has consistently served the same number of children with the same services. The school board has shown unwavering support for the preschool program by increasing funding annually, in spite of occasional resistance from ineligible families who do not understand the qualifications for entry and wonder why their children are not receiving comparable services.

The Los Alamitos Child Development Center offers two preschool classes (morning and afternoon sessions five days a week) for 20 children each. Parents are expected to volunteer in the classroom, go on field trips, and attend daytime workshops and discussions. Students from Laurel High School earn academic credit for their work as aides in the preschool. Bilingual aides assist Spanish-speaking parents and children. A toy-lending library circulates topic-related parent-child kits, developed by the staff to enhance learning at home. Developmental screening, a newsletter, home visits, and information and referrals to community agencies are integrated into family support services.

## Participants

Whites 43%

Blacks 11%

West Indians 1%

Asians 6%

Hispanics 39%

Following state guidelines, the Los Alamitos Child Development Center serves children ages three to five whose family incomes are at or below the ceiling approved for the year, with priority given to families with the lowest income. Participants come from a variety of ethnic backgrounds, many are from non-English-speaking homes, including Filipinos, Samoans, Vietnamese, and Mexicans. Twenty-five percent of the children speak Spanish. In 1988, the program served 54 mothers and children and 53 fathers; 2 percent were single parents.

*Resources continue to develop, says Ms. Halvorsen, who notes that at times you have to be "a little bit aggressive to get what you want" from agencies outside the school system.*

## Parent Education

Parent education sessions reflect the interests expressed on community surveys distributed during annual home visits. Speakers and group discussions focus on issues of developmentally appropriate behavior and behavior management, health and nutrition education, and the acquisition of learning skills.

## Curriculum

The program uses a developmental curriculum and relies heavily on experiential learning to reinforce verbal and auditory skills, spatial relations, classification, problem solving, sensory awareness, and visual discrimination. Materials are both prepackaged and developed by the staff, and the curriculum is tailored to match individual needs, age, and cognitive and social development. It is adapted to non-English-speaking families.

## Sites

The center has shifted location four times since 1972, a result of school closures and changing needs for space. In 1984, the center moved into the former kindergarten wing of a closed school site, which it shares with the continuation high school and district office. According to the director, the frequent moves have increased the program's visibility districtwide and made schools and residents aware of its presence.

## Parent Involvement

Parents serve on the advisory board, whose monthly meetings focus on increasing parent participation and networking. The board has a voice in curriculum, and spends a good part of the year becoming familiar with the educational objectives of the program.

**Outreach**

Recruitment is geared to low-income families. Personal contact, either with those already enrolled or with the community coordinator, remains the best strategy. Other outreach efforts include flyers sent home by the district and the program's own brochures.

**Staff**

| Job Title | PD | Vol | FT | PT | Educ Req | Status | Benefits |
|---|---|---|---|---|---|---|---|
| Teacher | 1 | - | 1 | - | College Degree | K-12 Contract | Yes |
| Bilingual Aide | 1 | - | - | 1 | High School Diploma | Hourly Contract | Yes |
| Instructional Aide | 1 | - | - | 1 | High School Diploma | Hourly Contract | Yes |
| Community Coordinator | 1 | - | - | 1 | High School Diploma | Hourly Contract | Yes |

**State/District Requirements**

For the teacher, elementary teaching credential; for the site supervisor, children's center supervision permit or administrative credential.

**Preferred Background**

None.

**Employee Education and Training Represented**

Prekindergarten and early childhood education; elementary education; parent educator; child care; nursing; speech therapy.

**Administration**

The director of classified personnel and pupil services of the Los Alamitos School District oversees the program director. The Child Development Division of the California Department of Education monitors the program.

**Relationship to the Schools**

Los Alamitos Child Development Center collaborates with the speech therapist, guidance counselor, and nurse in the special education department of the schools. Teachers make formal and informal referrals to the preschool. Transition to kindergarten is accompanied by an exchange of records and sharing of information.

**Community Links**

The preschool collaborates with outside social service agencies, referring families to food banks and local dental and medical professionals. Resources continue to develop, says Ms. Halvorsen, who notes that at times you have to be "a little bit aggressive to get what you want" from agencies outside the school system.

**Funding**

State preschool money, through the Child Development Division, and the California Department of Education, 72 percent; local school district, 28 percent.

**Funding History**

Grant money from the state has increased "somewhat" comments Ms. Halvorsen, but hasn't kept pace with salaries and the real cost of the program. The school district picks up the deficit because early intervention for special education has proved cost effective. "It has impressed the school board and community." Without this tangible show of support, the program would have closed or diminished in quality, she notes.

**Objectives**

The preschool's goals include providing an enriched environment that fosters the intellectual and social growth of each child. Parents' participation is viewed as essential to positive early development and later success in school.

**Evaluation**

The California Department of Education follows a three-year cycle of evaluation: a quality review followed by a compliance review, followed by a year off. In 1987, the program's compliance review was a positive experience, according to the director, and was useful in reinforcing good record keeping and internal organization.

**Replication**

The Los Alamitos Child Development Center follows the California State Preschool Initiative model, which is modeled after Head Start.

**Materials Available**

None.

# Project Hand-in-Hand

| | | |
|---|---|---|
| Preschool | Parent-child joint activities | Parenting/child development education |
| Networking | Health/nutrition education | Child care info/referral |
| Warmline | Resource center/library | Drop-in center |
| Newsletter | Biannual screening | Materials for school teachers |
| Toy lending | Community resource handbook | Teacher/parent workshops |
| Consultation | Developmental exams/screening | Community services info/referral |

**Contact:** Maria Richard, Early Childhood Coordinator

**Address:** Daniel Webster School
1456 Ocean Street
Marshfield, MA 02050
(617) 834-5048

**Established:** 1987, local initiative

**Budget '88-'89:** $108,200

**Sources:** Massachusetts Chapter 188 early childhood grant,
federal early childhood allocation funds,
Marshfield Public Schools, in-kind contributions

**Size:** 30 children in preschool, 1500 families use the resource center-library

**Area Served:** Marshfield Public Schools

**Auspices:** Early Childhood Department of the Marshfield Public Schools

**Community**

Marshfield is a small suburban "bedroom community" located 25 miles from Boston. The population is largely white; socioeconomic status ranges from low income to affluent. Project Hand-in-Hand targets the low- to middle-income group that is not income eligible for Head Start but cannot afford the expensive, private preschool programs available in the area. The group includes a large number of single-parent families who are eager for early intervention services.

**Philosophy and Goals**

The integrated early childhood program in Marshfield, part of which is Project Hand-in-Hand, is based on the developmental approach to early childhood education. According to this approach, children pass through a number of orderly stages in their growth while retaining a unique personality and an individual pattern of growth and development. For some families, Project Hand-in-Hand is the first contact with the school system; parents, especially those of special needs children, can be apprehensive. By highlighting accomplishments and encouraging parent networking, Project Hand-in-Hand stresses family inclusion to help parents feel good about their children and themselves. The project's name, "Hand-in-Hand," reflects its philosophy that families, schools, and communities all work together to support each other and promote the family.

**History and Origins**

Project Hand-in-Hand was established in response to a need recognized by primary-level teachers in the Marshfield Public Schools. The teachers found that increasing numbers of children were not meeting with success in kindergarten and first grade. Peter Noyes, principal of Daniel Webster School, was supportive of teachers' efforts to apply for an early childhood planning grant from Chapter 188 state funds. The

*Project Hand-in-Hand notes that its integrated format is not limited to a combination of developmentally delayed and typically developing children. A range of populations is represented, and Ms. Cipullo thinks the diversity helps families feel more at home in the classroom. She cites the example of a bilingual child, who recently arrived in the U.S. from Cameroon, saying that participation in the program helped both mother and daughter adjust to being in a new country.*

planning grant monies were used to hire an early childhood consultant to conduct a community-wide needs assessment. A 12-member advisory council composed of an administrator, teachers, parents, and community members worked with the consultant to develop a proposal for a Chapter 188 early childhood implementation grant. The Massachusetts Department of Education awarded the school $95,000 to hire an early childhood coordinator, establish a resource center for families and teachers of young children, and implement an integrated preschool program for three- and four-year-olds. Peter Noyes credits the immediate success of the program to the support of the teachers who originally recognized the need for preschool services.

### Features

Project Hand-in-Hand's preschool combines early intervention services for children having mild developmental delays with preventive services for children developing normally in two integrated classes of 15 preschool children each. The classroom is arranged in activity centers: blockbuilding, story writing, sand or water table, dramatic play, housekeeping, art, puzzles and manipulatives, and a gross-motor area. Materials are changed frequently to reflect a curriculum theme, reinforce skills, and respond to children's interests and different stages of development. Children spend time in individual and large group activities and in a language group led by a speech pathologist. The classroom reflects the philosophy that children learn best through interaction and experience.

Teacher recommendations guided the purchase of materials for the **resource center-library,** which provides educational toys, books, and instructional materials for use by children from birth to age eight, parents, and teachers in public and private schools. The resource center-library is open four days a week.

The Marshfield Special Education Department and private early childhood agencies collaborate to provide biannual screening to identify young children who are eligible for Project Hand-in-Hand and other special services.

Workshops, two-thirds for teachers in public and private schools, and one-third for public school teachers and parents together, are offered.

### Participants

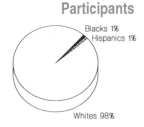

Blacks 1%
Hispanics 1%
Whites 98%

In 1988-89, Project Hand-in-Hand served 30 children in the preschool and 1,500 parents and children in the community (10 percent single parents). The program serves 5 percent of all children eligible for early childhood services. Children in Marshfield aged three or four by August 31 are eligible for the early childhood classroom; one-third are chosen for their mild developmental delays. For the remaining spaces, priority is given to children from low-income families and others who would benefit from a program prior to kindergarten.

### Parent Education

In 1987-88, Project Hand-in-Hand offered five workshops to parents: "Birth Order and Personality Development," "Helping Children Cope with Stress," "Building Self-Esteem," "Positive Discipline," and "Sensory Integration and Play." This year, a series on positive parenting and one on positive discipline were added. Past workshops have featured diverse child development topics.

**Curriculum**

Project Hand-in-Hand has developed its own preschool curriculum based on the developmental approach to early childhood education. The initial grant money included a large allowance to purchase new materials chosen by the coordinator and teacher. Materials are tailored to the different developmental needs of the children.

**Sites**

Classroom and offices are at the Daniel Webster School. Public school buses provide townwide transportation to preschool classes. Originally, the school system planned to offer programming in a community building, but space was unavailable. Former early childhood coordinator Martha Cipullo says that over time, the public school appears to be the appropriate home for Project Hand-in-Hand, since it uses many of the school's resources: the school nurse, the support staff, and materials. Also, she thinks the principal's support encourages community interest. Although legal constraints make field trips less possible, the program compensates by bringing the community into the building for events such as a speaker series.

*By highlighting accomplishments and encouraging parent networking, Project Hand-in-Hand stresses family inclusion to help parents feel good about their children and themselves.*

Ms. Cipullo warns that if a districtwide program is housed in a particular school, it must be careful to involve all eligible schools. To this end, Project Hand-in-Hand recently organized a four-part speaker series; the parent-teacher organizations of the four local elementary schools will each sponsor one evening.

The resource center-library is located in the office of the early childhood coordinator. Although the office is large, there is limited space to allow parents and children to work with materials. Staff members distribute library materials to teachers via interdepartmental mail. Ultimately, the project would like a large space both to accommodate more users and to create a drop-in center where parents, teachers, and families can interact comfortably.

**Parent Involvement**

Three parents, one of whom is co-chair, sit on the 12-person advisory council. The council is responsible for fundraising, project advocacy, member recruitment, and outreach in the community. Parents are encouraged to attend monthly parent-child activity days at the preschool with themes such as "Upside Down Day" and "Garden Planting Day." Some volunteer in the classroom, help construct classroom materials, or share a particular talent. Parents districtwide attend workshops and use the resource center-library. Parents help determine workshop topics and contribute to classroom planning. The teachers and coordinator have frequent contact with parents in classes and workshops and gather input in a survey at midyear and the end of the year. Parents also meet with teachers twice a year in conferences to discuss their children's development.

Project Hand-in-Hand publicizes itself in newspapers and on cable television, as well as through flyers and a newsletter. It exchanges referrals with nonpublic schools and public and private agencies. The project has children on a waiting list but continues to take referrals for the following school year.

**Staff**

| Job Title | PD | Vol | FT | PT | Educ Req | Status | Benefits |
|---|---|---|---|---|---|---|---|
| Early Childhood Coordinator | 1 | - | 1 | - | Post-Graduate Courses or Degree | K-12 Contract | Yes |
| Early Childhood Teacher | 1 | - | 1 | - | College Degree | K-12 Contract | Yes |
| Early Childhood Aide | 1 | - | 1 | - | Some College | Hourly Contract | Yes |
| Kindergarten Aide | 1 | - | 1 | - | Some College | Hourly Contract | Yes |
| Secretary | 1 | - | 1 | - | High School Diploma | Hourly Contract | Yes |
| Occupational Therapist | 1 | - | 1 | - | College Degree | Hourly Contract | No |
| Speech/ Language Pathologist | 1 | - | 1 | - | College Degree | Hourly Contract | No |
| Physical Therapist | 1 | - | 1 | - | College Degree | Hourly Contract | No |

**State/District Requirements**

A teacher's certificate for both the early childhood coordinator and teacher; two courses in early childhood education for the aides. The staff must participate in inservice training offered by the school, the project, and the Massachusetts Department of Education. Teacher surveys determine the focus of inservice training.

**Preferred Background**

For the coordinator, a master's degree in early childhood education and experience in grant writing, administration, and program design; for the teacher, experience with the developmental program model and preschool teaching.

**Employee Education and Training Represented**

Infant and toddler education; prekindergarten and early childhood education; elementary education; education, grades 7 to 12; special education; parent educator; child care; health and nutrition; home economics; nursing; occupational and physical therapy; speech therapy; psychology; counseling; child development and family studies; development and fundraising; research and evaluation.

**Administration**

Project Hand-in-Hand is a public school program overseen by the Early Childhood Advisory Council, which is composed of program staff members, school staff members, administrators, parents, and representatives. The 12-person board approves staff hiring, program services, and budget. Members also do fundraising, recruitment, and outreach.

The early childhood coordinator directs the program and reports to the advisory council, school administrators, and the school committee. Ms. Cipullo has especially close partnerships with the Daniel Webster School principal, Peter Noyes, the administrative representative on the advisory council, and several teachers and community resource people, all of whom are interested in her work with parents.

## Relationship to the Schools

The early childhood coordinator supervises special needs services at the preschool, acting as liaison between the project's therapists and the school's special education director. Ms. Cipullo has responsibilities besides Project Hand-in-Hand that increase her contact with teachers and administrators in the district: she directs the kindergarten curriculum committee that is working on a curriculum guide. She thinks having "fingers in other pies" increases her visibility in the district and makes the district staff more aware of Project Hand-in-Hand.

## Community Links

Martha Cipullo notes the crucial importance of networking within the community. To offset the potential for concern among private preschools over the possible loss of students, she offers her knowledge, the library, and inservice training as resources to private preschools and daycare centers. She wants to get out the message that many children and families are still not being served and that she is there to work with other schools and agencies, not to compete with them. Private school teachers use Project Hand-in-Hand as a link to the public schools.

*The project's name, "Hand-in-Hand," reflects its philosophy that families, schools, and communities all work together to support each other and promote the family.*

## Funding

State, 85 percent; school district, 6 percent; in-kind contributions, 6 percent; federal government, 3 percent.

## In-Kind Resources

Marshfield Public Schools provide facilities, some paid staff, transportation for the preschool, staff development, clerical support, access to equipment, and some supplies.

## Funding History

State funding decreased in the second year of programming, but new federal early childhood allocation funds and local school district money helped the program remain stable. The Massachusetts state fiscal crisis has prompted Chapter 188 to ask grantees to cut back costs without cutting services. Ms. Cipullo senses a commitment on the part of the state to Chapter 188, but since the legislative intent is for school districts to eventually take over the funding, that is an approaching concern.

## Objectives

For children, the objectives are to increase knowledge of the world and social relations, learn problem solving, and develop a positive self-concept and acceptance of others. For parents, the program hopes to increase knowledge of child development, early childhood education, and positive disciplining techniques. Early intervention for mildly delayed children and referral of such children to appropriate service agencies is an important goal, and outreach to all families of young children is crucial to its attainment. Project Hand-in-Hand hopes to decrease the number of children receiving special services from the school district; this reduction would make the program cost effective and, thus, a desirable adjunct to the school system, notes Ms. Cipullo.

**Evaluation**

The Massachusetts Department of Education requires a yearly evaluation. In 1988, Project Hand-in-Hand hired the early childhood coordinator from a nearby town to evaluate program implementation using the evaluation plan included in the grant proposal. After reviewing data and participant surveys, and meeting with teachers, parents, and the advisory council, the evaluator concluded that the program had met the proposed implementation goals. Specifically, the resource center-library and workshops were designed with teacher input, the preschool met the needs of all of the children, the project had established links to the community, and parent surveys showed that participants were pleased with the program.

**Replication**

The program has not been replicated.

**Materials Available**

None.

# Tacoma-Pierce County Council of Cooperative Nursery Schools

*One parent, whose four children all went through cooperative nursery schools, had held over the years a number of offices in the co-op framework. One year, she was elected president of the co-op and because of her interest and leadership abilities, served on a school district committee on communications. Last year, this empowered parent ran successfully for the Tacoma School Board.*

| | | |
|---|---|---|
| Resource library | Health/nutrition education | Parent-child joint activities |
| Networking | Developmental exams/screening | Parenting/child development education |
| Preschool | Newsletter | Child care info/referral |

**Contact:** Jackie Stenger, Associate Director

**Address:** Bates Vocational Technical College
Bates Ruston Campus
5219 North Shirley
Tacoma, WA 98407-6599
(206) 596-1760

**Established:** 1939, state initiative;
1959, Bates Vocational Technical College's involvement

**Budget '88-'89:** $361,600

**Sources:** State vocational funds, client fees, federal Carl Perkins funds (Public Law 98-542)

**Size:** 890 families

**Area Served:** Tacoma-Pierce County, Washington

**Auspices:** Home and Family Life Department of Bates Vocational Technical College

## Community

Tacoma, formerly a blue-collar, union-dominated industrial area, today has an extremely varied economy that ranges from banking to boat building. The Bates Vocational Technical College serves both the city of Tacoma, population 160,000, and the surrounding rural (increasingly suburban) county. The college is 50 years old and is well embedded in the middle-class community.

## Philosophy and Goals

Washington's Parent Education Model is based on the assumption that parents need help, advice, and support during their children's early years and that children benefit from the socializing experiences of nursery schools. Child development information and leadership training give parents the confidence to become actively involved in running their children's nursery school and to use community resources to enhance their personal and family lives.

## History and Origins

Fifty years ago, parent education in Washington began on the initiative of a group of women who approached the Seattle School System for help in setting up play schools for their children. Seattle led the state in funding cooperative nursery schools with money from vocational education and the local district. During World War II, the federal Lanham Act sponsored daycare for the children of working mothers, and after the war Seattle continued to take the lead in developing cooperative nursery schools with parents. The Bates Vocational Technical College became involved in 1959, in response to a request from mothers in the Tacoma School District. Four cooperatives had already been established in the Tacoma-Pierce County area as the movement gained momentum across the state.

**Features**

Twenty-five community colleges and five vocational technical colleges offer technical assistance to help parents start up cooperative nursery schools by providing facilitators to work with parents at the co-op sites and by receiving reimbursement from the state for parents' participation in the administration of the nursery schools, their work in the classroom, and their attendance at monthly parent education and support group meetings. Parents either enroll their children in an existing co-op or help establish a new neighborhood nursery school. Parents are assigned to work in the nursery school a minimum of twice a month; the community college or vocational technical college provides the parent education instructor. The latter is responsible for conducting monthly parent education classes, advising parents on nursery school operation, and helping parents become effective assistants in the co-op. Co-ops operate on a fee basis, with the exception of one in a women's correction center that enables incarcerated women to learn parenting skills. In this preschool for local children, the inmates are trained in child development and assist the teachers, as do parents in other co-ops; children attend free.

**Participants**

The majority of participants are white, middle-income families; 15 percent are single parents. In 1988, the co-op program served 890 families with children ages two to five.

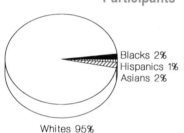

Blacks 2%
Hispanics 1%
Asians 2%
Whites 95%

*Ms. Stenger notes that since the state requires schools to provide special education services to children who are at risk for learning disabilities, the co-op is becoming a prime vehicle for service delivery. In addition, she adds, the co-ops mandate parent involvement, which gives parents skills that the public schools are finding essential to the later success of children.*

**Parent Education**

The Home and Family Life Department has eight sections; approximately 95 percent of these are involved in some kind of parent education. Other programs in the department, independent of the cooperative nursery schools and offered at the college to anyone in the Tacoma-Pierce County area, include: childbirth classes, a daycare advisory program, teen parent classes with an infant and toddler child care center, parent-infant and parent-toddler programs, the Effective Parenting Program, a child development program to train caregivers, clothes-making classes, and a high-risk parenting program. The Parent Education Model offers off-campus monthly classes in parenting and child development, health and nutrition education, and suggestions for joint parent-child activities; presentations include either a speaker or a film.

**Curriculum**

The curriculum is developed in house; it is tailored to suit particular groups of parents and children.

**Sites**

Bates Vocational Technical College has 21 co-ops in all (11 are located within Tacoma School District and 10 are within the county): 3 in public schools, 15 in churches, and 1 each in a Masonic temple, a community college campus, and a women's correction center. With the high cost of liability insurance, some agencies have been unable to continue to provide space. According to Ms. Stenger, public schools are increasingly interested in hosting cooperative nursery schools, but whenever there is a shortage of space, other uses preempt co-op classes. One co-op now occupies a portable site on the grounds of a middle school; here sixth, seventh, and eighth graders spend time interacting with the nursery schoolers.

**Parent Involvement**

The co-ops are parent organized and run. Parents serve on the working board, hire the teacher, work in the classroom, and are involved in the program's planning and implementation.

**Outreach**

The college prepares a flyer that is sent home with kindergartners and first to third graders in every elementary school in the city. In recent years, an annual week-long art show, held in a major shopping mall, exhibits the artwork of children in the co-ops. The college also advertises on the bulletin boards of local churches, groceries, and community agencies and through community newsletters. Although the program is a thirty-year-old initiative and well known in the community, it has been less successful in reaching inner-city and minority families. The supervisor feels that it is difficult for disadvantaged families who lack time and money to make the commitment, even though there is an extensive scholarship program.

**Staff**

| Job Title | PD | Vol | FT | PT | Educ Req | Status | Benefits |
|---|---|---|---|---|---|---|---|
| Nursery School Coordinator | 8 | - | 7 | 1 | College Degree | Other Contract | Yes |

**State/District Requirements**

Bates nursery school coordinators must have teaching and/or administrative experience in a cooperative nursery school and have completed college courses; vocational certification.

**Preferred Background**

Bachelor of arts degree.

**Employee Education and Training Represented**

Prekindergarten and early childhood education; elementary education; parent educator; adult vocational education; home economics; child development and family studies.

**Administration**

The Bates Vocational Technical College is part of the Tacoma School District. The co-op nursery schools and parent education programs are headed by the supervisor of the Home and Family Life Department of the college. The supervisor reports to the assistant superintendent of schools for vocational education and, through him, to the superintendent of schools and the Tacoma School District Board of Education. Each co-op has its own board, which interviews and selects teachers and has oversight of field trips, publicity, and fundraising efforts.

**Relationship to the Schools**

Although the co-ops run independently of the public schools, the co-op staff shares information with kindergarten teachers and invites them to spend an evening talking to participating parents whose children will be entering the elementary program in the fall. During kindergarten registration, the co-op provides child care and refreshments.

Ms. Stenger notes that since the state requires schools to provide special education services to children who are at risk for learning disabilities, the co-op is becoming a prime vehicle for service delivery. In addition, she adds, the co-ops mandate parent involvement, which gives parents skills that the public schools are finding essential to the later success of children.

## Community Links

In the Tacoma School District, a variety of programs for prekindergarten children are organized under the umbrella of the Early Childhood Education Council. Ms. Stenger serves as a council member, along with representatives from Head Start, personnel from special education services, and elementary school principals.

## Funding

State, 96 percent; client fees, 3 percent; federal government, 1 percent. Client fees pay for the co-op teacher, the facility lease, supplies, and equipment. State and federal monies support Bates nursery school coordinators who provide instruction and other resources.

## Funding History

Extra services have been reduced due to cutbacks on funds from the city, county, and state. Ten years ago, the health department provided a full-time social worker; today, hours have been reduced to quarter-time.

## Objectives

The Parent Education Model enhances individual and family development by giving parents the necessary skills and information to become leaders within the family and the larger community.

## Evaluation

Every five years, the state director of vocational education and family life programs reviews the program. Bates Vocational Technical College is accredited by the Northwest Association of Schools and Colleges. To gain accreditation, the program must be inspected over a three-year period, after which a repeat inspection is carried out every five years. The accreditation process gives schools the ability to offer programs through vocational education and to accept tax-deductible donations.

## Replication

The Cooperative Nursery School Program replicates the Parent Cooperative Nursery School in Seattle and is duplicated statewide in all five of the voc-techs and most community colleges.

## Materials Available

A brochure, *Parent Education Programs in Washington State,* is available free and the *Tacoma-Pierce County Council of Cooperative Nursery Schools Orientation Booklet* is available for a small fee. For details, contact the program director.

# Upper Tanana Regional
# Parent-Child Program — Head Start

*Claudia Shanley-Roberts says the Parent-Child Program is successful when it stimulates parents' personal growth. Women, in particular, who previously felt limited in their homes, have been motivated by program participation to reassess their personal and career goals.*

Networking
Warmline
Home visits
Newsletter
Preschool

Developmental exams/screening
Health/nutrition education
Family therapy
Resource library
Individual counseling

Parenting/child development education
Parent-child joint activities
Child care info/referral
Community services info/referral
Mother support groups

| | |
|---|---|
| **Contact:** | Claudia Shanley-Roberts, Parent-Child Program Director |
| **Address:** | P.O. Box 459<br>Tok, AK  99780<br>(907) 883-5157 or -5158 |
| **Established:** | 1977, local initiative |
| **Budget '88-'89:** | $102,000 |
| **Sources:** | State government (Head Start funds), in-kind contributions, private donations |
| **Size:** | 83 families |
| **Area Served:** | Upper Tanana Region, Alaska |
| **Auspices:** | Upper Tanana Development Corporation and Rural Community Action Program |

## Community

The Upper Tanana region includes Tok and six outlying villages in 36,000 square miles of rural Alaska. Two villages are not accessible by roads, but rely on airplane transport and riverboats in the spring. There are approximately 1,000 citizens in Tok and between 50 and 350 in each of the smaller villages. Tok's population is 65 percent white and 35 percent Athabascan Native American; in the outlying villages Athabascans make up 90 to 99 percent of the community. Tok is the first junction on the Alaska highway, 95 miles from Canada. People settled there in the 1940s when the highway was built, and it is now a tourist area, receiving 100,000 visitors annually. Residents make money in the summer tourist trade and government services provide income in the winter months. Health care is a matter of local concern. The Upper Tanana region has no doctor, but has a community clinic in Tok with a physician's assistant; each village has one or more community health aides trained in cardiopulmonary resuscitation (CPR), emergency care, and referral. The area has a high incidence of substance abuse and family violence.

## Philosophy and Goals

The Upper Tanana Regional Parent-Child Program educates parents to be their children's first and most important teachers. Parents learn to stimulate their children's development in the context of a healthy home environment. Parents volunteer and participate in early childhood classes, gaining a sense of self-esteem that they pass on to their children. Children, who may live in isolated homes, begin peer socialization in preschool; isolated parents benefit from frequent contact with their contemporaries. The program encourages parents to further their own personal goals and take an active interest in their children's education.

**History and Origins**

In 1977, the Upper Tanana Development Corporation, a private, nonprofit organization, began a preschool in the isolated Tok area where families were in need of early childhood services to improve their children's school performance. The corporation received state funds through its granting agency, Rural Community Action Program (Rural CAP). In 1979, Rural CAP obtained Head Start funds, also funnelled through the state. The preschool expanded to several villages, and the program added home visits and a comprehensive parent involvement effort.

**Features**

The Upper Tanana Regional Parent-Child Program offers programming from October 1 to April 30.

**Home-based Program** offers weekly 1½-hour home visits to children birth to age five and their parents. The visitor shares developmental information and models age-appropriate child activities for the parent.

**Preschool** is offered to children ages three to five, in five villages, including Tok. Hours vary from village to village, but a typical schedule is three times a week for two hours. The public schools provide breakfast and lunch to the preschool children as required by Head Start.

**Participants**

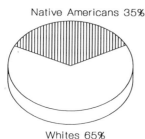

Native Americans 35%

Whites 65%

Eighty-three families throughout the region participated in the Upper Tanana Regional Parent-Child Program in 1987-88, an estimated 70 percent of the eligible population of families with young children. According to Program Director Claudia Shanley-Roberts, some poverty-level families with young children remain hard to reach because they live at such vast distances.

*Parents in the program have become more political in recent years in support of their children's education, writing letters to legislators and taking advantage of a toll-free number that allows constituents to express their opinions.*

**Parent Education**

Since parent volunteers play a large role in the preschool classroom, parents are included in staff training offered by agencies whenever possible. Many parents want to further their education beyond high school and may take early childhood classes offered by the University of Alaska at Fairbanks. Most of these classes are offered in Tok, either as weekend workshops or over a period of weeks via audio-conferencing; at least one series per year is offered in each of the outlying villages.

**Curriculum**

Although the program ran the preschool for several years without a set curriculum, it is now implementing the *Creative Curriculum*. There is no curriculum for the home-based program, but instructors combine the *Asper-Folta* and *The Portage Project* curricula, and *Life Skills for Little People*, a curriculum Ms. Shanley-Roberts helped develop. The program modifies materials to make them relevant to the Athabascan culture by using Athabascan symbols and language when appropriate; to this end, Athabascan elders volunteer in the preschool classroom.

**Sites**

In four villages the preschool meets in classrooms provided by the local elementary school. In Tok, where space is at a premium, the preschool meets in the community center, also the site of the program's offices. Parent groups may meet at a school or in a parent's home. College credit classes occur at the community center or at Tok's new university center.

**Parent Involvement**

A parent group meets monthly to plan fundraising and publicity. Parents who enroll their children in the preschool are required to volunteer; the classroom is staffed by one teacher and one parent volunteer. Parent volunteers also provide daily snacks. There are small parent groups in each village, usually mothers' groups, arranged around sewing or beading activities. Ms. Shanley-Roberts notes that parents in the program have become more political recently in support of their children's education, writing letters to legislators and taking advantage of a toll-free number that allows constituents to express their opinions. Because Alaska has such a small population, parents have found that as few as 10 letters or messages are extremely effective in swaying legislators' opinions.

**Outreach**

The most common outreach strategy is home visits to prospective participants. The program also uses potluck dinners to attract new families. The Tanana Chiefs Conference, a regional health agency for Native Americans, offers tuition assistance as an incentive to program participants who take early childhood courses. The program receives referrals from the Department of Health and Social Services. The local newspaper publicizes the program.

**Staff**

Alaska does not have licensure, certification, or training requirements for staff members in the program; however, the director expects that Head Start will soon require early childhood certification. Although she welcomes professionalization in the field, she is concerned that staff members do not have access to a university campus for regular courses; they rely on audio-conferencing and one-credit weekend workshops to complete early childhood coursework.

| Job Title | PD | Vol | FT | PT | Educ Req | Status | Benefits |
|---|---|---|---|---|---|---|---|
| Director | 1 | - | 1 | - | College Degree | Hourly Non-Contract | Yes |
| Secretary | 1 | - | 1 | - | High School Diploma | Hourly Non-Contract | Yes |
| Preschool Teachers | 5 | - | - | 5 | Some College | Hourly Non-Contract | Yes |
| Parent Volunteers | - | 66 | - | 66 | None | - | - |
| Home Visitors | 4 | - | - | 4 | Some College | Hourly Non-Contract | Yes |

**State/District Requirements**

None.

**Preferred Background**

Preschool teachers and village home visitors should have experience working with young children and be healthy role models for parents.

**Employee Education and Training Represented**

Infant and toddler education; prekindergarten and early childhood education; elementary education; bilingual education; special education;

parent educator; speech therapy; psychology; counseling; family therapy; social work; child development and family studies; development and fundraising.

## Administration

The Upper Tanana Regional Parent-Child Program is part of the Upper Tanana Development Corporation, a private, nonprofit organization that contracts with the statewide agency, Rural CAP, to provide early childhood and family services in the Upper Tanana region. The program director reports to the board of directors of the corporation, and Rural CAP monitors the program, requiring a yearly evaluation report.

## Relationship to the Schools

The Upper Tanana Regional Parent-Child Program is administered independently of the school district, but the district provides space for each village preschool, and there are formal means of coordination. Ms. Shanley-Roberts works closely with the assistant superintendent of schools, who is also the special education director, to coordinate joint staff training. Since 80 percent of area children have speech and language difficulties, there are channels for referring program participants to the district's Early Childhood Special Services Department. The village school principal or a teacher monitors each preschool classroom, and kindergarten teachers assist in referring families. The Alaska Department of Education certifies the program to operate in the public schools. Ms. Shanley-Roberts calls the village school a community gathering place and notes that parents experience a sense of ownership of the schools.

The Upper Tanana Regional Parent-Child Program will expand its partnership with the schools next year when it works cooperatively with a district-run preschool in Northway, which has seen declining enrollment and parent support. The district approached the program on the strength of its successful preschool component. The school will pay for the staff's time, and the program will provide technical assistance in implementing the Head Start model. In exchange for the aid, the program has insisted that local parents, in cooperation with the regional school board, take charge of the preschool.

## Community Links

The Family and Youth Services Division of the Department of Health and Social Services (DHS) provides the Upper Tanana Regional Parent-Child Program staff with training on detecting and preventing child abuse. In return, Ms. Shanley-Roberts offers family counseling to DHS clients. Alaska Crippled Children and Adult Services (ACCA) travels to Tok from Fairbanks to offer staff members training in speech, language, and physical therapy. A health educator from the Tanana Chiefs Conference gives presentations on a variety of health-related topics for the staff and parents. The University of Alaska at Fairbanks sends instructors to Tok, and occasionally to outlying villages, to complement courses delivered by audio-conference.

## Funding

Head Start funds, channeled through Rural CAP, 60 percent; in-kind contributions, 35 percent; private donations, 5 percent.

## In-Kind Resources

Facilities provided by school district and parents; staff development by school district, Tanana Chiefs Conference, and Alaska Crippled Children and Adult Services; screening by public health nurse and local physician's assistant; course instruction by University of Alaska at Fairbanks; parent and student volunteers; materials provided by Tanana Chiefs Conference.

**Funding History**

The director estimates that the program operates on one-fifth of a typical Head Start budget. For that reason, it cannot offer the full 4 1/2-hour day of preschool that Head Start recommends. The director has written a proposal to Rural CAP for increased funds for next year but expects that the program will have to cut back on preschool services next year. Two communities with no preschool-age children will have only home-based services, and unless new funding is found, preschool will not be reinstated here.

**Objectives**

The Upper Tanana Regional Parent-Child Program aims to raise parents' self-esteem, create a peer network of parents, help parents provide a healthy environment in the home, promote child development and stimulate learning, and involve parents in their own education and in that of their children.

**Evaluation**

Until 1989, a Rural CAP representative evaluated the program by studying administrative records of the number of staff members serving children and the degree of parent involvement. More recently, a Rural CAP evaluator conducted an on-site study looking at social services, parent involvement, screening, and instruction.

**Replication**

The Upper Tanana Regional Parent-Child Program is based on the Head Start model.

**Materials Available**

None.

# 2 Support for Special Needs Children and Their Parents

These programs respond to the needs of families having children with learning disabilities, physical or emotional handicaps, or developmental delays. Services vary but generally include early identification of risk factors through developmental screening and diagnostic evaluations, collaboration with parents on developing individualized education plans, home visits, therapeutic classrooms, parent support groups, resource libraries, referral services, and advocacy work. All are committed to informing parents about their children's needs and rights to intervention services. Parents are encouraged to become partners in the evaluation process and keen, appreciative observers of their children's progress. Six of the programs offer preschool as remediation, transition to a mainstream classroom, or preparation for continued special education services. The others offer intensive home- and center-based education, support, and referral services to families.

# Programs in Brief

**Cheshire Early Childhood Programs — p. 105**
*Connecticut state model preschool and consultation center for special needs children and their families*

**Consultation Center/Parent Child Program — p. 111**
*Early assessment and intervention for children birth to age five, with resources and support for their parents in Bridgeport, Connecticut*

**Early Developmental Awareness Project — p. 117**
*Screening services and parent education focusing on early childhood development and exceptional needs in Mequon, Wisconsin*

**Early Education Center — p. 121**
A Division of the Training and Evaluation Center of Hutchinson
*Support and education for handicapped and developmentally delayed children birth to age five and their parents, including detection of at-risk newborns, home- and center-based training, and toddler groups in Hutchinson, Kansas*

**Boston Institute for Art Therapies — p. 127**
*Art, music, and dance therapy for disadvantaged, special needs preschoolers in two Boston public schools, complemented by parent education and therapeutic support groups*

**Parent Resource Center — p. 131**
*Informational classes and home visits in Lewisburg, West Virginia to promote an understanding of special needs and special education services*

**Vermont College Preschool — p. 135**
*Preschool program in Montpelier serving special needs and at-risk children in mainstream classrooms*

**Willington Public Schools Early Childhood Services — p. 141**
*Screening and developmental preschool for identification and remediation, augmented by home visits and parent support groups in rural Connecticut*

# Cheshire Early Childhood Programs

| | | |
|---|---|---|
| Preschool | Parent support groups | Parenting/child development education |
| Resource library | Special education | Parent-child joint activities |
| Warmline | Speech/language therapy | Physical/occupational therapy |
| Networking | Home visits as needed | Referral/transition services |
| Newsletter | Crisis intervention | Developmental exams/screening |
| | Outreach professional training | Community services info/referral |

| | |
|---|---|
| **Contact:** | Lois Rho, Director |
| **Address:** | Stephen August Early Intervention Center |
| | 1686 Waterbury Road |
| | Cheshire, CT 06410 |
| | (203) 272-3577 |
| **Established:** | 1972, local initiative under Title III grant |
| **Budget '88-'89:** | $568,000 |
| **Sources:** | State and federal grants; local school district funds; client fees |
| **Size:** | 100 families |
| **Area Served:** | Cheshire public schools and nearby towns on a contract basis |
| **Auspices:** | Regional center directed by the public schools |

*For 2½ years, staff from the Cheshire Early Childhood Programs have worked with the family of a child tentatively diagnosed as having infantile autism. At each crucial stage of development, the center helps these parents cope with the enormous strain of working toward a breakthrough. Lois Rho sees progress, "I think this little boy is going to be O.K. . . . He can hug and kiss and make eye contact. He is learning."*

## Community

Cheshire (population 25,250) is a suburban, principally middle-class, professional community within easy commuting distance of three major cities in Connecticut. The 5,000 school children are served by one high school, one junior high, and four elementary schools. A recent survey in Cheshire showed that 17 percent of the school-age population had problems that predict school failure, indicating the need to provide remediation in the early years.

## Philosophy and Goals

Cheshire Early Childhood Programs are committed to the idea that children can overcome learning difficulties that stem from handicaps, including language and speech delays, emotional imbalance, physical impairments, hyperactivity, and psychological stress. The programs offer choices and alternatives for families, believing that respect for parents and children is essential for effective intervention. Staff members work with families in a transdisciplinary team approach, combining skills in development, psychology, speech pathology, and occupational and physical therapy, sharing perceptions with parents and engaging them in the process of observation, assessment, and planning for their children. Movement, interaction, and an experientially based curriculum with emphasis on the arts, music, and dramatic play in an architect-designed preschool setting are key to Cheshire's philosophy of early learning.

## History and Origins

In the early 1970s, Lois Rho, a former Head Start coordinator, Gwenette Caruthers, a school psychologist, and Stephen A. August, the superintendent of schools in Cheshire, combined their energies to develop a preschool intervention program. They began working together at the tail end of a Title III grant that provided high-risk three- and four-year-olds with a program of classroom activities and home visits. Without clearly articulated support from the superintendent the whole initiative would have failed, recalls Ms. Rho.

In 1973, the state, continuing funding under Title III, a special education grant, awarded the program $17,000 to work with six families in an in-depth program of joint classes for parents and children. By that time, says Ms. Rho, the early intervention center had established the four components that distinguish it today: parent involvement, a transdisciplinary team approach, an innovative learning environment, and observation as the primary tool for assessment.

In 1979, Cheshire Early Childhood Programs became a state-designated model and moved into the Stephen August Early Intervention Center. In 1983, it received federal funding from the Handicapped Children's Early Education Program and the Handicapped Preschool Incentive (Public Law 94-142) to develop a birth-to-three model called FIRST (Family Infant Resource Stimulation Team).

Today, the Cheshire center has six classrooms and supporting facilities, a birth-to-three area, a consultation center, and a home visit program. It is a model for similar programs throughout the state and in 1989 received a three-year federal outreach grant through the Handicapped Children's Early Education Program to train educators in Connecticut.

*"We take parents from where they are to the next step in a gentle and reassuring way. We help them get to know their child and to learn strategies for working with their child."*

**Features**

Cheshire Early Childhood Programs have three components that serve special needs children birth to age eight and their families.

**FIRST** consists of consultation, assessment, and programming for children birth to age three who need special education services.

**Preschool** for four- and five-year-olds and the **Non-Graded Primary Class** for five- to eight-year-olds serve children from two half-days to five full days a week, depending on their needs. Mothers come one to three days, spending an hour in the classroom and then participating in a group discussion of classroom dynamics, a workshop, or a planning session. Class capacity is six to eight children, with a minimum staff of one teacher and an aide.

**Consultation Center** offers screening, assessment, and planning for preschool children with special needs. Parents observe their children in guided play with a teacher. Staff members share their reactions with parents, whose concerns are addressed informally over coffee with the teaching and diagnostic team. A written report follows that includes general impressions, observations about fine and gross motor skills, learning and emotional development, and recommendations for an educational plan.

## Participants

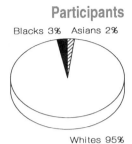

Blacks 3%   Asians 2%

Whites 95%

## Parent Education

## Curriculum

## Sites

## Parent Involvement

Cheshire Early Childhood Programs serve children with mild to severe physical handicaps, i.e., chronic physical or mental illness, developmental delays, prematurity, or any other factor indicating the need for a supportive environment. Children may be experiencing problems associated with a series of risk factors including abuse and neglect, poverty, inadequate support systems for the family, handicapped siblings, parental alcohol or substance abuse, or parental instability.

In 1988-89, the Stephen August Early Intervention Center served approximately 100 families, 100 percent of the eligible population that sought services.

Cheshire Early Childhood Programs seek active parent cooperation, feeling that effective participation occurs only through involving both the child and caregiver. Participation in the classroom several times a week teaches parents through observation and practice how to use and/or structure play situations to stimulate their children's development. Parents discuss their reactions to classroom activities and child development issues in group meetings with a staff person.

Ms. Rho notes, "When parents first come to the center they are already feeling like failures because they have an at-risk child. They feel their child can't do anything . . . . We take parents from where they are to the next step in a gentle and reassuring way. We help them get to know their child and to learn strategies for working with their child."

The curriculum approach is experiential and includes art, music, dramatic play, and gross and fine motor activities. Activities and materials have been developed by center staff over the past 16 years and are open-ended and responsive to the special needs of the children.

The intervention project started in one, and expanded to two kindergarten rooms in the Highland Elementary School. When the kindergarten population increased and the school needed additional space, the center moved to a closed school building and renovated the space with funds from the Connecticut Department of Education. The Stephen August Early Intervention Center at the former Darcey School is an architect-designed environment that includes six classrooms, offices, a consultation center, and a resource room. The board of education provides transportation to special education preschoolers who need it.

"We started with an empty room," reflects Ms. Rho, "with no equipment, except counter tops that served as low tables." The staff observed the six children in that first class and developed a setting based on their needs. According to Ms. Rho, the physical set-up and the center's philosophy are intertwined: Ideas of harmony and functionalism have shaped an environment which has both a therapeutic and an educational impact and is geared to encouraging early learning through playful interaction and skill mastery. Program literature states that the center is "more homelike than institutional . . . providing comfortable furniture, plants, carpeting, neutral colors, warm lighting . . ." Modular equipment creates child-sized spaces that can be adapted by children and offers a variety of sensory experiences.

According to the director, parents are highly motivated to meet with the school board, the advisory council, and the community to discuss the program's value and their own needs. In 1988, when the town was considering turning the Stephen August Early Intervention Center back into an active school, over 100 parents came to the town council to protest the move. Parents and grandparents are routinely involved in improving the center; in 1972, they built the first modular units, or child-sized areas.

**Outreach**

Special outreach efforts include letters sent home every spring to all parents with children under age five. The center welcomes visitors, holds open houses, and is in touch with area nursery schools and pediatricians.

**Staff**

A developmental optometrist, a pediatrician, and a child psychiatrist from outside the schools join the social worker, school psychologist, and others within the system who serve as support staff for the center's staff.

| Job Title | PD | Vol | FT | PT | Educ Req | Status | Benefits |
|---|---|---|---|---|---|---|---|
| Administrator | 1 | - | 1 | - | Post-Graduate Courses or Degree | Other Contract | Yes |
| Teaching Staff | 11 | - | 8 | 3 | Post-Graduate Courses or Degree | Other Contract | Yes |
| Aides | 8 | - | 4 | 4 | Varied | Hourly Non-Contract | No |
| Speech/Language Pathologists | 3 | - | 3 | - | Post-Graduate Courses or Degree | Hourly Contract | Yes |
| Occupational Therapists | 2 | - | 2 | - | Post-Graduate Courses or Degree | Hourly Contract | Yes |
| Physical Therapist | 1 | - | - | 1 | Post-Graduate Courses or Degree | Hourly Contract | Yes |
| School Psychologist | 1 | - | 1 | - | Post-Graduate Courses or Degree | Hourly Contract | Yes |
| Media Technicians | 2 | - | - | 2 | College Degree | Hourly Non-Contract | No |
| Secretaries | 4 | - | 2 | 2 | Some College | Hourly Contract/Non-Contract | Yes |
| Nurse | 1 | - | 1 | - | Post Graduate Courses or Degree | Other Contract | Yes |
| Music Therapist | 1 | - | - | 1 | Post Graduate Courses or Degree | Hourly Non-Contract | No |

**State/District Requirements**

Staff members meet Connecticut Department of Education certification standards.

| | |
|---|---|
| **Preferred Background** | For all positions, the ability to work as a team, as well as intelligence, flexibility, and sensitivity. |
| **Employee Education and Training Represented** | Infant and toddler education; prekindergarten and early childhood education; elementary education; special education; parent educator; nursing; occupational and physical therapy; speech therapy; psychology; child development and family studies; research and evaluation. |
| **Administration** | Cheshire Early Childhood Programs are part of the Cheshire Public Schools. The director reports to the superintendent, communicates with the coordinator of special education services, and sits on the administrative council. The Connecticut Department of Education and the U.S. Department of Education's Handicapped Children's Early Education Program monitor outreach. |
| **Relationship to the Schools** | Under Lois Rho's supervision, one elementary school has developed a kindergarten class using the center's Non-Graded Primary Class as a model. The intervention center's team-teaching approach and its style of involving parents are gradually influencing the school system as a whole, says Ms. Rho. The schools have also picked up on the center's use of specialists as consultants rather than as hands-on resources. This has proved an efficient use of the system's overextended staff, she explains. Ninety-five percent of the center's handicapped children go on to public kindergarten. To ease the transition, the center has hired a nurse practitioner to field questions from teachers and parents. She will get to know the children, says Ms. Rho, and is sensitive to problems in the schools. The center works with receiving teachers, who are now much better informed about incoming special needs students. |
| **Community Links** | This is a regional program serving area towns on a paying basis. Connecticut legislation requires towns to assess children from birth for learning disabilities and provide assessment and services for children from two years, eight months of age. Towns, therefore, pick up the tuition costs for nonresident children who attend Cheshire's center. Cheshire has an informal agreement with the Connecticut Department of Mental Retardation to provide additional services and occasionally refers families to the Child Guidance Clinic in Waterbury. |
| | With funding provided by a federal grant from the Handicapped Children's Early Education Program, the center distributes publications on developmentally appropriate environments for children birth to age five and offers three levels of training opportunities for teachers: guided observation; workshops throughout the year on topics that meet the needs of different groups (Head Start, daycare providers, special education teams); and in-depth training, involving hands-on experience at the Stephen August Early Intervention Center for five consecutive days. |
| **Funding** | Birth to three: client fees, 50 percent; state government, 25 percent; federal government, 15 percent; school district, 10 percent. Three to eight: tuition, 90 percent; federal government, 5 percent; school district, 3.5 percent; state government, 1.5 percent. Training throughout Connecticut: federal grant, 100 percent. |
| **In-Kind Resources** | Space and facilities are provided by the local educational authority and the program also receives transportation services. |

**Funding History**

Funding has remained stable and Ms. Rho considers it to be very secure.

**Objectives**

For parents, an understanding of child development and learning styles, better strategies for meeting their own and their children's needs, and the ability to communicate those needs to the extended family and community. For children, developing the capacity to make choices, gains in self-confidence and autonomy, and improvements in social, emotional, cognitive, physical, auditory, and visual skills.

*"Ideas of harmony and functionalism have shaped an environment which has both a therapeutic and an educational impact and is geared to encouraging early learning through playful interaction and skill mastery."*

**Evaluation**

From 1983 to 1986, Cheshire Early Childhood Programs evaluated the federally funded FIRST model using three different approaches: a pre- and posttest design questionnaire for parents that compared their satisfaction with the intervention program and another daycare program, an Early Learning Accomplishment Profile (E-LAP) study over three years, and open-ended interviews with parents who had participated for at least four months. The program director's final report in 1986 notes that talking and listening to parents provided the "best sense of both what the FIRST model is like and the meaning of the program to parents."

**Replication**

Aspects of the program have been adapted by local nursery schools and by the Brookfield and Monroe county boards of education. Other Connecticut towns replicating the program are Bridgeport, Branford, and Thomaston.

**Materials Available**

Slide presentations of *Developmentally Appropriate Environments* and training tapes are being duplicated for dissemination. They are currently available to those who participate in the center's outreach and training programs.

# Consultation Center/Parent Child Program

*A child whose parents were embroiled in a custody suit came to the center apparently suffering from multiple family stresses. Center staff members encouraged both parents and the child's daycare teachers to focus on his strengths. They helped him relax and enjoy his accomplishments. His mother gained confidence in the positive effects of her own more controlled behavior; his father let up on his threats of legal action.*

Home visits
Networking
Toy lending
Resource library

Parent-child joint activities
Parent support group
Child care info/referral

Parenting/child development education
Developmental exams/screening
Community services info/referral

**Contact:** Judith Hurle, Director of Early Childhood Programs
Ellen Cohen, Teacher Coordinator

**Address:** Franklin Education Center
389 Kossuth Street
Bridgeport, CT 06608
(203) 576-7410

**Established:** 1979, local school initiative

**Budget '88-'89:** $145,267

**Sources:** Local school district, federal grant

**Size:** 83 children, 81 families

**Area Served:** Bridgeport, Connecticut

**Auspices:** Bridgeport Public Schools

## Community

Bridgeport is situated in southwestern Connecticut, approximately 55 miles from New York City. The estimated urban population is 142,000 and the population of the metropolitan area is 440,000. According to the program's director, Judith Hurle, traditional blue-collar industries are moving out of the area, leaving only low-paying service-industry jobs for the undereducated segment of the population. The urban population is 20 percent black, 19 percent Hispanic, and 2 percent Native American and Asian, but the public school population has twice that percentage of minorities. Fifty-nine percent of the city residents are white. Nearly two-thirds of the white students attend parochial schools.

## Philosophy and Goals

The Consultation Center/Parent Child Program believes that parents should play an essential part in the process of identifying their children's special needs and in developing and implementing interventions. Parents' perceptions of their children's needs must be taken into account, even when they conflict with professionals' judgements. The program works with parents to plan their children's education and treatment. Parents are the essential link between their children and the professionals.

## History and Origins

The Consultation Center/Parent Child Program was begun by the Bridgeport Board of Education in 1979 in response to a need identified by a state compliance review to increase identification and intervention services provided to children from birth to age five.

The program replicated the Cheshire Early Childhood Program but modified it considerably to meet the needs of a large minority population in a lower socioeconomic urban community. Modifications included increased outreach and advocacy, more easily accessible program sites, and hiring teachers who had been involved in the community schools and were already familiar to families.

Factors that helped secure the program were its acceptance by the families and community referral agencies, the involvement and support of a number of people within the educational system and city government, and eventual formal recognition by the state of Connecticut under the Promising Practices Act.

Features

**The Consultation Center** involves parents in a process of screening, diagnosis, and referral for further intervention services.

A core assessment team is drawn from a staff that includes the school psychologist, speech and language clinician, special education teacher, early childhood education teacher, program aide, and if the child already attends preschool, the teacher as well. (A number of staff members are bilingual and sessions are conducted in Spanish or Portuguese when necessary.) A process of close observation of children during the intake session and discussions with parents leads to a considered interpretation of possible interventions. Children's personal histories and interactions at home and in school are also taken into account.

According to Ms. Hurle, throughout the discussion periods parents' perceptions of their children are respected. Consultation Center staff members strive to call attention to children's strengths and potential, as well as their possible problem areas. By helping parents to acknowledge something positive about their children, a firm starting point for intervention is established. After meetings, Consultation Center staff members put their observations and recommendations into written reports.

*The program works with parents to plan their children's education and treatment. Parents are the essential link between their children and the professionals.*

Once evaluated, children may be referred for more extensive testing, full-time preschool special education placement, or support services in a mainstream setting. Such services might include speech and language therapy or intervention and consultation by an itinerant special education teacher.

The **Parent Child Program** is a special program for children and parents. Groups of five to six children and their parents meet with the staff for approximately two hours a week. Parents, children, and staff members work in a flexible, open classroom setting. With support from the staff, parents focus on observing their children, extending their play, interacting positively, and helping to build new skills. Following this, parents meet with a facilitator while other staff members continue activities with the children.

In the fall of 1982, the center began an **Under Three's Group** to identify and serve children too young to receive state-mandated special education services. Parent participation is integral.

## Participants

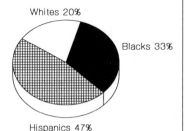

Whites 20%

Blacks 33%

Hispanics 47%

## Parent Education

## Curriculum

## Sites

## Parent Involvement

## Outreach

The Consultation Center and the Parent Child Program are open to all residents of the city of Bridgeport who have children under age five. Parent participation is mandatory. At present, the Parent Child Program serves children ages two years, eight months to four years, eight months, who may participate concurrently in regular nursery school, daycare, Head Start, or other preschool settings. During the 1987-88 school year, the program served 83 children from 81 families, 60 percent of whom were single parents and 8 percent of whom were teen parents. The program serves all families who apply, but Ms. Cohen estimates that this represents less than 30 percent of eligible families.

During the 1987-88 school year, 30 percent of the clients used the program at least once a week, 10 percent used the program monthly, and 60 percent participated one to five times a year.

In the second hour of the Parent Child Program, parents and educators use their observations from the previous hour to develop and refine intervention strategies. Parents offer each other support and insight. Information about child development and parenting comes via handouts, group discussion, videotapes, and staff modeling.

*Factors that helped secure the program were its acceptance by the families and community referral agencies, the involvement and support of a number of people within the educational system and city government, and eventual formal recognition by the state of Connecticut under the Promising Practices Act.*

The curriculum is based on the Cheshire Preschool Model. It consists of appropriate preschool materials adapted to the developmental and/or cultural needs of each child and family.

The program is situated at three sites, all of which have been relatively comfortable and stable places to complete child assessments and work with parents. All are easily accessible and familiar to families within the community. School personnel provide transportation when necessary.

The assessment procedure prepares parents to take a strong advocacy role in their children's education. Parents are not involved in the design or overall running of the program, but they do choose activities in the Parent Child Program. Whenever funding has been threatened parents have gone to the school board to voice their support for the program.

According to Teacher Coordinator Ellen Cohen, parents who have been or are involved in the program are the best referral sources. When professionals initiate a referral, it is essential that they be knowledgeable about the program and sensitive to parents' fears. Parents who initiate referrals themselves are most likely to participate actively in assessment and follow up.

The center has made an effort to work with professionals, such as pediatricians, to help them identify developmental delays and make use of available educational services. To develop credibility in the medical community and encourage referrals to the program, Ms. Hurle has met with a group of physicians and has participated in rounds at the pediatric unit of the local hospital. Annual mailings are made to social service agencies and preschool programs, as well as to the medical community.

**Staff**

| Job Title | PD | Vol | FT | PT | Educ Req | Status | Benefits |
|---|---|---|---|---|---|---|---|
| Teacher Coodinator | 1 | - | 1 | - | Post-Graduate Courses or Degree | K-12 Contract | Yes |
| Assistant Teacher Coordinator | 1 | - | 1 | - | Post-Graduate Courses or Degree | K-12 Contract | Yes |
| Program Assistant | 1 | - | 1 | - | College Degree | Other Contract | Yes |
| Speech Pathologist | 2-3 | - | - | 2-3 | Post-Graduate Courses or Degree | K-12 Contract | Yes |
| School Psychologist | 2-3 | - | - | 2-3 | Post-Graduate Courses or Degree | K-12 Contract | Yes |
| Preschool Teachers | 4 | - | - | 4 | College Degree | K-12 Contract | Yes |

**State/District Requirements**

All professional staff members are required to have state certification in their particular discipline.

**Preferred Background**

Knowledge of child development; nonjudgmental attitude; experience working with children birth to age five; ability to work in a team.

**Employee Education and Training Represented**

Infant and toddler education; prekindergarten and early childhood education; elementary education; special education; parent educator; child care; speech therapy; psychology; counseling; family therapy; child development and family studies; religion and clergy.

**Administration**

The program is administered exclusively within the Bridgeport Public School System and is under the supervision of the board of education. The Departments of Early Childhood, Psychology, Speech and Language, and Special Education collaborate to administer the Consultation Center/ Parent Child Program under the umbrella of the Early Childhood Program.

**Relationship to the Schools**

According to Ms. Cohen, the school system provides the program with credibility while the center offers a mandated service on behalf of the school board. Preschool and elementary teachers participate in workshops, assessments, and "internships" (three-day involvement in the program).

**Community Links**

The Consultation Center/Parent Child Program provides consultation to nursery school, daycare, and Head Start programs within the city of Bridgeport. The program also offers internships for staff members from these and other community agencies, as well as for teachers within the school system.

**Funding**

School system, 56 percent; federal grant under Public Law 99-457, 44 percent.

**In-Kind Resources**

The local school system and a church provide space and facilities; the school system also provides consultation and staff development, administrative and clerical support, telephone, utilities, materials, and supplies.

**Funding History**

Ms. Hurle reported that funding is very secure and has increased by 40 percent since the start of the program in 1979. Funding increases have been accompanied by increases in the levels of service: improved assessment equipment, increases in staff members who are now doing six evaluations per week instead of four, and promotion of a staff member to a parent coordinator position with increased responsibility for advocacy and outreach. Services have been extended to include a toy-lending library.

**Objectives**

In addition to identifying children with special needs and recommending direct services, the program aims to improve parent-child interactions, parents' advocacy skills, knowledge of child development, and parents' understanding of their children's particular needs. Also, by putting a high value on parent involvement, the program hopes to improve family-school relations.

**Evaluation**

No evaluations of the program have been completed.

**Replication**

The program replicated the preschool component of the Cheshire Early Childhood Programs in Cheshire, Connecticut.

**Materials Available**

None.

# Early Developmental Awareness Project

*A mother had been dealing with her young son's medical problems and suspected that he might be developmentally delayed. Her pediatrician disagreed. On the mother's request, Leesa Maxwell performed a developmental screening evaluation and found that indeed, the child had potential problems and needed help. Ms. Maxwell referred him to a diagnostic center for further evaluation, "putting the mother in touch with a person and a phone number to get the appropriate services."*

| | | |
|---|---|---|
| Newsletter | Individual counseling | Parenting/child development education |
| Warmline | Couple support groups | Parent-child joint activities |
| Home visits | Child care/preschool referral | Training in developmental screening |
| Networking | Community services info/referral | Developmental exams/screening |

| | |
|---|---|
| **Contact:** | Janet Ollech, Community Consultant and Coordinator |
| **Address:** | Donges Bay School |
| | 2401 West Donges Bay Road |
| | Mequon, WI 53092 |
| | (414) 242-4260 |
| **Established:** | 1986, school district initiative |
| **Budget '88-'89:** | $39,000 |
| **Sources:** | Federal government and local school district |
| **Size:** | 294 families |
| **Area Served:** | Mequon-Thiensville School District |
| **Auspices:** | Pupil Services of the Mequon-Thiensville School District |
| **1990 Respondent:** | Leesa Maxwell, Community Consultant and Coordinator |

## Community

Mequon, with a population of 19,857, is located in southeast Wisconsin on the shores of Lake Michigan. Formerly rural and wooded, this newly developed community is now populated by affluent professionals. Minorities make up 8 percent of the Mequon-Thiensville school population. The district participates in a voluntary school integration transfer program with the Milwaukee Public Schools.

## Philosophy and Goals

The Early Developmental Awareness Project (EDAP) operates on the principle that strong family units make strong communities and strong schools. Leesa Maxwell, former community consultant and coordinator for the project, asserts, "It is important for families to feel that they are supported by school systems." The program thus combines interagency communication and cooperation, parent education, and early developmental screening.

## History and Origins

In 1985, Dr. Thomas Balliet, the director of pupil services for the Mequon-Thiensville School District, became concerned about early identification of young children with significant learning difficulties. Area preschools, pediatricians, and parents of preschool children were making inappropriate referrals for exceptional educational needs (EEN) that required up to 90 days and from three to six people to process. Either children referred for EEN screening did not need special education, or those who did got overlooked. To revamp and streamline the process, he wrote a proposal to fund EDAP through the school district with Public Law 99-457 discretionary grant money. In August 1986, Leesa Maxwell was hired as community consultant to provide parent education and act as a liaison to other community resources in the school district.

**Features**

EDAP offers developmental screening and provides both direct services and referrals to families. EDAP coordinates community resources for parents of young children in the areas of child development information and diagnostic tests.

**Parent support** takes place through individual, biweekly counseling sessions with the community consultant.

**Parent education classes** meet in the afternoons and evenings for one to two hours.

**Networking** possibilities are advertised in the newsletter. Ms. Maxwell adds that "some parents call up and say that they would like to get together with other parents of preschoolers. I make the connections through the newsletter or simply supply phone numbers."

**Participants**

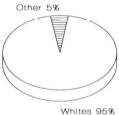

Other 5%

Whites 95%

In 1988-89, 294 families were served. Parents of children under age five are eligible to participate.

*"Some of my most important relationships are with the kindergarten teachers. I make a point of keeping up with their programs and new ideas so that I can relate those back to the preschools and daycare providers."*

**Parent Education**

EDAP is concerned with getting appropriate developmental information into parents' hands. Parents study communication with preschoolers, sexuality of preschoolers, health and nutrition, and guidance and discipline. The program prefers a combination of individual counseling and group discussion. EDAP puts parents in touch with appropriate community resources and encourages parents to link up with one another.

**Curriculum**

Ms. Maxwell is producing a videotape training module to teach preschool and child care providers how to use the Denver Developmental Screening Test (DDST), improve observation skills, assess problems, recognize immediate or long-term needs, talk with parents, and query the public schools. These skills are also taught by Ms. Maxwell in a series of five classes.

For parent education, Ms. Maxwell uses other nationally recognized curricula. "I am using *Active Parenting* for some group training. I also make presentations on children's learning and try to compile literature on developmentally appropriate practices from the National Association for the Education of Young Children [NAEYC]. I have adapted portions of the *Parents as Teachers* curriculum for parents of children birth to three." She also uses a variety of videotape materials from *Mister Rogers,* NAEYC, Educational Productions, and Practical Parenting.

**Sites**

EDAP's main office, in a public elementary school building, is shared with a school psychologist and a social worker. Classes are held in school buildings and the public library. Other sites include nine community preschool/child care programs.

**Parent Involvement**

Parents of preschoolers volunteered to conduct telephone interviews with their peers during the needs assessment phase of program development. Parents also evaluate the program by filling out one-page questionnaires.

**Outreach**

The program coordinator contacts child care providers and parents in the community to identify children who need screening for special needs. According to Ms. Maxwell, 80 percent of the area's children are enrolled in some kind of preschool program before kindergarten. A newsletter, sent to parents of preschoolers in the district as well as to child care providers and social service agencies, has been a successful outreach tool. In addition, Ms. Maxwell has used census information and advertisements in local newspapers to find parents whose children are not enrolled in any preschool program.

Ms. Maxwell comments on populations that are difficult to reach, "Mequon attracts many transient, corporate-type families who move, on, the average, every three to four years. The program adapts to their level of use, or ability to become involved. The newsletter, sent out to 600 parents, informs them about courses that will be offered, where and when. EDAP offers short- and long-term sessions geared to parents' interests."

**Staff**

| Job Title | PD | Vol | FT | PT | Educ Req | Status | Benefits |
|---|---|---|---|---|---|---|---|
| Community Consultant | 1 | - | 1 | - | College Degree | Other | Yes |

**State/District Requirements**

For the community consultant, preschool, kindergarten, and early childhood exceptional education teaching certificates.

**Preferred Background**

The community consultant should understand early development and handicapping conditions, know how to implement intervention strategies, be comfortable sharing information, and be able to work with parents and service providers.

**Employee Education and Training Represented**

Infant and toddler education; prekindergarten and early childhood education; elementary education; special education; parent educator; child care; child development and family studies; development and fundraising; research and evaluation.

**Administration**

The community consultant reports to the director of pupil services, who is responsible to the superintendent. The program is administered entirely within the public education system. The 21-member advisory board is made up of program participants, public school personnel, representatives from public and private agencies, community representatives, and members of the board of education. Meeting five times a year, its main tasks are to establish relationships with other agencies, raise public awareness, and give direction to project activities.

## Relationship to the Schools

According to Leesa Maxwell, the program fits into the school system well. Parents in the community trust their schools and are very concerned with their children's school-readiness. Ms. Maxwell notes the advantages of EDAP's close relationship with the schools, "They provide space and office support. All the necessary resource people are there, like the speech pathologist, guidance counselors, special needs teachers, and school nurses." She continues, "Some of my most important relationships are with the kindergarten teachers. I make a point of keeping up with their programs and new ideas so that I can relate those back to the preschools and daycare providers."

## Community Links

When starting the program, Ms. Maxwell interviewed kindergarten teachers, area preschool providers, and professionals in local diagnostic and treatment facilities and in public and private social service agencies to include them in a resource and referral file of family services. Referral to community resources is one of EDAP's top priorities.

## Funding

All of EDAP's funding originates at the federal level: 55 percent is allocated to the program through the school district's preschool entitlement funds and 45 percent comes directly from federal preschool discretionary grant monies.

## In-Kind Resources

The Mequon-Thiensville schools provide consultation and staff development, administrative and clerical support, and access to equipment, materials, and supplies. The Ozaukee County public health nurses provide periodic direct services to program participants.

## Funding History

EDAP won a grant to hire Ms. Maxwell in 1986 from funds allocated by Public Law 99-457. She expects that the district will pick up funding when grant money is no longer available.

## Objectives

EDAP seeks to conduct and facilitate appropriate developmental screening of young children and to train the preschool staff in screening skills. The program also identifies community resources that provide child development information and services to parents of young children and facilitates contact between early childhood resource people and community service agencies.

## Evaluation

Although there has been no formal evaluation, Ms. Maxwell's initial one-page questionnaire and telephone interviews have supported her belief that parent attendance is directly proportionate to their interest in particular subjects.

## Replication

The program has not been replicated.

## Materials Available

A manual and videotape that offer training in developmental screening are available.

# Early Education Center
A Division of the Training and Evaluation Center of Hutchinson

In a recent Early Education Center newsletter, one parent of a child with multiple handicaps recounts her experience in the program over a five-year period. She writes that EEC helped her and her husband to learn about their son's limits and potential in an atmosphere of encouragement and support. She learned to make informed decisions about his health and education and is happy to report that her son is now doing well in the public schools.

| | | |
|---|---|---|
| Home visits | Psychological testing | Monthly screening clinics |
| Preschool | Parent discussion group | Audiological/visual screening |
| Parent counseling | Speech/language therapy | Parenting/child development education |
| Lecture series | Health/nutrition education | Physical/occupational therapy |
| Hydrotherapy | Parent-child joint activities | Community services info/referral |

**Contact:** Lee Price, Director

**Address:** P.O. Box 399
Hutchinson, KS 67504-0399
(316) 663-2671

**Established:** 1967, local initiative

**Budget '88-'89:** $811,176

**Sources:** School district and county funds; state categorical aid; federal Chapter 1 funds; Public Law 99-457; corporate and business donations; fundraising; United Way; client fees

**Size:** 205 children and families

**Area Served:** Six school districts near Hutchinson, Kansas

**Auspices:** Jointly administered by a private agency and two public school special education cooperatives

**1990 Respondent:** Deborah Kraus Voth, Director

**Community**

Hutchinson, a city with a population of 40,000, is located in rural Reno County, an hour outside of Wichita. In the past five years, the county has seen the decline of the farming and farming support industries. The Early Education Center (EEC) serves a largely middle-class population, mostly in suburban Hutchinson and the outlying rural districts.

**Philosophy and Goals**

Recognizing that children learn more in the first years of life than at any other time, the Early Education Center's aims are early detection and treatment of handicaps and developmental delays. Its goal is to help every child reach fullest potential by eliminating delays, preventing secondary problems, and minimizing the effects of a serious and long-term handicap. EEC includes parents in the development of educational plans for children and teaches them how to provide a stimulating home environment to promote early learning.

**History and Origins**

In 1967, parents of handicapped children in Reno County began the Early Education Center, a preschool for handicapped children ages three to five, as a service to young parents. They hired a teacher and coordinator, but the preschool was staffed mostly by parent volunteers. In 1975, the program was incorporated into the Training and Evaluation Center for the Handicapped (TECH), a local nonprofit agency. At this time EEC began its Home-based Developmental Training Program component to provide support and education to parents and their young children. In 1978, in an effort to gain state and federal funds earmarked for school programs, EEC established an interagency agreement with six local school districts through their special education cooperative, the Reno County Education Cooperative (RCEC). The Hutchinson School

District later established a separate special education department with its own interagency agreement with EEC. Since 1980, EEC has provided screening to young children countywide and has diversified its services to provide family support and education in several formats, differentiated by age and the specific handicap of the child.

EEC services follow the handicapped child from birth to age five.

**Special Beginnings,** run in cooperation with the county health department, identifies newborns at risk for delayed development, checking them monthly to prevent risks from becoming permanent handicaps.

**The Home-based Developmental Training Program** is for children (birth to age three) with long-term or serious handicaps and their parents. Twice a week, a therapist meets with the family at home, demonstrates stimulation activities for the child, and helps the family incorporate these activities into the daily routine.

**The Center-based Developmental Training Program** is a preschool program for three-year-olds that meets five times a week, with both special needs and integrated classrooms.

**A Toddler Group** meets at the center weekly for 10 weeks in the spring to ease the transition of children from a home-based to a center-based group format.

There are also programs for children with specific developmental delays:

**Toddler Talk,** for children 12 to 30 months of age having expressive language delay as the only risk factor, offers monthly appointments at the center for children and their parents. The speech and language therapist works with the child while another therapist counsels each parent in turn.

**Outpatient speech and language** provides articulation therapy to children ages three to five, for half an hour twice a week.

In 1987-88, the Home-based Developmental Training Program served 47 families; the Center-based Developmental Training Program served 100 children; and other programs, 56 families. In 1988-89, EEC served 77 percent of the eligible population, but it anticipates reaching 100 percent of its targeted population in the coming year when transportation to the center will be provided throughout the county.

*EEC includes parents in the development of educational plans for children and teaches them how to provide a stimulating home environment to promote early learning.*

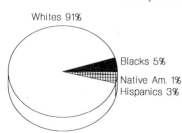

Whites 91%
Blacks 5%
Native Am. 1%
Hispanics 3%

**Parent Education**

EEC informs parents of their children's federal rights to special education. A bimonthly lecture series and discussion group features attorneys, doctors, and therapists who give parents professional guidance. The Home-based Developmental Training Program, Special Beginnings, and Toddler Talk teach parents stimulation activities to foster their children's development at home.

Federal law requires infant and toddler special education programs to draw up an Individual Family Service Plan (IFSP) that includes parents in their children's education. EEC educators and counselors provide child development information to help parents assess their children's development and set realistic goals for an educational plan. EEC director, Debbie Voth, thinks that parents can be intimidated by professionals, so she stresses that families are the child's best advocate.

**Curriculum**

EEC uses a combination of set curricula — the *Hawaii Early Learning Project* and the *Los Lunas Curricular System* — adapting them to particular handicapping conditions. As evaluation instruments, it uses the Brigance Inventory of Early Development and the Battelle Developmental Inventory.

**Sites**

Teachers and therapists deliver home visits to over 50 homes across Reno County. Center-based programming takes place in Hutchinson, which is less than a 35-minute drive from any corner of Reno County. The community donated EEC's original house, and last year the city of Hutchinson applied for a community block grant to build the present facility on a public elementary school campus. Transportation was once a problem, but next year EEC expects the last of the six districts to agree to bus its preschoolers to the center.

**Parent Involvement**

A parent advisory group incorporates parents from each component, and plans six lecture-discussion meetings per year. Ms. Voth is working on developing a more comprehensive parent-teacher organization, but she notes that parent groups are more cohesive and productive when the parents initiate them and also when parents share specific concerns. For instance, parents of children with hearing impairments have formed their own group to advise the public schools on curriculum for the hearing impaired.

**Outreach**

Each spring, EEC has a screening drive at 13 sites around Reno County. Full developmental, hearing, vision, and health screenings are also available at any time by request or referral. The Early Education Center receives referrals from physicians, the county health department, and the Kansas Department of Social and Rehabilitation Services and distributes brochures through pediatricians and hospitals. Interagency agreements with the public schools hold elementary school principals responsible for publicizing the screening clinics in their area.

*EEC educators and counselors provide child development information to help parents assess their children's development and set realistic goals for an educational plan.*

| Job Title | PD | Vol | FT | PT | Educ Req | Status | Benefits |
|-----------|----|----|----|----|----------|--------|----------|
| Director | 1 | - | 1 | - | Post-Graduate Courses or Degree | Other | Yes |
| Secretaries | 2 | - | 2 | - | High School Diploma | Hourly Non-Contract | Yes |
| Early Childhood Handicapped Teachers | 10 | - | 9 | 1 | College Degree | K-12 Contract | Yes |
| Para-professionals | 11 | 10 | 11 | 10 | High School Diploma | Hourly Non-Contract | Yes |
| Speech/ Language Therapists | 5 | - | 4 | 1 | Post-Graduate Courses or Degree | K-12 Contract | Yes |
| Occupational Therapists | 1 | - | 1 | - | College Degree | K-12 Contract | Yes |
| Physical Therapists | 3 | - | 3 | - | College Degree | K-12 Contract | Yes |
| Social Worker | 1 | - | 1 | - | Post-Graduate Courses or Degree | K-12 Contract | Yes |
| Custodian | 1 | - | 1 | - | Some High School | Hourly Non-Contract | Yes |

**State/District Requirements**

For the director, a Kansas Department of Education special education supervision certificate; for teachers, social workers, and speech and language therapists, state certification. The occupational therapist and physical therapist must be registered through the Kansas State Board of Healing Arts.

**Preferred Background**

All staff members should possess initiative, strong communication skills, and an interest in teamwork. The direct service staff should have experience with young children or a strong interest in children.

**Employee Education and Training Represented**

Infant and toddler education; prekindergarten and early childhood education; elementary education; education, grades 7 to 12; special education; parent educator; child care; health and nutrition; home economics; nursing; occupational and physical therapy; speech therapy; psychology; social work; child development and family studies; development and fundraising; research and evaluation.

**Administration**

The Early Education Center is jointly administered by TECH, the Reno County Educational Cooperative (RCEC), and the special education department of the Hutchinson School District. The EEC coordinator reports to the boards of TECH and RCEC and to the director of the Hutchinson Special Education Department, and meets with the three directors together every other month. Formal interagency agreements are reviewed annually. EEC employees are hired through RCEC and follow its personnel and evaluation procedures so that the program qualifies for state reimbursement money for certified staff members and paraprofessionals. The program is monitored by the Kansas Commission on Accreditation of Rehabilitative Facilities and the Kansas Departments of Education, Health and Environment, and Social and Rehabilitation Services.

## Relationship to the Schools

The Early Education Center coordinates the transition to kindergarten for participants entering elementary schools in the six county districts. The school principal, special education and kindergarten teachers, therapists, counselors, parents, and program staff members work together to decide a child's placement. Principals cooperate by allowing teachers to take time to observe children in the EEC classroom. The coordinator asks principals and teachers to be present at screening clinics for a postclinic review of the students in their districts.

*EEC director, Debbie Voth, thinks that parents can be intimidated by professionals, so she stresses that families are the child's best advocate.*

## Community Links

EEC offers Special Beginnings in cooperation with the Reno County Health Department. Hutchinson's Head Start program contracts with EEC for participant screening. Ms. Voth says educators think they don't have to sell their programs, but she is careful to win community support for EEC, since a county levy and local business donations constitute 17 percent of its funding.

## Funding

State categorical aid, 45 percent; federal Chapter 1, 18 percent; corporate and business donations, 9 percent; school districts, 9 percent; county tax levy, 8 percent; fundraising, 6 percent; United Way, 3 percent; client fees, 2 percent.

## In-Kind Resources

Staff development and some screening by RCEC; clerical support by RCEC and TECH.

## Funding History

Since EEC established an interagency agreement with six local school districts in 1978, its funding has diversified to include state and federal funds earmarked for school programs. EEC began as a local initiative using volunteers and has developed into a state and federally funded program.

## Objectives

The Early Education Center aims at early detection and treatment of developmental delays, minimizing delays due to handicaps, helping all children reach their fullest potential, and involving parents in their children's education.

## Evaluation

The Kansas Department of Education and the Commission on Accreditation of Rehabilitative Facilities require program evaluation. The most recent, conducted by a member of the EEC staff, evaluated the developmental growth of participating children, the ability of parents to articulate goals for their children's education, and general parent participation. She concluded that the program performed satisfactorily in all areas. Ms. Voth believes the lives of handicapped children and their parents in the county have been improved by their access to supervision, referral, and professional help. Some handicapped children who might have been institutionalized continue to live at home because of services available in the county. Constant stimulation of delayed children by parents and teachers has raised I.Q. scores considerably in short periods of time. She also notes increased identification of hearing disorders originally thought to be behavior problems.

**Replication**

This program has not been replicated.

**Materials Available**

None.

# Boston Institute for Art Therapies

Art therapy | Mother support groups | Parenting/child development education
Referral | Consultation with teachers | Parent-child joint activities
Networking

**Contact:** Ms. Ricky Stern, Ed.D., Executive Director
**Address:** 731 Harrison Avenue
Boston, MA 02118
(617) 262-6183
**Established:** 1987, local initiative
**Budget '88-'89:** $13,000
**Sources:** Private foundation grants, corporate grants
**Size:** 18 families in 1987-88; 8 families in 1988-89
**Area Served:** Two Boston inner-city schools
**Auspices:** Joint venture between Boston Public Schools and the Boston Institute for Art Therapies

*A single mother, living at home, felt overwhelmed by her daughter's acting out. The Boston Institute for Art Therapies' teachers helped her evaluate her relationship with her own mother and see her child's behavior as a plea for attention. She developed greater equanimity as a parent and real interest in her daughter, and gained the necessary emotional distance to appreciate her child's needs for respect, limitations, and empathy.*

## Community

Boston is a large, multiracial city on the eastern seaboard of Massachusetts. Employment opportunities are scarce and disadvantage is high in the inner-city neighborhoods and schools that the Boston Institute for Art Therapies serves.

## Philosophy and Goals

According to the program's director, Ricky Stern, one important goal of the parent-child component is to enable parents to "re-vision" their children. Parents are encouraged to enjoy their children's capacities, creativity, and level of competence. The program believes that support for the parent-child relationship has far-reaching effects. Ms. Stern asserts that parents often need support, especially when experiencing concerns associated with developmental delays in their children or cultural and/or familial stress. Inner-city communities often lack appropriate services, and the Boston Institute for Art Therapies believes school-based parent support services are an effective way to help parents and children and that therapeutic attitudes and modeling by clinicians are excellent vehicles for change. "The arts offer a safe, enticing connection between all parties concerned. Art is an involving process and creates a point of contact between parent, child, and therapist that is used to help participants reach important therapeutic goals," says Ms. Stern.

## History and Origins

By contractual arrangement with cooperating schools, the Boston Institute for Art Therapies (formerly the Center for Creative Art Therapies), an independent, nonprofit human service agency, brings programs in art, dance, and music therapy to disadvantaged children with special needs. The Boston Institute for Art Therapies began its early childhood special needs programs in the Boston Public Schools in 1983. In 1987, cooperating Boston Public Schools asked the institute to create a parent-child program to complement its other services. The institute complied with a summer pilot project, on which its present program is based.

## Features

Weekly sessions are offered at two sites for 16 weeks. A session consists of one hour of joint parent-child art activities followed by a one-hour support and education group. Clinicians also consult weekly with classroom teachers and program administrators.

**Parent-child joint activities** allow therapists to observe strengths and difficulties and provide support to the parent-child relationship. During this time parent and child interact around an art project or materials while the therapist observes, assessing the child's developmental skill level and the parent's response.

**Parenting support groups** and **child development education** grow out of the art activity. During the second hour, after children have returned to their classrooms, the therapist presents information about child development and conducts a short support session that allows parents to gain insight about their responses to and hopes for their children.

**Consultation to teachers** and **referral** are offshoots of the interactions among parents in the groups. Teachers are given insights on new ways to interpret and reach their students. Referrals for family support are given as needed.

**Participants**

Blacks 35%
Asians 5%
Hispanics 25%
Whites 35%

Children three to five years old who are Massachusetts residents and diagnosed as having special needs such as learning or language delays, Down's syndrome, or emotional distress are eligible. Daytime participation by parents is essential.

In 1987-88, 18 children and 18 parents received Boston Institute for Art Therapies services. This year the number has been reduced to eight because of a 65 percent decrease in funding. Most of the parents in the program are single mothers.

*"Art is an involving process and creates a point of contact between parent, child, and therapist that is used to help participants reach important therapeutic goals," says Ms. Stern.*

**Parent Education**

Therapists discuss parent-child interactions, child development, observed behaviors, and problem areas. Parent sessions also double as support groups.

**Curriculum**

The art therapist chooses from an array of teaching techniques. Activities are chosen to be relevant to the developmental needs of each child and to respond to family concerns, experiences, and issues. Projects include easel painting, body tracings, clay sculpture, print making, collage work, or found-object sculptures. Over the course of a semester, the curriculum is modified and enhanced to complement the developmental stages of participants.

**Sites**

During the 1988-89 school year the institute provided a morning program in one school and an afternoon program in another. Boston Institute for Art Therapies shares space at both sites. In one site participants work in a classroom, and in the other they use a small office area. The institute will remain at these sites as long as it can fund its own projects.

**Parent Involvement**

According to Ms. Stern, the best way to involve parents is to "give them something before you ask for something back. During the introductory party they experience what the program is going to be like, and only then are they asked to commit."

**Outreach**

In the beginning of the school year, the Boston Institute for Art Therapies meets with teachers and early childhood education specialists (liaisons) from the Boston Public Schools to discuss shared goals and determine which parents and children might benefit from the program. Teachers and early childhood liaisons send flyers home and make phone calls to prospective participants. The institute gives a party for children in the special needs program and their parents, including joint activities for parents and children based on an art therapy model. At the end of the party, parents are invited to commit to a 16-week program. If the parent agrees, the institute schedules an individual interview to discuss the family's situation.

**Staff**

| Job Title | PD | Vol | FT | PT | Educ Req | Status | Benefits |
|---|---|---|---|---|---|---|---|
| Administrator | 1 | - | 1 | - | Post-Graduate Courses or Degree | Other Contract | No |
| Art Therapist | 1 | - | 1 | - | Post-Graduate Courses or Degree | Hourly Non-Contract | No |
| Dance Therapist | 1 | - | 1 | - | Post-Graduate Courses or Degree | Hourly Non-Contract | No |
| Intern/ Student | - | 1 | - | 1 | Some College | - | No |

**State/District Requirements**

None.

**Preferred Background**

Staff members are creative art therapists with master's degrees in their fields. They have a minimum of two years post-master's experience, national certification in the art therapies, and experience in early childhood education.

**Employee Education and Training Represented**

Prekindergarten and early childhood education; special education; psychology; family therapy; child development and family studies; research and evaluation.

**Administration**

Early childhood liaisons from the Boston Public Schools, such as the early childhood coordinator from the special needs department, serve as links to the art therapists and families needing services.

**Relationship to the Schools**

The school is the center of the Boston Institute for Art Therapies' activities for its parent-child education program. Schools provide space and art materials. A staff member meets with teachers and the early childhood liaison on a weekly basis to discuss each family's progress. In turn, the teacher or liaison follows up with parents as needed.

Ms. Stern strongly advises, "As consultants, communication is the key. Put a lot of effort into staff support at the site, listen to their concerns and their opinions. Tell them what you can do and listen to their experience, involve them. Be up front and ask them what they do, then ask them what they want from the program. Make sure that everyone understands everyone else."

### Funding

Corporate and business donations, 60 percent; foundations or private agencies, 40 percent. The $13,000 budget for 1988-89 represents a 65 percent decrease from the 1987-88 budget due to cutbacks in the public school budget. Schools provide the sites and the institute provides the art materials.

### Funding History

The Boston Institute for Art Therapies' general funding has come from private foundations and grants as well as public agencies, among them the Bank of New England, the Boston Globe, the Ratshesky Foundation, IBM, the Millipore Foundation, Zayre's Corporation, Gillette, Polaroid, and Stride-Rite. The Boston Public Schools funded the parent-child component for one year (1987), enabling the institute to serve 17 families in three schools. Funding from the Boston Public Schools was discontinued for the 1988-89 year. To continue the parent-child component, the institute allocated grant dollars but services are now limited to two schools.

Ms. Stern comments on unstable funding, "Schools currently receive less creative art therapy than they need, but they would love to have more. Unfortunately, sources of funding vary from year to year and all sources must be reapproached for each new site or semester. Some individual schools have seized the initiative and have written proposals for Commonwealth Inservice Training to help teachers use more arts in the classroom, a service the Boston Institute for Art Therapies will soon provide."

### Objectives

According to Ms. Stern, "There is a need for parents to realize their child's capacities. This leads to lowered anxiety for parents and new self-esteem and self-respect for children." The institute's objectives for parents include self-acceptance, learning new ideas, and reframing their views of their children. Goals for children are improved language, coordination, and self-control; the acquisition of new cognitive skills; increased self-esteem; and clearer differentiation from parents.

### Evaluation

Liaisons and teachers responded to a questionnaire on program effectiveness.

### Replication

The Boston Institute for Art Therapies is unique.

### Materials Available

*A Point of Contact* is a videotape available through the Boston Institute for Art Therapies.

# Parent Resource Center

| | | |
|---|---|---|
| Home visits | Resource library | Community services info/referral |
| Newsletter | Drop-in center | Parenting/child development education |
| Networking | Warmline | Special needs info classes |

**Contact:** Jan Mayhew, Parent Coordinator

**Address:** Greenbrier County Schools
202 Chestnut Street
Lewisburg, WV 24901
(304) 647-6470

**Established:** 1987, state initiative

**Budget '88-'89:** $45,000

**Source:** School system

**Size:** 40 families

**Area served:** Greenbrier County School District

**Auspices:** District Departments of Special Education and Student Services

*When a low-income couple whose daughter was diagnosed as retarded approached Mrs. Mayhew about their child's speech impairments, she scheduled a reevaluation. Testing revealed their child was physically handicapped, not mentally deficient. They felt enormously relieved and developed a new, more hopeful outlook on their child's future and their own capacity to help her. In addition, the school board paid for the testing.*

## Community

Greenbrier County covers 1,022 square miles and has 40,000 residents, most of whom are white. The county, a mountainous area in the southeast part of the state, contains many tiny, isolated communities. A high-tech company, Combustion Engineering, and the Greenbrier, a world-renowned resort, are the area's major employers. Other county residents are involved in coal mining and subsistence farming; approximately 10 percent of the population is unemployed. Lewisburg (population 4,500), the home of the Parent Resource Center, is a tourist town famous for its crafts and historic landmarks.

## Philosophy and Goals

Federal law guarantees an appropriate educational program for all children over three years old. Although educators pursue this aim, parents have the responsibility for protecting their children's rights. The Parent Resource Center (PRC) is designed to help parents realize that children with special needs are eligible for services from the schools. The program seeks to provide training, resources, general assistance, and empathy to parents.

## History and Origins

The Parent Resource Center is modeled after a program called Parent Educational Advocacy Training Center (PEATC), which was started approximately five years ago by Dr. Nona Flynn in Alexandria, Virginia to provide services through the public school system to parents of children with handicaps and special needs. In 1987, PEATC got a contract from the West Virginia State Board of Education to train parents of handicapped children. They set up 24 resource centers in West Virginia and the state board of education has recommended that every county have one.

As a mother of a child with Down's syndrome, Jan Mayhew had actively pursued access to special needs programs in the Greenbrier County School District. In 1987, Thomas Long, the district's director of student services, and Dr. Tom Iles, supervisor of special education, hired her to be PRC's parent coordinator. Together with the educator coordinator, former teacher and principal Kermit Moore, she offers informational classes and home visits and has made herself available as a resource for parents of children with special needs.

Mrs. Mayhew advises leaders of programs just starting up, "Be patient. It's slow at first, but then it will take off. Have a 'What can I do to help you?' attitude, not, 'I have come to solve your problem.' Help parents to help themselves. The parents I have visited are happy to have someone who cares enough to come and visit, and who is interested in their child's education."

### Features

Jan Mayhew acts as the liaison between home and school and provides most of PRC's services. She defines her role as "being available to parents as someone who understands." The federal government mandates parent involvement in the formulation of an educational plan for children receiving special education services. Mrs. Mayhew coordinates the meetings between parents and teachers. Families frequently need several sessions, and the coordinator may meet with teachers, visit the home, meet again with parents and teachers together, and conduct follow-up visits to both parents and teachers. Since many participants are geographically isolated, the home visit is the central activity of the program. In these one-on-one sessions, Mrs. Mayhew provides parents with relevant books and materials. In addition, a parent resource library and drop-in center is open Monday through Friday from 8:30 a.m. until 3:00 p.m. Once a year PRC offers a six-hour course called "Understanding Special Education".

Parent-initiated groups focus on shared concerns around school-related issues. Home visits occur whenever problems arise. Mrs. Mayhew is vigilant about keeping in touch through what she calls a PTD, or pass-the-time-of-day visit, in which she'll stop by and inquire about progress, because she feels, "People like having someone caring. . . . Some parents are so upset and feel so isolated and helpless when they find out that their child is mentally or physically impaired." She tries to make them feel less alone by connecting them to other people and letting them know that she, too, has a child with special needs.

### Participants

PRC serves approximately 40 families, including parents and occasionally grandparents. The catchment area includes a preschool, 11 public elementary schools, 10 junior high schools, and 2 high schools. According to participant records, 20 percent of the parents in the program are single and 5 percent are teens.

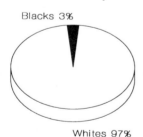

Blacks 3%

Whites 97%

*"The parents I have visited are happy to have someone who cares enough to come and visit, and who is interested in their child's education."*

### Parent Education

Formal parent education is delivered in the initial six-hour course, "Understanding Special Education," and Mrs. Mayhew provides supplementary information in the course of home visits. Parents may also use the parent resource library as a source of information and support.

| | |
|---|---|
| **Curriculum** | Books for families include: *Babies with Down's Syndrome, Choices in Deafness,* and *Children with Spina Bifida.* Mrs. Mayhew recommends special education books published by Brookes Publishing and Woodbine House. She also uses brightly colored five-by-nine-inch learning cards, which provide tips for parents and other family members on improving children's motor skills, concepts, and memory development through simple games. |
| **Sites** | The Maxwelton Center, where the Parent Resource Center is housed, includes the school district's textbook center, a tutoring center, and vocational rehabilitation offices. Mrs. Mayhew's work takes her in and out of the district's many schools on a daily basis; she also works out of her home. |
| **Parent Involvement** | Parents often initiate their own support groups for parents of children with similar handicaps. |
| **Outreach** | In 1988, Jan Mayhew gave a talk to teachers to introduce the Parent Resource Center. As a follow up, PRC sent a letter and a brochure describing the program to every principal and teacher in the county, and a local newspaper ran a feature story on the center. |
| | Mrs. Mayhew notes that veteran participants tend to attract new ones. "I have learned the age-old idea: if you want something done, get busy people to do it," says Jan Mayhew. "If a group wants to get together, it's usually the busy, already involved people who do the most. They'll recruit others." |

| Job Title | PD | Vol | FT | PT | Educ Req | Status | Benefits |
|---|---|---|---|---|---|---|---|
| Parent Coodinator | 1 | - | - | 1 | College Degree | Other Contract | No |
| Educator Coordinator | 1 | - | - | 1 | College Degree | K-12 Contract | Yes |

| | |
|---|---|
| **State/District Requirements** | The educator coordinator must be a teacher, principal, or the equivalent. The parent coordinator must be the parent of a handicapped child, communicate effectively, and know special education laws. |
| **Preferred Background** | None. |
| **Employee Education and Training Represented** | Education, grades 7 to 12; special education; parent educator. |
| **Administration** | Mrs. Mayhew shares most of the workload with the educator coordinator, although she makes more home visits than originally anticipated since they have proven so effective. There is no advisory board. Both Mrs. Mayhew and Mr. Moore are responsible to the director of special education for the Greenbrier County Public Schools. |
| **Relationship to the Schools** | PRC depends upon the schools for referrals. When a parent comes to Mrs. Mayhew to seek a change in a child's program, she has the board of education's sanction and the school's cooperation. Should testing for learning disorders be indicated, parent approval is required. Sometimes |

parents resist additional school-initiated testing, and Jan Mayhew acts as a mediator. Because of her own experience with special needs, parents are generally receptive to her. She calls herself "simply a public relations person, a parent who can help other parents." Frequently, she will drop into the schools spontaneously and check in with teachers about the progress of different children involved in the program. Officially, her school visits are on an "as needed basis."

## Community Links

Interactions with other agencies occur in special circumstances, as in the case of a child with impaired vision whose parents would not get an eye exam because they couldn't afford the glasses. "I found a doctor who would do the exam at a reduced rate and the special needs program paid. I asked the Lion's Club to pay for the glasses, which they did," says Mrs. Mayhew.

## Funding

All of the Parent Resource Center's funding comes from the Greenbrier County School District.

## In-Kind Resources

The board of education provides volunteer staff; access to equipment, materials, supplies, and books; reimburses for mileage; and pays for workshops.

## Funding History

The program coordinator is not involved with obtaining funds. Thus far funding remains constant. Mrs. Mayhew feels that the county is in good shape, and funding is secure.

## Objectives

The Parent Resource Center aims to help parents feel confident to use the special education services offered in the schools and community.

## Evaluation

Mrs. Mayhew keeps track of the number of home visits delivered to each family and enhances these reports with narratives about the participants.

## Replication

Based on the Parent Resource Center's success in the field of special education, the state legislature is looking at the overall benefits of parent involvement for all children. Mrs. Mayhew served on a committee formulating a policy to bring more support to parents, using the PRC model as a prototype.

## Materials Available

None.

# Vermont College Preschool

Newsletter
Preschool
Networking
Warmline
Home visits
Child care

Parent-child joint activities
Parent support groups
Resource library
Speech therapy
Health/nutrition education

Child care info/referral
Developmental exams/screening
Community services info/referral
Parenting/child development education
Physical/occupational therapy

**Contact:** Beverly Heise, Early Education Initiative Teacher/Coordinator

**Address:** Vermont College Preschool
Lower Level — Schulmaier Hall
Montpelier, VT 05602
(802) 828-8768

**Established:** 1965, Vermont College Preschool began; 1981, joint initiative between the Montpelier Public Schools and the Vermont College Preschool

**Budget '88-'89:** Vermont College Preschool, $46,142
Central Vermont Essential Early Education Program, $101,191
Early Education Initiative, $30,000

**Sources:** State and federal government, in-kind contributions, and client fees

**Size:** 84 families

**Area Served:** Montpelier, Vermont

**Auspices:** Vermont College of Norwich University and the Montpelier Public School System

*Two-year-old Lester was referred to Essential Early Education (EEE) with an attention deficit disorder, fetal alcohol syndrome, and developmental delays in all skill areas. An EEE teacher began home visits, and Lester entered the preschool at age three on a part-time basis, starting at just 20 minutes a day and working up to the full morning session. When he turned four, EEE staff began transition planning with Lester's local elementary school. The staff and Lester's parents agreed that an extra year of preschool with a gradual transition to kindergarten would be best. The transition, though rocky, was successful, and Lester now attends kindergarten full time.*

## Community

Montpelier, the capital of Vermont, has a predominantly white population of 8,000. Annual income levels range from welfare level to between $60,000 and $80,000. The major employers are the state and the National Life Insurance Company, without which Montpelier would lose its high-income group. Other employers include light industry, the granite industry, the school system, small businesses, and maintenance and factory work.

## Philosophy and Goals

The Vermont College Preschool is based on the concept that home and school share the responsibility of caring for and educating children. Preschool staff members help parents assess their children's needs and build on existing family strengths to enable parents to improve the quality of life for their children and for themselves.

## History and Origins

The Vermont College Preschool started in 1965 as a lab school for the education department at Vermont College. In 1981, Vermont College and the Montpelier Public Schools jointly established the Central Vermont Essential Early Education Program (EEE) to serve preschool children with handicaps in a separate program.

Since 1983, in a cooperative venture among three area supervisory unions (school districts) that serve eight towns in the Montpelier area, EEE allowed the mainstreaming of handicapped children into classrooms with their nonhandicapped peers.

Staff members from EEE and community volunteers screen children from Montpelier and other area communities (according to the Vermont special education specifications children ages three to five must have an 18-month developmental delay to qualify for services). Each year, 15 to 20 of the children screened appeared to have learning and behavior problems that, although not severe enough to qualify them as handicapped under the state guidelines, might hinder advancement in public school. Many of the families of these children did not have access to or could not afford private preschools and child care programs. The Early Education Initiative Program (EEI), a joint venture between the Vermont College Preschool and the Montpelier Public School System, was established in 1988 to meet the needs of these unserved or underserved children, based on the same integrated, mainstreamed model as EEE.

## Features

**Vermont College Preschool** offers child development training, preschool, and afterschool programs to 130 children and families. Children come to the Vermont College Preschool for two or four half-days per week. Some of the participants are also served by Head Start. Although the Vermont College Preschool has three separate programs in place, it provides services to special needs children in mainstream classrooms. "The classroom composition mirrors the diversity children will find later in society as adults," notes Beverly Heise.

In the **Central Vermont Essential Early Education Program,** specialists come into the classroom to provide services to the handicapped students. Other children are encouraged to participate.

In the **Early Education Initiative Program,** a full-time teacher and aide conduct a center-based classroom program in the mornings and spend afternoons with parents and children in a home-based program. Home visits address children's skills and assist parents in identifying family needs, goals, and possible means of support. Home visits last about one hour and are scheduled according to individual family needs. For families in crisis, home visits occur weekly; for stable families, they occur monthly. According to Ms. Heise, when the activities in school are reinforced with the parents at home, the difference for the child is significant. Parents are actively involved in both center- and home-based experiences with their children. Individual programs prepare children to enter kindergarten in the local school. The Montpelier Public School System provides transportation for EEE and EEI programs.

## Participants

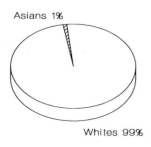

Asians 1%

Whites 99%

The entire program serves 84 children and families. Referrals come from the Montpelier Public Schools, Head Start, local librarians, physicians, and public health nurses. To participate, children must be three years old by September 1 of the school year. The preschool serves 60 percent of the families eligible for the program.

EEE participants must live in one of eight communities, range in age from birth to six years, and satisfy the special education eligibility criteria. This is a public school program without income restrictions. It serves 90 percent of the eligible population.

EEI participants must be three or four years old, be Montpelier residents, and meet the criteria in the Vermont College Preschool Early Education Initiative Screening Tool. Eighty-five percent of the families fall at or below the poverty level. The program serves 80 percent of the eligible families.

**Parent Education**

The curriculum of the parent component has a family focus derived from *Empowering and Enabling Families: Principles and Guidelines for Practice* by Carl Dunst and the *Nurturing Program,* designed by Family Resources of Eau Claire, Wisconsin and implemented by Parents Anonymous of Vermont. This combination of materials is modified according to the individual needs of the child or parent.

**Curriculum**

The Vermont College Preschool has developed a curriculum using the National Association for the Education of Young Children's (NAEYC) *Developmentally Appropriate Practices,* the *High/Scope* curriculum, and George Forman's "continuum of learning" philosophy and practice.

EEE uses the *Peabody Early Experiences Kit* and the developmental interaction approach to fundamental skills acquisition. Assistance is provided for children in this program by specialists in areas such as occupational therapy, physical therapy, speech and language therapy, hearing impairments, and the multihandicapped.

For EEI, a Child-Family Education Plan (C-FEP) is developed for each child based upon the child's individual needs. Brigance Inventory of Early Development is used to assess children's progress.

> *"We hope to enhance parents' awareness of developmentally appropriate activities and resultant expectations of their children."*

**Sites**

The program is located at the Vermont College campus of Norwich University. The three programs share space with other early childhood programs and are connected to the college's education department. Additional space for EEI brought the program up to three fully integrated classrooms.

**Parent Involvement**

Parents help "behind the scenes and in the classroom," says Ms. Heise. Parents have formed a volunteer network: they organize field trips and newsletters, arrange parent substitute teachers for teacher absences, and collect materials for the classroom. In addition, parents are actively involved in identifying goals and in the evaluation process.

**Outreach**

Participants are most likely to hear about the Vermont College Preschool through preschool screening, physicians, public school referral, newspapers, Vermont Social and Rehabilitation Services Department referral, parents of children enrolled or previously enrolled, health and social agencies, and Head Start.

The tuition-based Vermont College Preschool has a long waiting list. EEE has an extensive "child find" process that includes biannual public notices in all local newspapers and citywide preschool screenings, a referral network of local and state health programs and individuals (hospitals; ophthalmologists; ear, nose, and throat doctors; health department; and pediatricians), a referral network of human and social service agencies, and referrals from teachers, school administrators, and Head Start staff members.

*"It is our hope that parents will enjoy their children's developmental progress more and that the children served will be more successful and motivated in school."*

EEI sends out over 50 letters requesting referrals each spring to physicians, human service agencies, local child care and preschool professionals, and churches. The school system sends a note about the program home with students. The elementary school principal informs eligible families about the program. Parents of enrolled children suggest other families to contact. Often during a home visit, families in the neighborhood will express interest to the home visitor. Biannual preschool screenings also provide referrals.

**Staff**

| Job Title | PD | Vol | FT | PT | Educ Req | Status | Benefits |
|---|---|---|---|---|---|---|---|
| Supervisory Preschool | 1 | - | 1 | - | College Degree | Other Contract | Yes |
| Early Education Initiative Teacher | 1 | - | 1 | - | College Degree | Other Contract | Yes |
| Preschool Lead Teacher | 1 | - | - | 1 | College Degree | Other Contract | Yes |
| Preschool Assistant Teacher | 1 | - | - | 1 | High School Diploma | Hourly Non-Contract | Yes |
| Essential Early Education Teachers | 3 | - | 2 | 1 | College Degree | K-12 Contract | Yes |
| Essential Early Education Tutors | 2 | - | - | 2 | High School Diploma | Hourly Non-Contract | Yes |

**State/District Requirements**

All teaching positions require teacher certification with state endorsement in the specific field of practice. At least one teacher must be certified in cardiopulmonary resuscitation (CPR) and first aid.

**Preferred Background**

All staff members must have early childhood teaching experience; a strong belief in the benefits of an integrated, mainstreamed learning environment; a team-teaching approach; and commitment to family-focused intervention. Teachers must have the ability to supervise and direct practicum students from the college.

**Employee Education and Training Represented**

Infant and toddler education; prekindergarten and early childhood education; elementary education; special education; child care; speech therapy; counseling; research and evaluation.

**Administration**

The Vermont College Preschool is administered by Vermont College of Norwich University. EEE is administered by the Montpelier Public School System. The EEI advisory board includes members of the school administration, school staff members, parents, and other community members.

| Relationship to the Schools | Beverly Heise, an EEI teacher, reports that administrators from the Montpelier School District supported EEI and were involved in its conceptual development. All children who will attend local kindergartens in the fall visit the elementary school in small groups with a preschool teacher in the spring. In addition, the EEI holds transition conferences for all the children it serves. Parents, preschool teachers, and elementary school staff members participate in these conferences. |

The Vermont College Preschool is involved with several school services or departments, including guidance, Chapter 1, and special education.

**Community Links**

According to Ms. Heise, Montpelier residents have easy access to social services, since most agencies have headquarters in the city. The early childhood programs have well established links with Head Start, private preschools, child care centers, family daycare homes, parent groups, and human service organizations, all of which are actively involved in referring children to the program and providing information to interested parents. Some provide screening services, consultation, or staff development. Central Vermont Hospital provides occupational, physical, and speech therapy as related services to children's educational evaluations and programs. Washington County Mental Health provides psychological services when needed.

**Funding**

State, 66 percent; in-kind contributions, 16 percent; client paid fees, 10 percent; federal, 8 percent.

**In-Kind Resources**

Space and facilities; paid staff for service delivery; administrative and clerical support; equipment; materials; transportation; consultation and staff development; and periodic direct service to program participants (e.g., workshops, vision or hearing screening) from cooperating agencies such as Head Start, Montpelier Public Schools, Washington County Parent-Child Center, Kiwanis, Adult Basic Education, Parents Anonymous, and Vermont College campus of Norwich University.

**Objectives**

Vermont College Preschool: "We hope to enhance parents' awareness of developmentally appropriate activities and resultant expectations of their children," says Ms. Heise. Other expected changes will be in the areas of children's self-esteem, social skills and peer interactions, preacademic skills, and recognition of the importance and benefits of family participation.

Central Vermont Essential Early Education Program: "It is our hope that parents will enjoy their children's developmental progress more and that the children served will be more successful and motivated in school once they start. It is also hoped that the special needs children will remain in their local districts for school and will not be sent to regional programs."

Early Education Initiative Program: "The immediate objectives are to improve preacademic skills, enhance personal self-esteem, and promote the children's social skills development. We work to enhance parent and family self-esteem, to help families assess their personal and family needs, to define priorities, and to determine sources of support. Improved parent-child interactions and the development of parenting skills are also immediate objectives."

**Evaluation**

The Vermont Department of Education requires an evaluation, which is conducted annually by gathering information from parents, referral agencies, and teachers, and by assessing children's progress.

**Replication**

Central Vermont Essential Early Education Program: eight towns, which comprise three rural supervisory unions in Vermont, have recently drafted a proposal for an Essential Early Education Program, based on the Central Vermont EEE Program, for another area of the state.

Early Education Initiative Program: three programs, Oak Hill, Blue Mountain, and Kids' Place, have adapted parts of the Vermont College Early Education Initiative Program. The Vermont Department of Education has adapted the parent and community education evaluation forms for use statewide.

**Materials Available**

The program is in the process of producing a videotape.

# Willington Public Schools
# Early Childhood Services

*A family of five children, all of whom were placed in special education programs, seemed to be a classic case of cultural and environmental deprivation. The children received help for learning disabilities, and the family took part in the whole range of programs including home visits and developmental kindergarten. Last fall, the youngest passed the prekindergarten screening test brilliantly — the first in the family to do so.*

Preschool
Toy lending
Kindergarten
Home visits
Resource library

Parent discussion groups
Parent-child joint activities
Health/nutrition education
Developmental screening

Speech/vision/hearing exams
Consultation for nursery schools
Community services info/referral
Parenting/child development education

| | |
|---|---|
| **Contact:** | Vivian J. Carlson, Early Childhood Coordinator |
| **Address:** | Center School |
| | 12 Old Farms Road |
| | Willington, CT 06279 |
| | (203) 429-9367 |
| **Established:** | 1980, school initiative |
| **Budget '88-'89:** | $62,000 |
| **Sources:** | School district funds, state and federal government |
| **Size:** | 125 families |
| **Area served:** | Willington School District |
| **Auspices:** | Elementary Education and Early Childhood Education Departments of the Willington School District |

**Community**

Willington is a rural area whose population of 5,000 has traditionally included professionals from the University of Connecticut and working-class and farming families. In the last five years, the community has experienced tremendous growth and its agrarian character has taken on a suburban quality.

**Philosophy and Goals**

Willington Public Schools Early Childhood Services (ECS) is committed to working with young children before they experience failure in school. The program's two major goals are to strengthen school-community bonds by involving parents in the educational process and to provide extra help for children at risk of failure in school. All families are encouraged to engage more actively in shaping their children's educational development.

**History and Origins**

In 1980, responding to local needs, the school system developed a program of early childhood services that specialized in identifying and treating children with learning problems and providing opportunities for parent education. A federal block grant initially supported the salary of ECS early childhood coordinator, Vivian Carlson, who visited families in an effort to determine the range of local needs. The community quickly began requesting services.

**Features**

For at-risk three- to five-year-olds, ECS provides secondary prevention services through the Willington Early Childhood Education Program. ECS first performs extensive screening to identify at-risk preschool and kindergarten children. Those identified as having developmental delays or learning disabilities are eligible for the preschool kindergarten, which provides weekly home visits and a twice-weekly classroom program based on the developmental needs of individual children.

For handicapped children, the coordinator acts as a liaison and parent advocate, helping families obtain appropriate educational services. ECS staff members arrange child placements and monitor progress three to four times a year. To minimize the possibility of tension, Ms. Carlson conducts evaluations in the children's homes to demystify the screening process and develop an easy rapport with families. ECS also offers a weekly, 90-minute play group and parent discussion session, free to anyone in the community. The ECS coordinator provides consultation services to area nursery schools.

**Participants**

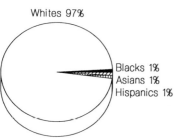

Whites 97%

Blacks 1%
Asians 1%
Hispanics 1%

Services are available to all residents with children from birth to age six. Approximately 70 percent of the eligible population takes advantage of screening services, and 50 parents participate in group discussions and social activities. Only children with developmental or learning delays are eligible for the preschool and kindergarten programs; 25 currently participate.

*Interagency cooperation helps familiarize parents and the community with Willington Public Schools Early Childhood Services and boosts interest and participation in the program.*

**Parent Education**

Home visitors concentrate on showing parents how to turn daily tasks into learning opportunities and household items into art or manipulative materials. During group sessions children play together while parents engage in discussions that focus on developing competence in areas related to childrearing and early learning.

**Curriculum**

ECS has adapted the curriculum material designed for the Early Education Program of the Ferguson-Florissant School District in Missouri. Additional materials are developed in house. Parent education programs include *STEP (Systematic Training for Effective Parenting), Active Parenting,* and others. Early childhood screening is based on the *Comprehensive Identification Process,* by R. Zehbach, and the *Early Screening Inventory,* by Meisels and Wiske.

**Sites**

Parent discussion and children's play groups take place at Firehouse Hall and screening takes place at the public library. Two private nursery schools participate in Willington's consultation program. The developmental preschool and kindergarten have sites at the public elementary school. In addition, services are delivered in 25 homes.

**Parent Involvement**

According to the director, parent involvement in the schools has increased across all grade levels since program implementation. At first, some teachers felt uncomfortable having parents in the schools on a daily basis. Inservice workshops honed in on specific areas for effective parent involvement, including reading aloud, tutoring, preparing materials for classroom use, and helping to run the "Publishing Center" where children's stories are bound and shelved.

All families with preschoolers are invited to receive developmental screening. Nursery schools, public schools, and the library distribute information about the program's services, and handouts are available at local functions. To increase visibility, Ms. Carlson has made presentations at school staff meetings, parent-teacher association meetings, and board of education meetings. She attributes successful recruitment to personal contacts within the community. ECS has had less success recruiting teen parents; Ms. Carlson feels this is due to the absence of a local high school, which would serve as a liaison between teen mothers and ECS.

**Staff**

| Job Title | PD | Vol | FT | PT | Educ Req | Status | Benefits |
|---|---|---|---|---|---|---|---|
| Early Childhood Coodinator | 1 | - | - | 1 | Post-Graduate Courses or Degree | K-12 Contract | No |
| Early Childhood Teacher | 1 | - | 1 | - | College Degree | K-12 Contract | Yes |
| Early Childhood Assistant | 1 | - | 1 | - | High School Diploma | Hourly Contract | Yes |

**State/District Requirements**

For the coordinator, a master's degree and state special education certification; for the teacher, a bachelor's degree and state special education certification.

**Preferred Background**

For teachers, flexibility, professionalism, and early childhood and parent education experience; for the assistant, early childhood experience and the ability to work with parents.

**Employee Education and Training Represented**

Infant and toddler education; prekindergarten and early childhood education; elementary education; special education; parent educator; child development and family studies.

**Administration**

ECS is administered exclusively within the public school system and involves the special services and early childhood education departments. The coordinator reports to the director of special services of the Willington School District. Referrals are made to the regional special education service.

**Relationship to the Schools**

Ms. Carlson acts as a consultant to the school's kindergarten team. She takes part in the weekly teachers' meetings, serves on the special education committee, and is part of the planning and placement team that determines eligibility for special education programs and develops recommendations for individual children.

**Community Links**

ECS maintains strong links with public health and nursing agencies, which perform auditory screening. The program shares staff, facilities, and equipment with private area preschools, to which Ms. Carlson acts as a consultant. Interagency cooperation helps familiarize parents and the community with ECS and boosts interest and participation in the program.

**Funding**

Federal government, 39 percent (Title IV, part B, federal flow-through funds, and Public Law 99-457, federal preschool handicapped funds);

state government, 37 percent (Connecticut handicapped reimbursement funds for at-risk children in the classroom); local and district, 22 percent.

**In-Kind Resources**

Space and facilities provided by the public library and fire department; screening for hearing impairments provided by the public health nursing association.

**Funding History**

According to Ms. Carlson, ECS provides highly visible community services at a low cost to the school system. Funding has risen from $7,500 in 1980 to $62,000 for 1988-89 and is secure for the next two years. Budget increases have gone toward expanding classroom services in the developmental kindergarten and the prekindergarten. The school system hires Ms. Carlson for 1½ days a week and, while she feels that funding for her position is secure, the work involved is constantly increasing.

**Objectives**

Since the program began, the number of children requiring special education services has declined. Ms. Carlson attributes this to the effectiveness of Willington's early education programs and to elementary school teachers who are less inclined to refer children to special education programs and more willing and confident to deal with at-risk children in the classroom.

**Evaluation**

Following its first year of operation, an educational consultant at the University of Connecticut evaluated Willington Early Childhood Services. Findings showed that although the program did not reach its entire target population, those who participated reaped considerable benefits. Motor, language, and cognitive skills were found to have improved after six months of involvement. Evaluation results helped validate the new initiative at school board presentations, says Ms. Carlson.

**Replication**

In Connecticut, the school districts of Coventry, Columbia, Stafford Springs, Windham, and Putnam have replicated the identification and screening components of Willington Public Schools Early Childhood Services.

**Materials Available**

None.

# 3 Parent-School Partnerships for School Readiness and Enrichment

These programs enhance academic achievement in school-age children by engaging parents in the educational process. Strategies for alerting parents to the need for intellectually stimulating and supportive family dialogue include joint parent-child classes in mathematics concepts and games, workshops on cognitive development and volunteer opportunities in the school, packaged resource "kits," bilingual home tutoring materials, a parent-child preschool, and peer-taught workshops on reading and studying skills. Two underlying goals — to develop and strengthen the connection between families and schools and to promote equal educational opportunities for all families — emerge in the effort to enhance parents' experience of school via more meaningful teacher conferences, telephone information lines, and meetings with school administrators.

# Programs in Brief

# Chapter 1/Parent Program

| | | |
|---|---|---|
| Kindergarten | Resource library | Parenting/child development education |
| Newsletter | Educational teaching aids | Parent-child joint activities |

**Contact:** Myrna L. DeBose, Administrator of Chapter 1

**Address:** 900 North Klein Street
Room 420
Oklahoma City, OK 73106
(405) 297-6569

**Established:** 1970, federal initiative

**Budget '88-'89:** $4,093,905

**Sources:** Chapter 1

**Size:** 5,000 children, 1,600 families

**Area Served:** Oklahoma City metropolitan area

**Auspices:** Oklahoma City Unified School District

**Community**

Oklahoma City, with suburbs extending into five counties, has the third largest metropolitan area of any city in the United States. The city's economic base includes livestock, farm produce, petroleum, and aircraft production. While the area was initially hard hit by the drop in oil prices during the 1980s, the city's economy has since diversified into the production of automobile parts and electronic and computer equipment.

The Oklahoma City Unified School District extends 30 miles beyond the city limits. The approximately 37,000 students in the district come from surrounding urban, suburban, and rural areas. While a number of schools have a high percentage of students who qualify for the free lunch program, the district also encompasses a number of very wealthy suburbs.

**Philosophy and Goals**

Chapter 1/Parent Program in Oklahoma City considers parents the main link in the academic success of their children and thus feels it is important to get parents interested and involved in their children's schools. The program urges schools to help parents become involved in a variety of ways and on numerous levels within the public education system.

**History and Origins**

The Chapter 1 preschool and its accompanying Parent Program began in 1970 as a federally funded, mandated enrichment curriculum targeting children in need of more intensive academic services.

**Features**

Program components include: extended-day kindergarten, remedial reading and math instruction, learning and resource centers (grades 1 to 8), and services for Chapter 1 students attending independent schools whose education is being paid with public education funds. Yearly parent orientation meetings are held at each of the Chapter 1 public and nonpublic schools. Districtwide meetings allow parents to bring their educational concerns and issues to the attention of system personnel. Parents have the opportunity to serve on project planning committees, which make budgetary and site selection decisions for the coming year, and can attend inservice training and workshops offered by Chapter 1 or by the Oklahoma Department of Education.

### Participants

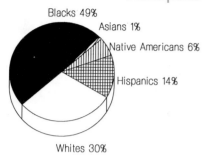

Blacks 49%
Asians 1%
Native Americans 6%
Hispanics 14%
Whites 30%

Under federal guidelines, once a school qualifies for Chapter 1 funds, as determined by the percent of students on the free lunch program, all eligible students and parents within that school have access to Chapter 1 services and the Parent Program. During the 1987-88 school year, 1,575 parents participated in inservice training sessions, orientation meetings, and visits to the resource center.

*Parent involvement is considered the "hub" of the Chapter 1 / Parent Program.*

### Parent Education

Each year, four to six inservice sessions provide training on academic and developmental topics. Parents also have the opportunity to participate in "Make and Take" workshops. The Parent Program provides a summer activities book that includes math, language, and spelling games for school vacations. The program's resource center and lending library circulates educational materials no longer used by the schools. For parents without transportation, a traveling resource center delivers materials to their homes or to their children's school.

### Curriculum

The curriculum for the training sessions and resource center consists of lectures, discussion groups, filmstrips, cassettes, educational kits that are either provided to parents or created by them, books, free informational materials, and educational supplies.

### Sites

Each school has to requalify annually to receive funding for Chapter 1 services. While sites for the program change from year to year, this has little effect on the design of the program and the quality of services delivered. During the 1987-88 school year, 38 public and 3 nonpublic schools participated in the Chapter 1 program. For public school students, all services occur within the building. According to Ms. DeBose, under federal regulations Chapter 1 services for independent school students whose education is provided by the district must be delivered on "neutral ground" outside the private school, a stipulation which creates some logistical difficulties.

### Parent Involvement

Parent involvement is considered the "hub" of the Chapter 1/Parent Program. According to Ms. DeBose, parents are involved in the planning, development, and evaluation of the program. They are given an opportunity to share their ideas on how the school can work with children and parents to achieve Chapter 1 objectives — formally, through their participation in the yearly school and districtwide needs assessment meeting, and informally, through parent conferences and personal contact with Parent Program staff members and Chapter 1 teachers. Many parents volunteer to serve on project planning committees, which oversee the budget and site selection. Parents are instrumental in determining target areas of academic need and setting budgetary priorities to address those needs. Parent volunteers are drawn from each of the schools and serve on parent advisory councils to represent Chapter 1 needs. Volunteers from different councils form another committee that represents Chapter 1 within the independent schools.

### Outreach

The identification of children for Chapter 1 services is carried out within the regular education programs. Parents whose children are new to Chapter 1 are contacted by newsletters, brochures, and personal letters and are encouraged by parent volunteers to attend Chapter 1 programs. Ms. DeBose reports that the outreach and response rate has been so successful that in many of the schools Chapter 1 parents have served as a "nucleus" for parent-teacher associations.

## Staff

| Job Title | PD | Vol | FT | PT | Educ Req | Status | Benefits |
|-----------|----|----|----|----|----------|--------|----------|
| Coordinator | 1 | - | 1 | - | Post-Graduate Courses or Degree | K-12 and Other Contract | Yes |
| Facilitator | 1 | - | 1 | - | Some College | Other Contract | Yes |

**State/District Requirements**

For the position of coordinator, state teacher certification is required.

**Preferred Background**

None.

**Employee Education and Training Represented**

Prekindergarten and early childhood education; elementary education; education, grades 7 to 12.

**Administration**

The program is administered exclusively within the public education system.

**Relationship to the Schools**

The Chapter 1/Parent Program is contained within the public school system. According to Ms. DeBose, the Chapter 1/Parent Program has been a source of increased parent involvement in the schools. Ms. DeBose notes that the Parent Program has helped schools review and adjust to the needs of working mothers. The program has demonstrated that while poverty and the need for remediation are not necessarily synonymous, children living in poverty are at greater risk for school failure.

> Ms. DeBose reports that the outreach and response rate has been so successful that in many of the schools Chapter 1 parents have served as a "nucleus" for parent-teacher associations.

**Community Links**

Chapter 1 programs have worked closely with Native American (Johnson-O'Malley Program, Indian Education Program) and bilingual programs. According to Ms. DeBose, community-based social service programs handle the cultural aspects of working with Native Americans and Hispanics, while Chapter 1 deals with their educational needs.

**Funding**

Federal support (Chapter 1 grant), 100 percent.

**Funding History**

Chapter 1 funding is determined by federal guidelines; the number of eligible schools changes yearly, depending on district demographics.

**Objectives**

The Chapter 1/Parent Program has three objectives — to promote and improve parents' understanding of their involvement in the Chapter 1 program, to provide training and resources for parents to help their children with school work, and to establish a naturally supportive partnership between parents and schools.

**Evaluation**

Under federal guidelines, the Parent Program (and staff training guidelines) is evaluated annually by the Oklahoma Department of Education to ensure that Chapter 1 educational objectives are being met.

**Replication**

The Chapter 1/Parent Program in Oklahoma City has been replicated in Buffalo, New York.

**Materials Available**

None.

# Waiahole Parent-Community Networking Center

| | | |
|---|---|---|
| Field trips | Drop-in center | Parent volunteer opportunities |
| Warmline | Home visits | Parent-child joint activities |
| Hotline | Networking | Parenting/child development education |
| Newsletter | Social events | Community services info/referral |
| | Parents as tutors | Health/nutrition education |

**Contact:** Linda Kamiyama, Principal,

**Address:** Waiahole Elementary School
48-215 Waiahole Valley Road
Kaneohe, HI 96744
(808) 239-8395 or -8626

**Established:** 1986, state pilot

**Budget '88-'89:** $5,900

**Sources:** State legislative appropriation

**Size:** 75 families

**Area Served:** Waiahole Elementary School

**Auspices:** Waiahole Elementary School

**1990 Respondent:** Raymond Sugai, Principal

*Since she started working as a parent facilitator, Pat Royos, previously an active volunteer in community organizations, quickly developed "people skills" and self-confidence. She now makes professional presentations about the program to the state legislature and other parent involvement groups. Her husband donates his time for repairs and handiwork at the school. Their fourth-grade daughter offers the clearest measure of success: once a shy child, her self-confidence "blossomed" and her participation in Learning to Read Through the Arts contributed to the dramatic increase in her reading score on standardized tests.*

## Community

The Hawaii school system is centralized at the state level; all public schools are divided into seven large districts managed by the Hawaii Department of Education. Waiahole Elementary School serves a small, rural area of 100 relatively low-income families who are generally employed in farming, although some commute to the Kaneohe town center or to Honolulu, a 45-minute drive. Of the 30 schools in its district, the school was ranked as having the second poorest population, with many single parents and 70 percent of the children eligible for free or reduced-price lunches. However, in 1987-88, Waiahole Elementary School won a contest sponsored by Frito-Lay, which named it the outstanding elementary school in the state.

## Philosophy and Goals

Waiahole's Parent-Community Networking Center (PCNC) operates on the theory that getting parents involved in the school system strengthens ties among school, home, and community and that when schools are part of a community network, both parents' and children's self-esteem and confidence improve, family relationships become stronger, and children perform better academically.

## History and Origins

In 1986, Waiahole Elementary School was chosen as one of six pilot sites for the Hawaii Parent-Community Networking Centers (PCNC), a state program designed to increase parent involvement in the schools and encourage a sense of local ownership of the school system. PCNC, created by the Hawaii Department of Education and funded by the legislature, initially paid only the salary of a part-time parent facilitator and provided training and guidelines on ways in which schools could increase parent involvement. Waiahole Elementary School's steering committee, the School Climate Improvement Committee (SCIC), composed of teachers, counselors, custodians, and administrators, created a task force to implement PCNC. Surveys to assess the school's and the community's needs determined that parents needed more opportunities to become involved in the school and wanted training in parenting skills; it also recommended that parents, represented by a parent facilitator, participate on the SCIC. Late that year, the newly hired parent facilitator began working with the existing parent organization, Ohana ("family" in Hawaiian), to plan activities to encourage parents to come into the schools. PCNC began with purely social activities, then expanded to include a wide variety of parent education and volunteer opportunities.

## Features

The PCNC program is based on grass roots community self-assessment; the state does not mandate a series of services but allows the individual school to develop programming adapted to its specific needs. Since PCNC began in 1986, Waiahole Elementary School has developed three programs that rely heavily on parent support and involvement.

**Learning to Read through the Arts** teaches children how to put on a dramatic production. Preparation for a school play, such as *The Wizard of Oz,* integrates reading, writing, and communication skills. Parent volunteers provide direction, creative support, and supervision.

The **tutoring program** is a parent-run program in which children who need help in reading receive assistance from PCNC parents during the daily half-hour reading period.

**Scoring High** is a test-taking skills program. Parents tutor and supervise children, proctor exams, and raise money to purchase incentives for high scorers.

Parents may also register in two series of parent education workshops, **Parent Effectiveness Training (PET)** or **Parents Anonymous**. PET meets weekly for nine weeks and Parents Anonymous for six weeks. Supplementary sessions target specific groups of parents for certain topics, such as a two-part workshop on adolescence for mothers of fifth- and sixth-grade daughters.

The parent facilitator acts as liaison between parents and the school administration. PCNC also staffs its own phone line to provide information on the program and to handle questions about parents' school concerns. The parent facilitator makes home visits to parents who lack a telephone when the school needs to get in touch with them or to families whose children have special concerns. Finally, PCNC, in cooperation with Ohana, organizes field trips and social events to bring parents and children together at school functions.

## Participants

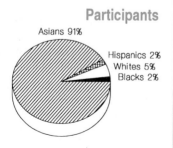

Asians 91%
Hispanics 2%
Whites 5%
Blacks 2%

PCNC is a family enrichment program for any parent of a Waiahole elementary student. In 1987-88, 50 mothers, 25 fathers, and 160 children participated in PCNC. Twenty-five parents attended the two parent education workshops. Approximately 26 percent of PCNC parents are single parents.

*Success came quickly to the program because of its ties to community organizations.*

**Parent Education**

Parents may attend the Parent Effectiveness Training or Parents Anonymous workshop series, which teach about parenting skills, child development, health, nutrition, and effective discipline. Other parent sessions, such as a two-part panel discussion on child abuse, supplement the basic curricula. The school offers training to parents who volunteer to tutor reading and holds inservices to teach the specific skills required for involvement in other parent volunteer activities, such as learning to tie-dye for the Learning to Read through the Arts program.

**Curriculum**

Waiahole follows the PCNC curriculum obtained from the Hawaii Department of Education. The Adult Community Schools Division provided the PET curriculum, and Waiahole obtained Parents Anonymous independently. Learning to Read through the Arts is an enhancement program of the basic language arts curriculum; it was developed in New York State and its developers came to Waiahole to train staff members and parents in its application.

*Surveys to assess the school's and the community's needs determined that parents needed more opportunities to become involved in the school and wanted training in parenting skills . . . .*

**Sites**

Waiahole Elementary School does not have the space for a parent center, but the parent facilitator has her own centrally situated desk and phone line and may use conference rooms to meet with parents when necessary. Former Principal Raymond Sugai thinks parents are more comfortable coming to the school when a parent facilitator is there to greet them at the door.

**Parent Involvement**

PCNC's primary goal is to involve parents in the school, and the facilitator's first effort was to organize potluck lunches so that parents could meet administrators without a formal agenda. Now social events are likely to have a component of parent education or planning. Ohana and PCNC memberships are nearly identical, and the two organizations meet together to plan fundraising and other activities every month. Parents can choose to volunteer as teachers' aides in the classroom in either the tutoring or Scoring High programs, or they may work on Learning to Read through the Arts production in either a creative or supervisory capacity. Parents accompany teachers and students on field trips and organize school functions to honor outstanding students. Waiahole PCNC plans labor-intensive fundraising activities like cookouts and luaus that both raise large amounts of money and encourage parents, teachers, and administrators to work together.

**Outreach**

PCNC puts out a monthly bulletin to keep parents up to date on school activities and notify them of monthly meetings. It also hosts open houses and potluck lunches to attract parents to the school. The Waiahole

Waikene Community Association (WWCA) and Ohana both encourage their members to participate.

| Job Title | PD | Vol | FT | PT | Educ Req | Status | Benefits |
|-----------|-----|-----|-----|-----|----------|--------|----------|
| Parent Facilitator | 1 | - | - | 1 | High School Diploma | Hourly Non-Contract | No |
| Parent Group Officers | - | 1 | - | 1 | None | - | No |

**State/District Requirements**

The parent facilitator must have a high school diploma and a driver's license and must undergo 15 hours of basic training and monthly inservices.

**Preferred Background**

Parent facilitators must be willing to work some evening and weekend hours, have organizational and people skills, and a genuine concern for people and their problems; no specific educational background is required.

**Employee Education and Training Represented**

None.

**Administration**

The parent facilitator works with the four officers of Ohana to develop PCNC programming and reports to the school principal, who directs the program. The principal is responsible to the district superintendent. The parent facilitator receives support services from the Office of Instructional Services in the Hawaii Department of Education and attends PCNC state conferences. The Hawaii Department of Education monitors the program.

**Relationship to the Schools**

The parent facilitator represents the parents on the School Climate Improvement Committee, which meets monthly to discuss progress toward goals set in the fall. Mr. Sugai thinks that having parents as a "role group" on the school steering committee sets them on an equal footing with teachers and counselors, giving them a sense of belonging and ownership in the school.

**Community Links**

Mr. Sugai feels that success came quickly to the program because of its ties to community organizations. When hired, the parent facilitator was already a member of WWCA; other parents had ties to the Lion's Club and a volunteer association called the Waiahole Key Club. These agencies were happy to provide volunteer workers for fundraising events to get the program off the ground. Many of their members were also parents and soon developed an allegiance to PCNC as well. Mr. Sugai says that when money is tight, either he or a parent can approach these clubs or the state legislature for a donation to a worthy project. He notes that it is important to take the initiative when developing community links. He and the parent facilitator often attend WWCA meetings together to maintain ties between programs.

**Funding**

The state provides $5,900 from a legislative appropriation for PCNC programs. This pays for the parent facilitator's salary, a phone and phone line, mileage reimbursement, and limited supplies.

**In-Kind Resources**

The Hawaii Department of Education, through Waiahole Elementary School, provides desk space and training for the parent facilitator, periodic direct service to program participants, administrative and clerical support, equipment, materials, and supplies. The volunteer staff is provided by the Waiahole Parent Group.

**Funding History**

PCNC is a new initiative.

**Objectives**

Waiahole's PCNC aims to increase parent involvement in the school, boost the numbers of people contacting the center for help, facilitate communication between the home and the school, improve student discipline, and establish a sense of community responsibility for and investment in the schools.

**Evaluation**

Every fall, Waiahole's SCIC sets goals for each of its participating groups. Its initial goal for PCNC was to increase parent involvement by 10 percent. PCNC exceeded that figure many times over. Attendance at Ohana meetings, for instance, has increased from 15 to 20 parents to 40 to 50 in an average month. In addition, SCIC does a self-evaluation of its progress each year; one factor measured, on a four-point scale, is the "school climate." Raymond Sugai credits PCNC with a score increase from 2.5 to an unprecedented 3.5 and notes that teachers have also had fewer discipline problems in the classroom because of the increased presence of teacher aides and because stepped-up communication between home and school has made children less likely to misbehave.

**Replication**

The PCNC curriculum model is based on *Parent Modules* by EPIC in Honolulu. The program is modeled on Ohana, a parent involvement project established in Hawaii in the 1970s. Waiahole was one of six initial pilot sites of PCNC; the program now exists in 101 schools, 54 funded by legislative appropriation and 47 operated by volunteer parent facilitators.

**Materials Available**

For more information about Parent-Community Networking Centers, contact Kenneth Yamamoto or Vivian Ing (the program's developers and administrators at the state level) at 595 Pepeekeo Street, Building H-2, Honolulu, Hawaii 96825.

# Mililani Waena Parent-Community Networking Center

Workshops
Open house
Warmline
Networking
Counseling

Drop-in center
Parent bulletin
Resource library
Newsletter

Parenting/child development education
Health/nutrition education
Community services info/referral
Parent-child joint activities

| | |
|---|---|
| **Contact:** | Gracie Aoki, Parent Facilitator |
| **Address:** | Mililani Waena Elementary School |
| | Parent-Community Networking Center |
| | 95-502 Kipapa Drive |
| | Mililani Town, HI 96789 |
| | (808) 625-1211 |
| **Established:** | 1987, state legislative initiative |
| **Budget '88-'89:** | $9,000 |
| **Sources:** | Hawaii Department of Education, local school district funds, and Mililani Waena's Parent-Teacher Group |
| **Size:** | 505 families (1,050 children) in one elementary school |
| **Area Served:** | Mililani Town, Hawaii |
| **Auspices:** | Mililani Waena Elementary School |
| **1990 Respondent:** | Aiko Eckerd, Parent Facilitator-Coordinator |

*A young mother who was new to the district wanted to be more involved in her elementary-age son's education. When the Parent Center opened in 1987, she volunteered her time as a parent facilitator to tutor special needs students and supervise student activities and became a team member on Project Self-Esteem. Through PCNC, she had the opportunity to explore her own potential and become more involved in her son's development. She is now considering returning to college to pursue a career in counseling.*

## Community

Mililani Town is a suburb 20 miles northwest of Honolulu on the island of Oahu. The town's population of 2,035 falls mostly within the upper- and middle-income brackets, although the community has its share of less affluent, single-parent families. Professionals, many of whom commute, work in education, business, and high technology; others hold jobs in the military reserves to the north and east of Mililani Town.

## Philosophy and Goals

With improving the education of children as their focus, Parent-Community Networking Centers (PCNCs) strive to develop a supportive network of parents, children, and teachers. Their overall goals are to raise children's academic achievement and to build their self-esteem and ability to interact successfully in a group setting.

## History and Origins

Aiko Eckerd, a retired teacher and administrator, started the Mililani Waena Elementary School's PCNC in 1987. The state legislature invited the school's participation and that of 53 other public schools in Hawaii. Ms. Eckerd became the parent facilitator and within the year implemented the project. All PCNCs have similar goals, with individual centers tailoring their programs to the specific needs of the community. Ms. Eckerd structured the Mililani Waena PCNC according to responses to a needs-assessment survey sent to parents. She is the district coordinator for 10 funded Parent-Community Networking Centers.

## Features

PCNC in Mililani Waena Elementary School sponsors parent involvement in the life of the school by organizing parent volunteers in the classroom as reading tutors, computer teachers, and resource people and at the administrative level in areas of clerical support, supervision, and fundraising. PCNC engages parents and their children in small, teacher-led workshops on activities for learning at home. Parents team teach the 12-week series "Project Self-Esteem."

**Participants**

Any family with children in the Mililani Waena Elementary School is eligible to participate in the Parent-Community Networking Center. In 1988-89, 505 families were served.

*Parent involvement is key to the success of the Parent-Community Networking Centers, says Ms. Eckerd. "We talk to them and they get the message: 'Parents, we need you — you're very important.'"*

**Parent Education**

Parent education takes place in workshops, lectures, group discussions, and parent-child activities. Workshop titles include "Parents as Reading Partners," "How to Help Your Child Develop Good Homework/Study Habits," "Grades K-2," "Fun Friday," "Ethnic Food Preparation," "Personality Styles," and "Basic Principles for Parents."

**Curriculum**

Although the curriculum for the PCNCs is based on *Parent Modules*, developed by the Hawaii Department of Education, each PCNC program offers workshops and events particular to the needs of its own community. The Mililani Waena PCNC also uses the Year of the Family in Education, created by the Wisconsin Department of Education.

**Sites**

Space for a parent center in most schools is a rarity, according to Aiko Eckerd, and the Mililani Waena PCNC is fortunate in having the use of a former teachers' lounge for theirs. She credits much of the Mililani Waena PCNC's success to the center's welcoming atmosphere.

**Parent Involvement**

Parent involvement is key to the success of the Parent-Community Networking Centers, says Ms. Eckerd. "We talk to them and they get the message: 'Parents, we need you — you're very important.'" According to Ms. Eckerd, the Mililani Waena PCNC has encouraged and given parents an opportunity to express their concerns and ideas and to suggest topics for workshops. Most parents participate in the center as volunteers, fundraisers, teachers, and learners. Many are involved in an active parent-teacher group executive board that meets monthly.

**Outreach**

The school district, community organizations, the Hawaii Community Education Association, and the Parent-Community Networking Center itself make broad outreach efforts through newsletters, press releases, newspaper advertisements, and flyers.

**Staff**

PCNCs are staffed by a half-time parent facilitator.

| Job Title | PD | Vol | FT | PT | Educ Req | Status | Benefits |
|---|---|---|---|---|---|---|---|
| Parent Facilitator | 1 | - | - | 1 | High School Diploma | Hourly Non-Contract | No |

**State/District Requirements**

Parent facilitators complete a 15-hour training course and attend inservice training once a month. Administrators and teachers involved in the PCNCs attend orientation and workshops and receive consultation as needed from the Adult and Early Childhood Section of the Hawaii Department of Education.

**Preferred Background**

Parent facilitators must have a genuine concern for people; an ability to communicate with, organize, recruit, and train volunteers; and must be able to build trust among participants in the PCNCs.

**Employee Education and Training Represented**

Prekindergarten and early childhood education; elementary education; special education; parent educator; counseling.

**Administration**

The parent facilitator reports to the school principal, who is the director of the program, and to the district superintendent of schools. Although teachers and other resource persons run the workshops, the parent facilitator sets them up, distributes flyers, prepares materials, and provides refreshments.

**Relationship to the Schools**

The Adult and Early Childhood Section of the Hawaii Department of Education provides training and technical services to the PCNCs and continues to help in assessing the programs. The district office specialists and resource teachers help train teachers to run workshops for parents. Ms. Eckerd admits having to sell the Parent-Community Networking Center concept to the school staff. "It's not just a question of what parents can do for the school, but what the school can do for parents," notes Ms. Eckerd.

Some teachers were more open to having parents in their classrooms than others. "We had to build trust," she says, adding that she spoke to the faculty about her role and responsibilities, explained the idea behind parent involvement, helped make instructional materials for parents, and provided a supportive framework for teachers running workshops.

**Community Links**

The Wahiawa Community School (which provides adult education in the community) provides resource people for workshops and hosts special adult education classes for parents. Its principal and vice principal are members of the PCNC planning team. Public and private agencies refer parents to the program, and informal publicity is provided by community organizations, businesses, and churches.

*"It's not just a question of what parents can do for the school, but what the school can do for parents," says Ms. Eckerd.*

| | |
|---|---|
| **Funding** | Hawaii Department of Education, 90 percent; local school district funds, 5 percent; local parent-teacher group, 5 percent. |
| **In-Kind Resources** | Parent volunteers and school staff members provide administrative support; consultation and staff development are provided by the adult education district and state offices; churches, libraries, and community centers also provide space and facilities. |
| **Funding History** | Funding for the PCNCs is stable and remained level for the 1988-89 school year. |
| **Objectives** | Parent-Community Networking Centers seek to help parents become partners with the schools and the community in the education of their children. The program fosters personal and community networks among parents, teachers, and children. Schools and parents together assess what parents and their children need, resulting in improved home-school relationships, increased parent involvement in the schools, and a stronger community. |
| **Evaluation** | Teacher and parent surveys of all state-funded programs examine implementation and outcome findings and make recommendations for future planning. |
| **Replication** | PCNCs exist throughout Hawaii. |
| **Materials Available** | A slide presentation and materials on Parent-Community Networking Centers are available from Mr. Kenneth Yamamoto, Administrator, Adult and Early Childhood Section, Hawaii Department of Education, 595 Pepeeko Street, Honolulu, Hawaii 96825. |

# Family Study Institute

Networking     Parent training workshops     Training for school staff
Couple support group     Mother/father support groups     Parenting/child development education
Parent-child joint activities

**Contact:**     Dr. Sam Redding, Executive Director

**Address:**     1603 South Michigan, Suite 402
Chicago, IL 60616
(312) 427-1692

**Established:**     1985, local school and agency initiative

**Budget '88-'89:**     $115,000

**Sources:**     Chapter 1 (through schools), foundations, corporate donations

**Size:**     In 1987-88, 1,000 families

**Area Served:**     Several communities in and around Chicago

**Auspices:**     Academic Development Institute and the Chicago Public Schools

### Community

The Family Study Institute (FSI) began in three Chicago public schools and has since expanded into schools in the black inner city; Hispanic neighborhoods; the rural, blue-collar community of Lockport; Polish neighborhoods; and an affluent Lake County suburb.

### Philosophy and Goals

The Family Study Institute feels that the family is a powerful influence on a child's academic development and that practices to enhance learning can be taught and shared.

### History and Origins

The Family Study Institute is a parent education program of the Academic Development Institute (ADI), a nonprofit research and development organization whose function is to help families cope with the academic and personal lives of their children. In the early 1980s, with pilot dollars from the Joyce Foundation and the Kemper Educational and Charitable Fund, ADI launched an experimental program, the Family Study Institute, based on prior research in three Chicago public schools selected to represent a cross-section of the city's school population. After evaluating and modifying the pilot, FSI expanded to operate out of 18 Chicago public schools in 1987-88. Funding sources now include 16 foundations and corporate sponsors.

### Features

FSI operates nine months of the year; a typical client attends six sessions per year. Two courses, "Studying at Home" and "Reading at Home," involve parents in helping their children establish habits of learning, reading, and studying and are taught to parents by peers. "Leadership Workshops," facilitated by an FSI representative, train the school's principal, two parents, and a school staff member to become coordinators for FSI in their school by teaching parent recruitment strategies and methods for maintaining motivation. Parent group leaders are recruited and meet in groups of 10 once a week for three weeks. Parents apply the program at home between sessions and return to their groups to discuss their progress.

## Participants

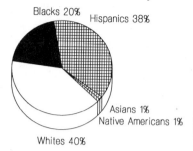

Blacks 20%  Hispanics 38%

Asians 1%
Native Americans 1%

Whites 40%

In 1987-88, the program served 1,000 families (800 mothers, 200 fathers, and 2,500 children); 25 percent were single parents.

*The program's PYRAMID model offers a broadening of the training base, as each person trained moves on to train others — a cost-effective method of disseminating the program.*

## Parent Education

FSI uses a peer-teaching, small-group approach and works directly with parents to help them boost their children's learning at home and in school.

## Curriculum

The FSI curriculum is based on research findings that describe conditions in the home that enhance learning and academic achievement. "Studying at Home" focuses on creating such a home environment and "Reading at Home" emphasizes parent-child interactions that are important in the development of verbal skills: active listening and the exploration of "reading for pleasure and reading to learn." Materials for these courses have been developed in house and are available in both English and Spanish.

## Sites

Twenty-three public schools (22 elementary), 2 private schools, and 2 neighborhood organizations host FSI.

## Parent Involvement

The original teaching models were based on parents' input. In three schools, FSI hosted workshops to gather ideas, meeting with principals and small groups of parents. The peer-teaching concept grew out of parents' positive experiences in small groups and became the PEER model. The program's PYRAMID model offers a broadening of the training base, as each person trained moves on to train others — a cost-effective method of disseminating the program.

## Outreach

Participants may hear about the program through the school via flyers or newsletters. Dr. Redding reports that the most effective outreach strategy is to ask teachers and other parents to telephone prospective participants.

## Staff

| Job Title | PD | Vol | FT | PT | Educ Req | Status | Benefits |
|---|---|---|---|---|---|---|---|
| Director of Program | 1 | - | 1 | - | Post-Graduate Courses or Degree | Other Contract | Yes |
| Chicago Director | 1 | - | 1 | - | Post-Graduate Courses or Degree | Other Contract | Yes |
| Administrative Assistant | 1 | - | - | 1 | High School Diploma | Hourly Contract | No |
| Program Facilitators | 9 | - | - | 9 | High School Diploma | Hourly Non-Contract | No |

| State/District Requirements | No formal requirements besides initial training. |
|---|---|
| Preferred Background | None. |
| Employee Education and Training Represented | Elementary education; education, grades 7 to 12; counseling; social work. |
| Administration | FSI is administered jointly by ADI and the public schools. FSI's director is also the executive director of ADI and reports to ADI's board of directors. The board, composed of public school personnel, representatives of public and private agencies, and members of the community, has decision-making powers in areas of staff hiring, budget, services, and curriculum. The principals of the schools and their parent councils are in close touch with FSI administration; there are also links to the school central office and teachers. All funders, including Chapter 1, play monitoring roles. |
| Relationship to the Schools | According to Dr. Redding, FSI director, the program gives parents new, enjoyable experiences in the schools. The schools, he observed, are not always receptive to building on the spirit of parent involvement that FSI cultivates. |
| Community Links | Community linkage occurs mainly through information sharing and participant referrals. FSI staff members have been involved with private interagency councils and have done joint fundraising with public and nonpublic schools. Some links with settlement houses have had positive results for recruitment. |
| Funding | Foundations and private agencies, 50 percent; local school district funds, 25 percent (75 percent of these funds are Chapter 1); corporate and business donations, 25 percent. The total fee assessed to each school per FSI course is $1,300. |
| Funding History | Funding has increased 400 percent since the first year and the director feels that funding is moderately secure. |
| Objectives | The program hopes to foster family-initiated study at home, family reading activities, parental monitoring of school progress, and positive parent-child communication about school. |
| Evaluation | FSI has tracked the achievement test scores of the first group of children involved in the program and supplements this data with surveys of parents who have participated. A preliminary evaluation report released in 1988 describes program implementation and draws tentative conclusions from the as yet incomplete data. It reports score increases as a result of FSI intervention and notes that parents express satisfaction with their experience in the program. This year FSI will publish a monograph with a two-fold goal: to report on daily program interactions with suggestions for improvement and to present a statistical analysis of the program's progress. |

| | |
|---|---|
| **Replication** | The FSI model has not been replicated outside the Chicago area. |
| **Materials Available** | FSI brochures and a descriptive videotape are available. Contact Dr. Redding for further information. |

# Project AHEAD

Home visits
Advocacy
Newsletter
Adult literacy

Group meetings
Resource library
Networking
Crisis intervention
Child care info/referral

Home educational materials
Health/nutrition education
Parent-child joint activities
Parenting/child development education
Community services info/referral

**Contact:** Genethia Hayes, Director

**Address:** Project AHEAD
4182 South Western Avenue
Los Angeles, CA 90062
(213) 295-8582

**Established:** 1977, collaborative venture between a private foundation
and the school district

**Budget '88-'89:** $479,199

**Sources:** Local school district, private foundations

**Size:** 750 families

**Area Served:** Ten schools in south central Los Angeles

**Auspices:** Private agency with contract to serve the
Los Angeles Unified School District

*A single head of household with four children in kindergarten through high school felt overwhelmed by her life. Project AHEAD's family educator visited her once every two weeks; the mother became a "frontline teacher" at home, making puzzles out of the back of Cheerio boxes, using flash cards, and playing games like Concentration with her children. Says Genethia Hayes, "Her children began to perceive education in a different light and her own self-esteem increased as she began to value herself and her role as a parent."*

## Community

Project AHEAD (Accelerating Home Education and Development) is located in south central Los Angeles, where the population is approximately 500,000. Two of the 10 schools participating in Project AHEAD are situated in the University of Southern California district and the others are in the Watts area. Project AHEAD works in a part of the Los Angeles community exclusively populated by Hispanic, black, and Asian families. The unemployment rate among Project AHEAD's participants (20 percent) is accompanied by a high incidence of substance abuse, poverty, and illiteracy. The community also has many female heads of household and teen mothers.

## Philosophy and Goals

Project AHEAD responds directly to a declining scholastic profile among blacks and Hispanics in the Los Angeles School District and attempts to rescue families from a degenerative cycle of poverty and illiteracy. Project AHEAD's primary goal is to increase children's competency and performance in school and to enhance the schools' potential to offer equal educational opportunities to disadvantaged children. Project Project AHEAD works to bring parents in closer touch with their children's academic lives both by engaging them in learning projects at home and by informing them of the schools' educational objectives.

## History and Origins

The model for Project AHEAD, a parent education, job-training, and empowerment program, was developed by Dr. Dorothy Rich of the Home and School Institute in Washington, DC in 1977. The Los Angeles Project AHEAD program was the brainchild of Marnessba Tackett, former director of the Southern Christian Leadership Conference of Greater Los Angeles (SCLC/LA), which sponsors the program. Her idea was to use Project AHEAD to reach children through their parents and to develop contacts with people inside the community to approach parents. Initial funding came from the Comprehensive Employment and Training Act (CETA), because Project AHEAD was designed to employ parents as family educators. Most of these men and women had never been in the work force prior to employment with Project AHEAD. The program provided black and Hispanic parents who were living below the poverty level or receiving welfare an opportunity to develop self-sufficiency.

In 1978, threatened by loss of CETA funds, Project AHEAD wrote a grant to the Los Angeles Unified School District, which subsequently funded the program beginning in the 1978-79 school year. The program in its present form was piloted in 22 schools, but budget cuts in 1980-81 reduced the number of participating schools to 10. Initial resistance came from the school district, which perceived the project's mission as opposite from that of the schools. According to Genethia Hayes, the project's director, "They viewed Project AHEAD as a job-training program and thought the staff less than professional." The schools have remained skeptical, but individual principals and teachers have lobbied the board of education. Churches and community activists have helped to further the project. Project AHEAD has been incorporated into the Ten Schools Program, a comprehensive program to increase minority children's chance of success in 10 Los Angeles schools.

*"We develop appetizers that teach parents how to engage in activities at home — different from those the children engage in at school — that will lead to the mastery of skills outlined by grade level in the district's curriculum . . . ."*

**Features**

Project AHEAD is a year-round, bilingual Spanish-English program mandated by SCLC to develop programming to educate black and Hispanic communities. It attempts to create a triangular partnership among parents, children, and teachers. Family educators or facilitators (more than half of whom are bilingual) visit homes twice each month to help strengthen the home-school partnership. Monthly "cluster meetings" bring parents to their children's schools to discuss special topics such as discipline, classroom observation skills, and nutrition.

Project AHEAD publishes "appetizers" (pamphlets) that are distributed through the schools and are aimed at increasing parent effectiveness. All of Project AHEAD's educational materials are in a simple, large-print, cartoon-like format and use animals as family characters.

Three special annual events — the **Parent Learning Factory,** the **Mid-Year Skills Event,** and the **Creative Family Fair** — are provided by the program to recognize and reward the work of parents to improve their children's academic achievement. All three programs take place in a public, competitive, and festive atmosphere. A fourth event, the **Summer Read-Off,** is the culminating event of the Summer Reading Program, which engages participants in educational activities during the summer months.

## Participants

Blacks 45%

Hispanics 55%

## Parent Education

## Curriculum

## Sites

## Parent Involvement

## Outreach

Project AHEAD serves low-income black and Hispanic families with children ages four to twelve. Home visits are discontinued for parents of fourth and fifth graders, but materials for them remain available in one of the schools served. The program is targeted at families whose children are at risk of dropping out of school. The average family participates on a monthly basis for up to three years. In 1988-89, Project AHEAD served 289 single mothers, 86 single fathers, and 375 two-parent families. Two percent of those served were teen parents. Mrs. Hayes estimated that the program reached 10 percent of the eligible families at each school site.

Family educators help parents develop opportunities for their children to learn at home, reaffirm the parents' role as their children's primary teachers, and pass on information from the schools to help parents make informed decisions about their children's schooling.

"Appetizers" are bilingual educational materials created by Project AHEAD to build literacy skills and help parents enhance their children's educational readiness at home. They deal with topics such as nonviolent parenting, nutrition, reading, and language development. Parent education messages are clear, step-by-step suggestions for becoming a "superparent" and a "reading-readiness teacher," for working on prekindergarten letter recognition, for sharpening classroom observation skills, and so on.

The district uses an innovative curriculum that mandates parent involvement and is tailored to the needs of each of the 10 schools served by Project AHEAD. Mrs. Hayes comments, " We develop appetizers that teach parents how to engage in activities at home — different from those the children engage in at school — that will lead to the mastery of skills outlined by grade level in the district's curriculum . . . . The curriculum for parents is uniquely our own, but draws upon the work and research of the past 15 years in the relatively new field of parenting education. " Appetizers and workshop materials are based on Dr. Reginald Clark's *Family Life and School Achievement: Why Do Poor Black Children Succeed or Fail?* Other materials used are: *School Power,* by Dr. James Comer and *Assertive Discipline for Parents,* by Lee and Marlene Cantor.

Project AHEAD has offices at the Martin Luther King Legacy Association and uses classrooms in 10 different schools for meetings and events.

Project AHEAD uses educational pamphlets to urge parents to take an active role in their children's schools and encourage increasing levels of involvement by: making annual classroom visits, joining the parent-teacher association, attending school events, sharing parenting skills and ideas, and working with Project AHEAD's staff to advise and recruit new staff.

In 1987, Project AHEAD served approximately half the number of families required by its 1988-89 contract. Since then, the program has intensified outreach efforts. The radio station most popular with the clientele targeted by Project AHEAD now regularly airs its public service announcements. Project AHEAD works with the schools, grass roots community organizations, religious leaders, community agencies, business people, and community educators to develop its parent constituency. Classroom teachers distribute a brochure each autumn with an attached consent form to be signed and returned to the school. Family educators make follow-up home visits to complete the enrollment process, do house-to-house recruitment, and network at parent meetings sponsored jointly by Project AHEAD and the schools.

Peer pressure and word-of-mouth draw some parents to the program. The most needy, among whom illiteracy and substance abuse is most prevalent, are the hardest to reach.

## Staff

The program's director holds a master's degree in education and has been a classroom teacher, curriculum specialist, and principal, as well as an editor and publisher of a language arts newspaper for elementary school students. About half of the family educators are male. According to Mrs. Hayes, Hispanic clients respond more "seriously" to men. "The age of the educator matters more than the parental status," explains Mrs. Hayes, adding that the community is reluctant to accept younger, unmarried people as authorities on childrearing. Even though many participants favor older women with considerable life experience, the school district and funders tend to value professional degrees more.

| Job Title | PD | Vol | FT | PT | Educ Req | Status | Benefits |
|---|---|---|---|---|---|---|---|
| Director | 1 | - | 1 | - | Post-Graduate Courses or Degree | Other Contract | Yes |
| Program Coordinator | 1 | - | 1 | - | College Degree | Hourly Non-Contract | Yes |
| Administrative Assistant | 1 | - | - | 1 | Some College | Hourly Non-Contract | Yes |
| Field Supervisor | 1 | - | 1 | - | Some College | Hourly Non-Contract | Yes |
| Family Educators | 10 | - | 10 | - | Some High School or More | Hourly Non-Contract | Yes |
| Graphics | 1 | - | 1 | - | College Degree | Hourly Non-Contract | Yes |

## State/District Requirements

None.

## Preferred Background

Family educators' credentials include a minimum of a high school diploma plus 12 units of coursework in child growth and development; bilingual staff members with a bachelor's degree are preferred (all have finished high school). Mrs. Hayes has all staff members take a Red Cross Parenting Specialty Course and become Red Cross certified parent educators. In addition, assertiveness discipline training, training in identification of suspected child abuse cases, a 32-hour Megaskills course, eight hours of monthly staff development, and participation in frequent discussions with classroom teachers, school counselors, and school psychologists are all mandatory.

## Employee Education and Training Represented

Prekindergarten and early childhood education; elementary education; parent educator; child care; social work.

**Administration**

The project is part of a larger outreach campaign of educational and social services developed by the Southern Christian Leadership Conference (SCLC) and the Martin Luther King Legacy Association (MLKLA). Project AHEAD's director reports to SCLC, which administers the program. The schools supply back-up staff members or liaisons appointed by the principals who facilitate Project AHEAD's interactions with the school staff.

**Relationship to the Schools**

Project AHEAD is funded through the district's Office of Student Integration Options and Traveling Programs. According to Mrs. Hayes, Project AHEAD addresses the district's obligation to provide programming that alleviates racial isolation due to low academic achievement, low self-esteem, interracial hostility and intolerance, and lack of access to postsecondary opportunities. Each school's liaison makes resources available to Project AHEAD, coordinates events to be held at the schools, and monitors the program as it unfolds throughout the year.

**Community Links**

Project AHEAD coordinates services between two programs that are part of the Ten Schools Program. The School-Readiness Language and Development Program is modeled on Head Start with a preschool and parent component; Parents Involved in Community Action (PICA) is geared to introducing newly arrived Hispanic families (but also serves black families) to the schools and to community resources. If the children are in elementary school, parents can participate in both the school readiness program and Project AHEAD. PICA encourages parents who attend its workshops and are not already active in Project AHEAD to join. PICA and Project AHEAD collaborate on workshops, staff development, and staff meetings four times a year.

*Project AHEAD addresses the district's obligation to provide programming that alleviates racial isolation due to low academic achievement, low self-esteem, interracial hostility and intolerance, and lack of access to postsecondary opportunities.*

**Funding**

Local and district, 95 percent; foundation, 5 percent.

**In-Kind Resources**

The SCLC, MLKLA, and the Los Angeles Unified School District provide space and facilities, paid staff for service delivery, consultation and staff development, periodic direct service to program participants, volunteer staff, administrative and clerical support, access to equipment, and materials and supplies.

**Funding History**

The program is funded by the Los Angeles Unified School District and the MLKLA, a nonprofit corporation of the Southern Christian Leadership Conference that was founded to promote educational projects within Los Angeles. Funding has been reliable for the last seven years, but Mrs. Hayes is concerned that the national emphasis on school performance in math and science may jeopardize the program, which focuses more on attitudes and subtle behavior changes than on grades.

**Objectives**

Mrs. Hayes hopes that Project AHEAD will turn parents into advocates of quality education for all children and that as more parents become involved, they will begin to view schools as a positive force for change within the community. " Project AHEAD changes people's attitudes and gives them the strength to make changes," she declares.

**Evaluation**

A 1985-86 evaluation consisted of staff and family questionnaires, telephone interviews with participating parents, records of parent involvement in Project AHEAD, and traditional school meetings and questionnaires administered to regional school administrators, teachers, principals, and family educators. This evaluation showed an ambivalence to Project AHEAD on the part of teachers in the school district. However, interviews with parents revealed that Project AHEAD is meeting its goals. Results showed that parents were taking more responsibility for their children's schooling, developing better attitudes toward the schools, spending more time talking with their children, and talking to the schools more readily about their children's welfare. The majority of parents in the evaluation felt that the program should expand to other schools, other parents, and other grades.

At the end of each school year, parents and family educators fill out parent progress reports detailing strengths and weaknesses of parents' participation throughout the year.

**Replication**

Although the program has not yet been replicated, Dr. Reginald Clark was hired as a consultant to focus program goals and to facilitate later replication.

**Materials Available**

Contact Genethia Hayes for samples of Project AHEAD's "appetizers."

# Activity, Book, and Toy Library

Toy lending            Resource library

| | |
|---|---|
| **Contact:** | David Campbell, Assistant Principal |
| **Address:** | New Market Elementary School<br>P.O. Box 284<br>New Market, MD 21774<br>(301) 865-5407 |
| **Established:** | 1979, statewide initiative; 1986, New Market program |
| **Budget '88-'89:** | $500 |
| **Sources:** | State start-up grant; funding continued through the PTA |
| **Size:** | 100 families using services every two weeks |
| **Area served:** | New Market, Maryland |
| **Auspices:** | Elementary Education |
| **1990 Respondent:** | Rebecca L. Karp, Assistant Principal |

## Community

New Market, formerly a farming community, is a middle-class town whose one main street is lined with antique stores. The area has limited cultural resources, yet the tiny population of approximately 500 is involved with many community-centered activities that take place in either the elementary school or the firehouse hall across the street. According to Rebecca Karp, assistant principal of the New Market Elementary School, this is a close-knit community with a history of commitment to the school.

## Philosophy and Goals

Recognizing that parents are their children's first teachers, the Activity, Book, and Toy (ABT) Library provides parents with the tools and skills to make the most of the time they spend with their children. The program encourages parents to become actively involved in the educational lives of their children and forges links between home and school. It provides parents with high-quality materials to reinforce skills and extend learning into the home in developmentally appropriate ways.

## History and Origins

In 1979 the Maryland Department of Education (MDE) offered 10 counties a $2,500 technical assistance grant to start activity-, book-, and toy-lending libraries as part of the Extended Elementary Education Program (EEEP) for four-year-olds in Chapter 1 schools. Dr. Frances O. Witt, a specialist within the MDE, designed the ABT program and initially provided technical assistance to schools. In each county, the program develops according to local needs. Local spin-offs include ABT-on-wheels, parent workshops, book clubs, preschool story hour, and play groups. In some cases, parents run the resource center; in others they are involved only as recipients of services. The ABT library concept matches services to local needs. In New Market, where few children come from disadvantaged families, the focus was on parent involvement—giving parents reasons to come into the school and helping them further their children's education. Ms. Karp notes that parents wanted to help their children but lacked confidence. Although New Market did not qualify for Chapter 1 funding, the state awarded financial aid on the strength of the community's history of parent involvement and enthusiasm for the initiative. Continued financial support comes through the parent-teacher association (PTA).

**Features**

The ABT library, open year-round, provides quality educational materials in the form of simple kits for parents to use at home with their children. Kits consist of a book, a toy, and an activity, catalogued by grade level and subject. Parents wishing to borrow a kit can consult with their child's teacher or browse through the catalogue.

**Participants**

Blacks 1%  Hispanics 1%

Whites 98%

The ABT library is open to residents of the community. In 1988-89, the program served 100 low- to middle-income families, an estimated 50 percent of those eligible. Five percent were single parents and participants' incomes ranged from $10,000 to $35,000.

*The ABT library concept matches services to local needs.*

**Curriculum**

Developed in house, kits utilize commercial and teacher-made materials coordinated with the language, art, science, and math curriculum for preschool through fifth grade.

**Sites**

The ABT library has moved several times. It is situated on the second floor of the New Market Elementary School, a convenient site that is private and easy for parents to find. The room is open during school hours (8:30 a.m. to 4:00 p.m.) and by appointment.

**Parent Involvement**

After meeting with Ms. Witt to discuss implementation and after visiting successful programs, Ms. Karp formed a steering committee of teachers and parents to set up the library at New Market. The PTA held a fundraiser which successfully matched the state start-up grant. Today, the program is run by two parent volunteers. Once the kits are created, the center "almost runs itself" says the assistant principal.

**Outreach**

Teachers refer children to ABT materials. Parents are contacted to initiate the checking out process. The center has had difficulty involving single-parent families and families in which both parents work, so the parent resource library hours have been extended (by appointment) to encourage these families to participate in the program.

**Staff**

The staff is composed of volunteers who maintain records of kits and keep the catalogue updated.

| Job Title | PD | Vol | FT | PT | Educ Req | Status | Benefits |
|-----------|-----|-----|-----|-----|-----------|--------|----------|
| Clerical | - | 2 | - | 2 | Some High School | - | No |

**State/District Requirements**

None.

**Preferred Background**

None.

| | |
|---|---|
| Employee Education and Training Represented | None. |
| Administration | The ABT library is administered through the public school system and is monitored by the state coordinator of Project "Accept and Challenge" and by the Early Learning Section of the Maryland Department of Education. An advisory board meets twice a year to approve the program's services and curriculum and maintains connection with the PTA. It is made up of participants, personnel from the school site, and community representatives. |
| Relationship to the Schools | The ABT library exists entirely within the framework of the school. Increasingly, the resource library has established credibility among teachers and parents, and Ms. Karp reports that the program has become a stable and integral part of the school's educational services. Its kits enhance the curriculum and help children take learning a step beyond the classroom. |
| Community Links | The ABT library in New Market has not established any links to local social service or community agencies. |
| Funding | The New Market PTA, 100 percent. After an initial start up grant of $2,500, the program has been able to run on a yearly operating budget of $500. |
| In-Kind Resources | Space, facilities, administrative and clerical staff, telephone, and other equipment are provided by New Market Elementary School. According to Ms. Karp, operating costs are very low because parents, feeling that the program belongs to them, take care of kits and donate new materials. |
| Funding History | Funding has dropped 80 percent since the first year of implementation but is secure at its present level for the next two years. |
| Objectives | The purpose of the ABT library is to provide parents and students with high-quality, school-related curricular materials and activities to use outside of school time. The program's designers hope increased exposure will result in improved performance in school and better understanding of the school's developmental curriculum. |
| Evaluation | Parent surveys were used in nine schools in five local districts where the ABT library was implemented. Parent responses indicated that the ABT library boosted children's performance in school, encouraged parents to take an interest in their children's homework, and improved their relations with their children. Each kit contains an evaluation form to be completed by parents. An end-of-year evaluation, aimed at improving the ABT library's services, is solicited from all participants. |
| Replication | The New Market program replicates the Maryland Department of Education's model, which operates at 15 sites in three counties. |
| Materials Available | The New Market ABT library has a slide-tape program, available free; write to the program address for information. A descriptive brochure of the model, *Activity, Book, and Toy Lending Program: A Vehicle for Home-School Cooperation,* is available from the Maryland Department of Education. |

# FAMILY MATH

Leader workshops        Parent-child learning activities
Training manual         Parenting/child development education

| | |
|---|---|
| **Contact:** | Virginia Thompson, Director |
| **Address:** | EQUALS Programs |
| | Lawrence Hall of Science |
| | University of California |
| | Berkeley, CA 94720 |
| | (510) 642-6859 |
| **Established:** | 1982, collaboration between federal government and state university research center |
| **Budget '88-'89:** | Subsumed under EQUALS |
| **Sources:** | Federal and state departments of education and private foundations |
| **Size:** | Information unavailable |
| **Area Served:** | Widespread dissemination in this country, Canada, and abroad |
| **Auspices:** | University of California, Berkeley EQUALS Program |

*A woman with a master's degree in anthropology, who had dropped out of math in eighth grade, was shocked when her first-grade daughter told her she hated math. Hoping to improve her daughter's experiences in math, the mother attended a FAMILY MATH class and decided to push to have the program implemented in her daughter's school. Her daughter, now in seventh grade, chose to take "Problem Solving" (a voluntary, high-level course) and the whole family works together on the weekly problems she brings home from school.*

## Community

FAMILY MATH has served nearly 100,000 parents and children since 1984. Its programs are now running in 30 states as well as in Sweden, Canada, Puerto Rico, Australia, Costa Rica, and New Zealand.

## Philosophy and Goals

FAMILY MATH helps parents assist their children with math and provides opportunities for students to develop problem-solving skills and an understanding of math concepts. The program was designed to involve families in their children's mathematics education and to demonstrate the relevance of mathematics to future career options. It addresses the traditionally poor performance of women and minorities on mathematics tests and their resultant waning interest in the subject during high school.

## History and Origins

Since 1977, the EQUALS program at the Lawrence Hall of Science, a science center and research and development unit at the University of California, Berkeley, has provided inservice training for kindergarten through twelfth-grade teachers to improve mathematics teaching and learning and to help students, particularly females and minorities, to succeed in math. Teachers who went through the training asked EQUALS to develop materials that parents could use with children at home. FAMILY MATH was the result of these requests. In 1982, initial funding for the program came from a three-year grant from the Fund for the Improvement of Post Secondary Education (FIPSE). In the first two years, funding supported a prototype program and pilot tests in two low-income, inner-city communities in Richmond, California; paid for expanded course offerings in Oakland, California; and sponsored two-day training sessions for future FAMILY MATH instructors. In the third year, EQUALS developed the manuscript for the *FAMILY MATH Book,* which detailed the curriculum and furnished information about establishing and conducting FAMILY MATH courses. After FIPSE funding ended, the program grew through a series of training sessions for FAMILY MATH teachers in the United States, which was funded by the Carnegie Corporation.

## Features

FAMILY MATH focuses entirely on parents and children learning math together. Courses taught by grade level run in a series of six or eight two-hour evening sessions. Topics include arithmetic, geometry, probability and statistics, measurement, estimation, and logical thinking. Instructors leave time for discussion, and in some courses each family is assigned a "buddy" family they can call during the week. Refreshments are often provided and babysitting is available.

**Leader workshops,** held at the Berkeley center, train teachers who plan to start FAMILY MATH courses in their communities. These two-day workshops were established during the program's first year to ensure that FAMILY MATH classes would continue to spread beyond the initial participants. Workshops include discussions about the philosophy of the program, suggestions for starting courses, ideas about what and how to teach, and opportunities to try FAMILY MATH activities.

## Participants

Primarily, courses are offered to all parents with children in grades K to 8. In some cases, students must either attend the local school or be a member of the organizing group that brought FAMILY MATH into the community.

*The director comments on instructor training, "We present the material in our training workshops for potential leaders and trainer-of-trainers the same way that we want them taught in classes, and we find that most instructors feel well prepared to teach courses."*

## Parent Education

Parents learn about home activities that reinforce mathematical concepts and are encouraged to adopt the instructor's teaching style, which accentuates empowering children, focusing on their accomplishments, establishing a comfortable learning pace, and incorporating strategies that generate enthusiasm for math.

## Curriculum

FAMILY MATH materials are developed for parent-child classes and include activities that can be duplicated at home with inexpensive household materials. Culturally relevant materials are added to the basic curriculum whenever possible. For instance, classes for Native Americans estimate measurements using units such as tepee poles, and the geometry sessions include discussions of traditional Native American designs.

Instructors focus on developing problem-solving skills by identifying patterns, drawing pictures, working backward, and eliminating possibilities. They use concrete objects such as beans, pennies, or toothpicks to illustrate concepts. According to the director, increasing the number of strategies at the students' disposal enhances their confidence and increases their willingness to tackle new problems.

**Sites**

FAMILY MATH is a spin-off of EQUALS and has offices at the Lawrence Hall of Science, a science museum on the Berkeley campus. Leadership workshops, staff development, and occasional FAMILY MATH courses are conducted here. In other areas around the world, commonly used sites include schools, churches, homes, and community centers.

**Parent Involvement**

Parents become involved as volunteers, participants, instructors, and supporters who see that the program becomes implemented in the school.

**Outreach**

Initially, workshops, talks, and papers about FAMILY MATH were presented at local, regional, state, and national teachers' conferences. A 17-minute film titled "We All Count in FAMILY MATH" enables thousands of people each year to see what actually goes on in the classes and how families use the ideas and materials. The *FAMILY MATH Book* also increases the demand for the program.

Participants hear about the program through schools, community-based organizations, and churches. The schools and organizations that present FAMILY MATH courses or sponsor leadership workshops do outreach on the program's behalf, but the director feels that Asian immigrants, Hispanics, blacks, and Native Americans are still underrepresented in leadership preparation workshops for instructors and trainer-of-trainers workshops. Special letters to potential participants and recruitment through community-based organizations have been used in efforts to increase the participation of these ethnic groups.

**Staff**

| Job Title | PD | Vol | FT | PT | Educ Req | Status | Benefits |
|-----------|-----|-----|-----|-----|----------|--------|----------|
| Director | 1 | - | 1 | - | College Degree | Other Contract | Yes |
| Networker | 1 | - | 1 | - | College Degree | Other Contract | Yes |

**State/District Requirements**

None.

**Preferred Background**

Network coordinators and class instructors should have good "people" skills, workshop presenters should have teaching skills and mathematics experience, and curriculum developers should have a math background appropriate for kindergarten through college.

**Employee Education and Training Represented**

Elementary education; education, grades 7 to 12; parent educator; mathematics; mathematics education.

**Administration**

Ultimate responsibility for the program and its dissemination lies with the director of EQUALS. A board of directors, made up of paid staff members and volunteers from the program, meets four to eight times a year and approves staff hiring, program services, and curriculum.

**Relationship to the Schools**

According to the literature, FAMILY MATH works best when classroom teachers become involved in training and recruiting parents of students. The program has captured the interest of teachers, as well as others, but remains outside the framework and jurisdiction of the public education system.

FAMILY MATH works with the National Urban Coalition and the American Association for the Advancement of Science (both funded by the Carnegie Corporation) to assist minority communities in upgrading the math and science skills of their youth. Individuals with math-based occupations who live in the community come to FAMILY MATH classes to talk about their jobs and to clarify the reasons for studying mathematics.

The FAMILY MATH budget is part of the EQUALS program budget; figures are unavailable.

Space and facilities are usually provided by schools; paid staff for service delivery is provided by school districts, museums, and community organizations; schools and community-based organizations provide volunteer staff, administrative and clerical support, access to equipment, materials, and supplies.

FIPSE provided a three-year grant to pilot-test the program, develop two-day training sessions for instructors, and compile the *FAMILY MATH Book*. The Carnegie Corporation of New York funded the publication of 5,000 copies of the book and a series of trainer-of-trainers workshops. Book sales fund additional reprints. A grant from the Women's Educational Equity Act Program enabled the production of the film, *We All Count in FAMILY MATH*. Funding for courses comes from a variety of state and local sources. In 1985, FAMILY MATH received a three-year National Science Foundation grant to work with community-based organizations. Most recently, a U.S. Department of Education grant funded FAMILY MATH to host inservice training for teachers who work with Spanish-speaking families.

FAMILY MATH seeks to involve parents in their children's mathematics education and to make the subject enjoyable by providing materials that parents can use at home with their children. In addition, the program expands the concept of mathematics for parents and their elementary-age children to include more than arithmetic and provides information about math and its role in the children's future schooling and careers.

The program was evaluated in accordance with National Science Foundation requirements. The evaluation goals were: to determine use of materials by participants in the courses, to monitor the courses taught by FAMILY MATH leaders, and to assess the extent of dissemination of the program in different sites. Follow-up questionnaires are sent to participants in the leadership workshops at the Lawrence Hall of Science each year to quantify dissemination. A study of the impact of the program on families, *Families of FAMILY MATH,* is forthcoming.

Evaluations conducted in the program's first year used interviews, observations, and surveys to determine reasons for participation, whether participants' goals were met, participants' enjoyment of different course components, and their use of activities at home. The directors commented, "Results reported in the year-one final summary showed that over 90 percent of the parents who attended courses regularly during the first year played math games with their children and helped them with their math homework; over 80 percent talked to their children's teachers about their math progress. It appeared that math-related activities begun during classes were sustained. Further, 75 percent of the parents attending the first year courses indicated they were able to help their children with math.

Replication

FAMILY MATH has been replicated around the country and abroad.

Materials Available

The *FAMILY MATH Book*, published in 1986 and translated into Spanish and Swedish, is available. *We All Count in FAMILY MATH*, a 17-minute film of scenes from FAMILY MATH classes, and the *FAMILY MATH Leadership Workshop* videotape are also available. Contact Ms. Thompson at the program address.

# Parents in Touch

*A single mother, whose child now attends one of the Chapter 1 programs, left home at age 17. "This mother is very keen on having her child benefit from all educational opportunities. We recently sent her to a National Coalition of Chapter 1 Parents Regional Meeting where she was selected to be an officer on the state steering committee. We view her commitment to her child and to our program as extraordinary. She sees what can be done and she does it."*
— *Izona Warner*

**Contact:** Dilynn Phelps, Dissemination Specialist
**Address:** Indianapolis Public Schools
SCIPS Building, 901 North Carrollton
Room 208
Indianapolis, IN 46202
(317) 226-4134
**Established:** 1979, school district initiative (public-private venture)
**Budget '88-'89:** $366,690
**Sources:** State and federal government, local school district, corporate and business donations, foundations, special events, fundraising, and in-kind contributions
**Size:** 50,143 children
**Area served:** Indianapolis Public School District
**Auspices:** Indianapolis Public Schools
**1990 Respondent:** Izona Warner, Project Director

## Community

Indianapolis, in central Indiana, has a population of approximately 731,000 and is about three-quarters white. Other than the government, the city's largest employers are the Methodist Hospital and Indiana Bell Telephone. Unemployment is at 5 percent. Black students comprise 49 percent of the public school population.

## Philosophy and Goals

Parents in Touch (PIT) enhances the learning process by developing channels of communication among parents, teachers, and students. The program strives to link the three, to strengthen bonds between home and school, and to develop a system of reciprocal accountability.

## History and Origins

Parents in Touch began in 1979. Its emphasis on parent involvement in the schools resulted directly from two needs assessments conducted within the Indianapolis Public School System (IPS) in 1975 and 1977. The assessments indicated teachers' and administrators' interest in encouraging parent participation in the schools. William Douglas, the assistant to the superintendent for Supplemental and Auxiliary Services, developed a proposal for the Lilly Endowment in response to their interest in funding a parent involvement program. PIT began offering services in the 1979-80 school year under the guidance of Izona Warner, the project director. Funding continues through the school district's Chapter 1 and Chapter 2 allocations. The program draws additional grant support from the Indianapolis Chamber of Commerce and business communities.

PIT involves the entire school district in its program, which is designed to create an awareness of the role parents can have in their children's education and to actively involve parents in the educational process.

**Parent-teacher conferences** are 20-minute one-on-one meetings scheduled on a day set aside for that purpose. In each school, a PIT building coordinator works with the staff to facilitate these conferences, sends out invitations to parents, and provides instructional materials for teachers to give to parents.

**Parents in Touch activity calendars,** for parents of children in kindergarten to sixth grade, include curriculum-related ideas and suggestions and information about holiday schedules, test dates, report cards, and references to community and school resources.

The **STP folder and contract** is an agreement among students, teachers, and parents. Parents promise to establish a regular time for homework, provide a well-lighted place to study, and make a commitment to having their children attend school regularly. The folders include a streamlined communication system for comments and suggestions between parents and teachers. A similar contract is offered to junior high school students and their teachers and parents.

**Dial-a-Teacher** is designed to provide homework assistance and information to students and parents. Two teams of specialists offer assistance in math, social studies, science, language arts, and elementary education.

**Homework Hotline** is a live, hour-long cable television program, broadcast once a week, that provides mathematics assistance and information to students in grades one through six and their parents.

The **Parent/Line Communicator** is a 24-hour-a-day call-in service that provides brief tape-recorded messages on a variety of school-related topics, including drug and alcohol abuse, school policies, options programs, magnet schools, parenting skills, adult education programs, and others.

**Parent Focus Series** is a parent education component of 90 special workshops the schools may request from PIT. Some workshops run as a series, others meet only once. Workshops include discussions, lectures, and videos. Participant interaction is encouraged and desired. Workshops are offered days and nights; child care is sometimes provided. Program director Izona Warner notes that workshops are not "formal support groups, but some sessions end up that way."

**Operation Pass Preschool,** a program begun in 1988 for three- and four-year-olds from low-income families living in a public housing project, uses an early childhood developmental model. Additional services for children in the preschool include: medical and dental care and developmental exams and screening. Parents of preschoolers participate in Graduate Equivalency Diploma (GED) and literacy classes and parenting workshops and are eligible for individual counseling. Each family in the preschool program receives at least one home visit; some families receive several follow-up visits, if necessary.

## Participants

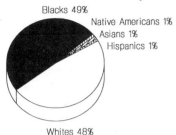

Blacks 49%
Native Americans 1%
Asians 1%
Hispanics 1%
Whites 48%

PIT serves 82 percent of the eligible population of families with children enrolled in the Indianapolis Public School District. Participants in Operation Pass Preschool are disadvantaged children, to whom the program offers both enrichment and prevention against future failure in school. During its first year, 44 children enrolled in Operation Pass Preschool, 98 percent of whom were black and 2 percent white. (Note: Data presented in the pie chart to the left reflects demographics for the entire school-age population.)

> *Ms. Warner notes, "There are no liabilities to being a school program. One strength is that a large number of students in Indianapolis attend the public schools, so we have an audience for our services that's already identified."*

## Parent Education

The Parent Focus Series offers a broad range of courses to parent-teacher organizations, clusters of schools, and parent groups on personal growth, child development, children's school experience, parent-child relationships, and parent-school relations. Parents of preschoolers learn to fulfill their role as their children's first teacher. Parent meetings, workshops, field trips, and home visits contribute to parent education.

## Curriculum

The Parent Focus Series uses specially designed materials, including *Good Touch / Bad Touch,* a series of child abuse workshops in which many parents share their own experiences about being abused; and *Picture This,* a therapeutic theater group that brings parents — and sometimes parents and students — together to share feelings, role play, and act out vignettes. *Parent Effectiveness Training, Active Parenting, Systematic Training for Effective Parenting (STEP),* and the *Nurturing Program* are also used.

Operation Pass Preschool uses an early childhood development curriculum designed by program staff members and a university consultant to emphasize parent involvement and the child's physical, social, emotional, and cognitive development.

Other curricula used are: *FAMILY MATH,* which provides training classes for elementary classroom and Chapter 1 remedial math teachers to work with families to improve students' math skills; *Triple P (Parents Participating for Progress),* which trains teachers and social workers in 10 schools and helps establish parent-teacher partnerships; and *Leadership Training Workshops,* which help parents, school staff members, and representatives of community services design a plan of action for home-school involvement geared to improving students' behavior, attendance, and achievement.

## Sites

The program runs parent-teacher conferences in all Indianapolis schools. The Parent Focus Series is offered in community centers, corporate administration buildings, and local businesses. The program's main site is in a school building, and has a parent resource center, an office for each of the three staff members and the secretary, and an auditorium that is used for some workshops. Izona Warner adds, "We even have a kitchen. Parents have baked cookies here with their children during some parent-child activities. We are very lucky to have wonderful facilities."

Operation Pass Preschool is housed in an elementary school adjacent to the housing project where the participating children live. The parent component takes place in the housing project's community center.

**Parent Involvement**

Parents were involved in the original needs assessment, and parent involvement continues to fortify the program, with 46 participants serving on the advisory board.

**Outreach**

The Indianapolis Chamber of Commerce has education as its top priority and has put together payroll inserts for businesses that emphasize the role of parents in education. It has also produced a videotape available to businesses at cost. The Indianapolis Chamber of Commerce urges business to give parents time off for conferences and school visits. PIT offers brown bag lunches and discussion at various workplaces.

**Staff**

| Job Title | PD | Vol | FT | PT | Educ Req | Status | Benefits |
|---|---|---|---|---|---|---|---|
| Consultant for Parent Involvement | 1 | - | 1 | - | Post-Graduate Courses or Degree | Other Contract | Yes |
| Dissemination Specialist | 1 | - | 1 | - | College Degree | Other Contract | Yes |
| Chapter 1 Parent/ School Liaison | 1 | - | 1 | - | College Degree | K-12 Contract | Yes |
| Secretaries | 2 | - | 2 | - | College Degree | Hourly Non-Contract | Yes |

**State/District Requirements**

Requirements vary for different components of the program.

**Preferred Background**

Project associates and trainers should have media and public relations training.

**Employee Education and Training Represented**

Prekindergarten and early childhood education; elementary education; education, grades 7 to 12; adult basic education; parent educator; health and nutrition; counseling; social work; child development and family studies.

**Administration**

PIT is administered within the school system's Department of Supplemental and Auxiliary Services, which is responsible for grants and special programs. The Division of Research, Testing, and Evaluation monitors Chapter 1 programs. A 46-member advisory board approves services, monitors the program, makes suggestions for improvement, participates in fundraising, and engages in community public relations. The director, Izona Warner, reports to William Douglas, the district's assistant superintendent.

Operation Pass Preschool teachers report to the school principal. PIT is the support system for the preschool's parent involvement component.

## Relationship to the Schools

According to Ms. Warner, the program has important links with school staff members, including nurses, guidance counselors, social workers, adult education teachers, early childhood specialists, IPS administrators, and instructional television staff members. Ms. Warner notes, "There are no liabilities to being a school program. One strength is that a large number of students in Indianapolis attend the public schools, so we have an audience for our services that's already identified."

## Community Links

The program has strong ties with the Family Services and Community Centers of Indianapolis, both of which provide inservice workshops, presentations, and sites. Many presenters from community organizations are brought in to run workshops for the Parent Focus Series.

## Funding

The program receives federal funds for Chapter 1 and Chapter 2 programs, state "at-risk" funds and discretionary grants, local school district funds, corporate and business donations, funding from foundation and private agencies, and in-kind contributions (no percentages given).

## In-Kind Resources

The Indianapolis Public Schools provide space and facilities, consultation and staff development, administrative and clerical support, and access to equipment. Chapter 1 and Chapter 2 provide paid staff for service delivery as well as materials and supplies. The Indiana Department of Education and the Marion County Health Association provide periodic direct service to program participants and parents provide the volunteer staff for special projects.

## Funding History

PIT was started with monies from the Lilly Endowment. State and federal government sources have provided funding in subsequent years.

## Objectives

The program seeks to improve students' attendance, behavior, and achievement; establish links with parents and teachers; provide school-related information to parents; and offer workshops to parents based on their selection and interests.

## Evaluation

Chapter 1 and Chapter 2 require program evaluation, conducted by an internal evaluator. Findings showed that 82 percent of parents of students in grades K to 12 attended parent-teacher conferences in the fall of 1987. Dial-a-Teacher processed 8,878 phone calls from students for homework assistance.

## Replication

PIT was modeled on a program in Philadelphia, Pennsylvania and has been replicated through national dissemination of packets of materials. PIT sponsored two national conferences, where educators had the opportunity to learn about the model. In addition, PIT staff members make frequent presentations at regional and national educational and social service conferences.

## Materials Available

*Methods of Achieving Parent Partnerships (MAPP); Maintaining Active Parent Partnerships (MAPP 2).* To order, contact PIT at the above address.

# Parent Child Preschool

Resource library
Networking
Toy lending
Home visits

Mother support group
Community services info/referral
Adult reading program
Health/nutrition education

Developmental exams/screening
Parent-child joint activities
Parenting/child development education

**Contact:** Sarah Howell, Director
**Address:** Preschool-Parenting Program
Fox Elementary School
3720 Fifth Avenue
Columbus, GA 31904
(706) 649-0740
**Established:** 1982, local initiative
**Budget '88-89:** $43,386
**Sources:** Local school district
**Size:** 55 families; 80 children
**Area Served:** Muscogee County, Georgia
**Auspices:** Fox Elementary School

*Many of the mothers participating in the Parent Child Preschool have not finished high school and regret that their parents did not encourage them to do so. Several have been inspired to study for their GED, and one went back to college to study early childhood. All intend to "stick with their children" throughout their school experience and pass on their recognition of the importance of education.*

**Community**

Columbus, with a population of just under 200,000, once belonged to Georgia's poor, rural south, an area of cotton plantations and smaller farms. Since a military base came to the area, the city's commercial interests have grown. Fox Elementary School serves 500 children. Of the 80 children who attend the Parent Child Preschool, most live in the nearby mill district. Many of the mothers are single women on welfare without high school diplomas.

**Philosophy and Goals**

The Parent Child Preschool hopes to create equality in educational opportunities for children whose poverty prevents them from attending preschool. Goals include helping parents value the relationship they have with their children, fostering their self-esteem, and creating a climate for positive interaction between home and school.

**History and Origins**

The principal of Fox Elementary School, Guy Sims, developed the Parent Child Preschool in response to discrepancies in ability and socialization experience among entering kindergartners. Although the preschool was conceived in 1981 as a conventional child-centered program, Mr. Sims shifted his direction based on research in the early 1980s that indicated the home environment was important to children's social and intellectual growth. In 1982, the preschool began on a half-time basis, targeting low-income families. Participants were identified by the school or referred through community agencies. In 1983, the district superintendent asked the school board to fund the program full time, and in 1985 the funding process stabilized.

**Features**

Parent Child Preschool meets once a week for an hour; children are grouped by age, with five or six in each class. The preschool provides the foundations for learning and the opportunity to develop language and motor skills that will put entering kindergartners on an equal footing with their peers. For the first half hour, the teacher demonstrates learning and play activities appropriate to the age and development of each child. In the second half hour, while the children continue their activities with an aide, Ms. Howell works with parents on parenting skills and child development. The program makes home visits when needed and provides evening parent workshops. It runs a toy- and book-lending library and has initiated an adult reading program through the volunteer efforts of a retired teacher. In addition, the Parent Child Program identifies children's developmental delays or disorders and provides remediation through referral to outside agencies.

## Participants

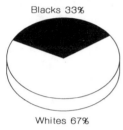

Blacks 33%

Whites 67%

Mothers with children birth to age five and children unexposed to preschool are targeted. The program is available to families throughout Muscogee County and 90 percent of the participants live within the school's attendance area. In 1987-88, 80 children and 50 mothers completed the program; 100 children and 70 parents received services. Six percent were teen parents and 70 percent single parents.

*"There are many more teacher conferences now, initiated by parents," notes the principal. "Parents didn't have positive experiences in school themselves, and for the first two years that was the biggest thing we had to fight against: school was not a place they wanted to be involved with."*

## Parent Education

"The success of the project may be attributed to the program's open and accepting attitude toward parents," notes the director. Parent workshops consist of lectures, handouts, and group discussions that focus on play and learning experiences in conjunction with child development and health and nutrition education. An adult reading program is available for mothers and extended-family members.

## Curriculum

Classroom materials include *Small Wonders! Kit,* levels 1 and 2, from the American Guidance Service; *Bowdoin Method,* a series of filmstrips, tapes, and books showing basic learning activities for preschoolers from Webster International Tutoring Systems, Inc.; *Growing Child* newsletters (one month to three years); *The First Three Years* videotapes, focusing on Burton White's seven phases of early development; *Understanding Children's Art Expression,* International Film Bureau, Inc.; and *Assertive Discipline for Parents.*

## Sites

The preschool occupies a frame house on the school campus and is part of, but not in, the Fox Elementary School. Parents come by foot, and participation decreases during heavy rains. The director makes every effort to keep in touch with absent parents through home visits and phone calls. "Parents know their participation is important," she said, "not taken for granted." In 1989, Parent Child Preschool will have a minibus for use in bad weather.

**Parent Involvement**

Each week, parents bring home materials necessary for the development of a particular skill. They keep a record of daily activities with their children and meet weekly with teachers to discuss the past week and set new objectives. Parents' needs shape the curriculum. Says the director, " It doesn't matter what their education and financial background is. It doesn't require expensive materials and equipment to turn everyday activities into learning experiences with children — modeling how to read to children and so on . . . . This gives parents confidence — never pushing them into anything, letting them plan what they want to do."

**Outreach**

Flyers, posters, word-of-mouth, and messages sent home from school comprise the major outreach efforts. Referrals come through the Department of Family and Child Services, the county health department and the Columbus Junior League. The program has received local television and newspaper coverage, but finds direct contact with people in the neighborhood the most effective means of recruitment. "Typically," observes the principal, "there is an invisible wall between teachers and parents. This program has helped to break that down . . . it's helped parents realize school is not off limits." Word-of-mouth, he said, has contributed to this new attitude, and "parents have become the best source of breaking down intimidation."

*"The success of the project may be attributed to the program's open and accepting attitude toward parents."*

**Staff**

The principal notes that the "right personnel" have the ability to relate not only to children, but to every type of parent "from the eager to the intimidated, the abused, and the insecure."

| Job Title | PD | Vol | FT | PT | Educ Req | Status | Benefits |
|-----------|----|----|----|----|----------|--------|----------|
| Teacher Director | 1 | - | 1 | - | College Degree | K-12 Contract | Yes |
| Teacher Aide | 1 | - | 1 | - | High School Diploma | Hourly Contract | Yes |

**State/District Requirements**

For the teacher-director, early childhood certification and 10 hours of staff development or college credit every five years; for the teacher-aide, 30 hours of staff development annually.

**Preferred Background**

Capacity to work with families of all races, backgrounds, ages, and abilities.

**Employee Education and Training Represented**

Infant and toddler education; prekindergarten and early childhood education; elementary education; parent educator; child care; child development and family studies.

**Administration**

The director reports to the principal of Fox Elementary School. On a day-to-day basis, the program director is in direct contact with the elementary and early childhood education teachers. The schools offer access to staff development opportunities and screening, research, and evaluation resources.

## Relationship to the Schools

According to Mr. Sims, it is vital for the school's faculty to understand the program's importance. By actively rechanneling funds from the elementary grades into the preschool, he has built teachers' awareness of the need for early education. "The program helps teachers realize that parents have to be involved in the educational process," he comments, adding that the program has smoothed communication between teachers and parents. Sixty to 70 parents, many of them graduates of the program, attend a monthly parent night at the school.

"There are many more teacher conferences now, initiated by parents," notes the principal. "Parents didn't have positive experiences in school themselves, and for the first two years that was the biggest thing we had to fight against: school was not a place they wanted to be involved with."

The program detraumatizes the transition into kindergarten for both parents and children by getting parents into the habit of coming to school for parties or for visits to the classroom. Says the director, "We help them through the — at times alarming — process of kindergarten registration." One mother put it this way: "I want my child to get used to the smell and feel of school with me going there with him."

## Community Links

Agencies such as the Columbus Health Department and the Department of Family and Child Services make referrals and share information with Parent Child Preschool. The Columbus College Early Childhood Department has adopted an advisory role, consulting on issues related to oral language delays and offering suggestions for remediation. The college makes its speech clinic available for testing and therapy and is interested in providing a research assistant to help with program evaluation.

## Funding

Muscogee County School District, 100 percent. Funds cover salary and benefits to the staff and director.

## In-Kind Resources

Materials are donated and the school provides for space and facilities, paid staff, consultation and staff development, periodic direct service to program participants, administrative and clerical support, and access to equipment.

## Funding History

Initially, the Parent Child Preschool was not an official line item in the school budget but came up annually for discretionary funding. Parents had to contact the superintendent to ask for his support. The school board began funding the project as a line item in 1985, and the director's position, initially half time, became a full-time job.

## Objectives

The program aims to help parents understand child development and learn ways to foster growth through interaction, play, and reading aloud. It gives parents a sense of the importance of their role in their children's education at home and in school, and provides children with exposure to activities that enhance intellectual, social, and physical development.

## Evaluation

The Parent Child Preschool has not yet been evaluated.

| | |
|---|---|
| **Replication** | The program is unique. |
| **Materials Available** | Contact the director for a list of program objectives. |

# Children with Teachers at Home (CWTAH)

| | |
|---|---|
| Toy lending | Parenting/child development education |
| Home visits | Parent-child joint activities |

**Contact:** Carolyn Gibson, Coordinator

**Address:** District One Schools
P.O. Box 218
Campobello, SC 29322
(803) 472-2846

**Established:** 1978, local initiative

**Budget '88-89:** $35,500

**Sources:** Local school district, state child development funds

**Size:** 340 families (368 children) served at five elementary school sites

**Area served:** District One, Campobello, South Carolina

**Auspices:** Elementary Education

*It has been six years since the home-school coordinator positions were eliminated in District One elementary schools. Gradually, the schools began to lose contact with parents, and new families entering the system were unfamiliar with the school program. Last spring, elementary school principals were asked, "If money were not a factor, what would you want most for your school next year?" The response from all five principals was to reestablish the home-school coordinator positions.*

## Community

Children with Teachers at Home (CWTAH) serves District One of Spartanburg County, a rural, mountainous area on the border between the Carolinas. Employment is primarily in the textile mills, other blue-collar industries, and agriculture. The population is approximately 15 percent black and 85 percent white.

## Philosophy and Goals

CWTAH provides parents with information about parenting skills, child development, and early learning patterns. The program presents materials and information by modeling so that the parent is not simply taught, but is exposed to alternative ways of interacting with children.

## History and Origins

In 1978, at the prompting of an elementary school principal, CWTAH began by supplying information about parenting skills and child development to parents of children birth to age four, both to improve kindergarten readiness and to help parents convey the importance of school to their children. The program was funded by the Charles Stewart Mott Foundation. The coordinator, Carolyn Gibson, joined CWTAH shortly thereafter. In 1981, the program received an additional grant from the Mott Foundation and expanded to the four other elementary schools in the district. Home-school coordinators in each of the schools were responsible for conducting outreach and working with families in their homes. Ms. Gibson feels that an important part of their responsibility was keeping the principals informed about their activities and making the school system aware of potential learning or adjustment problems. She notes that principals began requesting help with anticipated problems among incoming children, a sign of their growing acceptance of the program.

In 1983, a cutback in funding caused the loss of the five home-school coordinator positions. Home visits now occur only as needed. The program is school-based and focuses on educational programs for parents and a kindergarten readiness program to introduce children and parents to their teachers and schools in preparation for children's entry in the fall.

**Features**

Initially, home visits are used to assess the effectiveness of the parent-child relationship. In subsequent visits, workers bring books or activities to model interaction skills. If the parent is unable to read, picture books are available. Other approaches include taking the parent and child on a field trip within the community (to a supermarket or playground). Ms. Gibson stresses that for more needy parents this kind of activity provides an opportunity for rapport to develop among adults, and gives parents the confidence to engage with their children.

Before budget cutbacks, the program visited individual families two and three times a month for assessment and intervention. Home visits are now limited to those requested by school personnel and parents. Frequency of service varies from one to five times per year, depending on the needs of the family.

**Participants**

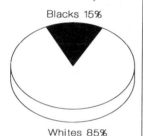

Blacks 15%

Whites 85%

During the 1987-88 school year, CWTAH served 386 children and 340 families, 15 percent black and 85 percent white. Sixty-six percent had an income under $20,000, 22 percent earned between $20,000 and $35,000, and 10 percent earned between $35,000 and $50,000.

*Carolyn Gibson suggests keeping the school board alerted to the time constraints of foundation grants so the schools and community can anticipate and make provisions for assuming financial responsibility.*

**Parent Education**

Parents are provided with information about parenting skills and child development, with a focus on social, emotional, and cognitive development. For example, parents are encouraged to read regularly with their children not only to promote reading, but to enhance the relationship between parent and child and to emphasize the importance of reading and school.

**Curriculum**

The curriculum is a combination of materials developed within the program and prepackaged curricula, such as *Systematic Training for Effective Parenting (STEP)*. Each of the educational programs is modified to meet individual needs.

**Sites**

Since home visits have been cut from the program, CWTAH activities take place in the local schools. Carolyn Gibson indicated that the schools are the best place to begin working with families, since this prepares them for their children's subsequent enrollment in kindergarten.

**Parent Involvement**

When the program was fully operational, parents actively served on the advisory council. They organized and distributed a newsletter and helped design "Fun Fair," a children's program held each year at the schools. Training for parents prepared them to volunteer as home visitors and in the six-week kindergarten orientation program each spring. Carolyn Gibson feels that one of the real strengths of the program was the involvement of parent volunteers. Since parent involvement was curtailed by funding cuts, many parents previously involved in CWTAH continue to run activities for children in the classroom.

## Outreach

Families are most likely to hear about the program either through children already enrolled in school or through the school's survey of families that is done each fall. Outreach strategies include media announcements, posters, and direct recruitment by teachers, counselors, and school administrators. The best source of referrals are parents participating in the program or teachers who have referred families in the past. Birth announcements from the local hospital target new parents (including teens), who receive program information and brochures about child development and parenting issues. The program also reaches teen parents through child development courses taught at the high school.

## Community Links

When the program first began, community agencies were invited to the parent and child development education programs to discuss their services and CWTAH made frequent referrals.

## Staff

| Job Title | PD | Vol | FT | PT | Educ Req | Status | Benefits |
|-----------|-----|-----|-----|-----|----------|--------|----------|
| Program Director | 1 | - | 1 | - | Post-Graduate Courses or Degree | K-12 Contract | Yes |
| Secretary | 1 | - | 1 | - | Some College | Other Contract | Yes |

## State/District Requirements

The full-time director is required to have teacher certification.

## Preferred Background

None.

## Employee Education and Training Represented

Infant and toddler education; prekindergarten and early childhood education; elementary education; parent educator; counseling.

## Administration

CWTAH is administered exclusively within the public education system. The program director reports to the district superintendent and works closely with the early childhood education, parent education, and guidance departments.

## Relationship to the Schools

Within the schools, CWTAH makes presentations at faculty meetings and attempts to work closely with teachers and administrators. Ms. Gibson feels that it is important to keep teachers informed about program issues and activities to secure their support. In collaboration with the kindergarten teachers, a special program for incoming kindergarten students occurs each spring.

## Funding

State child development grant, 60 percent; local and district, 40 percent.

## Funding History

In 1978, CWTAH obtained a demonstration grant from the Charles Stewart Mott Foundation and additional funding for expansion in 1981. In 1983, foundation support ended, and CWTAH experienced a 50 percent funding cut. The home-school coordinator positions in each of the schools were lost. In spite of reduction in the staff, CWTAH continues to serve the five elementary schools within District One. Carolyn Gibson suggests keeping the school board alerted to the time constraints of foundation grants so the schools and community can anticipate and make provisions for assuming financial responsibility.

**Objectives**

The primary intent of CWTAH is enrichment of child and family development. The program is designed to foster a partnership between home and school.

**Evaluation**

The last evaluation of the program was completed in 1983, as a funding requirement of the Mott Foundation. Ms. Gibson reports that evaluations are important to determine how effectively the program is meeting its goals and the needs of the population served. She indicates that evaluation should be built into the program's structure from the start, because there will be neither time nor money to get to it once the program is functioning.

**Replication**

The model developed by CWTAH was adopted and implemented by Laures, a neighboring school district. Carolyn Gibson reported that the South Carolina Department of Education was appropriating money to implement similar programs statewide. With renewed funding, Ms. Gibson hopes the full program, with its focus on prevention, will reemerge.

**Materials Available**

None.

# 4

# Home Visits for Parenting Support

The following six programs provide early childhood and parent education services to families with children from birth to ages three through five. Programs screen children to identify developmental delays early to anticipate intervention and prevent academic problems down the line. In addition, they have a strong parent focus and work to improve the home environment. Three of the programs are Parents as Teachers (PAT) initiatives in Missouri, two cite PAT as an inspiration or a model for curriculum, and one is a uniquely intensive response to the need for remediation in the early years. Parents as Teachers began in 1984 with the passage of Senate Bill 658 in Missouri, which legislated district-initiated parent education and screening services to families with children birth to age five. Burton White developed the initial curriculum, based on developmental theory and structured around a monthly home visit. Four of the directors interviewed mentioned declining test scores, increased numbers of dropouts, or children unprepared for school as motivation for implementing early childhood and family services.

# Programs in Brief

# Parents as Teachers

| | | |
|---|---|---|
| Drop-in center | Monthly home visits | Parenting/child development education |
| Resource library | Monthly group meeting | Mother/father support groups |
| Networking | Traveling library | Parent-child joint activities |
| Toy lending | Monthly newsletter | Child care info/referrals |
| | Warmline | Developmental exams/screening |

**Contact:** Frances Rittenhouse, Coordinator
**Address:** Box 846
Hollister, MO 65672
(417) 334-6482
**Established:** 1983, state legislative initiative
**Budget '88-'89:** $45,000
**Sources:** State funding authorized under Missouri Senate Bill 658; local school district contributions
**Size:** 300 families (352 children) from seven elementary school districts
**Area Served:** Seven school districts in the Hollister area
**Auspices:** Hollister Public Schools

*"A little boy came into the program at 15 months; he was not walking at the time and we had a little concern although he was still within normal developmental limits. We talked with his parents, and when his language acquisition didn't progress we suggested some intervention. They found out he was having seizures. He was subsequently put on medication and very soon after walked and talked. Now he's right on target."*
— Frances Rittenhouse

## Community

Parents as Teachers, based in Hollister, serves portions of Taney, Stone, and Barry counties in the rural Ozark Mountains along the Missouri-Arkansas border. State and national forests cover most of this 500-square-mile region. A busy tourist spot in summer, the area has a scant and in some cases erratic year-round population. Tourism forms the economic base. In winter, when tourism declines, many subsist on public welfare or unemployment compensation. Many families live in isolated areas without telephones or cars. At the same time, the area is experiencing rapid population growth with an increasing number of school-age children.

## Philosophy and Goals

PAT believes parents are their children's first teachers and offers them the opportunity to develop parenting techniques in the nonjudgmental, semistructured atmosphere of their own homes. The program cultivates a positive relationship between parents and parent educators, and teaches parents to have realistic goals for their children while offering access to resources that address developmental delays. PAT helps parents cope with stress by reducing their social isolation and giving them a second chance to learn new skills and acquire Graduate Equivalency Diplomas (GED).

## History and Origins

In 1983, Parents as First Teachers began in Hollister as a local initiative spearheaded by the superintendent. At his request, Frances Rittenhouse, then active in a parent involvement project in the Hollister Public Schools, visited Missouri's four PAT pilot sites and, together with the superintendent, presented the school board with a plan for developing a model program in Hollister. Funds then came from the state legislature and competitive grants through the Missouri Department of Education. Following Hollister's successful adoption of the program, neighboring school districts asked to join the venture.

Frances Rittenhouse attributes Hollister's sweeping acceptance of PAT in part to a previously existing parent involvement program that had established the idea of linking community, parents, and schools in the joint enterprise of raising children and enhancing family life. A community advisory board of local businessmen, farmers, and professionals and a strong core of support from the families of the local college faculty generated further community interest in PAT. Initially, parent councils in each school district shaped the program, but since then, Ms. Rittenhouse notes, "The resource center has become a community project."

**Features**

The core of the PAT program is the home visit, in which a teacher visits with a family for an hour, encouraging interaction and understanding between parent and child. Although the state and national PAT model requires only four home visits a year, the Hollister program visits families monthly. Teachers offer suggestions for activities that capitalize on the home environment and the objects found in it to stimulate ideas for parent-child interaction. Based philosophically on Burton White's seven stages of child development, monthly lessons emphasize realistic expectations and age-appropriate activities for children. Written materials offer backup information to parents and suggest phase-related skill-building through play to foster language acquisition, fine and gross motor skills, sensory discrimination, and so on. The program screens children for developmental lags and helps parents seek outside remediation.

**Participants**

The state requires PAT to serve 30 percent of the eligible population, which includes all families with children birth to five living within the seven elementary school districts. In 1988, 590 parents participated in PAT; of these less than 1 percent were single parents and 10 percent were teen parents.

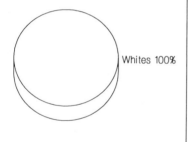

Whites 100%

*Initially, Parent Councils in each school district shaped the program, but since then, Ms. Rittenhouse notes, "The resource center has become a community project."*

**Parent Education**

Parents are taught how to use their homes and objects found within it to stimulate early learning. They attend an evening lecture and discussion series and have access to literacy tutoring and to SAT and ACT preparation materials.

**Curriculum**

PAT uses the curriculum prepared by the Parents as Teachers National Center in St. Louis, implemented by state mandate throughout Missouri.

**Sites**

PAT operates out of six area schools and has a free-standing resource center in a double-wide trailer on the grounds of the Hollister Elementary School. In addition to a resource library and drop-in center, the trailer houses PAT's office and separate play and learning areas for older siblings. In the summer all activities go on here; in the winter, workshops and parent discussions take place at neighborhood schools.

Space allocation has been stable since 1983, but the size of the county and the poverty and isolation of many families prevent frequent use of the resource center by all but four of the seven school districts. Other parents and children come only for scheduled monthly play times. One school is planning to develop its own satellite resource center in an available classroom.

**Parent Involvement**

Parents have been involved in PAT since its start-up, serving on the community advisory board to generate widespread community support for the program. Parents develop ideas for an evening speaker series, work as volunteers in the resource center, supervise play areas during drop-in hours, and help with screening activities.

**Outreach**

Word-of-mouth is the most successful outreach mechanism for PAT, but other strategies include screening in neighborhood preschools, sending videotapes and invitations to eligible families, distributing brochures in clinics, doctors' offices and hospitals, and displaying posters in Laundromats, utility offices, and city halls. A clothing exchange in the resource center also attracts parents. The schools, county health departments, Department of Family Services, and state regional developmental centers make referrals to PAT. Although PAT offers free child care for those attending evening workshops, it has been less successful in reaching single and teen parents. Outreach to teens has included dispensing with the conventional PAT logo; new posters targeted to adolescent parents resemble record album covers and carry a short message in small letters. This year, in an effort to reach isolated families, the program instituted a traveling library that brings books to families who have little access to outside resources. According to Frances Rittenhouse, this has been an "overwhelming success."

**Staff**

| Job Title | PD | Vol | FT | PT | Educ Req | Status | Benefits |
|---|---|---|---|---|---|---|---|
| Program Coordinator/ Parent Educator | 1 | - | 1 | - | College Degree | Other Contract | Yes |
| Parent Educators | 2 | - | 1 | 1 | Some College | Other Contract | Yes |

**State/District Requirements**

Parent educators are required to complete a state training program offered by the PAT National Center in St. Louis.

**Preferred Background**

For parent educators, two years experience working with young children, strong knowledge of early childhood development, active listening skills, and a compassionate, nonjudgmental style.

**Employee Education and Training Represented**

Infant and toddler education; prekindergarten and early childhood education; adult literacy; parent educator; health and nutrition; psychology; child development and family studies.

**Administration**

Locally, PAT is administered by the Hollister Public School District. The director reports to the superintendent of schools, and the program develops curriculum in conjunction with the divisions of Early Childhood Education and Elementary Instruction and the parent councils in each school. In addition, staff prepare kindergarten teachers for incoming students and have access to the expertise of the special education teachers, speech therapists, and guidance counselors. By state mandate, the program has access to materials for assessment, screening, and referrals. An advisory council, composed of paid staff, program participants, public school personnel, representatives from public and private agencies, and residents of the community at large, meets twice yearly and works to increase community awareness of the program, recruit participants, and enlist volunteers. The Missouri Department of Education, through its national center for Parents as Teachers, monitors local sites.

## Relationship to the Schools

In the rural Ozark Mountains, Frances Rittenhouse has made sure PAT not only belongs to the schools, but to the community as a whole. PAT's presence in the schools has made administrators more accountable to parents, and parents in turn have grown more aware of education issues in their district. PAT encourages parents to register to vote, so that when local levy questions appear on the ballot, they are ready to vote. Usually they vote pro-school, pro-children.

## Community Links

The advisory board is PAT's strongest link to the community. Agreements with outside agencies formalize information and referral exchange and joint ventures. PAT helped start a development center for handicapped children in the county. In an effort to acquaint people living in remote areas with its services, the program brings families with identified needs to visit the center. PAT collaborates with the Literacy Council by making the center available for tutoring. One room in the resource center resembles a school library, stocked with high school textbooks and ACT and SAT preparation materials, which are available to parents who want to earn the GED. Parenting and child development materials have been simplified for easier comprehension.

## Funding

State legislative appropriation, 96 percent; local school district, 4 percent.

## Funding History

Last year local school districts contributed 4 percent of the budget. Hollister funds the resource center, and other school districts are helping to pick up the bills for utilities, postage, telephone, and mileage. Frances Rittenhouse feels the program is "very secure" and attributes the good rapport between PAT and the Hollister Public School District to her monthly attendance and annual presentation at school board meetings.

*PAT encourages parents to register to vote, so that when local levy questions appear on the ballot, they are ready to vote. Usually they vote pro-school, pro-children.*

## Objectives

PAT hopes to give parents realistic expectations for their children's development, to enhance their self-esteem and ability to cope with daily stress, to encourage their involvement in the schools and in their children's learning, and to reduce the incidence of developmental delays in young children.

## Evaluation

The program coordinator and a state-level trainer evaluate PAT annually. In 1987, the home visit program and parent meetings received an "excellent" assessment; record keeping and school and community involvement and support were rated "good."

**Replication**

Representatives from 26 states have come to Missouri to learn about Parents as Teachers. Within the state, Frances Rittenhouse is a "trainer of trainers" and the regional coordinator of PAT.

**Materials Available**

PAT's curriculum can be obtained from the Parents as Teachers National Center in St. Louis, Missouri, listed in the Resource Section of this guide.

# Parents as Teachers

Part of Early Education Services of Brattleboro

| | | |
|---|---|---|
| Home visits | Health/nutrition education | Parenting/child development education |
| Toy lending | Resource library | Parent-child joint activities |
| Preschool | Crisis intervention | Mother/couple support groups |
| Warmline | Newborn workshops | Community services info/referral |
| | Child care info/referral | |

| | |
|---|---|
| **Contact:** | Judie Jerald, Director |
| **Address:** | Powers House |
| | 218 Canal Street |
| | Brattleboro, VT 05301 |
| | (802) 254-3742 |
| **Established:** | 1987, local initiative |
| **Budget '88-'89:** | $101,558 |
| **Sources:** | Special local tax, state funds, foundation grants, in-kind contributions, special events and fundraising |
| **Size:** | 103 families (50 to 60 at a time) |
| **Service Area:** | Windham County, Vermont |
| **Auspices:** | Brattleboro Public Schools |
| **1990 Respondent:** | Winsome Hamilton, Director |

## Community

Parents as Teachers (PAT), which is part of Early Education Services and not affiliated with the Missouri Parents as Teachers program, is situated in Brattleboro, a small town in southern Vermont with a lively, highly concentrated business district. In addition to a population of artists, faculty connected with Marlboro College and other professionals in Brattleboro, the town and outlying area has a substantial number of people living in poverty, whose level of education and expectations for their children are low.

## Philosophy and Goals

PAT's goals focus on parents and children together: the program seeks to promote the healthy development of young children and effective communication between parents and children. In addition, it seeks to help parents develop the confidence to make positive social, economic, and personal changes in their lives.

## History and Origins

The town of Brattleboro established the Parents as Teachers program in response to an alarming increase in the number of children with test scores well below the national average (the statistics rose from 20 percent in 1982 to 37 percent a few years later). The school district researched various school-based early intervention models, including the Missouri Parents as Teachers program, and hired a consultant to make community-wide presentations about the need for parent education. As a start-up suggestion, Dot Marsden, founding director, recommends an understanding of local politics and the ability to educate the community about the need for a family support program. In Brattleboro, 140 local business persons who served as town representatives voted on the budget that included PAT. Ms. Marsden had to rally support to create not only consensus, but active commitment to the program.

**Features**

Vermont's PAT program is based on Missouri's Parents as Teachers model. Home visits to families with children birth to age three form the core of the program. Ancillary support services include a toy- and book-lending library, Saturday workshops for parents with newborns and nine-month-olds, and support groups. PAT also operates the Early Education Initiative Preschool funded by the state for impoverished children at risk for developmental delays.

Home visitors meet with children and their parents, either weekly, biweekly, or monthly to educate parents about child development and to encourage interaction in play and learning activities. They also teach parents to make books and toys, bring activities for siblings, and frequently leave books behind for parents to share with their children in the intervening week. Educators are flexible and responsive to family needs. In extreme cases, says Dot Marsden, the home visitor's role becomes one of caregiver: she may have to wake parents up, help clothe and feed an infant, or extend the scheduled hour for an expedition to the park or children's museum. At Saturday morning workshops staff members offer presentations and encourage parents to talk about their children's development and establishing trust in the early years.

**Participants**

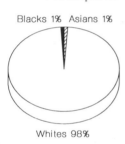

Blacks 1%   Asians 1%

Whites 98%

In 1987-88, PAT served 156 children (70 percent of the eligible population), 103 mothers, and 35 fathers. Fifteen percent were teen parents. Approximately half the families use PAT services several times a week, and the remainder, weekly. Children participating in the Early Education Initiative Preschool must meet income guidelines and be at risk for abuse and neglect or developmental delays.

*"Ideally, says Ms. Marsden, PAT should have its own free-standing facility, preferably in one of the less affluent sections of town, to make it more accessible to low-income families."*

**Parent Education**

Parent education goes on during home visits and Saturday workshops via group discussions, handouts, and presentations. Dot Marsden notes, "We're trying to help parents understand children. We hand out lots of materials concerning specific levels of child development and materials in response to parents' expressed concerns, such as setting limits, imposing discipline, age-appropriate activities, and coping with home situations."

**Curriculum**

PAT has an eclectic approach to curriculum. It uses the Missouri Parents as Teachers materials and High/Scope's cognitively-oriented early education curricula to build a program based on the developmental level and individual needs of the family.

**Sites**

Sites of service delivery include participants' homes, the public elementary schools, three preschools, and a church. Two of the preschools provide space for the Early Education Initiative Preschool. PAT's main office is located in Powers House, a building owned by the public schools which also houses special education and Chapter 1 staff, elementary school nurses, and special services personnel. The program provides transportation to preschool and parent educators offer rides to PAT events. The director feels the commute takes time away from other families who need PAT's services. Ideally, says Ms. Marsden, PAT should have its own free-standing facility, preferably in one of the less affluent sections of town, to make it more accessible to low-income families.

**Parent Involvement**

Three parents serve on PAT's advisory board, which meets monthly to approve staff hiring, budget, program services, and curriculum. The program relies on the active involvement of middle-income parents; families living on marginal incomes appear less willing or able to give the time, observes Ms. Marsden.

**Outreach**

In its first year, PAT sought and easily got referrals from social service agencies. In 1988, it sent out letters and brochures to all families with newborns, the Special Supplemental Food Program for Women, Infants, and Children (WIC), pediatricians, and public health home visitors. PAT reaches across all socioeconomic lines in Windham County, says the director, who feels that her program lacks sufficient staff to visit more than 37 percent of the eligible families with newborns. In addition, the program invites all families with children under age five to most Saturday workshops. All three elementary school principals include news about PAT in their weekly newsletters. School counselors make direct referrals; kindergarten and first grade teachers inform families with infants about the program.

**Staff**

| Job Title | PD | Vol | FT | PT | Educ Req | Status | Benefits |
|---|---|---|---|---|---|---|---|
| Program Director | 1 | - | 1 | - | Post Graduate Courses or Degree | Other Contract | Yes |
| Home Visitor/Parent Educators | 3 | - | - | 3 | High School Diploma | Hourly Contract | Yes |
| Secretary | 1 | - | - | 1 | High School Diploma | Hourly Contract | No |
| Psychologist/ Consultant | 1 | - | - | 1 | Post Graduate Courses or Degree | Hourly Non-Contract | No |

**State/District Requirements**

None.

**Preferred Background**

For the director, administrative experience in early childhood development and education, fundraising coordination, staff training, and public relations skills; for home visitors and parent educators, maturity, warmth, a nonjudgmental and positive attitude toward children, willingness to learn, and flexibility.

**Employee Education and Training Represented**

Infant and toddler education; prekindergarten and early childhood education; elementary education; special education; parent educator; child care; home economics; psychology; counseling; child development and family studies; development and fundraising; research and evaluation.

**Administration**

PAT works closely with the special education department of the public schools. The director reports to the assistant superintendent of schools in the Windham Southeast Supervisory Union, which consists of six towns, each with their own elementary schools and school boards, and one consolidated high school. Program administration occurs exclusively within the schools.

## Relationship to the Schools

PAT is sponsored by the schools and in a time of budget cuts the director feels this financial commitment represents an unusual show of support and confidence in the family initiative. PAT makes presentations to the schools and gets strong support from the kindergarten teachers and school principals. Dot Marsden has been invited to do case counseling for specific kindergartners and routinely meets with the Chapter 1 director to discuss recommendations for the 20 children involved in the preschool initiative. She claims that PAT's links to the public schools make families more receptive to home visitors than they would be if PAT were closely allied to social services.

## Community Links

PAT works closely with a variety of community agencies including Brattleboro Child Development and the Winston Prouty Center, both of which provide space and transportation for the preschool program, Brattleboro Family Counseling, Vermont Public Health, and Brattleboro Youth Services. If several agencies deliver services to the same family, they will meet every six weeks to discuss goals and objectives, and to avoid overlapping services. Agencies share information, referrals, and services. The agencies most directly involved in PAT have representatives on the advisory board. Dot Marsden observes that as the program has received more funding, tension over turf has risen. Maintaining a good collaborative relationship with Head Start, for instance, requires mediation.

## Funding

Local levy, 50 percent; Vermont Department of Education Early Education Initiative funds, 30 percent ($30,000 to fund preschool for 16 to 20 eligible three- and four-year-olds living in Brattleboro); foundations and private agencies, 15 percent; in-kind contributions, 4 percent; and special events and fundraising, 1 percent.

## In-Kind Resources

Brattleboro Town Schools provide space and facilities; administrative, clerical, and fiscal support; materials, supplies, and access to equipment.

## Funding History

In 1987, the town representatives voted to fund the final proposal for PAT with $45,000 from the local levy. The Turrell Foundation contributed an additional $25,000 to fulfill a $70,000 budget. PAT is seeking state and federal grants to expand services in the community and to develop a formal evaluation strategy. It is hoping to qualify for a new free-standing facility through the Vermont Department of Human Services, which is establishing parent-child centers across the state. Funding is up 30 percent from the first year of operation.

## Objectives

PAT aims to provide parent education and social and educational opportunities for children unable to attend private daycare or preschool programs. PAT works with other community agencies to give children and families all the support necessary for healthy functioning.

## Evaluation

Town taxpayers require evaluation procedures. Parents fill out a family satisfaction assessment form provided by the Vermont Department of Education. Preschool children take the McCarthy IQ tests. Pre- and post-attitudes are measured by the Minnesota Child Development Profile. Formal evaluation of the program's objective to teach parents to become better caregivers is a difficult task, notes Ms. Marsden.

This program used Parents as Teachers in Missouri as a model.

Consultation, staff training, and record-keeping forms are available from the program.

# Parents and Children Together (PACT)

*"What is success?" asks PACT Coordinator Mary Haust. She is satisfied to know that PACT has made a difference in the lives of families. She cites the example of a highly dysfunctional family that had been ordered by the courts to seek parent education. At the beginning of their three years with PACT, the parents were substance abusers. Now the father has "dried out," because he has decided that parenting is more important to him than drugs. Ms. Haust feels he has become more patient and less abusive toward his children and can be a good parent even in times of stress.*

Networking
Adult literacy
Resource library
Newsletter
Warmline

Health/nutrition education
Mother support group
Monthly home visits
Toy/book lending
GED preparation
Drop-in center

Parenting/child development education
Parent-child joint activities
Community services info/referral
Monthly parent meetings
Child care info/referral
Developmental exams/screening

| | |
|---|---|
| **Contact:** | Mary Haust, Project Coordinator |
| **Address:** | MacArthur School |
| | 1123 Vestal Avenue |
| | Binghamton, NY 13903 |
| | (607) 762-8197 |
| **Established:** | 1987, local initiative |
| **Budget '88-'89:** | $98,000 |
| **Sources:** | New York State Department of Education: Schools as Community Sites |
| **Size:** | 180 families |
| **Area Served:** | Binghamton, New York |
| **Auspices:** | School District |

## Community

Parents and Children Together (PACT) serves residents of Binghamton, a small city in central New York. As the area's industrial base declines, Binghamton's population is steadily decreasing, and fewer young families are moving into the area. Only an estimated one in four homes has school-age children. In general, the city schools serve a low- to middle-income population. The nearby state university gives research support to the school system, particularly in the area of adjustment to primary school.

## Philosophy and Goals

PACT considers parents the first and most important educators of children, yet recognizes that parents need appropriate developmental information to perform this task. PACT believes that despite the high incidence of dropouts and delinquency, every child starts out with a great deal of parental love. The program's role is to provide intervention and education as early as possible to nurture family and child development from the beginning.

## History and Origins

In 1983, the New York State Board of Regents strengthened its requirements for high school graduation. School administrators in Binghamton suspected that borderline students, unable to pass the new competency tests and unwilling to undertake required remediation, might drop out. Indeed, by 1986, this proved true. Nathan Bell, the school district's director of research, planning, and evaluation, was inspired by Burton White's New Parents as Teachers model to look at the early years as the origin of later school difficulties. Mr. Bell submitted a proposal to the Department of Occupational Education, outlining PACT, a preschool and parenting program based on home visits. He was awarded $150,000, of which $98,000 was allotted to the PACT component. The original grant also provided funding for a community resource center, shared by PACT and other district agencies. Mr. Bell worked independently to plan and fund a program based on his concern for families; he feels state initiatives should eliminate the need for locally started programs.

**Features**

PACT offers monthly home visits to parents of children birth to age three. During these visits, parents and educators observe the child and share appropriate developmental information. Educators also provide information about child care and community services. Screenings for vision and hearing as well as social, language, and general development are performed on a regular basis. Parents are included in the administration of the screening and receive the assessment results. Throughout the year, parents may attend group meetings offered at the community resource center. The center houses a lending library of parenting and child development books, videotapes, and age-appropriate toys. PACT distributes a seasonal newsletter, *PACT Digest*, which announces program events and includes excerpts from national publications with information relevant to parenting. It also suggests parent-child activities and instructions for making age-appropriate toys.

PACT chose to provide home visits in an effort to meet people on their own ground and out of concern for the difficulty young families might have in coming to the center. For families on marginal incomes, the staff provides transportation to group meetings by cab or bus.

**Participants**

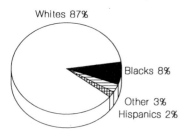

Whites 87%

Blacks 8%

Other 3%
Hispanics 2%

The program draws on the city school population, which includes many high-risk families. Alcoholism and substance abuse are common risk factors among participants. Coordinator Mary Haust estimates that 45 percent of PACT participants receive public assistance, 30 percent are either illiterate or poorly educated, and 40 percent have an annual income below $10,000. In 1987-88, PACT performed 501 screenings and visited the homes of 157 families, 40 percent of whom were single parents and 10 percent teen parents.

*Teachers spend a lot of time simply building a trusting relationship with parents and, as many families exhibit extreme stress, teachers may find themselves dealing with crises that preempt scheduled topics of discussion.*

**Parent Education**

While typical home visits focus on a single topic, such as teething, teachers begin every visit by checking children's general development, reviewing appropriate expectations with parents, and recommending activities and toys. PACT teaches parents to observe their children's development closely and to create an environment which fosters the acquisition of the skills and self-esteem necessary for a good start in school. *PACT Digest* offers safety and parenting tips and guidance in choosing age-appropriate activities. In 1988, PACT held 31 group meetings, ranging in size from a handful of parents to 15 families. This year, topics included toilet training, positive discipline, language development, play, sleeping patterns, and working parents. PACT teachers note that reading and language development are not popular elective topics with parents, so they try to work that information into the home visits, modeling ways in which illiterate or undereducated parents can improvise stories from picture books.

**Curriculum**

The PACT curriculum is based on the New Parents as Teachers model and adapts materials based on individual family needs, family structure, and literacy level. The Denver Development Chart provides norms of child development. There is a 36-month curriculum plan, but PACT teachers have found that they must be flexible in presenting it. Teachers spend a lot of time simply building a trusting relationship with parents and, as many families exhibit extreme stress, teachers may find themselves dealing with crises that preempt scheduled topics of discussion.

**Sites**

PACT's educational services are delivered to families in their homes; screening occurs either in homes or at the public elementary school. The community resource center houses the program's offices, resource library, and group meeting rooms.

**Parent Involvement**

Parents are involved in every aspect of PACT. They participate in home visits, attend group meetings, frequent the resource library, and even participate in screening. Three parents sit on the advisory council.

**Outreach**

PACT serves 27 percent of the eligible population and would eventually like to broaden its participant base, although staff are working to capacity. PACT sends humorous cards to parents of newborns in the community and follows up with a phone call. Outreach efforts halt temporarily when a waiting list develops for enrollment. The Departments of Social Services and Public Health help PACT locate impoverished families.

**Staff**

| Job Title | PD | Vol | FT | PT | Educ Req | Status | Benefits |
|---|---|---|---|---|---|---|---|
| Project Coordinator | 1 | - | 1 | - | College Degree | Other Contract | Yes |
| Clerk-Typist | 1 | - | 1 | - | High School Diploma | Other Contract | Yes |
| Parent Educator | 4 | - | 4 | - | College Degree | Other Contract | Yes |

**State/District Requirements**

Parent educators must be licensed teacher assistants.

**Preferred Background**

Parent educators should have parenting experience and tolerance for a variety of lifestyles; women are preferred.

**Employee Education and Training Represented**

Infant and toddler education; elementary education; parent educator; medicine; social work; child development and family studies; research and evaluation.

**Administration**

The project coordinator reports to the district director of research, planning, and evaluation and to the advisory council. The latter is composed of public school teachers and administrators, representatives of public and private agencies, program participants, and several community members. The council serves in an advisory capacity only.

In an effort to serve all eligible families and to maintain a record of children who have received services, PACT is designing a computerized case-management system to identify all children in the community eligible for the prekindergarten program.

## Relationship to the Schools

The program receives referrals from the school nurse, but otherwise functions separately from the schools' K to 12 departments. Nathan Bell, now PACT's director, recognizes that the school district may want to know how state-funded community programs like PACT will fit into the school organization. The teachers' unions, for instance, are uneasy about licensed K to 12 teachers who are technically overqualified for the job of parent educator. To curtail anxiety, PACT maintains a low profile, confident that it is difficult to argue with a program that is succeeding.

*Mary Haust advises program coordinators to keep in close touch with related agencies. She suggests making frequent phone calls until it seems natural to be calling back and forth.*

## Community Links

According to Ms. Haust, when PACT began she expected that private and public agencies and private preschools would express territorial concerns. To head off conflict and establish good relations, PACT hosted an interagency breakfast. Staff visited agencies to make sure they were not duplicating services, and checked that the Department of Public Health was giving compatible information to families. Mary Haust advises program coordinators to keep in close touch with related agencies. She suggests making frequent phone calls until it seems natural to be calling back and forth.

## Funding

State funds, 100 percent.

## In-Kind Resources

The school district provides facilities, materials, and equipment; the state and Department of Public Health provide consultation and staff development; local professionals donate screening services; and the Urban League provides some transportation services.

## Funding History

The state department administering PACT's funding has changed several times in the last two years. Nathan Bell says PACT must be attentive to the different interests of the various funding administrators. For example, the original request for proposals, under the administration of Community Renewal, asked that proposed community centers be located in a low socioeconomic area. Accordingly, the school system chose a neighborhood on the south side of town, and although the site is not easily accessible to the community at large, this choice helped secure state funding.

## Objectives

PACT anticipates that parents will have increased confidence and a more cooperative attitude toward the school, fewer developmental delays should go undetected, and children should enter kindergarten with improved socialization and language skills.

Ms. Haust maintains reasonable expectations for families, recognizing that some may always be under stress and will need constant monitoring. But she also thinks PACT families develop a more trusting relationship with social services and the school system and hopes this will continue down the line.

| | |
|---|---|
| **Evaluation** | Program staff performed an in-house evaluation at the end of the first year of service to assess the degree of parent satisfaction. Parents gave PACT a high approval rating, saying they felt more confident and found home visits reinforcing. They proposed changes that PACT is working to implement, such as publishing a clearer explanation of the screening process. PACT intends to perform a formal evaluation at the end of the three-year cycle to consider parental attitudes and children's outcomes in the areas of language and cognitive growth. In addition to the formal evaluation, PACT anticipates favorable feedback from teachers when the first set of three-year-olds enters kindergarten. |
| **Replication** | PACT is based on the Parents as Teachers model used in Missouri. |
| **Materials Available** | None. |

# Parent Early Education Center

| | | |
|---|---|---|
| Networking | Health/nutrition education | Parenting/child development education |
| Resource library | Child care info/referral | Community services info/referral |
| Parent groups | Monthly home visits | Teen parent groups |
| Newsletter | Parent-child joint activities | Developmental exams/screening |

**Contact:** Jean Tucker, Coordinator
**Address:** Newark High School
East Delaware Avenue
Newark, DE 19711
(302) 454-5955
**Established:** 1987, school initiative
**Budget '88-'89:** $107,800
**Source:** Section 166 of Delaware state budget
**Size:** 152 families
**Area Served:** Christina and Red Clay School Districts
**Auspices:** Christina School District Instruction Department
**1990 Respondent:** Mary H. Stokes

*One participating mother of a fifteen-month-old had an alcoholic husband and friends who were 'party animals' with careless lifestyles that were not conducive to raising children. She has learned to resist the negative influences of her environment and has taken charge of her son's early education by creating a strong and nurturing home life for him. Recently, she took custody of her three-year-old nephew and expressed shock at how little he knew about colors, shapes, and numbers. She had begun to take it for granted that exposure to learning and intellectual stimulation is an important part of childrearing.*

## Community

The Christina School District has approximately 17,000 students in an area of 90,000 residents. The district includes the cities of Wilmington and Newark and the surrounding suburbs. Industry and chemical companies form the economic base and source of livelihood for this community. The district operates under a 1978 court-ordered desegregation plan; the school population is approximately 25 percent minority and 75 percent white.

## Philosophy and Goals

The Parenting Early Education Center (PEEC) offers information, enrichment, and support to parents to indirectly improve the quality of life for children. PEEC uses the Parents as Teachers (PAT) curriculum, which is committed to enhancing and reinforcing parent-child interaction from birth through a series of home visits. Developmental examinations and screening facilitate early or preventive treatment for children.

## History and Origins

Seventeen years ago, Joe Cobb, an elementary school principal, founded Project Uplift, a school-based parent education program, in response to the wide variation in the readiness skills of incoming kindergarten students. Project Uplift consisted of school-based group meetings and originally received money from private and federal sources. When those funds ran out, Mr. Cobb secured funding from the state legislature, which created a separate section in the state budget to support the project, then renamed it the Parent Early Education Center.

In 1986, members of the Wilmington Junior League saw a presentation of the PAT program. They approached Joe Cobb, who was anxious to expand PEEC with a home visiting component. According to PEEC's coordinator Mary Stokes, "It was a case of perfect timing."

In 1987, PEEC adopted the PAT curriculum throughout the Christina and Red Clay school districts. PEEC's state funding was switched over to fund its new home visit format. The Wilmington Junior League provides a strong legislative lobby for this program at the state house.

**Features**

PEEC's format, based on Missouri's PAT model, includes monthly home visits and evening group meetings. Home visits are scheduled at the families' convenience, and materials are personalized to children and their environments. Group meetings take place in an elementary school. They address parents' concerns and provide the opportunity for formal instruction in child development. PEEC is looking into the need for child care during meetings.

PEEC also serves teen parents in group meetings that take place during the school day in the high school. Meetings are either conducted during 30-minute lunch periods or held when administrators allow students to be pulled out of classes to attend them.

**Participants**

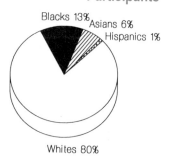

Blacks 13%  Asians 6%
Hispanics 1%

Whites 80%

To be eligible, parents of children from birth to age three must reside in the Christina School District or in the neighboring one of Red Clay. Because of the high pregnancy rate among students at the three vocational high schools that serve the county, administrators asked PEEC to set up a program to meet the parenting needs of these teenagers. PEEC had been interested in extending its services to teens. Ms. Stokes notes, "We saw it as a good partnership."

In 1987-88, 152 families were served; 20 percent single parents; 14 percent teen parents; 56 percent low- to middle-income families; and 23 percent earned between $35,000 and $50,000. PEEC serves 8 to 9 percent of the eligible population.

**Parent Education**

The PAT curriculum presents parents with the basic concepts of child development and teaches them how to stimulate early learning. Home visitors model appropriate behaviors for parents and show them how to make the home a learning environment. Group meetings provide supplemental information and support and allow parents to share their experiences with one another.

**Curriculum**

The curriculum combines prepackaged materials obtained from the PAT National Center in St. Louis, Missouri (see Resource Section) with those developed in house.

**Sites**

PEEC has had to move three times in the last two years. It began in Joe Cobb's elementary school and soon moved to a social service agency, the Hudson Center, for one year. Presently, PEEC is housed in Newark High School where Ms. Stokes says she expects to stay.

**Parent Involvement**

In addition to regular participation, parents also provide an ongoing evaluation of services by filling out frequent questionnaires.

**Outreach**

PEEC alerts new parents to the availability of its services with a brochure and follows up with a phone call. Health and nutrition clinics and some pediatricians receive PEEC's informational brochures to pass on to their clients. In addition, staff members make presentations at local high schools and teen pregnancy programs. Public health nurses also refer families to the program.

| Job Title | PD | Vol | FT | PT | Educ Req | Status | Benefits |
|---|---|---|---|---|---|---|---|
| Parent Educators | 8 | - | - | 8 | College Degree | Hourly Non-Contract | No |
| Coordinator | 1 | - | - | 1 | College Degree | Hourly Non-Contract | No |
| Secretary | 1 | - | - | 1 | High School Diploma | Hourly Contract | No |

**State/District Requirements**

For parent educators, a bachelor's degree in a field related to early childhood education and training in the PAT curriculum.

**Preferred Background**

Preference is given to applicants who are parents.

**Employee Education and Training Represented**

Prekindergarten and early childhood education; elementary education; special education; speech therapy; psychology; social work.

**Administration**

PEEC is administered exclusively within the public education system. The coordinator reports to an administrative assistant, who in turn reports to the assistant superintendent for instruction in the Christina School District.

**Relationship to the Schools**

Mary Stokes feels that the expansion of PEEC was readily accepted by the school system because staff felt the new services "fulfilled a previously recognized need." She thinks it helped that the original program was a school-based initiative.

**Community Links**

Ms. Stokes views PEEC's relationships with pediatricians, clinics, nutrition clinics, adolescent pregnancy programs, and public health nurses as a "partnership" and says that PEEC's educationally based preventive approach "doesn't threaten anyone's hegemony."

**Funding**

State, 100 percent.

**Funding History**

PEEC's funds, separate from the state education budget, come directly from Section 166 of the Delaware state budget, a funding source specifically designated for parent education programs in Delaware. Under these funds, programs can make discretionary decisions such as adding or dropping services. In 1989, PEEC was the only program using Section 166 funds.

*Mary Stokes feels that the expansion of PEEC was readily accepted by the school system because staff felt the new services "fulfilled a previously recognized need."*

**Objectives**

PEEC aims to involve parents with their children's learning; to improve children's language, cognitive, and social skills; to help parents enjoy parenting and view the public schools more favorably.

| Evaluation | A formal evaluation is in the planning stages. PEEC is a relatively new program, with an ongoing, informal evaluation process, soliciting parents' comments during home visits and evening meetings. PEEC tailors its program to their responses. |
| --- | --- |
| Replication | PEEC replicated the Missouri PAT model. |
| Materials Available | None. |

# Parkway Early Childhood Program

| | | |
|---|---|---|
| Home visits | Teen parent program | Parenting/child development education |
| Drop-in center | Health/nutrition education | Developmental exams/screening |
| Newsletter | Parent-child joint activities | Community services info/referral |
| Networking | Resource library | Preschool-daycare info/referral |
| Speaker series | PTO parent support group | |

**Contact:** Linda Hamberg, Coordinator, Early Childhood Education

**Address:** Parkway School District
14605 Clayton Road
Ballwin, MO 63011
(314) 391-4783

**Established:** 1985, state initiative

**Budget '88-'89:** $368,467

**Sources:** Missouri Department of Education as per Senate Bill 658 and local school district funds

**Size:** 2,852 families

**Area Served:** Parkway School District

**Auspices:** Parkway Public Schools

*The mother of an eighteen-month-old child feared her son was autistic and obtained a diagnostic work-up from a developmental pediatrician. The tests were inconclusive and the parents were distraught, searching for answers and further resources. The staff worked with the parents throughout the process and referred them to a speech and language specialist. The specialist concluded that the child was not autistic but needed intensive language therapy. She is currently teaching the parents to work with their child.*

## Community

The Parkway School District covers 68 square miles in the western corridor of St. Louis County. Its largely white, middle- to upper-middle-income population includes the often transient families of corporate executives. The Parkway Early Childhood Program is situated in the southern part of the district.

## Philosophy and Goals

The Parkway Early Childhood Program considers parents their children's first and most influential teachers and believes that parents who receive timely information and guidance can best foster their children's development and learning.

## History and Origins

In 1984, the Missouri Senate passed Bill 658, the Early Childhood Development Act, legislating parent education and screening services for parents of children from birth to age five through the Parents as Teachers (PAT) program. In 1985, revised legislation mandated and funded services for children birth to age three. Anticipating the mandate, Parkway established a task force of teachers, school administrators, and community professionals to study the need for early childhood programs. The task force recommended, but did not initiate, a series of programs even broader than the state would later require. In the fall of 1985, Parkway began offering Parents as Teachers, providing home visits, child screening, and group meetings to parents of children birth to age three. In the program's second year, the district itself funded the Three- and Four-Year-Old Developmental Screening Program. Late that year, the district faced budgetary cutbacks and parents worried that the Parkway Early Childhood Program would be affected. Others were concerned that their two-year-olds would "age out" of the home visit program. Parents formed an advocacy group called the Early Childhood Organization (EChO), whose support encouraged the district to maintain the Parkway program's funding and expand full services to parents of three- and four-year-olds. In 1987, Parkway also began the Teen Parent Program to serve young parents in high school.

**Parkway PAT** offers four home visits and one mandatory group parent session per year to families with children from birth to age three. PAT also provides hearing, vision, language development, and health screening through the **Three- and Four-Year-Old Program** to locate prekindergarten children with potential learning problems who might benefit from special education intervention. Parents are invited to a monthly speaker series treating parenting, reading, and school-readiness issues, and to one-hour parent-child sessions to learn about developmentally appropriate activities. Teen parents have the option of enrolling in the PAT program, in which case they are entitled to a fifth home visit instead of the group meeting, or they may choose the in-school **Teen Parent Program,** consisting of weekly or biweekly group meetings during school hours that provide parent education and support for pregnant and parenting teens. Parkway maintains a file of current articles and information on early childhood and parenting topics, available to parents at the Parkway Early Childhood Center. From 1985-88, the Parkway Early Childhood Program had a drop-in center for child play, parent networking, and information, which closed due to lack of available space. Parkway expects funds from a recent bond issue to expand its program and reinstate **Drop-In and Play** in 1989-90. The program recently piloted a **Fee-based Program** that parents and children attend together, with classes arranged according to the child's age.

**Participants**

In 1987-88, PAT served 1,192 families; the Three- and Four-Year-Old-Program served 1,503 families; the Teen Parent Program saw 37 teens; the Fee-based Program, 120 families. The state mandates service delivery to 30 percent of the eligible families each year before PAT can compile a waiting list. The program has consistently exceeded the ever-increasing quotas; its waiting list has reached as high as 310 families. Indeed, any Parkway resident may consult the center for referrals and information.

Whites 91%
Blacks 2%
Asians 5%
Hispanics 2%

*The intensity of parent involvement in the Parkway program through EChO and the Parent Council often carries parents into a long-term commitment to the schools.*

**Parent Education**

The parent education components in all four subprograms provide information about child development, health and nutrition, and parenting. The format encourages parents to interact to reduce their sense of isolation. Parent educators and the screening team carefully review the results of screening tests with parents and advise them to observe their children closely. If indicated, staff connect families to resources for remediation, follow up on referrals, and encourage parents to become advocates for their children.

**Curriculum**

Parkway uses the basic curriculum provided by the Parents as Teachers National Center in Missouri. Staff members supplement it with current articles, other published curricula, and their own expertise.

Harvard Family Research Project

**Sites**

The Parkway Early Childhood Program delivers services at 1,192 homes, four high schools, and the Early Childhood Center in Ballwin. The Early Childhood Center, a former elementary school building currently used as an annex for an adjoining high school, houses the program's offices, the Three- and Four-Year-Old Program site, and the PAT health screening. In April 1989, the program opened an additional site in the northern end of the district, which houses the fee-based program and part of the adult education component for parents of three- and four-year-olds.

**Parent Involvement**

The Parkway program has a parent council, designed to unify the large Parkway school district and increase awareness of the Parkway Early Childhood Program in the community. Council members represent each of the 17 elementary school attendance areas and meet three times a year with the program coordinator and a staff representative to make suggestions for program improvement. Although the parent council has no decision-making powers, each team serves as a link to the specific neighborhood it serves. EChO, an advocacy group run by parents, provides support to the Parkway Early Childhood Program, its center, and staff. This districtwide parent-teacher organization has high visibility with the board of education and district administrators. EChO does fundraising, helps with program development, publishes a newsletter, and prints a yearly "buzz book" of all families in the early childhood program. It also donates equipment to the program and plans social events for its members. In 1988-89, membership totaled 563 dues-paying families.

*Ms. Hamberg notes that it is very important not to put off establishing community linkages until the program is settled. She advises program directors to assign a staff member to be in charge of establishing resources and referrals and to maintain this important link to the community.*

**Outreach**

In addition to the parent council's outreach efforts, Parkway accepts referrals from private and public agencies, preschools, and elementary counselors and principals. The program places an article in the district newsletter each August, distributed to 50,000 Parkway residents. Flyers are sent home with children in kindergarten to grade 3. The program puts announcements in the St. Louis *Post Dispatch* and local newspapers. Area preschools and daycare centers send home brochures and flyers with children. Private and parochial schools also distribute literature as the program is open to all residents. Still, Ms. Hamberg calls word-of-mouth publicity from pleased participants the most successful recruiting strategy. Parent council representatives work with Welcome Wagon and Good Neighbors to reach new residents with young families and have redesigned mailings and stepped up strategies for broadening outreach.

| Job Title | PD | Vol | FT | PT | Educ Req | Status | Benefits |
|---|---|---|---|---|---|---|---|
| Parent Educators | 21 | - | - | 21 | College Degree | Hourly Non-Contract | No |
| Nurse | 1 | - | 1 | - | College Degree | Other Contract | Yes |
| Secretaries | 3 | - | 2 | 1 | High School Diploma | Hourly Non-Contract | Yes |
| Screening Facilitator | 1 | - | 1 | - | College Degree | Hourly Non-Contract | Yes |
| Center Facilitator | 1 | - | 1 | - | College Degree | Hourly Non-Contract | Yes |
| Screening Associates | 2 | - | 2 | - | College Degree | Hourly Non-Contract | Yes |

**State/District Requirements**

The Missouri Department of Elementary and Secondary Education requires parent educators to undergo a week-long training session and a yearly inservice program.

**Preferred Background**

Parent educators and the screening team should have an appropriate educational background, warm, caring, and sincere personalities, and some practical experience.

**Employee Education and Training Represented**

Infant and toddler education; prekindergarten and early childhood education; elementary education; education, grades 7 to 12; special education; parent educator; nursing; occupational and physical therapy; speech therapy; social work; child development and family studies.

**Administration**

The Parkway Early Childhood Program comprises the early childhood education department of the Parkway School District. The coordinator reports to the assistant superintendent for administrative services. Linda Hamberg attends elementary principals' meetings, which enhances communication between the program and the elementary schools and facilitates smooth transfer of children's records.

**Relationship to the Schools**

Parent educators are assigned cases by elementary attendance areas and are required to meet with the elementary principals. Once a year, the Parkway Early Childhood Program staff hosts a joint staff development session with kindergarten and first grade teachers, reading specialists, and elementary counselors. Staff members hand deliver records of entering kindergartners to elementary counselors and discuss individual cases. Ms. Hamberg believes the program is seen as an integral part of the district and thinks frequent formal contact with the elementary schools assures continuity between the early childhood department and the school instruction program. The intensity of parent involvement in the Parkway program through EChO and the parent council often carries parents into a long-term commitment to the schools. Ms. Hamberg says that elementary principals appreciate this and support the Parkway Early Childhood Program because of it.

**Community Links**

When appropriate, the Parkway Early Childhood Program makes referrals to the Special School District, which provides special education to all of St. Louis County; to private diagnostic centers associated with two major area hospitals; to speech and language pathologists; to occupational therapists; to pediatric specialists; and to training colleges at area universities offering medical and clinical services at low rates.

Parkway also exchanges referrals with Head Start and United Way agencies. Quarterly gatherings, yearly meetings, and annual phone contacts are made with each of the 93 area preschools and daycare centers. Ms. Hamberg notes that it is very important not to put off establishing community linkages until the program is settled. She advises program directors to assign a staff member to be in charge of establishing resources and referrals and to maintain this important link to the community.

**Funding**

State, 60 percent; Parkway district, 40 percent. The Teen Parent Program received a special Missouri Department of Elementary and Secondary Education grant of $6,640.

**In-Kind Resources**

Office space from the district and occasional volunteer help in the office.

**Funding History**

State funding is based on a quota established from a percentage of the birth to age three and the three- and four-year-old population in the district as reported in the 1980 census, and on the level of participation at each site. Parkway's rapid early childhood expansion resulted in part from annual increases in the funding quotas. This requires extensive documentation and record keeping; to assure a minimum level of state reimbursement, Ms. Hamberg makes one parent meeting mandatory.

**Objectives**

The program seeks to detect early developmental delays in young children, to provide the opportunity for maximum growth and development during the first three years of the child's life, and to enhance family bonding. Further, it assists parents in providing a good learning environment for children and builds their confidence by establishing a practical, community-based system of education and referral services. Finally, it facilitates early and continuing communication between parents and the schools.

**Evaluation**

The Parkway Division of Planning and Evaluation formally evaluated the program during the 1989-90 school year. Each program participant receives a yearly progress report as well. The program surveys participants; Ms. Hamberg says their suggestions are taken seriously and incorporated into the program if possible. In the past, parents have suggested topics for group meetings and have expressed great enthusiasm for Drop-in and Play. The coordinator meets with each parent educator individually three times a year to discuss the state of their caseloads, and each staff member receives an annual formal evaluation. There are plans to institute a tracking system to follow the progress of program participants as they move up through the grades.

**Replication**

The Parkway Early Childhood Program has replicated the Missouri PAT model with considerable modifications. Linda Hamberg advises school districts to tailor programs carefully to their needs.

**Materials Available**

Ms. Hamberg recommends two booklets developed by Parkway staff for general program use: *Special Moments* (a booklet for parents to check and list stages in their children's development), *Three to Get Ready . . . Four to Go . . . Ready for Five* (a resource guide for parents on the growth and development of three- and four-year-olds). To order, write to the program.

# At Home

Home visits                  Developmental screening      Parenting/child development education
Group meetings               Parent-child joint activities   Child care info/referral
                             Networking                   Community services info/referral

**Contact:**         Director of State and Federal Projects
**Address:**         Ridge School
                     650 Ridge
                     Elk Grove, IL  60007
                     (708) 593-4071
**Established:**     1985; local initiative
**Budget '88-'89:** $58,400
**Sources:**         Illinois State Board of Education's Preschool
                     At Risk of Educational Failure Program
**Size:**            30 families
**Area served:**     Parts of five towns in Community Consolidated School District 59
**Auspices:**        Instruction Department of the Public Schools
**1990 Respondent:** Mrs. Leone Mydill

*Leone Mydill mentions one little girl who tested poorly in certain developmental areas and seemed extremely timid. Noticing that her mother was highly critical and negative, the teacher tried to counteract this by encouraging the child to take risks and succeed. When she saw the results, the mother adopted a similar approach and indirectly picked up a new nurturing style. Modeling made it unnecessary for the teacher to criticize the parent's style and helped build good rapport.*

## Community

Community Consolidated School District 59 includes parts of five towns in a formerly rural area 30 miles northwest of Chicago. Following rapid growth in the 1960s and 1970s, the school population is declining again, forcing the shut-down of eight local schools. The surplus apartment complexes built in the years of expansion are now low-rental units, which attract a poorer population, many of whom are blue-collar workers in a nearby industrial park. The district also borders on O'Hare International Airport, whose employees make the area ethnically diverse; 32 languages are represented, many of them Asian. The population is predominantly white, with approximately 10 percent each of Asians, Pacific Islanders, and Hispanics.

## Philosophy and Goals

Though children progress through a similar sequence of stages in their growth, At Home holds that each child's development is unique. Children need activities that are both age and developmentally appropriate to stimulate cognitive, language, and social growth. At Home recognizes that some parents feel they lack the skills or the materials to help their children develop in areas of deficiency. By using the home as the classroom and modeling activities for parents, the program empowers parents to become the first and long-term teachers in their children's lives. At Home uses common household objects as learning materials so parents feel that no matter how humble their lifestyles, children's environments can be made to work effectively for development.

## History and Origins

In 1984, kindergarten teachers in District 59 found that many children were unprepared for the curriculum; to benefit from the school program and reach entry-level readiness, these children needed four to six months of remediation. Leone Mydill, the district kindergarten supervisor, investigated the community and found several competent daycare and preschool programs; she also discovered that the developmentally delayed children were often those kept at home or with a neighborhood babysitter. Ms. Mydill, who is also the district's director of state and federal projects, looked for funds on the state level to address her community's need. She found a state grant through the early childhood division and wrote a proposal for a developmentally delayed preschool home visit program. When designing the screening component, she was careful to assure that At Home's population would not overlap with the preexisting Handicapped Preschool or the Bilingual Preschool.

In 1985, after the program had begun, kindergarten teachers were still identifying delayed children, some of whom came from daycare situations that had no preschool component. Now, At Home also works with children in the homes of their daycare providers. At Home attributes its community and participant support to the fact that it serves a clearly underserved community. At Home was careful to articulate its specific target group and not to take over any other programs' territory.

## Features

All parents of children (ages three to five) in District 59 may request developmental screening. Children are considered eligible for At Home if they are at or below the twentieth percentile in one or more of the following areas: vocabulary, visual-motor integration, language, and fine or gross motor skills. The At Home preschool teachers visit participants two or three times a week for 45-minute sessions and play with the child while the parent or caretaker is present. Concept development is encouraged by using familiar objects in instructional activities easily practiced by parent and child in their daily setting. The two preschool teachers develop and update monthly individual assessment profiles for each student. These include the initial screening results, social information regarding the family, and plans and goals for the child's development. Several evenings each year, At Home holds parent discussion groups or lectures.

## Participants

In 1987-88, At Home served 30 children and 33 parents — 98 percent of the eligible population. Although all At Home children must be developmentally delayed, preference is given to those from at-risk families — impoverished families, families with inadequate parenting skills, or geographically or socially isolated families — factors that are determined by an interview with the parents at the time of screening. Families isolated by a language barrier are referred to the Bilingual Preschool. An estimated 20 percent of parents are single and 5 percent are teens. Last year several children were visited in the homes of their daycare providers; preschool teachers also worked with children and their babysitters together.

*At Home uses common household objects as learning materials so parents feel that no matter how humble their lifestyles, children's environments can be made to work effectively for development.*

## Parent Education

At Home insists that parents be present at all home visits, since a fundamental principle of the program is that parents can learn by example. Initially some parents expressed dissatisfaction with this requirement, preferring a center-based program that would give them respite time, but At Home overcame these protests. When the daytime caretaker is a babysitter or daycare employee, At Home staff will telephone the parents weekly to update them on their children's development. Three or four times a year, discussion groups or lectures are held that deal with parenting issues and community resources. At Home has discovered that many parents are grossly uninformed about normal child development; some who request screening are worried that their child cannot read at age four. At Home reassures those parents their children are fine by providing developmental information.

**Curriculum**

The instrument used for screening is a combination of EARLY and the Preschool Language Scale. The early childhood program component uses *Pots and Pans* and the *Brigance Readiness and Practice Book*. Daily activities focus on tasks that take place regularly in most homes. Teachers explain each play activity and supplement the explanation with simple illustrated handouts to explain its developmental relevance.

**Sites**

At Home delivers services in 30 homes, including the homes of daycare providers. The teachers share an office in a public elementary school with the bilingual and handicapped preschools. Shared space gives At Home teachers a chance to interact with one another, says Mrs. Mydill, and this alleviates the isolation of a home visit schedule.

**Parent Involvement**

In addition to participation in the home visit component, parents are asked to evaluate the program on a yearly basis.

**Outreach**

Notices describing At Home and its free screening component are sent home with all elementary school students in the district and placed in apartment complexes, trailer parks, and stores in low-income neighborhoods. School principals are informed of At Home's activities and often refer families. The program exchanges referrals with the bilingual and the handicapped preschools. The district parent-teacher organization lets At Home do an annual presentation, which contributes to word-of-mouth advertising. Local hospitals, private doctors, and the parks service also do outreach on its behalf. To become eligible for At Home, parents must request screening, and At Home suspects that some hard-to-reach parents fail to do so because they fear their children will be diagnosed as abnormal.

**Staff**

| Job Title | PD | Vol | FT | PT | Educ Req | Status | Benefits |
|-----------|----|----|----|----|----------|--------|----------|
| Director | 1 | - | - | 1 | Post-Graduate Courses or Degree | Other Contract | Yes |
| Teachers | 2 | - | 2 | - | College Degree | K-12 Contract | Yes |

**State/District Requirements**

For the director, state administrative certification; for teachers, state early childhood certification.

**Preferred Background**

At Home prefers its teachers to be mature, sensitive, well-informed about child development, and experienced parents.

**Employee Education and Training Represented**

Infant and toddler education; prekindergarten and early childhood education; elementary education; bilingual education; special education;

parent educator; child care; health and nutrition; home economics; psychology; counseling; family therapy; social work; child development and family studies; research and evaluation.

## Administration

Leone Mydill, the program director, reports to the District 59 superintendent. The Illinois State Board of Education and the local school board monitor the program.

## Relationship to the Schools

The program is located in the instruction department and shares inservice programming with the bilingual and the handicapped preschools. School principals learn about the program through newsletters and informal contact with teachers and superintendent. The district now offers a summer transition-to-kindergarten program for At Home students and other children who score poorly on the screening test. At Home preschool teachers design the curriculum but the program is taught by separate school staff. Even after the At Home child participant has entered kindergarten, preschool teachers telephone kindergarten teachers to monitor the child's progress and offer advice.

*At Home has discovered that many parents are grossly uninformed about normal child development; some who request screening are worried that their child cannot read at age four. At Home reassures those parents their children are fine by providing developmental information.*

## Community Links

At Home has strong links to the city parks and public libraries. The park staff members keep them aware of free services such as swimming lessons, and At Home prompts participants to take advantage of them. The preschool teachers also encourage parents to use the public libraries, letting them know they lend puzzles and games as well as books. Some parents request screening even though their work prevents them from participating in the program. Since kindergarten teachers found that a number of children who virtually grew up in daycare situations were not developmentally on target, At Home offers home visits to providers on site. According to Ms. Mydill, the initial meetings were tense; daycare providers feared they would lose children and the income they provided. But At Home made it clear that teachers would work with the children in cooperation with the provider.

## Funding

At Home is entirely funded by the Illinois State Board of Education's Preschool At Risk of Educational Failure Program.

## In-Kind Resources

Office space for teachers, all special service personnel, staff development programs, psychological services, screening for vision and hearing, clerical support, and access to all district equipment is available to the program.

## Funding History

Leone Mydill feels that the state is committed to early childhood programs. Her budget has increased 30 percent since implementation.

She is confident of continued funding because her program costs are lower than other state-funded initiatives. Ms. Mydill notes the cost-effectiveness of her program. She says that bus transportation is the single biggest expense for schools, and At Home eliminates this. Also, the program has neither classroom nor material costs since the *Pots and Pans* curriculum utilizes items found in the home. All funds support direct services to families, which pleases the district.

**Objectives**

At Home aims to teach parents that they can foster their children's growth in areas of developmental deficiency. It provides parents with developmental information and teaches them how to make their homes stimulating learning centers.

**Evaluation**

Pre- and posttests of children show that all have improved in their areas of deficiency. Teachers of kindergarten, first, and second grades are asked to evaluate At Home graduates in several areas. The longitudinal study has thus far shown that students have made progress and have reduced chances of developing later school problems. The Illinois State Board of Education has done several favorable on-site inspections of the program. Finally, parents are asked to assess their own participation and satisfaction with the program; so far they have given At Home a very high approval rating.

Leone Mydill considers herself accountable to the taxpayers and is a strong believer in thorough and well-conducted evaluations. She also finds it useful to have evaluative data to back up her claims of success. The local school board publishes the program's evaluation, and newspapers report on At Home.

**Replication**

The Illinois State Board of Education has recommended that the program be replicated by other districts in the state, and many similar programs have developed based on the At Home model.

**Materials Available**

None.

# 5

## School- and Center-based Parenting Support

Education and support for parents of school-age children, through resource libraries, peer networks, English language workshops, evening discussion groups, advocacy work with disenfranchised populations, Adult Basic Education, home visits, counseling, and a range of formal and informal channels for information, referral, and crisis intervention form the substance of these programs. Four of the eight programs operate under the auspices of the adult or community education departments of the public schools; one is a collaborative venture of the public schools and the Linn-Benton Community College in Oregon and one is the project of a private, nonprofit social service agency in Seattle, Washington. Where services for children do occur, they are offered as a medium for family enhancement.

# Programs in Brief

**Jefferson County Parent Support Team — p. 243**
*Parent support network in suburban Colorado for parents of children who receive special education services*

**Practical Parent Education — p. 249**
*Suburban Texas parent education groups for parents of children of all ages, co-sponsored by the local business community*

**Citizens Education Center**
**Parent Leadership Training Project — p. 255**
*Seattle-based social service agency offering educational program with rural outreach, targeted to migrant Hispanic parents with limited English language proficiency*

**Parent/Child Program — p. 261**
*Suburban Maryland program serving middle-income, teen, single, and impoverished families with gymnastic workout and child development classes, and parent education and support groups*

**Parent Education Groups in the Schools — p. 267**
*School-based parent education and family enhancement workshops in rural Oregon*

**Parent Education Resource Center — p. 273**
*Resource library and special services for at-risk families in suburban Utah*

**Community Education Home and Family Development Program — p. 277**
*Metropolitan community education center offering home visits, Adult Basic Education, counseling, and teen parenting support to five outlying rural areas in Pennsylvania*

**Parenting Education Center — p. 283**
*Countywide adult community education program based in Falls Church, Virginia, offering parent-child classes, parenting sessions, daycare, and academic courses for teen mothers*

# Jefferson County Parent Support Team

| | Hotline | Networking | Crisis intervention |
|---|---|---|---|
| | Warmline | Referral services | Parent support groups |
| | | | Parenting/child development education |

| | |
|---|---|
| **Contact:** | Dr. JoAnn Fujioka, Central Area SERS Manager |
| **Address:** | 10500 W. 25th Avenue |
| | Lakewood, CO 80215 |
| | (303) 232-2275 |
| **Established:** | 1984, local initiative |
| **Budget '88–'89:** | $400 |
| **Sources:** | County school district |
| **Size:** | 150 parents (100 families) |
| **Area Served:** | Jefferson County School District |
| **Auspices:** | Administered by central area of the district |

*When a child's special education assessment is complete, many parents have a difficult time accepting the label "handicapped." Parents of "borderline" children are especially vulnerable. Says Dr. Fujioka, "They wonder, will it harm their child in the long run? Will it hurt their job prospects down the line? Their chance in the armed services? College acceptance? . . . . Parents on the Parent Support Team are able to give the particulars about the confidentiality of records. They see newly referred parents in the denial stage of the grief process . . . and can empathize because they've gone through it themselves."*

## Community

The Jefferson County School District covers 794 square miles, stretching from the Rocky Mountains to the suburbs of Denver. The largest district in the state and the twenty-seventh largest in the country, its 120 schools serve 76,000 students and are divided among four geographically determined areas. The central area has 24 schools, the oldest school buildings, a declining enrollment, a large percentage of elderly residents, and a needy population of single-parent families, many of whom live in motel bedrooms. About one-third of the schools in the central area serve children of low-income families, and the rest serve a broader middle- and high-income population. The west area has a similar population but has the added element of the foothills and mountain segments of the districts. The north and south areas are the largest, the fastest growing, and the wealthiest areas; together they comprise two-thirds of the total enrollment. It is the higher-income segment that tends to request the Jefferson County Parent Support Team's services.

## Philosophy and Goals

The Jefferson County Parent Support Team (PST) believes that parents of handicapped children undergo similar periods of emotional pain and adjustment, which can be mitigated by mutual support and understanding. Better adjusted and informed parents can become effective advocates for their children. PST also works to promote understanding between schools and families under stress. The uniqueness of the program is that it is a buddy system and information network with an informal air. Dr. Fujioka notes that "parents of handicapped children are up to their ears in professionals, or else the whole idea of special education is new and scary to them. In either case, they don't need another professional. They need someone who has lived in their shoes."

## History and Origins

PST began in 1981 when JoAnn Fujioka, special education and related services manager of the Jefferson County School District's central area, marshalled parents of special education students, who felt their concerns were neglected by the school administration. Twenty-five interested parents went on a weekend retreat to develop a mechanism for helping the parents of handicapped children. They discussed creating a support network of parents who shared the emotional trials, practical difficulties, and legal concerns of raising handicapped children. Over the next three years, little was accomplished; Dr. Fujioka thinks that these parents needed time to feel confident as parents of handicapped children before they felt secure about helping others. In 1984, a smaller group revived the ideas of the original task force and planned a series of workshops on three consecutive Saturdays. Out of these emerged a core of 50 parents who were ready to support others during the special education review and staffing process. The school board approved the concept of a parent support team and made it a part of the special education advisory committee. The committee in turn formed a parent support task force with JoAnn Fujioka as administrative liaison. The task force established annual Saturday workshops and developed a PST telephone directory and guide to services.

**Features**

Parents of students in the Jefferson County Schools who have been referred for special education services can participate either as clients or providers of services. PST holds annual one- to three-day workshops that provide emotional support and information and train parents to work with other parents. Parents who have completed the workshop may then be included in the Parent Support Team directory, which links veterans of the special education review process with those who are new to it. The directory is distributed to parents of students who are identified as potentially in need of special education services, and includes a mail-in card that parents can fill out if they wish to be contacted by a PST member. A PST member may make home visits to parents in need of services, or they may choose to meet at a restaurant. PST's parents provide information, counseling, and support and may accompany another parent to district meetings to "interpret" the jargon and to be an objective listener.

*"Parents of handicapped children are up to their ears in professionals. They don't need another professional. They need someone who has lived in their shoes."*

**Participants**

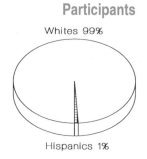

Whites 99%

Hispanics 1%

In 1987-88 PST served parents from 100 families. This is a small fraction of the more than 6,000 students who receive special education services in the district. Any parent of a handicapped child or of a child who has been referred for evaluation in the Jefferson County Schools is eligible for services. About one-fourth of PST participants are single parents. Low-income and transient families are underrepresented; PST finds that middle- to upper-middle-income families tend to request services. Dr. Fujioka also notes a fairly high rate of decline in PST membership, which she feels reflects the general instability and lack of time in families who have handicapped children.

**Parent Education**

PST modeled its workshop format on the Colorado Department of Education's Parents Encouraging Parents program but later changed the emphasis from specific categories of need to a more generic approach, focusing on issues relevant to all parents of developmentally delayed school-age children. A psychosocial perspective prevails in small group discussions of motivation, grief and loss, support tactics, conflict resolution, family dynamics, and counseling tactics. The workshops also stress the importance of being a well-informed advocate for one's child. Parents learn about special education laws and specific district procedures.

**Curriculum**

PST no longer uses a packaged curriculum, but instead draws on the knowledge and training of the schools' guidance and special education staff and professionals from community groups who work with handicapped populations. Parents' own insights on parenting handicapped children are discussed and integrated into the curriculum.

**Sites**

PST does not have a formal headquarters, but PST directories and information packets are available at all elementary, middle, and high schools. Workshops are held in community buildings or public schools, wherever donated or inexpensive space can be found.

**Parent Involvement**

PST enlists parents on one of three levels: as a phone contact, a public relations source, or a companion to parents who are going through the schools' special education procedures "to go along and be the ears, if nothing else," says Dr. Fujioka. Six parents and two administrators sit on the task force that guides PST activities, and members of the task force occasionally make presentations in the community.

**Outreach**

Informational packets about workshops are distributed to parents of special education students in all of the schools in Jefferson County, and notices are put in local newspapers and school newsletters. Brochures about the PST are available in all the schools. School administrators may tell parents who are new to the special education review process about PST, but parents must request services in order for a PST member to contact them. Responses are sporadic, and Dr. Fujioka attributes the lack of response to "the somewhat frustrating dynamic that parents at that stage are not yet able to reach out."

**Staff**

| Job Title | PD | Vol | FT | PT | Educ Req | Status | Benefits |
|---|---|---|---|---|---|---|---|
| Task Force Members | - | Varies | - | Varies | None | - | No |
| Administrative Liaison | 1 | - | - | 1 | Post-Graduate Courses or Degree | Other Contract | No |

**State/District Requirements**

The administrative liaisons must have special education teaching or related service certification and be endorsed by the district's director of exceptional student services.

**Preferred Background**

The administrative liaison should have excellent skills for working with parents and volunteers.

**Employee Education and Training Represented**

Special education.

## Administration

The two administrative liaisons report to the central area superintendent. Administrative liaison is an unpaid position filled by a full-time district employee. The PST's advisory board is a special task force of the district's special education advisory committee. The task force meets eight or nine times a year to plan and evaluate program activities.

## Relationship to the Schools

Although this program is administered exclusively within the schools, it is nonetheless essentially devoted to parent advocacy. The administrative liaison's role is sometimes to bridge the interests of the school system and the parents. Dr. Fujioka says that the school system may have originally feared that a parent advocacy group would assume an adversarial relationship between parents and staff, but she feels that this has not happened. Dr. Pamela Mills, director of exceptional student services and former advisor to the PST, says that instead "the school board sees the parents as a resource." Dr. Fujioka feels that "our value to the district is that parents are available for support and can offer an objective perspective on the system. It is a unique alternative for troubleshooting and heading off parents dissatisfied with the district. It opens up lines of communication that might otherwise be closed."

## Community Links

PST arranges speakers and presenters for its workshops, drawing on community groups like the Association of Retarded Citizens, the state legislature, and local universities. In turn, PST members give presentations on parenting handicapped children to classes of prospective special education teachers in area colleges.

## Funding

The Jefferson County Schools pay 100 percent of the PST's expenses.

## In-Kind Resources

Space for workshops and meetings from community groups and the schools; food from area supermarkets for snacks during meetings; door prizes from local businesses to encourage attendance at meetings; services from district staff.

## Funding History

Funding has decreased more than 50 percent in the five years of PST's existence, but Dr. Fujioka feels that the level of funding is moderately secure and has not affected the program's services. The budget includes rental space for workshops, presenters' fees, and child care.

## Objectives

PST provides support to parents of handicapped students when they are in crisis or in need of information. Parents involved gain knowledge about special education and become active participants in their children's programming.

## Evaluation

The task force periodically sends questionnaires regarding the program's services to PST's members. Results are evaluated by the group. From 1984 to 1988, the initial training workshop was offered every fall, but steadily declining enrollment (despite positive evaluations from parents) tipped off PST's task force that something new was needed. A survey showed that participants felt both well informed and competent and would prefer more topical workshops alternating on an annual basis with the introductory course. The 1988 workshop emphasized stress and stress management, and Dr. Fujioka hopes that in the future PST workshops will continue to address parents' changing needs.

| Replication | PST has not been replicated. |
| Materials Available | None. |

# Practical Parent Education

| | | |
|---|---|---|
| Warmline | Family resource library | Parenting/child development education |
| Networking | Child care referral | Community services info/referral |
| | Parent support groups | |

**Contact:** Linda Leslie-Johnston, Executive Director

**Address:** 1517 Avenue H
Plano, TX 75074
(214) 519-8254

**Established:** 1986, local initiative

**Budget '88-'89:** $119,400

**Sources:** Business donations, foundation grants, special events and fundraising, private and religious contributions, client fees

**Size:** 10,000 parents during three-year pilot

**Area Served:** Plano, Texas

**Auspices:** Plano Independent School District Student Services Department and a community-based board of directors

## Community

Plano, with a population of approximately 135,000, is an upper-middle-class bedroom community outside Dallas. Plano neighborhoods range from those with multimillion-dollar homes to those in the poverty range. Plano has a significant multiethnic population, and bilingual programs in the schools are common.

## Philosophy and Goals

Practical Parent Education believes that through community support and parenting training, parents will be able to raise responsible, self-confident, and mentally healthy children. By supporting adults in their critical role as parents, Practical Parent Education hopes parents will be able to relax and enjoy their children more. Educators encourage parents to explore options in parenting techniques and to choose those that are most comfortable for them and their children. The program emphasizes that there are no "quick fixes" for the job of parenting and is designed to offer a series of classes throughout parents' childrearing years.

## History and Origins

Practical Parent Education was the inspiration of the superintendent of Plano schools, Dr. H. Wayne Hendrick, and Joe Collins, a respected businessman and long-time area resident. Both were concerned with the phenomena of teen suicide, school dropout rates, drug and alcohol abuse, teen pregnancy, and the break-up of the family. They envisioned a program that would not wait for families and young people to reach a crisis, but would prevent such problems through education and community support. They agreed that the school district would administer the program, but that the most effective support and funding could be found through the community. A strong partnership between the schools and the community was developed. The board of directors represents a cross-section of the community, including educators, medical and mental health professionals, clergy, business professionals, and community leaders.

The board spent three years studying established parent education programs. From their research the members drew three conclusions that guided the design of Practical Parent Education. First, they postulated that parents are less eager to come to a central parenting center and would be more likely to attend classes at familiar sites in their local neighborhoods. Second, the board concluded that parents may not enjoy and often do not complete assignments from a textbook. Finally, their research convinced them that parent education must be ongoing to bring about positive, enduring changes. In October 1986, with financial support from community organizations and businesses throughout Plano, the program hired two parent educators and began offering classes to parents at various sites, including schools, churches, daycare centers, and apartment complexes.

### Features

Practical Parent Education offers weekly classes usually in clusters of four- and six-week sessions. In any given week, as many as 15 different series may be offered throughout the community. The program originally focused on specific age groups of children, but as parents suggested, it now also offers a wide range of classes to address the specific concerns of single parents, stepparents, working parents, and parents of children with special needs such as adopted children, children with handicaps, and those with attention deficit disorder.

The program provides a warmline for parents to call for information and support. A referral service gives information about local mental health professionals and community services for families. Practical Parent Education also has a family resource library where parents have access to over 1,400 books on parenting and child development, video- and audiotapes, periodicals, parenting kits, and books for children.

### Participants

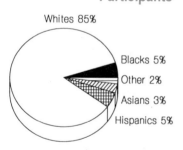

Whites 85%

Blacks 5%

Other 2%

Asians 3%

Hispanics 5%

An estimated 56,000 parents in the Plano community are eligible to take classes. In 1987-89, Practical Parent Education served 4,000 parents (2,500 mothers and 1,500 fathers). Executive Director Linda Leslie estimates that 10 percent were single parents, 5 percent were stepparents, and 1 percent were teen parents. The program charges a small fee for each series, but fees are waived on the basis of need.

*The program emphasizes that there are no "quick fixes" for the job of parenting and is designed to offer an ongoing series of classes throughout parents' childrearing years.*

### Parent Education

Practical Parent Education teaches child development and effective parenting skills in an informal, supportive environment. Class agendas are established by parents and deal with such topics as self-esteem, effective problem-solving skills, communication, and expressing emotions. The emphasis is placed on group interaction and empowerment of parents. All topics are designed from within the framework of a curriculum developed by Practical Parent Education. The 1½-hour group meetings are very informal, less oriented toward lecturing, and more concerned with parent involvement and interaction. Parents discuss topics in small groups, do role-playing exercises, and practice communication skills. Parent educators have found that the more parents are actively involved, the more they retain and carry over to their home behavior.

**Curriculum**

Practical Parent Education spent three years designing a curriculum that would include child development theory and offer choices in parenting techniques, minimizing book learning and maximizing parent interaction. The curriculum is based on a family systems approach and draws on the studies of healthy families by Jerry Lewis and John Gossett, and studies of family atmospheres by Diana Baumrind. It is designed as a flexible tool for use with all parents.

*A strong partnership between the schools and the community was developed. The board of directors represents a cross-section of the community, including educators, medical and mental health professionals, clergy, business professionals, and community leaders.*

**Sites**

Classes meet at various locations across Plano, including public and private schools, local businesses, religious facilities, and individual homes. The program has two office bases, one in a public elementary school, the other in the district administration building. The resource library is housed in a local church.

**Parent Involvement**

Parental input determines the character of Practical Parent Education class offerings. Parents make frequent use of the family resource library and the warmline. Nearly everyone involved in the program — the board of directors, the associate parent educators, and the resource library volunteer staff — is a parent and has taken at least one series of classes.

**Outreach**

One of Practical Parent Education's primary goals is to reach parents where they feel most comfortable in the community. When the program first began, it contacted schools, churches, and community organizations throughout Plano to ask permission to offer classes at those sites. The program targets a specific community by going to the institutions already serving that group. For instance, to reach the black community in Plano, it contacted key people in the local ministries, won their support, and offered classes through those ministries. To reach the Asian and Hispanic populations, the program turned to bilingual programs in public elementary schools.

The community organization hosting the classes usually takes the responsibility of publicizing, with materials provided by Practical Parent Education and through their own public relations vehicles. The program has little trouble reaching healthy parents who are eager to enhance their parenting skills and who are the target group of the primary prevention program. Many other families are referred through the courts, mental health professionals, educators, and ministers.

| Job Title | PD | Vol | FT | PT | Educ Req | Status | Benefits |
|---|---|---|---|---|---|---|---|
| Coordinator | 1 | - | 1 | - | Post-Graduate Courses or Degree | Other Contract | Yes |
| Parent Educator | 1 | - | 1 | - | Post-Graduate Courses or Degree | Other Contract | Yes |
| Parent Educator | 1 | - | - | 1 | Post-Graduate Courses or Degree | Hourly Contract | No |
| Secretary | 1 | - | - | 1 | Some High School | Hourly Contract | No |
| Associate Parent Educators | - | 32 | - | 32 | Some College/College Degree | - | No |
| Librarians | - | 20 | - | 20 | None | - | No |

**State/District Requirements**

The director and the parent educators must hold a college degree in education, counseling, social work, or nursing.

**Preferred Background**

Parent educators should have exemplary teaching skills, good people skills, and experience in group facilitation. Volunteer associate parent educators should have a college degree and some practical experience in dealing with families. Associate parent educators undergo a 38-hour training program and continue inservice training for three hours per month indefinitely.

**Employee Education and Training Represented**

Infant and toddler education; prekindergarten and early childhood education; elementary education; education, grades 7 to 12; special education; parent educator; child care; home economics; speech therapy; psychology; counseling; family therapy; social work; child development and family studies; development and fundraising; research and evaluation; religion and clergy.

**Administration**

The program is administered jointly by the Plano Independent School District student services department and the program's own board of directors, which includes program staff, public school personnel, community representatives, local politicians, clergy, medical professionals, and representatives of local businesses. An executive board of 15 meets monthly, and a larger advisory board of 50 meets approximately quarterly. The executive board approves the budget, staff hiring, and program planning and coordinates fundraising, outreach, and community relations. The Practical Parent Education director reports to the director of student services and the board of directors.

**Relationship to the Schools**

A large portion of programming takes place at public schools in the Plano district. Linda Leslie says this is a natural partnership, since most teachers and administrators feel parents need more support. The program has multiple contacts throughout the school system, including counselors, truancy officers, drug counselors, and racial relations staff. Practical Parent Education frequently provides inservice programs for school personnel. Ms. Leslie feels that teachers are grateful to know they can refer families to Practical Parent Education.

The Plano schools have been cited as a model school system in Texas, and the district superintendent, a principal founder of Practical Parent Education, is well known in the state. The executive director believes that this strong reputation may attract schools and parents to the program.

## Community Links

The classes have proved so successful that many sites now contact Practical Parent Education themselves to request further programming. To accommodate the huge demand for classes, Practical Parent Education asks local volunteers to train as associate parent educators and offer classes on their own sites. There were 30 trained volunteer educators in 1988, including religious personnel, teachers, school administrators, and members of community service organizations. Practical Parent Education considers itself a community organization that could not exist without the financial and moral support of Plano businesses, organizations, and residents. The family resource library, for instance, is entirely funded and staffed by volunteers of the local Junior League, which has donated over $8,000 to the library.

## Funding

Corporate and business donations, 30 percent; foundations or private agencies, 30 percent; private donations, 15 percent; client paid fees, 10 percent; contributions from religious institutions, 10 percent; fundraising events, 5 percent.

## In-Kind Resources

The public schools provide two offices and space for training workshops, clerical support, access to materials and equipment, and staff development. Other community organizations and churches provide space, volunteer staff, and outreach services.

## Funding History

Funding remains stable.

## Objectives

To foster the development of responsible, self-confident, mentally healthy children through parent education and support.

## Evaluation

After each series of classes, parents rate the program's effectiveness. The great majority report improvement in family communication, confidence, and problem solving. Linda Leslie explains that the program has not done an extensive evaluation both because of lack of funds and because the board feels appropriate long-term evaluative instruments are unavailable.

## Replication

Practical Parent Education has recently joined forces with the Texas Association of School Boards (TASB) to replicate the program in school districts across the state of Texas. TASB expects that 140 school districts and communities will adopt the program in 1990.

## Materials Available

*Practical Parent Education Curriculum* and a child development text; *Parenting Today,* a guide for parents; *Administrative and Parent Educator Training,* quarterly newsletter for parent educators. To obtain any of these materials, contact: Texas Association of School Boards, P.O. Box 2947, Austin, Texas 78768-2947.

# Citizens Education Center
# Parent Leadership Training Project

| | | |
|---|---|---|
| Networking | Monthly radio show | Parenting/child development education |
| | Spanish language materials | Community services info/referrals |

**Contact:**       Jacque Shayne, Project Director
                   Citizens Education Center Northwest

**Address:**       310 First Avenue, South
                   Suite 330
                   Seattle, WA 98104
                   (206) 624-9955

**Established:**   1986, joint initiative

**Budget '88-'89:**  $96,437

**Sources:**      Corporate and business donations, foundations, or private agencies

**Size:**         150 families

**Area Served:**  Public schools in Wapato, Toppenish, and Seattle

**Auspices:**     Citizens Education Center Northwest and the schools

**1990 Respondent:**  Mary-Louise Alving, Assistant Director

*Parents participating in PLTP are the success stories of the program. Even though most of them work extremely hard during the week, they still ask for reading classes on Saturday afternoon. When told they could approach teachers, one parent responded, "You mean I can talk to my kid's teacher anytime I want, not just in conferences?" High school dropouts who have returned to school come to talk to parents' groups. Parents who can't read get their children's older siblings to work with them. One parent who had never been inside a school before now serves on a parent advisory board.*

## Community

The Parent Leadership Training Project (now called Families and Schools: Powerful Partners) runs workshops and is working in the Wapato, Toppenish, and Seattle public schools. Both Toppenish and Wapato are small, rural towns located in the Yakima Valley, in south central Washington where produce is an important industry. Wapato's population of 3,307 is mostly Hispanic (41 percent) and Native American (27 percent), with 28 percent whites. Toppenish has a population of 6,517 made up of 56 percent Hispanics, 26 percent whites, and 16 percent Native Americans. Seattle (population 500,000) is situated in the northwestern part of the state along the Puget Sound. Residents are mostly white; minorities make up less than 10 percent of the population.

The Parent Leadership Training Project (PLTP) serves mostly Hispanic, migrant, and minority families. Agriculture is the major source of livelihood for the migrant population. Many families have "settled-out" in the valley and seek citizenship, home ownership, and intrastate employment.

## Philosophy and Goals

PLTP believes that parent involvement in children's educational process is critical to children's success in school and that parents will embrace this role if they are given the information and skills necessary to fulfill this responsibility. The program teaches parents to be effective advocates for their children and to work with schools on improving student performance. The program focuses on promoting academic success among children of migrant families at risk of school failure. The program affirms the parental role by helping parents realize the extent to which they have already contributed to their children's well-being. Similarly, it "tries to build a bank of positive experiences" for families that may have had negative experiences with schools.

In the Yakima Valley, the Hispanic dropout rate ranges from 50 to 80 percent, according to the Citizens Education Center Northwest (CECN), and families typically feel very isolated from the public school system. The Washington State Migrant Council (WSMC) provides Head Start and state-funded preschool programs for Hispanic children; it invited the CECN to work in its Sunnyside and Mabton preschools with Hispanic parents whose children were making the transition from preschool to the K to 12 school system. The CECN accepted, and the Parent Leadership Training Project in Sunnyside began in 1986 as a follow-up program to Head Start. In 1988, PLTP expanded and offered workshops in other school districts in the Yakima Valley. PLTP also developed training for parents of children in special education in the Toppenish School District. They began a smaller program in a Seattle school in 1987 for low-income parents, many of whom had failed in school themselves. In 1989, the project moved to a multiracial school in central Seattle. The school is in an inner-city area undergoing redevelopment. It serves many children living in public housing. The fact that the school was new made it an attractive setting. An average of 30 parents, representing mixed groups, participate in the six spring training sessions.

**Features**

The PLTP course consists of 12 to 14 weekly sessions held over an eight-month school year and during summer school. The parent discussion groups generate a lot of conversation and networking among parents that help build self-confidence and break isolation barriers. Parents formulate recommendations to the school on how to improve communications. The program also teaches parents the value of engaging in games and activities with their children. Parents learn how to help their children prepare to learn to read and capture the joy of books.

**Participants**

In 1988, PLTP served 150 parents, primarily low-income families living in high-risk neighborhoods. Thirty percent of the participants are single, and 10 percent are teens. PLTP serves parents with limited proficiency in English.

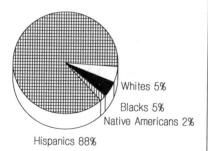

Whites 5%
Blacks 5%
Native Americans 2%
Hispanics 88%

*Hispanic fathers have become very involved in the program. Traditionally in the Hispanic culture, mothers are responsible for educating and nurturing young children.*

**Parent Education**

Parent Leadership Training Project sessions include these topics: "What is a Public School?," "Rights and Responsibilities of Parents," "Parents' Role in Education," "Parent-Teacher Conferences," "The Kindergarten Program," "Who Works in Public Schools," "The School Program," "Helping Your Child at Home," "Learning through Play," and "How to Help Your Child Enjoy Reading."

**Curriculum**

PLTP uses easy-reading or bilingual materials and graphics to reach parents of all literacy levels. Curriculum materials are developed by the PLTP staff and have been adapted for Spanish-speaking parents. Small group oral evaluations and activity sheets without written directions have been provided to Spanish-speaking parents. In 1988, PLTP began working on a manual for trainers and a bilingual handbook for parent participants for use by groups working with Hispanic parents in Washington and nationwide.

PLTP develops innovative ways of integrating English as a Second Language (ESL) lessons within civics courses, which are offered at night and required for migrants applying for United States citizenship. Rather than take up another week night, the program has incorporated English language workshop sessions with civics courses on the structure and hierarchy of schools.

## Sites

The number and location of sites used by the PLTP varies as the program adjusts to meet the needs of parents and school districts. Sites include preschools, public elementary schools, neighborhood or community agencies, alternative schools, or religious facilities. The program has office space in Grandview in the Yakima Valley and in Seattle.

## Parent Involvement

Parents are the primary participants in the program and help determine topics offered during each session. They also participate in the evaluation process of the program and act as trainers. Hispanic fathers have become very involved in the program. Traditionally in the Hispanic culture, mothers are responsible for educating and nurturing young children, said Ms. Candanoza.

## Outreach

Schools participating in PLTP assist the program's outreach efforts with flyers, phone calls, and radio announcements. In one school district, children made invitations for their parents, and videotapes of the class were shown during the first PLTP session. PLTP is also seeking funding to reach the Asian language communities in Seattle and "those profoundly alienated from the urban school system," says Ms. McTaggart.

## Staff

| Job Title | PD | Vol | FT | PT | Educ Req | Status | Benefits |
|-----------|----|-----|----|----|----------|--------|----------|
| Director | 1 | - | - | 1 | Post-Graduate Courses or Degree | Other Contract | Yes |
| Coordinator | 2 | - | 1 | 1 | High School Diploma | Other Contract | Yes |
| Instructor | 1 | - | - | 1 | High School Diploma | Hourly Contract | Yes |

## State/District Requirements

None.

## Preferred Background

All staff members are required to have parenting experience, sensitivity to other cultures, and a commitment to and belief in the ability of parents to make a difference in their children's educational success. Staff members in the Yakima Valley sites must have proficiency in Spanish.

## Employee Education and Training Represented

Prekindergarten and early childhood education; education, grades 7 to 12; parent educator; child development and family studies.

## Administration

PLTP is a project of the Citizens Education Center Northwest (CECN). The program is administered by Mary-Louise Alving, assistant director of the CECN. Ms. McTaggart serves as overall director and reports to CECN's board of trustees.

## Relationship to the Schools

PLTP is administered independently of school systems, but seeks their cooperation and shares staff, facilities, and equipment. The program works with schools to facilitate children's success in the K to 12 system by arranging parent meetings with kindergarten teachers and principals. PLTP maintains links with the principal, teachers, and school resource people. In Seattle, PLTP videotaped certain school specialists like the nurse, speech therapist, and counselor and then presented the videotape at parents' meetings to show parents what kind of services are available to their children. PLTP works hard at building trust between the parents and the schools by bridging the gap between communities and schools. The Seattle Public Schools, for example, have received negative media coverage for failing to meet the needs of black children. The schools also realize that they have neglected to involve parents. PLTP instructors in Seattle have spent time becoming familiar with teachers and videotaping classes to present at the first session of PLTP courses.

School support of the program has varied. Some districts have welcomed the program and supported efforts to increase parent involvement. Others have not. When schools or districts have recruited parents half-heartedly, it plays into the myth that parents do not care about education. Trainers have learned that nothing is farther from the truth. Being asked and encouraged to be involved and having meaningful information at meetings has been the core of PLTP success.

## Community Links

PLTP sees itself as filling a gap in the wider family support and social service arena by providing a unique orientation and set of services. Toward this end it has made its work visible in the community and collaborates with other agencies providing services to low-income, disadvantaged residents. "To be hooked up to an agency that provides additional services is wonderful," said Ms. McTaggart. She believes that it takes a while to build trusting relationships with other groups and organizations, but said, "To be able to go into a place with a strong parent constituency speeds along the process."

## Funding

In 1988-89, foundations or private agencies, 90 percent; corporate and business donations, 10 percent.

## In-Kind Resources

Washington State Migrant Council and school districts contribute services, space, staff, and access to equipment.

## Funding History

Funding for the program has increased several times since it began, and Ms. McTaggert said funding is secure for the next two years. Among those who have supported PLTP are ARCO, the Fred Meyer Charitable Trust, the Haas Foundation, the John D. and Catherine T. MacArthur Foundation, the Medina Foundation, the Murdock Charitable Trust, the New World Foundation, and the Titcomb Foundation.

## Objectives

The program expects that parents will provide a positive environment for their children, accept their role as participants in their children's education, and become involved in their children's school experience.

## Evaluation

The Fred Meyer Charitable Trust visited PLTP in the Yakima Valley in 1988 and awarded it a grant of $76,000 over a two-year period to support its work, increase its staff, and develop an evaluation component. "They thought it very important that we document what we do," said Ms. McTaggart, "so that others can replicate our efforts." PLTP began an evaluation of the program in January 1989 to determine its impact on schools, parents, and students, which will be completed in August 1990.

**Replication**

In August 1989, 12 school communities sent teams to a two-day training of trainers workshop conducted by CECN. Teams will go on to offer PLTP sessions throughout the year with support and technical assistance from the CECN staff.

**Materials Available**

Materials are being prepared.

# Parent/Child Program

Counseling
Networking
Job training
Resource library
Adult literacy

Teen parenting classes
Child care info/referral
Parent-child joint activities
Health/nutrition education
Free transportation
GED preparation

Parenting/child development education
Community services info/referral
Support groups for teen parents
Motor development classes
Developmental exams/screening
Support groups for battered spouses

**Contact:** Teena L. Broadrup, Parent-Child Specialist

**Address:** Governor Thomas Johnson High School
1501 North Market Street
Frederick, MD 21701
(301) 694-1829

**Established:** 1976, joint venture between the Adult Education Department and community group

**Budget '88-'89:** $41,485

**Sources:** Local, state, federal governments; client fees

**Size:** 1,375 families

**Area Served:** Frederick County, Maryland

**Auspices:** Frederick Public Schools
Frederick County Adult Education Department

### Community

Frederick is a bedroom community of both Washington, DC and Baltimore, Maryland. Housing prices have doubled since 1980 and rents have risen 75 percent. The majority of residents come from middle- and working-class backgrounds. Although the city is experiencing gentrification of its historic district, accompanied by an influx of new money and new values, there remains a significant low-income population. The area population is 74 percent white, 20 percent black, 3 percent Hispanic, and 3 percent Asian.

### Philosophy and Goals

The Parent/Child Program provides opportunities for parents to share their common interests, concerns, and accomplishments with one another in small discussion groups. "Part of our goal," says Teena Broadrup, "is to educate parents not to push their children too much; that's where early childhood education comes in handy." In the belief that parents need nurturing to maintain a constructive level of energy and commitment to their role in the family, the program supports and encourages the personal growth of parents by boosting their self-concept and providing information about community resources.

### History and Origins

In the late 1970s, interest in early childhood education and family life swept through a generation of educated, professionally ambitious parents in Frederick County. Requests for classes on childrearing from middle-class families filtered into Frederick County Public Schools. An active community leader and mother of 10, Ann Hall Marshall began independently run tuition-based classes geared to parents of infants. In 1976, these became the prototype for the Parent/Child Program, a joint venture between Ms. Marshall's organization and the local school board. Teena Broadrup then assumed leadership. In 1985, the program expanded to include a motor development and exercise program for children, and in 1987 a program for disadvantaged teen and single parents was established.

**Features**

The Parent/Child Program classes meet for an hour and a half on weekday mornings, afternoons, evenings, and some Saturday mornings for six to eight weeks. During weekly and biweekly meetings, parents and children participate in joint activities devoted to the visual arts, music, language development, role playing, readiness skills, or gross motor skills. The Parent/Child Program offers 20 general parenting classes differentiated by the ages of the children.

The **Wee Workout Exercise Program** is a series of motor development classes during which time children (infants through age 10) learn gymnastics and parents become acquainted with the stages of physical growth and ways to foster continued development of motor skills at home.

A program for teen, single, and low-income parents provides parenting and child development information to parents of high-risk children. This free program is geared to encouraging participants to enroll in adult education or vocational skills development classes. Classes are scheduled during evening hours, and child care and free transportation encourage attendance.

The Parent/Child Program also publishes a series of booklets titled *Your Home is a Learning Center* that provide suggestions for turning daily activities such as cooking, gardening, shopping, and pet care into opportunities for cognitive learning.

Three additional programs affiliated with the Parent/Child Program (available at six elementary schools), FAMILY MATH, Family Reading, and Family Computers, offer opportunities for intergenerational learning to students in kindergarten to grade 8 and their families.

**Participants**

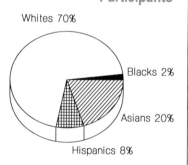

Whites 70%

Blacks 2%

Asians 20%

Hispanics 8%

The program serves infants, toddlers, and preschoolers in its regular classes and infants to ten-year-olds in its motor development classes. Pregnant women, as well as any adult residents of Frederick County accompanied by children, are welcome. The average family participates weekly or biweekly for two to three years (usually until their child enters school). In 1987-88, 686 children, 650 mothers, and 36 fathers participated in various programs.

*"Part of our goal," says Teena Broadrup, "is to educate parents not to push their children too much; that's where early childhood education comes in handy."*

**Parent Education**

The parent education component acquaints parents with the emotional, intellectual, and physical needs of early childhood and offers a flexible forum for discussing childrearing issues. Each class is divided into two segments. The first consists of joint parent-child activities that are developmentally appropriate for infants, toddlers, and preschool children. The second is an informal discussion group focusing on childrearing techniques and developmental stages, personal goals, survival tips, time management, budget, children's literature, and building self-esteem.

**Curriculum**

The teen- and single-parent program uses *Choices and Challenges,* job training and equity manuals by Bingham, Edmondson, and Stryker, and *FAMILY MATH,* by Stenmark, Thompson, and Cossey. Other curricula are developed in house for specific courses.

**Sites**

Initially, classes met in churches, but within two years the school board offered the Parent/Child Program rooms in the Elm Street School Annex, an alternative high school. It has since moved to a middle school, but continues to offer some of its programs in the old building.

**Parent Involvement**

Ninety-five percent of staff members are parents who have participated in the Parent/Child Program with their own children.

**Outreach**

News of the program spreads through parents. Flyers are distributed in OB-GYN clinics, hospitals, and children's clothing stores; mass mailings accompany adult education program materials; and local newspaper articles contribute to publicity. In addition, Ms. Broadrup addresses various community groups and church-sponsored forums, describing the program's opportunities and discussing topics relevant to childrearing and family interactions.

**Staff**

The staff and administration meet once a month to exchange ideas and concerns about the program.

| Job Title | PD | Vol | FT | PT | Educ Req | Status | Benefits |
|---|---|---|---|---|---|---|---|
| Parent/Child Specialist | 1 | - | - | 1 | College Degree/ Post-Graduate Courses or Degree | K-12 Contract | Yes |
| Teachers | 4 | - | - | 4 | Some College/ College Degree | Hourly Non-Contract | No |
| Aide | 1 | - | - | 1 | High School Diploma | Hourly Non-Contract | No |
| Saturday Special Teachers | 6 | - | - | 6 | College Degree | Hourly Non-Contract | No |

**State/District Requirements**

The parent-child specialist must have a bachelor's degree. Ms. Broadrup has a master's in education, with certification in early childhood education and administration.

**Preferred Background**

Teachers must be friendly and understanding; they must be parents with some early childhood education training.

**Employee Education and Training Represented**

Infant and toddler education; prekindergarten and early childhood education; elementary education; education, grades 7 to 12; special education; adult literacy; parent educator; adult basic education; adult vocational education; child care; home economics; psychology; counseling; family therapy; social work; child development and family studies.

**Administration**

The superintendent of the Frederick County Public Schools is ultimately responsible for the Parent/Child Program. Teena Broadrup reports to the coordinator of the Adult Education Department, who is responsible to the director of vocational education. The Maryland Department of Education monitors the program. An advisory board for the Adult Education Department, comprised of representatives from public (noneducational) and private agencies and the community, also serves the Parent/Child Program. The board meets four times a year and functions in advisory and community public relations capacities.

**Relationship to the Schools**

Ms. Broadrup noted that Parent/Child's programs give Frederick's growing middle-class families a sense of having a voice in their own school system. She added, "It's usually their first contact with the schools, and they get a low-key, positive view of the system." According to Ms. Broadrup, teen, disadvantaged, or disturbed parents often find schools threatening places. The Parent/Child Program minimizes the school link in programs directed at those parents.

In addition, being housed in the Adult Education Department affords the Parent/Child Program easy access to collaborations with Evening High School and Adult Basic Education, which would be difficult to arrange if the program were under the auspices of early childhood education.

**Community Links**

In collaboration with the Department of Social Services and Heartly House (a shelter for abused women), the Parent/Child Program has developed a series of free discussion and support groups for teen parents, abusive parents, and battered spouses. It also offers a combination of evening high school, child care, and support groups for students with young children.

The program participates in the Frederick Festival of the Arts by sponsoring a staff display, a children's art show, and a day-long free program of movement, art, and literature for toddlers through ten-year-olds. In 1987, the Parent/Child Program took part in Frederick's third annual women's fair.

**Funding**

Local and district, 61 percent; federal, 18 percent; state, 12 percent; client fees, 9 percent. Tuition ranges from $20 to $33 for a weekly series of six to eight parent-child classes; $50 to $66 for the biweekly series; $14 to $19 for the six-week Wee Workout sessions; the six-week summer preschool costs $50 for 12 meetings.

**In-Kind Resources**

Speakers, supplies, equipment, and space are all donated by the board of education and local churches.

**Funding History**

The program started with funds from the federal government, funnelled through the school district's adult education program. Ms. Broadrup's position is funded by the school district's board of education and the state. Funding is considered moderately secure and has increased by 50 percent since the program began. Ms. Broadrup says the program has won local support because of parent interest and because the Adult Education Department is so responsive to community needs.

**Objectives**

The Parent/Child Program seeks to provide opportunities for parents to share concerns, to become acquainted with young children's developmental needs, to nurture parents through support and information services and counseling, and to foster personal growth in parents and children.

**Evaluation**

The Maryland Department of Education evaluates the Adult Education Department as a whole. The program was commended for enabling 35 young women, participants in the single-parent program, to enroll in adult education or vocational skills development classes. The Parent/ Child Program conducts its own in-house evaluation, including parent evaluation sheets distributed at the end of each class series. Staff discussions emphasize teamwork and problem solving.

**Replication**

The Parent/Child Program has been replicated in Baltimore and Montgomery County.

**Materials Available**

Curriculum and programming information and *Your Home is a Learning Center (Parts 1, 2, 3)*. Contact the Parent/Child Program for information on how to order.

# Parent Education Groups in the Schools

| | | |
|---|---|---|
| Networking | Community services info/referral | Parent resource fair with child care |
| Resource library | Parenting/child development education | Parent-child joint activities |

**Contact:** Bobbie Weber, Chair
**Address:** Linn-Benton Community College
Department of Family Resources
6500 SW Pacific Boulevard
Albany, OR 97321
(503) 928-2361, ext. 383

**Established:** 1983, local initiative
**Budget '88-'89:** $23,500
**Sources:** State Juvenile Services Commission grant;
school district funds; community college funds
**Size:** 467 mothers, 146 fathers, 120 children
**Area Served:** Linn and Benton Counties, Oregon
**Auspices:** Linn-Benton Community College, Department of Family Resources,
and four school districts

*Bobbie Weber recalls a mother who first came to PEG classes expressing hysterical concern that she was losing her daughter and that her husband refused to acknowledge the problem. In class, the mother gradually developed listening skills and became more comfortable in her own parenting. Her husband, intrigued by the change in his wife, started coming to classes while she worked as a parent volunteer. Together, they learned that they have options and now feel capable of trying out new approaches in their family. Their daughter, who was on the verge of moving out, stayed at home, and the couple now feels family communication is a common endeavor.*

## Community

Linn and Benton counties occupy a valley between the Coastal Mountains and the Cascade Mountains. Albany, in Linn, has a manufacturing base, but in general Linn County is a region of poor, rural communities inhabited by a blue-collar population that makes its living in lumbering, fishing, or farming. Work is seasonal and erratic; extremes of poverty can alternate with relative prosperity within a year. The rate of child abuse in Linn ranks among the highest in the country. The adjacent county of Benton is more prosperous. Home to the land-grant university and several prestigious industrial engineering firms, it boasts some of the best schools in the state. There are, however, several pockets of poor, small, rural towns adjacent to the more prosperous city of Corvallis.

## Philosophy and Goals

Linn-Benton Community College and the public schools share the goals of reducing the number of children who get into trouble, fail in school, and drop out of both school and their parents' lives. Parent Education Groups in the Schools (PEG) provides educational support for parents of children who are not thriving in school. The program's goal is to strengthen family relationships by increasing parents' awareness of their own importance in the lives of their children. PEG aims to support parents by bolstering their self-confidence and social connectedness and increasing their knowledge of children's developmental needs.

## History and Origins

Linn-Benton Community College's Department of Family Resources began offering parent education classes and courses related to childrearing in 1973. In the early 1980s, parents asked Linn-Benton's parent education program to expand its offerings to specifically address the concerns of parents of school-age children. Meanwhile, in 1981, the Oregon court system, overwhelmed by the numbers of convicted adolescents in the system, instituted the Juvenile Services Commission, the goal of which was to keep youth out of the justice system by expanding local community-based resources. At this point, the administration of the Albany Public Schools thought that educational support for parents could also combat increasing absenteeism and generalized negative behavior of students toward the schools. The goals of Linn-Benton and the public schools merged in 1983 in their joint proposal to the Juvenile Services Commission to fund Parent Education Groups in the Schools. The JSC provided $6,000 in implementation funds to pay a coordinator and instructors to lead parent education workshops and parent-child activity sessions for families with young adolescents. PEG has since expanded to serve several school districts, with increased financial support from the community college and participating schools in the Albany, Corvallis, Scio, and Sweet Home districts.

*PEG offers several approaches to parent education; classes vary by population and mission.*

**Features**

PEG classes run from six to eight weeks, one evening a week, and may or may not have a small registration fee. Scholarships are readily available. PEG offers several approaches to parent education; classes vary by population and mission. There are classes for families with specific needs such as those of stepparents, single parents, or parents of teens. A school or district may also opt to plan basic parenting skills classes open only to parents of its students. There are limited opportunities for family enhancement workshops that parents and children attend together; these workshops use pottery, math, or computer projects to build closer family relationships. Finally, PEG may organize classes for school personnel, either to discuss community issues or to familiarize the school staff with the PEG project. In 1987-88, PEG piloted a workshop series and discussion group for parents of early elementary children enrolled in one school's special language-activity classroom. Head Start has commissioned PEG to provide separate parent education classes for its parents. PEG also sponsors the annual Parent Resource Fair for residents of Linn and Benton counties, a day-long series of over 40 presentations, workshops, and informational displays offered by community resource organizations and social service agencies. An inexpensive lunch and child care are provided.

**Participants**

In 1987-88, PEG served 120 children in parent-child classes and 613 parents in classes and at the Parent Resource Fair, which generally attracts over 200 parents. Forty percent of PEG participants are low-income rural families, and the rest are a more affluent mix of middle- to upper-middle-income families. Approximately 20 percent are single parents, and 1 percent are teens. Although PEG began by serving mostly impoverished families of troubled children, the current participants are a representative mix of at-risk and healthy families. PEG serves approximately 4 percent of the eligible families of school-age children in Linn and Benton counties.

**Parent Education**

Most PEG classes teach a core set of basic parenting skills and convey information about child development, communication, guidance, and discipline. Classes have a discussion format that encourages parents to interact with each other and the instructor. PEG emphasizes the importance of careful listening, both in class and in family relationships. Discussion topics vary according to the issues of the specific population; for example, the series for parents of students in a special language-based classroom focuses on language acquisition and delay and suggests how parents can further their children's education at home.

**Curriculum**

PEG's curriculum includes concepts from many authors and theorists in the areas of family dynamics and education such as Ginott, Gordon, Driekers, Faber, Mazlish, Illsley-Clark, and Briggs. Staff members build upon their own knowledge of human development, communication, guidance, and family life and use prepackaged curricula such as *Systematic Training for Effective Parenting (STEP), STEP-TEEN, Strengthening Step Families, Parenting on Your Own,* and *Unplug the Christmas Machine* as resources. Parents help define the issues that will be addressed in any series of classes. PEG materials are organized in a computerized file system under 400 topics of interest to parents.

**Sites**

PEG covers four school districts; classes meet at four preschool buildings, eight elementary schools, six middle schools, and two private schools. Classes take place in school libraries, faculty rooms, and classrooms. The resource fair is held on the community college campus. The program director, Bobbie Weber, says space is sufficient and that reception at the public schools is welcoming.

**Parent Involvement**

Each participating school or district has its own PEG advisory committee of parents who work with the school principal or administrator and the PEG staff to determine the character and content of PEG offerings. In addition, five parents serve on the program's overarching advisory committee, a 17-member group that plans and approves PEG programming. Parents provide input for curriculum design through surveys, usually taken during the first meeting of each series of classes. PEG places a strong emphasis on the importance of parents volunteering their time to help other parents. Twenty-five parents, who have had considerable experience in PEG, now lead or help teach PEG classes.

**Outreach**

PEG classes are listed in the community college's class schedule, mailed to all residents of the two counties. Parents are also notified through flyers, in notices that are included in school mailings, and through parent-teacher organizations. Bobbie Weber says the most effective way of getting parents involved is to invite them to design the curriculum and help publicize PEG classes. When PEG targets specific populations within a school or district, principals and counselors refer appropriate families to the program.

**Staff**

| Job Title | PD | Vol | FT | PT | Educ Req | Status | Benefits |
|---|---|---|---|---|---|---|---|
| Chair | 1 | - | 1 | - | Post-Graduate Courses or Degree | Other Contract | Yes |
| ESD Coordinator | 1 | - | 1 | - | Post-Graduate Courses or Degree | Other Contract | Yes |
| PEG Coordinator | 1 | - | - | 1 | Post-Graduate Courses or Degree | Other Contract | Yes |
| PEG Instructors | 15 | - | - | 15 | College Degree | Hourly Non-Contract | No |
| Parent Volunteers | - | 25 | - | - | None | - | No |

**State/District Requirements**

None.

**Linn-Benton Community College Requirements**

Instructors must have experience working with groups of children. Linn-Benton faculty have a master of arts or science degree. Part-time instructors should have a bachelor of arts or science degree in human development, education, social work, or a related field.

**Preferred Background**

The coordinator should have knowledge and experience in adult education and working with the public schools. Instructors should have experience teaching parents.

**Employee Education and Training Represented**

Prekindergarten and early childhood education; elementary education; education, grades 7 to 12; special education; parent educator; home economics; counseling; social work; child development and family studies; research and evaluation.

**Administration**

PEG is administered jointly by the Greater Albany Public Schools, Corvallis Public Schools, Scio Public Schools, Sweet Home Public Schools, Head Start, and Linn-Benton Community College (LBCC). The public schools are represented for administrative purposes by the umbrella district for Linn and Benton counties, the Education Services District (ESD), within its Behavior Management Division. PEG administrative staff members are Linn-Benton faculty. PEG is housed within the parent education program of LBCC's Department of Family Resources. PEG's coordinator, the chair of the Department of Family Resources, is the ESD behavior management coordinator, and designated staff members from the two major school districts meet regularly approximately six times a year to make decisions about programming and planning. In addition, an advisory committee is responsible for community networking, planning, and monitoring community feedback. It includes PEG staff members, public school representatives, members of community agencies, and program participants. The Juvenile Services Commission monitors the program.

**Relationship to the Schools**

PEG was specifically designed to enhance communication between parents and the schools, and only the parents of public school students are eligible to attend many classes. Each school or district to offer PEG classes designates a staff member to be its liaison to PEG. PEG's staff therefore plans its programming with principals, superintendents, or representatives from specific departments such as counseling, drug abuse, or family advocacy.

**Community Links**

PEG is a cooperative venture of Linn-Benton Community College, the Education Services District (the umbrella district of the public schools), the individual schools and districts, and the Juvenile Services Commission. In addition, PEG has invited representatives of several community agencies to serve on its advisory committee. This means that a cross-section of the community is involved and invested in PEG. Ms. Weber advises similar programs to garner a base of support by being respectful listeners and by having a flexible approach to program delivery. Focusing on the cooperative nature of the endeavor maximizes available resources.

*PEG emphasizes the importance of careful listening, both in class and in family relationships.*

**Funding**

Linn-Benton Community College, 36 percent; local school district funds, 34 percent; state Juvenile Services Commission grant, 30 percent. (The community college budget is made up of revenues from local property taxes, tuition, and state reimbursements.) Some PEG classes have small fees, with a reduction for the second parent. Classes that have required reading carry a small materials fee. Scholarships are readily available, and classes for targeted families are free.

**In-Kind Resources**

Public schools, private schools and local agencies provide meeting space for PEG classes; the Education Services District and the public schools provide coordination, participant referrals, publicity in school newsletters, clerical support, printing, and postage.

**Funding History**

Funding has remained stable.

**Objectives**

PEG aims to support parents of children who are not thriving in school, to bolster the self-confidence of parents, to promote better understanding of children's developmental needs, and to foster parents' sense of their own importance in the lives of their children.

**Evaluation**

The Linn County Juvenile Services Commission requires a descriptive report of PEG activities. The evaluation, whose format is set by the Juvenile Services Commission, measures parent satisfaction, as reported in parent surveys and anecdotal evidence, and instructor performance, as determined by coordinator evaluation, and requires a detailed report of meetings and activities. PEG integrates this information into report form on an ongoing basis. The overall PEG advisory committee and the local committees also constantly monitor and evaluate PEG. Ms. Weber relays evaluative information to the program's sponsors, school principals, and parent organizations, to increase the sense of ownership of PEG that she says these organizations already feel. Ms. Weber notes the lack of longitudinal or hard data in PEG evaluations. She does not feel the PEG staff is qualified to perform such a study, but is concerned that future funding sources might require it.

**Replication**

PEG was inspired by an earlier project of the Department of Family Resources called Between Parents and Teens. PEG has been adapted by Portland Community College and the Eugene Education Services District.

**Materials Available**

Ms. Weber offers PEG's curricular materials. Contact her at the program address. Materials include the *Parent Education Coordinator's Manual,* which includes policies and procedures; *Educating Parents: Instructor Handbook,* for parent-only instruction; *Educating Parents and Children Together: Instruction Handbook,* for instructors and facilitators of parent-child classes; and *Parent Education Curriculum Topic Resource File System,* which includes articles, handouts, and materials organized by topic, for computer or manual searches.

# Parent Education Resource Center

| | | |
|---|---|---|
| Resource library | Child care info/referral | Parenting/child development education |
| Home visits | Individual counseling | Community services info/referral |
| Toy lending | Health/nutrition education | Parent aide volunteer program |
| Evening classes | | |

**Contact:** Kathy Shaw, Director

**Address:** 120 West 3000 North
Layton, UT 84041
(801) 774-7427

**Established:** 1977, state pilot

**Budget '88-'89:** $41,388

**Sources:** Local school district; Davis County Social Services

**Size:** Approximately 1,000 parents

**Area Served:** Davis County, Utah

**Auspices:** Adult Education Department, Davis County School District

**1990 Respondent:** Beverly Dawson, Director

*A parent volunteer met regularly with a mother of two children who lived rural, isolated lives and were regularly abused by the husband. The wife accepted the abuse passively and would not seek help. One night, her husband called to say he was coming home with a gun. She and PERC's parent volunteer sought intervention from the police and a clergyman. Since then she has started to read about parenting and family issues, and as her confidence has increased, she has agreed to let her husband live with the family as long as he refrains from abuse.*

**Community**

Davis County is a narrow strip of suburbia stretching between Ogden and Salt Lake City, two metropolitan centers in northern Utah. Farmington, a bedroom community 18 miles from Salt Lake City, represents the more affluent segment of the county's population. The communities to the north are socially more diverse, with many families employed at an air force base and with more low-income and at-risk families. Ninety percent of the county's population is white. Davis County as a whole has suffered economically in recent years; many major industries have either moved out or closed down. The school system, the third largest in the state and overburdened by the rapid transformation from rural to suburban population, has had less money to spend on nonacademic programs.

**Philosophy and Goals**

The Parent Education Resource Center (PERC) believes that parents want to raise responsible, happy children but often lack appropriate knowledge of child development and parenting skills. By educating parents, PERC helps them raise their own self-esteem and take a more positive and effective approach to parenting.

**History and Origins**

In 1976, at the urging of its director of pupil personnel services, the Davis County School District responded to a request for proposals from the Utah Department of Adult Education, volunteering Davis County as a pilot site for a fledgling parent resource program. The Davis County School District's social work department worked with the parent-teacher association (PTA) and other community agencies to develop the model for the Parent Education Resource Center. It included a drop-in lending library for parents and children, parent education groups, counseling, and referrals. After a year and a half of programming, Utah State University conducted an extensive evaluation of the pilots; parent evaluations and self-assessments contributed to the overall conclusion that Davis County PERC had a significant effect on increasing parents' understanding of child development. In 1979, the state set up eight other parent resource centers modeled on the Davis program. Although the state continues to be supportive of PERC, the school districts became responsible for funding the program after 1979. At that time, the Davis County Social Services Department funded PERC to train parents to provide home-based remedial services to abusive and neglecting parents.

## Features

The Parent Education Resource Center offers an extensive lending library of books, toys, filmstrips, pamphlets, and education kits on child development and parenting, which are available on loan to parents and children at no charge. A drop-in play area allows children to explore the toys quietly while their parents browse. The center is open all day on school days and until 7 p.m. one day a week. PERC staff members are available during open hours to match the resources of the program and the community to parents' needs and requests. The PERC coordinator provides short-term crisis counseling to parents who need it and may refer participants to additional sources of counseling. During the school year PERC sponsors a variety of fee-based evening classes for parents, both single sessions and series. PERC's Parent Aide Volunteer Program trains volunteer parents to offer home-based remedial services and support to abusive and neglectful families in the community at least once a week for as long as is needed.

## Participants

In 1987-88, 650 parents used the lending library and 495 attended parent education classes; eight volunteers served eight at-risk families. Any parent in the county may use PERC services; some parents attend only classes that address specific needs, and some have been in the library lending pool for as long as 10 years. There is a small fee per parent per evening class session, but waivers are available to low-income participants. Participation has decreased in the 10 years of PERC's existence. The program director, Mrs. Beverly Dawson, attributes this largely to the growing number of dual-career families who do not have time during the day to take advantage of the resource center.

*Volunteer home visitors help parents see ways to raise their children without abuse and encourage them to recognize and relate to their children's developmental and emotional needs.*

## Parent Education

PERC's resource library provides a wealth of information to parents in the areas of discipline, self-esteem, language development, special needs, surviving divorce and remarriage, and others. Evening classes for parents consider such topics as gifted children, handicapped children, how to cope with learning disabilities, and stress management. The center's staff worked with PTA volunteers to develop an educational program about sexuality for parents of elementary students.

## Curriculum

PERC frequently uses the nationally recognized *Systematic Training for Effective Parenting (STEP)* curriculum, but class presenters may design their own programs on a variety of topics. Parent volunteers develop a curriculum catering to the needs of abusive and neglectful families, with the help of the PERC staff and library resources.

**Sites**

The main resource center is located at the Monte Vista center in Farmington, a public school that serves handicapped and nonhandicapped students. PERC runs parent education classes at the school one night a week and is free to use any part of the building for its evening programs. The program has two smaller satellite centers in the Cook and Washington elementary schools that are open 1½ days a week and offer lending library services only. Both sites are more easily accessible to parents in Syracuse and Bountiful than the central Farmington location.

**Parent Involvement**

Parents have not been involved in PERC's administration since Mrs. Dawson's early efforts to encourage a strong parent advisory board failed. Parents do, however, play a large role in its outreach into the community. Potentially abusive and neglectful parents, identified by the county's social services, receive home visits once a week from parents trained by PERC to provide parent support and education. Volunteer home visitors help parents see ways to raise their children without abuse and encourage them to recognize and relate to their children's developmental and emotional needs. They must attend five two-hour training sessions taught by a certified social worker.

**Outreach**

The Davis County PTA provides outreach for PERC, announcing classes and services in its newsletters and at meetings. Public school teachers may refer families to the center. PERC contracts with the Davis County Social Services Department to provide home-based services to potentially neglectful or abusive parents. The program also advertises in the newspaper, hosts orientation programs, distributes brochures, and commissions public service announcements.

**Staff**

| Job Title | PD | Vol | FT | PT | Educ Req | Status | Benefits |
|-----------|----|-----|----|----|----------|--------|----------|
| Director | 1 | - | - | 1 | Post-Graduate Courses or Degree | K-12 Contract | Yes |
| Secretary/ Coordinators | 2 | - | 1 | 1 | High School Diploma | Hourly Contract | Yes |
| Volunteer Coordinator | 1 | - | - | 1 | College Degree | Hourly Contract | No |
| Volunteers | - | 9 | - | 9 | High School Diploma | - | No |

**State/District Requirements**

None.

**Preferred Background**

The director and secretary-coordinator must be parents and should have either training or experience in social work, child development, and family relations. The coordinator of volunteer services should have a bachelor's degree. Parent aide volunteers are screened for family problems and must undergo five two-hour sessions of training by a licensed social worker before they can visit abusive and neglectful families.

**Employee Education and Training Represented**

Prekindergarten and early childhood education; parent educator; counseling; family therapy; social work; child development and family studies.

| | |
|---|---|
| **Administration** | A part-time director and two paid staff members administer the PERC. Satellite centers are run by volunteers, with some support from the Farmington staff. The program director, Beverly Dawson, oversees the program and counsels families in crisis. Other staff members run the library and coordinate volunteer services. PERC staff members are hired and paid by the district, and the director reports to the director of curriculum of the Davis County Public Schools. |
| **Relationship to the Schools** | PERC is a public school program, although any parent may take advantage of its services. Over the years, PERC has added evening courses that deal directly with children's performance in school in the hope, Mrs. Dawson says, that school-oriented classes would make PERC an indispensable part of the district's services. PERC notifies elementary school principals of its events and services and, last year, sent packets of information to all elementary school teachers. Teachers often use the PERC library as a resource for curriculum and problem solving, and PERC staff members meet monthly with the school's social workers and counselors to discuss general issues and specific cases. PERC also helps the PTA develop educational services for parents. |
| **Community Links** | PERC exchanges referrals with the social service community. |
| **Funding** | Resource library, $24,660 from the school district; parent aide volunteers, $16,728 from Davis County Social Services Department. |
| **In-Kind Resources** | The Davis County School District provides space, utilities, phone service, materials, and access to equipment. |
| **Funding History** | Funding increased steadily until 1986, when a fiscal crisis in the state and the district's budgetary cutbacks caused funds to decrease sharply. The director's position, once full time, has been cut to 1½ days per week. Mrs. Dawson continues to be available at the center every day but has other assignments in the district as well. Since 1986, PERC has shortened its hours slightly but has not significantly altered services. |
| **Objectives** | Participants improve their parenting skills, strengthen family relationships, gain knowledge of their children's social, emotional, and academic development, and increase their own self-esteem. PERC functions as an ongoing resource for all parents, available in crisis situations for counseling and referral. |
| **Evaluation** | After its first 18 months PERC was evaluated by the state university. The study found that parents' knowledge of child development had increased as a result of participation. For the first several years, PERC performed annual self-evaluations and kept careful statistics, but reductions in budget and staff limit the time available for evaluation, and Mrs. Dawson admits that the staff has not made it a priority. She says the staff's day-to-day experience suggests that PERC is meeting parents' needs. |
| **Replication** | Davis County PERC is the result of experimentation with the basic model proposed by a state initiative. Subsequent sites to implement the program have used Davis County's PERC as a model. |
| **Materials Available** | None. |

Harvard Family Research Project

# Community Education Home and Family Development Program

*A woman contacted Connie Schulz after hearing her speak about parenting. She was having problems with both her daughter and her husband, who was struggling with his job but didn't approve of his wife going to work to help out. Connie helped set up appointments with the school guidance counselor for the daughter, then worked with the husband to design a manageable family budget. The information and help that Connie provided helped this family to make changes that improved the quality of their lives.*

| | | |
|---|---|---|
| Consultation | Adult literacy | Health/nutrition education |
| Child care | Counseling | Community services info/referral |
| Home visits | GED services | Teen parent support groups |
| Warmline | Parent support groups | Parent-child joint activities |
| Networking | Newsletter | Developmental exams/screening |
| | | Parenting/child development education |

**Contact:** Nancy Desmond, Director of Community Education
Constance E. Schulz, Family Outreach Specialist

**Address:** State College Area School District
411 South Fraser Street
State College, PA 16801-5289
(814) 231-1061

**Established:** 1965, Chapter 1, federal program

**Budget '88-'89:** $220,000

**Sources:** State, federal, and local school district funds; client fees

**Size:** 700 families

**Area Served:** State College Area School District

**Auspices:** State College Community Education Department

**Community**

The State College Area School District (SCASD), in a mountainous region of central Pennsylvania, includes five rural townships and a "metropolitan community in a rural setting." A 1980 census revealed that 7 percent of the population had not completed high school. Pennsylvania State University employs the majority of the work force; other employers include a defense industry plant and small businesses. An increasing population of black and Asian graduate students (approximately 9 percent of the population) is changing the demographics of this mostly white community.

**Philosophy and Goals**

The Community Education Home and Family Development Program is designed to equip parents with positive parenting skills that build communication among family members and reduce parental stress. In addition, the program involves families in schools, believing that cooperative efforts between parents and teachers help children succeed in school.

**History and Origins**

Since the 1960s the SCASD adult education program has focused on individual and family development, homemaking and artistic skills, and management of resources. During the War on Poverty, the program broadened to include the Community Education Department, with its long-standing interest in parenting. Parent education programs have been offered through home economics since the mid-1960s, directed by the homemaking consultant. When Constance Schulz, the homemaking consultant, was hired by the Community Education Department in 1983, she saw a need to update courses in child development and parent education.

Ms. Schulz joined the Centre County Human Services Planning Offices Task Force to determine community needs. Concern for teen parents emerged from the study as a major issue. As a result, 20 agencies teamed up to develop an ideal program for teen parents which, following the Missouri Parents as Teachers (PAT) model, would utilize existing community services and hire a home visitor to work with teen parents. When funding through vocational education became available, the model became a home-based program called Teen Parents as Teachers (TPAT). The Homemaking Consultant Program and other existing programs fall, with TPAT, under Community Education Department auspices.

**Features**

The Community Education Department offers parents an array of home-based and center-based services 12 months a year.

The **Home and Family Development Program** is an umbrella for the Homemaking Consultant Program, two teen parent programs, the Home Management Outreach Program, and the Adult Basic Education and GED programs. It targets low- and middle-income families and is offered free to parents of children in the school district and to teen parents. In addition to the free services, it offers fee-based parent education classes to the community.

The **Homemaking Consultant Program** provides opportunities for adults within the school district to work with a home economist to improve their home management and parenting skills and coordinates instruction with the Adult Basic Education and GED programs.

**Teen Parents as Teachers (TPAT)** provides monthly home visits from parent educators to teen parents, helping them prepare for childbirth and learn about childrearing and child development.

**Parenting and Childbirth for Teens (PACT),** a school-based program for teens, offers child care, counseling, support groups, health education and monitoring, transportation for infants, vocational counseling, and parent education classes (available for academic credit) to teens enrolled in school. If the mother is unable to obtain daycare for her newborn, PACT also provides home instruction for up to six weeks following childbirth, when the child can begin to attend daycare.

The **Home Management Outreach Program** assists single parents, disabled parents, and the elderly with homemaking and family management skills and career planning, and makes linkages with other social service agencies.

**Participants**

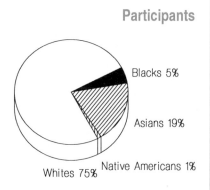

Blacks 5%

Asians 19%

Whites 75%   Native Americans 1%

In 1987-88, the Homemaking Consultant Program component served 70 individual parents and 93 parents in groups; 40 percent of the participants served were single parents and 15 percent were teens. TPAT served 54 teen parents and PACT served 11 teen mothers; the Home Management Outreach Program served 17 single parents. One hundred and fifty-nine parents enrolled in fee-based parenting classes and 74 parents attended a one-day Focus on the Family conference. According to Ms. Schulz, only 25 percent of the eligible parents in the district have been reached, the majority of whom came from low- and middle-income brackets. The Home and Family Development Program participants must be parents of children enrolled in the school district or teen parents, though not necessarily "at risk." TPAT is offered to parents under 21. The Home Management Outreach Program is offered to single parents, disabled parents, and the elderly. The Adult Basic Education and GED programs are offered to parents or teens over 16 years of age who have withdrawn from school.

**Parent Education**

Some classes are free, others are fee-based. Free miniclasses varying in subject matter from cooking lessons to computer literacy are conducted in participants' homes once or twice a week for six weeks. The fee-based classes are geared to parents with infants, toddlers, or small children and focus on child development and parents' needs. The cost has risen ($45 to $56 per person, and $77 to $95 per couple) due to cutbacks in funding from the school board. Ms. Schulz feels that home visits are the core of the parent support program and are crucial for parents who are unable or unwilling to attend classes. "We meet needs as they arise through referrals from the school staff to the home economist. We individualize, treat everyone differently. Sometimes we call parents up and invite them to a small group, sometimes we make home visits for those who don't want to come to group. There is a range, some people will pay for services, some can't. All are served."

**Curriculum**

Every fee-based class and miniclass begins by determining the concerns of participants. A variety of packaged curriculum materials are used, including *Active Parenting,* PAT materials, *Responsive Parenting,* and other curricula available through the Center for Early Adolescence in Carrboro, North Carolina. Guest speakers from local organizations like WIC (Special Supplemental Food Program for Women, Infants, and Children) speak to parent groups about foods and supplements to breast feeding.

**Sites**

Programs are offered in a preschool, public elementary schools, other public schools, neighborhood or community agencies, a religious facility, homes, and a housing project.

Unstable siting arrangements are a common problem for the community education programs and the location of the program office changes periodically. Courses meeting at night have easier access to school classrooms, but in the daytime there is a severe shortage of space. A refurbished school building that houses a kindergarten is used for parent-toddler courses. An unsatisfactory, temporary solution had been renting space from a church. Although church sites can be convenient outreach locations, they are not rent-free and add to the cost of parenting education classes.

**Parent Involvement**

Parents are the recipients of services and host programs in their homes.

**Outreach**

Program outreach takes place at job fairs and in cooperative educational programs with other agencies. The Christian Mission, Food Bank, and County Adult Services Program actively make referrals.

| Job Title | PD | Vol | FT | PT | Educ Req | Status | Benefits |
|---|---|---|---|---|---|---|---|
| Homemaking Consultant | 1 | - | 1 | - | College Degree | Hourly Contract | Yes |
| Teen Parent Educator | 1 | - | - | 1 | College Degree | Hourly Contract | Yes |
| Home Management Outreach Specialist | 1 | - | 1 | - | College Degree | Hourly Contract | Yes |
| Assistant Director/ABE Supervisor | 1 | - | 1 | - | College Degree | Other Contract | Yes |
| Adult Parenting Education Instructors | 5 | - | - | 5 | College Degree | Hourly Non-Contract | No |
| ABE Instructors | 8 | - | - | 8 | College Degree | Hourly Non-Contract | No |

**State/District Requirements**

The home management outreach consultant, teen parent educator, and homemaking consultant are certified home economics teachers. Although the state does not require it, all staff members have college degrees.

**Preferred Background**

Sensitivity to a variety of socioeconomic levels.

**Employee Education and Training Represented**

Infant and toddler education; prekindergarten and early childhood education; elementary education; education, grades 7 to 12; bilingual education; special education; adult basic education; parent educator; adult vocational education; child care; home economics; child development and family studies.

**Administration**

The program has always been administered through the school district of State College. The homemaking consultant reports to the program director of the Community Education Department who is responsible to the superintendent of schools, the program advisory committee, and the school board. The Community Education Department's advisory board, composed of five paid staff members, five program participants, and five members of the community, meets six times a year to approve program services and curriculum, suggest courses, establish relationships with other agencies, and help with recruitment.

**Relationship to the Schools**

Free facilities and participant referrals are the two chief benefits derived from being attached to the school system, according to Ms. Schulz. The program director feels that parenting programs belong in the schools, making schools a place with something to offer everyone. The schools appreciate working with parents who are alert to their children's developmental needs.

Pupil-Personnel Services alerts the homemaking consultant about families who may need assistance. The district's Chapter 1 program also works closely with the homemaking consultant in planning parent activities.

**Community Links**

Centre County Council for Human Services, a consortium of community agencies, arranges monthly lunch meetings for its members to make program announcements and share information. Each month a different group makes a presentation of its services.

**Funding**

Local school district, 47 percent; participants' fees, 30 percent; state, federal, and local government services, 23 percent. Parent education funding is moderately secure and has increased by 65 percent since the program's first year of operation. The Home and Family Development Program has a budget of $50,000; TPAT, $40,000; the Home Management Outreach Program, $40,000; and Adult Basic Education, $55,000.

**In-Kind Resources**

The State College area schools provide space and facilities, access to equipment, materials, and supplies.

**Funding History**

Initially, funding for parent education programming came from the federal vocational education program and filtered down to the State College Area School District Community Education Department through the Pennsylvania Department of Education.

In 1986, the school district created a special budget for parent education components. At that time the Home Management Outreach Program, PACT, and TPAT were self-supporting through grants, and Education for Parenthood classes were supported by fees. The school district funded the Homemaking Consultant Program. In 1988-89, however, the school district cut back the parenting budget, and the teen programs have suffered staff time cuts. The homemaking consultant is now paid through the Vocational and Community Education Departments.

*The program director feels that parenting programs belong in the schools, making schools a place with something to offer everyone. The schools appreciate working with parents who are alert to their children's developmental needs.*

**Objectives**

The program hopes to increase families' confidence in their abilities to meet their own needs by enhancing knowledge of child and family development, school procedures, and community resources.

**Evaluation**

There are no formal evaluations. Surveys, participant evaluations, community task forces, advisory committee studies, and information about similar programs are used to plan new courses.

**Replication**

TPAT is based on the Missouri Parents as Teachers model.

**Materials Available**

None.

# Parenting Education Center

*Project IMPACT and the Minority Student Achievement program's bilingual, bicultural presentations fulfill a unique need, notes Nancy Scesney. She feels that translation cannot communicate the nuances of parents' concerns; non-English speakers especially enjoy question-and-answer sessions with professionals who speak their own language.*

| | | |
|---|---|---|
| Networking | Health/nutrition education | Parenting/child development education |
| Newsletter | Multilingual presentations | Technical assistance to schools |
| Life skills classes | Teen parenting classes | Child care info/referral |
| GED services | Mother support group | Community services info/referral |
| Resource library | Parent/couple support groups | Teen parent career center resource room |
| Crisis intervention | Individual counseling | Parent-child joint activities |

**Contact:** Karen Willoughby, Coordinator and Program Specialist

**Address:** 7510 Lisle Avenue
Falls Church, VA 22043
(703) 506-2221

**Established:** 1974, local initiative

**Budget '88-89:** $50,000 plus class tuition

**Sources:** Carl Perkins Vocational Act; Minority Student Achievement grant; client fees

**Size:** 5,650 families

**Area served:** Fairfax County, Virginia

**Auspices:** Office of Adult and Community Education, Fairfax Public Schools

**1990 Respondent:** Nancy Scesney, Adult Education Program Specialist

**Community**

Fairfax County spans 30 miles of the Washington, DC metropolitan area. The 125,000 students in the public schools come from families of widely varying income levels and ethnic groups including blacks, Spanish-speakers, and Asians speaking Vietnamese, Cambodian, or Korean. An army base contributes highly transient families to the mix. The school district is the tenth largest in the country, with 160 schools. In recent years the school system has identified many of these schools as "special needs" schools that, due to the high number of students whose primary language is not English, the high rate of student mobility, and the large number of students receiving free or reduced-price lunch, receive additional funding, staff, and resources.

**Philosophy and Goals**

The Parenting Education Center believes the schools and the community have a mutual goal of helping families reach their fullest potential, and it attempts to make information and education easily accessible to parents in a large county. The center holds that there is no single best parent education technique; schools need technical assistance and resource information to match program content and delivery to the needs and characteristics of specific communities.

**History and Origins**

In 1974, the Office of Adult and Community Education of the Fairfax County Public Schools added tuition-based parent-child classes to its roster of educational programming. In 1979, a local group asked the office to take over the coordination and administration of Project IMPACT, a program that had been sponsored by several community agencies, offering a series of parenting sessions for hard-to-reach parents. Under the auspices of the Office of Adult and Community Education, the program has expanded to four sites throughout the county and is offered in several languages.

In 1985, the office received a local school grant through its Minority Student Achievement (MSA) program. The original $8,000 grant, twice renewed and since increased to $15,000, allows special needs schools to request technical assistance to develop parent education classes and parent involvement programs.

In 1988, the department started Project Opportunity, which offers daycare and high school credit to teen mothers who participate in classes in parent education, life management skills, and sex equity issues. That same year, the Office of Adult and Community Education established the Parenting Education Center at the Pimmit Hills Adult Education Center as a clearinghouse for parent education resources in the county.

**Project IMPACT** offers programs to parents of children from birth to age nine in low-income areas twice a year, in the fall and spring, at four different sites. Parents preregister and child care is provided.

**Minority Student Achievement (MSA)** helps individual special needs schools design parent education and involvement programs. Depending on the needs of the school, MSA might organize a series of classes following the IMPACT model or hold a one-night parent involvement workshop to attract parents to the parent-teacher association or other parent groups. When appropriate, programs are held in English, Spanish, Vietnamese, Korean, Cambodian, Laotian, Chinese, or Farsi.

**Project Opportunity** offers high school credit for classes taken through the Teen Parent/Career Center at the Bryant Adult and Community Education Center. Teens may earn five credits per semester taking classes in life skills management, parenting, early childhood, and a course in sex equity and gender issues.

The **Parenting Education Center** continues to offer nearly 100 tuition-based parenting classes per year, some with a parent-child activity format, and publishes the *Fairfax County Guide to Parenting Programs,* a comprehensive guide to parent services offered by the department and nonprofit community agencies throughout the county. It also coordinates the Speakers Bureau, which provides professional speakers to community groups for a fee. Topics include parenting issues.

Project IMPACT targets low-income parents of young children who may need information on basic child development issues or who may be experiencing any of several risk factors, including family violence, marital instability, or isolation. Project IMPACT also serves court-ordered clients. Although programming takes place in low-income neighborhoods, any parent in the county is welcome to attend; 1,050 parents participated in 1987-88.

Minority Student Achievement (MSA) served approximately 875 parents last year, in half of the special needs schools that requested programming. By definition, special needs schools have large populations of racial and ethnic minorities and high numbers of students for whom English is a second language. Project Opportunity served 29 teen mothers, mostly in the Bryant center area. Although transportation assistance is available in the form of bus tickets or mileage reimbursements, only 10 percent of those eligible took advantage of the program. Tuition-based classes and the Speakers Bureau served 2,500

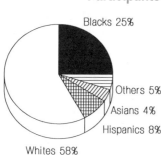

Blacks 25%

Others 5%

Asians 4%

Hispanics 8%

Whites 58%

adults in the community in 1987-88; these were generally middle- to upper-income families.

## Parent Education

Tuition-based parenting classes cover a wide variety of topics for parent education and parent-child participation, such as building children's self-esteem, parenting a shy child, discipline issues, and sibling rivalry. Summer courses teach parents activities that are designed to reinforce academic skills acquired during the school year. Most tuition-based classes focus on a particular age group. Project IMPACT and MSA provide information about child development, family communication, discipline, stress management, and child and family self-esteem. Project Opportunity helps teen parents complete their high school education and gain marketable skills. It also explores the concepts of sex-role stereotyping and vocational equality.

*When the center begins working with a school under the MSA grant, it emphasizes that parents need both passive and active ways of being involved as teachers, learners, and educational advocates.*

## Curriculum

At each of the four Project IMPACT sites, a committee of agency and school representatives chooses topics (from a list of over 40 from past programs), presenters, and language of presentation. MSA is likewise tailored to the needs of the parent community in the individual school, as determined by the principal, school counselors, English as a Second Language (ESL) teacher, and parent requests. Project Opportunity follows the Fairfax County Public Schools home economics and marketing curricula, adapting materials on parenting to the special needs of teen mothers. The job-skills component of the curriculum emphasizes gender equity.

## Sites

Local committees decide on the delivery sites for Project IMPACT. Currently, it is offered at public elementary and high school buildings and community buildings such as churches. MSA programming is delivered at 19 elementary and 7 other public schools. Project Opportunity meets at the Bryant Adult and Community Education Center, where a room is set aside as the Teen Parent/Career Center. Tuition-based programming meets at public elementary schools, neighborhood centers, public libraries, and a religious facility. The district has integrated its adult programs at a former elementary school that now houses the Parenting Education Center classes, ESL, GED, and several tuition-based adult education classes. Space is at a premium because the county population has continually increased. According to Ms. Scesney, the center has decreased its parent-child activity classes because they require so much space and has requested community centers and churches to donate facilities that it cannot afford to rent.

## Parent Involvement

The Parenting Education Center has identified a wide range of opportunities for parent involvement in the county, but parents do not participate in center administration. The purpose of the MSA grant, however, is to get parents involved in their children's schools, whether by participating in parent education or the PTA, or using a parent resource library.

When the center begins working with a school under the MSA grant, it emphasizes that parents need both passive and active ways of being involved as teachers, learners, and educational advocates.

**Outreach**

The Parenting Education Center coordinates the publishing of the *Fairfax County Guide to Parenting Programs (GTPP)* and distributes 4,000 copies to school and agency personnel. Costs prohibit distributing a guide to every parent in the county, but the GTPP Coordinating Committee has put together a single-page parenting resources telephone list, which has been translated into Spanish, Vietnamese, Korean, and Cambodian. The Office of Adult and Community Education and other agencies include these lists in mailings to parents. The center's outreach philosophy for the Project IMPACT and MSA programs is to free school and community agencies from routine administrative details so that they can identify and recruit parents who need these programs. The center publicizes them in local newspapers and district newsletters, and the Fairfax County Council of PTAs has been vocal on behalf of the center. The center approaches professionals who are familiar with minority cultures and asks them to suggest local cultural groups whose sponsorship, listed in program literature, would legitimize parenting programs.

**Staff**

The Parenting Education Center relies on part-time professionals paid (no benefits) by the hour. This system saves the center money and seems better suited to employees' schedules.

| Job Title | PD | Vol | FT | PT | Educ Req | Status | Benefits |
|---|---|---|---|---|---|---|---|
| Lead Program Specialist | 1 | - | 1 | - | College Degree/ Post-Graduate Courses or Degree | K-12 Contract | Yes |
| Classes Program Specialist | 1 | - | 1 | - | College Degree/ Post-Graduate Courses or Degree | Hourly Non-Contract | Yes |
| MSA Grant Program Specialist | 1 | - | - | 1 | College Degree/ Post-Graduate Courses or Degree | Hourly Non-Contract | Yes |
| Project Opportunity Coordinator | 1 | | - | 1 | College Degree/ Post-Graduate Courses or Degree | Other | Yes |
| IMPACT Program Specialists | 2 | - | - | 2 | College Degree/ Post-Graduate Courses or Degree | Hourly Non-Contract | Yes |
| Instructors | 40 | - | - | 40 | College Degree | Hourly Non-Contract | No |

| State/District Requirements | The lead program specialist is certified as an adult home economics teacher; the coordinator of Project Opportunity is a guidance counselor with a degree in vocational education. |
|---|---|
| Preferred Background | For any position, a bachelor's degree in a helping profession; a self-directed, hard-working, detail-oriented individual with experience working with children and parents, both individually and in groups. |
| Employee Education and Training Represented | Prekindergarten and early childhood education; parent educator; adult vocational education; home economics; counseling; child development and family studies. |
| Administration | The Parenting Education Center is part of the Office of Adult and Community Education of the Fairfax County Public Schools. The center coordinator reports to the director of adult and community education. The center coordinates Project IMPACT, but regional advisory groups, composed of local sponsoring agencies, have decision-making powers over Project IMPACT's budget, services, fundraising, publicity, and the language of service delivery. The MSA program is monitored by the MSA office of the public schools' Department of Instructional Services. Project Opportunity is monitored by the Virginia Department of Education. |

*The center approaches professionals who are familiar with minority cultures and asks them to suggest local cultural groups whose sponsorship, listed in program literature, would legitimize parenting programs.*

| Relationship to the Schools | The Minority Student Achievement grant is the Parent Education Center's closest tie to individual schools. The center sends memos to principals of special needs schools, notifying them of the availability of assistance. The principal will usually assign a teacher or a counselor to coordinate with the center. Although Ms. Scesney hesitates to give the Parent Education Center credit, she notes that all district schools, not just MSA schools, have been increasingly concerned with parent contact in the past few years. Every elementary school must now have a trained counselor to work with parents and children, and Ms. Scesney says that these counselors turn to the center as a resource. |
|---|---|
| Community Links | Local agencies share the cost of publishing the *Guide to Parenting Programs* and refer parents to programs listed therein. The Parenting Education Center runs Project IMPACT in cooperation with several community agencies, including Fairfax County's Departments of Social Services and Health, a mental health center, and the Fairfax Cooperative Extension. All Project IMPACT speakers volunteer from different agencies. |
| Funding | Client paid fees, third-party reimbursement (insurance, etc.), other local governments, private donations, local school district funds, state government, special events, and fundraising activities. More specifically, Project Opportunity received $35,000 through the Carl Perkins Vocational Act, Virginia Department of Education. The Minority Student Achievement grant of $15,000 is used to provide coordination, staffing |

and babysitting for up to 100 programs. Other parenting classes are self-supporting through class tuition and Speakers Bureau fees.

**In-Kind Resources**

Office space and classroom space provided by the school district, neighborhood centers, a religious facility, and a public library.

**Funding History**

The original MSA grant has nearly doubled since 1974.

**Objectives**

The Parenting Education Center aims to make parents in Fairfax County aware of the diverse opportunities for adult education and involvement and help them realize they share concerns and frustrations about the education and development of their children. It fosters strong relationships among parents, community agencies, and community schools, caters to the specific needs of parent groups, and provides technical assistance and guidance.

**Evaluation**

Parenting Education Center staff members have observed that parents involved in Project IMPACT and MSA are more likely to become involved in their school parent organizations. Eighty-two percent of the principals and school counselors who responded to an evaluative survey of the MSA grant indicated that parents who participated are developing a better rapport with teachers; 64 percent feel that these parents are improving their relationship with their children. A formal evaluation, to identify MSA's role in increasing parent involvement in the schools, was planned for 1988-89.

**Replication**

Parenting Education Center programs are based on widely held concepts of child development and childrearing, but none was based on a specific model and none has been replicated.

**Materials Available**

For information on individual programs, a copy of the *Guide to Parenting Programs* or the parent resources telephone list, please contact Nancy Scesney.

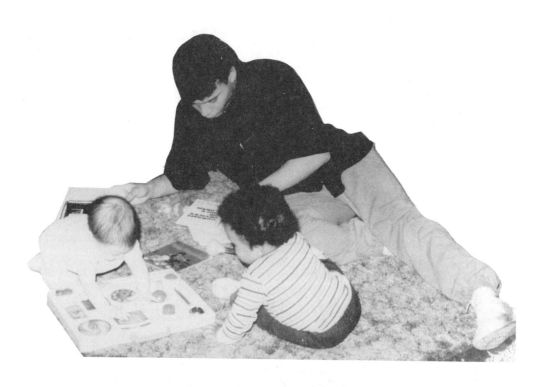

# 6

## Teens, Parenthood, and Child Development

This chapter begins with two preventive programs that teach child development and family life issues to young adolescents. They aim to give students the self-respect, knowledge, and experience necessary to make responsible decisions.

The remaining programs focus exclusively on providing parent education, support, health and advocacy services, and daycare to pregnant and parenting teens and their infants. As alternatives to regular high school, many offer academic coursework with a career orientation. They may be bona fide high school degree granting programs, like the Quincy Teen Mothers Program in Quincy, Massachusetts, or function as bridges for teens who will return to their schools. Uniformly, these programs aim to keep adolescent parents engaged in completing high school and looking toward their futures and to give them the skills to become effective parents.

# Programs in Brief

Sullivan County Health Department/
Kingsport City Schools Family Life Education Program — p. 295
*A preventive model of sex and human development education for young adolescents in Blountville, Tennessee*

Child Development — p. 299
*Suburban New Jersey program of preschool and intergenerational parenting classes for upper-middle-class families*

Jefferson County Teen Parent Program — p. 303
*Rural Oregon program for low-income teen parents offering parent education and support in a school setting*

New Futures School — p. 309
*Alternative school in Albuquerque, New Mexico offering comprehensive services for low-income adolescent parents and their infants*

CEC Child Care Center — p. 315
*Daycare programs and seminars on parenting and child development in Iowa City, Iowa for adolescent parents with children birth to age three*

Project Hope — p. 321
*An inner-city program in Warwick, Rhode Island, offering middle- and low-income teen mothers the opportunity to finish high school*

Off Campus Alternative Class — p. 327
*Urban alternative high school in Sacramento, California, providing education and support to pregnant and parenting teens and child care for their infants*

Quincy Teen Mothers —p. 333
*Urban alternative academic and self-development program serving pregnant and parenting students and their children*

Preschool/Parenting Learning Center — p. 339
*Tennessee state model of alternative education for pregnant and parenting teens of low-income families*

# Sullivan County Health Department/ Kingsport City Schools Family Life Education Program

*Seeing a list of sexually transmitted diseases on the chalk board, one seventh grader queried, "You know, it's really best not to be sexually active, isn't it?" When students draw their own conclusions from the material presented in family life education, Debbie Dotson feels, "That's a sign of the best teaching. It's not that we want to be negative about sex," she adds, "but we're scared because of the emotional immaturity and vulnerability of the children."*

| Academic credit | Individual counseling | Teen pregnancy prevention |
|---|---|---|

**Contact:** Debbie Dotson, Health Educator

**Address:** Sullivan County Health Department
Kingsport City Schools Family Life Education Program
P.O. Box 630
Blountville, TN 37617
(615) 323-7131

**Established:** 1983, local initiative

**Budget '88-'89:** $18,264

**Source:** School district

**Size:** 1600 students

**Area served:** Kingsport, Tennessee

**Auspices:** Sullivan County Department of Health and Education and the Kingsport City Schools

## Community

Sullivan County covers a sprawling rural area; its two urban centers, Kingsport and Bristol, each have their own school boards and their own city governments. Blountville, the centrally located county seat, is home to the Sullivan County governmental offices and the school board. Kingsport has a high concentration of the county's 1 percent minority population.

## Philosophy and Goals

The Family Life Education Program adopts a preventive focus, providing comprehensive family life and sex education in an open and nonjudgmental, professional atmosphere. Its aims include strengthening family communication, delaying premature sexual activity, preventing teen pregnancy and its associated problems, strengthening adolescents' self-esteem, and improving their ability to set goals and make responsible decisions.

## History and Origins

The Family Life Education Program initiative grew out of a pilot family life education course offered to eighth graders at a Sullivan County school. Bill Clark, principal of Ross Robinson Middle School in Kingsport, first had the idea of running the program for sixth graders. He contacted Debbie Dotson, a health department educator who offered to provide instructors and materials (paid for by the county health department) if the school agreed to pick up the cost after three years. Both the Robinson Parent-Teacher Association and the district superintendent responded enthusiastically, as did the community. "The timing was good," comments Ms. Dotson, "The religious right was not so well organized and the school had a matter-of-fact attitude. It didn't make a big deal out of the course, just said this is what we're doing." Kingsport School District has been paying for the program since 1986 and in 1989 purchased supplementary materials and started to teach the course in its second middle school. The district shares one instructor between the two schools. Selected as a state model in 1987 and 1988, the Family Life Education Program has been showcased in Nashville, Knoxville, and Jackson. Tennessee has just passed legislation mandating family life education in the schools, but the curriculum, says Ms. Dotson, is a bare skeleton, leaving lots of latitude for school systems to interpret the ruling as they wish.

Programs offering family life and sex education have to know how to deal with right-wing controversy, states Ms. Dotson. She suggests, "The key is to know what to expect; others can clue you into that. Realize which curriculum areas will be a problem and make them palatable. Also realize that no matter how much you compromise, it will, for some people, never be enough. So, develop a good, strong, well-rounded curriculum and then leave it up to the parents to decide whether or not their children will participate."

**Features**

The Family Life Education Program is a seven- to nine-week classroom series designed for sixth, seventh, and eighth graders. It focuses on such topics as puberty, reproduction, family planning, parenting, sexually transmitted diseases, AIDS, sexual abuse prevention, teen pregnancy, communication, and relationships. Decision making and responsible action are underlying themes. The program is available to all middle school children with permission from parents. The course culminates in a test (with academic credit given to students enrolled in home economics), which according to Ms. Dotson, helps impress students with its importance. Test results are given immediately, and answers are discussed in class. The program runs during the school day, using time otherwise allocated for home economics, band, or orchestra. The teachers of these courses, says Ms. Dotson, take a real interest in the Family Life Education Program and in their students' performance and attitude.

**Participants**

Since 1983, about 1,600 students per year, ages 12 through 14, have participated in the Family Life Education Program; all but 2 percent of the eligible population. Nonparticipants are those whose parents have refused permission.

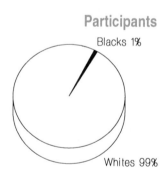

Blacks 1%

Whites 99%

*"Teachers can tell which students have taken the course," says Ms. Dotson, "because it shows up in their level of maturity."*

**Parent Education**

The Family Life Education Program works exclusively with young adolescents on issues related to teen sexuality and parenting, with a focus on prevention. Instructors are always available for parental consultations and presentations.

**Curriculum**

The program uses five lessons from the *Values and Choices* curriculum developed by the Search Institute in Minneapolis, Minnesota. In addition, the instructor uses films, videos, and handouts from the health department, Coronet Films, Intermedia Films, Children's Society of California, Planned Parenthood, American Red Cross, New Day Films, and others.

**Sites**

Classes are offered at the Robinson Middle School and more recently at the John Sevier Middle School. Students assigned to an "alternative" school program for discipline problems and those in the special education program also participate in family life education classes.

**Parent Involvement**

When the initiative emerged as a priority in 1983, the parent-teacher association cooperated in a low-key publicity campaign by talking about the curriculum in their immediate neighborhoods. Parents who want to know more about the course can consult with the teacher. The majority approve without question, said Ms. Dotson. Recently, parents expressed their good opinion of the course by requesting a continuation of the Family Life Education Program into high school.

**Outreach**

Special recruitment efforts are unnecessary as the Family Life Education Program is part of the school curriculum.

**Staff**

| Job Title | PD | Vol | FT | PT | Educ Req | Status | Benefits |
|---|---|---|---|---|---|---|---|
| Family Life Educator | 1 | - | 1 | - | College Degree | Hourly Contract | Yes |
| Public Health Educator | 1 | - | - | 1 | College Degree | Hourly Non-Contract | Yes |

**State/District Requirements**

None.

**Preferred Background**

The family life educator should be able to give classroom presentations with comfort, ability, and professionalism, have the ability to deal with potentially controversial issues, and know how to establish an atmosphere of rapport and mutual respect.

**Employee Education and Training Represented**

Elementary education; education, grades 7 to 12; health and nutrition; psychology; counseling.

**Administration**

Debbie Dotson reports to the assistant superintendent of Kingsport City Schools and the director of the Sullivan County Health Department. The program is administered jointly by the schools (school board, superintendent, and two middle school principals) and the health department. The schools provide funds for the educator's salary, and the health department provides the program. Cooperating school departments include home economics, band, orchestra, and living skills. Within the schools, the program also shares information with guidance, the school nurse, special classes for pregnant teens, school administrators, and teachers.

**Relationship to the Schools**

"Teachers can tell which students have taken the course," says Ms. Dotson, "because it shows up in their level of maturity." The course appears to have had a positive impact on student attitudes toward their academic work, goals, and aspirations.

**Community Links**

The Family Life Education Program is offered within the schools through a cooperative partnership between the Sullivan County Health Department and the Kingsport City Schools. No other agencies are involved.

**Funding**

The local school district provides 100 percent of the funding.

**In-Kind Resources**

The Sullivan County Health Department provides consultation and staff development, periodic direct service to program participants, administrative and clerical support, as well as access to equipment, materials, and supplies.

**Funding History**

When the Family Life Education Program started, the Sullivan County Health Department covered costs for salary and materials. Since 1987, the Kingsport School District has fully funded the program. The Family Life Education Program has a good base of local support and a strong sense of autonomy, notes the director.

*Ms. Dotson advises building an evaluation component into the course and utilizing the ideas and suggestions of former students.*

**Objectives**

Objectives include increased knowledge of family life and sexuality issues, improved communication between children and parents about sexuality, more effective decision-making skills, increased sense of responsibility, fewer teen pregnancies, delayed onset of sexual activity, and familiarity with methods of contraception.

**Evaluation**

Follow-up surveys with high school seniors who took the course in their middle-school years show they are less likely to be involved in a pregnancy and are less sexually active than peers who were not exposed to the program. Ms. Dotson advises building an evaluation component into the course and utilizing the ideas and suggestions of former students. But, "don't put the whole weight of the evaluation on the number of subsequent pregnancies . . . . You have to know what you're comparing these statistics with . . . . It's very hard to measure prevention. Evaluation should also include a survey of sexual activity, knowledge, and attitudes among Family Life Education Program graduates."

**Replication**

The Family Life Education Program has not been replicated.

**Materials Available**

None.

# Child Development

*One senior girl, raised in a family of athletic boys, never felt she fit in anywhere. Her success in working with the children at the Child Development preschool helped her develop self-esteem and forge her own identity. She is now making a career in child care.*

Preschool     Health/nutrition education     Community services info/referral
Networking     Parent-led discussion groups     Parenting/child development education
Newsletter

**Contact:**     Mrs. Mercina Simeonidis, Teacher and Program Director
**Address:**     Northern Highlands Regional High School
               Hillside Avenue
               Allendale, NJ 07401
               (201) 327-8700, ext. 17
**Established:**     1977, local initiative
**Budget '88-'89:**     $5,000
**Sources:**     Local school district funds
**Size:**     100 teens, 25 preschool children; 125 families
**Area Served:**     Allendale and Upper Saddle River, New Jersey
**Auspices:**     Northern Highlands Regional High School

**Community**

The two towns served by the Northern Highlands Regional High School, Allendale and Upper Saddle River, are comparable upper-middle-class communities within easy range of New York City. Both attract highly educated, professional families. An estimated 92 percent of the high school graduating class goes on to college.

**Philosophy and Goals**

Child Development is designed to teach the skills, knowledge, and responsibilities involved in parenting. High school seniors study child development in the context of the family and society. For preschoolers, learning activities are guided by the learning lab's three central goals: the development of self-image, independence, and socialization skills. In the interests of intergenerational cooperation in education, parents of preschoolers offer their insights to the high school students.

**History and Origins**

In 1976, in the face of radically declining high school enrollment, Mercina Simeonidis revamped the home economics program in an effort to attract more students. With a planning grant from the New Jersey Department of Vocational Education, she designed a program in child development and received approval from the district board of education and the superintendent to create a parenting curriculum for high school students in conjunction with a preschool learning lab. Once the proposal was complete and state, municipal, and school approvals had been secured, the district received a $7,000 implementation grant from the New Jersey Department of Education.

**Features**

The preschool runs on a semester basis concurrently with a class in child development and practicum offered to high school seniors. In the preschool learning lab, fine-motor activities using beads and lacing cards foster the development of finger dexterity and eye-hand coordination; play telephones and dress-up kits teach children to communicate words and feelings and to relate to their peers, teens, and adults; books and videotapes are used to promote a conceptual understanding of grammar; a jungle gym, balance beam, and play tunnel encourage large-muscle development; plant and animal care teaches health, nutrition, and nurturance.

For seniors, this is primarily a learning-by-doing course, but they also follow an academic course of study in child development theory. They conduct weekly planning sessions, maintain records of daily activities in the lab, and assess the progress of individual children's mastery of skills.

## Participants

In 1977, the program attracted 10 children and 10 female high school students. Subsequently, due to its popularity, the program has expanded to five classes of 10 seniors each semester, nearly half of whom are boys. The program is free to preschoolers whose families are residents of Allendale and Upper Saddle River.

Whites 100%

*Parents contribute to the seniors' instruction while participating in their children's education. Mercina Simeonidis feels they develop an enthusiasm and respect for the program that carries over to other aspects of the school system.*

## Parent Education

High school seniors are the primary recipients of parent education in this program. They receive classroom instruction in child development theory, including units on child abuse and neglect, parenting, changes in family structure, handicapped and gifted children, genetic screening, child care careers, and nutrition. Parents of the preschool children lead discussion groups with seniors on special topics in their area of expertise or experience.

## Curriculum

The preschool learning lab uses a variety of materials, both prepackaged and developed in house. Packaged kits include *My Friends and Me* and the *Peabody Language Kit*. Animal care is an important part of the curriculum, and the classroom is home to hamsters, gerbils, fish, and turtles.

## Sites

The theory class and the preschool learning lab are located in adjacent classrooms at the regional high school. A one-way mirror between the rooms allows nonintrusive observation of the children at play. This is a permanent site. The parents of preschoolers arrange their own transportation.

## Parent Involvement

Mercina Simeonidis considers the high school students her primary target for instruction and treats parents as a resource group who lead discussions in their areas of expertise. Past topics include "Being a New Parent," "Problems of a Single Parent," and "Symptoms of Child Neglect." They also provide input on their children's needs through casual contact with the students and teacher while dropping off children. They observe their children at play and follow their progress through teacher conferences several times a year. Parents contribute to the seniors' instruction while participating in their children's education. Mercina Simeonidis feels they develop an enthusiasm and respect for the program that carries over to other aspects of the school system.

**Outreach**

At the outset, to fill the first class, Mrs. Simeonidis used her personal contacts with families in the community and the home and school administration. Since then, encouragement from parents and former students continues to attract a sufficient number of preschoolers and high school students to the program.

**Staff**

| Job Title | PD | Vol | FT | PT | Educ Req | Status | Benefits |
|-----------|-----|-----|-----|-----|-----------|---------|----------|
| Teacher | 1 | - | 1 | - | College Degree | K-12 Contract | Yes |

**State/District Requirements**

New Jersey Department of Education certification for the teacher.

**Preferred Background**

For the teacher, experience in child development, a friendly, articulate, poised, professional attitude, and an understanding of young children.

**Employee Education and Training Represented**

Prekindergarten and early childhood education; home economics; child development and family studies.

**Administration**

The program director reports to the supervisor of the Home and Industrial Technology Department, formerly home economics, which establishes enrollment of the preschool children. Within the regional high school, Child Development has a very high profile. The whole staff tries to cooperate with the program. The science teacher lets the children visit his planetarium, the art teacher conducts projects like making plaster footprints, and the children often attend musical assemblies or make trips to the school cafeteria and the library. The school newspaper and newsletter publicize learning lab activities.

**Relationship to the Schools**

Every year the kindergarten teachers in the two local districts meet with the local nursery schools, including Child Development's preschool, to apprise teachers of the skills they would like children to have when entering kindergarten. Child Development has adapted its curriculum accordingly; now students teach children to print their names with lowercase letters, and listening exercises have increased.

**Community Links**

Child Development is self-contained within the school system.

**Funding**

Local school district, 100 percent.

**In-Kind Resources**

Classrooms and access to support staff, materials, school nurse, and guidance services. The Home and School Association did some outreach in the first few years and now donates classroom materials, such as an Apple computer.

**Funding History**

For 10 years this program was funded by a state grant. When the grant ended, the local school district picked up the costs. Child Development's budget is lower than in its first year, but the director does not feel program services have been affected. Without start-up expenses, the only costs are consumable products.

**Objectives**

High school seniors learn that home and family serve as the background for growth and development of children. They should recognize signs of possible child abuse and neglect, gain knowledge of child development and parenting, handle emergencies with assurance, and find out about careers in early childhood education. Preschoolers gain the benefits of an integrated program including opportunities for the development of fine and gross motor skills, and communication, computer, and social skills.

**Evaluation**

Child Development has received several awards for excellence from the Kellogg Foundation, the Middle Atlantic States evaluation team, and the New Jersey Department of Education. When the program received external funds, those grants required progress reports and a summative evaluation. The program has used letters from student alumni and parent comments to supplement these reports. Student graduates have written from college to tell Mrs. Simeonidis that her program led them to a career in early childhood, special, or elementary education. Parents' testimonies suggest that the Child Development preschool is a stimulating, positive experience for both parents and children. A five-year postsurvey of alumni drew little response, but the teacher and students are now developing a time-lapse survey of alumni parents, children, and students that they hope will elicit more information.

**Replication**

This program has not been replicated. Mrs. Simeonidis stresses the necessity of adapting a program to the needs of the community. She realizes that her program would not work everywhere; for instance, other school systems might require a daycare program for student parents.

**Materials Available**

None.

# Jefferson County Teen Parent Program

| | | |
|---|---|---|
| Networking | Mother support group | Prenatal/postnatal care info |
| Home visits | Parent support group | Personal counseling/problem solving |
| Warmline | Child care info/referral | Community services info/referral |
| Crisis intervention | Job training assistance | Parenting/child development education |
| High school credit | Health/nutrition education | |

**Contact:** Lisbet Hornung, Program Coordinator

**Address:** 390 Southeast 10th Street
Madras, OR 97741
(503) 475-7265

**Established:** 1987, local initiative

**Budget '87-'88:** $30,000

**Budget '88-'89:** $7,200

**Sources:** Oregon Student Retention Initiative, federal Johnson O'Malley tribal funds

**Size:** 25 teen parents

**Area Served:** Jefferson County, Oregon

**Auspices:** Jefferson County Public Schools

*Lisbet Hornung offers the example of a young woman whose half-credit from the Teen Parent Program allowed her to graduate from high school. With the support of her peers and Ms. Hornung, she became determined to go to college. Her participation in the program gave her the confidence to get out of an abusive relationship and set her own goals. She is considering counseling as a profession, and Lisbet Hornung calls her an exemplary parent.*

## Community

The small town of Madras is located in central Oregon in the center of Jefferson County, which encompasses 1,800 square miles of rural, high desert landscape and has a population of 12,150. Agriculture and forestry are the county's major industries. The Warm Springs Reservation, 15 miles outside the town, has its own elementary school, but students from the sixth grade on attend school in Madras. Native Americans comprise 35 percent of the 25,000 students in Jefferson County. The Hispanic population is also sizeable. Nineteen percent of the births in the county in 1986 were to teens between 15 and 19 years old. Forty-five percent of high-school-age teens were not enrolled in school, and 42 percent of female dropouts were either pregnant or had a child at home when they left school.

## Philosophy and Goals

The primary goal of the Jefferson County Teen Parent Program (TPP) is to encourage pregnant and parenting teens to stay in school and earn a high school diploma. TPP addresses the social barriers and isolation that can discourage adequate parenting. The program provides teens with a network of peers and the support of a caring counselor. Program Coordinator Lisbet Hornung says the program stresses that real life means going to work and school and making arrangements for child care. She believes that home tutoring during a pregnancy is merely enabling; the Teen Parent Program is empowering.

## History and Origins

TPP began in response to the high rate of pregnancy and the resulting abandonment of school among adolescents in Jefferson County. Four individuals, representing the public schools and various Jefferson County agencies, began a countywide effort to address the problem. Teresa Hogue of the Oregon State University Extension Service; Darrell Wright, the school superintendent; Linda Allen of the Jefferson County Health

Department; and Guy Crawford of the Central Oregon Intergovernmental Council's (COIC) Job Training department applied for funds through Governor Neil Goldschmidt's Student Retention Initiative (SRI). They were awarded grants for three different dropout programs, among them a one-year grant to implement the Teen Parent Program. Lisbet Hornung was hired to design a two-year curriculum providing parent education, counseling, and support to pregnant and parenting teens enrolled in school. The Jefferson County Teen Parent Program, modeled on the YWCA Teen Parent Program in Salem, Oregon, began in the fall of 1987 and is directed by the four founders and available to students for credit.

## Features

Pregnant or parenting teens may register in one of four sequential half-credit classes that meet every day during school hours. Upon joining the program, teens sign a contract agreeing to attend all classes on time and obey school rules. The program coordinator agrees to arrange for child care for the students' children. The program includes pre- and postnatal classes, parenting education, a peer support group, job-training assistance, and information about community services. Lisbet Hornung says she establishes a personal relationship with each of the TPP students to provide individual counseling that addresses their personal and family issues. Participants utilize bus transportation provided to all students by the district.

## Participants

Whites 35%

Hispanics 5%

Native Americans 60%

In 1988-89, 15 students participated in classes and an additional 10 received services. Teens must be enrolled in school to be eligible for the program. The courses are designed to accommodate a maximum of 20 students.

*Program Coordinator Lisbet Hornung says the program stresses that real life means going to work and school and making arrangements for child care. She believes that home tutoring during a pregnancy is merely enabling; the Teen Parent Program is empowering.*

## Parent Education

Pregnant and parenting teens study pre- and postnatal care, parenting education, job training, and life skills that will help them become good parents and responsible, employable members of the community. Students learn about labor and delivery, child development and nutrition, family dynamics, child abuse, career decisions, problem solving, time management, goal setting, and related topics. The four courses are designed to be taken sequentially. The classroom atmosphere encourages trust and the development of self-esteem as individuals and parents. Ms. Hornung conducts the classes behind closed doors and stresses the importance of confidentiality within the classroom group. She does make it clear, however, that she is required by law to report any incidence of abuse of minors.

## Curriculum

Lisbet Hornung developed the program curriculum using the existing pre- and postnatal class offered by the health department, the *Footsteps* parenting curriculum available through the Oregon State University

Extension Service and the *Pre-Employment Training (PET)* course from COIC. All other materials are found in the school library or acquired by the program. The curriculum incorporates audio-visual materials.

**Sites**

The classes are held in the sewing room of Madras High School. Ms. Hornung finds this site satisfactory and notes that the school principal is eager to make it available to her each semester.

**Parent Involvement**

Besides their agreement to attend school faithfully and meet TPP class requirements, teens are also responsible for monitoring their children's daycare situation. Once TPP makes child care arrangements, the teen must inspect the daycare site and monitor the provider. Ms. Hornung says this encourages teens to demand good care and to be advocates for their children. The coordinator also tries to include the teens' parents when possible. Recently, TPP teens conducted a panel discussion on sexuality before an audience of parents.

**Outreach**

The Teen Parent Program conducts outreach through the school counseling department, teachers, administrators, and the school nurse. The Special Supplemental Food Program for Women, Infants, and Children (WIC), health clinics, and the health department also refer pregnant teens to the program.

**Staff**

| Job Title | PD | Vol | FT | PT | Educ Req | Status | Benefits |
|---|---|---|---|---|---|---|---|
| Program Coordinator | 1 | - | - | 1 | College Degree | Hourly Contract | No |
| Registered Nurse | - | 1 | - | 1 | College Degree | Other Contract | No |
| Job Placement Specialist | - | 1 | - | 1 | High School Diploma/ Some College | Other Contract | No |

**State/District Requirements**

The outreach and education coordinator must have a teaching certificate in secondary (grades 7 to 12) education.

**Preferred Background**

The outreach and education coordinator must have an appropriate educational background, parenting insight and experience, and an understanding of teens.

**Employee Education and Training Represented**

Education, grades 7 to 12; bilingual education; parent educator; child care.

**Administration**

Initially, the four founding county representatives managed TPP as a team. Ms. Hornung made monthly reports and the team had the power to approve hiring. Since implementation, the management process has been simplified, and Ms. Hornung reports only to the superintendent of schools. The program coordinator has autonomy in designing the program; the superintendent helps her arrange the program budget. Ms. Hornung says she also consults frequently with the high school principal about program activities and her intervention on behalf of TPP teens in dealings with teachers and counselors.

Ms. Hornung notes the importance of direct contact with the school administration from the top down. She says she is careful to make the principal aware of the goals and means of the program, both to get approval for her actions and win his support. She thinks her previous role as teacher at the high school facilitates program-school relations. Since the preoccupations of pregnancy and parenting are often at the root of her teens' academic difficulties, Ms. Hornung acts as a liaison among parents, teachers, and teens about attendance and school performance. She is also a resource to pregnant and parenting teens who may not have room in their school schedule to enroll in the program. Ms. Hornung consults with the high school's liaison to the reservation's tribal government for advice on tribal culture that may affect home visits to Native American teens.

## Community Links

This program began as a countywide effort, and its curriculum still relies on contributions from several agencies. A registered nurse from the Jefferson County Health Department teaches the pre- and postnatal care segment of the curriculum. The health department also provides information about family planning, birth control, and Lamaze. A representative of COIC teaches the PET job skills course. The Education Services District (ESD), the administrative arm of the county school district, is under contract to arrange child care for program participants' children. Adult and Family Services, a county agency, pays for child care if teens are on public assistance. Ms. Hornung contacts a local medical clinic for information and advice when needed. She also maintains a relationship with the obstetrics department of the county hospital, so she can check on teens' health concerns and facilitate the students' communication with hospital staff.

Ms. Hornung stresses the importance of initiating a productive relationship with community agencies and advises program coordinators to make personal visits with agency directors. She brings materials and an introductory letter and says she is very clear about what her program does and how the other agency can fit in. She wants to let them know she is there to do more than drink their coffee. Ms. Hornung registers TPP participants in Together for Children, a state-sponsored community parent education program she also directs. This entitles them to home visits and a monthly speaker series.

## Funding

Johnson O'Malley tribal funds, 56 percent; the remainder is covered by cooperation with another local program (of which Ms. Hornung is also coordinator), Together for Children, which serves families with children birth to age three.

## In-Kind Resources

Classroom, materials, and some clerical support from the schools; desk space from the Education Services District.

## Funding History

The original Student Retention Initiative (SRI) funding was a one-year implementation grant for the 1987-88 school year and was not renewed. Going into the 1988-89 academic year, TPP had no funds, so students registered in the fall semester's TPP classes were forced to withdraw and find other classes. Fortuitously, Lisbet Hornung was hired at this time to be the coordinator of another state-funded parent education program, Together for Children, in which she could enroll her teen parents, still provide some services, and be available as a resource. In November 1988, the Warm Springs Reservation donated $4,000 of federal Johnson

O'Malley tribal funds to resume programming. For the rest of the fall semester, TPP classes met after school. In January, SRI provided $3,200 in unclaimed funds, and the program resumed a regular classroom schedule. TPP has a commitment from the county for $5,000 for the 1989-90 school year, and SRI is considering a large grant as well. Lisbet Hornung suggests program directors secure funding at least a year ahead of time to prevent disruptions in programming.

**Objectives**

TPP's primary goal is to keep adolescent parents enrolled in school until graduation. The program wants to foster responsibility and realistic expectations in teen parents so that they can become productive, employable members of the community. Participants gain knowledge of pregnancy, childbirth, and birth control, and develop the skills and self-esteem of confident, informed parents.

**Evaluation**

Ms. Hornung conducted an evaluation of the program after the first year as required by the SRI grant. She based her results on her own statistics and the results of student surveys. Every student enrolled in the program successfully completed the school year. The surveys showed that students found the program useful and supportive. Ms. Hornung suggests program directors be self-critical and heed the suggestions of participants. She, for instance, learned from the surveys that some of the students found her approach overly aggressive and has toned down her initial contact.

**Replication**

TPP is modeled on the YWCA Teen Parent Program in Salem, Oregon.

**Materials Available**

None.

# New Futures School

Networking
Meals
Work-study
Home visits
Child care

Crisis intervention
GED services
Prenatal health care
Support groups
Academic courses

Health/nutrition education
Parenting/child development education
Individual/group counseling
Community services info/referral
Job-training program

| | |
|---|---|
| **Contact:** | Sandy Dixon, Director |
| **Address:** | New Futures School |
| | 5400 Cutler, NE |
| | Albuquerque, NM 87110 |
| | (505) 883-5680 |
| **Established:** | 1970, local initiative |
| **Budget '88-'89:** | Approximately $1,000,000 |
| **Sources:** | Local school district, state, corporate, and foundation funds |
| **Size:** | 475 teen mothers, 150 infants, annually |
| **Area Served:** | Albuquerque, New Mexico |
| **Auspices:** | Albuquerque Public Schools and New Futures, Inc., a community-based organization |
| **1990 Respondent:** | Veronica Garcia, Director |

The Albuquerque School District, one of the largest in the nation, has a substantial minority population. The schools and the University of New Mexico are the major employers, followed by Sandia Weapons Lab and Kirtland Air Force Base.

## Philosophy and Goals

The New Futures School aims to assist and motivate teen parents to complete their secondary education; to make responsible, informed decisions; to have healthy pregnancies and healthy families; and to become responsible parents and contributing community members.

## History and Origins

The New Futures School was initiated in 1970 by Albuquerque YWCA volunteers, who wanted to provide a means for pregnant adolescents to continue their high school education and have access to good health care. The public school system agreed to grant credit for classes taught by certified volunteer teachers and the program opened in the basement of the YWCA in January 1970 with two students. In 1976, the YWCA ceased sponsorship, and the Albuquerque Public Schools, which had steadily increased their involvement and financial commitment, assumed primary responsibility for the program. At the same time, New Futures, Inc., a community-based organization, was formed. This organization not only provides links to the community, but also reaches beyond the school to other parts of New Mexico and other states to promote awareness of the needs of adolescent parents and provide technical assistance about services related to adolescent pregnancy.

## Features

The New Futures School's in-school program has two departments:

The **Perinatal Program** serves teens during pregnancy and until the end of the semester in which their children reach three months of age.

The **Young Parents' Center** serves teen mothers and fathers who cannot successfully participate in the regular school program in the year following the birth of their child.

**New Futures Education Services** offers courses in special education, postnatal care, vocational opportunities, and parenting and child development in addition to the academic subjects required for high school graduation. Perinatal health and parenting classes and a course in personal and child health, which meets daily for 18 weeks, are required. All classes carry credit toward graduation and are taught by accredited teachers. Academic levels range from basic skills to college preparatory; counseling and a Graduate Equivalency Diploma (GED) pretest determine skill levels. GED preparation is available if a diploma is an inappropriate goal.

**Work Experience Program** students may enroll in a job-training class for one semester and earn a semester's credit for each 90 hours of work experience. Student jobs are partially subsidized to encourage the participation of potential employers.

**Child care** is provided at four child care facilities operated by the New Futures School on its premises for participants' children. Each is licensed to serve 25 children. Developmental activities are included in the daily program; care is provided only while the child's mother is in class or participating in the Work Experience Program.

**Home tutoring** was added in 1987-88 for students who are ill or have sick children.

Open enrollment in the New Futures School is available throughout the school year. Pregnant or parenting teens aged 12 to 20 who are not yet high school graduates are eligible to participate. Forty-five of the participants have an income below $10,000; 45 percent have an income between $10,000 and $20,000. In 1987-88, the New Futures School served 475 teen mothers and children, approximately 70 percent of those who were eligible.

*This organization not only provides links to the community, but also reaches beyond the school to other parts of New Mexico and other states to promote awareness of the needs of adolescent parents and provide technical assistance about services related to adolescent pregnancy.*

### Participants

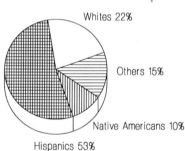

Whites 22%

Others 15%

Native Americans 10%

Hispanics 53%

### Parent Education

Beyond the structured classes, which are the core of the New Futures School program, mothers and fathers also have opportunities to interact with their children in the child care facilities, where staff members observe and assist with hands-on parent-child interaction.

### Curriculum

The New Futures School combines materials developed in house with prepackaged curricula and modifies them for a Hispanic population and for single-parent families and unplanned pregnancies. The basic text is *Teenage Pregnancy: A New Beginning* and the accompanying teacher's guide, *Working with Childbearing Adolescents*. This text was developed by the New Futures School staff. Other materials used are published by Morning Glory Press in California.

## Sites

The New Futures School is located in a free-standing facility and shares space with the Public Health Department's Special Supplemental Food Program for Women, Infants, and Children (WIC) and child immunization clinics, the University of New Mexico Medical School's prenatal care, family planning, and family practice clinics, and the New Mexico Department of Human Services' Project Mainstream. Transportation is provided to the site either by the Albuquerque Public Schools, a Pueblo Indian tribe, or the Economic Opportunity Board. Students often have long rides and bus schedules may require them to leave before the school day ends.

## Parent Involvement

Parents of the teen participants serve on the board of New Futures, Inc. and occasionally volunteer in the program. Parent volunteers are few because the program serves many dysfunctional families. Those families functioning more successfully work at salaried jobs and have little time for volunteering.

## Outreach

The former program coordinator, Caroline Gaston, stresses the importance of being responsive when organizations request speakers; she notes that participants are the program's best spokespersons. Special outreach strategies include placing public service announcements on radio and television and distributing posters and flyers in places where students congregate. Counselors, nurses, and many other medical and social service providers refer clients.

## Staff

| Job Title | PD | Vol | FT | PT | Educ Req | Status | Benefits |
|---|---|---|---|---|---|---|---|
| Teachers | 15 | - | 15 | - | College Degree | K-12 Contract | Yes |
| Nurses | 3 | - | 3 | - | College Degree | K-12 Contract | Yes |
| Counselors | 6 | - | 6 | - | Post-Graduate Courses or Degree | K-12 Contract | Yes |
| Child Care Workers | - | 3 | - | - | High School Diploma | Other Contract | Yes |
| Volunteers | - | 12-15 | - | - | No Requirement | None | No |
| Clerical | 1 | - | 1 | - | High School Diploma | Other Contract | Yes |
| Cooks | 3 | - | 3 | - | High School Diploma | - | Yes |
| Volunteer Coordinator | - | 1 | - | 1 | High School Diploma | - | Yes |

| State/District Requirements | State licensure is required for teachers, counselors, and nurses; administrative licensure is required for the director. |

| Preferred Background | Social agency experience and background is stressed. |

| Employee Education and Training Represented | Infant and toddler education; education, grades 7 to 12; bilingual education; special education; adult basic education; parent educator; adult vocational education; child care; health and nutrition; home economics; nursing; speech therapy; counseling; social work; child development and family studies. |

| Administration | New Futures School's program coordinator is a principal in the Albuquerque Public Schools and reports to the assistant superintendent for high schools. She is also the executive director of New Futures, Inc. and reports to their board. The program is administered primarily by the school system with linkages to health services, special education, counseling services, and categorical programs. Other organizations involved include the University of New Mexico Medical School and health center, the city library system, and the Public Health Department. New Mexico Department of Human Services, the New Mexico Health and Environment Department, the New Mexico Department of Education's Vocational Education Unit, New Futures, Inc., the Albuquerque Public Schools, and foundation funders all monitor the program. The New Future's advisory board includes ex officio program staff, ex officio public school personnel, community representatives, and parents of participants. It meets eight to ten times a year and has decision-making powers with respect to the program budget and program services and curriculum. The board also helps with outside agency contacts, development of enrichment activities, and volunteer recruitment. |

| Relationship to the Schools | The schools' original agreement to grant credit for New Futures School courses made the proposed program a reality. Ms. Gaston indicates the important role school board members and school administrators played in recognizing the merits of the alternative school concept and encouraging its growth. She stresses the benefits of providing comprehensive services; a cooperative community plus school system support provides a firm basis for a wide range of services. In turn, the New Futures School has helped to decrease the school dropout rate. Ms. Gaston feels that being in charge of staff recruitment and selection helps her maintain a balance of cooperation with the schools and enhances program autonomy. |

| Community Links | The New Futures School receives services from the Albuquerque Public Library. In return for broad community cooperation, the New Futures School provides speakers upon request to local agencies and organizations, and several New Futures School staff members serve on advisory committees and boards of local organizations, such as the mayor's Child Abuse Council and the Albuquerque Primary Prevention Task Force. The University of New Mexico School of Medicine's Maternity and Infant Care Project operates a free weekly prenatal clinic in the school. |

| Funding | Local school district, 75 percent; state, 10 percent (federal funds via state government); foundations, 10 percent; corporate donations, 5 percent. State funds come from the following sources: social services block grant, maternal and child health block grant, Perkins vocational |

education funds, and welfare reform monies from the New Mexico Department of Human Services.

**In-Kind Resources**

The New Mexico Department of Human Services provides a social worker and, in cooperation with the Economic Opportunity Board, provides buses for welfare clients. The Albuquerque Public Schools and the New Mexico Department of Human Services host workshops, the Public Health Department and the University of New Mexico Medical School provide WIC and health services, and the city library system supplies materials.

**Funding History**

The New Futures School's chief funder during the 1987-88 school year was the Albuquerque Public School System. Funders include the Ford, Levi Strauss, Albuquerque, and Flinn Foundations. Agency funding came from the New Mexico Department of Human Services and the New Mexico Health and Environment Department. Funding has increased 400 percent since the program's inception.

**Objectives**

The New Futures School hopes to improve parenting by ensuring the health of mothers and babies, imparting knowledge about responsible interpersonal relationships, and encouraging a more positive attitude toward education. Expected outcomes include increasing the number of high school graduates and reducing the rate of repeat unplanned pregnancies.

**Evaluation**

The Work Experience Program has undergone two different third party evaluations. In 1987, an independent evaluator conducted a follow-up study of a randomly selected sample of students who attended the New Futures School between 1980 and 1985. The study indicated repeat pregnancy rates of 6 to 11 percent at one year postpartum, contrasted with a national average of 18 to 25 percent. Seventy-three percent of participants had finished high school and 54 percent had gone on to get postsecondary training or education.

**Replication**

The New Futures School has been replicated in Carlsbad and Roswell, New Mexico; Fort Worth, Texas; and Phoenix and Tucson, Arizona. Ms. Gaston has provided consulting services, including workshop presentations, on-site visits, and telephone technical assistance to several sites.

**Materials Available**

Educational materials published by New Futures, Inc. include *Teenage Pregnancy: A New Beginning* with study guide; a teacher's guide, *Working with Childbearing Adolescents;* a supplementary textbook of basic math, *Math Applications in the Home;* and videotapes. Staff training workshops are available for $300 per day, plus expenses; on-site program evaluations are also available for $300 per day. Contact Caroline Gaston at the above address for more information.

# CEC Child Care Center

Child care
Networking
Respite care
Resource library

Teen parenting classes
Mother support groups
High school credit

Parenting/child development education
Community services info/referral
Individual counseling

| | |
|---|---|
| **Contact:** | Lori Powell, Center Director and Lead Teacher |
| **Address:** | 115 Wright Street<br>Iowa City, IA 52240<br>(319) 339-6879 |
| **Established:** | 1987, collaborative effort among school district and social service agencies |
| **Budget '88-'89:** | $106,085 |
| **Sources:** | State government, school district, in-kind contributions, foundations, federal government, private donations, client fees |
| **Size:** | 22 children and 21 parents |
| **Area Served:** | Iowa City, Iowa |
| **Auspices:** | Iowa City Community School District's alternative high school |

*When Jodie started coming to the child care center in the fall of 1988, she was pregnant, had many health problems, and was living in a group youth home. She attended parenting classes and worked at the center, where staff members helped her formulate a plan for her new life as a mother. Jodie returned to school after giving birth and brought her baby to CEC. She has since moved into her own apartment and attends a support group for teen parents. She graduated from high school in 1989, receiving a scholarship from the alternative high school to pursue an education in nursing.*

### Community

Iowa City, located in east central Iowa, is a university town with a population of 79,000. The majority of residents are white; most of the minority population is affiliated with one of the town's two major employers—the university and the teaching and research hospital.

### Philosophy and Goals

The Community Education Center (CEC) Child Care Center recognizes that children enter the program with a variety of needs, abilities, backgrounds, and interests and that development and readiness occur at different rates. The infant and toddler program therefore provides a climate that is both supportive and individually challenging, allowing children to develop and learn at their own pace and in their own style. The program is designed to provide an environment in which children experience success and become well-rounded, self-confident individuals. In an effort to keep teen parents in school the center has a community teen pregnancy prevention program that provides child care and parenting and child development education.

### History and Origins

In the spring of 1987, Jean Gehrig, a graduate student at the University of Iowa, was working as assistant to the superintendent of schools in Iowa City. She and three other women from the community (a teacher at the alternative high school, a representative from an advocacy program for teens, and a teacher in the school district) recognized the need for a daycare center for teen mothers that would enable them to finish high school. Under the auspices of the alternative high school, they applied for funding from the Iowa Adolescent Pregnancy Prevention and Services grant and received $48,000 in the fall of 1987 to open the doors of the CEC Child Care Center. CEC began offering child care in a church-donated site (which they rent). Lori Powell was hired shortly thereafter as full-time lead teacher and the center's director.

### Features

The CEC Child Care Center is a licensed daycare provider. There are never more than 12 children in a group and the staff/child ratio is one to three. Teen parents are required to work in the center 45 minutes each day and receive academic credit for those hours. Parenting classes and weekly parent meetings are provided for both teen parents and Title XX families. Parent education classes meet three times a week for 45 minutes in the afternoons while child care is provided. Additional weekly meetings offer social opportunities and support, exclusively for pregnant teens and teen parents.

### Participants

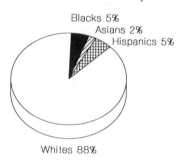

Blacks 5%
Asians 2%
Hispanics 5%
Whites 88%

Enrollment is open to all adolescent parents under age 21 who are working toward a Graduate Equivalency Diploma (GED) or high school diploma, to families who qualify for Title XX funds (federal child care aid for low-income families), and to Iowa City Community School District employees. The CEC Child Care Center serves children ages two weeks to three years. While families do not have to be at risk to enroll, the program serves many who are. Risk factors include economic disadvantage, inadequate parenting skills, and open protective service cases. Seventy-eight percent of the program's participants in 1987-88 were single parents.

*"We're going to try and identify pregnant girls in the school system, not just the alternative high school. We want to reach them early so that they know they can return to school after delivery and receive child care."*

### Parent Education

Parenting classes provide students with information and discussion time on topics such as child development, appropriate discipline, realistic expectations for young children, and decision making. Students talk about the kind of parenting they received and qualities they would like to change or carry over into their own parenting. Classes stress the notion that in most cases, parents tried their best. The program tries to mesh theoretical and experiential learning; for instance, a class studying self-esteem might focus on learning to accept responsibility.

Mother support groups offer parents cardiopulmonary resuscitation (CPR) training with a school nurse, presentations by a community nurse on safety in the home, and a four-week session on violence in relationships. Weekly parent meetings also include speakers on topics such as child-proofing your home, accident prevention, and assertiveness training.

Ms. Powell reflects that "a lot of 'modeling' of child care providers' behavior takes place during the 45 minutes the teen moms spend at the CEC Child Care Center each weekday. They watch the aides and learn child care informally. We give parents positive information about their child and praise good interactions."

### Curriculum

The CEC Child Care Center uses *Positive Parenting: First Steps,* by local authors Jenson, Funk, and Nelson; *Parenting: A Guide for Young People,* by Gordon and Wollin; and *Parenting Today,* edited by Jerelyn B. Shultz (Iowa University Press).

**Sites**

The CEC Child Care Center rents a church, but this is a temporary arrangement. "We are moving to a privately owned space in a renovated railroad depot. We need to be near the alternative high school so that students can work in the daycare center during school hours. The new building is a half block from the school. The school's physical plant staff renovated the space to meet licensing requirements and made an outdoor play area . . . . The rent for the new space is $625 per month. This comes out of the grant money. It would certainly be helpful if the school would pay our rent or find a place for us in one of their buildings, but that hasn't happened . . . ."

**Parent Involvement**

Adolescent parents must work in the center for 45 minutes each day as a way of paying for child care, and receive school credit for doing so. One teen mother serves on the advisory board. Mothers participated in a program evaluation conducted by the University of Iowa.

**Outreach**

Ms. Powell notes that the best outreach is word-of-mouth from participants. "Also, it is important to keep talking to community people who have contact with teen mothers or work in pregnancy prevention, like doctors and nurses. We're going to try and identify pregnant girls in the school system, not just the alternative high school. We want to reach them early so that they know they can return to school after delivery and receive child care." In addition, to reach dropouts who might be influenced to return to school, staff members network with community agencies, visit high schools to talk to students about the program, and visit low-income apartment complexes.

**Staff**

| Job Title | PD | Vol | FT | PT | Educ Req | Status | Benefits |
|---|---|---|---|---|---|---|---|
| Director/ Teacher | 1 | - | 1 | - | College Degree | K-12 Contract | Yes |
| Teacher Aides | 4 | - | 3 | 1 | High School Diploma | Hourly Contract | Yes |
| Teen Mothers | - | 9 | - | 9 | None | - | No |

**State/District Requirements**

The head teacher and director is required to have a teaching certificate and early childhood certification.

**Preferred Background**

The director should be a good parenting role model. Teaching aides should have a concerned and caring attitude and an ability to work with children and adults.

**Employee Education and Training Represented**

Infant and toddler education; prekindergarten and early childhood education; special education; child care; occupational and physical therapy.

**Administration**

The principal of the alternative school is ultimately responsible for the program. Funding procedures go through the school board. The program is administered within the public school system and involves both the elementary and secondary curriculum coordinators and two outside community service agencies that share in the program's funding. A 16-member advisory board meets three to four times a year to share criticism and suggestions with the staff.

| | |
|---|---|
| **Relationships to the Schools** | The program maintains links with school counselors, nurses, home economics teachers, and high school health aides. According to Ms. Powell, the alternative school principal is more than the titular head of the program. He takes an active role in counseling the teen parents involved in the CEC Child Care Center. The director attends staff inservice training with other school district teachers. |
| **Community Links** | The program shares its funding and administrative structure with Youth Homes, Inc. (which provides care for pregnant and parenting teens) and United Action for Youth (which provides counseling for teens). All three share the Iowa Adolescent Pregnancy Prevention and Services grant, although the CEC Child Care Center receives the largest amount. The center is licensed by the Iowa Department of Human Services. |
| **Funding** | State, 45 percent; local and district, 27.3 percent; in-kind contributions, 22 percent; foundations, 3 percent; federal, 1 percent; private donations, 1 percent; client fees, 0.7 percent. |
| **In-Kind Resources** | The Iowa City Community School District, United Action for Youth, and Youth Homes, Inc. provide administrative and clerical support and access to equipment. The school matches the state grant with in-kind services: for example, the principal and school counselors spend time working with the teen mothers and that portion of their salary is regarded as an in-kind contribution. |
| **Funding History** | The Iowa Department of Human Services grant of $500,000 was made available in 1987 for service programs and prevention projects for adolescent pregnancy. Initially, the CEC Child Care Center received $48,000, which it shared with Youth Homes, Inc. and United Action for Youth. The three organizations continue to apply for state funding jointly. Funding has remained stable, but according to Mrs. Powell, "We are currently waiting to see if a third year of funding from the state is approved in the legislature." |
| **Objectives** | The CEC Child Care Center strives to strengthen the parent-child bond. It helps parents form more realistic expectations of their children, develop positive parenting techniques, gain self-confidence and self-esteem, and complete their high school education. |
| **Evaluation** | Iowa State University conducted an evaluation of mothers participating in the CEC Child Care Center, using the same criteria at two different times during the program: after starting the program, and upon completion of the school year. Measures concentrated on the adjustment of the young mother and her performance in the parenting role; criteria included levels of self-esteem, depression, and social maturity. Aspects of parenting performance studied included parenting self-confidence and efficacy, knowledge of child development, optimal parenting practices, and aspects of competence in the parenting role. The students' advisors at the CEC Child Care Center assessed social maturity. |
| **Replication** | The program has not been replicated. |
| **Materials Available** | The CEC Child Care Center will soon release a videotape about teen pregnancy and parenting, produced in collaboration with teen mothers. It is also developing an infant and toddler curriculum for parents. |

# Project Hope

*"Wendy, a good student, got pregnant in her senior year and felt her life was over. I let her know that she could continue to pursue her educational goals, which included college, and that her relationship with the father could continue even if marriage was inappropriate. After delivery, Wendy wanted to return to school, but needed daycare. Her family resisted state-assisted daycare, but she overrode them, stayed in school, and later enrolled in college. Project Hope empowered Wendy by letting her know she had options."*

*— Maria Toro-Hollis*

| | | |
|---|---|---|
| Home visits | Grandmother support group | Teen support group |
| Networking | Crisis intervention | Parenting/child development education |
| Child care | Family services | Parent-child joint activities |
| Newsletter | Medical care referrals | Community services info/referral |
| Warmline | Homemaker services | Child care referrals |
| Hotline | Individual counseling | Health/nutrition education |
| | Resource library | Adult literacy/GED referrals |

**Contact:** Sonya Murphy, Coordinator

**Address:** Pilgrim High School
111 Pilgrim Parkway
Warwick, RI 02888
(401) 737-3300 ext. 373

**Established:** 1986, joint venture between school department and mental health facility

**Budget '88-'89:** $76,829

**Sources:** City of Warwick (funds from federal demonstration grant, three years); Rhode Island Department of Human Services

**Size:** 56 mothers; 25 fathers; 46 children

**Area Served:** Warwick, Rhode Island

**Auspices:** Kent County Medical Health Center and the public schools

**1990 Respondent:** Maria Toro-Hollis, Coordinator

## Community

Covering 49.1 square miles on the state's eastern coast, Warwick is the second largest city in Rhode Island. Of Warwick's 87,000 residents, 98 percent are white, 1,725 are single parents, 5,697 people live below the poverty line, and 2,725 are unemployed. Most of the population is composed of blue-collar workers employed in the shellfishing, jewelry, and textile industries. Affordable housing and adequate health care are major problems for this group, which earns just enough to be ineligible for federal and state assistance.

## Philosophy and Goals

Project Hope views the extended family as a potential source of support for teen mothers. Uniquely, it tries to engage the family in its services, making therapeutic referrals when necessary. Project Coordinator Maria Toro-Hollis feels that working effectively with families means respecting confidentiality, concentrating on good communication, presenting teens and their families with appropriate information, and letting participants know that the project is there to help them make informed decisions.

## History and Origins

The head of the Warwick Department of Human Services, Paula Crombie, started Project Hope in 1986. By surveying one of Warwick's high schools Ms. Crombie determined a direct relationship between teen pregnancy and the rising student dropout rate. Ms. Crombie, former director of a teen parent program in Providence, worked with Superintendent Clyde Bennett to develop Project Hope and apply for federal demonstration grant monies. The city of Warwick was awarded funding and subcontracted the Kent County Mental Health Center (KCMHC) to administer the funds and provide services.

**Features**

Social workers and psychologists in the schools act as liaisons between pregnant teens and Project Hope. The teen first meets with a liaison when she suspects she is pregnant. After pregnancy has been confirmed, and if the teen decides to have her baby, she is either referred to Project Hope, or the project seeks her out with the help of the liaison and assesses her home situation, offering to accompany her when she tells her parents about her pregnancy.

Students are visited in their homes, schools, or community settings during pregnancy and shortly after delivery and are encouraged to talk about parenting issues. Young mothers bring their babies to weekly support groups and receive information about child development and growth. Project Hope has a library and gives free information to participants on sexual decision making, contraception, and other health issues.

According to new state policy, pregnant students are eligible for home tutoring. Project Hope has encouraged the school system to develop a consistent policy for providing tutoring. Previously, some students stayed out of school for several months, receiving occasional visits from tutors; others remained in school until delivery. Regular tutoring allows a student to remain at home and receive tutoring from the eighth month of pregnancy to two months following birth. "Now schools are more consistent," says Ms. Toro-Hollis. "Our program has forced faculty to accept pregnant teen parents. They can't ignore them. We don't necessarily have more teen parents, but more of them stay in school. Schools look at home tutoring differently. Instead of letting girls drop out and being lax about providing home tutoring, they now use home tutoring as a way of meeting students' needs."

**Weekly support groups** are offered to the mothers of teens. Some grandmothers attend more frequently in the beginning, when they are trying to accept what has happened, and again around the due date. The biggest challenge for grandmothers is dealing with issues of discipline and responsibility now that their children are mothers.

**Participants**

Project Hope serves three very different populations from three high schools: students with a scholastic-athletic orientation, a vocational focus, and a mixture of both. Ninety-three percent of all participants served in 1988 were single parents.

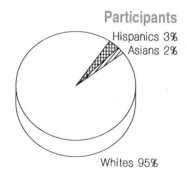

Hispanics 3%
Asians 2%
Whites 95%

*"We work as a partner with the schools," says Ms. Toro-Hollis, "communicating with teachers and principals, helping the student get the extra help she needs, whether it's making up a test or completing work she's missed due to her pregnancy."*

**Parent Education**

Educating and supporting adolescent parents is the core of Project Hope.

**Curriculum**

According to the program coordinator, teen mothers know little about contraception and sexuality even though health education courses teach these subjects in school. The two main books Project Hope recommends are *Parent Making* and *Choices and Challenges*. Project Hope's curriculum combines parenting and child development information with lessons on informed decision making in careers and future relationships.

**Sites**

Project Hope has a secure home, including two private offices and a group space, in the annex of Pilgrim High School. A school-based daycare center called Child, Inc., attended by the infants of Project Hope participants, is adjacent to the project's office and the school psychologist's and social worker's offices. The project shares space with social service staff of hospitals, mental health centers, and community agencies.

**Parent Involvement**

Neither teens nor their parents were involved in implementing Project Hope, nor do they participate in its administration. However, participants will testify to the state legislature in support of Project Hope's continued funding.

**Outreach**

For community outreach, Project Hope frequents social service agencies and speaks to service providers in churches, teen pregnancy organizations, and homeless shelters. Weekly networking lunches with other community service providers promote sharing of resources and stimulate new approaches. Project Hope provides transportation to appointments.

Maria Toro-Hollis asserts that she has to be creative to involve pregnant teens and their parents. "Some people won't be receptive. Don't give up. Just give them the time and space and they may be more receptive. Be mobile. We'll go to a Burger King if they don't want to meet us at home or come to the office. I'll bribe students with baby clothes and diapers. If they aren't receptive to counseling, they will be receptive to learning about how their baby is developing inside them." Once she wins their trust, she easily coaxes them into counseling.

**Staff**

| Job Title | PD | Vol | FT | PT | Educ Req | Status | Benefits |
|---|---|---|---|---|---|---|---|
| Coordinator | 1 | - | 1 | - | College Degree | Hourly Non-Contract | Yes |
| Case Manager | 1 | - | 1 | - | College Degree | Hourly Non-Contract | Yes |
| Administrator | 1 | - | - | 1 | Post-Graduate Courses or Degree | Other Contract | Yes |

**State/District Requirements**

None.

**Preferred Background**

For the coordinator and case managers, good communication and organizational skills, flexibility, experience with teens, and a sense of humor.

**Employee Education and Training Represented**

Infant and toddler education; elementary education; special education; child care; medicine; health and nutrition; home economics; speech therapy; psychology; psychiatry; counseling; social work.

| Administration | The coordinator reports to the program manager. Both are responsible to the executive director of the administering agency, Kent County Mental Health Center, Inc. The program coordinator also reports to a team of social workers and school psychologists who provide a link to school administration. |
| --- | --- |

**Relationship to the Schools**

"We work as a partner with the schools," says Ms. Toro-Hollis, "communicating with teachers and principals, helping the student get the extra help she needs, whether it's making up a test or completing work she's missed due to her pregnancy." According to Ms. Toro-Hollis, "Some of the teachers have a certain amount of denial about the usefulness of the program. Each year, at least once, we present ourselves to the health classes of all three high schools and to the faculties." Sexuality, decision making, and contraception are stressed at these presentations. Project Hope reinforces the school's health curriculum.

**Community Links**

Project Hope maintains good relationships with the three state adoption agencies, local mental health counseling services, and alcohol abuse support groups. Local hospitals, social service agencies, and the welfare office hand out Project Hope brochures. When a referral to another agency is necessary, the program coordinator accompanies the student for the first visit. The coordinator feels that this allows the social service agency to see the program's work and ensures that clients keep appointments and follow through with necessary services.

**Funding**

Rhode Island Department of Human Services, 60 percent; city of Warwick (grant from U.S. Department of Health and Human Services, Office of Adolescent Pregnancy), 40 percent.

**In-Kind Resources**

The Warwick School System provides space, facilities, paid staff for service delivery, transportation services, and consultation and staff development, as well as access to equipment. The Kent County Visiting Nurse Association provides periodic direct service to program participants; the Kent County Mental Health Center provides administrative and clerical support.

**Funding History**

Paula Crombie originally applied for federal monies in the hope that another funder would pick up and continue support when the initial three-year grant ended. Special legislation is being proposed at the statehouse for continued funding, since all other teen pregnancy programs in the state have been maintained. Project Hope participants will testify in the state senate on behalf of the program.

**Objectives**

Project Hope tries to help participants by providing prenatal, medical, emotional, and parenting education. Ms. Toro-Hollis describes the project's main objective: "We strive to teach our clients healthier parenting skills. We try to teach our clients about making choices through informed decision making and to assist them in breaking the cycle of poverty, abuse, or teen parenting."

**Evaluation**

The project coordinator is required by the federal government to do follow-up interviews with participants for two years. An intake interview focuses on relationships with the child's father and the mother's own family and on knowledge of contraception and sex education. Later interviews take place after the birth of the child, at 6, 12, and 24 months.

| Replication | Project Hope bases its services on other teen programs and has served as a model itself. |
| --- | --- |
| Materials Available | None. |

# Off Campus Alternative Class

A Laotian-Mien student, enrolled in gifted classes after entering the program, had her first child at age 12, which is not unusual within her culture. At age 14 she testified before the state legislature on behalf of all California students and the program on the importance of keeping pregnant and parenting teens in school. That summer she started working in the legislature. Now, at age 16, she is married and has a second child. After graduation, she plans to attend Stanford or one of the state universities on scholarship.

| | | |
|---|---|---|
| Academic courses | Health/nutrition education | Parenting/child development education |
| Networking | Mother support group | Parent-child joint activities |
| Home visits | Crisis intervention | Developmental exams/screening |
| Child care | Group counseling | Child care info/referral |
| Newsletter | Resource library | Community services info/referral |

**Contact:** Sandy Young, Teacher-Coordinator

**Address:** 4701 Joaquin Way
Sacramento, CA 95822
(916) 277-6394

**Established:** 1982, school initiative

**Budget '88-'89:** $75,000

**Sources:** Local school district, foundation

**Size:** 75 teen mothers and 35 children

**Area served:** Sacramento, California

**Auspices:** Sacramento Unified School District

**1990 Respondent:** Michele Hobza, Teacher-Coordinator

## Community

Sacramento has a diversified industrial and service economy, including several medical and educational institutions, a large computer industry, two military bases, agricultural interests, and government services. The population of the school district covers the whole socioeconomic spectrum and diverse ethnic backgrounds, including a large number of Laotian refugees, Mien or Hmong.

## Philosophy and Goals

Through the resources available within the public school system, the Off Campus Alternative Class focuses on the academic, physical, and social needs of pregnant and parenting teens. The program tries to foster a safe, supportive, and nonjudgmental environment. The staff seeks to instill a sense of inner strength and to help each student build his or her own support system. They would like to see students increase their repertoire of strategies for success and learn to become their own advocates.

## History and Origins

The Off Campus Alternative Class was started in 1982 to fill a gap created by a state regulation that forbade pregnant and parenting teens under age 16 from attending a continuation high school designed for students identified as having academic difficulties and unable to participate in a regular high school program. While the Off Campus Alternative Class is entirely separate from the middle school, high school, and continuation high school programs, it constitutes an accredited program from which students may return to their referring schools after age 16.

According to Ms. Hobza, the program's teacher-coordinator, while there has been no organized opposition to the program, periodically someone will ask why so much money is spent on such a small population. She feels it is important to understand that the money goes a long way toward helping young women complete their education and preventing short- and long-term adverse medical consequences of pregnancy. It keeps them off Aid to Families with Dependent Children (AFDC) and in the work force and has a substantial impact on the quality of their childrearing and their children's prospects of academic success. She reported that once these long-term costs and benefits are understood, questions about the short-term costs disappear.

### Features

The Off Campus Alternative Class offers voluntary educational and social service support to pregnant and parenting teens in an academic setting within the Sacramento City Unified School District (SCUSD). Off Campus Alternative Class students remain in school while pregnant and return to school after delivery. The program provides child care during school hours for infants from birth to one year old. Teen mothers work in the child care program, which is virtually a lab providing them with practical experiences in parenting. The program is offered during school hours for the academic year.

### Participants

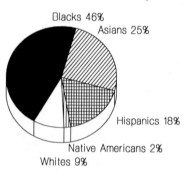

Blacks 46%
Asians 25%
Hispanics 18%
Native Americans 2%
Whites 9%

The program targets pregnant and parenting teens who are under age 16 and residents of the school district. Attendance is voluntary. Ms. Hobza reported that for some of the minority students, particularly the Mien or Hmong Laotian refugees, early marriage and childbearing is a part of their cultural traditions. The program's staff accommodates and works with the cultural practices of a diverse ethnic population.

*Periodically someone will ask why so much money is spent on such a small population. The money goes a long way toward helping young women complete their education and ... has a substantial impact on the quality of their childrearing and their children's prospects of academic success.*

### Parent Education

Parent education is built into the overall academic curriculum and the child care practicum provided by the teaching staff. Staff members from outside agencies provide additional parenting and Lamaze classes. Child abuse prevention is emphasized.

### Curriculum

The integrated curriculum consists of course work in mathematics, English, physical education, family and consumer education, social science, and science, with a special emphasis on the anatomy and physiology of pregnancy, fetal and child development, and information about conception and contraception. The mathematics course is individualized, based on a basic skills diagnostic pretest that is used to find the student's appropriate skill level. The English program provides students with basic literacy skills as well as practice in effective writing, speaking and listening, grammar, vocabulary, and the elements of literature. Students are required to maintain a daily journal throughout their course work. They are encouraged to read for pleasure, to read to their infants (Lap Reading Program), and to enter the SCUSD Real Women Writing Contest and Project Picture Book. According to Ms. Hobza, six students within the program won prizes in the 1989 contest.

Ms. Hobza would like to see the program expand to include additional electives in social science, computer lab, and laboratory sciences.

**Sites**

The Off Campus Alternative Class has learned it will have to move; its future location is uncertain.

**Parent Involvement**

The students' parents have not been involved with the design, implementation, or function of the program. However, a lengthy, personalized orientation for parents and students is included during the intake registration. Telephone contact is ongoing.

**Outreach**

Information from the California Vital Statistics Branch concerning births to teens during a three-year period reports over 900 births, with only 200 accounted for within the district's schools. Ms. Hobza feels this indicates that more intensive outreach within the community is needed to reach pregnant teens who are falling through the cracks in the system. The program generates publicity through brochures, public speaking engagements, television, public service announcements, and newspaper articles. Most referrals are generated through the public schools.

**Staff**

| Job Title | PD | Vol | FT | PT | Educ Req | Status | Benefits |
|-----------|-----|-----|-----|-----|----------|--------|----------|
| Teachers | 2 | - | 2 | - | Post-Graduate Courses or Degree | K-12 Contract | Yes |
| Instructional Aide | 1 | - | - | 1 | Some College | Hourly Contract | Yes |
| Instructional Aides | 2 | - | - | 2 | High School Diploma | Hourly Non-Contract | No |
| School Nurses | 1 | - | - | 1 | Post-Graduate Courses or Degree | K-12 Contract | Yes |
| Student Interns | - | 3 | - | 3 | Some College | - | No |
| Parapro-fessional Social Workers | 2 | - | - | 2 | College Degree | Hourly Contract | No |
| Lamaze Instructor | 1 | - | - | 1 | College Degree | Hourly Non-Contract | No |
| Tutors | 1 | 1 | - | 2 | Some College | Hourly Non-Contract | No |
| Therapists | 4 | - | - | 4 | Post-Graduate Courses or Degree | Other Contract | No |

**State/District Requirements**

For all teaching staff, appropriate teaching credentials within their field of expertise; for the school nurse, a state nursing license.

**Preferred Background**

None.

**Employee Education and Training Represented**

Infant and toddler; prekindergarten and early childhood education; elementary education; education, grades 7 to 12; bilingual education; special education; child care; health and nutrition; nursing; counseling;

family therapy; social work; child development and family studies; research and evaluation.

The Off Campus Alternative Class is administered exclusively within the Sacramento public education system. The coordinator of the program reports to the off-site school principal who is responsible to an assistant superintendent.

The Off Campus Alternative Class provides a state-mandated service on behalf of the public school system. No other public school departments are involved with the program.

A number of community groups, such as LINKS (a professional black women's oganization), Kappa Delta Gamma Teacher's honorary society, women's clubs, and other civic groups have adopted the program.

Ms. Hobza feels that family support programs should be embedded within the community and that staff members need to learn to feel comfortable networking. She reports that it is important to build relationships that provide the program with some leverage to safeguard the needs of the target population and the program.

The Off Campus Alternative Class subcontracts for services from the following agencies: the Child and Family Institute provides weekly sexual abuse therapy groups; pregnant students participate in Lamaze classes for two hours a week; weekly parenting classes are taught by outreach staff from Mercy Hospital. In addition, the Off Campus Alternative Class provides educational services to pregnant teens participating in the state-funded Adolescent Family Life Program.

*An evaluation should focus on the social support aspects and their long-term effect on the participants' ability to support themselves and care for their children.*

Ninety-nine percent of the funding for the entire program comes through the school district's general fund; 1 percent comes from private grants.

The school district provides three classrooms, occasional workshops for consultation and staff development, administrative support and access to equipment (such as media resources). Volunteer staff members, tutors, and interns are provided by various groups and universities.

According to Ms. Hobza, funding for resources other than staff (i.e., curriculum, instructional supplies, text books, clerical supplies) has not increased since 1983, even though the population served has tripled and infant care has been added to the program. Continued funding from the school district may be in jeopardy. She would like to see agencies outside the school provide support for the program and is approaching health agencies, social service agencies, and the private sector to develop new sources of support.

In addition, she thinks the program should offer services until students have graduated from high school. At age 16, teen mothers either have to return to the high school or enter an alternative academic program. The school system provides subsidized daycare for students in the Off Campus Alternative Class and the two continuation (alternative) high schools.

**Objectives**

The objectives of the program are to improve low-achieving students' basic academic skills by at least two grade levels; improve parenting skills; establish realistic developmental expectations for their children; improve the students' self-esteem, decision-making ability, and advocacy skills, and encourage each student to complete school.

**Evaluation**

While the Off Campus Alternative Class has not undergone formal evaluation, Ms. Hobza states that program evaluation helps ensure continued funding. In addition to looking at academics, she thinks an evaluation should focus on the social support aspects and their long-term effect on the participants' ability to support themselves and care for their children.

**Replication**

The Off Campus Alternative Class is an original design and has not been replicated.

**Materials Available**

*Concrete to Abstract* (curriculum), $5.00; program description, $4.00; the flyer, *We Are Here to Help,* free. Contact the Off Campus Alternative Class for details.

# Quincy Teen Mothers

| | | |
|---|---|---|
| Child care | Academic curriculum | Child care info/referral |
| Home visits | Transportation | Parent-child joint actitivies |
| Counseling | Crisis intervention | Health care education |
| Warmline | GED services | Parenting/child development education |
| Newsletter | Parent support groups | Community services info/referral |
| Hotline | Resource library | Developmental exams/screening |

**Contact:** Janice Walsh, Coordinator

**Address:** Bethany Congregational Church
18 Spear Street
Quincy, MA 02169
(617) 984-8704

**Established:** 1978, school initiative

**Budget '88-'89:** $130,000

**Sources:** Local school district, state government, private donations

**Size:** 31 teen parents (15 children)

**Area Served:** Quincy, Massachusetts

**Auspices:** Quincy Public Schools

**1990 Respondent:** Gail Rowerdink, Coordinator

**Community**

Quincy, with a population of 84,300, is a predominantly white, blue-collar city bordering Boston. It has a small-town atmosphere, with established families and a strong community identity. Because of its proximity to Boston, the demographics of Quincy are changing. There has been an influx of new families from other communities and a rise in the median income level and real estate prices.

**Philosophy and Goals**

The Quincy Teen Mothers (QTM) program is based on the belief that pregnant and parenting teens need to complete their education in an academic setting rather than through home-based instruction. The program tries to provide not just a high school education, but a warm, sheltering environment in which students learn self-respect, self-discipline, and self-reliance. The goal is to help students pass on to their children the care and thoughtfulness they have received from the program.

**History and Origins**

In 1978, at the suggestion of Assistant Superintendent Carol Lee Griffin, Dr. Linda Shapiro, a clinical psychologist with the Quincy Public Schools, designed a program for pregnant and parenting teens. Dr. Shapiro interviewed pregnant girls receiving home tutoring and others who had dropped out of school. She found them, as a group, to be lonely, depressed, and isolated. They expressed an interest in seminars rather than counseling. The Bethany Church, across the street from the high school, offered space for classes and a nursery for a modest rent and, in March 1978, the Quincy Teen Mothers pilot program began with one teacher, a child care provider, and four young women. By June, the program had enrolled 6 students and by September, 21 had enrolled.

**Features**

As an alternative high school within the Quincy Public School System, the Quincy Teen Mothers program offers educational and social services to teen mothers and pregnant students. The program allows students to remain in school while pregnant and facilitates their return to school after delivery by providing nursery care during school hours. The program helps locate prenatal care to minimize the health risks for mother and infant and offers courses in nutrition, child development, and parenting, as well as academic, business, and vocational education classes. QTM operates three days a week during school hours from September to June, offering an academic curriculum, child care, and group and individual counseling. A support group continues over the summer.

**Participants**

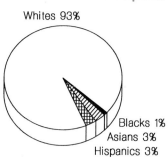

Whites 93%

Blacks 1%
Asians 3%
Hispanics 3%

Pregnant high school students or young mothers from Quincy who are younger than age 22 and have not completed high school are eligible. Their children must be under two years, nine months old. The program averages 27 students per year, and participation can vary from six months to three or four years. All of the students enrolled attend with their infants. The school provides transportation. While the program is designed to serve teen mothers, fathers have also begun to take part in discussion groups and individual counseling. In 1987-88, 15 children, 29 mothers, and 2 fathers participated. All were single parents.

*Many of the problems the staff sees are not those of becoming or being new parents, but are those of adolescence: issues of identity, wanting to be independent, and finding employment.*

**Parent Education**

The family life education course focuses on parenting and child development and covers such topics as preparation for childbirth, discipline, and behavior management. Ms. Rowerdink notes that information is provided both in formal settings within the classroom and through more informal channels, saying that "incidental remarks from the nursery staff to the parent, observations of the 'did you notice' variety can be just as effective."

Individual counseling treats practical issues such as applying for welfare, finding health care, and choosing a daycare program. The coordinator and counselor run weekly discussion and support groups that offer therapy in the guise of a social event. Discussions range from future plans to drugs, sexual abuse, alcohol dependency and its effect on the family, and raising children. Many of the problems the staff sees are not those of becoming or being new parents, but are those of adolescence: issues of identity, wanting to be independent, and finding employment.

**Curriculum**

Teachers devise an individualized academic curriculum for each student, many of whom have fallen behind in school. Five basic subjects — English, functional competency, math, business skills, and family life education — make up the core of the program, with a variety of other optional courses, including computer literacy, French, algebra, geometry, earth science, and United States history. Students work at their own level, pursuing either a Graduate Equivalency Diploma (GED) or a high school diploma in a course of study designed to prepare them for the working world.

QTM rents approximately 2,000 square feet in the Bethany Congregational Church, directly across the street from the high school. The site includes a large classroom, nursery, full-size bathroom, kitchen access, and a comfortable meeting room.

**Parent Involvement**

Teen parents play no role in the design, implementation, or operation of the QTM. They do, however, define their own short- and long-term goals within the program. Two graduates are on the QTM advisory board and another works in the nursery.

**Outreach**

Potential students are identified by participants, high school personnel, or community health and social service agencies. Because pregnant and parenting teens often drop out of sight, the program adopts an aggressive but sensitive approach to outreach through home visits and phone contact. In an effort to find prospective students and to inform local agencies about the program, the coordinator contacts the Department of Social Services; the Special Supplemental Food Program for Women, Infants, and Children (WIC); the welfare office; Quincy Family Planning; local health centers; the middle schools; and the high school. QTM has received recognition in the *Boston Globe* and other local newspapers and has been named an exemplary program by the Massachusetts Department of Education and featured on local television.

**Staff**

While the staff may be available full time to the students, QTM officially operates only three days a week. Full-time positions are actually three-fifths full-time employment.

| Job Title | PD | Vol | FT | PT | Educ Req | Status | Benefits |
|-----------|----|----|----|----|----------|--------|----------|
| Program Coordinator | 1 | - | 1 | - | Post-Graduate Courses or Degree | Other Contract | Yes |
| Head Teacher | 1 | - | 1 | - | College Degree | Other Contract | Yes |
| Teacher | 1 | - | 1 | - | College Degree | Other Contract | Yes |
| Social Worker | 1 | - | - | 1 | Post-Graduate Courses or Degree | K-12 Contract | Yes |
| Head Nursery Teacher | 1 | - | 1 | - | High School Diploma | Hourly Contract | Yes |
| Nursery Aides | 4 | - | 3 | 1 | High School Diploma | Hourly Contract | Yes |
| Volunteers | - | 4 | - | 4 | High School Diploma | - | No |

**State/District Requirements**

The program coordinator is certified as a school adjustment counselor and guidance counselor and is a licensed certified social worker. Each teacher is certified by the state.

| | |
|---|---|
| **Preferred Background** | Staff members should possess a nonjudgmental attitude toward different lifestyles and have experience in special education. |
| **Employee Education and Training Represented** | Prekindergarten and early childhood education; education, grades 7 to 12; special education; parent educator; child care; psychology; counseling; family therapy; social work; child development and family studies. |
| **Administration** | QTM is administered exclusively within the Quincy Public Schools and is under the direct supervision of the assistant superintendent of schools, Dr. Carol Lee Griffin. Although the program is not under the auspices of the high school administration, participants do have access to any and all of the services provided by the Quincy High School and the Quincy Public School System. An advisory board provides community outreach to help the public understand the multifaceted problems of pregnant and parenting teens. |
| **Relationship to the Schools** | QTM is an alternative school within a school under the jurisdiction of the superintendent and building principal. It maintains a strong degree of independence and autonomy. |
| **Community Links** | Ms. Rowerdink reported that because Quincy is a close-knit community, building and maintaining links with community agencies and services has not been difficult. She feels that the program has positive relations with the Massachusetts Department of Social Services, local hospitals, community health programs, and social service agencies. |
| **Funding** | Local and district, 52 percent; state, 44.5 percent; private donations, 3.5 percent. State funding flows from a vocational education grant from the Massachusetts Department of Education and two teen-parenting grants from the Massachusetts Department of Social Services. |
| **In-Kind Resources** | The school system funds the educational staff, supplemental tutoring, a child care aide, and the part-time services of a guidance counselor and nurse, in addition to lunches, transportation, and learning materials. The Massachusetts Department of Social Services funds the coordinator-social worker position. Continued financial support has also been provided by local churches and community groups. Individual donations usually take the form of cribs, baby and maternity clothes, and toys. |
| **Funding History** | When the program first began in 1978, financial support came from the Quincy Public Schools and a grant from the Massachusetts Office for Children. The Junior League of Boston made a three-year commitment of volunteers and financial aid to help develop the program, and the Flexible Children's Fund of the Massachusetts Department of Mental Health gave the Family Service Association of Greater Boston a grant to hire a social worker to coordinate the program and provide social services. In the summer of 1978, the Quincy School Committee voted the program its unanimous support. QTM now operates under the collaborative sponsorship of the Massachusetts Department of Education, the Department of Social Services, and the Quincy Public Schools. |
| **Objectives** | The program is designed to help teen mothers complete high school, reduce the chance of future unplanned pregnancies, enhance parenting skills, and provide an enrichment program for infants. The curriculum prepares mothers for employment. |

**Evaluation**

Each year QTM performs an internal evaluation, the results of which appear in an annual report. Of the 29 mothers enrolled during the 1987-88 school year, 10 graduated from high school or earned their GED, 14 returned in the fall, 2 dropped out of school, and 3 moved away from Quincy during the school year.

**Replication**

QTMP has served as a model for others but remains unique.

**Materials Available**

None.

# Preschool/Parenting Learning Center

*A pregnant ninth-grader entered the Preschool/Parenting Learning Center's program, had her baby in February, and continued in the program with her infant until she graduated four years later. She has gone on to a state technical college on scholarship, while her son James attends Head Start. "She absolutely defeats the stereotype of dropping out and remaining dependent," comments Lyn Overholt, Director of the Preschool/Parenting Learning Center.*

| | | |
|---|---|---|
| Child care | Individual counseling | Parenting/child development education |
| Resource library | Health/nutrition education | Developmental exams/screening |
| Warmline | Parent-child joint activities | Routine medical care for children |
| Networking | Child care info/referrals | Routine medical care for enrolled teens |
| | | Community services info/referral |

**Contact:** Tracy Barbra, Director

**Address:** West High School
Preschool/Parenting Learning Center
3326 Sutherland Avenue
Knoxville, TN 37919
(615) 594-4487

**Established:** 1984, school initiative

**Budget '88-'89:** $65,000

**Sources:** Tennessee Department of Education budget, client fees, in-kind contributions

**Size:** 74 high school students and 12 preschool children

**Area Served:** Knox County School System

**Auspices:** Vocational Home Economics Department

**1990 Respondent:** Lyn Overholt, Director and Teacher

## Community

The Knoxville metropolitan area is the seat of Knox County in eastern Tennessee. The city has a diversified economy based on manufacturing, the textile, clothing, and chemical industries, and tobacco and livestock. The presence of the state university brings an academic subset to the city. The Knoxville metropolitan area population is over 500,000 (13 percent minority).

## Philosophy and Goals

The Preschool/Parenting Learning Center (PPLC) emphasizes the individuality and self-worth of each participating student by fostering the development of problem-solving skills, self-discipline, and constructive methods of learning, and imposing discipline. For children, it builds on their natural eagerness to learn and become competent.

## History and Origins

Lyn Overholt, the PPLC's former director, reports that she began working in the public schools setting up a peer tutoring program. Based on her experience in a University of Tennessee class, she designed the Preschool/Parenting Learning Center to address the problem of adolescent pregnancy at Rule High School in Knoxville. She presented it to the curriculum coordination committee at the Knoxville City Schools and the program was approved on the condition that outside funding sources be found. Initial funding was obtained through a Title II competitive grant and a grant from the Levi Strauss Foundation. Funding is now a line item in the Tennessee Department of Education budget. The program adopted the Vocational/Home Economics Department as a fiscal agent through the public schools and continues to operate under a state grant. No county or city funds are used for the program.

Since PPLC opened, the Knoxville City Schools have been incorporated into the Knox County School System. The program has also expanded beyond the community that it originally served and is now getting referrals from other schools. For the last three years it has been designated as a model by the Tennessee Commission on Children and Youth and has been showcased throughout the state. In 1989, PPLC was named an ongoing or permanent model program.

Ms. Overholt thinks it essential to create a foundation of support prior to launching a program. She indicates that in the South the support of an influential preacher helps sway local opinion. She also emphasizes the importance of the daycare component, not only as a source of child care for teen mothers, but also as a realistic forum for teaching parenting skills as an academic course.

*One of the primary guidelines is to protect participants' feelings and use positive reinforcement to change or redirect behavior.*

### Features

PPLC, a demonstration school for children of adolescent teens and a parent education center, operates five days a week during the academic year. The center provides child care while students attend high school and offers a series of required classes that focus on parenting skills, child development, and family life education. Teen parents continue in the parenting learning center while enrolled in high school, as long as their children attend the preschool. Students interested in early childhood education who may elect to take parenting classes are required to participate in the preschool.

Whenever possible, PPLC makes an effort to get to know its students' extended families and to develop rapport with parents, grandparents, and siblings.

### Participants

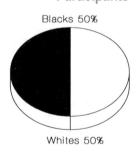

Blacks 50%

Whites 50%

The preschool program serves children (between the ages of 6 weeks and 36 months) of participating high school students; however, classes in the parenting learning center are open to all high school students, many of whom are not parents.

Ms. Overholt reports that during the 1987-88 school year there were 113 identified student pregnancies within the Knox County School System. During the same year, the program served 19 children in the preschool, 16 mothers, and 3 fathers in the parenting learning center and 55 students who were not parents. Seventy-five percent of participants came from families with an average yearly income of less than $10,000 and 25 percent came from families whose income ranged between $10,000 and $20,000.

### Parent Education

Program staff members model good parenting techniques. They reinforce discipline by redirecting children's behavior, stating things positively, and responding enthusiastically to responsible behavior. One of the primary guidelines is to protect participants' feelings and use positive reinforcement to change or redirect behavior. Students are given responsibility for seeing that rules are followed and, as a result, experience a sense of program "ownership." Participating teens realize that "it is a privilege to be in the program," says Ms. Overholt.

**Curriculum**

The curriculum for the parenting and child development education classes is a combination of prepackaged curricula and materials developed within PPLC.

**Sites**

PPLC, formerly housed at Rule High School, is now housed at West High School. Ms. Overholt thinks many students want to stay in their community schools because of established social patterns; if they have to participate in another school's program it is important to have an attraction. To widen outreach, she believes the program should be replicated in other high schools.

**Parent Involvement**

Participants serve on the program's advisory board, which meets at least twice a year. Board members are responsible for public relations and offer support in making the program acceptable to the community. Many grandparents of preschool children have served as advocates for the program with the local community and county school system.

**Outreach**

The Knox County School System has an at-risk identification system called "Child Find," which targets high-risk children for special needs services and alleviates problems with recruitment.

**Staff**

| Job Title | PD | Vol | FT | PT | Educ Req | Status | Benefits |
|-----------|-----|-----|-----|-----|----------|--------|----------|
| Teachers | 2 | - | 1 | 1 | College Degree | K-12 Contract | Yes |
| Aide | 1 | - | 1 | - | High School Diploma | Other Contract | Yes |

**State/District Requirements**

All professional staff members are employed under the regular school contract. The school district and the Tennessee Department of Education require certification for all teachers.

**Preferred Background**

Experience with children in a variety of settings; flexibility, creativity, communication skills, patience, warmth, sensitivity, and stamina are desired.

**Employee Education and Training Represented**

Infant and toddler education; prekindergarten and early childhood education; elementary education; education, grades 7 to 12; parent educator; child care; health and nutrition; home economics; psychology; child development and family studies.

**Administration**

The program is administered exclusively within the Knox County School System through the supervisor's office of the Vocational/Home Economics Department. The staff is also responsible to the principal and to the superintendent and school board of the Knox County School System.

**Relationship to the Schools**

PPLC formed a coalition between school and community groups; school board members are frequently invited to visit the program and close contact is maintained with the school counseling network. Credibility within the community, Ms. Overholt says, "can go a long way toward winning local favor."

**Community Links**

The program maintains contact with public and private social service agencies, the Knox County Health Department, and the courts. It provides field experience for education, nursing, health and human services, and social work programs at the University of Tennessee. Expectant mothers at the Florence Crittendon Agency come weekly to the preschool to gain maternal experience.

Lyn Overholt notes the importance of collaboration with professional organizations. She has made presentations to, or been involved with, the East Tennessee Education Association, the Adolescent Pregnancy Task Force, the Tennessee Commission on Children and Youth, the Tennessee legislature's Task Force on Adolescent Pregnancy and Parenting, and the American Home Economics Association.

**Funding**

Tennessee Department of Education, 80.7 percent; local and school district, 16.8 percent (in-kind contributions and transportation); client fees, 2.5 percent ($5.00 per week per child in the preschool program).

**In-Kind Resources**

The Knox County School System provides space and facilities, consultation and staff development, administrative and clerical support, phones, utilities, and facility maintenance. The Knox County Health Department sponsors the Well Baby Clinic and tuberculosis screening for all class participants; and a private physician donates his time to conduct physical examinations for all class participants.

**Funding History**

Funding has increased since 1983, but only at a pace that maintains the status quo. Ms. Overholt expresses concern that the program's success may cause competition for funding with other communities eager to begin similar ventures.

**Objectives**

PPLC provides students with a realistic understanding of parenthood and child development in an effort to reduce child abuse. It gives guidelines for home management, promotes good health practices for adolescent parents and their children, and enables students to finish high school by offering quality daycare.

**Evaluation**

The preschool is licensed by the Tennessee Human Services Department. The entire program is evaluated by the Tennessee Department of Education. Past evaluations have been used to strengthen the program, increase community support, and gain funds. Ms. Overholt would like to find some way to tie the evaluation into ongoing research on the program's impact on the students, their children and extended family, the community, and the schools. She recommends planning an evaluation procedure from the outset to measure the long-range impact of the program on participants.

**Replication**

In Tennessee, PPLC is being replicated in two Memphis city schools and a Rutherford city school. In addition, the Tennessee Department of Education has chosen one rural school system in which to replicate the model in the fall of 1989. Because state money is scarce, Ms. Overholt urges schools to write programs into their district budgets at the outset.

**Materials Available**

Program staff members have written the *Exportability Manual* (Year I, Year II, and Year III) to help others replicate the program model, and a six-week communication skills unit.

# 7

# Family Literacy and Intergenerational Skill Development

The following programs focus on giving mothers and children the opportunity to share the experience of learning to read. They target a migrant or multicultural adult population whose low literacy level and English-speaking proficiency inhibits their taking necessary steps toward self-sufficiency, hampers their understanding of their children's rights to equal educational opportunities, and contributes to their sense of powerlessness in the system. Many programs supplement or combine literacy skills classes with child development education, career counseling, and Graduate Equivalency Diploma (GED) preparation. Their hope, as Kentucky PACE founders have stated, is to "break the cycle of intergenerational illiteracy."

# Programs in Brief

# SHAPE Plus

## Part of South Hennepin Adult Programs in Education

| | | |
|---|---|---|
| Networking | Resource library | Parenting/child development education |
| Toy lending | Career counseling | Child care info/referral |
| Child care | Transition services | Community services info/referral |
| Adult literacy | GED services | Parent-child joint activities |
| Home visits | High school diploma | Postsecondary training |

**Contact:** Kevin Byrne, Coordinator SHAPE

**Address:** Bloomington Education Center
8900 Portland Avenue South
Bloomington, MN 55420
(612) 885-8550

**Established:** 1987, collaborative venture between Community Education and Early Childhood Family Education

**Budget '88-'89:** $62,381

**Sources:** Minnesota Adult Basic Education (ABE), local tax levy

**Size:** 99 families

**Area Served:** Four school districts

**Auspices:** Community Education Department of the public schools

*Kathy, a single mother of two, enrolled in SHAPE classes to earn her high school diploma. She also took advantage of the free parenting classes offered and observed the daycare provided by SHAPE. Discouraged by a third pregnancy, Kathy contemplated how she could continue her education once her baby was born. Her growing sense of scholastic accomplishment and her awareness of quality daycare options gave her the confidence to pursue postsecondary training as an occupational therapist.*

## Community

SHAPE (South Hennepin Adult Programs in Education) Plus serves the Bloomington, Richfield, Edina, and Eden Prairie school districts, all of which are suburban communities outside the Minneapolis-St. Paul area. Although it is the third largest city in Minnesota (population approximately 84,480), Bloomington lacks a cohesive set of municipal services. All four communities are mainly white and middle class with pockets of low-income families; all suffer from poor public transportation.

## Philosophy and Goals

SHAPE Plus targets single mothers with literacy problems who are vulnerable to the stigma of receiving welfare. The program encourages them to view welfare as a means toward an end and to think about their careers in terms of personal growth and future self-sufficiency. Participants need to think of themselves as "winners and bread winners," says Coordinator Julie Williams, "a goal that is particularly difficult when their sense of self-worth is tied to their role as mother . . . . This can make them unwilling to arrange for the child care that would allow them to participate in training or to ask older children to share responsibilities. We help them see the potential that training and work have for increasing family stability and the opportunities their children will have. We provide support when parents and children experience stress from the changes that growth engenders."

## History and Origins

The roots of SHAPE Plus are in an Early Childhood Family Education (ECFE) pilot program begun at two sites in Bloomington in 1975 and 1977. Sponsored by the Council of Quality Education (CQE), each site served a single elementary attendance area in Bloomington, offering center-based child development activities along with parent and family education workshops. In 1984, state legislation shifted responsibility for ECFE to the community education department of each school district, and three years later the idea for SHAPE Plus emerged as a logical collaboration between the existing SHAPE program that provided Adult Basic Education (ABE) and Graduate Equivalency Diploma (GED) classes through the Community Education Department and the ECFE parent education program. SHAPE Coordinator Kevin Byrne submitted the proposal to Community Action for Southern Hennepin, a granting mediator and community council that receives proposals and acts as a transfer and screening agency for the federal government.

## Features

SHAPE Plus combines adult education and GED classes with parent education training. Unique to the program is the free sibling care service it extends to mothers while they attend GED classes, with the stipulation that they participate in an ECFE parent-child class. Those involved in its administration call SHAPE Plus a "key to reaching the family that may be at risk." SHAPE Plus participants attend GED classes three afternoons a week and take ECFE parenting classes less frequently. Graduates are eligible for transition services to postsecondary training including counseling, daycare, and transportation subsidies.

## Participants

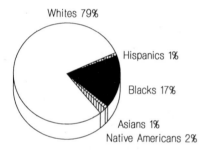

Whites 79%

Hispanics 1%

Blacks 17%

Asians 1%
Native Americans 2%

SHAPE Plus targets low-income parents, usually single, who have neither a GED nor a high school diploma. Typical families are those with a high incidence of risk factors including adult illiteracy, divorce or separation, poverty, and educational disadvantage. In 1987-88, the program served 99 single parents, 4 percent of whom were teens. SHAPE Plus reached 50 percent of the eligible population, 98 percent of whom had incomes below $10,000.

*Participants need to think of themselves as "winners and bread winners," says Coordinator Julie Williams, "a goal that is particularly difficult when their sense of self worth is tied to their role as mother . . . ."*

## Parent Education

ECFE classes use lectures, speakers, handouts, group discussions, films, and field trips to facilitate parent training.

## Curriculum

SHAPE Plus combines prepackaged materials with those developed in house. SHAPE curriculum has been developed by public school teachers and counselors. Parenting materials are adapted by ECFE to fit the special needs and literacy level of low-income, single parents and emphasize self-esteem and personal growth. The focus is less on passive learning and more on verbal exchange with particular focus on use of community resources.

## Sites

Program sites include nine classrooms at seven public schools and rented space in a commercial building, a technical institute, and a community college. School and program share audio-visual equipment, xerox machines, and computers. Libraries offer one-on-one tutoring. Space is an ongoing issue for SHAPE Plus.

## Parent Involvement

Parents articulated the need for child care and transportation to the SHAPE Plus director. They routinely get involved in evaluations and discussion groups, and they are expected to play important roles in the advisory council, which is currently in the planning stages. Informal parent surveys support the program concept in grant applications.

## Outreach

A public relations person on the SHAPE Plus staff combines standard public relations with direct outreach, including a door-to-door campaign in public housing projects. Generally, parents hear about the program through a direct mailing strategy coordinated with the Aid to Families with Dependent Children (AFDC) office. Underemployed parents who need skill development to advance at work and low-level readers are hardest to reach, says the director. Public health groups, drug and alcohol counselors, food commodity centers, and emergency food-shelf outlets make referrals. Three times a year, SHAPE Plus includes information about programming in welfare checks and surplus commodities sacks.

## Staff

The SHAPE Plus staff and public school staff share inservice training workshops that emphasize maintaining motivation among at-risk families.

| Job Title | PD | Vol | FT | PT | Educ Req | Status | Benefits |
|---|---|---|---|---|---|---|---|
| Coordinator | 1 | - | 1 | - | College Degree | Other Contract | Yes |
| Counselor | 1 | - | - | 1 | Post-Graduate Courses or Degree | Other Contract | No |
| Volunteer Tutors | - | 25 | - | 25 | High School Diploma | Other Contract | No |

## State/District Requirements

For counselors, active secondary or elementary teaching license; for the coordinator, college degree in a related field.

## Preferred Background

Experience with low-income clients and good written and verbal communication skills are preferred for both coordinator and counselor positions.

## Employee Education and Training Represented

Prekindergarten and early childhood education; bilingual education; adult literacy; child care; psychology; counseling; social work; development and fundraising; research and evaluation.

## Administration

The SHAPE Plus coordinator reports to the SHAPE coordinator, who is based in the Community Education Department serving the four participating school districts. Community Action for Suburban Hennepin monitors the program.

## Relationship to the Schools

SHAPE Plus coordinates its programming with public school departments including ECFE, special education, and guidance. SHAPE Plus participants are eligible for elective credit toward a high school diploma or GED for participation in a SHAPE program called "Parent to Parent," in which volunteers work with parents once a week to help them prepare their three- to five-year-old children for kindergarten, while the children participate in school readiness activities.

**Community Links**

SHAPE Plus subcontracts with ECFE to get child care, and with the Special Supplemental Food Program for Women, Infants, and Children (WIC) for health screening and outreach services.

**Funding**

State grant (through ECFE funding for SHAPE), 60 percent; special local tax levy, 40 percent.

**In-Kind Resources**

The public schools provide space, facilities, consultation and staff development, equipment, and access to computers and telephones; the Community Education Department provides periodic direct service to program participants through workshops and classes.

**Funding History**

Originally, SHAPE received a grant to start SHAPE Plus, but Adult Basic Education state and federal funds have funded the pilot since July 1988. Funding has increased by 25 percent over the program's first year of operation and is moderately secure.

**Objectives**

SHAPE Plus aims to reduce the social isolation of low-income, single parents, foster their parenting skills and self-esteem, and boost their interest in further education and career opportunities.

*"We provide support when parents and children experience stress from the changes that growth engenders."*

**Evaluation**

In an external evaluation required by the community education director and Community Action for Suburban Hennepin, 30 percent of the 43 surveys were returned, and of these, half the respondents had completed the program. (Follow-up efforts revealed that half the participants' telephones had been disconnected.) Staff members are researching more effective evaluation tools to use with this highly transient group.

**Replication**

SHAPE Plus has served as a model for a plan submitted to the Minnesota legislature by the state planning agency, Jobs and Training, and the Minnesota Department of Education. Robbinsdale Adult Basic Education has collaborated with ECFE to adapt the SHAPE Plus model to its community.

**Materials Available**

*SHAPE Diploma Curriculum Guide* and outreach materials are both available at cost of reproduction. Contact Julie Williams at the above address.

# Home Instruction Program for Preschool Youngsters

*Sally, a twenty-four-year-old single mother of four boys, was having difficulty talking to her children. She enrolled in HIPPY and through the curriculum learned to set aside individual time with each child every day and to set her own goals. She now has a cosmetology business and has encouraged her mother and two brothers to complete their GEDs.*

| | | |
|---|---|---|
| Home visits | Mother support groups | Health/nutrition education |
| Networking | Medical care referrals | Holiday workshops |
| Resource library | Child care info | Parent-child joint activities |
| Counseling | Adult literacy/GED referrals | Warmline/welcome calls |
| Newsletter | Family therapy | Parenting/child development education |
| | Developmental exams/screening | |

**Contact:** Marian Shead, Supervisor

**Address:** 1401 Scott Street
Little Rock, AR 72202
(501) 324-2266

**Established:** 1985, state initiative; 1986, Little Rock program

**Budget '88-'89:** $140,000

**Sources:** City and federal funds

**Size:** 240 families

**Area served:** Little Rock, Arkansas

**Auspices:** HIPPY in Israel, part of state pilot project through the governor's office

**Community**

Little Rock, the capital of Arkansas, has a mixed socioeconomic population of 190,000. The HIPPY program serves families in the lower-income bracket. Small factories and AT&T are the chief employers of this group; the unemployed receive welfare and Aid to Families with Dependent Children (AFDC).

**Philosophy and Goals**

HIPPY's philosophy that home instruction can effectively improve learning stems from a belief in the power of home socialization patterns. The goal of the program is to help children become more responsible, responsive, and successful in school and to help mothers attain a positive self-image and attitude toward education by encouraging them to increase their awareness of their own strengths and potential as home educators. "We try to instill self-esteem and self-worth and start with small goals, then move to larger ones," says Marian Shead, supervisor of HIPPY in Little Rock.

**History and Origins**

In 1969, Dr. Avima Lombard at Hebrew University in Israel developed Home Instruction Program for Preschool Youngsters (HIPPY) as part of a research project that examined the feasibility of home-based educational intervention with mothers of disadvantaged preschool children, with the aim of preparing these children for school. By 1975, the program was operational in Israel and had been adopted into the national educational welfare program. Studies of the program assert that its participants are less likely to repeat grades, are less likely to be identified as needing special education, are less likely to drop out of school, and are more successful students overall. HIPPY has now spread to Turkey, Canada, Chile, Holland, South Africa, and several locations in the United States.

In 1984, Hillary Rodham Clinton approached the Arkansas Department of Education about implementing the HIPPY model throughout the state. In September 1986, HIPPY was launched in Little Rock and three other sites; currently 14 communities sponsor the program. The Little Rock School District paid for representatives to go to Israel to take the HIPPY training course; when they returned, they recruited others to work in the program. In 1986, Marian Shead, a substitute teacher in the school system, was hired as program coordinator and later became supervisor in Little Rock. For its first two years the program was funded by the Little Rock Job Training Partnership Act (JTPA) and Chapter 2.

### Features

HIPPY is a home-based parent education program designed to show mothers how to read, play games, and complete daily worksheets with their four- and five-year-olds so the children will be prepared for the rigors of kindergarten and first grade. Families join the program when their child turns four. They make a two-year commitment to allot 15 minutes a day for 30 weeks to work through a packet of structured learning activities.

Paraprofessionals or instructional aides who reside in the target neighborhoods are hired and trained to teach the HIPPY curriculum to parents of four- and five-year-old children. In Little Rock, these home visitors are mothers who are enrolled in the program. Aides are assigned 12 to 18 families and visit each participant's home every other week for one hour to instruct parents in the use of learning materials.

The program is two-tiered: aides develop their own skills as community service providers and then train their peers to become more effective home educators and parents. Upon completion of the 30-week program, aides are employed through the JTPA training agent of the school district.

Parents attend a monthly group meeting with their aide to review the curriculum, look at materials covered in the previous weeks, and discuss individual progress. Meeting times accommodate parents, and those who attend are exempt from receiving a home visit on that particular week.

### Participants

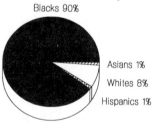

Blacks 90%
Asians 1%
Whites 8%
Hispanics 1%

In the first year (1986-87) 240 students participated in the Little Rock initiative. Program participants are primarily low-income mothers and their prekindergarten four- and five-year-olds who are viewed as high risk and educationally deprived. Families participating in the four-year-old program are expected to continue into the five-year-old program. All 24 instructional aides and their children are participants of the HIPPY program. In 1987-88, 60 percent of these women were single parents and 20 percent were teen mothers.

### Parent Education

Parent education classes are offered to aides as part of their job training. These classes take place once a week and last for 6 1/2 hours. Aides learn to instruct participants more effectively; they are taught basic English, writing, and communication skills.

### Curriculum

Prepackaged curriculum materials are prepared by the program's developers in Israel. Expanded and adapted to suit Little Rock, they are enhanced by activities and books appropriate to African-American culture. The HIPPY staff offers ideas to aides about making the HIPPY curriculum relevant and playful.

**Sites**

HIPPY is headquartered in an adult education building. Parent education classes and group meetings are held in public elementary schools, religious facilities, and neighborhood community centers. According to Marian Shead, "The school system provides the main site, other locations for group meetings are donated. There has never been a problem with available space. We even meet in the public library occasionally. The community is very cooperative." The most important site for the HIPPY program is the home.

**Parent Involvement**

Parents are involved as participants and as instructional aides. Most instructional aides are parents who are already working with their own children on the HIPPY curriculum. Marian Shead writes, "HIPPY has a parent involvement component, so the PTA [parent-teacher association], Parent Association Council, and the in-school parent involvement group work closely together on enrichment workshops for the advancement of parents."

**Outreach**

Outreach occurs principally through participants' recommendations. However, television spots, radio talk shows, school newsletters, and school flyers advertising the program have all been helpful in recruiting participants. Mrs. Shead feels that it is especially important to attend orientation meetings at the beginning of the school year, since teachers can help her identify children who may have younger siblings eligible for HIPPY. She notes that she also contacts human service agencies, "I make them aware that we are here and that we could be of service to them."

**Staff**

The aides are trained in the HIPPY curriculum, writing, and oral communication skills, personal and social development, parent education, and cultural enrichment.

| Job Title | PD | Vol | FT | PT | Educ Req | Status | Benefits |
|---|---|---|---|---|---|---|---|
| Supervisor | 1 | - | 1 | - | College Degree | Other Contract | Yes |
| Coordinators | 2 | - | 2 | - | College Degree | Other Contract | Yes |
| Secretary | 1 | - | 1 | - | Some College | Other Contract | Yes |
| Instructional Aide | 1 | - | 1 | - | Some College | Other Contract | Yes |
| Instructional Aides | 24 | - | - | 24 | High School Diploma | Hourly Contract | No |

**State/District Requirements**

The city requires that HIPPY instructors be certified to participate in the training program. Aides must have a referral from JTPA stating their eligibility; job performance forms filled out by HIPPY's coordinator are required. HIPPY evaluates each aide's performance.

**Preferred Background**

HIPPY instructional aides must be parents whose background is similar to the parents they teach. This is a job-training program as well as a parent education program.

**Employee Education and Training Represented**

Prekindergarten and early childhood education; counseling; social work; child development and family studies; religion and clergy.

## Administration

Mr. James Jennings, associate superintendent for desegregation, is responsible for oversight of HIPPY in the Little Rock School District. Marion Shead supervises the program; Little Rock School District, the superintendent, and the school board are responsible for approving the budget and program services.

## Relationship to the Schools

HIPPY maintains linkages with school personnel, counselors, and curriculum supervisors and with a school-based preschool attended by many of the children who are participants of HIPPY. There is some sharing of staff, staff development, and facilities, as well as both informal and formal participant referrals. Mrs. Shead makes presentations about HIPPY and frequently attends meetings with the school counselors, administration, superintendent, and elementary school principals.

*In HIPPY's second year in Little Rock, pre- and posttesting of children was completed at the kindergarten level to assess academic growth. There was a 30-month increase in learning following 9 months of involvement with HIPPY.*

HIPPY is very important to the schools and vice versa, asserts Mrs. Shead. "It is a springboard for a positive experience in school . . . After HIPPY, kids enter school better prepared and parents are more involved. For us, being in the school system is a safety margin because everything we do has to be approved by the district administration. Schools monitor our plans, curriculum, and instruction. We are kept in line with the district's goals and HIPPY's goals. We have to plan our programs ahead and keep up with the school bureaucracy. I see this as positive. Even for purchases, we make requisitions and the district approves them. This takes time, but it keeps us within our budget and we don't overspend. We have access to school facilities and equipment such as the media center services, which keeps our budget at a minimum."

## Community Links

Watershed Human Services refers likely candidates to HIPPY for the instructional aide and job-training program. The Arkansas Department of Human Services and the Community Organization for Poverty Elimination (COPE) both make referrals to the program.

## Funding

Federal, 80 to 85 percent; city, 15 to 20 percent. Federal money comes from Chapter 2 funding; city money is allocated from JTPA for instructional aides' salaries.

## In-Kind Resources

The school district provides space and facilities, consultation, staff development, periodic service to program participants (workshops, vision and hearing screening), and access to equipment.

## Funding History

Funding is very secure and has increased by 50 percent since the program's first year in Little Rock.

**Objectives**

HIPPY helps children academically and gets parents involved in the beginning stages of their children's education which, according to Mrs. Shead, is necessary with high-risk children. It seeks to affect test scores directly, to increase children's feelings of self-worth, and to make children more responsive and successful when they enter school.

**Evaluation**

JTPA evaluates the program at the end of each year. Mrs. Shead describes their requirements: "They have milestones that must be reached, based on our ability to teach aides the curriculum and prepare them for employment. JTPA monitors the aides' files to ensure they have fulfilled the necessary requirements."

In HIPPY's second year in Little Rock, pre- and posttesting of children was completed at the kindergarten level to assess academic growth. There was a 30-month increase in learning following 9 months of involvement with HIPPY.

**Replication**

The HIPPY program has been replicated all over the world and in 14 locations in the state of Arkansas.

**Materials Available**

HIPPY materials are available from the HIPPY USA Office, National Council of Jewish Women, 15 East 26th Street, New York, New York 10010, telephone (212) 532-1740. Contact Dr. Miriam Westhiemer, Director.

# Literacy and Basic Skills
# Family Literacy Project

| | | |
|---|---|---|
| Networking | Parent-child joint activities | Parenting/child development education |
| Adult literacy | Mother support groups | Health/nutrition education |
| Newsletter | Individual counseling | Child care info/referral |
| Home visits | Resource library | Community services info/referral |
| GED services | Adult Basic Education | Preemployment preparation |
| Preschool | Father support groups | |

**Contact:** Sue G. Thorne-Crytzer, Director of Literacy Education

**Address:** Fayetteville Technical Community College
ABE programs
2201 Hull Road
P.O. Box 35236
Fayetteville, NC 28303
(919) 678-8491

**Established:** 1988, collaborative venture

**Budget '88-'89:** $46,500

**Sources:** Kenan/SREB Family Literacy Project Foundation and in-kind contributions

**Size:** 24 families

**Area Served:** Fayetteville, North Carolina

**Auspices:** Kenan Trust Family Literacy Project, Southern Regional Education Board, Fayetteville Community College

**Community**

In Fayetteville, local shopping malls and services cater to military personnel from the nearby Fort Bragg and Pope Air Force Base. Low-level literacy is perceived as a problem in this city with its high proportion of adults (close to 46,000) who do not possess a high school diploma. Currently, the community is making an effort to attract large, northern businesses.

**Philosophy and Goals**

The Literacy and Basic Skills Family Literacy Project (formerly the Kenan/SREB Faimily Literacy Project), located in Chapel Hill, North Carolina and administered by the Southern Regional Education Board (SREB) in Atlanta, Georgia, seeks to break the intergenerational cycle of undereducation by improving parents' basic skills and attitudes toward education, improving children's learning skills, and uniting parents and children in a positive educational experience.

**History and Origins**

In July 1988, Dr. Sharon Darling, director of the Kenan Trust Family Literacy Project, presented the goals of the Kenan Charitable Trust's model programs to Dr. R. Craig Allen, president of Fayetteville Technical Community College (FTCC), and Dr. Jack Britt, superintendent of Cumberland County Schools. Both administrators were enthusiastic and immediately formed a partnership to promote the concept of family literacy in Fayetteville. The Family Literacy Model Program is funded and operated through the cooperative efforts of the community college and the school system.

## Features

The Literacy and Basic Skills Family Literacy Project offers services during the nine-month school year. It provides parents with an opportunity to earn a Graduate Equivalency Diploma (GED) while giving their children constructive preschool activities. To maintain motivation among participants, classes for parents meet three days a week; two days are set aside for parents to volunteer or take job training courses at their schools and in the community. The four major components of the model are early childhood education, adult education, parenting education, and vocational education. Parents and children both receive free breakfast and lunch.

## Participants

At this time, the program can serve a maximum of 24 eligible students — parents who lack a high school education or equivalent skills — and their three- and four-year-old children. Eighty-three percent earn less than $10,000; the remainder earn less than $20,000.

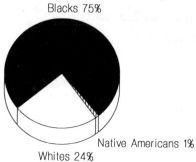

Blacks 75%

Native Americans 1%

Whites 24%

*". . . it is important for the agencies to recognize that the Kenan literacy program can perform an important service for them by enabling parents to pursue job skills and by raising their educational levels."*

## Parent Education

The program emphasizes strong socialization skills — helping parents take control over their lives. Workshops and discussions identify parental needs and help parents plan ways to meet those needs. According to the program's directors, group support contributes to a "tight bonding" that evolves among parents; the group envelops new members, adding to their sense of security and reducing their fears, including anxieties about school.

## Curriculum

The Literacy and Basic Skills Family Literacy Project uses the Adult Basic Education and GED preparation curriculum recommended by the North Carolina Department of Community Colleges, including: the *Cambridge Pre-GED Programs in Reading and Math,* the *Cambridge Skill Power Series, Math for Adult Living, Strategies for Success in Reading, Strategies for Success in Writing,* and *Contemporary's Building Basic Skills in Reading.* The instructor often needs to "translate" reading materials to make them easier to understand.

## Sites

The program is housed at a single school site.

## Parent Involvement

Parents attend the program three days a week and are expected to work, volunteer, or participate in job training during the rest of the week. Parents also learn how to help their children with homework and keep diaries recording their children's growth and behavior.

## Outreach

Outreach strategies used include: bulk brochure mailings to targeted areas; dissemination of information through the North Carolina Department of Social Services; contact with the Council of Ministers, the American Indian Association, and Project Head Start; and community service announcements on radio, television, and in the newspapers. Fayetteville Urban Ministries, Vocational Rehabilitation, and the

Employment Security Commission distribute brochures. The community college, the public school system, and other local agencies explain the opportunities offered by the Literacy and Basic Skills Family Literacy Project to potential students.

## Staff

| Job Title | PD | Vol | FT | PT | Educ Req | Status | Benefits |
|---|---|---|---|---|---|---|---|
| Coordinator | 1 | - | - | 1 | Post-Graduate Courses or Degree | Other Contract | Yes |
| Recruiter | 1 | - | - | 1 | Post-Graduate Courses or Degree | Other Contract | Yes |
| Adult Education Instructor | 1 | - | - | 1 | Post-Graduate Courses or Degree | Hourly Contract | No |
| Early Childhood Instructor | 1 | - | - | 1 | College Degree | K-12 Contract | Yes |
| Early Childhood Instructor Aide | 1 | - | - | 1 | Some College | Other Contract | Yes |
| Volunteer | - | 1 | - | 1 | High School Diploma | Other Contract | No |

**State/District Requirements**

Minimum of a bachelor's degree; master's degree in education preferred.

**Preferred Background**

Experience in adult education, special education, or human resource development.

**Employee Education and Training Represented**

Prekindergarten and early childhood education; adult basic education; adult literacy; parent educator; adult vocational education; health and nutrition; home economics; counseling; social work; research and evaluation; administration; supervision; curriculum.

**Administration**

The Literacy and Basic Skills Family Literacy Project is monitored by Dr. Andrew Hayes, the evaluator for the Kenan Charitable Trust. Ms. MacGregor, the coordinator, is responsible to Sue Thorne-Crytzer, director of literacy education at the community college, and Dr. Sharon Darling, national director of the Kenan Trust Family Literacy Project. The coordinator manages the team efforts of instructors and offers counseling and referral services to participants in the program. Within the school system, Dr. Tryon Lancaster, associate superintendent of the Cumberland County Board of Education, shares responsibility in this partnership. Fayetteville Technical Community College (FTCC) provides an adult education instructor; the Cumberland County Board of Education provides an early childhood education instructor. The program is administered jointly by the public school system, FTCC, and Cumberland County Board of Education. Frequent phone calls maintain continuous communication among the partners. The literacy education advisory board includes: seven staff members from the program, one representative from the host school, ten representatives from public agencies, twenty from private agencies, and three from the community.

| | |
|---|---|
| **Relationship to the Schools** | The director says that the academic community was prepared for parents to start coming to school sites because of extensive media coverage when the program began. The teachers have gained a new appreciation of the importance of home life to the success of children. The only liability for this school-based program is the long Christmas break. The director notes that parents can fall back into bad habits over several weeks, and the program has to re-recruit to draw parents back into the program. |
| **Community Links** | Time to Read volunteers assist in Adult Basic Education instruction to parents. When children reach kindergarten age, parents are referred to Fayetteville Technical Community College for further adult education or to appropriate job-training agencies. The program maintains close ties with several agencies for support, recruitment, information exchanges, and interagency staff participation. Ms. Thorne-Crytzer, the literacy education director, notes that it is important for the agencies to recognize that the Kenan Trust Family Literacy Project can perform an important service for them by enabling parents to pursue job skills and by raising their educational levels. |
| **Funding** | Kenan Trust Family Literacy Project Foundation, 98 percent; in-kind contributions, two percent. |
| **In-Kind Resources** | Volunteer staff is provided by Time to Read and the Cumberland County School Club provides clothes, toys, and food. |
| **Funding History** | The program has been in operation for one year. |
| **Objectives** | The program seeks to improve academic proficiency in adults and preschoolers while fostering the adults' independence, sense of self-discipline, and potential for economic success. Directors anticipate an increase in the value placed on education within the home, greater success in academic as well as vocational endeavors, and improved parenting skills. |

*The program emphasizes strong socialization skills — helping parents take control over their lives . . . group support contributes to a "tight bonding" that evolves among parents.*

| | |
|---|---|
| **Evaluation** | A representative of the Kenan Charitable Trust collects data for a longitudinal study on three- and four-year-olds. The literacy education director advises collecting data right from the start. |
| **Replication** | Three other family literacy programs have been established in North Carolina through the Kenan Charitable Trust. |
| **Materials Available** | Order the *Kenan/SREB Family Literacy Guidebook* and *Family Literacy Video* from Dr. Sharon Darling, Director, Kenan Trust Family Literacy Project, Suite 1063, Starks Building, Louisville, Kentucky 40202. Samples of press coverage are available from Sue Thorne-Crytzer at the program address. |

# Family Literacy Center

| | | |
|---|---|---|
| Adult literacy | Parent-child joint activities | Parenting/child development education |
| Resource library | Consultation for adult educators | Technical assistance for adult educators |
| Networking | Video training for adult educators | Community services info/referral |

**Contact:** Kay Taggart, Coordinator

**Address:** El Paso Community College
P.O. Box 20500
El Paso, TX 79998
(915) 542-2745

**Established:** 1985, community college initiative

**Budget '88-'89:** $123,000

**Sources:** Federal Title VII, Office of Bilingual Education and Language Minorities

**Size:** 60 families in five schools

**Area Served:** El Paso and environs

**Auspices:** El Paso Community College

**1990 Respondent:** Betsy Quintero, Project Director

*Vicky came to the United States from Mexico four years ago with her family, unable to speak or read English. She and her preschool-age daughter, Sandra, were invited to attend the program's first classes. Vicky recalls, "At first I was afraid that I would seem stupid because I was an adult in a child's classroom. But I have two older children in high school and I wanted to read enough English to be able to help them. The program surprised me because it was fun. I didn't feel strange. Everyone was in the same situation."*

## Community

El Paso, located in southwestern Texas on the Mexican border, is a Hispanic city of approximately 400,000, with a large concentration of people living in poverty. Twenty-eight percent of the adult population has completed less than eight years of school, the unemployment rate is 11.6 percent, and the annual per capita income averages $5,000. The Family Literacy Center of El Paso Community College is situated in downtown El Paso. The school districts served by the college's Family Literacy Center, formerly Project FIEL (Family Initiative for English Literacy), are in rural and urban areas, populated largely by migrant families, within half an hour of the city. Other residents work at the local factories or comprise a relatively unskilled labor force doing piece work, farming, and domestic labor.

## Philosophy and Goals

The Family Literacy Center aims to help promote family literacy and break the intergenerational cycle of undereducation.

## History and Origins

The Family Literacy Center is an offshoot of the Literacy Education Action (LEA) program established by the president of El Paso Community College, Dr. Robert Shepack, in the fall of 1985 as a plan of social action that, at the college level, merged the disciplines of reading, sociology, and English as a Second Language (ESL). In 1986 LEA opened the literacy center, which offered drop-in literacy tutoring, computer-assisted instruction, and small group instruction. That same year, LEA initiated family literacy classes at the community college literacy center with funds from the Texas Education Agency. The project's director, Betsy Quintero, has a background in early childhood and bilingual education. The Center offers technical assistance and consultation for teachers who conduct bilingual literacy classes for parents and their preschool or elementary-age children.

**Features**

The Family Literacy Center offers 12 weekly literacy classes in five public schools in the El Paso area. Taught by kindergarten teachers who have participated in an eight-hour training session, classes follow a five-step language experience curriculum that emphasizes role modeling, home activities, classroom participation, and cultural reinforcement. Learning is based on daily experience, and English is taught in a bilingual setting. Class capacity is approximately five parents and five children. Following the initial teacher training sessions at the literacy center, Betsy Quintero and three part-time trainers provide both on-site visits and consultations with adult educators who make suggestions for revising and improving the model based on their own experiences.

**Participants**

Hispanics 99%

Blacks 1%

The Family Literacy Center participants are parents and children within school districts receiving funds for students with limited proficiency in English. Participants are at risk for illiteracy, poverty, lack of parenting skills, and developmental delays. In 1988, the project served 50 children, 43 mothers, and 2 fathers; 71 percent were single parents, 8 percent teens; 98 percent had incomes below $10,000.

> *Taught by kindergarten teachers who have participated in an eight-hour training session, classes follow a five-step language experience curriculum that emphasizes role modeling, home activities, classroom participation, and cultural reinforcement. Learning is based on daily experience, and English is taught in a bilingual setting.*

**Parent Education**

A preventive model for parents at risk due to low English language proficiency, the Family Literacy Center offers parent education and encourages peer support as a by-product of its literacy course, interjecting useful tips on childrearing and helping parents develop a strong rapport with their children through projects that engage them in shared activities.

**Curriculum**

The Family Literacy Center uses a five-step curriculum developed by LEA. The steps used in each class include an oral language activity, a hands-on learning activity, a language experience approach activity in family teams, a story time that encourages interaction, and suggestions for home activities for the family. The model, Ms. Quintero says, has been adapted over time to reflect teachers' classroom experiences. The shift from Spanish to English is more gradual in largely migrant communities and classroom content changes to match parents' skills and interests. The themes of the five-step curriculum similarly reflect local concerns.

**Sites**

The Family Literacy Center is working with five school districts and plans to increase that number to eight by January 1990. Because the outlying school districts are rural, transportation is a problem, says Ms. Quintero, so much so that one staff member has been picking up parents on her way to work.

**Parent Involvement**

Parents serve on an advisory board made up of project staff and school personnel that meets twice yearly to approve services and curriculum.

**Outreach**

Outreach is carried on through teachers and aides at the schools and through other parents. Parents, who might be suspicious of the Rio Grande campus literacy center because of its urban situation and college affiliation, feel comfortable with their children's kindergarten teachers. In 1986, LEA ran a pilot program for parents and children at the literacy center. "Logistics were a nightmare," says Ms. Quintero, because recruitment was very difficult. "Now teachers play a large part in recruitment, parents get to know their child's teacher; there is an element of trust and familiarity to build on . . . ."

**Staff**

| Job Title | PD | Vol | FT | PT | Educ Req | Status | Benefits |
|-----------|-----|-----|-----|-----|----------|--------|----------|
| Director | 1 | - | 1 | - | Post-Graduate Courses or Degree | Other Contract | Yes |
| Assistant Director | 1 | - | - | 1 | Post-Graduate Courses or Degree | Hourly Contract | Yes |
| Teacher Trainers | 2 | - | - | 2 | Post-Graduate Courses or Degree | Hourly Contract | Yes |
| Counselor | 1 | - | - | 1 | Post-Graduate Courses or Degree | Hourly Contract | Yes |
| Teachers | 12 | - | - | 12 | College Degree | Hourly Contract | No |
| Aides | 12 | - | - | 12 | High School Diploma | Hourly Contract | No |

**State/District Requirements**

None.

**Preferred Background**

Teachers should have experience and interest in working with parents and an openness to new findings in literacy research; for aides, classroom experience and knowledge of and rapport with the local community are very important.

**Employee Education and Training Represented**

Infant and toddler education; prekindergarten and early childhood education; elementary education; education, grades 7 to 12; bilingual education; special education; adult basic education; adult literacy; parent educator; adult vocational education; child care; psychology; counseling; family therapy; applied linguistics; child development and family studies; development and fundraising; research and evaluation.

**Administration**

The project's director is employed by the community college and works directly with teacher trainers and counselors. Administratively, the project is split between on-site teachers and aides and the community college literacy program, which steers curriculum development, articulates program philosophy, provides teacher training and evaluation, and takes responsibility for program replication.

| | |
|---|---|
| **Relationship to the Schools** | According to Ms. Quintero, "The project is keyed into participating teachers (kindergarten through second grade): it has a good relationship with the administration, personnel, and counselors to whom it makes referrals in individual situations." The Family Literacy Center has received a lot of support from the schools, she notes. Teachers, too, are supportive, although some have had difficulty accepting the whole language approach and a curriculum that engages parents and children together on projects. "In general," says Ms. Quintero, "teachers take to what we're doing beautifully, and learning occurs both ways." Teachers are adapting to a holistic approach to learning, while parents are developing new skills in reading and parenting. "The biggest hurdle," she notes, "is getting teachers to realize that the project has the same goals they do, only our approach is different, based on experiential learning, on more involvement with the family." Teachers are also learning that reaching out to families is not trespassing. Occasionally, she observes, a parent will come to class for a couple of weeks and then disappear. The program urges teachers to follow up, visit the home, find out what is going on. This more active orientation toward families has resulted in discovering problems and making referrals to appropriate social service agencies. |
| **Community Links** | The Literacy Education Action program has developed a network of collaborative relationships resulting in seed money for pilot programs and links with mutually supportive community literacy groups. A grant from the Levi Strauss Foundation enabled LEA to buy an Apple II computer for computer-assisted instruction and pay additional tutors at the center. The college developed the El Paso Literacy Coalition and assisted the El Paso public libraries in seeking grants to support library-based ESL and family literacy classes. The college has also published a clearinghouse directory listing all literacy-related classes in the city and a computerized referral system for residents who are seeking programs and services in the county. |
| **Funding** | The Family Literacy Center is a federally funded demonstration model under a three year grant from Title VII for Family Literacy from the Office of Bilingual Education and Language Minorities. |
| **In-Kind Resources** | Administrative and clerical support are provided by El Paso Community College. |
| **Funding History** | Funds for LEA, from which the Family Literacy Center sprung, have come from the El Paso Community College, state and federal grants, and private foundations. |
| **Objectives** | The Family Literacy Center aims to foster literacy and biliteracy development, promote verbal fluency and reading proficiency in English, encourage better parenting techniques, open avenues of communication between family members, alleviate potential delays in learning or development in children, and give parents the tools to further their careers and education. |
| **Evaluation** | The federal government evaluates the program for continued funding. Internally, the Family Literacy Center uses participant and nonparticipant narrative evaluations, classroom videos, pre- and postinterviews with parents, samples of work, and pre- and poststandardized tests for children. |

**Replication**

This intergenerational literacy approach has been replicated in numerous Adult Basic Education programs throughout Texas. The bilingual approach is currently being used as a demonstration model for various bilingual methodologies.

**Materials Available**

None.

# Parent and Child Education

| | | |
|---|---|---|
| Toy lending | GED services | Mother support groups |
| Transportation | Occasional home visits | Community services info/referral |
| Networking | Parent-child joint activities | Parenting/child development education |
| Adult literacy | Health/nutrition education | Developmental exams/screening |
| Preschool | Homemaker services | Child care info/referral |

**Contact:** Patty D. Vaughn, Supervisor of Instruction

**Address:** Butler County Public Schools
Box 339
Morgantown, KY 42261
(502) 526-5624

**Established:** 1987, state initiative

**Budget '88-'89:** $100,000

**Sources:** Kentucky Department of Education, Division of Adult Education

**Size:** 25 families

**Area Served:** Butler County, Kentucky

**Auspices:** Butler County Public Schools

*As an example of success in the PACE program, Ms. Vaughn cites the case of two sisters who were determined to get their high school diplomas and give their children a preschool education. They had to approach their boss at a local factory to obtain permission to work a split shift around the class day. They have completed the program and are taking vocational courses to improve their job prospects. Ms. Vaughn feels PACE has helped them realize the role of education in planning for the future.*

**Community**

Butler County is a rural area with a widely scattered population of approximately 12,000, of which 2,500 live in Morgantown, the county seat. Most inhabitants are employed either in farmwork or light industry. The area suffered an economic depression in the early 1980s; jobs were scarce and most high school graduates left town in search of work. The situation has improved over the last three years; three small companies have relocated to Butler County, somewhat alleviating unemployment.

**Philosophy and Goals**

Parent and Child Education (PACE) is based on the belief that the school performance of children is closely linked to their family's educational attainment and economic status. The program's philosophy is that parent involvement in children's education is crucial to their academic success, but that parents feel unqualified to play an active role. PACE therefore encourages parent involvement by focusing first on the educational needs of the parents and demonstrating how children benefit from their parents' schooling. The program's goal is for parents to value education to improve their own lives, and to develop a positive attitude toward the school system and their children's school experience.

**History and Origins**

The Kentucky Department of Education developed PACE in response to the high number of adults in the state who had not completed their high school education. In 1986, seeking to break Kentucky's intergenerational cycle of illiteracy, the General Assembly of Kentucky passed a bill offering funds to school districts to implement PACE, a program that combines preschool for three- and four-year-olds with Adult Basic Education and parenting education in a daytime format. The Kentucky Department of Education sent out a request for proposals in 1986 and the Butler County School District responded immediately; two out of three adults in the county lacked a diploma. Its grant request was initially denied because there was no classroom space available in the public schools. However, the district reapplied in 1987, having arranged to rent a classroom in a local church's educational center, and was awarded $100,000 to offer PACE in that school year. Patty Vaughn, the district's supervisor of instruction, was appointed to direct the program.

**Features**

PACE meets three days a week during regular school hours throughout the academic year. In the mornings parents are taught by adult educators while preschool instructors work with children. Parents work on individualized lesson plans that prepare them for a Graduate Equivalency Diploma (GED). One hour is devoted to parent-child activities and directed play. PACE provides free breakfast, lunch, and snacks. After lunch, while the children rest, parents participate in the parent support curriculum. PACE also provides child screening: instructors perform a full screening in the fall and continue to note the rate of acquisition of key skills throughout the year. PACE instructors may perform a variety of informal services, such as referrals to community resources and counseling, help in obtaining financial assistance, coordination with substance-abuse programs, and transportation to doctor's appointments.

This year, the district implemented a statewide innovation, offering home visits every other week to parents who need time to build self-confidence before entering the program. An early childhood educator and an adult educator visit each family as a team and present a condensed version of the PACE curriculum.

**Participants**

In 1987-88, PACE served 27 children, 23 mothers, and 2 fathers in the regular program and 8 families in the home visit component. Approximately 50 percent of these were single parents. Ms. Vaughn estimates that PACE serves 20 percent of the eligible population: parents of preschoolers who lack a high school diploma. This figure is based on a 1980 census report that revealed two out of three adults in Butler County had not completed high school.

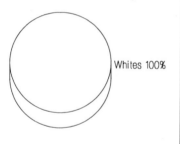

Whites 100%

*In addition to participation in the program, parents have formed informal support groups; Ms. Vaughn says parents have been isolated for a long time and are thrilled to finally have a chance to meet people who share their problems.*

**Parent Education**

PACE classes develop parents' literacy and basic academic skills, preparing them to earn the equivalent of a high school diploma. The parent education component of the program focuses on child development, health care, and nutrition and effective methods of discipline. Parents discover ways that they can help their children learn at home and participate in their children's formal education; parents also learn how to talk to teachers and administrators and how to act as advocates for their children. Ms. Vaughn stresses the flexibility of the adult education instructors; she says they are prepared to teach a variety of subjects when needed, such as personal hygiene and access to community resources.

| | |
|---|---|
| **Curriculum** | The preschool component uses the *High / Scope* curriculum, recommended by the state PACE director, and the Child Observation Record (COR) and Child Assessment Record (CAR) as screening instruments. Adult and early childhood educators use the *Family-Oriented Structured Preschool Activity* (FOSPA) curriculum and the district's Adult Basic Education and GED materials. |
| **Sites** | Butler County PACE rents the educational annex of a local church building. The site is conveniently located near a school building, where parents and children are bused for breakfast and lunch. Ms. Vaughn thinks being in a church gives the program more freedom than if PACE were in a public school. Parents feel free to leave the building to smoke or relax and need not adhere to school rules. |
| | Most PACE participants need transportation to the program. Since they are widely distributed across the county, public school buses bring both parent and child to the church site as part of the regular school bus runs. The large distances between Butler County homes limit the number of home visits a teaching team can reasonably make. |
| **Parent Involvement** | Parents have a voice in the curriculum; the current emphasis on disciplinary issues is at the request of participants. In addition to participation in the program, parents have formed informal support groups; Ms. Vaughn says parents have been isolated for a long time and are thrilled to finally have a chance to meet people who share their problems. |
| **Outreach** | PACE publicizes its services on the radio, in newspapers, and through flyers distributed in banks and supermarkets. Staff members set up displays at community functions and host an open house to attract participants. School personnel, Head Start, social services, and the health department refer eligible parents. PACE may deliver a home visit to an eligible family referred by an agency to invite the parents to participate. Ms. Vaughn notes that the participants have become the program's best recruiters, "selling" PACE to their families and friends. |

**Staff**

| Job Title | PD | Vol | FT | PT | Educ Req | Status | Benefits |
|---|---|---|---|---|---|---|---|
| Early Childhood Teachers | 2 | - | 2 | - | College Degree | K-12 Contract | Yes |
| Preschool Co-Teachers | 2 | - | - | 2 | High School Diploma | Hourly Contract | Yes |
| Adult Teachers | 2 | - | - | 2 | College Degree | Hourly Contract | Yes |
| Volunteers | - | 2 | - | - | None | - | None |

| | |
|---|---|
| **State/District Requirements** | Preschool teachers must be approved by the Kentucky Department of Education. Adult education teachers must be certified. Teacher assistants must have a minimum of a high school diploma. All PACE staff members must undergo PACE training. |
| **Preferred Background** | PACE staff members should be caring and tolerant of many lifestyles. Teachers who are also parents are preferred. Ms. Vaughn praises her |

staff members for their independence and competence, noting that this frees her to perform her role as instructional supervisor.

**Employee Education and Training Represented**

Prekindergarten and early childhood education; elementary education; adult literacy; adult vocational education; health and nutrition; home economics; child care.

**Administration**

Program Director Patty Vaughn reports to the superintendent of Butler County Schools. All PACE programs are overseen by Jeanne Heberle, the PACE state coordinator.

**Relationship to the Schools**

PACE is a public school program intended by the state to be administered exclusively within the system. Ms. Vaughn says the schools benefit from early contact with students; before a child moves into kindergarten, the program does health, vision, and developmental screening with the parent present. This information and previous PACE records go into the child's school file. PACE also does an orientation to acclimate both parent and child to the new kindergarten classroom and teacher. If necessary, the child may also be oriented to the school bus. Ms. Vaughn believes PACE's place in the school system is an advantage because it allows for continuity between children's experience in preschool and the K to 12 program. For instance, she likes the *High/Scope* curriculum and was able, because she is the instructional supervisor, to ask the kindergarten teachers to be trained in it.

**Community Links**

PACE maintains close ties to community agencies and resources because their participants are often in need of government assistance. The public housing office notifies PACE when a new family moves in, and PACE may contact social services, the health department, or a substance-abuse program on a participant's behalf. PACE takes advantage of a nearby municipal park and brings parents and children to story hour at the public library. While a storyteller occupies the children, teachers show parents how to choose books for children and introduce them to the library's many resources.

**Funding**

PACE's $100,000 budget is provided in full by a state grant. The Kentucky Department of Education provides half of the money up front and reimburses the rest quarterly as the program director's financial reports demonstrate need.

**Funding History**

The Kentucky Department of Education funded the initiative in 1987-88, with no changes in funding since.

**Objectives**

The high incidence of high school dropouts, teen pregnancy, and illiteracy in Kentucky originally sparked the PACE project. PACE aims to help those parents without a high school diploma get a GED, give parents the resources and literacy skills to help their children learn, improve their attitude toward school, achieve self-sufficiency, and therefore be able to provide their children with a more positive outlook toward education and the future.

**Evaluation**

The Kentucky Department of Education grant allows funds for an independent evaluation of PACE. The 1989 evaluation praised Butler County's PACE classroom and the rapport between parents and staff. Ms. Vaughn intends to track the children through their school years. PACE's internal self-evaluation is ongoing. Each staff member has one day a week to record children's and parents' progress, consider parental input, and evaluate his or her own performance.

**Replication**

The Kentucky PACE program has been replicated by the Kenan Trust Family Literacy Foundation in North Carolina.

**Materials Available**

None.

# Literacy/Curriculum Connections

| | | |
|---|---|---|
| Forums | Resource library | Parent-child joint activities |
| Field visits | Workshops | Demonstration classes |
| Networking | Kindergarten | Parenting/child development education |
| Preschool | Newsletter | Outreach programs |

**Contact:** Lynne Hall, Project Leader
Sheli Wortis, Outreach Coordinator

**Address:** Cambridge Public Schools
159 Thorndike Street
Cambridge, MA 02141
(617) 349-6485

**Established:** 1986, local initiative

**Budget '88-'89:** $138,750

**Sources:** Massachusetts Chapter 188 early childhood grant

**Size:** 500 families, 500 children

**Area Served:** Maynard and Tobin School Districts in Cambridge, Massachusetts

**Auspices:** Public Schools and Early Childhood Advisory Council

**Community**

Cambridge is an urban, ethnically diverse, academic community of 86,865. The proliferation of hi-tech industries has accelerated gentrification and the accompanying displacement of older neighborhoods. The school system serves 7,797 students, 50 percent white, 50 percent minority.

**Philosophy and Goals**

Literacy/Curriculum Connections, a state Chapter 188-funded program, provides young children with a positive introduction to literacy, encourages them to become enthusiastic readers and writers, and reduces later school failure. To achieve this, the program models developmental literacy theory and practice in preschool and kindergarten classrooms, establishes communication between home and school in an effort to involve families in their children's literacy development, trains preschool and kindergarten teachers in developmental theory and practice, and cultivates linkages between neighborhood preschools and public kindergartens to help make the transition into public school easier for children. The program has developed a multicultural curriculum that reflects and supports their students' diverse ethnic backgrounds.

**History and Origins**

In 1983, as part of the Cambridge-Lesley College Literacy Project, New Zealand educator Don Holdaway trained Cambridge teachers to implement a developmental literacy model (or "whole language" approach), which placed a high priority on reading and writing through purposeful activities and strongly emphasized integrating the arts. American educators recognized the value of children seeing themselves as readers and writers and determined to develop a preschool program based on the New Zealand model. In 1986, the Early Childhood Advisory Council, a policy-making board concerned with Cambridge educational issues, joined Lynne Stuart, coordinator of primary education, in applying for a Chapter 188 grant to establish a program that combined the best of the New Zealand program with a home-school component to meet the special multicultural needs of Cambridge preschool and kindergarten children.

**Features**

Services and curriculum stem from the basic concept that children learn to read naturally and easily when sharing this activity with important people in their lives. The approach makes print an exciting part of the children's lives as they are introduced to stories, poems, and songs. Program staff members stress the child's natural inclination to repeat pleasing phrases and believe reading and writing comes from this "storehouse of loved material." Children participate in "shared book experiences," through reading "Big Books" (enlarged texts of favorite children's literature) with accompanying songs and poetry. Follow-up activities include drama, puppet making, art and imaginative games, tape recordings of stories read together, and individual reading time. These self-selected activities provide an opportunity for children to express the meaning and practice the language of their favorite stories.

Workshops, forums, meetings, and activities bring together parents, teachers, administrators, and adults from the preschool, afterschool, public school, and human service communities. There are two distinct sets of forums, one focusing on multicultural identity, the other on promoting linkages between public and private preschools and kindergartens. All forums are open to the public and well publicized. Aimed at parents, teachers, early childhood program providers, administrators, and community workers, they recently have focused on "developmentally appropriate practices for young children." College credit is available through Bunker Hill Community College; inservice and Master's Plus credit can be earned by public school teachers.

Cambridge Partnerships, a group of business and university representatives, sponsor field visits by subsidizing substitute teachers, thus giving classroom teachers time to visit other classrooms. Workshops and courses include "Training of Trainers," parent workshops, whole language, and developmental education classes.

**Participants**

Participants are children three to five years old, many of whom are from low-income families of diverse cultural backgrounds.

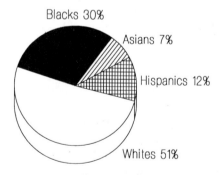

Blacks 30%
Asians 7%
Hispanics 12%
Whites 51%

*The program's emphasis on cultural diversity and the whole language approach requires parent involvement. Children may come from homes that are quite unlike the school community, notes Sheli Wortis, and parents' attitudes are vital to their successful integration in school.*

**Parent Education**

Parent workshops provide opportunities for parents to talk with teachers about child development issues, and forums expose parents to issues of child care, cultural diversity, and developmentally appropriate practices for children. Parents and teachers work together with the Literacy/Curriculum Connections staff to gather verse, songs, poems, chants, and short stories in the children's own languages and put them into "Big Books" or charts. The Home Reading Program encourages parents to read with their children to reinforce classroom activities.

**Curriculum**

Literacy/Curriculum Connections is based on developmental learning theory and works in collaboration with Don Holdaway and the Cambridge-Lesley College Literacy Project. The whole language approach to reading and writing is a self-paced interactive process occurring in a social context and based on concrete experience. It involves emulating people who model reading as a daily skill. During the three-year life of the program, the multicultural Early Childhood Advisory Council has urged a more thematic curriculum and sought materials that support the notion of diversity and ethnicity. Ideas for change and revision filter into the program from the rapidly growing Whole Language Teachers Association.

**Sites**

Literacy/Curriculum Connections has classroom sites in the Maynard and Tobin elementary schools and in 10 preschool settings, including five Head Start classrooms and five private schools and daycare sites.

**Parent Involvement**

Throughout the year, parents participate in hands-on workshops, serve on the advisory council, act as program proponents, lobby to be included in the school budget, and fill out evaluation forms of all program components. The program's emphasis on cultural diversity and the whole language approach requires parent involvement. Children may come from homes that are quite unlike the school community, notes Sheli Wortis, and parents' attitudes are vital to their successful integration in school.

**Outreach**

Participants hear about the program through newspaper advertisements, letters and flyers, television announcements, word-of-mouth, school notices, newsletters, and referrals. The program reaches only two targeted neighborhoods, but forums and workshops are open to the entire community.

**Staff**

| Job Title | PD | Vol | FT | PT | Educ Req | Status | Benefits |
|-----------|-----|-----|-----|-----|----------|--------|----------|
| Project Leader | 1 | - | 1 | - | Post-Graduate Courses or Degree | K-12 Contract | Yes |
| Outreach Coordinator | 1 | - | - | 1 | Post-Graduate Courses or Degree | Other Contract | Yes |
| Staff Developer | 1 | - | 1 | - | Post-Graduate Courses or Degree | K-12 Contract | Yes |
| Secretary | 1 | - | - | 1 | Some High School/ High School Diploma | Hourly Contract | Yes |

**State/District Requirements**

The project leader should have principal and teacher certification; the staff developer should have teacher certification.

**Preferred Background**

Multicultural education and community action for the outreach coordinator; computer expertise for the secretary.

| | |
|---|---|
| **Employee Education and Training Represented** | Prekindergarten and early childhood education; elementary education; education, grades 7 to 12; special education; parent educator; child care; psychology; child development and family studies; research and evaluation. |
| **Administration** | The director's immediate superior is the coordinator of primary education in the Cambridge Public Schools. The program is administered jointly by the public school system and the Early Childhood Advisory Council, which meets monthly and plays an active decision-making role with regard to staff hiring, program budget, approval of program services, and curriculum. The council, composed of five early childhood providers, seven public school personnel, nine representatives from public agencies, one community representative, three parents, and the project director, is co-chaired by the coordinator of primary education. |
| **Relationship to the Schools** | Literacy/Curriculum Connections is sponsored by a Massachusetts Chapter 188 grant to the Cambridge Public Schools. Directors and staff members are employees of the school system. The program offers opportunities for curriculum enrichment and collaboration, and supports the needs of a multicultural community whose diversity has not been consistently addressed. Special needs teachers observe the preschool and a variety of inservice workshops, and demonstration classes keep elementary school and preschool colleagues in touch with one another and informed of new curriculum ideas. |
| **Community Links** | Literacy/Curriculum Connections represents a network of community linkages with child, family, and multicultural agencies and advocacy groups. All share a common goal in wanting to bridge the gap between private preschools and public elementary schools and between teachers and parents. Forums, inservice courses, workshops, and field visits strive to develop educational continuity for children. "Exploring Cultural Diversity" forums are organized by the Multicultural Committee of the Cambridge Council for Children, which includes representatives from at least six child and family advocacy groups (among them are the Cambridge Somerville Child Care Alliance, the Child Care Resource Center, Concilio Hispano, and the Cambridge Council for Children). Early Childhood Community Forums are a collaborative effort of the Cambridge child care and public school communities. Initiated in 1987 through a Chapter 188 grant, forums are currently funded through a Commonwealth Inservice Institute grant of the Massachusetts Department of Education. |
| **Funding** | State funds (Chapter 188), 100 percent. |
| **In-Kind Resources** | From the school district, facilities, paid staff, and equipment; from Lesley College, consultation and staff development; public and private agencies provide volunteer staff. |
| **Funding History** | Funding is applied for annually and, because of a state fiscal crisis, has decreased 25 percent since the program's first year. |
| **Objectives** | Literacy/Curriculum Connections aims to integrate community needs into its curriculum and services, create an active flow of information and education between school and home, and heighten multicultural understanding as well as literacy. |

| | |
|---|---|
| **Evaluation** | The program follows 40 children each year to document their literacy development. An end of the year report summarizes the results. |
| **Replication** | The program trains local educators to use the Literacy/Curriculum Connections curriculum in other early childhood programs. |
| **Materials Available** | A lending library of big books, small books, audiotapes and charts, a slide and tape show, bibliographies, informational packets, and staff training materials are available for free for use by Cambridge early childhood and public school teachers. Training video: $10 rental fee. Contact Sheli Wortis, outreach coordinator, at the above address. |

# 8 Family Resource Centers

These programs have in common a pattern of services that balances the importance of adult education and support with learning environments for preschool children. Most make a special effort to nurture the nontraditional household, including dual-career families, parents requiring literacy training and Graduate Equivalency Diploma (GED) preparation, incarcerated or abused parents, family caregivers, and single-parent, racially isolated, and educationally deprived families. All offer neighborhood center-based services such as drop-in times and parent-child classes and make a considerable effort to seek out and design programming for disadvantaged families.

# Programs in Brief

### The Family Center — p. 385
*Multifaceted suburban Missouri program, serving families with children birth to age five, with drop-in hours and a wide range of scheduled classes*

### Early Education Program — p. 391
*Suburban Missouri program, with a state-mandated Parents as Teachers component, emphasizing parent involvement and early detection of learning problems*

### Barbour County Community Education — p. 397
*Rural Alabama initiative offering preschool with parent support, remedial summer school, adult literacy training, and parent education*

### Working Families Center of the Parent Education/Family Support Programs — p. 403
*Education, training, and support for families and daycare providers in suburban Washington, DC*

### Parent Resource Center — p. 409
*Port Washington, New York, resource center run for and by parents, with outreach to at-risk families*

### Parent and Child Education Centers (PACE) — p. 415
*Ohio state initiative offering comprehensive parent education and joint parent-child activities*

### Stratford Parents Place — p. 421
*Suburban resource and support center in Stratford, Connecticut, providing parent education to all parents*

# The Family Center

Workshops
Preschool
Newsletter
Networking
Home visits
Family therapy

Dinner groups
Child care info & referral
Resource library
Family life classes
Individual counseling
Health & nutrition education
Drop-in center

Parent & couple support groups
Parent-child joint activities
Parenting & child development education
Counseling for special needs families
Screening for special needs families
Developmental exams & screening
Special education services

**Contact:** Mary Jo Liberstein, Director

**Address:** 301 North Gay Avenue
Clayton, MO 63105
(314) 725-1350

**Established:** 1975, school district initiative

**Budget '88-'89:** $219,000

**Sources:** Local school district, state government, federal government, corporate and business donations, fundraising activities, client-paid fees

**Size:** 425 families

**Area Served:** Clayton, Missouri

**Auspices:** Family Center of the Clayton School District

*In her first year of preschool, the fourth of five children was feisty, independent and willful. Her mother worried about her daughter's ability to cope. A conference at the preschool revealed the little girl was doing well. Her mother was surprised. She thought she would never get good reports and told the staff at the Family Center that they were responsible for pointing out her daughter's strengths and helping her relax.*

### Community

Clayton is a small, upper-middle-class suburb of St. Louis, with a population of 45,000, whose inhabitants are predominantly white, well-educated professionals. Washington University in St. Louis brings foreign scholars into the community, contributing to cultural and ethnic diversity.

### Philosophy and Goals

The Family Center cultivates the relationship between parent and child. The center supports parents in their roles as caregivers and encourages understanding of family dynamics and developmental stages. The center believes that support for families is most effective when it is based in the communities where those families live and work.

### History and Origins

This program was inspired in the early 1970s by the research of early childhood educators and the White House Conference on Education's recommendation that "local school districts develop comprehensive programs for parents and young children that focus on the understanding of child development." The Clayton School District's Board of Education became committed to establishing a multifaceted early childhood parent education program. A local committee was formed in January 1975, both to review Clayton's summer program designed to prepare children for kindergarten and to research a more comprehensive early childhood program. In May 1975, the Clayton early childhood initiative got underway with funds from Title IV C, Innovative Programs. Parenting classes met twice a week for nine-week sessions, with a drop-in center for parents and infants. The program became known as the Family Center in 1985.

The center provides services to parents with children from birth to age five and offers parents a place to share information, receive support in solving everyday problems, and gain confidence in their own parenting abilities. Open 10 1/2 months a year, the program also offers a summer session. "The Family Center spirit is most evident during Open Times, a drop-in program of lightly supervised activities for parents and children," says program coordinator Mary Jo Liberstein. Frequent drop-in times (three mornings, one afternoon, and some evenings, as well as selected weekend mornings) are opportunities for parent networking and informal consultation with staff members.

**Parent and child development classes** are courses for parents and their young children, appropriate to the child's developmental level. Staff members lead discussions on parenting skills and child development. Classes meet for 18 sessions, once or twice a week.

**Parents as Teachers (PAT)**, a statewide program, is both home-based and center-based and offers support, education, and resources in the form of home visits for parents and child screening; evening visits and programs accommodate the hectic lives of working parents.

The **Lunch Bunch** and **Supper Bunch** are informal discussions for parents and staff in a support group format. After a shared meal, child care is available while parents and staff members participate in group discussions and workshops.

**Parent workshops** run from two to eight weeks and focus on relevant topics.

**Middle and senior high school classes** in child development and family life teach students theoretical backgrounds in child care and human development. Students also work with young children in the various Family Center programs.

The **Special Services Program** provides developmental screening, diagnostic evaluations, an early childhood special education program, individual and family counseling, and observation and consultation services.

The **Community Outreach Program** includes workshops and inservice training for early childhood educators, speakers for interested groups, and the educational publication, *Growing Times*.

Participants come to the center twice weekly for an average of 2½ years. The center seeks to support nontraditional families, dual-career families, single parents, and families experiencing multiple stresses. Ms. Liberstein added that, "There are people within the community who are isolated, either geographically, or because they are transient, or they are in a lower-income bracket. In the past we hadn't reached those families. Fees posed a barrier. We have made an effort to inform those people about free programs and we offer them PAT services, which are free and based on home visits." The Family Center offers members a payment plan. Participants can defray tuition by volunteering. The parent-teacher organization offers some scholarships. The school district has authorized Ms. Liberstein to make tuition discounts based on family need. Of the

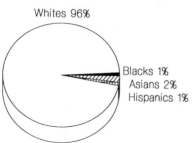

Whites 96%

Blacks 1%
Asians 2%
Hispanics 1%

parents participating in 1987, 3 percent were single parents, and 3 percent were minorities (black, Hispanic, or Asian).

*"There are people within the community who are isolated, either geographically, or because they are transient, or they are in a lower-income bracket. In the past we hadn't reached those families. Fees posed a barrier. We have made an effort to inform those people about free programs and we offer them PAT services, which are free and based on home visits."*

**Parent Education**

The Family Center gives parents information and support through classes, workshops, support groups, and center activities. Some classes focus on child development and guided play. Other topics for classes and workshops include: Raising Siblings, Issues in Single-Parent Families, Stepparenting, Forming a Parenting Partnership, For Fathers Only, and Discipline. Joint activities for parents and children include gymnastics, music, and hands-on math and science forchildren ages 3½ to 5 years.

In an effort to carry its philosophy of parent education and support into the elementary years, the center uses some of its lunch discussion groups as an opportunity for parents of four- and five-year-olds to talk about the transition into grade school. The school district is currently developing a comprehensive K-12 parent education and family resources program.

**Curriculum**

Materials are developed in-house by the Family Center staff. Special classes and workshops are designed to address the interests of participants. New programs, some of which are based on the PAT model, are being developed for transient, less affluent, working and single parents.

**Sites**

The Family Center operates out of three sites and, according to Ms. Liberstein, is seen by the community and the schools as an indispensable part of the school's educational services. The main center, located in a school building, houses the administration staff, the *Growing Times* office, and a large room for the drop-in center, cooperative child care, classes, programs, and library. Satellite centers are in an elementary school and a former primary school building. The Family Center had planned to move to a single site in 1990.

**Parent Involvement**

The Family Center's parent-teacher organization serves in an advisory capacity.

**Outreach**

In addition to conventional approaches, to attract more families the center has increased its late afternoon, evening, and weekend workshops and discussion groups and initiated the supper-time format to target fathers and working parents.

**Staff**

| Job Title | PD | Vol | FT | PT | Educ Req | Status | Benefits |
|-----------|-----|-----|-----|-----|----------|--------|----------|
| Director | 1 | - | 1 | - | Post-Graduate Courses or Degree | Other Contract | Yes |
| Parent Educator/ Counselor/ Coordinators | 2 | - | 2 | - | Post-Graduate Courses or Degree | K-12 Contract | Yes |
| Special Education Teacher | 1 | - | 1 | - | Post-Graduate Courses or Degree | K-12 Contract | Yes |
| Speech Pathologist | 1 | - | - | 1 | Post-Graduate Courses or Degree | K-12 Contract | Yes |
| Occupational Therapist | 1 | - | - | 1 | College Degree | Hourly Contract | No |
| Parent Educators | 3 | - | - | 3 | College Degree | Hourly Contract | Yes |
| Child Care Teachers | 16 | - | - | 16 | Some College | Hourly Non-Contract | No |
| Secretaries | 2 | - | 1 | 1 | High School Diploma | Other Contract | Yes |
| Child Care Assistants | - | 40 | - | - | None | - | None |

**State/District Requirements**

For the special education teacher, speech pathologist, and parent educator, certification in their field; for Parents as Teachers educators, national PAT training.

**Preferred Background**

Parent educators should have a background in child development, early childhood education and/or family counseling, parenting experience, and strong communication skills. Child care teachers should be skilled with young children and have parenting experience.

**Employee Education and Training Represented**

Infant and toddler education; prekindergarten and early childhood education; elementary education; education, grades 7 to 12; bilingual education; special education; parent educator; child care; occupational and physical therapy; speech therapy; psychology; counseling; family therapy; child development and family studies; development and fundraising; research and evaluation.

**Administration**

The director of the center reports to the superintendent of schools. Ms. Liberstein has the administrative status of an elementary school principal.

**Relationship to the Schools**

Although the Family Center is administered within the school system, it is considered a department unto itself and comprises all the early childhood components of the school district. The center keeps school staff and maintenance people informed of the program's progress and offers resident rates to all faculty families. The parent-teacher organization does fundraising, provides opportunities for social networking, and acts as a liaison between the center's staff and participants.

A representative of the Family Center serves on the prekindergarten screening team; another representative takes part in kindergarten parent orientation meetings. The Family Center offers a workshop on transition to kindergarten for interested parents. When appropriate, the center shares the records from its special education component with elementary school personnel.

**Community Links**

Consultations with other community services and early childhood educators in Clayton and in nearby St. Louis are constant. "The Family Center is a referral agency," comments Ms. Liberstein. "At times we have brought in representatives from the community for ad hoc consultations."

**Funding**

Local school district, 60 percent; client fees, 21 percent; state (S.B. 658) Parents as Teachers program and a vocational education grant, 16 percent; federal 94-142 Education Handicapped Act, 1 percent; corporate and business, 1 percent; fundraising and special events, 1 percent.

Center membership includes drop-in privileges and discounts on class tuition. Fees range from $32 per semester ($57 for nonresidents) to $65 per semester ($119 for nonresidents) for the year. Parent classes cost $44 for members ($88 for nonmembers); Lunch Bunch for parents with children costs $63 per year ($33 for each additional child); parent and parent-child workshops range from $10 to $25. The fees have remained constant for three years and will be stable for at least another year.

**In-Kind Resources**

Although Ms. Liberstein has not calculated the dollar amount, she comments that volunteer hours provided by participating parents greatly offset the cost of the program.

**Funding History**

Ms. Liberstein considers funding to be secure; the school district budget has increased from $60,000 in the program's first year to $219,000 for 1988-89.

**Objectives**

The center hopes that parents will expand their knowledge of child and family development in an environment that bolsters their confidence. By enhancing early childhood experiences, the Family Center expects to increase children's chances for subsequent success in school and in life.

**Evaluation**

External and internal evaluators are currently completing evaluations that focus on the populations served and not served, the relationship between the program and the school district as a whole, children's transition from preschool into elementary school, and a needs assessment for parent education and support beyond the birth to age five range.

**Replication**

Several family support projects across the country have replicated the Family Center and utilized its curricula. These include Parents and Children Together, Ladue, Missouri; the Parenting Center, New Orleans, Louisiana; and the Parent Center, Springfield, Missouri.

**Materials Available**

A free descriptive brochure; *Growing Times*, a nationally distributed, bimonthly newsletter; a curriculum and workshop outline for three classes available for $10; *Workshops for Parents* and *Individual Services Handbook*, $7.50 each.

# Early Education Program

| | | |
|---|---|---|
| Home visits | Toy lending | Child care info & referrals |
| Family therapy | Group meetings | Developmental exams & screening |
| Child care | Resource library | Health & nutrition education |
| Networking | Drop-in center | Parenting & child development education |
| Newsletter | Individual counseling | Parent & couple support groups |
| | Parent-child activities | Community services info & referral |

| | |
|---|---|
| **Contact:** | Marion M. Wilson, Director of Early Education |
| **Address:** | 1005 Waterford Drive<br>Florissant, MO 63033<br>(314) 831-8809 |
| **Established:** | 1971, local initiative; state legislation |
| **Budget '88-'89:** | PAT, $195,000; LINK, $17,600; Child Development, $237,000;<br>Saturday School/Special Education $900,000 |
| **Sources:** | Local school district; client fees; state government;<br>federal government |
| **Size:** | 1,822 children, 1,700 families |
| **Area Served:** | Ferguson-Florissant School District |
| **Auspices:** | State program administered by the school district |

*Families note that home visitors are warm and friendly. They focus on learning but value a trusting and accepting environment. One mother commented, "I hope this isn't the only time in my daughter's education that she is considered special."*

**Community**

The Ferguson-Florissant School District is predominantly middle class. It is located in the heart of North County, adjacent to the Lambert-St. Louis International Airport. The district serves all or part of 11 municipalities and a portion of unincorporated St. Louis County. The municipalities, say school administrators, have "all the advantages of a small town against the backdrop of a major metropolitan area and its diverse offerings." Several major highways provide quick access to St. Louis, Clayton, University City, Washington University, and Webster University.

**Philosophy and Goals**

The Early Education Program (EEP) believes that parents are their children's most important teachers and that support for young families helps parents become more effective and independent. Marion Wilson has a strong commitment to addressing family conditions and believes, "You can't isolate a child from the family if learning is to occur."

**History and Origins**

In 1971, the assistant superintendent for elementary education in the Ferguson-Florissant School District became concerned about the lack of available preschool services. He wrote a proposal for federal Title III money to fund a preschool program for four-year-olds. The federal government granted the funds needed to implement Saturday School but required the district to provide services to the handicapped as well. In 1974, Saturday School became, and has since been, a developer-demonstrator project through the United States Office of Education. Two years later in response to a desegregation mandate, two small school districts were added to the system, which made the EEP's population more socioeconomically heterogeneous. Also in 1976, EEP was moved under the school district's instruction umbrella and the program's staff was placed on a regular school district salary scale. In 1981, Ferguson-Florissant became one of the four pilot sites in Missouri used to develop Parents as Teachers (PAT) which is now a mandated program for every Missouri school district. Additional subprograms were added in response to needs assessments.

## Features

**Saturday School** provides an educational program to prepare four-year-olds to succeed in school. It involves parents in teaching their children and provides related services directly to the family. Children receive a one-hour weekly home teaching visit to supplement the three-hour Saturday School. Screening and skills assessments help individualize the curriculum for each child. Parents participate in home teaching visits, attend parent group meetings, and may assist as teachers in Saturday School.

**Special Services** provides home visits and some classroom sessions to children identified as at risk for physical handicaps, chronic illness, developmental delay or learning/language/motor problems. A curriculum guided by an Individual Educational Plan (IEP) helps children develop skills appropriate to their age.

**Child Development Centers (Daycare)** is a Title III Innovative Program begun in 1974 to provide developmental child care to children ages two to four, run in part by high school students enrolled in child development classes. Children participate in age-appropriate learning activities as high school students acquire practical learning experiences in early childhood development. This year-round program also includes parents in group meetings and offers them consultation services.

**LINK** offers cooperative child care and extensive parent education courses to parents with children from birth to age five. Resource centers provide meeting places for a variety of short courses for parents and for parents and children together. Screening and counseling services are also available. LINK began in 1976 with a grant from the Danforth Foundation.

**Parents as Teachers (PAT)** began in 1981 to offer parent education and support for parents with children from birth to age three. Families receive home visits from a parent educator every four to six weeks and attend group meetings with other parents monthly. PAT provides developmental screening and runs a parent resource center that stocks learning materials for parents and children.

The Early Education Program provides home visits to 50 families in Special Services, 570 in Saturday School and 975 in PAT. Residents of the district and their children (birth to age five) are eligible.

*Marion Wilson has a strong commitment to addressing family conditions and believes, "You can't isolate a child from the family if learning is to occur."*

## Participants

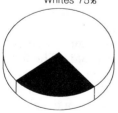

Whites 75%

Blacks 25%

## Parent Education

The Early Education Program offers parent education courses in resource centers through LINK, home visits through PAT, group meetings and consultation to parents through the child development centers, and parent meetings through Saturday School. All combine theoretical knowledge of child development and education with training in the practical skills of childrearing.

**Curriculum**

The Early Education Program adapts the High/Scope cognitively oriented curriculum and its developmental curriculum to the needs of each subprogram's population and often develops its own materials, such as those for Special Services, in-house. Parents as Teachers uses the state-mandated PAT curriculum which the Ferguson-Florissant staff helped Dr. Burton White develop when PAT was in its pilot phase. The Early Education Program modifies curriculum materials for parents with limited reading ability and for teen parents.

**Parent Involvement**

The Early Education Program establishes a partnership between home and school which involves parents in oversight and teaching. In Saturday School, parents take turns assisting in classrooms every four to six weeks and serve on the advisory council.

**Sites**

The Early Education Program has facilities at the administrative building and at the Vogt Center, and its staff members provide home visits to over 1,000 families.

**Outreach**

According to Ms. Wilson, the best outreach is word-of-mouth, particularly parent to parent. The program gains visibility through announcements in elementary school offices and press releases in the district newsletter and local newspapers. Brochures are left in doctors' offices, private daycare centers, and churches. Ms. Wilson recommends that programs keep lists of their original participants and make parents aware of continued offerings.

**Staff**

| Job Title | PD | Vol | FT | PT | Educ Req | Status | Benefits |
|---|---|---|---|---|---|---|---|
| Teachers | 18 | - | 16 | 2 | College Degree | K-12 Contract | Yes |
| Parent Educators | 18 | - | - | 18 | College Degree | Hourly Contract | No |
| Day Care Staff | 9 | - | 9 | - | Some College | Hourly Contract | Yes |
| LINK Parent Leaders | 12 | - | - | 12 | None | Hourly Non-Contract | No |

**State/District Requirements**

For teachers, an early childhood certificate or early childhood special education certificate; for parent educators, state certification; for child care workers, a two-year child associate degree.

**Preferred Background**

Teachers and parent educators are selected on the basis of their ability to relate well to people and their understanding of working with parents.

**Employee Education and Training Represented**

Infant and toddler education; prekindergarten and early childhood education; elementary education; special education; parent educator; child care; home economics; occupational and physical therapy; speech therapy; psychology; counseling; family therapy; social work; child development and family studies.

**Administration**

Director Marion Wilson reports to the assistant superintendent for instruction of the Ferguson-Florissant School District. The program is monitored by the Missouri Department of Education. An advisory board is composed of three paid staff and/or volunteers from the program, three public school personnel, three representatives from public agencies (noneducational), three from private agencies, and six people from the community. It has decision-making powers regarding approval of program services, curriculum, and public relations strategies.

## Relationship to the Schools

The Early Education Program keeps the school system informed of its activities through a regular newsletter which includes a column directed to principals. The program also has an early childhood committee composed of teachers, principals, counselors, and representative personnel from Special Education, Child Development centers and LINK. Children's school records are started at the preschool level. Preschool teachers share information with kindergarten teachers and meet jointly with parents to explain the transition into elementary school. School district inservice programs and joint problem-solving meetings provide contact between the program staff, kindergarten teachers, and the primary staff. The program also relates closely to the guidance department.

## Community Links

The Early Education Program maintains a continuous flow of information among the circle of public and private schools and agencies through informal and formal participant referrals, joint planning, training and evaluation activities, and participation on interagency councils.

## Funding

Local school district, 62 percent; state government, 20 percent; client fees, 15 percent; and federal government, 3 percent. Federal funding is composed of Title XX funds (social service), grants, and entitlement funds. State funds come through Exceptional Pupil Aid and State Senate Bill #658 for PAT and screening for children through age four.

## In-Kind Resources

The schools provide space and facilities, paid staff for service delivery, and consultation and staff development.

## Funding History

Funding has increased 90 percent since the program's first year of operation and, according to Ms. Wilson, appears to be moderately secure for the future.

## Objectives

The Early Education Program anticipates that through participation, parents will gain greater understanding of child growth and development, sharpen their observational skills, interact more effectively with their children, and link up with other community resources, if needed. Goals for children include age-appropriate development and detection of developmental delays.

## Evaluation

The program staff performs ongoing internal review. In 1987, a team representing several Missouri colleges and universities and the Missouri Department of Elementary and Secondary Education evaluated the program. A summary of staff responses to questions related to mission and goals, learner objectives, and staff development noted the need to increase contact with families to 11 monthly home visits, to provide alternative services to at-risk families, including respite time for mothers and joint parent-child activities in a playroom setting, to develop peer groups for children with special needs and, overall, to vary levels of program intensity to meet the needs of individual children and families.

The evaluation also noted the need for expanded facilities for LINK, for Parents as Teachers, and for teachers working with small groups of children. Increasing funds per family, reducing the case load for parent educators, and augmenting services to parents (particularly to adolescent and single parents) were other recommendations.

**Replication**

Parents as Teachers is replicated throughout the state and in various parts of the country. Other components of the Early Education Program are unique to the Ferguson-Florissant School District.

**Materials Available**

A complete set of brochures describing all five subprograms is available by writing to Marion Wilson at the above address.

# Barbour County Community Education

| | | |
|---|---|---|
| Preschool | Home visits | Parenting & child development education |
| Adult literacy | GED services | Parent-child joint activities |
| Tutoring | Summer school | Child care info & referral |
| | Evening seminars | Mother support group |

**Contact:** Frazelma Pugh, Coordinator of Community Education

**Address:** Barbour County Schools
P.O. Box 219
Clayton, AL 36016
(205) 775-8946

**Established:** 1982, local initiative

**Budget '88-'89:** $10,000 plus fundraising and contributions

**Sources:** Federal funds, Alabama community education funds, local businesses, private donations, local school district, in-kind contributions

**Size:** 502 families

**Area Served:** Barbour County, Alabama

**Auspices:** Community education

**1990 Respondent:** Eloise Hall, Coordinator of Community Education

*A young, single mother of an extremely slow-developing child despaired over her daughter's lack of progress, felt isolated from sources of help and incapable of teaching her daughter even the most basic skills to prepare her for school. Ms. Hall began transporting mother and daughter to Evening Outreach groups. The mother participated in PAL, where she learned to make her home into a learning environment. She is now much more confident of her ability to contribute to her daughter's growth, and the girl has caught up to her appropriate grade level.*

### Community

Barbour County has a small population sparsely distributed over a large area. The community has few recreational facilities and many isolated homes. Farming is the chief occupation, and unemployment is high; many families receive public assistance. Single-parent families are common. The school system serves 2,500 students in five elementary and two high schools.

### Philosophy and Goals

Barbour County Community Education's philosophy is that public schools belong to the people and that human resources can be developed locally to extend education into the community throughout the year. The program considers early childhood education necessary to give children from economically and educationally disadvantaged families a fair chance when they enter school, and that parents should be made aware of their important role as their children's first teacher. The community education department is equally concerned with older students and adults in the schools and community, believing that no age group should be excluded from learning opportunities.

### History and Origins

Eloise Hall was appointed coordinator of community education in the Barbour County School System in 1981 and began her tenure by visiting homes in the county to assess the community's needs. She was appalled to discover young children who did not understand the most basic concepts of colors and shapes or even know their parents' true names. Ms. Hall developed a four-week summer program for three- and four-year-olds and, with the help of her advisor in the Alabama Department of Education, designed a curriculum in which parents and preschoolers worked in tandem. The next year, the superintendent, impressed by the progress of the summer students, funded a one-day-a-week public prekindergarten program taught by a paraprofessional who traveled to each of the five elementary schools to work with parents and children together. In 1986, a federal Chapter 2 grant allowed the preschool to expand to a five-days-a-week format. Parents were no longer expected to accompany their children to class regularly, so Ms. Hall developed the Parents and Learning (PAL) program, which combines evening seminars and volunteering in the classroom, to continue parent involvement. Meanwhile, in 1982, she had begun another summer program, Remedial Summer School, in which students in prekindergarten through sixth grade could reinforce the skills they acquired during the school year. The same year, Ms. Hall also initiated the Community Education Adult Literacy Program to attract participants to the existing adult basic education (ABE) program and to provide much-needed coordination and walk-in support. She also began delivering home visits to at-risk families with young children.

*Ms. Hall says her measure of the program's success is the school district's declining enrollment in special education. After the first few years of Barbour County Community Education, the number of young children enrolled in special education decreased by 100 each year. She calls her program the "ounce of prevention that beats a pound of cure."*

**Features**

The federally funded preschool program has its own administration, but its parent support component, **Parents and Learning (PAL)**, is still under the auspices of community education. PAL offers evening seminars or workshops once a week to parents of the preschoolers at each of the five elementary schools in the county. The seminars cover parenting and educational topics, emphasizing the parent's role as home teacher. PAL also offers extensive opportunities for parent involvement, parent-child interaction activities and volunteerism.

**Home Visitation** offers home visits to at-risk families with young children. The program director visits particularly needy families twice a week and others less regularly, demonstrating home activities that parents can use with their children and checking for signs of abuse or neglect.

**Evening Outreach**, led by retired teachers, provides an hour of tutoring after school three days a week to students in kindergarten through eighth grade, both as academic support and to extend the school day for latchkey children.

**Remedial Summer School** teaches noncredit classes in reading and math for students in kindergarten through sixth grade who need reinforcement in the skills acquired during the academic year. The summer school meets for four hours Monday through Friday for a month.

**Adult Literacy** coordinates outreach and drop-in services for the state-funded adult basic education (ABE) program. Adults can drop in during evenings for academic support and to use Graduate Equivalency

Diploma (GED) study materials, attend formal classes once a week, or make arrangements for one-on-one tutoring.

The **Community Education Center** is open several evenings a week for parents of preschoolers and older children to drop in and discuss their concerns with the staff.

In 1987-88, PAL served 275 parents, with a small core group attending every seminar; Home Visitation, 70 families; Evening Outreach, no records; Remedial Summer School, 100 kindergarten through sixth grade students; Adult Literacy, no records.

PAL's participants are generally at risk because of family problems, economic disadvantage, or a child's handicap or developmental delay. Home Visitation serves at-risk families, some referred by teachers or school truant officers. Ms. Hall estimates that 72 percent of all participants in 1987-88 were single parents and 15 percent were teen parents.

Barbour County Community Education is committed to parent education. The coordinator, Eloise Hall, designates a set of basic skills, such as naming family members, color identification, and knowing left from right as "home skills" that she holds parents responsible for teaching their young children before they enter kindergarten. PAL and Home Visitation are designed to show parents how they can be successful first teachers of their children. Teachers demonstrate home activities that parents can use to help children learn and discuss topics such as child development, health care, nutrition, and discipline. Barbour County Community Education also emphasizes the importance of adult literacy and education. Ms. Hall says participants in the several community education programs have overlapped over the years; often the parents of preschoolers take advantage of the ABE program and its adult literacy drop-in support component.

Fannie Easterling, Barbour County's special education director and Ms. Hall's advisor, has made site visits to several successful early childhood education programs with substantial parent involvement around the country. Most recently, they have adopted the Beginning Milestones curriculum and the Sunburst computer programs, in use at the Ysleta School for four-year-olds in El Paso, Texas. The other subprograms use a similar variety of materials, with the exception of Remedial Summer School, which uses the texts recommended by the state.

PAL meets at the five elementary schools where preschool takes place. Evening Outreach is held at the Community Education center, formerly the vocational center, in Clayton. The summer school has four sites, at two elementary schools and two social service agencies. Barbour County Community Education delivers home visits to 70 homes across Barbour County. Adult literacy meets at six public and private schools. It is too costly to provide comprehensive transportation service within this rural area, so whenever possible, Ms. Hall, staff members, and volunteers transport parents to PAL meetings, ABE training and the center. Two staff members are licensed bus drivers and periodically transport program participants on field trips and program events.

**Participants**

Blacks 98%

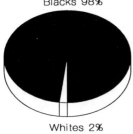

Whites 2%

**Parent Education**

**Curriculum**

**Sites**

Parent involvement is the heart of the PAL component. Parents not only learn how to become teachers at home, but are encouraged to volunteer in the preschool program either as classroom aides or by baking snacks. Remedial Summer School also relies heavily on the presence of parents in the classroom. The program's literature boasts that additional adults in the classrooms means increased individual attention to the children: teachers may work intensively with a small group while parents lead the others in a separate activity. Adult Literacy creates teams of participants who offer peer support. Parents are also involved in fundraising and outreach activities.

**Outreach**

Barbour County Community Education publicizes its services and events on the radio, in the newspaper, and in flyers distributed through the schools. Teachers and school administrators may refer families to a particular program, and Ms. Hall conducts home visits as part of outreach efforts. The program holds an open house to attract families to the Clayton center.

**Staff**

Staff members are all employed by the Barbour County Board of Education. Evening Outreach staff members are retired teachers from the district. Remedial Summer School teachers are regular school-year employees.

| Job Title | PD | Vol | FT | PT | Educ Req | Status | Benefits |
|-----------|----|----|----|----|----------|--------|----------|
| Supervisor | 1 | - | 1 | - | Post-Graduate Courses or Degree | K-12 Contract | Yes |
| Teachers | 10 | - | 10 | - | College Degree | K-12 Contract | Yes |
| Retired Teachers | - | 3 | - | 3 | College Degree | - | No |
| Parapro-fessional Aide | 10 | - | 10 | - | High School Diploma | Other Contract | Yes |
| Health Aide | 1 | - | - | 1 | High School Diploma | Other Contract | Yes |
| Bus Drivers | 2 | - | - | 2 | High School Diploma | Other Contract | Yes |
| Secretaries | 2 | - | - | 2 | High School Diploma | Other Contract | Yes |
| Volunteers | - | 20 | - | 20 | High School Diploma | - | No |

**State/District Requirements**

Teachers must be certified by the state; the Alabama Department of Education requires training for teacher aides.

**Preferred Background**

Staff members should have a suitable educational background, be experienced in working with the community and have appropriate personality characteristics.

| | |
|---|---|
| **Employee Education and Training Represented** | Prekindergarten and early childhood education; elementary education; education, grades 7 to 12; special education; adult basic education; adult literacy; parent educator; health and nutrition; nursing; occupational and physical therapy; speech therapy; child development and family studies. |
| **Administration** | The Barbour County Community Education director, Eloise Hall, reports to the superintendent of Barbour County Schools and to the Barbour County Board of Education. She works closely with Fannie Easterling, the director of special education in the district, and with the administration of ABE. The Alabama Department of Education monitors the program and serves in an advisory capacity. |
| **Relationship to the Schools** | Barbour County Community Education has its own department within the school district, and Ms. Hall feels it is accepted as a valuable component of the school program. She has held the summer school in each of the district schools at some point and knows the staff and administrators well. She feels she gets excellent support from the principals and, because the same teachers teach year round, she says she communicates well with them. The truancy office uses Barbour County Community Education as a liaison to families, asking Ms. Hall to investigate reports of delinquency, which she does during home visits. Often, teachers will approach Ms. Hall about absent students before they are labeled truants. Barbour County Community Education gives the schools a direct link into the home, increasing parent involvement and students' chances of success in school. |
| **Community Links** | Barbour County Community Education receives information and materials from the county extension agent on topics such as nutrition, physical fitness, and stress management. Home visitors report child abuse and neglect to the local welfare department. PAL takes advantage of the county's parks when arranging picnics and field trips. |
| **Funding** | The total budget for the preschool program is $933,000, of which a small fraction is available to the PAL component. The Alabama Department of Education matches local contributions for Barbour Community Education; in 1987-88, the state provided $10,000 to match Barbour County's fundraising efforts. Barbour County Community Education is funded for the most part by fundraising activities and contributions from its Adopt-a-School program. Adopt-a-School, recommended on the state level for use by school districts, asks local businesses to sponsor individual schools. Businesses visit the schools and assess their needs; they can earmark donations for specific purposes, such as playgrounds or video equipment. Eloise Hall has modified this strategy for Remedial Summer School; she estimates that tuition for each student is ten dollars and asks corporations to sponsor as many students as they can afford. Participants rarely pay tuition themselves and could not afford to do so if required. |
| **In-Kind Resources** | The Barbour County Board of Education provides space, clerical support, equipment, and materials to Community Education. Because the program's staff members are district employees, the board pays their salaries. The Adopt-a-School program is another source of equipment and materials. |
| **Funding History** | PAL started out funded by the local school board and by 1986 became a federally funded project. |

The program aims to improve parents' attitudes toward education; prepare children for kindergarten; increase self-esteem of parents and children; decrease the need for remedial and special education; and foster closer links among home, school, and community.

Barbour County Community Education is evaluated yearly by the Alabama Department of Education, as is Eloise Hall for her contribution both to community education and to ABE. The evaluations have been consistently favorable, and Chapter 2 funding to the preschool has more than doubled since 1986. Barbour County Community Education was cited as an exemplary program in Alabama in 1986.

Ms. Hall says her measure of the program's success is the school district's declining enrollment in special education. After the first few years of Barbour County Community Education, the number of young children enrolled in special education decreased by 100 each year. She calls her program the "ounce of prevention that beats a pound of cure."

Barbour County Community Education has not been replicated.

None.

# Working Families Center of the Parent Education/Family Support Programs

*The Working Families Center attracts extended family members as well as babysitters and day care providers. One of its great charms, and an unexpected bonus, according to Ms. Lewis, has been the opportunity to exchange intergenerational ideas about child rearing. One grandfather, whose grown child is fully employed, attends a parent center with his grandson almost daily and talks often about his delight in this role which is something of a novelty for him. He felt that he missed out on his own child's upbringing by having to work full-time.*

| | | |
|---|---|---|
| Warmline | Drop-in center | Parent-child joint activities |
| Newsletter | Resource library | Evening & Saturday seminars |
| Networking | Child care training | Developmental exams & screening |
| Baby basics | Parent-infant play group | Parenting & child development education |
| Home visits | Health & nutrition education | Groups for incarcerated parents |
| Toy lending | Child care info/referral | Parent program at a homeless shelter |
| Adult literacy | GED services | Community services info/referral |

| | |
|---|---|
| **Contact:** | Georgia Lewis, Parent Education Specialist |
| **Address:** | 12518 Greenly Street |
| | Silver Spring, MD 20906 |
| | (301) 929-2025 |
| **Established:** | 1977, local initiative |
| **Budget '88-'89:** | $92,000 |
| **Sources:** | Local school district; client fees; in-kind contributions; and third-party reimbursement |
| **Size:** | 5,000 families served |
| **Area Served:** | Montgomery County, Maryland |
| **Auspices:** | Adult education department of the Montgomery County Public Schools |

## Community

Montgomery County, an affluent suburb of Washington, DC, is a somewhat diverse and transient community of high-ranking civil servants, lawyers, government, embassy, and World Bank employees, as well as refugees and immigrants. The population of this former farming area has exploded from 164,000 in the 1950s to 635,000 in 1989. Its ethnic makeup includes: 67 percent white, 15.6 percent black, 10.6 percent Asian and Pacific Islander, 6.6 percent Hispanic, and 0.2 percent Native American.

## Philosophy and Goals

The Parent Education Program offers information, support, and resources to help parents build their skills and strengths. The program encourages participants to learn about child development and endeavors to identify and help children and families with special needs. In addition, all of the parent education programs provide opportunities for parents to discuss issues, share ideas, and address family life concerns. The Working Families Center aims to provide information and support to family daycare providers and to promote parent-provider partnerships in caring for children.

## History and Origins

In the early 1970s, local parents asked the Montgomery County school board for funds to support parent education. The board hired an education specialist who initiated parent-child development classes within the adult education department of the community education system. As family patterns and neighborhoods changed, the need arose for a center. In 1977, Public Law 94-142 mandated public education for special needs children, and the local schools received money for a parent education training and demonstration project. As a result, the adult education department in Montgomery County set up a parent education resource center in 1977, ostensibly for parent educators but increasingly used by the public. The program now has four centers for children and parents. These centers focus on the special needs of parents and family daycare providers.

The newest center, the Working Families Center (WFC), targets family daycare providers and employed parents. In 1984-85, the Parent Education Program established a permanent site for the WFC in Rockville, Maryland, to strengthen educational continuity and develop firm links between parents and their children's caregivers.

Features

The **Working Families Center**, one of four parent education centers that offer education, training, and support, specifically helps working parents and child care providers develop a closer alliance in the shared task of raising children. The center is a model learning environment for preschool children and a meeting ground for caregivers who are isolated from other adults and lack professional growth opportunities and exposure to new concepts in their field. During free drop-in hours, parents, grandparents and family daycare providers are welcome to bring their children, or the children in their care, to play and learn together.

**Working Parents Saturday Special** allows parents to bring their preschool children for art, music and play activities and meet other employed parents with young children. The program takes place monthly and registration is required.

The **Family Daycare Enrichment Program** offers weekly classes for family daycare providers and the children in their care. Each class session includes art, music, snack, play activities for children, and discussion time for adults. Evening programs for daycare providers offer opportunities to learn more about child development, behavior management, and activities for young children.

A **monthly newsletter** (October to May), *The Parent-Provider Exchange*, includes information about child development, parenting, child care and local activities of interest to parents. It also provides a forum for exchange between parents and family daycare providers. The newsletter is distributed to all participants in the Family Daycare Enrichment Program and is available at all Montgomery County public schools parent resource centers and at the Working Families Center.

The **Worksite Parent Education Program** offers lunch-hour seminars in parent education at various places of employment in Montgomery County.

**Parent resource centers**, including the Working Families Center, are open to families on a drop-in basis. Their programs and services are free and include play areas for children, books and resources for parents, toy-lending libraries, parent discussion groups, age-appropriate activities for preschoolers, and field trips for toddlers.

**Parent education classes** are held in various county locations and, depending on topic, range from one to seven sessions each; tuition is based on the number of participants. Fees are waived for low-income residents.

| Participants | WFC's participants are parents, daycare providers and children from birth to age five. The Parent Education Program as a whole serves 5,000 families. A babysitter training program serves 50 teens, the nanny program serves 36 adults and the Family Daycare Enrichment Program serves 140 adults and children. Typically, participants use the program's services once a week. |

> *The program tries to strengthen family relationships, promote positive, confident attitudes toward parenting, create an awareness of the parents' power to effect change, and increase the use and development of formal and informal service networks.*

| Parent Education | The Parent Education Program includes parent-toddler and parent-child development classes, parent resource centers, workshops, and seminars. One program, Helping Your Child Succeed in School, focuses on topics such as: "Motivation and Learning"; "Helping with Homework"; "School Problems: What Parents Can Do"; "Testing"; "Beyond the 'Three R's'"; "Enrichment Possibilities;" "Out-of-School Time: A Balanced 'Diet'"; "Child Stress"; and "New Issues in Education." |

| Curriculum | Most materials are developed in-house. The program uses modified versions of *Systematic Training for Effective Parenting (STEP)*, *How to Talk so that Kids Will Listen* and *Parentmaking*, as well as various books and videos. Georgia Lewis, the parent education specialist, writes: "We change the order of lessons and add information [such as developmental information to *STEP*] or use examples and anecdotes that our students can relate to." |

| Sites | The four parent resource centers and all parent education programs use school buildings. WFC shares a former school building, taken over by the county, with a variety of social services, including a child care referral service and a daycare program. In addition, the program offers services at a shelter for the homeless and at a county detention center. |

| Parent Involvement | Parents helped start the program by requesting services and continue to participate in the ongoing process of program evaluation. |

| Outreach | The Parent Education Program publicizes its activities and services through a quarterly adult education brochure that reaches all homes in the county. In an effort to encourage participation of low-income parents, fees for classes are waived. Flyers distributed to libraries, hospitals, and parent centers and press releases in local papers heighten program visibility. New outreach activities include lunchtime parenting seminars scheduled at work sites. |

| Job Title | PD | Vol | FT | PT | Educ Req | Status | Benefits |
|---|---|---|---|---|---|---|---|
| Parent Education Specialist | 1 | - | 1 | - | College Degree | Hourly Non-Contract | Yes |
| Teacher/ Parent Educators | 12-18 | - | - | 12-18 | College Degree | Hourly Non-Contract | No |
| Teacher Assistants | 7 | - | - | 7 | High School Diploma | Hourly Non-Contract | No |
| Parent Center Coordinators | 6 | - | - | 6 | College Degree | Hourly Non-Contract | No |

**State/District Requirements**

None.

**Preferred Background**

For all positions, staff members should possess human relations skills, communication and listening skills, parenting experience, and the ability to work independently and as part of a professional team. Parent educators should have a minimum of a bachelor's degree.

**Employee Education and Training Represented**

Infant and toddler education; prekindergarten and early childhood education; elementary education; education, grades 7 to 12; special education; adult education; group dynamics; parent educator; child care; health and nutrition; home economics; nursing; psychology; counseling; child development and family studies.

**Administration**

The program is administered exclusively within the adult education department of the Montgomery County Public Schools. The program's director reports to the director of adult education. The Maryland Department of Education monitors the county adult education department.

**Relationship to the Schools**

Staff members from the Parent Education Program assist the school system's "child find" effort to screen all preschool children for delays and disabilities. Adult literacy, Graduate Equivalency Diploma (GED), and English as a Second Language (ESL) staff members interact with the Parent Education/Family Support Program; all four are components of the adult education department.

**Community Links**

When the WFC and the Family Daycare Enrichment Program were getting underway, the Parent Education Program enlisted the aid of the county Family Daycare Association, the Department of Social Services, the Department of Family Resources, and the Health Department, all of which advertised the new program in their newsletters.

**Funding**

Local/district, 50 percent; client fees, 44 percent; in-kind contributions, 5 percent; third-party reimbursement/insurance, 1 percent. The Parent Education Program is part of the adult education department of Montgomery County and its budget is fluid, not a fixed line-item figure. The 1988-89 budget of approximately $92,000 represents the school system's budget for the Parent Education Program's salaries. Fees range from a $5 materials fee for children in the Family Daycare Enrichment Program to a $60 parent fee for classes (the exact amount depends on the number of sessions and participants). Activities and classes offered through the Working Families Center are free, with a $5 materials fee.

| | |
|---|---|
| In-Kind Resources | The school system provides space and facilities, paid staff for service delivery, consultation and staff development, administrative and clerical support, equipment, materials, and supplies. |
| Objectives | The Working Family Center seeks to increase parents' and daycare providers' knowledge of child development, awareness of child, adult and family issues, and parenting skills. In addition, the program tries to strengthen family relationships, promote positive, confident attitudes toward parenting, create an awareness of the parents' power to effect change and increase the use and development of formal and informal service networks. |
| Evaluation | Participant evaluation is ongoing and the parent education staff conducts annual self-evaluation. |
| Replication | The program has not been replicated. |
| Materials Available | None. |
| Update | The program has changed its name to Parenting Education/Family Support Programs. |

# Parent Resource Center

Transportation
Warmline
Networking
Newsletter
Home visits
Drop-in center
Adult literacy

Special events
Nursery school guide
Bilingual presentations
Music and dance classes
Parenting advice hotline
Summer day camp
Resource library

Child care info/referral
Parent-child joint activities
Community services info/referral
Guide to local preschool services
Parent support groups
Parenting/child development education
Health/nutrition education

**Contact:** Susan Cappon, Coordinator

**Address:** Flower Hill Instructional Center
99 Campus Drive
Port Washington, NY 11050
(516) 767-4428

**Established:** 1980, local initiative

**Budget '88-'89:** $76,550 (PRC, $65,050; Community Outreach, $11,500)

**Sources:** New York Department of Social Services, fundraising, client fees, in-kind contributions, private donations, private agency

**Size:** 400 families

**Area Served:** Port Washington, New York

**Auspices:** Port Washington Public Schools

## Community

Port Washington, on a peninsula in Manhasset Bay, Long Island, has some light industry in a nearby industrial park but is essentially a bedroom community to New York City. Housing costs range between $100,000 and $400,000, and most residents are homeowners. The median income is $20,000. Of the total population of 30,000, 90 percent are white, 4 percent are Hispanic, and 3 percent are black.

## Philosophy and Goals

The Parent Resource Center (PRC) provides members with opportunities for discussion among themselves and with professionals and mutual support in sharing the challenges and rewards of parenthood. Parents become familiar with educational activities and experiences available for their children in the community through networking and group participation. The center aims to improve parenting skills, to expose preschool children to educational materials and give them the chance to learn socialization skills in preparation for school. Parents gain awareness of nutritional needs and safety hazards and children reap the benefits of improved parenting.

## History and Origins

Lynn Patterson, Ed.D., former director of a mother-child program for low-income families, was the driving force behind the PRC. The idea for the program came from her conversations with middle-class mothers who had volunteered in the mother-child program and wanted a preschool program that would allow them to network, enjoy the parenting experience and give their children a chance to mix with peers. Port Washington school administrators felt the program would enhance the community and promised their support. The Mertz Community Foundation provided initial funding of $5,000, which enabled Lynn Patterson to implement the project. Two programs were instituted simultaneously: a parent-run early education center and a community outreach program to meet the needs of low-income families. Today, the Parent Resource Center is run for and mainly by a volunteer parent board of directors, most of whom have no formal training in early childhood education.

*"These parents are not going to be passive. This is good for the school; the more parents are educated about the way the school system runs, the more they can contribute. The school administration sees parents as an asset—the center enhances the school and the school is essential for the center."*

**Features**

The Parent Resource Center and Community Outreach Program operate throughout the year and offer the following:

**Mommy and Me classes**, a 12-week series led by mothers under the direction of a coordinator. Classes include crafts, singing, story, snack, music, and exercise.

**Parent support groups**, offered to the general public in 12-week sessions led by professionals. Discussion topics include: "Surviving Motherhood," "New Mothers," "Toddler Topics," "Mothers of Two-Plus," and "Beyond Infancy." Classes are repeated on demand.

**Workshops** on various aspects of childrearing and parenting as well as hands-on sessions for parents and children are offered twice a year, in January and June.

**Movement to Music** classes for age two and up led by a professional dance instructor with early childhood credentials.

The **Community Outreach Program** brings low-income and minority mothers and children to the school one morning a week by bus. Mothers participate in discussions run by a parent educator while children enjoy free play. Since most of the mothers in this program are Spanish speaking, discussions are in Spanish and focus on childrearing issues, use of community resources such as free dental care, and negotiating the public school system. Following the discussion mothers and children take part in a Mommy and Me session run by an early childhood educator.

The **summer program** component of the Community Outreach Program, a two-day-a-week camp for 30 to 50 pairs of mothers and children. Elementary-age siblings are invited to take part in this program.

**Participants**

The program serves two distinct client types. The primary participants of PRC are middle-class families with children from birth to 3 1/2 years. In 1987-88, 350 families in the Port Washington area took part in the center's activities. One percent of these were single parents and 0.01 percent teen parents. The Community Outreach Program serves a low-income, mostly Hispanic population with preschool children. The program targets families struggling with social and emotional problems. In 1987-88, 50 families were served, 25 percent of the eligible population.

**Parent Education**

All of the programming focuses on parent education through discussions and activities. Ms. Cappon reflects that in Port Washington many of the mothers are over 30, have just had their first baby, and stopped work and/or moved to the suburbs. The center gives them an outside interest, something that is not a job but is challenging and important. They feel what they are doing is both good for them and vital for their children. She feels the center bridges the gap between childbirth and returning to work for many mothers. The center also offers programs for working parents.

**Curriculum**

Curriculum is developed in-house for particular classes. Materials and content are adjusted to participant response. Successful lesson plans are kept in a resource library available to group leaders.

**Sites**

The Parent Resource Center is situated in an unused public school building. For the last 10 years, the building has served as a community center that houses, in addition to the Parent Resource Center, a daycare center, a prekindergarten program, a senior citizen program's administrative offices and adult education classes.

**Parent Involvement**

Since the center began, parents have been involved in every phase of its development. Once Lynn Patterson had secured funding and the promise of three child care workers, she ran an advertisement in the local newspaper inviting parents to a planning meeting. Response was overwhelming. Parents were ready to pay for services and wanted to plan and have a voice in the center's programs and administration. Today, an annually elected volunteer parent board of directors is responsible for all aspects of implementation from program development, writing and circulating the newsletter, to fundraising and recruitment. Parents make presentations to local organizations to bring the center and its work into the community consciousness and pave the way for later fundraising efforts.

**Outreach**

Outreach strategies include the center's newsletter, newspaper publicity, flyers about special events, and word-of-mouth.

**Staff**

Volunteer mothers who lead the Mommy and Me classes receive two-hour training sessions from a childhood educator. A parent educator, employed by the schools' prekindergarten program, coordinates the Community Outreach Program, assisted by an early childhood education teacher. Additional aides are employed in the Community Outreach Program during the summer.

| Job Title | PD | Vol | FT | PT | Educ Req | Status | Benefits |
|---|---|---|---|---|---|---|---|
| Coordinator | 1 | - | 1 | - | None | Hourly Non-Contract | No |
| Child Care | 3 | - | - | 3 | None | Hourly Non-Contract | No |
| Volunteers | - | 15+ | - | 15+ | None | - | No |

| | |
|---|---|
| State/District Requirements | None. |
| Preferred Background | None. |
| Employee Education and Training Represented | Infant and toddler education; elementary education; parent educator; health and nutrition; child psychology; social work; child development and family studies; research and evaluation. |
| Administration | The Parent Resource Center and Community Outreach Program are administered by an elected parent board within the public school system. The superintendent of schools is kept informed of the center's activities, which are planned and run by the Parent Board of Directors. An advisory board includes psychologists, social workers, health care professionals, and educators. |
| Relationship to the Schools | Susan Cappon, the coordinator, reports close collaboration between the public schools' prekindergarten program and the Parent Resource Center. Last year, parents and the school system joined forces to construct an innovative playground with activity areas specially designed for toddlers. |
| | Ms. Cappon asserts that the program gives parents a reason to be involved in their children's school early on. "These parents are not going to be passive. This is good for the school; the more parents are educated about the way the school system runs, the more they can contribute. The school administration sees parents as an asset—the center enhances the school and the school is essential for the center." |
| Community Links | Some classes are run by staff from local service agencies, including psychologists, social workers or community business people for whom this provides a novel means of publicizing their services. The Continuing and Community Education program lists the center's activities in its biannual brochure. |
| Funding | Client fees account for 48 percent of the budget; special events and fundraising activities, 20 percent; New York Department of Social Services, 15 percent; in-kind contributions, 11 percent; the Community Chest of Port Washington, 4 percent; private donations, 2 percent. The Parent Resource Center is a fee-based enrichment program; the Community Outreach Program is a secondary prevention program funded by special legislative grants. The annual center membership costs $30, 12-week courses cost $30 to $50, minicourses are $10 and one-time workshops are $5. |
| In-Kind Resources | Port Washington Public Schools provide space and facilities, consultation, and staff development as well as access to equipment. Private agencies contribute by providing speakers for workshops. |
| Funding History | The budget has grown from start-up funding of $12,000 in 1980, to $76,550 for 1988-89. Increased monies come from rising membership, stepped-up programming and services, and active fundraising. Funding from the Community Chest of Port Washington has remained stable at $4,000. Funding of the Community Outreach Program fluctuates; at present it is $11,000. |

| | |
|---|---|
| **Objectives** | The Parent Resource Center is dedicated to developing active, interested and informed parents. The program aims to diminish the barriers between home and school. |
| **Evaluation** | Program evaluation is an ongoing process. The coordinator states that she depends on feedback from participants. At the end of each course or workshop participants evaluate the course content and suggest useful changes and topics of future interest. |
| **Replication** | The Parent Resource Center began as a replication of the Mother/Child Home Program in Freeport, New York, but developed its distinct programs in response to participants' needs. |
| **Materials Available** | For more information on how to order materials mentioned in the curriculum section, write to Susan Cappon. |

# Parent and Child Education Centers (PACE)

*It was a year before Tina, a 17-year-old married with two children, revealed that her husband abused her. She had been abused as a child and thought it was normal. Tina went into counseling but her husband refused. She realized that she had to save herself and her children, who were becoming increasingly aggressive. She entered a child development class through Adult Education. This led to a job as a Montessori aide and a scholarship to earn her teaching certificate. She now leads workshops on early childhood education.*

| | | |
|---|---|---|
| Preschool | Individual counseling | Community services info/referral |
| Networking | Resource library | Parenting/child development education |
| Home visits | Parent support groups | Parent-child joint activities |
| Drop-in center | Developmental screening | Child care info/referral |
| Warmline | Toy lending | Health/nutrition education |

**Contact:** Aurelia Zoretich, Coordinator

**Address:** Martin School
1253 Third Street, SE
Canton, OH 44707
(216) 454-6877

**Established:** 1974, state initiative

**Budget '88-'89:** $180,000 (Parent-Child, $120,000; Preschool, $60,000)

**Sources:** Federal and state government, local school district, foundations

**Size:** 450 families (1028 adults and children)

**Area Served:** Stark County, Ohio

**Auspices:** Community Educational Services of the Canton Public Schools

## Community

Canton, with a population just under 100,000, has recently experienced an industrial exodus and rise in unemployment. Parent and Child Education Centers (PACE) functions out of inner-city sites but serves families from across Stark County, a farming and industrial area with a racially mixed population of many religious and ethnic backgrounds. The area's population is evenly divided between whites and blacks, with small numbers of Native Americans and Asians.

## Philosophy and Goals

PACE educates parents, teaching observation, moderation, and empathy through social dynamics. The program addresses a comprehensive list of problems including: domestic violence and child abuse, developmentally delayed infants, underachievement and failure in schools, unemployment, juvenile delinquency, teen pregnancy, and families in crisis.

## History and Origins

In 1974, the Ohio Department of Education channelled funds from the Division of Home Economics into Adult Vocational Family Life Programs. Canton Public Schools applied for this funding through its community education department, and Aurelia Zoretich, now the program coordinator, wrote the proposal for a comprehensive parent-child education project. The program design, influenced by early childhood educators Burton White, Uri Bronfenbrenner, and Ira Gordon, emphasized the importance of adult education, learning environments for children, and meeting parents' needs.

## Features

PACE offers programming 10 months a year and, depending on the availability of funding, for 8 to 12 weeks during the summer. Parent-child classes run in 15-week cycles, and families may attend daily. The daily, two-hour classes begin with songs, followed by joint parent-child activities; a short transition includes snack, story, and art activity and leads into staff-supervised play for children, while parents participate in discussions, speaker sessions, or workshops.

**Parent education topics** include self-concepts of parents and children, language development, communication skills, nutrition, early sensory and motor learning, human sexuality, prenatal care, and child care. When appropriate, families receive referrals to therapeutic, educational, medical, legal, and welfare services in the community. PACE staff may also make home visits to families in crisis.

**Evening seminars** have focused on family law, couples communication, sex education, discipline, and self-defense for women.

**Monthly luncheons**, featuring a guest speaker, are sponsored by a parent advocacy group called Mother's Kiss (Keeping Infant Stimulation Strong).

A **preschool program**, developed along prevention-model guidelines and using the High/Scope curriculum, began operating in the fall of 1988. Special features include bimonthly parent-child joint activities and parent discussions. The present enrollment is 100 children (25 at each site) and their parents (110 adults).

### Participants

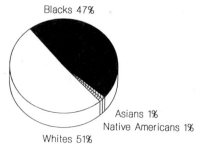

Blacks 47%

Asians 1%

Native Americans 1%

Whites 51%

When PACE began in 1974, it served 70 families. During 1987-88, PACE served approximately 450 families. Participants include parents, grandparents, foster parents, and extended-family members, as well as babysitters and friends. There is an emphasis on children from birth to age six, and a special focus on birth to age three. Approximately 25 percent of the participants were single mothers and 5 percent teens. The preschoolers come from lower-income families who live in the Canton school district and are at risk for developmental delay.

*Ms. Zoretich feels, "It takes at least two years to impact the life of a family."*

### Parent Education

The center is open on a drop-in basis. Parents write their own schedules and are encouraged to come in as often as they like. Most use the center several times a week. According to Ms. Zoretich, group discussions nurture awareness and thoughtful authority in parents, while teaching the practical skills of childrearing and family interaction. Ms. Zoretich feels, "It takes at least two years to impact the life of a family."

### Curriculum

Ms. Zoretich has developed and modified curriculum materials based on her 15 years of experience as program director. She noted, "In the early years it was necessary to develop our own handouts and slide presentations because we couldn't find appropriate or affordable materials. Much more is available now, but we still develop our own, based on our philosophy and target population." The curriculum integrates lectures, speakers, handouts, group discussions, and modeling of parent-child interaction. Hands-on workshops on toy making and nutrition supplement the regular curriculum.

Harvard Family Research Project

**Sites**

At its outset, PACE occupied a large kindergarten space and had use of a gym and outdoor play area in an unused school building, rent-free. In 1985, the program's central site moved to the Martin School, a larger, rent-free school building. New facilities include a child development room, library, parent discussion area, workshop, and storage area. Three satellite sites are scattered around Canton: an elementary school and two churches. "We try to place centers on bus routes and within walking distance of large numbers of participants . . . but there will always be transportation problems for someone," comments Ms. Zoretich.

**Parent Involvement**

Fifty-four percent of PACE parents volunteer in school, are active in the parent-teacher association (PTA), and regularly attend school activities. One program participant serves on the advisory board.

**Outreach**

PACE relies on personal contacts, newspaper articles, telephone calls, and door-to-door recruitment to draw in participants. Ms. Zoretich remarks, "We are at a high-water mark at our main center; the three new sites will require time to gain credibility and increase enrollment."

**Staff**

| Job Title | PD | Vol | FT | PT | Educ Req | Status | Benefits |
|---|---|---|---|---|---|---|---|
| Coordinator | 1 | - | 1 | - | Post-Graduate Courses or Degree | Hourly Non-Contract | Yes |
| Teachers | 4 | - | - | 4 | College Degree | Hourly Non-Contract | Yes |
| Teachers Assistants | 9 | - | 9 | - | High School Diploma/ Some College | Hourly Non-Contract | Yes |

**State/District Requirements**

The program coordinator and teachers must have a bachelor of arts degree, a standard vocational certificate and prekindergarten certification; teacher assistants need a minimum of 45 hours of early childhood training.

**Preferred Background**

PACE requires that its staff be able to work with both adults and young children and be knowledgeable about child development and community resources. Flexibility, creativity, dependability, and the ability to work in a team are valued.

**Employee Education and Training Represented**

Infant and toddler education; prekindergarten and early childhood education; elementary education; education, grades 7 to 12; bilingual education; special education; adult basic education; adult literacy; parent educator; adult vocational education; child care; health and nutrition; psychology; counseling; family therapy; social work; child development and family studies; development and fundraising; research and evaluation.

**Administration**

PACE's coordinator reports to the director of Community Educational Services, who is responsible to the superintendent of the Canton Public Schools. The entire program is accountable to the Ohio Department of Education. The advisory board, made up of one program participant, two public school personnel, three representatives from noneducational public agencies, two representatives from the community, and one legislative representative, functions as a "braintrust" and is mainly responsible for linkages with other agencies.

## Relationships to the Schools

PACE maintains strong relationships with Canton's community and vocational education programs. Within the school system proper, PACE integrates itself with instruction and development programs, the instructional media department, special education, art and music, guidance counselors and Chapter 1 programs. Ms. Zoretich notes that some school personnel are particularly helpful. "The school nurses, psychologists, and PTA members have all proven themselves willing allies."

*"We try to place centers on bus routes and within walking distance of large numbers of participants . . . but there will always be transportation problems for someone."*

## Community Links

The Parent and Child Education is an essential part of an extensive family support network in Stark County that includes, among others, area hospitals, Planned Parenthood, family physicians and pediatricians, Siffran Housing for Retarded Citizens, Family Counseling Services, Urban League, Stark County Mental Health, Stark County Intercollaborative Early Intervention Council, and the Community Action Center.

Area nursing schools participate in inservice and on-site observation, as do secondary school and college students studying child development, sociology and psychology. The program has also given workshops at regional conferences of La Leche International and National Association for the Education of Young Children and has participated in two national conferences for community education.

## Funding

The program receives Carl Perkins funds through the Ohio Department of Education and vocational education funds. In 1988-89 the federal government provided 40 percent; state government, 30 percent; local school district, 20 percent; and 10 percent came from grants.

## In-Kind Resources

Space and facilities are provided by two churches in the Canton area and the school system, which also provides paid staff, periodic direct service to program participants (as do the health department and SERRC Center), administrative and clerical support and access to equipment.

## Funding History

Funding is moderately secure, although vocational education must constantly lobby to maintain its presence as a line item in the federal budget. Unit funds have not kept up with cost of living increases. PACE must apply for competitive grants to maintain level funding.

## Objectives

PACE offers parent education as a means of nurturing the family; provides a supportive environment for a diverse inner-city clientele; and fosters understanding, individual growth, and awareness of options.

**Evaluation**

PACE conducted a longitudinal study in 1982 in which 83.5 percent of the participants reported that family communications and discipline had improved as a result of their involvement in the program. Seventy percent of the parents reported that their children were doing very well. This was reflected in the overall Normal Curve Equivalent of all participating students, regardless of the year tested: 56.54 percent, compared to the city average of 48.43 percent. The children in this study retained their gains through each school year.

The staff performs needs assessments with parents who are newcomers to the center. Their children are given the Denver Developmental Screening Test. PACE's advisory board monitors the program's progress, and parent evaluations provide immediate feedback to the staff. Once a year, state supervisors make site visits, as do the granting officers from the Children's Trust Fund. In 1987, the Triangle Research Institute, from North Carolina, performed an evaluation and recommended that PACE expand its services to four quadrants of the city. In response, PACE has developed three new sites.

**Replication**

The program was an original design and has not been replicated.

**Materials Available**

Handouts, curriculum materials, slides, and training assistance; write to Aurelia Zoretich at PACE for information.

# Stratford Parents' Place

| | | |
|---|---|---|
| Newsletter | Workshops/events | Community services info/referral |
| Networking | Parent support groups | Parent-child joint activities |
| Toy lending | Health/nutrition education | Parenting/child development education |
| Resource library | Child care info/referral | |
| | Technical assistance, consultation, and training to service providers | |

**Contacts:** Priscilla Long, Program Coordinator
Patricia Naylor, Executive Director of Stratford Community Services

**Address:** 719 Birdseye Street
c/o Johnson House, Stratford Academy
Stratford, CT 06497
(203) 386-9668

**Established:** 1987, local initiative

**Budget '88-'89:** 43,957

**Sources:** Connecticut Department of Children and Youth Services
and client paid fees

**Size:** 400 families

**Area Served:** Stratford, Connecticut

**Auspices:** Cooperative project of Stratford Community Services
and Stratford Public Schools

*A mother and son had been participating in the program sporadically for a year. The mother did not really network with other parents. Recently, she had a second child. A few weeks ago, she broke down and cried during a support group meeting. Her husband was giving her no support, making too many demands, and she had no family in the area to help her. The other mothers in the group rallied and for several nights they brought dinner to her family. Their response to her situation made me feel our program really works.*
*— Priscilla Long*

**Community**

This Fairfield County city, with a population of approximately 52,000, is situated on Connecticut's southeast coast. In recent years Stratford's affordable housing has attracted a growing number of younger families. Stratford Parents' Place (SPP) is in a Chapter 1 magnet school, located near a low-income housing project.

**Philosophy and Goals**

Stratford Parents' Place is committed to strengthening families and promoting the positive, healthy development of young people.

**History and Origins**

Stratford Parents' Place developed out of recommendations from a youth and family services advisory board, composed of representatives from churches, schools, the police department, parents, and youth. White Plains Parents' Place, in White Plains, New York, served as a model for the initiative. When funding became available through the Connecticut Department of Children and Youth Services in June of 1986, a planning committee comprised of representatives from the Stratford Public Schools, Parent-Teacher Association (PTA) Council, Stratford Community Services, and others was formed to develop a proposal. With the support of the school superintendent, the committee decided to develop a school-based program.

**Features**

Stratford Parents' Place is a cooperative project of Stratford Community Services and Stratford Public Schools. Its emphasis is two-pronged: the project offers education, training, support, and information to parents and technical assistance, consultations, and training to service providers. The program is open four mornings a week from 9 a.m. to 2 p.m. Parent education and support programs and other special events are scheduled during evening and weekend hours. From

September to June Stratford Parents' Place operates on a school schedule. In July and August, special programs are offered during an abbreviated summer schedule.

**Parent Support Services** schedules parent-child activities three mornings a week, including a weekly Baby Steps program for parents and infants. One Saturday a month, SPP schedules "Especially for Fathers." The focus is on parent-child interaction in an informal, yet structured, atmosphere. The activity sessions involve play with educational toys, arts and crafts projects, singing and movement. Time is arranged for parents to meet informally for discussion on parenting topics. Additional parent-child programming occurs in cooperation with the public library and may be expanded to other sites.

**Information and Coordination Services** include a resource library, parent bulletin board, and resource file, with materials about community agencies, organizations, and events.

SPP is open to all Stratford parents of children from birth to age 18. Specific programs and outreach efforts are aimed at parents of preschool and kindergarten children, lower-income families, young parents, single parents, dual-career families and new parents. Special efforts are also made to involve fathers in the program.

*"We are aware that some parents are ambivalent about school, but we feel that their involvement at the preschool level will give them a chance to develop positive attitudes about the future." To that end, SPP cosponsored a program with the PTA addressing the positive educational benefits of parent involvement.*

### Participants

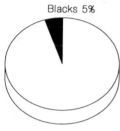

Blacks 5%

Whites 95%

### Parent Education

Established parent education and training programs that have formal curricula are scheduled throughout the year. These include *Systematic Training for Effective Parenting (STEP)*, *STEP-TEEN* for parents of teens, and *Developing Capable Young People*. In addition, several shorter programs are offered including *How to Talk So Your Kid Will Listen*, *Assertive Discipline*, and *Sibling without Rivalry*. Weekly two-hour sessions combine information and discussion and cover such topics as child development, communication, and discipline. In autumn 1989, SPP will pilot *Preparing for the Drug Free Years* for parents of students in fifth to eighth grade, in an effort to involve more families with school-age children.

### Curriculum

SPP uses established parent education curricula (see above, Parent Education).

### Sites

The program occupies one room at Stratford Academy, a Chapter 1 magnet school. To serve as many people as frequently show up for classes (on occasion up to 60) the program anticipates the need for more space in the near future.

**Parent Involvement**

The parent advisory committee, open to all parents registered at SPP, meets monthly as a forum for parent input. Parents assist with fundraising, publicity, and family-oriented events, coordinate the quarterly newsletter and organize resource- and lending-library materials. "We are aware that some parents are ambivalent about school, but we feel that their involvement at the preschool level will give them a chance to develop positive attitudes about the future." To that end, SPP cosponsored a program with the PTA addressing the positive educational benefits of parent involvement. Ms. Naylor continues, "A lot of parents don't realize that their involvement in schooling and school activities —from helping with homework to interacting with teachers and principals—can have an impact on their child's success."

**Outreach**

SPP coordinates its outreach efforts with the Stratford School System (pupil services, nurses, teachers and administrators) and local community agencies. Flyers about the program are distributed to these organizations on an annual basis as part of a resource packet. Publicity is included in Stratford Community Services' tri-annual newsletter.

**Staff**

| Job Title | PD | Vol | FT | PT | Educ Req | Status | Benefits |
|---|---|---|---|---|---|---|---|
| Program Coordinator | 1 | - | - | 1 | College Degree | Hourly Contract | Yes |
| Parent Consultant | 2 | - | - | 2 | College Degree | Hourly Contract | No |
| Early Childhood Educator | 1 | - | - | 1 | College Degree | Hourly Contract | No |

**State/District Requirements**

None.

**Preferred Background**

For the program coordinator, administrative and community experience.

**Employee Education and Training Represented**

Infant and toddler education; prekindergarten and early childhood education; elementary education; parent educator; home economics; counseling; family therapy; child development and family studies; development and fundraising.

**Administration**

The program coordinator reports to the executive director of Stratford Community Services, who coordinates youth services in Stratford.

**Relationship to the Schools**

SPP provides the parent involvement component mandated for Chapter 1 schools and by attracting families to Stratford Academy, a magnet school, helps restore the city's racial balance. Through presentations at staff meetings and professional development days and distribution of flyers, SPP keeps the schools informed of its resources. In 1987-88, SPP and the Chapter 1 coordinator, Lynette Baroni, helped establish the Stratford Early Childhood Council, which provides a forum for educators to share information and encourage cooperation between preschool and elementary school personnel in an effort to prepare children and parents for the transition into kindergarten.

Stratford Community Services director Pat Naylor feels strongly that the program's affiliation with the schools makes it more approachable for high-risk families.

**Community Links**

SPP is linked to the community through its parent organization, Stratford Community Services, which provides counseling and positive youth development programs for children and families.

**Funding**

The Connecticut Department of Youth Services, 97 percent; client fees, 3 percent to cover the cost of books and other educational materials. This fee is discussed with parents in confidence when they register. No one is turned away because of inability to pay.

**In-Kind Resources**

The Stratford Public Schools provide space and assistance with public relations and staff support through a liaison.

**Funding History**

The original grant funded the project for six months during 1988-89, at $15,000; it was extended to a full year at $30,000. In 1987-88, minimum fees were charged for special events and high attendance indicated that fees could be increased.

**Objectives**

Stratford Parents' Place seeks to involve families with children from infancy through the elementary grades in the common goal of education and self-development.

**Evaluation**

SPP is participating in a three-year evaluation initiative (1987-1990) in cooperation with the Connecticut Department of Children and Youth Services and the University of Southern Maine. A list of knowledge and behavior indicators have been developed and several instruments, including a new registration form, pre- and posttests, and a questionnaire, are being field tested. A positive outcome will be helpful in public relations and fundraising efforts, says Pat Naylor.

**Replication**

Stratford Parents' Place is modeled on a similar project in White Plains, New York, and Stratford has itself served as a model for others interested in starting school and center-based programs.

**Materials Available**

None.

# *9* Family, School, Community Partnerships

The following programs operate in a broadening arena that links social services to the schools. They concentrate on low-income families whose children are considered at risk for educational disadvantage. In general, these programs see themselves as integral to a larger community effort. Collaboration with other agencies and with the professional, medical, and educational communities is extensive. Projects in Washington, Oregon, and Vermont represent examples of newer legislative initiatives. In Oregon, several nonprofit social service agencies won state Together for Children grants to offer preschool and parent education in collaboration with the schools. By contrast, the Minnesota legislature created the Council on Quality Education to develop the innovative Early Childhood Family Education (ECFE) program at the local district level. Launched as a pilot project in the early 1970s, ECFE has since expanded from an original 34 sites to 310 and in 1988 received over 7 million dollars in state funds.

# Programs in Brief

### Birth to Three School Collaboration Program — p. 429
*Private social service agency serving low-income, high-risk families in urban Oregon, offering parent education and support groups and a teen outreach program; partially supported by the Together for Children initiative*

### Family Focus — p. 435
A Program of Crisis Intervention Services
*Urban Oregon social service agency serving outlying suburban and rural communities; offering comprehensive parenting classes and support groups to teen, migrant, and at-risk families; a Together for Children initiative*

### Together for Children — p. 441
*Pilot state-funded initiative in suburban and rural Oregon serving low- to middle-income families with children birth to age three through home visits and comprehensive education and support services*

### Avancé Family Support and Education Program — p. 447
*Urban, community-based, nonprofit social service agency in San Antonio, Texas providing parent education workshops in the schools for low-income Mexican-American families*

### Addison County Parent/Child Center — p. 455
*Comprehensive family support and education project in rural Vermont, targeting low-income families with special services for teen and at-risk parents*

### Aberdeen Preschool Project — p. 463
*Suburban and rural school-based program for disadvantaged families, offering Developmental Preschool for children with disabilities and Open Preschool for four- and five-year-olds, augmented by state ECEAP funds*

### Early Childhood Education and Assistance Program — p. 469
*Early intervention curriculum for low-income families with preschool children at risk for school failure in Seattle, Washington*

### Early Childhood Family Education — p. 475
*Citywide initiative in Duluth, Minnesota, serving low- to middle-income families with parent support and education classes, neighborhood centers, and intensive Family School*

# Birth to Three School Collaboration Program

| | | |
|---|---|---|
| Newsletter | Networking | Parenting/child development education |
| Warmline | Crisis intervention | Parent/couple support groups |
| Home visits | Informal counseling | Health/nutrition education |
| Child care | Parent-child joint activities | Teen parent panels in the schools |
| | | Community services info/referral |

**Contact:** Minalee Saks, Executive Director

**Address:** 3411-1 Willamette
Eugene, OR 97405
(503) 484-5316

**Established:** 1984, agency; 1988, Oregon Department of Education's Together for Children initiative

**Budget '88-'89:** Make Parenting a Pleasure, $20,000; Birth to Three for Teenage Parents Program, $36,324

**Sources:** Oregon Department of Education

**Size:** Make Parenting a Pleasure, 30 parents; Birth to Three for Teenage Parents Program, 56 parents

**Area Served:** Eugene and Springfield school districts

**Auspices:** Cooperative venture between Birth to Three, the schools, and the Oregon Department of Education

## Community

The Birth to Three School Collaboration Program serves Lane County, an area in the Willamette valley bordered on one side by mountains and on the other by the Pacific Ocean. Its School Collaboration Program works with the school districts of Eugene (population 105,000) and adjacent Springfield (population 40,000). Many residents of the Willamette valley work in the lumber industry or for the University of Oregon. There is a high incidence of poverty, social isolation, and unemployment.

## Philosophy and Goals

The Birth to Three School Collaboration Program aims to alleviate stresses on families that contribute to abuse, neglect, and future school failure, including low self-esteem, isolation, poor coping skills, lack of resources, poverty, lack of parenting skills, and resultant unrealistic expectations for themselves and their children.

## History and Origins

Birth to Three is a private, nonprofit organization that offers prevention and early intervention services to families with young children. It was one of three recipients of the state's Together for Children grant. The School Collaboration Program, funded by Together for Children, provides school-based services through Make Parenting a Pleasure, based on an earlier collaboration between Birth to Three and the Eugene Family YMCA, and through the Birth to Three for Teenage Parents Program, an expansion of an earlier teen program. The teen parents program is situated in an alternative high school and also offers outreach to teens who are no longer enrolled in school, providing emotional support and parent education on an individual or group basis.

| | |
|---|---|
| **Features** | **Make Parenting a Pleasure** consists of a 10-week series of parenting classes led by a salaried staff member, followed by a three-month support group led by a trained volunteer. Parenting classes offer information about normal child development, discipline, communication, and stress management. In addition, the program offers an exercise class to reduce tension, led by an instructor from the Eugene Family YMCA, child care during parenting and exercise classes, a follow-up support group led by a trained facilitator, individual counseling, crisis intervention, and referrals.

**Birth to Three for Teenage Parents Program** runs year-round and serves low-income parents under age 21, many of whom have inadequate parenting skills or were abused as children. The program provides a support network for teens, who receive high school credit for participating. Weekly meetings concentrate on self-esteem, communication skills, and parenting techniques. The emphasis is on adolescent issues, particularly education and career preparation. Individual attention to teens includes home visits, telephone contacts, informal counseling, and crisis intervention. Birth to Three distributes donated formula and baby clothes and offers child care on site, provided in collaboration with the Eugene and Springfield school districts. Both the teen parents program and Make Parenting a Pleasure use peer support as a mechanism for sustaining participants whose access to overburdened mental health services is limited. |
| **Participants** | Oregon's Together for Children initiative funds programs that serve the families of children from birth to age eight assessed as at risk for failure in school because of low income, parent illiteracy, poor health, and mental or emotional stress. Make Parenting a Pleasure targets low-income, high-risk populations in Eugene and Springfield and serves 5 percent of all eligible families, 18 percent teen parents, and 30 percent single parents. Participant records show that the majority have an annual income of less than $10,000. Birth to Three for Teenage Parents serves 15 percent of the eligible teen parents between the ages of 12 and 21, including single mothers, young married couples with children, low- and moderate-income families, teen parents enrolled in school, and those who have either completed school or dropped out; the majority live in poverty. |
| **Parent Education** | Make Parenting a Pleasure offers parent education through group discussions, parenting classes, home visits, and peer support groups. Birth to Three for Teenage Parents offers individualized parent education as well as group meetings that focus on health care, parent-child activities, parenting skills, and developing self-sufficiency. |
| **Curriculum** | Make Parenting a Pleasure uses *Make Parenting a Pleasure: A Program Guide and Curriculum for Parents Under Stress,* developed by Birth to Three's director, Minalee Saks, with help from program staff, local professionals, and parents. Birth to Three for Teenage Parents uses a combination of prepackaged and in-house materials, adapted to the needs of individual participants, including *Dynamics of Relationships: A Prevention Program for Teens and Young Adults,* by Patricia Kramer. |

**Sites**

Make Parenting a Pleasure has sites in two public elementary schools. Birth to Three for Teenage Parents shares a building with the Opportunity Center in Eugene, an alternative school program for pregnant and parenting teens. Parent educators also offer individual counseling in the teens' homes.

**Parent Involvement**

Parents serve on an advisory board that determines programming. Parents also help promote visibility and recruit participants for the School Collaboration Program and serve as volunteer leaders in peer support groups.

**Outreach**

Referrals come from the Eugene and Springfield public schools; the Boys and Girls Aid Society; Adult and Family Services; physicians; Special Supplemental Food Program for Women, Infants, and Children (WIC); community and mental health departments; and other local human service agencies. Birth to Three produces a community resources poster that is distributed to all new parents in the community through local hospitals. When it comes to recruiting teens, the program has found that teen parents can be reluctant to attend group meetings. Some prefer home visits, workshops, or special events. The director reports that it can sometimes take up to six months of work to bring a teen parent into the group.

**Staff**

| Job Title | PD | Vol | FT | PT | Educ Req | Status | Benefits |
|-----------|----|----|----|----|----------|--------|----------|
| Executive Director | 1 | - | - | 1 | Post-Graduate Courses or Degree | Other Contract | Yes |
| Assistant Director | 1 | - | - | 1 | Post-Graduate Courses or Degree | Hourly Non-Contract | Yes |
| Program Coordinators | 2 | - | - | 2 | Post-Graduate Courses or Degree | Hourly Non-Contract | Yes |
| Program Staff | 4 | 8 | - | 12 | College Degree | Hourly Non-Contract | Yes |
| Office Manager | 1 | - | - | 1 | College Degree | Hourly Non-Contract | Yes |

**State/District Requirements**

The program coordinator and staff members are required to have good communication skills, parenting experience, child development background, and training in group dynamics.

**Preferred Background**

Staff members should have a nonjudgmental attitude and knowledge of child abuse indicators and community resources; a master's degree is preferred.

**Employee Education and Training Represented**

Infant and toddler education; prekindergarten and early childhood education, elementary education; education, grades 7 to 12; parent educator; child care; psychology; counseling; family therapy; social work; child development and family studies; development and fundraising; research and evaluation.

**Administration**

Birth to Three contracts with Eugene School District 4-J and in Springfield works in the schools through a contract with the juvenile services department. In both settings, the program coordinator meets regularly with the school staff and principals. The executive director of Birth to Three meets with the school district superintendent. The School Collaboration Program reports to the Oregon Department of Education as part of the Together for Children early childhood initiative.

**Relationship to the Schools**

Birth to Three is a private, nonprofit agency. Both components of its School Collaboration Program report to the Oregon Department of Education. Make Parenting a Pleasure is a cooperative effort of Birth to Three, the Eugene and Springfield school districts, and the Eugene Family YMCA. The schools provide neighborhood meeting facilities, referrals, personnel resources, medical assistance, and a van. Birth to Three provides the 10-week parenting class and three months of support services, including group meetings run by a parent facilitator and leadership training to a volunteer who runs the follow-up support group. An advisory committee of administration, staff, and participants meets quarterly to monitor program services and budget and support outreach efforts through personal contacts. The Birth to Three for Teenage Parents Program has a cooperative arrangement with the alternative high school; students receive academic credit for participating. The teens involved in the program share their parenting experiences with home and family life classes throughout Lane County in the program's effort to educate students about the responsibilities of parenthood.

**Community Links**

Birth to Three networks actively with 50 other community groups and agencies. It makes cross-referrals and shares resources with the community health department, Adult and Family Services, the Children's Services Division, Family Services, local hospitals, Legal Aid, Womenspace, and the University of Oregon, among others.

*When it comes to recruiting teens, the program has found that teen parents can be reluctant to attend group meetings. Some prefer home visits, workshops, or special events. The director reports that it can sometimes take up to six months of work to bring a teen parent into the group.*

**Funding**

The School Collaboration Program is funded entirely through the Oregon Department of Education's Together for Children early education initiative.

**In-Kind Resources**

Space and facilities are provided by community centers, churches, school districts, and the YMCA; transportation services by the Springfield Park and Recreation Department and the Lane Transit District; consultation and staff development by other nonprofit organizations, businesses, hospitals, and local professionals; Planned Parenthood, Community Health Division, WIC, Adult and Family Services, local hospitals, Legal Aid, and other resources provide periodic direct service to program participants; volunteer staff is provided by the Springfield Parks and Recreation Department, the University of Oregon, and Portland State University; the Eugene Education Association provides administrative and clerical support; school districts, the YMCA, and other private agencies supply access to equipment; materials and supplies are provided through churches, private businesses, and service clubs.

**Funding History**

At the outset, prior to the School Collaboration Program, Make Parenting a Pleasure was financed for two years by grants from the Fred Meyer Charitable Trust and the Oregon Community Foundation. Other funding comes through the United Way, private foundations, and the Active 20/30 Club. The Birth to Three for Teenage Parents Program first received funds through the Junior League and Churchwomen United. Supporting funds also come from the Juvenile Services Commission and private and public donations.

**Objectives**

The program aims to reduce the risk factors associated with abuse and neglect, and to give parents the information and support necessary to enhance family life and ensure a brighter educational future for children. Birth to Three also provides the opportunity for early identification of abuse and neglect, substance abuse, health disorders, stress, and potential school failure. In addition, the Birth to Three for Teenage Parents Program aims to decrease the number of unplanned pregnancies and to encourage teen parents to return to school and complete their high school education.

**Evaluation**

The Oregon Department of Education plans to evaluate the School Collaboration Program.

**Replication**

There are two other Together for Children initiatives in the state, each unique in its style of service delivery.

**Materials Available**

The following manuals are available from Birth to Three: *Make Parenting a Pleasure: A Program Guide and Curriculum for Parents Under Stress; Parents Helping Parents: A Volunteer Manual for Parent Support Groups; Meeting the Teen Parent Crisis: A Program Model for Young Parent Groups; Understanding and Enjoying Your Toddler; From the Editor's Desk: Readings for Parents and Instructions on Newsletter Production;* and *Fundraising for Nonprofits.* The following book is also available: *Birth to Three: Educational Materials for New Parents.* To place an order, contact the program directly.

# Family Focus

## A Program of Crisis Intervention Services

*Sue, a single mother of four with a serious medical condition, was referred to Family Focus by her children's elementary school. When Sue first attended classes she admitted relying on threats to enforce discipline at home. She felt out of control and seemed grateful to attend parenting sessions. The outreach counselor provided additional services, obtained food when the family had none, and visited their home when Sue felt ill.*

| | | |
|---|---|---|
| Home visits | Adult literacy | Mother support groups |
| Hotline | Parent-child activities | Child care info/referral |
| Newsletter | Resource library | Health/nutrition education |
| ESL classes | Networking | Parenting/child development education |
| Child care | Parent support groups | Community services info/referral |

**Contact:** Catherine Fleshman, Executive Director

**Address:** P.O. Box 819
Medford, OR 97501
(503) 779-1111

**Established:** 1976, local initiative; state funding awarded 1988

**Budget '88-'89:** $66,000

**Sources:** State funds: Together for Children grant

**Size:** 301 families (260 children)

**Area Served:** Medford, Oregon

**Auspices:** Family Focus, a program of the umbrella agency, Crisis Intervention Services

## Community

Medford is one of the largest cities in southern Oregon. It is isolated from other metropolitan areas and surrounded by suburban and rural communities. Located on the I-5 highway corridor between Mexico and Canada, Medford has a large transient population of manual laborers. Employment for many is seasonal, and the overall yearly unemployment rate is high. The ethnic makeup of the community is 85 percent white, 7 percent Hispanic, and 8 percent Native American.

## Philosophy and Goals

Family Focus offers support, information, and alternative approaches to the understanding of parenting and child development. Participants develop improved parenting skills and confidence in their ability to use these skills. The program provides parents with alternatives and supports them in making appropriate choices for themselves and their families.

## History and Origins

Crisis Intervention Services is the umbrella agency for four human service programs: Family Focus, a child abuse prevention program; Dunn House, a shelter for battered women and their children; Rape Crisis, a sexual assault program; and Helpline, a 24-hour crisis, information, and referral line.

Prior to receiving the state Together for Children grant in 1988, Family Focus had been offering community involvement and parent support services for 12 years. The grant has allowed Family Focus to expand existing services, to evaluate and assess clients' parenting needs, and to offer home visits as a mechanism for providing support of long-term changes.

From the start, Family Focus had an on-going relationship with many schools in the community. Initial support came from cooperating community agencies, including the Children's Services Division, Adult and Family Services, a drug and alcohol program, a shelter for battered women, and a women's center.

Family Focus cosponsors six programs: parent education and support groups, Crossroads Teen Parenting Program, Master Parent Volunteer Program, Moms of Migrant Students (MOMS), and community workshops.

**Parent education and support groups** offer group meetings and home visits to parents of children from birth to age eight. Although services are available to all parents, the program targets parents of children at risk of school failure and high absenteeism, economically disadvantaged families, or those with a potential for child abuse or neglect. An outreach counselor assigned to at-risk families is available to make home visits to parents between group meetings to help reinforce the skills acquired in class. She is also a resource during times of stress.

The **Crossroads Teen Parenting Program** offers parenting and child development education to pregnant and parenting teens. The program takes a pragmatic approach to working with this population and constantly revises its curriculum on the basis of perceived needs. Group discussion and parent-child joint activities take precedence over more traditional didactic approaches to teaching. In addition to providing information about parenting skills and child development, the program increases the affective bond between parent and child, helps parents develop behavioral management skills by improving family management skills, and helps teen parents identify and develop strategies to meet their own needs. Attendance at the weekly one-hour classes held during alternative school hours is credited toward a high school diploma or Graduate Equivalency Diploma (GED).

The **Master Parent Volunteer Program** (offered by the Oregon State University Extension Service) trains volunteers to present parenting classes. The curriculum is based on the FOOTSTEPS program produced by the Institute for Child Study of the University of Maryland. Volunteers are given 25 hours of training and are asked to present parenting information either to groups of parents or to individuals.

**Mothers of Migrant Students (MOMS)** provides services to migrant Hispanic mothers through a contract with the Jackson Educational Service District's migrant education program. The curriculum is based on the experience of migrant teachers and a survey of the parenting skills and needs of Hispanic mothers. The curriculum consists of support and social networking to address the needs of isolated and frequently transient families. It focuses on parenting and living skills, English as a Second Language (ESL) classes, and children's programming. Generally, participants neither drive nor have access to cars; the program teaches the use of public transportation, a skill which reconnects participants to their community.

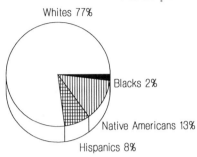

Whites 77%

Blacks 2%

Native Americans 13%

Hispanics 8%

In 1987-88, Family Focus served 285 mothers, 48 fathers, and 324 children, 68 percent of the eligible population. Twenty-one percent were single parents, and 21 percent teen parents; approximately 50 percent had an income under $10,000.

*Catherine Fleshman reported that, "there are core parenting issues or an agenda that each group brings with them. We try to identify these issues and address them."*

## Parent Education

Family Focus offers parenting classes and parent support groups during the entire year. The program's flexible format covers topics ranging from child development and communication to nonviolent behavior management and self-esteem. Modifications are continually made in response to the needs and parenting skills of participants, whose level of education and English proficiency vary considerably. Catherine Fleshman reported that "there are core parenting issues or an agenda that each group brings with them. We try to identify these issues and address them." The children's program runs concurrently with the adult classes and provides a parallel curriculum to facilitate effective changes in families.

## Curriculum

The program has adopted an "eclectic approach" to curriculum, using a variety of sources including: *Person to Person,* by John Taylor; *Children's Services Division Parent Education Manual; Systematic Training for Effective Parenting (STEP)* material; and *Self-Esteem: A Family Affair,* by Jean Clark. The curriculum is modified by the knowledge and experience of the staff to fit the needs of participants.

## Sites

Family Focus classes take place in four public schools, three churches, and one private agency. Parenting class sites are stable, but because parent support groups meet throughout the year, placement is more problematic. Public schools close for vacations and churches are beginning to charge fees for space, which increases program costs.

Since child care is offered during parenting classes, Family Focus requires at least two rooms for all parent meetings. The director explains that if 25 parents show up, as many as 75 children may come along as well.

## Parent Involvement

Parents serve on an advisory board that helps assess parent needs. They also participate in program evaluation and assist in topic selection and workshop planning.

## Outreach

Families are most likely to hear about the program from guidance counselors, newspaper and television announcements, other participants, and school notices. Following referral, an outreach counselor performs an intake evaluation in the home and familiarizes parents with support services. The program provides transportation to the education and support groups.

The Family Education Resource Network, a coalition of parent educators and local agency personnel, acts as an information network, encouraging clients to attend classes and support groups. Catherine Fleshman notes it is important to establish a strong network with other service provider agencies and to be prepared when outreach works. She emphasizes the importance of maintaining relationships with parents once you have reached them. Parents who have had previous contact with social service agencies experience some initial anxiety, which Family Focus allays by carefully building trust between participants and parent educators.

The program has a liberal and discrete sliding fee scale that allows all families to participate. At the beginning of each session parents receive an envelope on which they check off their fee. If they have money they put it in, if not they hand in an empty envelope. Payment is strictly confidential.

**Staff**

| Job Title | PD | Vol | FT | PT | Educ Req | Status | Benefits |
|---|---|---|---|---|---|---|---|
| Program Administrator | 1 | - | 1 | - | College Degree | Hourly Non-Contract | Yes |
| Program Coordinator | 1 | - | 1 | - | College Degree | Hourly Non-Contract | Yes |
| Family Services Coordinator | 1 | - | - | 1 | College Degree | Hourly Non-Contract | Yes |
| Parent Educators | 2 | - | - | 2 | College Degree | Hourly Contract | No |
| Children's Program Coordinator | 1 | - | 1 | - | College Degree | Hourly Non-Contract | Yes |
| Child Care Providers | 1 | 6 | - | 7 | High School Diploma | Other Contract | No |
| Group Facilitators | 1 | 5 | - | 6 | College Degree | Other Contract | No |
| Outreach Counselor | 1 | - | - | 1 | College Degree | Hourly Contract | No |
| Clerk Typist | 1 | - | - | 1 | Some High School | Hourly Non-Contract | Yes |

**State/District Requirements**

None.

**Preferred Background**

The majority of program staff members have a college degree. In addition, all personnel have experience working with abusive families and in group facilitation, child development, and stress and crisis management.

**Employee Education and Training Represented**

Infant and toddler education; prekindergarten and early childhood education; elementary education; education, grades 7 to 12; bilingual education; parent educator; child care; psychology; counseling; family therapy; social work; child development and family studies; development and fundraising; research and evaluation.

**Administration**

The Together for Children grant is administered entirely by the program manager of Family Focus, an arm of Crisis Intervention Services, a private, nonprofit social service agency that is independent of the public school system. Family Focus is the service provider for all services under the Together for Children grant, with the exception of the

Master Parent Volunteer Program of Oregon State University Extension Service and the MOMS program of the Educational Service District's migrant education program. Family Focus is monitored by the Oregon Department of Education. Crisis Intervention Services has a board of directors and Family Focus has its own advisory council.

## Relationship to the Schools

The director of Family Focus meets monthly with the migrant program coordinator to monitor and supervise service delivery and with school principals about referrals and the progress of the parent classes. Initially, Ms. Fleshman said, the schools cooperated with the design and goals of Family Focus because its main thrust was enhancing students' school performance by working with parents.

## Community Links

Collaboration with outside agencies serves as a source of referrals, as well as an opportunity to share resources, inservice training, and information. Given the limited financial resources for parent support programs, cooperation among the social service and parent education agencies is essential to avoid duplication and gaps in services.

## Funding

Oregon's Together for Children grant funds Family Focus entirely.

## In-Kind Resources

Space and facilities are provided by three churches, two schools, and two private agencies. Paid staff for service delivery is provided for the Master Parent Volunteer Program (home economist), the Crossroads Teen Parenting Program (director of the alternative school) and the MOMS program (coordinator for migrant education); the volunteer staff is provided by Crisis Intervention Services.

## Funding History

This is the first year Family Focus has operated under a Together for Children grant.

## Objectives

Family Focus hopes that parents will learn to communicate more effectively with their children, gain an understanding of the relationship between behavior and psychosocial development, and develop strategies for managing stress. To help children succeed in school and build interfamily support, the program tries to provide parents with a comfortable setting in which to share concerns and issues, to recognize and enhance the skills and strengths parents bring with them, and to emphasize the importance of reaching out to others to extend the fabric of social support.

## Evaluation

The program is in its first year of operation so evaluation is forthcoming.

## Replication

Family Focus is one of three Together for Children pilot sites in the state.

## Materials Available

*Together for Children Parent Training Curriculum,* from Family Focus.

# Together for Children

| | | |
|---|---|---|
| Home visits | Group meetings | Parenting/child development education |
| Toy lending | Child care info/referral | Developmental exams/screening |
| Resource library | Monthly newsletter | Community services info/referral |
| Networking | Parent-child joint activities | |

**Contact:** Lynette Patterson, Program Coordinator

**Address:** 520 NW Wall Street
Bend, OR 97701
(503) 388-1014

**Established:** 1988, state pilot project collaborating with the local school district

**Budget '88-'89:** $143,575

**Sources:** State government

**Size:** 125 parents

**Area Served:** Madras, Pineville, La Pine, Sisters, and Bend, Oregon

**Auspices:** Oregon Department of Education and Central Oregon Community College (COCC)

*A single mother with a two-year-old had left an abusive situation and moved into a place of her own where she had minimal sanitation, no phone and no transportation. TFC concentrated on the mother's efforts to improve her life, helping to identify and market her considerable secretarial skills. During home visits, the facilitator drove her to a pay phone, stayed with her child, and provided additional child care during job interviews.*

## Community

The tri-county area of Jefferson, Crook, and Deschutes lies east of the Cascade Mountains in central Oregon, isolated from the urban centers on the Pacific coast. The region's population is mostly white, with some Native American and Hispanic communities. Logging, cattle ranching, farming, and tourism are the main industries. Madras is a farming area with a large Native American population; Pineville and La Pine are both sparsely populated smaller communities; Sisters is a resort; and Bend is a sophisticated college town.

## Philosophy and Goals

Together for Children (TFC) aims to give children the best possible start in life by fostering parenting skills, helping parents understand more about child development, and maximizing the pleasures of parenting. Part of the TFC philosophy involves parents helping each other and sharing resources. Brita Gould, the program director, feels that "there are some aspects of parenting that everyone does well and can share. Very early on we verbalize to parents where their strengths lie. Then the family facilitator [a TFC staff member or parent educator] encourages parents to share their strengths with others."

## History and Origins

Together for Children is one of three pilot family support initiatives funded through the Oregon Department of Education. The Central Oregon Human Care Needs Assessment Study, completed in 1988, revealed that increasing numbers of children would soon be at risk of failure in school due to a series of factors, including: a growing school-age population with increasing numbers of disadvantaged minority students, a decrease in family incomes, an increase in unemployment and teen pregnancy, and a rise in reported child abuse. The study indicated a great need for parenting education among the parents of children birth to age three to prevent potential problems among children. Based on these findings, the state sent out a request for proposals. Representatives from the Central Oregon Parent Partnership, a coalition of agencies and individuals in the tri-county area, wrote one of three winning grant proposals. Carol Stiles, selected by the coalition as budget administrator of the grant, hired Brita Gould to coordinate the program.

The program director, Brita Gould, feels that it is important to determine the specific needs of a community before starting a program. She adds, "Become familiar with preexisting materials, look to the experts, don't reinvent the wheel. For example, Oregon State Extension and Central Oregon Community College had been teaching parent education and early child development; TFC used some of their materials as guides when designing the programs."

### Features

Offered during the nine-month school year, Together for Children emphasizes family education and enrichment. The program offers handouts, speakers, videos, parent support groups, and play groups for children that are designed to encourage social development.

Home visits occur monthly. Each TFC staff facilitator is responsible for three groups of six to seven families each, which meet twice a month for drop-in play groups. Once a month, classes and lectures are offered to all participants on topics requested by parents.

Parents meet in small groups to discuss age-specific problems and in larger groups to address parenting issues. Children under one year old stay with their parents during group meetings. Older children receive child care in a different setting. Guest speakers address parent groups on child development, parenting, and health care. Each month a calendar of planned events goes to participants. Time for socializing following lectures and presentations is an important component of TFC. In this informal atmosphere parents get acquainted and build alliances for mutual support.

### Participants

TFC serves normal and moderately at-risk families overlooked by social service and educational programs that target highly or borderline dysfunctional families. To participate, it is not necessary that every child and family be at risk, but 60 percent of the total participants must be at risk of possible school failure. Approximately 60 percent of the participants use TFC's services once a week and approximately 40 percent use them every two weeks. At the time the interview was conducted, the program had only been in operation a few months and had reached 125 of the 145 families targeted.

### Parent Education

During home visits, the facilitator looks for age-appropriate behavior and deviations from the norm (for example, the development of eye-hand coordination). If a child's development is delayed, the facilitator suggests guidelines and activities for parents, indicating things to watch for and ways to stimulate development. In group meetings, to complement speakers and lectures, the facilitator uses slides, videos, and written materials. Recent topics for the monthly groups have included discipline and setting limits. The program coordinator notes that discussion is lively.

Much of the learning is experiential and hands on. One facilitator uses picture books without words to teach language development and to encourage parents to do the same at home with their children. Parents role-play, dramatizing parent-child encounters. Facilitators also teach parents how to construct books using materials found in the home to create stories with their children.

442

## Curriculum

TFC uses several curricula. *Parents as Teachers: Missouri Model (PAT)* includes lesson plans and parenting materials covering developmental issues for the first 36 months of life; *FOOTSTEPS / Master Parenting* is a series of videotapes dramatizing parenting issues; *Stress Management Curriculum* and *Looking at Life,* from Head Start, focus on stress management. All materials are modified to meet participants' needs. Facilitators design their own presentations or call in specialists.

*"Become familiar with preexisting materials, look to the experts, don't reinvent the wheel."*

## Sites

Services are delivered at public elementary schools in five community education buildings (part of the COCC system), at a Head Start agency, and in participants' homes. Each community holds large group meetings at the same site every month, but small groups change locations. Play groups usually take place in preschools, elementary school classrooms, or churches. If sites are unavailable, participants meet in someone's home. Facilitators work out of their homes, keeping records, toys, and other materials in portable cases.

The Redmond Evergreen School houses the program's central office. The school shares some of its library materials and gives the program mailing and photocopying privileges. Two facilitators use the Head Start office in Bend as a message center, and as a place to store materials and have access to office equipment. Community education centers share their office space, take messages, allocate space for meetings, and share office equipment.

## Parent Involvement

Half of the advisory council is composed of parents, one of whom tracks the prevailing issues and needs of participating families. In this way, parents design their own curriculum. For example, when one group of parents of newborns expressed interest in infant massage as an alternative way of calming and touching babies, the facilitator found a masseur to demonstrate.

## Outreach

At the outset, TFC made presentations to educational districts to promote the program and increase visibility in the community. Outreach strategies TFC has found successful include: putting TFC brochures into "newborn" kits at the hospital, having facilitators address Lamaze classes, and alerting the professional community to TFC's services. In addition, the program utilizes public media channels, circulates posters, and gives talks to social service agencies, ministerial committees, and school faculties. In one school, teachers refer to the program during parent conferences. Head Start promoted the program in several newsletters mailed to parents. Parents in the program who have experienced dynamic changes in their families provide the best outreach. Typically, these parents will ask for pamphlets to bring to work or other activities. The main outreach strategy has been to build up the strengths of participants: they sell the program.

| Job Title | PD | Vol | FT | PT | Educ Req | Status | Benefits |
|---|---|---|---|---|---|---|---|
| Budget Administrator | - | 1 | - | 1 | College Degree | - | No |
| Program Coodinator | 1 | - | 1 | - | College Degree | Other Contract | Yes |
| Family Facilitators | 6 | - | 1 | 5 | Some College | Hourly Contract | Yes |
| Administrative Secretary | 1 | - | - | 1 | High School Diploma | Hourly Contract | Yes |

**State/District Requirements**

The program coordinator must have a bachelor's degree in early childhood education, child development, or a related area. The state requires that family facilitators have an associate's degree in early childhood education or child development or a Child Development Associate (CDA) certificate or equivalent educational background.

**Preferred Background**

Family facilitators should have effective communication skills, knowledge of child development, and an ability to teach adults with diverse backgrounds. The program director should have two years of experience as an administrator at a social service agency, school, or early childhood education program or similar agency; knowledge of fiscal management, administration, and personnel management; and an awareness of early childhood development.

**Employee Education and Training Represented**

Infant and toddler education; prekindergarten and early childhood education; elementary education; education, grades 7 to 12; bilingual education; special education; parent educator; social work; child development and family studies; development and fundraising; research and evaluation.

Every two months, facilitators have a curriculum day to review materials in the main office that are not available in their communities. The center's family facilitators conduct "minitraining" sessions to make the program's output consistent. Staff training focuses on speech and language development, the efficacy of home visits to empower or create dependency, recognition of different kinds of child abuse, and bonding and attachment.

**Administration**

When TFC started, a Head Start program was already administered through Central Oregon Community College (COCC). Dean William H. Lindeman of COCC agreed to participate in a similar arrangement with TFC. Together for Children has a complex administrative structure linking the Oregon Department of Education with Central Oregon Community College, which acts as the fiscal agent and receives 8 percent of the TFC budget for their indirect services. The program director reports to Randy Hitz, early childhood education specialist for the Oregon Department of Education, which is the grantor.

The administrative staff includes a budget administrator, Carol Stiles, who is director of Crook-Deschutes Head Start and who also helped develop the proposal for TFC. Although she is not paid by TFC, Ms. Stiles attends board meetings and goes to conferences for which TFC reimburses her. The rest of the staff members are salaried and include the program coordinator, six family facilitators, and an administrative secretary.

| Relationship to the Schools | School guidance counselors refer families to TFC and frequently speak at TFC events. In Madras, where TFC is working with teen mothers, the facilitator sees the school nurse almost daily. Nurses from the school and the health department speak about health and nutrition at TFC events and dispense health information to parents. Both nurses and counselors publicize the program in the schools. |
|---|---|
| | According to the program coordinator, schools in central Oregon like to have a lot of activities going on, since they are the primary community gathering place. The schools benefit from parent education because parents' increased self-esteem has a positive effect on children. |
| Community Links | TFC is part of the community college and belongs to the Central Oregon Parents Partnership. The advisory board has 14 members: the program coordinator, 7 parents, 2 elementary school guidance counselors, a special education instructor, a preschool director, a director of an alternative school, and a curriculum director from Bend schools. The board acts as a steering committee, establishes relationships with other agencies, and participates in fundraising and recruitment. |
| Funding | A grants-in-aid initiative of the Oregon Department of Education provides 100 percent of the funding. The original bill funded the program for one year. Senate Bill 780, passed in 1989, re-funded the program for two more years, with annual budget increases of 6 percent (cost of living) biannually. |
| In-Kind Resources | The Redmond School District provides space, facilities, consultation, and staff development; Head Start contributes paid staff for service delivery; periodic direct service to program participants comes from New West Educational Services, a nurse practitioner, and COCAAN; Head Start, community education, and the Redmond School District contribute equipment or access to equipment. |
| Funding History | Program has been in operation one year. |
| Objectives | TFC seeks to enhance the family's capacity to help itself. It expects parents will gain insight about strengths and new interests, meet other parents with similar needs, gain understanding of child development and normal pacing, and learn about community resources. If the program aids parents in these areas, Ms. Gould feels that children's needs will be met more frequently, resulting in school success. |
| Evaluation | Plans include an evaluation by families and facilitators. In turn, the advisory board will evaluate its own usefulness and the program coordinator will evaluate the facilitators. |
| Replication | One of three pilot sites for Together for Children, the program was adapted from a Parents as Teachers program at the Redmond School. |
| Materials Available | None. |

# Avancé Family Support and Education Program

| | | |
|---|---|---|
| Home visits | Center-based activities | Bilingual programming |
| Networking | Mother support groups | Parenting/child development education |
| Child care | Father support groups | Child care info/referral |
| Resource library | Individual counseling | Community services info/referral |
| Toy lending | Crisis intervention | Developmental exams/screening |
| GED services | Homemaker services | Medical care for children |
| Adult literacy | Health/nutrition education | Parent-child joint activities |

**Contact:** Gloria Rodriguez, Executive Director
Carmen Cortez, Associate Director

**Address:** 301 South Frio, Suite 310
San Antonio, TX 78207
(210) 270-4630

**Established:** 1973, joint initiative between individuals and a private foundation

**Budget '88-'89:** $992,826

**Sources:** Foundations, local city government, fundraising, in-kind contributions, state and federal government, private donations

**Size:** 1,318 children; 1,045 mothers; and 35 fathers

**Area Served:** San Antonio, Texas

**Auspices:** Avancé, a nonprofit agency

*At the end of the nine month program, the parents show an appreciable gain in knowledge and parenting skills. Hundreds continue their education (80% of them had dropped out of school); approximately sixty have gone on to pursue a college education. Other parents have obtained jobs, become leaders in the community and schools; many are proud to report that their children are on the honor roll and have received achievement awards.*

## Community

The city of San Antonio is divided into four sections and has approximately 800,000 residents. The affluent, mostly white population lives on the north side; a lower-income group (primarily Mexican-American and black) live on the east and west sides; the south side's population is middle-income Mexican-American. Five military bases provide employment for many of the south side's blue-collar workers. The nonskilled workers tend to have low-paying service jobs, a significant high school dropout rate, and early pregnancies and marriages. Avancé is situated in a low-income area of the city, characterized by high unemployment, underused social services, and crowded housing conditions.

## Philosophy and Goals

The goal of Avancé is to break the cycle of poverty for parents and children by strengthening the family. Avancé emphasizes both parents' personal development and the acquisition of specific parenting skills.

## History and Origins

In 1972, Ann Willig and Bonnie Park, graduate students at Cornell University under Dr. Urie Bronfenbrenner, received funding from the Zale Foundation to start an early childhood intervention program in Dallas, Texas that provided home visits, tutoring, and parent education. A second program, Avancé — San Antonio, Inc., was established in 1973 by Gloria G. Rodriguez as a private, nonprofit, community-based organization to serve local, predominantly low-income Hispanic mothers and children in the Mirasol Housing Project. The Avancé Dallas program dissolved in 1976.

The Parent-Child Education Program, a center-based service, is the core of all Avancé services, from which other complementary projects have evolved. One of those projects was the Community Workshops Program, a school-based effort to prevent adolescent pregnancy initiated in 1986 that was made possible through a special national demonstration project funded through the Coalition of Spanish Speaking Mental Health and Human Services Organizations (COSSMHHSO). The Avancé staff developed the Community Workshops Program at the elementary school level to work with parents of school-age children.

In 1987, Avancé initiated a fatherhood project with grants from the Mailman, Hasbro, and Hazen Foundations. Avancé has four centers in San Antonio funded by the city government and United Way. In 1988, Avancé replicated the comprehensive community-based model in Houston, Texas with a grant from the General Foods Fund, Inc.

**Features**

The core of Avancé is the **Parent-Child Education Program,** which familiarizes educators and parents with the basic social, emotional, physical, and cognitive needs of young children. The program offers weekly three-hour center-based activities and bimonthly home visits for nine months. Daily class capacity is approximately 15 mothers and up to 45 children. Transportation and child care (in a separate part of the building) are provided. The first hour of classes consists of bilingual lessons in child development, based on the Avancé parenting education curriculum. The second hour is a toy-making class, which focuses on learning through play. The third hour features outside speakers who represent community resources. Avancé also provides one-on-one counseling and makes social service referrals available to parents. Staff members videotape and observe parent-child play in the home; these tapes are discussed in the third hour of the center-based classes.

Children whose mothers attend Avancé's classes receive free lunch. Holiday celebrations and field trips are regular features of the program. Both parents and children, dressed in cap and gown, participate in graduation ceremonies at the local university.

**Avancé's Basic Literacy and Advanced Education Program** for parents who have completed the nine-month program, offers on-site classes for Graduate Equivalency Diploma (GED), English as a Second Language (ESL), and college classes and assists clients with job placement. Avancé brings the existing underutilized services to the parents in their community.

The **Homebound Parenting Education Program** for families with confirmed cases of abuse and neglect. Services include weekly home visits, individualized parenting classes, and social activities. After the families stabilize, they join the center-based program.

The **Community Workshops Program** includes school-based programs initiated by invitation from a school principal. Each class has between 10 and 15 parents; numbers are kept small to facilitate group discussions and maximize individual attention. Weekly two-hour classes are scheduled both in the mornings when parents drop children off and just before the end of the school day.

The **Avancé Hispanic Fatherhood Project** meets once a week for father support groups, as well as for field trips, films, and outings with their children and the whole family.

Avancé's Parent-Child Education Program serves approximately 100 mothers and their children at each center each month. The parent must have one child under the age of three years and be a community resident; both parent and child must participate. In 1987-88, 1,318 children, 1,045 mothers, and 35 fathers were served; of those participants, 56 percent were single parents and 3 percent were teens. There were 519 individuals who served in the Community Workshops Program.

**Participants**

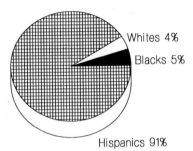

Whites 4%

Blacks 5%

Hispanics 91%

*"The best relationship has been for Avancé to be independent from the school; either to contract out with the school or for Avancé to find the funds and provide the needed services. Avancé has the experience and expertise in reaching parents, a proven curriculum, and can serve as the liaison between the school and the home."*

**Parent Education**

The Parent-Child Education Program acquaints parents with the cognitive and developmental needs of their children. Home visits stress stimulation of children's language development. The Community Workshops Program offers two kinds of classes: child development and child development plus toy making. Child development classes consist of group discussions around issues of discipline and children's behavior. In the toy-making classes, mothers learn to make toys and books from Avancé-designed materials. Parents are also encouraged to complete or continue their own academic education.

**Curriculum**

The Avancé parent education curriculum has gone through many revisions in 16 years. The associate director, Carmen P. Cortez, with input from the Avancé staff, is revising and enhancing the original curriculum written by Ann Willig and Gloria G. Rodriguez. Basic ideas are translated into the daily practical life situations of the target population. The curriculum stresses topics of urgent concern and interest to each group.

**Sites**

Avancé delivers its parenting programs in low-income federal housing projects, a vacant church building, a former daycare center, and a community center. All centers are located in the communities they serve. Community workshops are given at public elementary schools, medical facilities, mental health facilities, community agencies, public social service agencies, and housing projects. Other Avancé workshops take place in the centers. Mercedes Perez de Colon, the director of programs, noted that "one of the problems we have with the schools is space; some schools just don't have room for us." The other need is more monies to hire and train more staff members to respond to the requests for services.

**Parent Involvement**

Staff members actively seek parents' feedback to enhance the curriculum. Families participating in Avancé programs must contribute volunteer hours. Most of the employees are Avancé graduates who serve as bus drivers, cooks, home visitors, toy instructors, aides, and occasionally advance to center managers, teachers, research assistants, or coordinators of child abuse projects. Some are hired in the administrative offices as secretaries and accounting assistants. Avancé requires that all employees must have their high school diploma or GED and must agree to pursue college education. Two program participants serve on the board of directors.

**Outreach**

Most participants hear about the program by word-of-mouth from people in the community, through door-to-door recruitment by the staff, or over radio and television. Avancé submits flyers to schools, clinics, and community service agencies and puts posters in community businesses like neighborhood stores, laundromats, bakeries, and shopping malls. The schools publicize the community workshop by sending notes home with students. Principals set up bulletin boards that display toys and books made by Community Workshops Program participants to advertise the program to other parents. In addition, some teachers may telephone parents to tell them about the program. The workshops are listed in the local telephone directory under "Community Support for Children and Families" and in the local United Way directory.

**Staff**

| Job Title | PD | Vol | FT | PT | Educ Req | Status | Benefits |
|---|---|---|---|---|---|---|---|
| Executive Director | 1 | - | 1 | - | College Degree/ Post-Graduate Courses or Degree | Other Contract | Yes |
| Associate Director | 1 | - | 1 | - | College Degree/ Post-Graduate Courses or Degree | Other Contract | Yes |
| Director of Programs | 1 | - | 1 | - | College Degree/ Post-Graduate Courses or Degree | Other Contract | Yes |
| Program Coordinators | 2 | - | 2 | - | College Degree/ Post-Graduate Courses or Degree | Hourly Contract | Yes |
| Research Coordinator | 1 | - | 1 | - | College Degree/ Post-Graduate Courses or Degree | Other Contract | Yes |
| Comptroller | 1 | - | 1 | - | College Degree/ Post-Graduate Courses or Degree | Other Contract | Yes |

**Staff**
(continued)

| Job Title | PD | Vol | FT | PT | Educ Req | Status | Benefits |
|---|---|---|---|---|---|---|---|
| Child Development Teachers | 5 | - | 5 | - | College Degree/ Graduate Courses or Degree | Other Contract | Yes |
| Day Care Supervisors | 2 | - | 2 | - | Some College/ College Degree | Hourly Contract | Yes |
| Home Visitors | 7 | - | 7 | - | Some College/ College Degree | Hourly Contract | Yes |
| Field Interviewers | 5 | - | 3 | 2 | College Degree | Hourly Contract | Yes |
| Secretaries | 4 | - | 4 | - | High School Diploma | Hourly Contract | Yes |
| Day Care Aides | 6 | 6 | - | 12 | High School Diploma | Other Contract | Yes |
| Bus Drivers | 2 | - | 1 | 1 | Some High School | Other Contract | Yes |
| Toy Instructors | 2 | - | - | 2 | Some High School | Other Contract | Yes |
| Cooks | 2 | - | - | 2 | Some High School | Hourly Non-Contract | No |

**State/District Requirements**

None.

**Preferred Background**

Sensitive, caring individuals who are bilingual and knowledgeable about the culture and the community are preferred. A large percentage of the staff should be from the target community to provide participants with an opportunity to grow and be both a source of support and a role model for other parents. Professional staff members should have teaching experience and be knowledgeable about child growth and development.

**Employee Education and Training Represented**

Infant and toddler education; prekindergarten and early childhood education; elementary education; education, grades 7 to 12; bilingual education; special education; adult basic education; adult literacy; parent educator; child care; health and nutrition; home economics; social work; child development and family studies; development and fundraising; research and evaluation.

**Administration**

Avancé's programs are administrated primarily by the executive director, Gloria G. Rodriguez, who reports to the agency's board of directors. She also works cooperatively with associate director, Carmen P. Cortez, and the director of programs, Mercedes Perez de Colon, in the creation and implementation of programs. Avancé is also monitored by the city of San Antonio's Department of Human Resources, the United Way of San Antonio and Bexar County, and the Texas Department of Human Services. Up to 30 individuals can serve on the board of directors, which meets 11 times a year to set policies, approve the budget and program services, and fundraise.

**Relationship to the Schools**

According to Ms. Rodriguez, parents involved in the program have greater self-assurance, attend more parent-teacher association (PTA) meetings, and become people the schools can depend on. In turn, the schools have often been cooperative. Frequently, school principals provide refreshments and materials for the community workshops. Program coordinators and participating parents make presentations to the PTA to discuss the program and show the books and toys they've produced. Mrs. Perez de Colon commented, "We have good ties with these schools, and we were invited to come into them. We haven't experienced too many problems. Each school is different and has a social behavior all its own; we have to be aware of that. Some are outstanding in their commitment to parent involvement; others are just learning." Gloria G. Rodriguez states, "The best relationship has been for Avancé to be independent from the school; either to contract out with the school or for Avancé to find the funds and provide the needed services. Avancé has the experience and expertise in reaching parents, a proven curriculum, and can serve as the liaison between the school and the home."

## Community Links

Avancé has working relationships with many social service agencies and it also makes referrals. During the third hour of the weekly program, individuals from other agencies are invited to make presentations to supplement the Avancé curriculum. Speakers are also invited to come to the schools to address specific concerns.

## Funding

Foundations and private agencies, 54 percent; local government, 32 percent; federal, 10 percent; state, 4 percent; in-kind contributions, private donations, and special fundraising events further supplement the budget.

## In-Kind Resources

The city of San Antonio Housing Authority provides classroom and office space. Medical evaluations on the participating children are performed by nursing students from Incarnate Word College. The Region XX Education Service Center and St. Philips College provide ESL, GED, and college courses and various social service agencies provide workshops. The volunteer staff provides daycare; furniture, audio equipment, and other miscellaneous goods are contributed by CBM Business School and individuals; AT&T provided a parade float.

## Funding History

In 16 years, funding has increased from $50,000 to $1.2 million and is considered moderately secure. Avancé now has diversified its funding sources. In 1976, the Dallas program lost its funding, but San Antonio, under Ms. Rodriguez's direction, received money from the Texas welfare department to continue its center-based parent education and home visit components. Between 1974 and 1976, Avancé offered a two-year program with home visits and two hours a week of center-based parent education. In 1976, with additional support from the Zale Foundation and the Texas welfare department, the Avancé staff decided that a one-year, three-hour a week program was more efficient. The Zale Foundation provided additional support, and the budget was supplemented by the Texas welfare department. Between 1978 and 1980, the city of San Antonio provided matching funds to meet the welfare department's regulations. Welfare funds were withdrawn in 1980 and the city assumed responsibility for Avancé's parent education program. Since 1981, the United Way has substantially funded Avancé's activities, along with the city of San Antonio's general revenue funds. Avancé aggressively seeks foundation, corporate, and federal funding for new demonstration projects.

| Objectives | Parents will increase their knowledge of their young children's social, emotional, physical, and cognitive needs and will develop new attitudes and perceptions about their own roles. |

**Objectives**

Parents will increase their knowledge of their young children's social, emotional, physical, and cognitive needs and will develop new attitudes and perceptions about their own roles.

**Evaluation**

Avancé is evaluated annually by each of its main funders and also by those from whom it has received special demonstration grants (COSSMHHSO, Parent-Teen, Levi Strauss, and the Texas Department of Human Services). The programs are assessed for the achievement of articulated objectives and the fulfillment of parents' perceived needs. In 1979, Avancé was evaluated by Project CAN Prevent and in 1987 received a $750,000 grant from the Carnegie Corporation of New York to evaluate the program.

**Replication**

In 1979, the program was replicated in a different part of San Antonio. In 1983, Avancé provided technical assistance and help in curriculum development to the Texas Migrant Council in Laredo, Texas, and in 1988, the program was replicated in Houston, Texas.

**Materials Available**

Videotapes presenting an overview of the Avancé services and various publications are available at the cost of reproduction and shipping. The curriculum is presently being revised and will be available in the near future.

# Addison County Parent/Child Center

*A mother of four who endured the sporadic, abusive visits of her alcoholic husband joined Intensive Parent Training. Threatened by group interaction, she spent weeks working silently at tasks around the Center. Gradually, she gained the confidence to forbid her husband's visits, move to a new home and obtain counseling for her children. When she decided to go back to school, the Center helped her find child care and offered tuition assistance.*

| | | |
|---|---|---|
| Newsletter | Respite child care | Drop-in-center activities |
| Networking | Health/nutrition education | Parent-child joint activities |
| Home visits | Individual counseling | Medical care/referral for children |
| Transportation | Social opportunities | Community services info/referral |
| GED services | Vocational activities | Weekly fee-based parent education |
| Warmline | Crisis intervention | Mother/father/couple support groups |
| Hotline | Drop-in center | Developmental exams/screening |
| Child care | Resource library | Parenting/child development education |
| Driver training | Adult literacy | Child care info/referral |

**Contact:** Howard Russel and Susan Harding, Codirectors

**Address:** P.O. Box 646
Middlebury, VT 05753
(802) 388-3171

**Established:** 1980, local initiative

**Budget '88-'89:** $500,000

**Sources:** State, federal, county government, client fees, memberships, foundations, local school district, religious contributions

**Size:** 1,600 families

**Area served:** Addison County, Vermont

**Auspices:** Partnership between schools and health and human services

**1990 Respondent:** Cheryl Mitchell, Codirector

## Community

Addison County is a sprawling rural area composed of 23 small towns in west central Vermont. Sparsely populated, the county is home to 32,000 people; the largest town has a population of 6,000. The area's major occupations have traditionally been agriculture and logging, but both industries have declined in the past seven years, resulting in the displacement of many families who have lost their small farms. The area's dropout rate is above the national average, as is that of the entire state. A vocational program associated with the school district is meant to encourage students to stay in high school, but many drop out in the ninth and tenth grades before they are eligible for vocational education. Adolescent pregnancy has declined in the 10 years since the Addison County Parent/Child Center opened; fewer parents are married, however, and the area has a large number of young single-parent families struggling to make a living.

## Philosophy and Goals

The center provides opportunities for parents to experience success in the belief that helping people feel good about themselves empowers them to develop gratifying and independent lives. Whether it is a task as simple as volunteering at the center or as difficult as completing a high school education, the center bolsters parent education with activities that allow parents to develop self-confidence and pride.

## History and Origins

The Addison County Parent/Child Center grew out of a community committee in 1979. A group of parents and representatives of health and human service agencies in the county sat down to look at the concerns of young families related to abuse and neglect, adolescent pregnancy, and parenting issues. They determined that Addison County needed a broad-based program to serve the entire county with home visits, infant daycare, and a preschool learning lab. The original funding came from the Turrell Foundation, which funds programs in Vermont and New Jersey. The center started out in donated space in a church and health center. In 1980, with a grant of $500,000 ($150,000 a year for five years) from the federal Office of Adolescent Pregnancy, the center expanded its services to teen parents. The program now provides a comprehensive set of services (including child care, parent education, counseling, screening, special education, and referral) to teen parents, at-risk parents, abusive families, and other families in the community, with funding from more than 20 federal, state, and local sources.

In 1982, at the request of teen parents in the program, the Addison County Parent/Child Center began a partnership with the school system to provide preventive services to junior and senior high school students. Teen participants go into schools as speakers and panelists to tell their peers what parenting is like and to encourage them to delay pregnancy until they have completed high school. The center now runs annual series of family life education classes and the Alternatives for Teens program to provide social activities and peer support to teens in junior and senior high school.

*Cheryl Mitchell notes that the strongest influence the center has had on the school system is in the area of special education services. She says the center's Developmental Child Care Program provides a model for the schools to move toward mainstream programming in the early grades.*

Features

The Addison County Parent/Child Center provides a wide battery of services, some open to all parents and some targeted to specific groups of families.

The **Learning Together Intensive Parent Training Program** serves targeted families with six months of daily classes in parenting and communication. Families receive home visits and their children receive preference for placement in developmental child care. Participants earn a small stipend to encourage them to complete the program.

The **Adolescent Pregnancy Program** targets pregnant and parenting teens from ages 11 to 21. Teens receive preference for participation in the Learning Together Intensive Parent Training Program and receive support services, counseling, home visits, prenatal care, labor and delivery support, and extensive vocational education opportunities.

The **Developmental Child Care Program** serves infants and handicapped children from birth to age six.

The **Early Education Initiative** is a partnership with one of the schools in the county to provide services to children ages three to five who require mild special education services but do not qualify for special education. Children receive attention through home visits or through participation in a neighborhood play group or receive indirect service in the form of tuition assistance to local preschools. The center also acts as an advocate for these children and for handicapped children in the Developmental Child Care Program during their transition to school.

**Play groups** in nine different towns serve parents and their children birth to age six.

The **Family Life Education Program** provides two weeks of classes per year to adolescents in 11 schools, with concurrent seminars for parents.

The **Alternatives for Teens Program** arranges drug- and alcohol-free events in 11 participating schools. The program is run by teens and a center facilitator who meet for planning, leadership training, and peer support.

**Daycare home training** provides on-site training to daycare providers in the county.

In general, the center gives priority to teen parents and their families, families of handicapped children, violent and disturbed families, and families at risk for other reasons (e.g., low-income and single-parent families). The Intensive Parent Training Program can serve 25 families at a time, and the Developmental Child Care Program can serve 45 children. There are always waiting lists of infants and handicapped children for daycare and parents who need intensive training. The play groups serve from 8 to 50 families each. The Adolescent Pregnancy Program serves over 300 teens per year, or 98 percent of those eligible who want services. Alternatives for Teens includes 130 teens in 11 junior and senior high schools. Fee-based parent education classes reach 600 families each year. Family Life Education Program classes reach 800 students and 200 parents. Altogether, the center provides services to 1,600 families per year.

## Participants

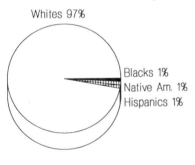

Whites 97%

Blacks 1%
Native Am. 1%
Hispanics 1%

## Parent Education

Much of the parent education offered at the center is hands-on. Teen parents and the parents in intensive training work, often with their own children, in the developmental child care unit, which doubles as a learning lab. Staff members teach effective parenting methods by modeling and meeting in discussion groups and in supervised parent-child activities. Parents who receive home visits similarly learn from the modeling of parent educators and from discussion. Parents of handicapped children receive special guidance in their legal rights regarding their children's education.

## Curriculum

The Addison County Parent/Child Center uses sets of materials developed in house for each component.

Most of the center's services take place either in the homes of participants or at the center's free-standing facility, a huge house built in 1988 with the proceeds of a capital-fund drive and a matching community block grant. Neighborhood play groups take place in two elementary schools, three churches, two town halls, and a public library. Family Life Education Program classes are offered at 11 area public schools. The school system's vocational center gives the Addison County Parent/Child Center space to pursue projects for young fathers. Some early education initiative services are delivered at the Family Center, a school site comanaged by the school district and the center.

The center owns two vans and has two licensed driver-mechanics to bring participants in isolated areas to the center; staff members and parent volunteers also help transport families when necessary. The center provides driver education to participants when appropriate and teaches parents to utilize public transportation.

*Ms. Mitchell sees a high degree of cooperation among county services and notes that the Family Support Team inspires the social service community to adapt its delivery system. "Changes and improvements get made on behalf of a particular family."*

A crucial component of participation in the Addison County Parent/Child Center is the development of self-esteem, confidence, and communication skills. To this end, parents are put to work as volunteers in all areas of the center: working in the daycare center, doing clerical work in the office, and improving the center facility. In the Parent Aide Program, parents help each other work on communication skills and prepare for the Graduate Equivalency Diploma (GED). Parents teach workshops, lead support groups, and run vocational projects. They serve on the volunteer board of directors which makes hiring, budgetary, and programming decisions. Parents are the major source of feedback and evaluation for the center's staff.

Families may hear about the center through its publicity efforts, such as newspaper coverage, but are most often attracted by positive reports from family and friends. Ms. Mitchell believes the play groups in nine communities are a good opportunity for parents to "check out" the program without commitment and then come forward for further services on their own. The schools, the health and welfare departments, the Social and Rehabilitation Services Department, the county's adult education program, and local employers are sources of referral to the program. The center actively recruits families with handicapped infants or toddlers and pregnant and parenting teens. The center staff members feel they are reaching everyone in the community they should but not at the level of intensity they would like.

| Job Title | PD | Vol | FT | PT | Educ Req | Status | Benefits |
|---|---|---|---|---|---|---|---|
| Caregiver/ Educators | 5 | - | 4 | 1 | College Degree | Other Contract | Yes |
| Outreach Workers | 5 | 6 | 2 | 9 | College Degree | Other Contract | Yes |
| Nurses | 3 | - | 1 | 2 | College Degree | Other Contract | Yes |
| Child Care Aides | 2 | 20 | 1 | 21 | High School Diploma | Other Contract | Yes |
| Van Driver/ Mechanics | 2 | - | 1 | 1 | Some High School | Other Contract | Yes |
| Administrators | 4 | 2 | 3 | 3 | High School Diploma, Some College, or College Degree | Other Contract | Yes |
| Alternatives Coordinators | 1 | 6 | - | 7 | College Degree | Other Contract | Yes |
| Education and Support Group Leaders | 1 | 20 | 1 | 20 | Some College | Other Contract | Yes |
| House Mothers | 1 | 2 | - | 3 | College Degree | Other Contract | Yes |

**State/District Requirements**

Vermont has no training or certification requirements for staff members of the Addison County Parent/Child Center.

**Preferred Background**

Staff members should have an appropriate educational background, parenting experience, joyousness, drive, flexibility, resourcefulness, and cars that work.

**Employee Education and Training Represented**

Infant and toddler education; prekindergarten and early childhood education; elementary education; education, grades 7 to 12; special education; adult basic education; parent educator; adult vocational education; child care; medicine; health and nutrition; home economics; nursing; speech therapy; psychology; counseling; family therapy; social work; child development and family studies; development and fundraising.

**Administration**

Codirectors Ms. Mitchell and Ms. Harding report to a volunteer board of directors composed of three program participants, plus representatives of the public schools, public and private agencies, and the community. The board has decision-making powers with respect to staff hiring, budget, and program services. The board provides the community with a voice in the center's activities and is also responsible for fundraising and community support.

**Relationship to the Schools**

The Addison County Parent/Child Center has written service agreements with the schools to guide their cooperative efforts; center and district personnel meet annually and update their agreements every other year. They have further contact at meetings of the Addison County Children's Task Force. The center's staff members teach family life education classes and lead Alternatives for Teens. At the school they maintain personal contacts by conferring with guidance counselors, special education staff members, science teachers, and home economics teachers. Occasionally, the schools allow teens to bring their children on the bus to the high school near the center (with permission from the subcontracted bus companies), and the vocational center provided much needed space when the center was overcrowded in its old building.

Cheryl Mitchell notes that the strongest influence the center has had on the school system is in the area of special education services. She says the center's Developmental Child Care Program provides a model for the schools to move toward mainstream programming in the early grades. Also, the schools have increased parent involvement in planning the education of special students. Previously, parents were not consulted when the school developed Individual Education Plans (IEPs) but were merely invited to the school "to sign on the dotted line." Now, since the center works with many of these families in the Developmental Child Care Program, the center's staff acts as their advocate, going to the IEP consultations with parents to get them more involved.

## Community Links

The center's strongest link with the community is its seat on the Addison County Children's Task Force, which is made up of representatives of county agencies, the schools, churches, community groups, and businesses, and performs a community needs assessment every spring. The center has written service agreements with most of these agencies that outline referral exchanges, shared inservice training, and shared testing or screening services. A similar group, the Family Support Team, invites parents to its meetings to put forward their particular problems in obtaining services, which are then solved cooperatively among the agencies and organizations present. Ms. Mitchell sees a high degree of cooperation among county services and notes that the Family Support Team inspires the social service community to adapt its delivery system. "Changes and improvements get made on behalf of a particular family."

The center relies on the Vermont Department of Employment and Training to provide counseling and job training to participants. The health department monitors the center's records, and the mental health department provides billing, administrative, and supervisory support.

## Funding

State government, 30 percent (Departments of Education, Health, Social and Rehabilitation Services, Drug and Alcohol Abuse, Agriculture, Transportation, and Social Welfare); client fees, 30 percent; federal government, 15 percent (Department of Health and Human Services); foundations, 10 percent; county government, 10 percent; local school district, 2 percent; religious contributions, 2 percent; memberships, 1 percent.

## In-Kind Resources

Space for play groups from schools, churches, town halls, and libraries; crossover staff from Foster Grandparents, Senior Community Service Employment Program, Community Work Experience Program, On the Job Training, and the Retired Senior Volunteer Program (RSVP); staff development at the University of Vermont; services from the health department, adult education, mental health, and community volunteers; volunteers from colleges and high schools; clerical support from United Way, businesses, RSVP, Work Study, and the chamber of commerce; and supplies from various businesses.

**Funding History**

In 1987, when the five years of federal funding from the Office of Adolescent Pregnancy expired, support from parents in Addison County and in other counties that have replicated the Addison County Parent/Child Center, encouraged the Vermont legislature to make parent-child centers line items in the state budget.

**Objectives**

The center aims to increase parents' knowledge of child care, parenting skills, and personal and child health; to bolster self-esteem and self-perception; to help participants develop communication skills and improve relationships; to encourage parents to complete or continue their education; and to reduce teen pregnancy, child abuse, and dependence on state and federal aid.

**Evaluation**

Since 1983, a professor at the University of Vermont has conducted annual longitudinal evaluations of the center. Findings show that as a direct result of the program's work, significant progress has been made in the prevention of adolescent pregnancy, repeat pregnancy, low birth weight, infant mortality, child abuse, and family violence. The center is committed to having an annual external evaluation whether or not the program receives special funding for this purpose. Ms. Mitchell believes the University of Vermont study was a decisive factor in the state's decision to provide line-item funding for parent-child centers.

**Replication**

The positive results of the University of Vermont's evaluation have led to the replication of the Addison County Parent/Child Center, or aspects of its services, in every county in Vermont.

**Materials Available**

*Life Skills for Teens,* a group leader's guide to alternatives for teens published by the Addison County Parent/Child Center is available for $15. Send prepaid orders to the attention of Irma McCreary. Add $2 postage and handling for the first book and $.75 for each additional book. Vermont residents, add 4 percent tax. The center can provide technical assistance and in 1989 hosted its first summer institute to train professionals to replicate the center's program.

# Aberdeen Preschool Project

Preschool
Newsletter
Networking
Resource library
Home visits
Adult literacy

Medical care for children
Parent education
Parent support groups
Transition services
Kindergarten
Individual counseling

Developmental exams/screening
Kindergarten screening
Health/nutrition education
Special needs summer session
Parenting/child development education
Parent-child joint activities
Community services info/referral

**Contact:** Dr. Paula Akerlund
Educational Assistance Coordinator

**Address:** Aberdeen School District No. 5
216 North G Street
Aberdeen, WA 98520
(206) 538-2000

**Established:** 1973, local initiative with state Early Childhood Education Assistance Program (ECEAP) components

**Budget '88-'89:** Total, $635,600; Open Preschool, $102,000; ECEAP, $148,400; Developmental Preschool, $385,200

**Sources:** Federal, state, and local funding

**Size:** 298 children, 296 mothers, and 150 fathers

**Area Served:** Grays Harbor County, Washington

**Auspices:** Aberdeen School District, Department of Pupil Services

*One mother whose child quali-fied for an ECEAP slot in the Open Preschool was refereed by the Parent Options Program staff to adult literacy classes. She improved her literacy skills and wanted to attend the com-munity college but remained too unsure of herself to enroll alone. The home educator accompa-nied her on her first visits to the college, talked to the counselor about appropriate courses and helped to secure financial aid for her studies. Today, this mother serves on the program's policy council.*

## Community

Aberdeen, on the southwest coast of Washington, has a population of 17,000. This economically depressed area is supported by the highly unstable fishing and lumber industries. The area has many low-income families and high rates of unemployment, alcoholism, teen pregnancy, and child abuse.

## Philosophy and Goals

The Aberdeen Preschool Project is geared to the development of healthy, motivated students. Both the preschool and the parent program support, empower, and collaborate with families in an effort to foster the cognitive, social, and physical growth of children.

## History and Origins

The Aberdeen School District has offered early childhood programs through its Department of Pupil Services since 1973. Current programs include a developmental preschool, which offers early intervention services and education for disabled children from birth to age six, and since 1986, an open preschool for all four- and five-year-olds in the district, which began in response to literature that encouraged early intervention for at-risk families. Both programs incorporate the Parent Options Program, which encourages parent involvement and education. The two preschool programs share activities twice a week in an effort to integrate or "blend" students. Since 1988, the state's Early Childhood Education and Assistance Program (ECEAP), which is modeled on Head Start and targets at-risk children of low-income families, has funded 54 slots in the Open Preschool. ECEAP also entitles families to participate in the Parent Options Program. The Aberdeen School District invited Head Start to participate in the planning and implementation phases of program development for the Open Preschool.

The **Developmental Preschool** uses an interdisciplinary approach for children who are at risk for delayed development, including sensory, physical, vision, speech, hearing, and language impairments, and emotional difficulties. Infants and their families are served primarily through weekly home visits from a teacher and a developmental therapist. Toddlers and prekindergartners come to a center-based classroom three or four days a week for 2-hour sessions and receive monthly home visits. Services include physical and occupational therapy, speech and language therapy, and audiology. Evaluations of children suspected of having developmental delays are carried out through the Grays Harbor Pupil Services Cooperative Assessment Clinic. Assessment, recommendations for services, placement, and an individualized educational plan are developed with parents.

The **Open Preschool** offers an individualized program for normally developing children.

The **Parent Options Program** includes three monthly home visits by trained home educators, a monthly home or school visit with the child's preschool teacher, opportunities to observe or volunteer in the classroom, informational or training meetings, and referrals to Project Even Start for literacy and basic skills training.

The district encourages interaction between the two groups of children through structured and spontaneous play. Twice a week for 30-minute sessions, children from both preschool initiatives come together to share materials and play. In addition, Aberdeen operates one integrated preschool classroom for a mixed group of "typical" children and those with developmental delays. For this class, children with special needs receive support services from itinerant specialists.

*The director feels the program has sensitized the school staff to the complex needs of families and to the need to act in part as social workers, reaching out to parents to encourage their involvement. Elementary school teachers have started doing home visits and networking for families who are in need of community services.*

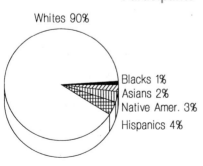

Whites 90%

Blacks 1%
Asians 2%
Native Amer. 3%
Hispanics 4%

Aberdeen Preschool Project serves families with children birth to age six who live in Grays Harbor County. Children attending the Developmental Preschool have handicapping conditions as defined by Public Law 94-142, including physical handicaps, chronic illness, mental illness, prematurity, and developmental delays. Families qualify for ECEAP preschool scholarships by meeting federally established poverty-level income guidelines. The overall population served is mixed income with many low-income families and is largely white; 75 percent are single parents and 2 percent are teen parents. From 1987-88, the program served 298 children, 296 mothers, and 150 fathers, an estimated 100 percent of the eligible population.

**Parent Education**

The Parent Options Program offers education and support to parents, encourages parent involvement, and makes referrals to social service agencies and adult literacy programs. Parents of developmentally delayed children receive special guidance in formulating an Individualized Education Plan (IEP) with the school district for their children.

**Curriculum**

The curriculum is eclectic and incorporates materials provided by the High/Scope Foundation with elements of parent education programs such as *Systematic Training for Effective Parenting (STEP)* and *Responsive Parenting*. Established developmental theory guides the individualized education program for each child. Classroom activities combine structured and unstructured play, stories, sharing, fine and gross motor activities, art, and music. Activities are designed to facilitate cognitive, language, social, emotional, fine and gross motor development, as well as self-help skills.

**Sites**

The preschool program uses nine classrooms in three public elementary schools, offering morning and afternoon sessions. Aberdeen preschool teachers are certified and therefore entitled to classroom space, and the school system provides the program consistent commitment.

**Parent Involvement**

Parents were involved in the program's initial planning committees and the Parent Options Program remains flexible and responsive to parents' suggestions. ECEAP has a formal policy council that includes parents of participating children.

**Outreach**

The Early Childhood Interagency Planning and Advisory Council, composed of representatives of agencies that serve families, distributes information about the program. Radio, television, and newspapers are also used for publicity.

**Staff**

| Job Title | PD | Vol | FT | PT | Educ Req | Status | Benefits |
|-----------|----|----|----|----|----------|--------|----------|
| Coordinator | 1 | - | 1 | - | College Degree | K-12 Contract | Yes |
| Teachers | 13 | - | 10 | 3 | Some College | K-12 Contract | Yes |
| Teaching Assistants | 10 | - | 10 | - | High School Diploma | Other Contract | Yes |
| Home Educators | 3 | - | 3 | - | Some College | Other Contract | Yes |

**State/District Requirements**

For teachers, certification in early childhood elementary education and/or special education and training and/or experience in early childhood education; for home educators, an associate's degree in human services and two years' experience or a bachelor's degree in adult education or development, social work, or psychology and one year of practical experience.

**Preferred Background**

Teachers and home educators must have the ability to work with families and perform as a part of a multidisciplinary team.

Infant and toddler education; prekindergarten and early childhood education; elementary education; education, grades 7 to 12; special education; adult basic education; adult literacy; parent educator; health and nutrition; nursing; occupational and physical therapy; speech therapy; psychology; counseling; child development and family studies; research and evaluation.

On Friday mornings, staff members share information, discuss issues, and make programmatic plans. Inservice training focuses on building a spirit of teamwork and joint decision making among staff members.

## Administration

The Aberdeen Preschool Project is administered within the Aberdeen School District through the Department of Pupil Services. The project director reports to the Aberdeen superintendent of schools. The district manages Grays Harbor Pupil Services Cooperative, which in turn runs the developmental preschool. An advisory board for the overall program meets monthly and is composed of representatives from the ECEAP Policy Council, the Aberdeen School District, and members of the staff. The Aberdeen School Board oversees hiring, budget, program services, recruitment, and fundraising. The Office of the Superintendent of Public Instruction, the Washington State Department of Community Development, and Educational Service District 113 all monitor the program.

## Relationship to the Schools

Families involved with the Aberdeen Preschool Project have access to all available services in the schools, including the school psychologists, communication disorders specialists, an audiologist, occupational and physical therapists, a special education nurse, and the teachers, staff members, and administrators. The boundaries between the preschool project and the elementary school are flexible; preschool children can visit the kindergarten class, children in grades 3 through 6 help out in the preschool.

Teachers are considered part of the school staff. The district central office coordinates scheduling and acts as a liaison with building principals. The director feels the program has sensitized the school staff to the complex needs of families and to the need to act in part as social workers, reaching out to parents to encourage their involvement. Elementary school teachers have started doing home visits and networking for families who are in need of community services.

## Community Links

The district staff designed the program to link parents to education, health, social service, and community agencies, community preschools, daycare providers, Head Start, and the local community college. The Early Childhood Interagency Planning and Advisory Council meets monthly to share information, make referrals, and coordinate services. The Aberdeen project subcontracts with the Coastal Community Action Council to provide the staff, consultation services, transportation, and screening services for the parent involvement and social services component of ECEAP. Other cooperating public agencies include Grays Harbor Pupil Services Cooperative, which provides the Developmental Preschool, and Grays Harbor County Health Department, which offers on- and off-site medical care.

| | |
|---|---|
| **Funding** | State government (ECEAP and Handicapped Excess Cost Funding), 85.74 percent; federal government (special education preschool grants), 8.83 percent; local school district funds, 5.43 percent. |
| **In-Kind Resources** | The Aberdeen School District provides space and facilities; other resources such as paid staff for service delivery, transportation services, consultation and staff development, periodic direct service to program participants, administrative and clerical support, and materials and supplies are provided by a combination of sources including the Aberdeen School District, the Coastal Community Action Council, the Grays Harbor Pupil Services Cooperative, and the Grays Harbor County Health Department. |
| **Funding History** | Funding has increased by 20 percent since the first year of operation. ECEAP funds will continue through 1991. |
| **Objectives** | The Developmental Preschool provides educational intervention to any child who is at risk for delayed development. It supports families by building on their strengths to promote self-esteem and achievement for all children. Aberdeen Open Preschool and ECEAP offer children the opportunity to participate in an integrated program of classroom and home-based experiences in which teachers and parents collaborate to provide the experiences that are necessary for future success in school. Children gain familiarity with school personnel, facilities, and activities, and those with special needs have immediate access to professionally trained staff members. Parents become involved in positive relationships with school staff members. The program strengthens and supports families as parents become partners in the educational process. |
| **Evaluation** | All aspects of the Developmental Preschool were monitored for compliance with state and federal laws governing the education of handicapped children. ECEAP is evaluated in compliance with the Office of the Superintendent of Public Instruction and the Washington State Department of Community Development guidelines. Internally, the project seeks an objective assessment of its effects and is using a locally designed research model to conduct a longitudinal study of children who participated in the first Open Preschool classes. The study uses standardized instruments to measure children's performance in areas of cognitive and social development. Parent reactions are culled from informal reports by parents and formal surveys. |
| **Replication** | The Aberdeen Preschool Project is unique, although the ECEAP component is a statewide initiative. |
| **Materials Available** | None. |

# Early Childhood Education and Assistance Program

A very talented single mother with three sons—ranging in age from four to eleven—came from a dysfunctional family and was close to suicide. Throughout her deep depression, she continued to receive home visits and became increasingly involved with programs at ECEAP. Now she contributes to the policy board, volunteers in the classroom, and has started her college education with support from a grant. During her two-year involvement with ECEAP, she came to recognize each of her sons and herself as an individual with unique needs.

**Contact:**  Barbara Brauer, Director

**Address:**  200 South Dayton Avenue
Kennewick, WA 99336
(509) 736-2286

**Established:**  1988, state initiative

**Budget '88-'89:**  $203,230

**Sources:**  Local school district funds; state government

**Size:**  52 families

**Area Served:**  Benton County, Washington

**Auspices:**  Kennewick School System and Washington Department of Education

## Community

Kennewick, Pasco, and Richland comprise a tri-city area surrounded by rural farming country in Benton County in southeastern Washington. Kennewick's population of 30,000 includes a select scientific community affiliated with the Hanford Atomic Reservation, as well as farmers and migrant agricultural workers employed by the local food processing industries. In the tri-city area, 27 percent of the population is minority.

## Philosophy and Goals

The Early Childhood Education and Assistance Program (ECEAP) is an early intervention initiative that focuses on the whole family. It operates on the premise that all young children need socializing experiences and that children at risk for failure in school require a comprehensive developmental preschool curriculum. ECEAP legislation mandates adult education and is philosophically committed to helping low-income parents become self-sufficient and proactive.

## History and Origins

In 1985, the Washington Department of Community Development and a 30-member advisory board comprised of early childhood experts developed ECEAP, which was funded for $2.97 million through the governor's Early Childhood Assistance Act. In its first year, ECEAP successfully served over 1,000 children; the 1987 legislature increased the budget to $12.1 million which allowed the statewide program to serve 4,000 children.

In 1987, a modest home-based parent education program functioning in Kennewick's school system for 18 years applied for and received state ECEAP funds. Kennewick's grant proposal was written by Barbara Brauer, coordinator of the home-based program since 1979, and her supervisor, the federal projects coordinator for the district. Additional support came from the district's superintendent and from the Washington Department of Community Development, in charge of distributing ECEAP funds across the state.

**Features**

ECEAP offers four days of preschool and targets two populations: bilingual children of migrant workers and low-income English-speaking children. Each class has 18 children, a lead teacher, and 2 instructional assistants. In addition, parent educators make weekly home visits engaging parents and children in activities that enhance early development. Two kinds of skills are stressed: intensive language development for bilingual children and social skills for all children. Field trips and nature walks are integral to ECEAP's weekly activities. The program provides free medical and dental screenings, links families with social services, and helps parents gain access to community resources such as literacy training, general education, and job training. ECEAP operates on a nine-month school calendar.

**Participants**

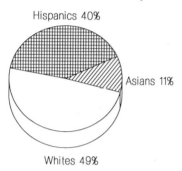

Hispanics 40%

Asians 11%

Whites 49%

Eligibility is based on income level, age, and state residency requirements: children must be four years old and come from families living at or below the poverty level; single-parent families and children with a history of poor scholastic performance also qualify. In 1988-89, Kennewick served 72 families, over half of which qualified for ECEAP; 54 percent of the children came from single-parent households; 50 percent were children of migrant parents.

*ECEAP solicits local grass roots support by inviting businesses and service organizations to volunteer in classrooms or coordinate food events, assist with site improvement, donate equipment for classrooms and playgrounds, sponsor services or lunch programs, raise funds to purchase transportation vehicles, and provide money for scholarships to involve more children in the program.*

**Parent Education**

The program offers weekly home visits and monthly parenting meetings featuring 20-minute lectures on requested topics followed by open discussion and social activities. Barbara Brauer, the program director, noted that one of the most successful recent meetings featured presentations by district kindergarten teachers. "Make It and Take It" workshops are scheduled bimonthly, both mornings and evenings.

Parents and ECEAP staff members are trained in child development as well as learning techniques for guidance, including positive reinforcement, anticipation, and methods for eliminating potential problems.

**Curriculum**

Much of ECEAP's curriculum is developed in house and is based on activities derived from a variety of sources modified and adapted to four- and five-year-olds. These include: *Whole Language Learning,* which focuses on small group learning centers, *Total Physical Response,* which targets children with limited English proficiency, *Creative Curriculum for Early Childhood, High/Scope,* and *Math Their Way.* Developmentally appropriate activities from less well known curricula are also used.

**Sites**

ECEAP offers services in two preschool classrooms in a public elementary school and in participants' homes. The main office is located in a building owned by the school district.

**Parent Involvement**

A parent policy council, which includes at least seven program participants (one selected from each parent educator's caseload), is mandated by ECEAP. This council has the authority to make programmatic changes. Parents are encouraged to volunteer in the program, but participation is not a precondition for a child's enrollment. Home visits, or an equivalent number of contact hours, are required to fulfill the ECEAP administration's standards. ECEAP encourages parents to meet with teachers and other program staff members to discuss their children's individual needs.

**Outreach**

The program canvases door-to-door and conducts neighborhood recruitment campaigns. The local newspaper publishes frequent articles about ECEAP activities. Staff members visit local civic organizations to educate the community about program services. Interagency networking, which is mandated in the ECEAP legislation, provides the best source of overall coverage of services for all disadvantaged parents. Head Start, elementary school principals, and kindergarten teachers make direct referrals to the program. Brochures are left in the community library, local health department, and food bank, and in the Department of Human Services office. The program is highlighted at parent-teacher organization meetings. The school district shares information about the program at school board meetings and makes referrals through all elementary schools and teen parent programs.

**Staff**

The entire staff meets weekly to discuss dysfunctional families, drug problems, child abuse, or issues of child development, as well as to plan themes for parent educators to use during upcoming home visits. The Kennewick district central office makes the staff aware of all local, state, and national opportunities in the field of early childhood education.

| Job Title | PD | Vol | FT | PT | Educ Req | Status | Benefits |
|---|---|---|---|---|---|---|---|
| Director | 1 | - | 1 | - | College Degree | Other Contract | Yes |
| Parent Educator Coordinator | 1 | - | 1 | - | College Degree | Other Contract | Yes |
| Parent Educators | 7 | - | 7 | - | Some College | Hourly Contract | Yes |
| Secretary | 1 | - | - | 1 | High School Diploma | Hourly Contract | Yes |
| Nurse | 1 | - | - | 1 | College Degree | Hourly Contract | Yes |
| Health Assistant | 1 | - | - | 1 | High School Diploma | Hourly Contract | Yes |

**State/District Requirements**

Parent educators are required to have an associate's degree and two years experience pertinent to direct involvement with low-income families and preschool children (or a bachelor's degree and one year relevant experience). Nurses are required to have an educational staff associate certificate of endorsement.

| | |
|---|---|
| **Preferred Background** | For parent educators, bilingual experiences with South Asian refugee families and migrant families and bicultural awareness of Hispanic and South Asian cultures and traditions. |
| **Employee Education and Training Represented** | Infant and toddler education; prekindergarten and early childhood education; elementary education; education, grades 7 to 12; bilingual education; special education; adult basic education; adult literacy; parent educator; child care; medicine; health and nutrition; home economics; nursing; psychology; counseling; family therapy; social work; child development and family studies; development and fundraising. |
| **Administration** | The ECEAP director reports to the Kennewick School District assistant superintendent and to the Washington Department of Community Development. The program is administered exclusively within the public education system through the Early Childhood Education and Federal Projects/Special Programs departments. Both the Department of Community Development and the state auditor's office monitor the program. The program's parent council meets eight times a year and has decision-making powers on issues related to hiring, budget, services, and curriculum. The council helps with recruitment, fundraising, field trips, and interagency networking. |
| **Relationship to the Schools** | In April, kindergarten teachers are included at the ECEAP parent meeting for an informal exchange of expectations, ideas, and concerns. Parents are invited to visit kindergarten classes in May and schedule informal conferences with teachers. ECEAP parent educators keep a line of communication open with kindergarten teachers regarding children's medical and dental screenings. |
| **Community Links** | ECEAP solicits local grass roots support by inviting businesses and service organizations to volunteer in classrooms or coordinate food events, assist with site improvement, donate equipment for classrooms and playgrounds, sponsor services or lunch programs, raise funds to purchase transportation vehicles, and provide money for scholarships to involve more children in the program. Clinics and private physicians donate professional services including screening exams, physicals, and follow-up consultations; others offer job training experience for parents. |
| **Funding** | Washington Department of Community Development, 91.5 percent; local school district, 8.5 percent. |
| **In-Kind Resources** | The schools provide office space and classrooms; busing, staff training, and development opportunities; physical education, music, and library services; equipment and materials; and a breakfast and lunch program. |
| **Funding History** | This is a new program. |
| **Objectives** | ECEAP seeks to enhance parents' awareness of their role as their children's primary educator and to help both parents and children develop self-esteem. ECEAP aims to develop language skills in children with limited English proficiency and help children prepare for kindergarten. |

| | |
|---|---|
| **Evaluation** | A full evaluation, required by the state of Washington, is pending. |
| **Replication** | ECEAP, still in a pilot phase, was modeled on various aspects of Head Start and encouraged by the National Association for the Education of Young Children in Washington, DC. |
| **Materials Available** | ECEAP has not yet developed marketable materials. |

# Early Childhood Family Education

*A social service agency referred Nancy, a mother with a history of mental illness and family violence, to ECFE's Family School. She remained withdrawn during the first several weeks of contact with ECFE, aloof and hostile to staff. Into the fifth week, she suddenly opened up, made friends and according to Ms. Larson, developed a softer tone and appearance. After the fourteen-week program, Nancy continued in a follow-up group. Staff observed her sharing with others and acting in a freer, more relaxed manner with her children.*

| | | |
|---|---|---|
| Newsletter | High school credit | Community services info/referral |
| Networking | Crisis intervention | Parenting/child development education |
| Child care | Parent-child activities | Child care info/referral |
| Advocacy | Toy lending | Health/nutrition education |
| Resource library | Discussion groups | Developmental exams/screening |
| Drop-in center | Parent support groups | Home visits to at-risk families |

**Contact:** Marilyn Marsh, Manager, Community and Student Services

**Address:** 215 North First Avenue East
Duluth, MN 55802
(218) 723-4149

**Established:** 1977, state initiative

**Budget '88-89:** $948,455

**Sources:** State, federal, local district, client fees, foundations

**Size:** 1,800 families

**Area Served:** Duluth, Minnesota

**Auspices:** Elementary education department of the Duluth Public Schools

**1990 Respondent:** Marilyn Larson, Supervisor

## Community

Duluth, in northeastern Minnesota on the shores of Lake Superior, is the fourth largest city in the state (population 83,065) and is socioeconomically stratified. The west side has a predominantly blue-collar, working-class population, most of which has completed high school; central Hillside is low income, with many educationally disadvantaged, transient, and welfare families; the east end is home to professional, often dual-income families. The city, like the state, has a mostly white population.

## Philosophy and Goals

The primary purpose of Duluth Early Childhood Family Education is to strengthen families by helping parents meet the developmental needs of their children. Recognizing that the home is a child's first learning environment and that parents are the primary influence in a child's life, the program believes that all parents can benefit from information and support relating to their parental role.

## History and Origins

In the early 1970s, the Early Childhood Family Education (ECFE) concept began as a state initiative, with state funds available to pilot sites through the Council on Quality Education. According to Marilyn Larson, the supervisor of ECFE in Duluth, "Head Start was already successfully operating in the schools, and early childhood and family education were a fact of life." The Duluth ECFE program began in 1977 with one pilot project in an inner-city elementary school. A second site in a similar low-income neighborhood was added in 1979. These two programs were tailored to meet the needs of parents in the community, rather than following the middle-class model of the ECFE prototype. In 1983, the state legislature allowed school districts that had community education programs to establish districtwide ECFE centers. The following year, Duluth set up a steering committee to implement ECFE's rapid expansion throughout the city. By 1985, the steering committee recommended to the school board that seven neighborhood sites form the axis of the program. Additional outreach efforts bring services to hard-to-reach populations in alternative sites.

ECFE provides discussion groups for parents, early childhood education for their children, and informal creative learning experiences for parents and children together.

**Neighborhood centers** bring parents and children together for 10 weekly 90-minute sessions. The curriculum includes joint activities, parent discussions, and supervised early learning experiences for children. Parent groups average 10 participants; children are grouped by age.

**Family School** is an intensive 14-week preventive program involving parents with children birth to age three, whose multiple stresses threaten their children's well-being. The program meets for five hours a day, twice a week. A three-phase program, Family School begins with home-based services, then moves to a center-based school for parents and children, and finally, into ECFE classes at a neighborhood center.

The **Habitat Program** grants high school credit for participation in child and family development education classes, 10 hours per week. On-site child care and health screening assessment are provided.

The **Parent-Infant Program** offers single sessions and a series of classes to first-time parents on-site at two local hospitals. A parent-infant educator visits prenatal classes to discuss the transition to parenthood and invites parents to attend an "Amazing Newborn" class before parents take their first child home. They may also join eight-week blocks of parenting classes offered during day or evening hours. Infants remain with their parents during all activities.

**Special programs** provide the same services on location to parents of children (birth to kindergarten) with special needs, as well as to single parents, retarded mothers, incarcerated fathers, residents of a women's shelter, residents of transitional housing, and residents of low-income housing projects — populations unable to get to neighborhood centers.

Duluth's Early Childhood Family Education program serves an economically diverse inner-city population. All parents in Duluth with children from birth to kindergarten-age are eligible. In 1987-88, approximately 1,470 children, 2,317 mothers and fathers, and 1,800 families took part in various ECFE programs. Twenty percent of these participants were single parents and 14 percent teen parents.

*"We have several pilot programs going that involve school personnel (principals, kindergarten teachers, and social workers) in working with parents the year before children enter kindergarten to begin the process of transition to school."*

**Features**

**Participants**

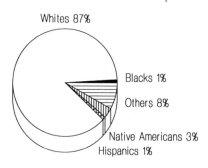

Whites 87%

Blacks 1%

Others 8%

Native Americans 3%
Hispanics 1%

**Parent Education**

Parent education includes child and family development information, nutrition counseling, and advice on the care of newborns. Since 1985, ECFE has adapted its program for at-risk, hard-to-reach populations. ECFE does not try to resolve family problems, but rather gives families an environment in which they can increase their self-esteem, coping skills, and perspectives on their life options.

**Curriculum**

ECFE maintains an extensive library and employs a parent education specialist to develop sessions based on topics of interest to parents.

**Sites**

Since 1985, ECFE has been bringing services into homes, two hospitals, one housing project, seven neighborhood drop-in centers, prisons, and facilities for children with special needs.

**Parent Involvement**

Nineteen program participants serve on the advisory board. Parents help expand the program by spreading the word about its positive effects.

**Outreach**

ECFE relies on word-of-mouth referrals from satisfied participants to promote its activities. The program runs the annual "Family Affair" at a shopping mall, does outreach at the maternity wards of both local hospitals, and conducts open houses at the schools. In addition, it publishes a quarterly newsletter, hands out flyers, buys television time, and receives newspaper coverage.

**Staff**

The staff includes a management team with Marilyn Larson as director. A specialist, who must be a nonteaching teacher, heads each subprogram. Volunteers include seven foster grandparents.

| Job Title | PD | Vol | FT | PT | Educ Req | Status | Benefits |
|-----------|----|----|----|----|----------|--------|----------|
| Supervisor | 1 | - | 1 | - | Post-Graduate Courses or Degree | Other Contract | Yes |
| Parent Educators | 17 | - | - | 17 | College Degree | K-12 Contract | Yes |
| Early Childhood Teachers | 15 | - | - | 15 | College Degree | K-12 Contract | Yes |
| Specialists | 4 | - | - | 4 | College Degree | K-12 Contract | Yes |
| Teaching Assistants | 28 | - | 2 | 26 | High School Diploma | Hourly Contract | Yes |
| Social Workers | 2 | - | - | 2 | Post-Graduate Courses or Degree | K-12 Contract | Yes |
| Secretaty | 2 | - | 1 | 1 | High School Diploma | Hourly Contract | Yes |
| Foster Grandparents | - | 4 | 4 | - | None | - | No |
| Nurses | 3 | - | - | 3 | College Degree | K-12 Contract | Yes |

**State/District Requirements**

The state requires parent educators to be licensed in family or parent education. Early childhood teachers must be licensed in prekindergarten or early childhood education. Social workers are licensed, and the supervisor is a licensed administrator.

**Preferred Background**

Early childhood teachers should have experience with infants, toddlers, and parents; parent educators should be experienced group facilitators with knowledge of child development.

**Employee Education and Training Represented**

Infant and toddler education; prekindergarten and early childhood education; elementary education; education, grades 7 to 12; special education; parent educator; adult vocational education; child care; medicine; health and nutrition; home economics; nursing; psychology; counseling; social work; child development and family studies.

**Administration**

ECFE is housed in the Early Childhood Division within the Department of Elementary Education of the Duluth Public Schools. Marilyn Larson reports to the director of elementary education. The Minnesota Department of Education monitors ECFE. The 42-member advisory board meets quarterly and has the power to recommend program policies and services, establish relationships with other agencies, and appoint smaller task forces to support program components such as recruitment, fundraising, and special events.

**Relationship to the Schools**

Ms. Larson feels that the schools approve of the program, but notes that there have been problems in the past. The schools influence ECFE's hiring practices and pressure the program to conform to the school calendar. Ms. Larson commented that relations have improved since the program has become districtwide. ECFE staff members make a point of attending elementary principals' meetings and share inservice training with Head Start. The early childhood special education program collaborates with ECFE on special programming.

**Community Links**

Ms. Larson comments that ECFE sees itself as performing the function of "an informal coordinating body for all social service agencies" in Duluth. ECFE exchanges referrals with hospitals; social service, public health, and special education groups; free clinics; Special Supplemental Food Program for Women, Infants, and Children (WIC); and various counseling services. The program also maintains links with the Duluth Clinic, a private medical facility that provides sessions for pregnant women, their partners, and expectant grandparents. "We have several pilot programs going that involve school personnel [principals, kindergarten teachers, and social workers] in working with parents the year before children enter kindergarten to begin the process of transition to school," comments Ms. Larson. Parents visit classrooms, develop reasonable expectations about the schools, and learn what will be expected of them. Children ride the bus and visit classrooms after school hours.

**Funding**

State (aid for ECFE), 78 percent; local and/or school district, 19.9 percent; client fees, 2 percent; foundations, 0.07 percent; federal (Child Care Food Program), 0.03 percent. Additional funds come from County Child Care Services. Parent-infant sessions and the first 10-week session at neighborhood centers are free; after that, fees are charged on a sliding scale beginning at $30 per quarter for families. Some special programs require a minimal fee, but most are free and no parent is ever denied the chance to participate due to an inability to pay. There is no fee for Family School.

**In-Kind Resources**

The school district and hospitals provide space and facilities; paid staff is provided by the building engineer; the school district also provides transportation services, consultation and staff development, periodic direct service to program participants (as do the local health department and Duluth Food/Nutrition), administrative and clerical support, and access to equipment.

**Funding History**

Funding has increased by 96 percent since the program began and is now considered moderately secure.

**Objectives**

ECFE's main objective is to stimulate parents' interest in meeting the social, emotional, intellectual, and physical needs of their children. The program hopes to help parents clarify their goals and values and develop stronger connections to their communities.

**Evaluation**

ECFE conducted an internal, formative evaluation in 1986. Plans for the future include hiring a professional to help design an evaluation system and a framework for developing policy procedures and personnel manuals. Ms. Larson would like to see the state evaluate subtle differences among ECFE programs to study outreach strategies.

**Replication**

This program is one of the original 36 pilot programs of ECFE, now replicated throughout the state.

**Materials Available**

*Living with Children* (parent education) and *Being with Children* (early childhood education) are both available for $15 each.

# Resource List

*Where to Look for Information, Advocacy, and Research*

## Academic Development Institute

Contact: Sam Redding
1603 South Michigan Avenue
Chicago, IL 60616
(312) 427-1692

*A not-for-profit organization founded in 1984 to assist families, schools, and communities with the academic and personal development of children.*

**Resources Available**

*Alliance for Achievement: Building the Value-based School Community,* description of a project in 29 Illinois and 3 Wyoming schools that use school councils to build school communities based on educational values. Includes an action plan to guide parents and educators in building school communities.

*School Community Journal,* three issues per year.

Offers the Family Study Institute, a parent education program that helps parents to establish a home environment that encourages learning and academic achievement. The institute assists schools in developing supportive communities that nurture the learning of all children. Courses available include "Studying at Home" and "Reading at Home."

**Publication is available on request.**

## Active Parenting Publishers

Contact: Dr. Michael Popkin
810 Franklin Court, Suite B
Marietta, GA 30067
(800) 825-0060 or (404) 429-0565

*Designs curricula and materials for video-based parenting education.*

**Resources Available**

*The Active Parenting Discussion Program,* video-based, six-session parent education program designed for group discussion. Includes videotape, *Leader's Guide, Parent's Handbook,* and *Action Guide* and promotional materials. Available in an all-video format.

*Free the Horses,* self-esteem program.

*Windows: Healing and Helping through Loss,* how to deal with loss program.

*Family Talk,* family communication program.

*Active Parenting of Teens,* for parents of teens, with special units on substance abuse and sexuality.

Audiotapes and books available on numerous subjects including parenting, self-esteem, suicide, and sex.

**Materials are available on a 30-day approval by calling the toll-free number or writing to the program address. Catalog is also available.**

## American Association of Colleges for Teacher Education (AACTE)

Contact: David G. Imig, Chief Executive Officer
One Dupont Circle, NW, Suite 610
Washington, DC 20036-1186
(202) 293-2450

*A national organization of over 700 schools, colleges, and departments of education, with over 5,000 education deans and faculty participating. Represents and serves the nation's researchers and practitioners. Runs the ERIC Clearinghouse on Teacher Education, an extensive database of scholarly writings on education topics.*

### Resources Available

Leadership Training Program.

New Deans' Institute.

*Journal of Teacher Education.*

Extensive publications are also available in the areas of minority recruitment, public policy, and school issues.

**Call AACTE for a publications brochure.**

## American Federation of Teachers (AFT)

Contact: Claude Duncan

555 New Jersey Avenue, NW

Washington, DC 20001

(202) 879-4458

*Conducts research and develops programs in areas of school restructuring and educational reform to meet the needs of educators and consumers of public education.*

### Resources Available

The Learning Line, a toll-free hotline with daily learning activities, (800) 242-5465.

Summer Learning Calendar and the "Home Team" Learning Activities Guide.

Issue papers and publications related to timely educational reform and restructuring issues.

**Contact the AFT's public relations or order departments.**

## American Home Economics Association

Contact: Mary Jane Kolar, Executive Director

1555 King Street

Alexandria, VA 22314

(703) 706-4600

*Tracks the involvement of home economists in parent education.*

### Resources Available

*Action,* newsletter, five issues per year.

*Journal of Home Economics,* four issues per year.

*Home Economics Research Journal,* scholarly publication.

**Write or call to order.**

## The ASPIRA Association, Inc.

Contact: Ronald Blackburn Moreno, National Executive Director
National Office
1112 Sixteenth Street, NW, #340
Washington, DC 20036
(202) 835-3600

*A national, nonprofit organization serving Puerto Rican and Hispanic youth through leadership development and education. The oldest and largest Hispanic youth organization in the United States, ASPIRA advances the socioeconomic development of the Latino community by providing emotional, intellectual, and practical resources to help students remain in school and contribute to the community.*

**Resources Available**
*ASPIRA Five Cities High School Dropout Study: Characteristics of Hispanic High School Students.*
*ASPIRA Five Cities High School Dropout Study: Focus on Parents.*
*Making the Most of Your Child's Education: A Parent's Guide .*
*Making the Most of Your Child's Education: More Topics for Parents.*
*ASPIRA News*, quarterly newsletter.
**Order from the Publications Department at the above address. Further publications and sponsorship information is available.**

## Association for Childhood Education International (ACEI)

Contact: Gerald Odland, Executive Director
11501 Georgia Avenue, Suite 315
Wheaton, MD 20902
(301) 942-2443

*An association of teachers, parents, and other adults that promotes good educational policies for children in infancy through early adolescence. Informs the public of the needs of children through publications, conferences, workshops, advocacy projects, and networking with other childhood organizations. Current issues include developmentally appropriate curriculum, assessment and evaluation of children, and parent-school partnerships in education.*

**Resources Available**
*ACEI Exchange,* newsletter, six issues per year.
*Childhood Education,* five issues per year.
*Journal of Research in Childhood Education,* two issues per year.
Professional Division newsletters (four issues per division: Infancy, Early
Childhood, and Later Childhood/Early Adolescence).
Annual Study Conference each spring.
**Contact ACEI headquarters for information about ACEI membership, conferences, and a free publications catalog.**

## The Association for Persons with Severe Handicaps (TASH)

Contact: Frank Laski, Executive Director
11201 Greenwood Ave., N.
Seattle, WA 98133
(206) 361-8870

*Advocates for comprehensive, high quality, integrated education and rehabilitative services and provides support for parents, educators, and service providers, with the goal of enabling people with disabilities to*

*participate fully in an integrated community. Forty TASH chapters
promote involvement in regional concerns.*

**Resources Available**

 TASH publishes several monographs, a newsletter, and a journal. Its
information department can refer callers to a register of professional
contact people available to assist with specific problems in education or
training.

**Contact the information department for ordering and referral.**

## Association for the Care of Children's Health

Contact: Dr. William Sciarillo, Executive Director
7910 Woodmont Avenue, Suite 300
Bethesda, MD  20814-3505
(301) 654-6549
(301) 986-4553 FAX

*A multidisciplinary, international membership organization of
professionals and parents that promotes the psychosocial well-being of
children and families in health care settings through education, research,
and advocacy.*

**Resources Available**

 Resource catalog listing books, videotapes, films, position papers, and
bibliographies in the areas of health care, hospital programming, special
needs children, and more.

 Quarterly peer review journal.

 Annual educational conference in May.

 Consultations available on family-centered, psychosocial,
developmentally supportive services.

**Write or call for more information or to order catalog.**

## Association for Supervision and Curriculum Development (ASCD)

Contact: Dr. Gene Carter, Executive Director
1250 North Pitt Street
Alexandria, VA  22314
(703) 549-9110

*A professional membership organization of principals, superintendents,
supervisors, teachers, professors, and school board members. Apolitical in
nature, ASCD is committed to developing leadership for quality in
education for all students. Has affiliates in all 50 states, Canada, Europe,
and the Caribbean.*

**Resources Available**

 *Education Leadership,* eight issues per year.

 *ASCD Update,* eight issues per year.

 *Curriculum Update,* eight issues per year.

 *Journal of Supervision and Curriculum,* four issues per year.

**Write or call for more information.**

## Bank Street College of Education

Contact: Edna Shapiro
610 West 112th Street
New York, NY  10025
(212) 875-4400

*Bank Street is a school for 500 children (6 months to 13 years); a graduate
school of education for 700 students; and an active group of researchers*

*focusing on improving the lives of children, youth, and families as well as influencing the social institutions that have an impact on them.*

**Resources Available**

*The Public School Early Childhood Study,* a three-volume report of a two- and-a-half year study of public school programs for prekindergarten children.

*Teenage Parents and Their Families: Findings and Guidelines from a Collaborative Effort to Promote Family Competence.*

*Working with Teenage Fathers: A Handbook for Program Development.*

*Reaching and Serving the Teenage Father.*

Curriculum materials and training for early childhood educators (birth to third grade).

**Direct orders to Patricia Landrum, Research Division. Request complete publication list and curriculum information.**

## Barbara Bush Foundation for Family Literacy

Contact: Benita Somerfield, Executive Director
1002 Wisconsin Avenue, NW
Washington, DC 20007
(202) 338-2006

*The foundation's mission is to establish literacy as a value in every family in America by helping parents understand that the home is the child's first school, the parent is the child's first teacher, and reading is the child's first subject. The foundation aims to break the intergenerational cycle of illiteracy by supporting the development of literacy programs that build families of readers.*

**Resources Available**

*First Teachers* (1989), examples of successful family literacy programs.
**Write for ordering information. Inquiries by mail only.**

## Bush Center in Child Development and Social Policy

Contact: Matia Finn-Stevenson, Associate Director
School of 21st Century Programs
310 Prospect Street
New Haven, CT 06511-2188
(203) 432-9944

*Performs case studies on the School of 21st Century programs and other school-based child care programs and provides technical assistance for implementation of School of 21st Century programs.*

**Write to Matia Finn-Stevenson at the above address for more information.**

## Carnegie Foundation for the Advancement of Teaching

Contact: Hinda Greenberg, Director
Information Center
5 Ivy Lane
Princeton, NJ 08540
(609) 452-1780

*A public policy educational research institute which conducts studies devoted to strengthening American education at all levels.*

**Resources Available**

*An Imperiled Generation: Saving Urban Schools* (April 1988), reviews conditions of schools in urban centers and makes recommendations for improvements.

*Student Service* (February 1987), examines high school community service programs and provides guiding principles for teachers and administrators contemplating the introduction of service units in their schools.

**Order titles from Princeton University Press, 3175 Princeton Pike, Lawrenceville, NJ 08648 (609) 896-1344.**

## Center for Early Adolescence

Contact: Frank Loda, Director
University of North Carolina at Chapel Hill
D2 Carr Mill Town Center
Carrboro, NC 27510
(919) 966-1148

*A national center providing research, training, and consultation to agencies and individuals who have an impact on the lives of ten- to fifteen-year-olds.*

**Resources Available**

The center produces over 40 books, curricula, audio-visual aids, and other resources.

**Contact the center for a free catalog.**

## Center for Law and Social Policy (CLASP)

Contact: Allan Houseman
1616 P Street, Suite 150
Washington, DC 20036
(202) 328-5140

*Represents the poor and minorities in family policy issues including child support, child care, public benefits, and education and employment training programs. Represents legal services programs and the Legal Services Corporation (LSC).*

**Resources Available**

Reports and publications in the areas of legal services, family policy, advocacy tools, education, and welfare reform.

*Family Matters,* quarterly publication.

*The Partnership,* a new publication promoting exchange and partnership between welfare, education, and job training (limited availability).

*State Update,* provides continuous news on welfare issues as well as policy analysis on emerging topics. Designed for those intimately involved in welfare policies and programs. Includes copies of *Family Matters,* 10 issues per year.

**Request a list of publications in your area of interest.**

## Center for Parent Education

Contact: Dr. Burton L. White
81 Wyman Street
Waban, MA 02168
(617) 964-2442 (617) 965-8827 FAX

*Assists professionals concerned with the education of children during the first three years of life. Provided assistance to the Missouri, South Carolina, Alabama, and Louisiana New Parents as Teachers Program (1982-85), now implemented in 40 states and several foreign countries. Educates the public about early childhood through the media and provides support services through workshops and material design.*

**Resources Available**

*The First Three Years,* a videotape series of eight 25-minute programs plus a summary program. Focuses on the seven phases of early development during the first three years of life (available on VHS, BETA, or other formats including those for the hearing impaired).

*Center for Parent Education Newsletter,* bimonthly.

Bibliography of articles, research reports, and manuals.

Consulting services, speakers for conferences, and evaluation of written and audio-visual materials.

Comprehensive training and materials available for New Parents As Teachers.

**Call or write to order. Send self-addressed, stamped envelope for bibliography. Call for more information about services.**

## Center for the Study of Social Policy

Contact: Frank Farrow, Director
Children Services Policy
1250 I Street, NW, Suite 503
Washington, DC 20005
(202) 371-1565

*Analyzes the effects of contemporary policy issues in the areas of poverty, family support, and children and youth services on states, communities, and families. Provides technical assistance to states in areas of service organization, finance, and delivery.*

**Call or write for publications list.**

## Center on Families, Communities, Schools, and Children's Learning and Center for Research on Effective Schooling for Disadvantaged Students (CDS)

Contact: Dr. Joyce L. Epstein
The Johns Hopkins University
3505 North Charles Street
Baltimore, MD 21218
(410) 516-8800

*The Center on Families, Communities, Schools, and Children's Learning and CDS conduct research on the effects of alternative school and classroom structures that may help improve students' learning and development. The centers' programs include research on teachers' practices of parent involvement and family-school-community connections, to better understand all of the resources in key institutions that can help students succeed.*

**Resources Available**

A list of reports, articles, and materials for educators, policy leaders, and researchers on parent involvement.

**Write for list at the above address.**

## Chapin Hall Center for Children

Contact: Ms. Susan Campbell, Director of Communications
University of Chicago
1155 East 60th Street
Chicago, IL 60637
(312) 753-5900

*A research institution that studies the needs of children and children's policy. While the center's primary focus is on Illinois, its research illuminates the condition of children nationwide. The center develops policies and programs to improve child care and services, especially in the areas of mental health, foster care, special education, public assistance, and community resources.*

**Resources Available**

Low-priced discussion papers and free descriptive brochures available. **Contact Susan Campbell for current publications list and order form.**

## Child Welfare League of America

Contact: Susan Brite, Director of Publications
440 First Street, NW, Suite 310
Washington, DC 20001-2085
(202) 638-2952

*A privately and publicly supported membership organization devoted to the improvement of care and services for deprived, dependent, and neglected children, youth, and families. Conducts agency and community surveys; develops standards for services; and publishes newsletters, books, a scholarly journal, and a magazine.*

**Resources Available**

Publications concerning administration, developmental disabilities, AIDS education, adoption, child care, child abuse and neglect, adolescent pregnancy, and family foster care. **Write for publications list.**

## Systems Reform Initiative

Contact: Margaret E. Rawle, State Director
Governor's Office for Children, Youth, and Families
300 West Lexington Street, Suite 306
Baltimore, MD 21201
(410) 333-4285

*Maryland's Children and Family Services Reform Initiative restructures the way services are delivered to children and families. The reform effort is built upon several principles: family preservation and self-sufficiency; interagency planning and budgeting; early intervention and prevention; noncategorical, community-based, family-focused services; flexible funding; and consistent case management.*

**Call or write to the above address for more information.**

## Children's Defense Fund

Contact: Marian Wright Edelman
25 E Street, NW
Washington, DC 20001
(202) 628-8787

*A child advocacy organization that conducts research and provides state and local technical assistance in the areas of child welfare, child care, public education, family services, and adolescent pregnancy prevention, among others. Drafts legislation and monitors federal agencies. Convenes annual conference.*

### Resources Available
*The State of America's Children,* an analysis of the status of America's children, with projections to the year 2000. Annual report.
*The Health of America's Children,* annual publication.
*CDF Reports,* monthly newsletter.
*Adolescent and Young Adult Fact Book,* a landmark study of the nation's 10- to 24-year-olds covering their health, education, living arrangements, family formation, childbearing, crime, victimization, substance abuse, employment, and income.
**Write or call for publications list or for additional selections.**


## Clark University Department of Education
Contact: Tom Del Prepe
950 Main Street
Worcester, MA 01610
(508) 793-7221

*Studies literacy-focused program for families with children from age three to adolescence; includes school- and community-based programs.*

### Resources Available
"An Examination of Programs That Involve Parents in Efforts to Support Children's Acquisition of Literacy," paper.
**Order from the above address.**


## Committee for Economic Development (CED)
Contact: Sandra Hamburg
477 Madison Avenue
New York, NY 10022
(212) 688-2063

*A private, nonprofit research and education organization composed of business leaders and educators who develop policy recommendations to improve the American economy and quality of life.*

**Write for further information.**


## Congress of National Black Churches
Contact: Reverend H. Michael Lemmons, Executive Director
1225 I Street, NW, Suite 750
Washington, DC 20005
(202) 371-1091

*Includes major black denominations in the United States and Africa. Seeks answers to problems that confront blacks in the areas of economic development, family support, social support, and education. Compiles statistics.*

**Call or write for more information.**

## Connecticut Department of Children and Youth Services

Contact: Dave Dearborn
Division of Planning and Program Development
505 Hudson Street
Hartford, CT 06106
(203) 550-6506

*Administers Parent Education and Support Centers (PESCs) and School-Home Liaison Projects. PESCs seek to improve parenting skills and enhance family functioning by offering information, training, and support services in centers located in a variety of settings including the public schools. Liaison projects combine the influence of families and schools to reduce truancy and promote academic achievement.*

### Resources Available

Program guidelines and descriptive information for both programs. Provides ongoing training and technical assistance to both initiatives. Evaluation report available.
**Write for more information.**


## Coordinating Council for Handicapped Children

Contact: Charlotte DesJardins
20 East Jackson Boulevard, Room 900
Chicago, IL 60604
(312) 939-3513

*The Coordinating Council for Handicapped Children provides free weekly training sessions on special education rights for parents and professionals. Also runs workshops on advocacy, assertiveness, organizing, and coalition building.*

### Resources Available

*How to Organize an Effective Parent/Advocacy Group and Move Bureaucracies.*
*How to Get Services by Being Assertive.*
*Does Your Child Have Special Education Needs?* also available in Spanish (free).
*How to Prepare for a Successful Due Process Hearing,* also available in Spanish (free).
*How to Participate Effectively in Your Child's IEP Meeting* (free).
**Write for further information on ordering and membership.**


## Cornell Family Matters

Contact: Mon Cochran/Christiann Dean
Department of Human Development and Family Studies
Martha Van Rensselaer Hall
Ithaca, NY 14853-4401
(607) 255-2260

*A research and outreach program that focuses on support for families with young children. Includes three workshop programs for parents and people who work with families: The Employed Parent; Empowering Families: Home Visiting and Building Clusters; and Cooperative Communication Between Home and School. All three are based on an empowerment approach to building on families' strengths.*

### Resources Available

Each workshop kit includes facilitators' manuals, handbooks, activity cards, and other materials.

*Family Matters,* documentary on how the social service system affects families (available on film or videotape, for rental or purchase).
**Write for ordering information.**

## Council for American Private Education (CAPE)

Contact: Joyce McCray, Executive Director
1726 M Street, NW, Suite 1102
Washington, DC 20036
(202) 659-0016

*A coalition representing elementary and secondary private schools. Comprised of 13 national private school associations serving 15,000 private schools and 4.1 million students. Members are nonprofit and nondiscriminatory.*

### Resources Available

*CAPE Outlook,* monthly newsletter for private schools with legislative update.
*Exemplary Schools, 1986,* report about recognized secondary schools.
**Write or call for more information.**

## Council for Exceptional Children (CEC)

Contact: Barbara Sorenson, Information Director
1920 Association Drive
Reston, VA 22091
(703) 620-3660

*The only professional organization dedicated to improving the quality of education for all exceptional learners, both handicapped and gifted. Provides information through its journals and publications program. Coordinates a political action network. Offers academies and conferences.*

### Resources Available

*Life-Centered Career Education: A Competency-based Approach.*
*Preparation for Special Education Hearings: A Practical Guide to Lessening the Trauma of Due Process Hearings.*
*Survival Guide for the First Year Special Education Teacher.*
**Contact CEC for prices. Discounts on quantity orders of the same title to one address are as follows: 10 to 49 copies, 20%; 50 or more, 25%. Direct orders to Publications Sales ER69.**

## Council of Chief State School Officers (CCSSO)
## Resource Center on Educational Equity

Contact: Paula Delo
1 Massachusetts Ave., NW, Suite 700
Washington, DC 20001-1431
(202) 408-5505

*A nationwide, nonprofit organization of the 57 public officials who head departments of public education in every state, the District of Columbia, the Department of Defense Dependent Schools, and five extrastate jurisdictions. The CCSSO Resource Center on Educational Equity provides services designed to achieve equity in education for minorities, women, and girls as well as for disabled, limited English proficiency, and low-income students. The center manages and staffs a variety of CCSSO leadership initiatives to provide better educational services to children and youth at risk for school failure.*

**Resources Available**
*Early Childhood and Family Education: Foundations for Success* (free).
*A Guide for State Action: Early Childhood and Family Education.*
*State Profiles: Early Childhood and Parent Education and Related Services.*
*State Education Indicators 1988.*
*Families in School* (October 1991).
*Family Support Education and Involvement: A Guide for State Action* (November 1989).
**Write for more information.**

## Council of Great City Schools
Contact: Michael Casserly, Executive Director
1301 Pennsylvania Ave., NW, Suite 702
Washington, DC 20004
(202) 393-2427

*An association of large city school districts. Studies problems shared by urban schools and provides informational support to legislative activities in the areas of discrimination, financing, testing, and teacher preparation.*

**Resources Available**
*Challenges to Urban Education: Results in the Making,* a report of self-examination by 44 large urban districts.
*Teaching and Leading in the Great City Schools.*
*Pre-Kindergarten Programs in Urban Schools.*
*Results 2000: Progress in Meeting Urban Education Goals.*
*Minority Student Access to and Preparation for Higher Education.*
**List of further publications is also available.**

## Council on Children and Families
Contact: Frederick Meservey, Executive Director
5 Empire State Plaza, Suite 2810
Albany, NY 12223-1553
(518) 474-6293

*A state agency that coordinates services to children and families. Facilitates discussion and resolution of interagency issues and initiates programs and policies at the state and local levels.*

**Resources Available**
*Parent's Resource Guide,* a bibliography of literature on family life.
*State of the Child in New York State.*
*Welcome to Parenthood: A Family Guide.*
The council has further publications in the areas of nutrition, child abuse and neglect, family policy, and early childhood education.
**Write to the council for ordering information and a complete list of publications.**

## Division of Adult Education and Literacy
Contact: George Spicely, School to Work Information Services
U.S. Department of Education
600 Independence Ave., SW
Washington, DC 20202
(202) 205-9872

*Works with federal and state agencies and the private sector on literacy projects and events. Coordinates with an extensive network of organizations involved in literacy efforts to oversee adult education and literacy programs and events. Disseminates information through a clearinghouse and publishes a bimonthly newsletter.*

**Resources Available**

*A.L.L. (Adult Literacy and Learning) Points Bulletin,* bimonthly newsletter (free).

*A Model for Rural Schools to Involve Parents in the Education of Their Children.*

Family literacy bibliography.

**Write for publication requests.**


## Early Childhood Family Education (ECFE)

Contact: Lois Engstrom
Minnesota Department of Education
991 Capitol Square
550 Cedar Street
St. Paul, MN 55101
(612) 297-2441

*A statewide parent-child program for children from birth to kindergarten and their parents, administered by the Department of Education.*

**Resources Available**

*Guide for Developing Early Childhood Family Education Programs* (October 1989).

Free information packets, posters, a descriptive brochure, and a videotape (free on loan).

**Contact ECFE office for more information.**


## Early Literacy Research and Teacher Training Program
## Erikson Institute for Advanced Study in Child Development
## (affiliated with Loyola University)

Contact: Joan Brooks McLane/Gillian Dowley McNamee
420 North Wabash Ave.
Chicago, IL 60611
(312) 755-2279 or (312) 755-2281

*Works with teachers, administrators, parents, and children from a variety of cultural backgrounds, usually in inner-city communities, to understand how literacy develops in children and adults in family, community, and school settings.*

**Resources Available**

*Bringing Home and School Together: Written Dialogue between Teachers and Parents.*

*Parent Handbook on Early Literacy Development.*

*Teacher's Manual: Erikson Institute's Early Literacy Project.*

*Learning to Read and Write in an Inner City Setting: A Longitudinal Study of Community Change.*

*Writing as a Social Process.*

*Early Literacy Development in Preschool and Kindergarten Classrooms,* a videotape.

Available from publisher: *Early Literacy,* McLane and McNamee, Harvard University Press, 1990.

**Written requests only.**

## Education Commission of the States (ECS)

Contact: Sherry Freeland Walker, Editor
707 Seventeenth Street, Suite 2700
Denver, CO 80202
(303) 299-3600

*A nonprofit, nationwide, interstate compact formed to help governors, state legislators, state education officials, and others develop policies to improve the quality of education at all levels.*

### Resources Available

*What States Can Do,* summarizes recommendations for family involvement in the schools (PI-88-4).

*Drawing in the Family,* looks at the state role in encouraging home-school relationships (PI-88-2).

*Family Diversity and School Policy,* (AR-87-4).

*ECS Survey of State Initiatives for Youth at Risk: Parental Involvement* (AR-87-53).

*Parent Involvement: Selected Readings* (PI-884).

**Contact the ECS Distribution Center at the above address or at (303) 830-3692 to order or to request a complete list of publications.**


## Education Development Center, Inc. (EDC)

Contact: Sharon Pickett
55 Chapel Street
Newton, MA 02158
(617) 969-7100, ext. 300

*An international, nonprofit research and development organization that applies education strategies to solve social problems. EDC develops education and training materials, provides training and technical assistance to support program diffusion, and evaluates results. Over 60 projects are currently in progress. The Division of School and Society Programs focuses on promoting health, strengthening children and families, building work skills and careers, and improving schools and colleges.*

### Resources Available

*Exploring Childhood,* a high school curriculum on child development and parenting.

*Family and Community Health through Caregiving,* a high school health promotion program with a strong family component.

**Call (800) 225-4276 for ordering information. In Massachusetts, call (617) 969-7100, ext. 215. Or write to Millie LeBlanc, Publications Coordinator, at the above address.**


## ERIC Clearinghouse on Elementary and Early Childhood Education

Contact: Norma Howard, Information Services Coordinator
University of Illinois
805 West Pennsylvania Avenue
Urbana, IL 61801-4897
(217) 333-1386

*An information system and clearinghouse containing publications on early childhood development, education, theory, research, curricula,*

*programming, and administration. Treats early childhood (birth to age 7)
and the middle years (ages 8 to 12).*

**Resources Available**
 *Resources from ERIC,* description of the ERIC system (single copies
free).
 Single copies of *Digests,* concise two-page summaries of current topics in
elementary and early childhood education (free).
 *Working with Families.*
 Topical resource lists available.
**Request *Resources from ERIC* or a list of *Digest* titles from the
above address.**

## Even Start
Contact: Janet Anderson
Office of Adult Education and Literacy
State Board for Community and Technical Colleges
P.O. Box 42495
Olympia, WA 98504-2495
(206) 664-9403

*A Washington State adult literacy initiative that selects and funds local
programs that fulfill the parenting and family education needs of the
community.*

**Write for more information.**

## Family Development and Self-Sufficiency
# Demonstration Grant (FDGG)
Contact: Karen McCarthy, FDGG Contact
Department of Human Rights
Division of Community Action Agencies
Lucas State Office Building
Des Moines, IA 50319
(515) 242-5845

*Iowa's state legislated demonstration grant, in its third year.*

**Resources Available**
 *Family Development and Self-Sufficiency in Iowa.*
 Progress reports.
**Write for more information.**

## Family Development Resources, Inc.
Contact: Family Development Resources, Inc.
3160 Pinebrook Road
Park City, UT 84060
(800) 688-5822 or (801) 649-5822
(801) 649-9599 FAX

*Produces programs and materials to assess, prevent, and treat child abuse
and neglect by promoting and building nurturing skills in families.*

**Resources Available**
 *Nurturing Program for Parents with Special Learning Needs and Their
Children: Engage Families in Home-Based or Group-Based Programs.*
**Write or call for more information.**

## Family Focus

Contact: Maureen Patrick, Executive Director
310 South Peoria Street, Suite 401
Chicago, IL 60607
(312) 421-5200

*Develops community-based resource programs designed to strengthen families of children from birth to age three and promote the optimal development of young adolescents and teenage parents. Family Focus fosters a national commitment to children and families through its model programs, public education efforts, and parent and professional advocacy. Programs build on the strength of families, link families to needed resources, and enable parents to draw on the ethnic, racial, and economic characteristics of the community.*

### Resources Available

*Creating Drop-in Centers: The Family Focus Model.*
*Deep Blue Funk and Other Stories: Portraits of Teenage Parents .*
*Working with Teen Parents.*
*Caring for America's Children.*
*Family Focus Update,* newsletter (free).
Annual Reports (free).
**Write or call to order.**


## Family Resource Coalition (FRC)

Contact: Linda Turner, Technical Assistance Coordinator
200 South Michigan Avenue, 16th floor
Chicago, IL 60604
(312) 341-0900

*A national organization representing preventive, community-based family resource and support programs. Provides technical assistance on all aspects of program development; publishes books, resource kits, periodicals, and newsletters; sponsors local, regional, and national conferences; operates the only national clearinghouse of these programs and advocates on behalf of issues and legislation affecting families. Parent Action, a division of FRC, is a national parent advocacy organization.*

### Resources Available

*Programs to Strengthen Families,* a resource guide.
*Family Resource Program Builder: Blueprints for Designing and Operating Programs for Parents.*
*Building Strong Foundations: Evaluation Strategies for Family Resource Programs.*
*Creating Parent-School Partnerships,* special focus issue of the FRC Report.
*Developing Parent Support Groups and Drop-in Centers,* parent resource kit.
**Write or call for further information.**


## The Family Academy

Contact: Christina Giammalva
220 West 121st Street
New York, NY 10027
(212) 749-3558 or (212) 678-2869

*The Family School is a small, intimate public school in Harlem that is carefully designed to meet the needs of the neighborhood families as well as its students. The school aims to create a place where children, families, and staff can learn, work, and grow together. The school operates extended-day and year programs, evening classes for parents, and has social workers in the building available for families. It seeks to involve parents in their children's education.*

**Resources Available**
  Program Description (free).
**Write or call to order.**


## Free the Children

Contact: Sara Lewis, Executive Director
1192 Peabody
Memphis, TN 38104
(901) 276-0843

*A private, nonprofit initiative working to break the cycle of poverty for the residents of a target area of Memphis. Works comprehensively to coordinate social services of all types for neighborhood residents.*

**Resources Available**
  Free the Children target area census.
  Monthly work plan updates.
  *Free the Children: Breaking the Cycle of Poverty,* summary report, 1987.
  *Free the Children: Breaking the Cycle of Poverty,* videotape.
**Write or call for more information or to order.**


## Friends of the Family

Contact: Linda Gaither, Deputy Director
1001 Eastern Avenue
Baltimore, MD 21202-4364
(410) 659-7701

*A partnership of private organizations, public agencies, and local communities committed to strengthening and supporting families with children from birth to age three. Provides training, technical assistance, evaluation, and program enhancement to Maryland's Family Support Centers. Advocates for family support.*

**Resources Available**
  *Maryland Family Support Centers' Manual.*
**For more information, write to the above address.**


## Growing Up Strong: A Mental Wellness and Substance Abuse Prevention Program for Young Children

Contact: Ann O'Bar
Center for Child and Family Development
Continuing Education and Public Service
The University of Oklahoma
555 East Constitution Street, Room 221
Norman, OK 73072-7820
(405) 325-1446

*A mental wellness and substance abuse prevention program for young children. The Center for Child and Family Development provides technical assistance.*

**Resources Available**
*Growing Up Strong Basic Kit,* a curriculum for preschool through sixth grade. Deluxe kit offers posters and puppets in addition to the basic kit.
*Spanish Bilingual Growing Up Strong Supplement,* for preschool through first grade.
*American Indian Growing Up Strong Supplement.*
**Write or call to order.**

## Harvard Native American Program
Contact: Jeffrey Hamley, Director
Harvard Graduate School of Education
Read House, Appian Way
Cambridge, MA 02138
(617) 495-4923

*A resource center dedicated to assisting Native Americans in obtaining advanced degrees from the Harvard Graduate School of Education.*

**Resources Available**
*A Bibliography on Contemporary Native American Education.*
**Order from Jeffrey Hamley at the above address.**

## Head Start Bureau
Contact: Head Start Bureau
201 North Union Street, Suite 320
Alexandria, VA 22314
(703) 739-0875

*The national headquarters for Head Start programs.*

**Resources Available**
*Easing the Transition from Preschool to Kindergarten: A Guide for Early Childhood Teachers and Administrators* (free).
**Write to order.**

## High/Scope Educational Research Foundation
Contact: Lawrence Schweinhart
600 North River Street
Ypsilanti, MI 48198-2898
(313) 485-2000

*Performs extensive educational research and curriculum development.*

**Resources Available**
*Policy Options for Preschool Programs.*
*Early Childhood Programs in the Eighties: The National Picture,* from the High/Scope Early Childhood Policy Papers series.
**Write or call for a catalog of curricular materials and research and policy papers.**

## Hispanic Policy Development Project
Contact: Mildred Garcia
1001 Connecticut Avenue, NW, Suite 538
Washington, DC 20036
(202) 822-8414

*Encourages policy analysis relating to Hispanic Americans, especially in the areas of education, employment, and family formation.*

**Resources Available**

*Together is Better: Strategies and Techniques for School-Parent Relationships*, includes 100 copies of *La Escuela Es Nuestra Tambien — It's Our School, Too,* in Spanish; a message to Hispanic parents that they are important in schools. Appropriate for low literacy adults.
**Write to order.**

## Home and School Institute, Inc., Special Projects Office

Contact: Dorothy Rich
MegaSkills Education Center
1500 Massachusetts Ave., NW
Washington, DC 20005
(202) 466-3633
(202) 833-1400 FAX

*A nonprofit center, begun in 1964, that develops educational partnership programs for parents and teachers and provides home learning recipes for families to help children succeed in school and beyond. Works with policy makers and community leaders to design community-wide education programs focusing on the family's role in education. Has conducted the MacArthur Foundation-funded New Partnerships for Student Achievement program with eight national organizations. Project AHEAD in Los Angeles is an institute model.*

**Resources Available**

*MegaSkills: How Families Can Help Children Succeed in School and Beyond* (Houghton Mifflin). This book is now also a series of eight community-based workshops. The institute trains workshop leaders at sites across the nation.
*The Forgotten Factor in School Success: The Family. A Policy-Maker's Guide.*
*Job Success Begins at Home.*
*Special Solutions,* a special education program with audiotape.
*Families Learning Together,* learning activities for both adults and children.
*101 Activities for More Effective School-Community Involvement.*
**Write for more information.**

## Illinois Prevention Resource Center

Contact: Barbara Allen, Communications Specialist
822 South College Street
Springfield, IL 62704
(217) 525-3456

*A nonprofit organization funded by the Illinois Department of Alcoholism and Substance Abuse which provides training, information, and research services to the state of Illinois.*

**Resources Available**

*Prevention Forum,* periodic update on people, projects, programs, issues, and research related to prevention (free).
**Address orders to Prevention Forum Subscription Services at the above address.**

## Institute for Responsive Education

Contact: Tony Wagner, Director
605 Commonwealth Avenue
Boston, MA 02215
(617) 353-3309

*Studies and advocates parent and citizen involvement in education. Special interest in promoting equity for poor and minority parents. Researches family involvement and provides information, consultation, and technical assistance to schools and state and local education agencies nationwide.*

### Resources Available

Numerous reports, working papers, resource guides, and videos available.
**Direct orders to publications department.**

## International Reading Association

Contact: Dr. Alan E. Farstrup, Executive Director
800 Barksdale Road
PO Box 8139
Newark, DE 19714-8139
(302) 731-1600
(302) 731-1057 FAX

*A membership organization to improve the quality of reading instruction and to encourage lifelong reading habits.*

### Resources Available

Offers subscriptions to up to four journals with membership. There is also an extensive catalog of publications in areas such as early reading, adult literacy, reading for special students, administration, and staff development and reading for students whose first language is not English.
**For membership information, direct inquiries to the membership services coordinator at the above address. For a catalog, write to the order department.**

## Literacy Council of Alaska

Contact: Mary Matthews, Executive Director
823 Third Avenue
Fairbanks, AK 99701
(907) 456-6212
(907) 456-4302 FAX

*The Literacy Council of Alaska is an educational agency that trains volunteers to teach adults to read, sponsors summer tutoring for children, and directs other literacy projects.*

### Resources Available

The council has a large selection of low level reading books, books on child care, teaching aids, posters, and other materials, some with Alaskan themes. Offers summer cross-age tutoring program.
**Write or call to request a materials catalog.**

## Morning Glory Press

Contact: Jeanne Lindsay
6595-B San Haroldo Way
Buena Park, CA 90620-3748
(714) 828-1998
(714) 828-2049 FAX

*Morning Glory Press publishes books on adolescent pregnancy and parenting and produces exhibits for conferences.*

**Resources Available**

*In School Together — School-based Child Care Serving Student Mothers: A Handbook.*

Publications catalog available.

**Write for more information.**

## National Association for the Education of Young Children (NAEYC)

Contact: Ms. Pat Spahr
1509 Sixteenth Street, NW
Washington, DC 20036-1426
(202) 232-8777
(202) 328-1846 FAX

*Advocates for young children, facilitates improvements in professional practice of early childhood education, and provides support for quality programs for young children and their families. Produces publications in the areas of children and family policy and early childhood education.*

**Resources Available**

*Parent Involvement in Early Childhood Education,* by Alice S. Honig.

*Families and Early Childhood Programs,* a research monograph by Douglas Powell.

*Young Children,* a journal.

Sponsors conferences, workshops, and seminars.

**For a catalog or ordering information call NAEYC's toll-free number: (800) 424-2460.**

## National Association of Elementary School Principals (NAESP)

Contact: Ronald Areglado, Director of National Principals Academy
1615 Duke Street
Alexandria, VA 22314-3483
(703) 684-3345
(703) 549-5298 FAX @RES-DEF = A professional association of principals engaged in administration and supervision of elementary and middle schools, whose goal is to improve elementary education by improving principals.

**Resources Available**

Sponsors seminars, fellowships, and workshops.

*A School Administrator's Guide to Early Childhood Programs.*

*Family Focus: Reading and Learning Together,* a kit.

*The Little Things Make a Big Difference,* videotape and booklet shows parents how to help kids to succeed.

**For information regarding NAESP's programming, write to NAESP National Principals Academy at the above address. For a publications catalog, write to the NAESP Educational Products Center at the same address.**

## National Association of Partners in Education (NAPE)

Contact: Janet Cox
209 Madison Street, Suite 401
Alexandria, VA 22314
(703) 836-4880
(703) 836-6941 FAX

*A nonprofit membership organization of businesses, schools, community groups, and individual volunteers who work together to help establish and strengthen education partnership programs throughout the nation.*

### Resources Available

*A Practical Guide to Creating and Managing School/Community Partnerships,* from needs assessment to program evaluation.
*Partners for the Eighties: Business and Education,* 24 program models.
**Call or write to request publications catalog, order form, and membership information. Membership discounts of 25 to 30% available.**

## National Association of School Psychologists

Contact: Susan Gorin
8455 Colesville Road, Suite 1000
Silver Spring, MD 20910
(301) 608-0500

*Represents over 20,000 school psychologists (practitioners, trainers, administrators, and researchers) by promoting the rights, welfare, education, and mental health of children and youth and by advancing the profession of school psychology. This is accomplished through education, service, research, and policy development.*

### Resources Available

Position statements. *School Psychology Review,* four issues per year.
*Communique,* eight issues per year.
Publications list available.
**Write to order and for further publications.**

## National Association of Secondary School Principals (NASSP)

Contact: Dr. Timothy J. Dyer, Executive Director
1904 Association Drive
Reston, VA 22091
(703) 860-0200
(703) 476-5432 FAX

*Sponsors secondary school honor societies and studies curriculum. NASSP Assessment and Development Center works with principals from 34 states, Australia, Germany, and England to better their skills.*

### Resources Available

Newsletter, journals, and an annual convention.
**Write for more information.**

## National Association of Social Workers (NASW)

Contact: Isadora Hare
The NASW Building
750 First Street, NE, Suite 700
Washington, DC 20002
(202) 408-8600
(202) 336-8310

*NASW has 123,000 members in 55 chapters nationwide and abroad, many of whom work with the school-age population. School social workers act as a link between family, school, and community, and NASW links social workers in the public schools.*

### Resources Available

*Achieving Educational Excellence for Children at Risk.*
*Expanding School Social Work: Through Federal Funding in P.L. 100-297.*
*The Family Caregiving Crisis.*
*Painful Passages: Working with Children with Learning Disabilities.*
*Caring Families.*
*Lesbian and Gay Issues: A Resource Manual for Social Workers,* includes a discussion of lesbian and gay adolescent issues.
*Analyzing Social Work Practice by Fields,* includes a discussion of school social work.
*School Social Work Information Bulletin* (free).
*Social Work,* a journal, six issues per year.
*Social Work in Education,* four issues per year.
*Social Work Speaks: NASW Public Policy Statements,* second edition.
**Send publications requests to the attention of Carmen Cajulis.**


## National Association of State Boards of Education (NASBE)

Contact: Brenda Welburn, Executive Director
1012 Cameron Street
Alexandria, VA 22314
(703) 684-4000
(703) 836-2313

*NASBE attempts to strengthen state leadership in education policy making, promote excellence in the education of all students, advocate equality of access to educational opportunity, and assure responsible governance of public education. Helps the state boards of education by providing technical assistance, legislative updates on educational issues, publications, and conferences.*

### Resources Available

*Right from the Start: The Report of the NASBE Task Force on Early Childhood Education.*
*Joining Forces* (Education and Human Services).
*Female Dropouts: A New Perspective.*
*What's Promising: New Approaches to Dropout Prevention for Girls.*
*Partners in Educational Improvement: Schools, Parents, and the Community.*
*Effective Accountability: Improving Schools, Informing the Public.* Free issue briefs.
**Address inquiries to Publications.**

## National Black Child Development Institute

Contact: Evelyn K. Moore, Executive Director
1023 Fifteenth Street, NW, Suite 600
Washington, DC 20005
(202) 387-1281
(202) 234-1738 FAX

*A national, nonprofit, charitable organization dedicated to improving the quality of life for black children and youth in the areas of health, child welfare, education, and child care. Provides direct services on the local level and monitors policy issues. Organizes and trains grass roots affiliates to advocate for the black child.*

### Resources Available

*Beyond the Stereotypes: A Guide to Resources for Black Girls and Women.*
*Child Care in the Public Schools.*
*Excellence and Equity . . . A Report on Civil Rights, Education, and Black Children.*
*The Black Child Advocate,* a periodical.
*Keeping Your Baby Healthy.*
*Giving Your Child a Good Start in School.*
*Parental Drug Abuse in Foster Care.*
**Call or write for an order form.**

## National Center for Children in Poverty

Contact: Lawrence Aber, Director
National Center for Children in Poverty
154 Haven Avenue
New York, NY 10032
(212) 927-8793
(212) 927-9162 FAX

*The center's goal is to strengthen programs and policies for young children and their families living in poverty in the United States. The center seeks to achieve this goal though interdisciplinary analysis and dissemination of information about public and private initiatives in the areas of early childhood care and education, maternal and child health, and the integration and coordination of services for young children and their families.*

### Resources Available

*Past Caring: A History of U.S. Preschool Care and Education for the Poor, 1820-1965* (1989).
*Five Million Children: A Statistical Profile of Our Poorest Young Citizens* (1990).
*Alive and Well? A Research and Policy Review of Health Programs for Poor Young Children* (1991).
*Community-based Family Support and Education Programs: Something Old or Something New?* (1991).
*Child Welfare Reform.*
*Urban Poverty Database Inventory* (1991).
Library and information services are available to professionals, policy makers, and researchers.
**Also available are slide sets, annotated bibliographies, special reports, and issue briefs. Write for a free publications list. Call for a descriptive brochure of services.**

## National Center for Clinical Infant Programs

Contact: Sharon Godsey, Coordinator
EMC2 1477 Chain Bridge Road, Suite 200
McLean, VA 22101
(703) 356-8301
(703) 528-6848 FAX

*A national, nonprofit organization concerned with promoting the healthy development of children and families in the first three years of life. Activities and publications are designed primarily for professionals from a range of disciplines; for policy makers and administrators; and for parents working in family resource and parent support settings.*

### Resources Available

*Zero to Three,* a bulletin published five times a year.
Booklets, policy position papers, and monographs.
National training institute held in Washington, DC in odd-numbered years.
Technical assistance to selected states, in the areas of health care, early intervention, and child care services.
**Write to request publications list or more information.**

## National Center for Education in Maternal and Child Health (NCEMCH) and National Maternal and Child Health Clearinghouse (NMCHC)

Contact: Olivia Pickett, Librarian, NCEMCH
Tom Mullarkey, NMCHC 2000 Fifteenth Street, N.,Suite 701
Arlington, VA 22201
(703) 524-7802 (NCEMCH) (703) 821-8955 (NMCHC)

*The center responds to information requests, maintains a reference collection of program materials, develops publications on maternal and child health topics, and provides technical assistance in educational resource development, program planning, and topical research. The clearinghouse collects and provides current information to agencies, volunteer organizations, health professionals, and consumers.*

### Resources Available

Each month the clearinghouse distributes more than 50,000 publications to over 2,000 requests nationwide.
**Contact the clearinghouse for a publications catalog and the center for information about technical assistance.**

## National Center for Family Literacy

Contact: Sharon Darling
325 West Main Street, Suite 200
Louisville, Kentucky 40202-4251
(502) 584-0172

*The centers' model programs focus on early family intervention to break the cycle of illiteracy. Undereducated parents and their three- and four-year-old children come to school together for individual and shared learning experiences. The center's broader purpose is to provide direction and staff development training to others who are replicating the model.*

### Resources Available

*Final Report* and *Research Report.*
*Kenan Family Literacy Project and Program Model,* a brief description (free).

*Executive Summary* (free).
*Kenan Trust Family Literacy Model Program Guidebook.*
*Funding Sources for the Kenan Trust Family Literacy Model Programs,*
a guide to funding literacy programs.
*Breaking the Cycle,* a 14-minute film on VHS format.
**Write for more information.**

## National Coalition of Advocates for Students (NCAS)

Contact: Co-Director
100 Boylston Street, Suite 737
Boston, MA 02116
(617) 357-8507
(617) 357-9549

*A national network of 22 experienced child advocacy organizations working to improve access to quality public education for all children, especially those who are most vulnerable to school failure — minorities, low-income, immigrant, and handicapped students. NCAS provides technical assistance to its member groups as they work to inform and empower local parents and communities and collaborates with its members to implement national projects that inform and validate local efforts at school improvement.*

### Resources Available

NCAS *Analysis of the 1986 U.S. Department of Education, Office of Civil Rights, Elementary and Secondary School Survey.*
*Barriers to Excellence: Our Children at Risk.*
**A complete list of publications is available.**

## National Coalition of Title I Chapter 1 Parents (NCTCP)

Contact: Betty Hawkins
Edmonds School Building
Ninth & D Streets, NE, #201
Washington, DC 20002
(202) 547-9286
(202) 544-2813

*Encourages community participation in development of educational programs and agendas for disadvantaged children. Assists Title I parents.*

### Resources Available

Newsletter available.
Annual national conference featuring state and national speakers, workshops, and reports on legislation and action.
**Contact NCTCP for more information.**

## National Community Education Association

Contact: Starla Jewell-Kelly, Executive Director
3929 Old Lee Highway, Suite 914
Fairfax, VA 22030-2401
(703) 359-8973
(703) 359-0972 FAX

*A membership organization that promotes and supports community involvement in K-12 education, creates interagency partnerships to address community needs, and provides life-long learning opportunities to everyone in a community.*

**Resources Available**

*Community Education Journal,* quarterly journal.

*Community Education Today,* monthly newsletter.

*The Learning Community,* an introduction to community education.

*Parents as Tutors.*

*Minority Vitabank.*

Hosts an annual conference and training workshops on parent involvement.

Provides information and referral. Conducts a spring institute on the latest, most poignant issues in education.

**Community Education Development Centers in most states distribute training materials. Write to the above address for the center nearest you. Membership is open to all. Contact the national office for membership and publications information and orders.**

## National Conference of State Legislatures (NCSL)

Contact: Constance L. Koprowicz
1560 Broadway, Suite 700
Denver, CO 80202
(303) 830-7200
(393) 863-8003 FAX

*An association of state legislators and legislative staff devoted to improving the quality and effectiveness of state legislatures. Ensures the states a strong voice in federal decision making. Compiles data and performs research studies focusing on a wide variety of education issues of interest to state legislators, including at-risk youth, restructuring schools, school finance, AIDS education, school counseling, and job training.*

**Resources Available**

Can develop mailing lists of legislators concerned with specific issues (fee).

Publishes directories of legislative staff and legislative committees.

Publishes *State Legislatures* magazine and other books and reports on issues of interest to state legislators.

Conducts meetings and seminars.

**Publications and mailing lists can be purchased through NCSL's marketing department at the above address and phone number. Publications catalog with prices and order forms are available through the marketing department. Call with any questions.**

## National Council of Jewish Women, Center for the Child

Contact: Amy Baker
53 West 23rd Street, Sixth Floor
New York, NY 10010
(212) 645-4048
(212) 645-7466

*The center works to increase public awareness and understanding of children's issues; improve children's programs having and emphasis on preventions; and influence public and private policy affecting the welfare of children and families. Conducts research on issues such as mothers in the workplace, family daycare, child abuse prevention, and the prosecution of child sexual abuse cases. Continues implementation and evaluation of the Home Instruction Program for Preschool Youngsters (HIPPY) in more than 20 sites across the country.*

**Resources Available**

Newsletter, brochures, training manuals, fact sheets, and working papers.

Distributes HIPPY materials.

**Write for a complete list of publications and materials available.**

## National Council of Jewish Women
## National Affairs/Community Service Department

Contact: Naomi Fatt
53 West 23rd Street, Sixth Floor
New York, NY 10010
(212) 645-4048

*Develops and implements community service, advocacy, and educational projects, such as the National Family Daycare Project and the Work/Family Project, that address national and local problems such as child homelessness, child development, child care, and juvenile justice.*

**Resources Available**

*Washington Newsletter,* quarterly publication concerning legislative issues.

*Community Service* newsletter.

Background papers on social issues affecting families (free).

How-to manuals for a variety of community services.

**Write for ordering information.**

## National Council of La Raza

Contact: Charles Kamasaki
810 First Street, NE, Suite 300
Washington, DC 20002
(202) 289-1380
(202) 289-8173 FAX

*Conducts applied research and policy analysis; advocates on behalf of Hispanic Americans; provides technical assistance and capacity-building support to community-based Hispanic organizations, Hispanic entrepreneurs, and elected officials in areas of high Hispanic population; and provides public information to Hispanic communities and the broader American public.*

**Resources Available**

*Parent Power in the Migrant Education Program: How to Make a Difference* (1980), in Spanish and English (56 pages).

**Contact Mr. Kamasaki at the above address.**

## National Education Association (NEA)

Contact: Warlene Gary
Center for the Revitalization of Urban Education
1201 Sixteenth Street, NW
Washington, DC 20036-3290
(202) 822-7091
(202) 822-7997

*Provides materials on family education issues through the Education and Outreach Program and the NEA Professional Library.*

**Resources Available**
Distributes videotapes and public education leaflets.
**For catalog, write to: NEA Professional Library, P.O. Box 509, West Haven, CT 06516.**


## National Governors' Association

Contact: Raymond C. Scheppach, Executive Director
444 North Capitol Street, NW, Suite 267
Washington, DC 20001
(202) 624-5300
(202) 624-5313 FAX

*Provides a voice for governors to influence national policy. Facilitates sharing of information on innovative programs among states.*

**Resources Available**
*Time for Results: The Governors' 1991 Report on Education* (Order #3049).
*Results in Education: 1987* (Order #3084, editions from 1987-89 also available).
*The First Sixty Months: A Handbook of Promising Prevention Programs for Children Zero to Five Years of Age,* evaluates promising prevention programs (Order #3087).
*From Rhetoric to Action: State Progress in Restructuring the Educational System* (Order #08080).
*The Next Steps: A Guide to Implementation* (Order #3838).
Many other publications in the areas of educational issues and policy, school dropouts, adult literacy, teen pregnancy, and parenting.
**Order from Matthew Davis at the above address or call (202) 624-7880.**


## National Head Start Association (NHSA)

Contact: Linda Likins, Director of Government Affairs
201 North Union Street, Suite 320
Alexandria, VA 22314
(703) 739-0875
(703) 739-0878 FAX

*NHSA is a membership organization representing the 600,000 children, 100,000 staff members, and more than 1,900 Head Start programs in the United States. NHSA is governed by a board of directors composed of representatives from each of the 12 Head Start regions and includes equal numbers of staff, parents, directors, and friends. Activities include education and advocacy, policy and legislative updates to affiliated organizations, networking through state and regional Head Start organizations, and an annual national training conference.*

**Resources Available**
*Tell the Head Start Story.*
*NHSA News,* quarterly (annual subscription includes legislative updates and special information).
*NHSA Journal,* quarterly.
*Head Start Staff Salary Survey.*
*Head Start: The Nation's Pride — The Report of the Silver Ribbon Pane.*
*Head Start: The Nation's Pride* (videotape).
Annual training conference.
Position and policy papers.
**Write for more information.**

## National Indian Training and Research Center

Contact: Cecil Corbett, Executive Director
2121 South Mill Ave., Suite 216
Tempe, AZ 85282-2136
(602) 967-9484
(602) 921-1015

*Provides services in program development, curriculum design, evaluation, organizational development, training for administrators, teachers, boards of education, and education committees. Also provides technical assistance and consulting services in management and administrative services for Indian schools, boards of education, and special Indian projects on a national front.*

### Resources Available

Services can include proposal writing, training, career development, leadership and managerial training, and technical assistance. Costs depend upon the type of services required and the agreement reached between the center and the client.
**Write for more information.**

## National Mental Health Association Information Center

Contact: Dutch Gennings
1021 Prince Street
Alexandria, VA 22314-2971
(703) 684-7722
(703) 684-5968

*The center provides information on mental health topics and issues through publications and referrals to service organizations that are capable of responding to clinical, technical, and specific questions.*

### Resources Available

*NMHA Prevention Advocate* (free).
*FOCUS-NMHA,* quarterly publication.
*Invisible Children Report,* a resource kit based on an investigation into emotionally disturbed youth.
**For more information, write to the attention of the publication division.**

## National Middle School Association

Contact: Sue Swaim, Executive Director
2600 Corporate Exchange Drive, Suite 370
Columbus, OH 43231
(614) 895-4730
(614) 895-4750 FAX

*Designed to promote middle schools and provide forums for sharing ideas and innovations in middle school education for students in grades five through nine.*

### Resources Available

NMSA currently has 35 titles in print, including monographs, videotapes, and research studies on young adolescents and other issues including curriculum and other school programs for middle grades learners.
**Write or call to request comprehensive publications catalog or membership information.**

## National PTA

Contact: Joe Sampson, Director of Program Outreach Division
330 North Wabash, Suite 2100
Chicago, IL 60611-3690
(312) 787-0977

*A volunteer membership association working for the education, health, and safety of all children. Addresses issues that cross state lines, such as missing children, needs of working parents, and child safety. Provides publications, programs, and services to help members be effective advocates for children.*

### Resources Available

*PTA Today,* each issue focuses on a topic such as communicating with your child and strengthening the family, seven issues per year.
*What's Happening in Washington,* newsletter, six issues per year.
*Help Your Child Get the Most Out of Homework,* available in Spanish and English (single copy free).
*School is What WE Make It! A Parent Involvement Planning Kit.*
**Write to request complete publications list.**

## National School Boards Association

Contact: Dr. Thomas Shannon, Executive Director
1680 Duke Street
Alexandria, VA 22314
(703) 838-6722
(703) 683-7590

*Provides information on curriculum development and monitors court and legislative decisions affecting educational and school policy.*

### Resources Available

*American School Board Journal* (monthly).
*Executive Educator* (monthly).
*School Board News* (bimonthly newspaper).
**Write for ordering information.**

## North-Central Indian Education Technical Assistance Center II

Contact: Francis Tobias, Director
United Tribes Technical College
3315 University Drive
Bismarck, ND 58504
(701) 258-0437 or (800) 437-8054 (701) 258-0454 FAX

*The Indian Education Technical Assistance Center II is one of five regional resource centers established in the United States to provide training and technical assistance for education programs serving American Indians and Alaskan Natives. Specialized educational services are provided in particular for Indian Education Act Title V programs in the states of Iowa, Kansas, Minnesota, Nebraska, North Dakota, South Dakota, and Wisconsin.*

### Resources Available

The center provides workshops, on-site visits, summer institutes, and professional consultants along with resource materials in the areas of: home-school relations, Indian students' learning styles, Title V/JOM parent committee development, school board development, K-12 cultural curriculum resource materials, Indian student self- esteem development, education needs assessment, Indian teacher-aide development, education

program design and management, program evaluation, and IEA federal grant application assistance.
**Write for resource materials, newsletters, or more information on technical assistance.**

## ORBIS Associates

Contact: Gwen Shunatona, President
1411 K Street, NW, Suite 700
Washington, DC 20005
(202) 628-4444
(202) 628-2241 FAX

*A Native American, nonprofit organization which provides training, assistance, evaluation, and management advice to schools, tribes, government agencies, and corporations.*

**Resources Available**
Training programs for inservice staff training, individual classroom training, or volunteer assistance training for work in family-school partnerships, especially from a multicultural perspective.
**Contact ORBIS for more information and training fee quotes.**

## Oregon Community Children and Youth Services Commission (OCCYSC)

Contact: Dianne Walton, Director
530 Center Street, NE., Suite 300
Salem, OR 97310
(503) 373-1283
(503) 378-8395 FAX

*The 11-member commission was established to bring together under one organization the responsibility for supporting community efforts aimed at children from birth to age 18. The commission also administers all of the state community grant programs, including Juvenile Services, Student Retention Initiative, and Great Start programs. Community development is also an important aspect of the commission's focus.*

**Resources Available**
Legislative report (free).
Various pamphlets and brochures (free).
**Order by calling Gretchen Clark at the OCCYSC.**

## The Ounce of Prevention Fund

Contact: Sandra Lightfoot
188 West Randolph Street, Suite 2200
Chicago, IL 60601
(312) 853-6080
(312) 853-3337

*Serves infants, children, adolescents, and families at risk throughout Illinois. Provides training, development, funding, or technical assistance to Head Start, Parents Too Soon, Toward Teen Health, and the Center for Successful Child Development, among others.*

**Resources Available**
*Ounce of Prevention,* magazine, four issues per year.
*Heart to Heart Survey,* a survey on sexual abuse in Parents Too Soon participants.

**Individual copies will have no charge. Bulk orders may negotiate a price. Written inquiries only.**

## Parent and Child Education (PACE)

Contact: Sara Calloway
Workforce Development Cabinet
Capitol Plaza Tower
Frankfort, KY 40601
(502) 564-3921
(502) 564-5316

*A family support and education program that focuses on family literacy. While children are in a model preschool setting, adults take classes that improve their basic skills and parental skills. During part of the day, parents act as children's teachers in their classroom; when children nap, parents work on life and employment skills. The program takes place in public schools for at least three days a week.*

### Resources Available
Brochure, fact sheet, and bibliography.
**Write to request materials.**

## Parents as Teachers National Center

Contact: Mildred Winter, Director
9374 Olive Blvd.
St. Louis, MO 63132
(314) 432-4330
(314) 432-8963 FAX

*The Parents as Teachers (PAT) program supports parents in their role as their children's first and most influential teacher in order to strengthen families and give children optimal beginnings. Offers professionals training in the PAT model and consultation on program implementation. Consults on public policy. Parents receive timely information on enhancing development from birth to age three through home visits by professional educators and group meetings. Results of an independent evaluation of the PAT pilot project showed project children to be significantly more advanced than their peers at age three in language, intellectual, and social development. PAT is now offered to families in all Missouri public school districts. As of October 1991, there were 220 replications in 36 other states, Australia, and England.*

### Resources Available
Free descriptive brochure.
Comprehensive packet of information on the PAT program.
Evaluative report on the PAT pilot project by Research and Training Associates.
*Second Wave Study of the Parents as Teachers Program*, Executive Summary.
PAT training institutes, PAT consultation and observation services.
**Write to order or for more information.**

## Vermont Agency of Human Services

Contact: Ted Mable, Director of Planning
Vermont Agency of Human Services
103 Main Street
Waterbury, VT 05671-0203
(802) 241-2227
(802) 241-2979 FAX

*A statewide community services system that addresses the multifaceted needs of children and families. Each center is designed to offer services in child care, parent support, parent education, drop-in programs, resource and referral, and more.*

### Resources Available

*Parent-Child Centers in Vermont: A Report to the State Legislature.*
**Direct orders to Ted Mable at the above address.**


## Parent-Child Programs

Contact: Ellen S. Kearns
District 742
820 Eighth Avenue South
St. Cloud, MN 56301
(612) 253-5828
(612) 252-0245 FAX

*Parent-Child Programs provide center-based early childhood family education programs for parents and their children birth through age four.*

### Resources Available

*Parents and Adolescents Communicating (PAAC): A Complete Curriculum to Be Used with Both Parents and Adolescents (11-14 Years) Together.* This curriculum is divided into eight sections, complete with activities, games, and discussion outlines for both parents and adolescents.
**Order through MCSC, Capitol View Center, 70 West County Road B2, Little Canada, Minnesota 55117. Write to Parent-Child Programs or call for more information.**


## Parent Educational Advocacy Training Center (PEATC)

Contact: Sherri Takemoto
10340 Democracy Lane, Suite 206
Fairfax, VA 22030
(703) 836-2953 or (800) 869-6782 (for parents calling long distance)
(703) 836-5869 FAX

*The Parent Educational Advocacy Training Center believes that children reach their greatest potential when families and service providers enjoy an equal, respectful partnership. PEATC builds upon parents' expertise to make effective educational choices with and for their children. The center strives to motivate education systems to be responsive to the dignity, dreams, and integrity of individuals with disabilities and their families. PEATC provides information and assistance to individuals in problem solving and identification of services needed; consultation to help organizations develop programs and policies; and community collaboration to advocate for the inclusion of families' perspectives and responsive community resources.*

**Resources Available**

*Negotiating the Special Education Maze: A Guide for Parents and Teachers* (available through Woodbine House Publishers (800) 843-7323.

*The Partnership Series,* 10 training workshops for teachers and administrators to strengthen their skill in working effectively with parents of children in special education.

*The PEATC Press,* newsletter (four issues per year).

Sponsors workshops for parents and educators.

**Call or write for more information.**

## Portage Project

Contact: Julia Herwig, Director, Portage Project Cooperative Educational Service Agency No. 5
Box 564
Portage, WI 53901
(608) 742-8811
(608) 742-2384 FAX

*The Portage Model is a delivery system of high quality, early intervention services to young children and their families that is utilized by more than 140 U.S. sites and over 30 countries.*

**Resources Available**

*Portage Classroom Curriculum,* designed for children ages two to six, including children with mild to moderate handicaps. This multilevel teaching system assists the teacher in individualizing for all children within the classroom.

*Portage Guide to Early Education,* a developmental approach to the early education of children birth to age six, including children with handicapping conditions. Everything needed to implement this educational model is included.

*Portage Home Teaching Handbook,* detailed plan for implementing a successful home-based program using the *Portage Model of Early Education.*

*Get a Jump on Kindergarten,* presents practical suggestions for helping children become successful and independent in their kindergarten experience.

*Special Training for Special Needs: A Competency-based Training Program for Personnel Working with Young Children Who Have Special Needs,* includes information on parent involvement.

*A Parent's Guide to Early Education.*

**Write or call for more information.**

## Project Spectrum

Contact: Mara Krechevsky
Harvard Project Zero
Longfellow Hall, Appian Way
Cambridge, MA 02138
(617) 495-4342

*Project Spectrum is an innovative approach to early school curriculum and assessment. The areas covered by Spectrum include music, science, movement, language, art, mathematics, and social intelligence, which includes interpersonal and intrapersonal intelligence.*

**Resources Available**

*Project Spectrum Activities Handbook* (available in 1992).

*A New Look at Intelligence through Project Spectrum.*

Mentorship program brings experts in music, science, movement, language, art, and mathematics into first grade classrooms.
**For a complete list of publications related to Project Spectrum and information about reprints and costs, write to Howard Gardner at the above address.**

## Public Education Fund Network

Contact: Wendy Puriefoy, President
601 Thirteenth Street, NW
Suite 290 North
Washington, DC  20005
(202) 628-7460
(202) 628-1893  FAX

*Provides technical assistance and nurturing to grantees of the Public Education Fund and other organizations and individuals interested in the local education fund approach.*

### Resources Available

*Public Education Fund Five Year Report.*
*Local Education Fund Handbook and Resource Guide.*
*Small Grants for Teachers Handbook and Materials Packet.*
*Principal Grants Handbook and Materials.*
*PERFORM,* a quarterly newsletter.
Technical assistance in the organization and development of local education funds, including on-site assistance. Priority for on-site assistance in communities whose school systems have significant minority and low-income populations. Assistance in developing networks of local education funds on a state, local, and national level.
**There is currently no charge for publications or services. Publications may be requested by mail or telephone.**

## Push Literacy Action Now (PLAN)

Contact: Anthony Kroll, Executive Director
1332 G Street, SE
Washington, DC  20003
(202) 547-8903

*Community-based nonprofit literacy training and advocacy group.*

### Resources Available

*The Ladder Newsletter,* six issues per year.
*Laying the Foundations: A Parent-Child Literacy Training Kit.*
*A Look at Illiteracy Today: The Problems, the Solutions, the Alternatives.*
*From the Crib to the Classroom* (videotape).
**Write for ordering information.**

## Reading Is Fundamental, Inc. (RIF)

Contact: James Wendorf, Director of Programs
600 Maryland Avenue, SW, Suite 600
Washington, DC  20024-2520
(202) 287-3220
(202) 287-3196 FAX

*A national, nonprofit organization that seeks to inspire youngsters to read. Works through local programs in thousands of communities throughout the country.*

**Resources Available**
  Guide for Parents series of brochures includes the following titles:
  *Family Storytelling, Summertime Reading, Choosing Good Books for Your Children,* and more.
**Complete publications list available.**

## School-Age Child Care Project

Contact: Michelle Seligson, Director, or
Lisa Cowley, Research Administrator
Wellesley Center for Research on Women
Wellesley College
Wellesley, MA 02181
(617) 283-2547
(617) 283-3657

*Provides information and assistance on developing options for school-age child care services and policies.*

**Resources Available**
  *School-Age Child Care: An Action Manual*
  *School-Age Children with Special Needs*
  *No Time to Waste*
  *Action Research Papers*
  Videotapes.
  Technical assistance and consultation on school-age child care.
**Write for a complete list of publications.**

## The School Improvement Council Assistance (SICA)

Contact: Dr. Jean M. Norman, Executive Director
College of Education, Suite 023
University of South Carolina
Columbia, SC 29208
(803) 777-7658
(803) 777-0023 FAX

*Provides training, technical assistance, and publications to South Carolina School Improvement Councils. Provides state, regional, and local training in effective schools research and practice and analyzes student achievement and survey data.*

**Resources Available**
  *SIC: Guide to Effectiveness* (100 pages).
**Call or write to order or for more information about services. An invoice will be mailed with requested materials.**

## School Development Program

Contact: Dr. James Comer, Director or Etta Burke
Child Study Center
School Development Program
230 South Frontage Road
P.O. Box 207900
New Haven, CT 06520-7900
(203) 785-2548
(203) 785-3359

*A child development-based school improvement program, known as the Comer Process, that aims to increase parent involvement in the actual management process of the school. This school-based management approach attempts to change working relationships between principals, teachers, counselors, and parents.*

**Write for more information.**

## Southwest Indian Education Technical Assistance Center IV

Contact: Shirley Hendricks, Director
2121 South Mill, Suite 216
Tempe, AZ 85282-2195
(602) 967-9428
(602) 921-1015 FAX

*Operated by the National Indian Training and Research Center under contract with the U.S. Department of Education. One of six regional centers authorized by Public Law 95-561 to provide technical assistance and training to funded Indian Education Act grantees, Indian organizations, Indian tribes, and Indian institutions. Serves the states of Arizona, California, Colorado, Hawaii, Nevada, and New Mexico.*

**Resources Available**
Monthly newsletter available to eligible clients in the region. Technical assistance and training are provided at no cost upon specific request to eligible organizations as described above.
**Written requests only.**

## TARGET

Contact: N/A
PO Box 20626
Kansas City, MO 64195
(816) 464-5400

*A service of the National Federation of State High School Associations helping students cope with alcohol and other drugs; includes a national resource center, leadership training, and an interactive video project teaching refusal and coping skills.*

**To order TARGET product catalog, write to the order department at the above address, or call (800) 366-6667.**

## Together for Children

Contact: Anita McClanahan
Early Childhood Education
Department of Education
255 Capitol Street, NE
Salem, OR 97310-0203
(503) 378-5585
(503) 373-7968 FAX

*Together for Children is a competitive grant program to establish parent education and family support programs through nonsectarian organizations in Oregon.*

**Resources Available**
"Off to a Good Start," a descriptive brochure.
*Together for Children: Oregon Parent Education Program, Progress Report,* Winter, 1989.
**Write or call to order.**

## United Indians of All Tribes Foundation

Contact: Roxanne Finney
1945 Yale Place East
Seattle, WA 98102
(206) 325-0070
(206) 328-1608 FAX

*Advocates the interests of Native Americans. Helps to develop and expand Native American education and curricula. Develops model programs and community education services and provides technical assistance.*

### Resources Available

Offers family counseling, minority groups counseling, foster care services, and healing and anger discussion groups.

Native American curriculum materials for the public schools.

**Write or call Sharon Patacsil (206) 285-4425 for more information.**

## Wellesley College Center for Research on Women

Contact: Susan M. Bailey, Director
Woment's Research Center
Wellesley College
Wellesley, MA 02181
(617) 283-2500
(617) 283-2504 FAX

*Studies women's and girl's issues such as stress, child care, and educational curricula. Special emphases on the economic condition of black women, teen parenting, and women in science careers.*

### Resources Available

Newsletter, research reports, luncheon seminar series, and working papers.

Publishes *Women's Review of Books.*

**Write or call for more information.**

## Wheelock College Center for Parenting Studies

Contact: Cindy Blumsack
200 The Riverway
Boston, MA 02215
(617) 734-5200

*Offers programs and services that respond to the changing needs of families. Offers seminars that incorporate strategies for enhancing individual and group work with parents to professionals at the workplace and / or at Wheelock College; executive seminars for educators and other professionals on working with parents and children; and consultation for human resource professionals. The programs are designed for those who conduct seminars and workshops or consult with parents in setting such as schools, corporations, private practice, churches, or other organizations.*

### Resources Available

*Helping Parents in Groups: A Leader's Handbook,* by Braun, Coplon, and Somenschein.

*Building Home-School Partnerships,* by Braun and Swap, a practical multimedia resource kit for course instructors and parent-teacher trainers.

**Write or call to order or for more information.**

## Women's Action Alliance, Inc.

Contact: Tanya Nieri, Administrative Assistant
370 Lexington Avenue, Suite 603
New York, NY 10017
(212) 532-8330 x110 (212) 779-2846 FAX

*Develops educational programs and services to assist women and girls in achieving full equality. Currently studies the educational experience of children of single-parent families. Maintains an information services program that provides information and referrals and disseminates publications on women's issues and programs.*

### Resources Available

*Beginning Equal: A Manual about Nonsexist Childrearing for Infants and Toddlers.*

*Nonsexist Education for Young Children: A Practical Guide.*

*Equal Play,* a monthly journal on nonsexist education.

*Bibliography of Materials for Equal Early Education.*

*A Guide to Educational Materials,* an annotated listing of AIDS prevention and educational materials for women.

**Address orders to the catalog department or request a complete catalog. Bulk discounts available.**

# PROGRAM LISTINGS BY DIFFERENT CHARACTERISTICS

## Alphabetical Listing of Programs

## State-by-State Listing of Programs

## State-Sponsored Programs

## Program Listing by Location

-Urban Programs
-Suburban Programs
-Rural Programs

## Demographic Characteristics of Participants

-Programs with a Service Component Serving 50% or More Low-Income
  Families (Under $10,000 per year)
-Programs with 25% or More Hispanic Participants
-Programs with 25% or More Black Participants
-Programs with 10% or More Single Parents

## Sources of Funding

-Programs with Three or More Funding Sources
-Programs with 50% or More Funding from State/Federal Sources
-Programs with 50% or More Funding from Local Sources
-Programs with 10% or More Funding from Business or Corporate Sources

## Administrative Relationship to the School District

-Programs Administered Exclusively by the School
-Programs Administered Collaboratively by the School and an Outside
  Organization
-Programs Administered Exclusively by an Outside Organization

## Program Service Components

-Regular Weekly Child Care Experience
-Development Exams or Screening
-Home Visits
-Support Groups
-Adult Literacy and/or GED Services
-Crisis Services
-Newsletter

## Program Service Delivery Sites

-Exclusively School Sites
-Combination of School and Home Sites
-Combination of School and Non-School Sites
-Exclusively Non-School Sites

DEMOGRAPHIC CHARAC-TERISTICS OF PARTICI-PANTS

## SOURCES OF FUNDING

### PROGRAMS WITH THREE OR MORE FUNDING SOURCES

### PROGRAMS WITH 50 PERCENT OR MORE FUNDING FROM STATE AND/OR FEDERAL SOURCES

## PROGRAMS WITH 50 PERCENT OR MORE FUNDING FROM LOCAL SOURCES

## PROGRAMS WITH 10 PERCENT OR MORE FUNDING FROM BUSINESS OR CORPORATE SOURCES

**ADMINISTRATIVE RELATION-SHIP TO SCHOOL DISTRICTS**

## PROGRAMS ADMINISTERED EXCLUSIVELY BY THE SCHOOL

## PROGRAMS ADMINISTERED COLLABORATIVELY BY THE SCHOOL AND AN OUTSIDE ORGANIZATION

Harvard Family Research Project

## PROGRAMS ADMINISTERED EXCLUSIVELY BY AN OUTSIDE ORGANIZATION

## REGULAR WEEKLY CHILD CARE EXPERIENCES

## SCREENING/DEVELOPMENTAL EXAMS

PROGRAM SERVICE DELIVERY SITES

Harvard Family Research Project

## COMBINATION OF SCHOOL AND NONSCHOOL SITES

## EXCLUSIVELY NON-SCHOOL SITES

# CONTRIBUTORS

**Project Director**

Heather B. Weiss

**Research Coordinators**

Kathryn Parsons · Ann Rittenburg

**Writers**

Nancy Cardwell · Zara Fisher · William McMullen
Kathryn Parsons · Kristine Puopolo · Paula Rhodes
Doris Scheff · Mary Uscilka · M. Elena Lopez
Mia MacDonald · Angela Shartrand · Mona R. Hochberg

**Editors**

Kathryn Parsons · J. Anne Pender · Katherine Wrean

**Production Coordinator**

Angela Shartrand

**Research/Production**

Miriam Avins · Tangee Burrell · Alejandra Carvajal
Margaret Dowley · Carolyn Dymond · Juliette Fay
Cinqué Hicks · Steven Hite · Ellen Mayer · Kate Ouderkirk
Jon Silverman · Jim Somers · Laura Stephens-Swannie · Julia Van

**Design**

Helen Owens · Jim Somers